EX LIBRIS

MACRO ECONOMICS

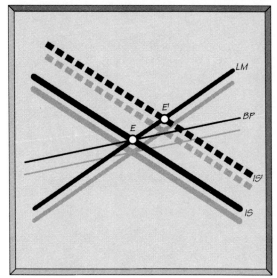

FOURTH CANADIAN EDITION

Study Guide to accompany **Macroeconomics**

ISBN 0-07-551404-4

Answers to even-numbered problems at the end of each text chapter can be found in the Study Guide, a valuable learning aid for students of macroeconomics.

Available now in your campus bookstore!

MACRO ECONOMICS

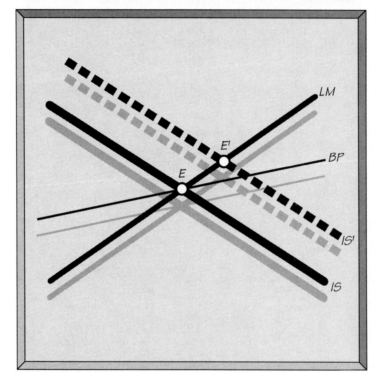

FOURTH CANADIAN EDITION

Rudiger Dornbusch
Massachusetts Institute of Technology

Stanley Fischer
Massachusetts Institute of Technology

Gordon R. Sparks
Queen's University

McGraw-Hill Ryerson Limited
Toronto Montreal New York Auckland Bogotá Caracas Lisbon London Madrid Mexico
Milan New Delhi Paris San Juan Singapore Sydney Tokyo

MACROECONOMICS
Fourth Canadian Edition

ISBN: 0-07-551403-6

1 2 3 4 5 6 7 8 9 0   RRD   2 1 0 9 8 7 6 5 4 3

Printed and bound in the United States of America by R.R. Donnelley (Canada) Limited

Care has been taken to trace ownership of copyright material contained in this text. The publishers will gladly accept any information that will enable them to rectify any reference or credit in subsequent editions.

Sponsoring editor: Jennifer Mix

Supervising editor: Rosalyn Steiner

Copy editor: Kate Forster

Cover design & text: Mireault Images

Canadian Cataloguing in Publication Data

Dornbusch, Rudiger
  Macroeconomics

4th Canadian ed.
Includes index.
ISBN 0-07-551403-6

1. Macroeconomics. I. Fischer, Stanley.
II. Sparks, Gordon R.   III. Title.

HB172.5.D78 1993   339   C92-095128-7

To the memory of Douglas D. Purvis, 1947–1993

Summary of Contents

Contents

Preface

This fourth edition of *Macroeconomics* remains faithful to our basic approach, presenting the relevant theory while at the same time showing both its empirical relevance and its policy applications. We have stayed with our general eclectic outlook on macroeconomics, but there have been changes in details of the presentation and the weight given various topics in light of the changing emphasis of macroeconomic issues and theory over the last few years.

There are five major changes in this edition:

- The basic treatment of aggregate supply has been reorganized and greater emphasis has been placed on the new classical macroeconomics. The introductory discussion of aggregate supply and demand is followed by a new chapter on aggregate supply in the short run that develops and compares the Lucas supply curve and a Keynesian short-run supply curve based on wage stickiness.

- The open economy chapters (5 and 6) have been reorganized and expanded. Rather than treating fixed and flexible exchange rates in separate chapters, the material is divided between an introductory discussion that excludes capital flows and a treatment of the model with capital flows. With this change, direct comparisons between the fixed and flexible exchange rate cases can be made. In addition, there is an expanded treatment of the case of flexible exchange rates with a positively sloped *BP* curve.

- The discussion of price level determination in an open economy is moved up from the present Chapter 19 to a new Chapter 9 that follows the discussion of the closed economy case. This chapter provides a detailed derivation of the aggregate demand curve that relates it directly to the *IS-LM-BP* model of Chapter 6.

- The discussion of the money supply process has been extensively revised in light of the zero reserve requirement system recently implemented by the Bank of Canada.

- The discussion of current issues has been expanded to provide more emphasis on the new classical macroeconomics. The dynamic aggregate supply and demand model, developed in Chapter 15 of the current edition, is used to compare the operation of policy rules in the adaptive versus rational expectations cases. This discussion leads to a derivation of the "policy ineffectiveness proposition" and the "Lucas critique" of econometric policy evaluation.

An Instructor's Manual, prepared by Patricia Pando and Gordon Sparks, is available to accompany this edition. It is an updated and improved version of the manual that accompanied the previous edition and now includes an extensive test bank of multiple-choice questions. The test bank is available on disk from the publisher.

To the Student

Macroeconomics is not cut and dried. There are disputes over basic issues such as how much weight should be given to fighting inflation. This makes macroeconomics unsatisfying if you are looking for clear-cut definite answers to all the economy's problems, but it should also make it more interesting because you have to think hard and critically about the material being presented.

Despite the disagreements, there is a substantial basic core of macroeconomics that we present in this book, and that will continue to be useful in understanding the behaviour of the economy. We have not hesitated to say where we think theories are incomplete, or where the evidence on a question is not yet decisive. Because we have not shied away from important topics even if they are difficult, parts of the book require careful reading. There is no mathematics except simple algebra, but some of the analysis involves sustained reasoning. (An asterisk denotes more difficult concepts and problems.)

A Study Guide prepared and updated by Frank Atkins and Richard Startz is available to accompany this edition. It contains a wide range of questions, starting from the very easy and progressing in each chapter to material that will challenge the more advanced student. Included in this edition of the Study Guide is a new section in each chapter called "Thinking Like an Economist," which will broaden and deepen your understanding of the chapters' key theories. Also included are suggested answers to the even-numbered end-of-chapter problems in this text. It is a great help in studying, particularly since active learning is so important.

Acknowledgments

We are indebted to many users of our book who have given us the benefit of their teaching experience and offered comments and suggestions. In particular we would like to thank Stephan Kaliski, Manfred Keil, Stuart Landon, Isidore Masse, Kanta Marwah, Duncan McDougall, Angela Redish, Peter Sephton, Connie Smith, and Peter Stemp. We have also benefited from detailed reviews of the fourth edition manuscript provided by the following economists:

Frank Atkins (University of Calgary)
Russell Boyer (University of Western Ontario)
Bram Cadsby (University of Guelph)
Douglas Curtis (Trent University)
Michael Peters (University of Toronto)
Jan van Vliet (Government of the Northwest Territories)
Catherine Wankel (University of Calgary)

Gordon Sparks
Rudiger Dornbusch
Stanley Fischer

PART I

Determination of National Income

CHAPTER 1 *Introduction*

Macroeconomics is concerned with the behaviour of the economy as a whole: booms and recessions, the economy's total output of goods and services and the growth of output, the rates of inflation and unemployment, the balance of payments, and exchange rates. To study the overall performance of the economy, macroeconomics focuses on the economic policies and policy variables that affect that performance, such as monetary and fiscal policies, the money stock and interest rates, the public debt, and the federal government budget. In brief, macroeconomics deals with many of the major economic issues and problems of the day.

Macroeconomics is interesting because it deals with important issues, but it is also fascinating and challenging because it reduces complicated details of the economy to manageable essentials. Those essentials lie in the interactions among the goods, labour, and assets markets of the economy.

In dealing with the essentials, we have to disregard details of the behaviour of individual economic units, such as households and firms, or the determination of prices in particular markets, or the effects of monopoly on individual markets. These are the subject matter of microeconomics. In macroeconomics we deal with the market for goods as a whole, treating all the markets for different goods, such as the markets for agricultural products and for medical services, as a single market, and treating all these different goods as a single good. Similarly, we deal with the labour market as a whole, abstracting from differences between the markets for, say, migrant labour and medical services. We deal with the assets markets as a whole, abstracting from the differences between the markets for provincial bonds and Rembrandt paintings. The cost of the abstraction is that omitted details sometimes matter. The benefit of the abstraction is increased understanding of the vital interactions among the goods, labour, and assets markets.

Despite the contrast between macroeconomics and microeconomics, there is no conflict between them. On the contrary, the economy in the aggregate is nothing but the sum of its submarkets. The difference between microeconomics and macroeconomics is, therefore, primarily one of emphasis and exposition. In studying price determination in a single industry, it is convenient for microeconomists to assume that prices in other industries are given. In macroeconomics, in which we study the price level, it is for the most part sensible to ignore changes in relative prices of goods among different industries. In microeconomics, it is convenient to assume that the total income of all consumers is given and to then ask how consumers divide their spending of that income among different goods. In macroeconomics, by contrast, the aggregate level of income or spending is among the key variables to be studied.

Macroeconomics has always been closely related to the economic problems of the day. *Keynesian* economics developed during the great depression of the 1930s and showed the way out of such depressions. *Monetarism* developed during the 1960s, promising a way of solving the inflation problem. *Supply-side* economics became the fad in the United States of the early 1980s, promising an easy way out of the economic mess of the time by cutting taxes, but supply-side economics promised too much and there was no easy way out. Today an influential school of thought, led by Robert Lucas, questions the effectiveness of policy. Even so, the scope for and limits of policy remain at the centre of debate. Beyond a questioning of policy effectiveness, the 1980s have also brought a renewed interest by macroeconomists in economic growth. The basic questions here are: What factors help explain the increase in a country's standard of living over time, and what role can economic policies play in speeding up economic progress?

Because macroeconomics is closely related to the economic problems of the day, it does not yield its greatest rewards to those whose primary interest is theoretical. The need for compromise between the comprehensiveness of the theory and its manageability inevitably makes macrotheory a little untidy at the edges. The emphasis in macroeconomics is on the manageability of the theory and on its applications. This book uses macroeconomics to illuminate economic events from the great depression to the 1990s. We refer continually to real world events to elucidate the meaning and the relevance of the theoretical material.

Controversies and the Research Agenda

There are three central issues on the research agenda in macroeconomics. First, how do we explain periods of high and persistent unemployment? For example, in the 1930s unemployment was more than 20 percent for several years, and the postwar period has also seen high unemployment rates on several occasions. In Canada, unemployment reached 12.8 percent in 1982 and rose above 11 percent in 1992. Several European economies, including the United Kingdom and France, suffered double-digit unemployment during much of the eighties.

Macroeconomic research focuses on persistent unemployment as a central question. There are many theories of why persistent high unemployment is possible, and we shall develop the most important in this book. There is also the research question of what should be done about unemployment. Some say not much, arguing that the government should put in place appropriate unemployment compensation schemes[1] but otherwise not undertake any special policies, such as cutting taxes, to deal with unemployment. This view, which may seem extraordinary to someone new to economics (and even to many who have spent a lifetime in the field), is persuasively argued by Robert Lucas, one of the the leaders in the profession.[2] Others argue that the government should pursue an active fiscal policy, for instance by cutting taxes and/or raising government spending when unemployment is high.

A second major research issue is how to explain inflation: Why did prices in Canada rise by more than 10 percent a year in 1981 and 1982, and by less than 4 percent in 1984 and again in 1991? What causes hyperinflations, when prices rise by more than 1000 percent per year — for instance, the more than 11 000 percent increase in prices in Bolivia in 1985? The policy issues here are how to keep inflation low, and, if it is high, how to reduce it without raising unemployment.

The third major research question is: What determines the rate of growth of output? Why has output per person risen more or less steadily in Canada at an annual rate of 2 percent, doubling every 35 years, and why has output grown more rapidly in Japan than in Canada or the United States over the past century? Will the Japanese economy keep growing more rapidly when income per person reaches the North American level, as, by some measures, it already has?

The questions of whether the government can and should do something about unemployment and what is best to do have been at the centre of macroeconomics for a long time. These questions continue to divide the profession, and every generation develops its own debate, reinterpreting past events, such as the great depression of the 1930s and more recent episodes. Similarly, views about inflation differ among economists. Some believe that inflation can be controlled by keeping money growth low and that the way to stop rapid inflation is to stop the money growth that certainly accompanies the inflation; others argue that the links between money and inflation are at best imprecise, and that merely cutting money growth in a high-inflation economy will also cause a recession that could be avoided by more sophisticated policies. There are still many unresolved questions but fewer controversies about the causes of growth.

We should also bear in mind that while the unemployment, inflation, and growth issues are central problems of macroeconomics, there are many others. Among the important issues are the international dimensions of macroeconomics, as the world economy becomes increasingly integrated and a stock market crash one day in New York spreads almost instantly to London, Tokyo, Frankfurt, Sydney, Hong Kong, Toronto, and every other stock market. Among the apparently less important issues is the question of why wages are so "sticky"; that is, why they change slowly, rather than quickly as does the price of fish. However, even the answers to such an apparently unimportant question may help in understanding how unemployment can emerge.

---

[1] These are schemes that make some payments to unemployed workers as compensation to them for losing their jobs; the worker is required to look for a new job, and the compensation usually lasts for a specified period. After that, if the worker still does not have a job and needs income, he or she has to depend on some form of welfare assistance.

[2] See Robert Lucas, *Models of Business Cycles* (Oxford: Basil Blackwell, 1987).

In the remainder of this chapter we present an overview of the key concepts with which macroeconomics deals. Section 1-1 examines the main macroeconomic variables, and relationships among them are discussed in Section 1-2. Section 1-3 presents a diagrammatic introduction to aggregate demand and supply and their interaction; it gives a very general perspective on the fundamentals of macroeconomics and the organization of this book. Section 1-4 introduces stabilization policy, and Section 1-5 reviews the major competing views of macroeconomic theory and policy. In Section 1-6 we outline the approach of the book, present a preview of the order in which topics are taken up, and offer some brief remarks on how to use the book.

1-1 Key Concepts

Gross Domestic Product

Gross domestic product (GDP) is the value of all goods and services produced in the economy during a given time period. GDP is the basic measure of economic activity prepared by Statistics Canada.[3]

Figure 1-1 shows two measures of GDP: *nominal*, or *current dollar*, GDP; and *real*, or *constant dollar*, GDP.[4] Nominal GDP measures the value of output at the prices prevailing in the period the output is produced, while real GDP measures the output at the prices of some base year. At present, 1986 serves as the base year for real output measurement. GDP statistics become available quarterly.

Figure 1-1 shows that nominal GDP was equal to $667.8 billion in 1990 and $505.7 billion in 1986. Thus nominal GDP grew at an average rate of 7.3 percent during that period. On the other hand, real GDP was $563.1 billion in 1990 and $505.7 billion in 1986,[5] implying an average annual growth rate of real GDP of only 2.7 percent over the period.

Inflation and Nominal GDP

Figure 1-1 shows that nominal GDP has risen much more rapidly than real GDP. The difference between the growth rates of real and nominal GDP occurs because the

---

[3] An alternative measure of output, gross national product (GNP), is sometimes used. The difference between GDP and GNP is explained in Chapter 2.

[4] Notice that the scale for GDP in Figure 1-1 is not linear. For example, the distance from 100 to 200 is bigger than the distance from 200 to 300. The scale is logarithmic, which means that equal ratios are represented by equal distances. For instance, the distance from 100 to 200 is the same as the distance from 200 to 400, since GDP doubles in both cases. On a logarithmic scale, a variable growing at a constant rate (e.g., 4 percent per annum) is represented by a straight line.

[5] Did you notice that real and nominal GDP are the same in 1986? This is because we use 1986 prices to calculate real GDP.

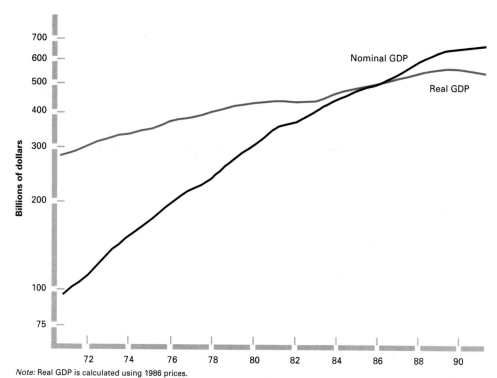

Figure 1-1 *Real and Nominal GDP, 1971–1991*

(*Source:* Adapted from Statistics Canada, 13-201, 11-010)

prices of goods have been rising, or there has been *inflation*. The inflation rate is the percentage rate of increase of the level of prices during a given period.

Real GDP grew at an average rate of 3 percent over the 10 years from 1980 to 1990, while nominal GDP grew at an average annual rate of 8 percent. Because real GDP is calculated holding the prices of goods constant, the difference is entirely due to inflation, or rising prices. Over the 10-year period, prices were on average rising at 5 percent per year. In other words, the average rate of inflation over that period was 5 percent per year.

With 1986 as the base year for the prices at which output is valued, we observe in Figure 1-1 two implications of the distinction between nominal and real GDP. First, in 1986 the two are equal because, in the base year, current and constant dollars are the same dollars. Second, with inflation, nominal GDP rises faster than real GDP and therefore, after 1986, nominal GDP exceeds real GDP. The opposite is true, of course, before 1986.

Growth and Real GDP

We turn next to the reasons for the growth of real GDP. The growth rate of the economy is the rate at which real GDP is increasing. Anytime we refer to growth or the growth rate without any qualifying word, we mean the growth rate of GDP. On average, most economies grow by a few percent per year over long periods. For instance, Canadian real GDP grew at an average rate of 3.7 percent per year from 1970 to 1990.

What causes GDP to grow? The first reason real GDP changes is that the available amount of resources in the economy changes. The resources are conveniently split into capital and labour. The labour force, consisting of people either working or looking for work, grows over time and thus provides one source of increased production. The capital stock, including buildings and machines, likewise has been rising over time, thereby making increased output possible. Increases in the availability of factors of production — the labour and capital used in the production of goods and services — thus account for part of the increase in real GDP.

The second source of real GDP growth is *productivity* increase. Over time, the same factors of production can produce more output. These increases in the efficiency of production result from changes in knowledge, including learning by doing, as people learn through experience to perform familiar tasks better.

Employment and Unemployment

The third source of change in GDP is a change in the employment of the given resources available for production. Not all the capital and labour available to the economy are actually used at all times.

The *unemployment rate* is the fraction of the labour force that cannot find jobs. For example, in 1982, a reduction in the employment of labour, or a rise in unemployment, shows up in Figure 1-1 as a fall in real GDP. Indeed, in that year unemployment rose to 12.8 percent, the highest unemployment rate in the post–World War II period. More than one person out of every eight who wanted to work could not find a job. Such unemployment levels had not been experienced since the great depression of the 1930s.

Inflation, Growth, and Unemployment: The Record

Macroeconomic performance is judged by the three broad measures we have introduced: the *inflation* rate, the *growth rate* of output, and the rate of *unemployment*. Because they affect our daily lives, news of these three variables makes the headlines.

When the inflation rate is high, the prices of goods people buy are rising. Partly for this reason, inflation is unpopular, even if people's incomes rise along with the prices. Inflation is also unpopular because it is often associated with other disturbances to the economy, such as the oil price increases of the 1970s, that would make people worse off even if there were no inflation.

When the growth rate is high, the production of goods and services is rising, making possible an increased standard of living. Along with the high growth rate typically goes lower unemployment, and more jobs. High growth is a target and hope of most societies.

For the long run, the growth rate of real GDP per person is the most important of all the macroeconomic performance indicators. Per capita GDP doubles every 35 years if it grows at 2 percent a year. In that case, each generation could look forward to a material standard of living double that of its parents. If per capita GDP grows at 1 percent per annum, it takes 70 years to double. Over long periods, small differences in growth rates mount up to big differences in the material standard of living.

High unemployment rates are a major social problem. Jobs are difficult to find. The unemployed suffer a loss in their standard of living, personal distress, and sometimes a lifetime deterioration in their career opportunities. When unemployment exceeds 10 percent — and even well short of that — it becomes the number one social and political issue.

Table 1-1 shows that economic performance in Canada deteriorated sharply from the decade of the sixties to the seventies. Inflation and unemployment increased and growth fell. In the eighties the inflation rate came down, but this was accompanied by a large increase in unemployment.

As we develop macroeconomics in this book, we are looking for answers to the questions that recent macroeconomic performance raises. Why did the inflation rate rise from the fifties to the seventies and then fall? Will the growth rate return to levels of the sixties? Can the unemployment rate be brought down, and what economic policies, if any, can produce low inflation, low unemployment, and high growth?

The Business Cycle and the Output Gap

Inflation, growth, and unemployment are related through the *business cycle*. The business cycle is the more or less regular pattern of expansion (recovery) and contraction (recession) in economic activity around the path of trend growth. At a cyclical *peak*, economic activity is high relative to trend, and at a cyclical *trough*, the low point in

Table I-I *Macroeconomic Performance, 1952–1991*

Period	Inflation (% per annum)	Growth (% per annum)	Unemployment (%)
1952–1961	1.0	4.7	5.0
1962–1971	3.1	5.6	4.8
1972–1981	9.3	3.4	7.0
1982–1986	6.1	2.9	10.6
1987–1991	4.4	2.0	8.5

Source: Statistics Canada, 13-001, 11-210, 11-206.

economic activity is reached. **Inflation, growth, and unemployment** all have clear cyclical patterns, as we will show below. For the moment we concentrate on measuring the behaviour of output or real GDP relative to trend over the business cycle.

Figure 1-2 shows as the straight line the trend path of real GDP and the fluctuations around this trend over the business cycle. During an *expansion* (or *recovery*) the employment of factors of production increases, and that is a source of increased production. Output can rise above trend because people work overtime, and machinery is used for several shifts. Conversely, during a *recession* unemployment develops and less output is produced than can in fact be produced with the existing resources and technology. The wavy line in Figure 1-2 shows these cyclical departures of output from trend. Deviations of output from trend are referred to as the *output gap*. The output gap measures the gap between actual output and the output the economy could produce at full employment given the existing resources. Full-employment output is also called potential output.

$$\text{Output gap} = \text{potential output} - \text{actual output} \qquad (1)$$

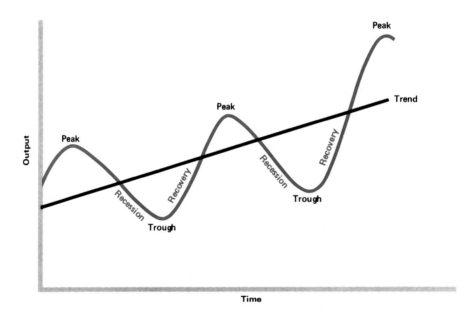

Figure 1-2   *The Business Cycle*

Output or GDP does not grow smoothly at its trend rate. Rather, it fluctuates irregularly around trend, showing business cycle patterns from trough, through recovery, to peak, and then from peak, through recession, back to the trough. Business cycle output movements are not regular in timing or in size.

The output gap allows us to measure the cyclical deviations of output from potential output. Figure 1-3 shows actual and potential output for Canada.

The figure shows the output gap growing during recessions, such as in 1982 and 1990. More resources become unemployed, and actual output falls below potential. Conversely, during an expansion, such as occurred in the early 1970s, the gap declines and ultimately even becomes negative. A negative gap means that there is overemployment, overtime work, and more than the usual rate of utilization of machinery.

Establishing the level of potential output is a difficult problem. In the 1960s it was believed that full employment corresponds to a measured rate of unemployment of 4 to 4.5 percent of the labour force. Changes in the composition of the labour force toward younger workers, and female workers who change jobs more frequently, raised the estimate of the full-employment rate of unemployment to a range above 6 percent

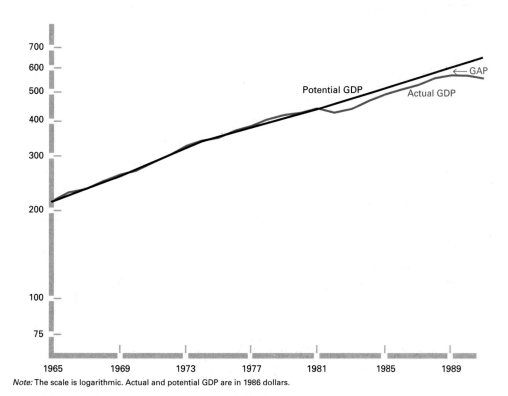

Note: The scale is logarithmic. Actual and potential GDP are in 1986 dollars.

Figure 1-3 *Actual and Potential Output, 1965–1991*

Potential output is the full-employment level of output. It grows like trend output in Figure 1-2. Actual GDP fluctuates around potential, falling below potential during recession and rising back toward the potential level during recoveries.

(*Source:* Adapted from Statistics Canada, 13-201)

in the 1970s. This is a benchmark for calculating what potential output or full-employ-ment output is, but it is only a benchmark, not a rigid, undebatable rule. Even so, the output gap provides an important indicator of how the economy is performing and in which direction policies should try to move the level of activity.

Seasonal Variation

Figure 1-4 shows the actual monthly unemployment rate from October 1990 to November 1991 together with the *seasonally adjusted rate*, as calculated by Statistics Canada. The seasonally adjusted series is obtained by correcting the raw data for the typical seasonal pattern observed in the past and is a measure of the underlying cyclical movement. For example, from March to June 1991 the unadjusted rate fell from 11.7 to 9.8 percent, but this was consistent with the decrease typically experienced in the spring of the year. Thus, when seasonal factors are removed, the seasonally adjusted rate remains the same at 10.5 percent.

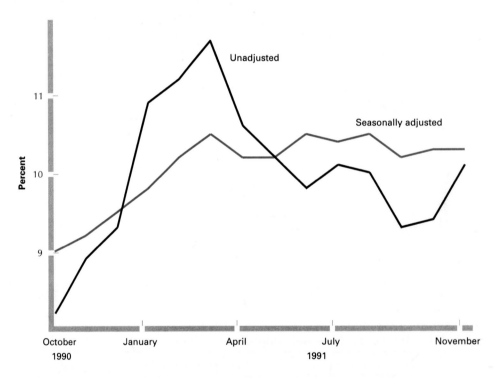

Figure 1-4   *Actual and Seasonally Adjusted Unemployment Rate*

(*Source:* Adapted from Statistics Canada, 11-010)

Balance of Payments

The *balance of payments* is the record of transactions of the economy with the rest of the world. It includes borrowing and lending and exchange of assets between countries as well as imports and exports of goods and services. Trade in goods is recorded in the merchandise trade balance. Figure 1-5 shows Canada's trade balance for 1971 through 1991. There have been wide swings, but exports exceeded imports in every year except 1975.

Exchange Rates

An exchange rate is the relative value of the currencies of two countries. For example, at the beginning of 1991 the Canadian dollar traded for about 86.5 U.S. cents, or equivalently one U.S. dollar cost $1.16 in Canadian funds. The British pound was worth $2.24 and the German mark was worth $0.77.

Under a *fixed exchange rate*, the external value of the country's currency is pegged within narrow bounds around a preannounced value. This system was followed by

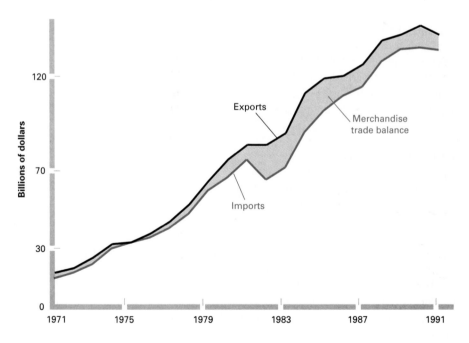

Figure 1-5   *Merchandise Trade Balance, 1971–1991*

(*Source:* Adapted from *Bank of Canada Review*)

Canada from 1962 to 1970 when the Canadian dollar was fixed at 92.5 U.S. cents. If a country allows the value of its currency to be determined by market forces, it is said to have a *flexible* or *floating* exchange rate. This practice was followed by Canada in the 1950s and from 1970 to the present. Since 1950, the value of our dollar has fluctuated between a high of about 105 U.S. cents and a low near 70 cents.

1-2 Relationships Among Macroeconomic Variables

The preliminary look at the data presented above, and our discussion of the business cycle, correctly suggest that we should expect to find simple relationships among the major macroeconomic variables: growth, unemployment, and inflation. There are indeed such relationships, as we now document.

Growth and Unemployment

We have already noted that changes in the employment of factors of production provide one of the sources of growth in real GDP. We would then expect high GDP growth to be accompanied by declining unemployment. That is indeed the case, as we observe from Figure 1-6. On the vertical axis, Figure 1-6 shows the growth rate of output for each year; on the horizontal axis it shows the change in the unemployment rate. For example, 1965, 1966, and 1973 were years of rapid expansion with growth rates of output in excess of 6.5 percent and declining unemployment. By contrast, in years such as 1970, 1975, 1982, and 1991, the economy was in recession with low growth and rising unemployment rates.

Inflation and the Cycle

Inflation is the rate of increase of prices. An expansion of aggregate demand tends to produce inflation, unless it occurs when the economy is at high levels of unemployment. Protracted periods of low aggregate demand tend to reduce the inflation rate. Figure 1-7 shows one measure of inflation for the Canadian economy for the period since 1960. The inflation measure in the figure is the rate of change of the *consumer price index*, the cost of a given basket of goods, representing the purchases of a typical urban consumer.[6]

The rate of inflation shown in Figure 1-7 fluctuates considerably. Just as we could tell much about the recent history of the economy from looking at Figure 1-3's picture

---

[6] By contrast, the measure of inflation obtained in Figure 1-1 by comparing nominal and real GDP is the rate of change of the GDP implicit price index. The consumer price index (CPI) is most frequently used to measure inflation, and the GDP implicit price index is the next most popular. Chapter 2 presents more details on different price indexes.

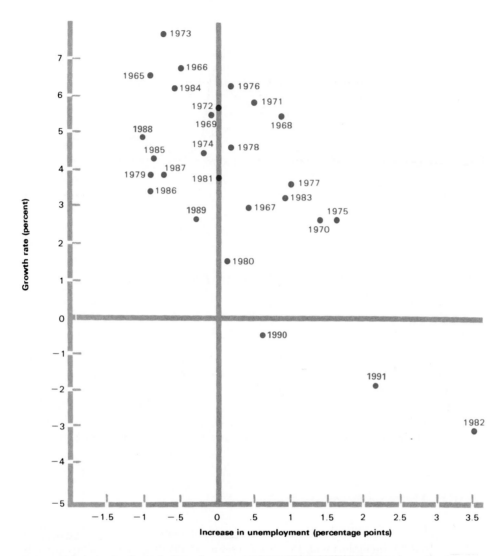

Figure 1-6 *Growth and the Change in the Unemployment Rate, 1965-1991*

High rates of growth cause the unemployment rate to fall, and low or negative rates of growth are accompanied by increases in the unemployment rate. The relationship shown by the scatter of the points in this figure is summarized by *Okun's law*, linking the growth rate to the change in the unemployment rate.

(*Source: Bank of Canada Review*)

of the course of actual and potential GDP, we can likewise see much of recent economic history in Figure 1-7. In particular, there is the long period of steady inflation from 1957 through 1964 when the inflation rate hovered around the 2 percent level.

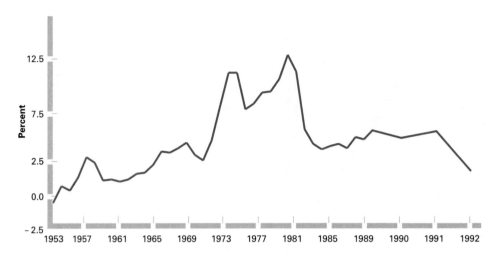

Figure 1-7   *The Rate of Inflation of Consumer Prices*

(*Source:* Department of Finance, *Reference Tables*)

Then there is a slow climb in the inflation rate in the late 1960s followed by the inflationary bursts of the 1970s. Finally there are the sharp declines in inflation in 1983 and 1992 under the impact of deep recessions.

Figure 1-7 shows the rate of increase of prices. We can also look at the level of prices. All the inflation of the 1970s and 1980s adds up to a large increase in the price level. From 1972 to 1986, the price level tripled so that a product that cost $1 in 1972 cost $3 in 1986.

Inflation–Unemployment Tradeoffs

The *Phillips curve* describes a relationship between inflation and unemployment: The higher the rate of unemployment, the lower the rate of inflation. The Phillips curve is an empirical relationship that relates the behaviour of wage and price inflation to the rate of unemployment. It was made famous in the 1950s in Great Britain and has since become a cornerstone of macroeconomic discussion. Figure 1-8 presents a typical downward-sloping Phillips curve showing that high rates of unemployment are accompanied by low rates of inflation and vice versa. The curve suggests that less unemployment can always be attained by incurring more inflation and that the inflation rate can always be reduced by incurring the costs of more unemployment. In other words, the curve suggests there is a tradeoff between inflation and unemployment.

Figure 1-9 shows that the Phillips curve broadly describes Canadian experience in the period 1956–1966. However, we can see also that subsequent economic events, particularly the combination of high inflation and high unemployment, are not consistent with the curve traced out in the earlier years.

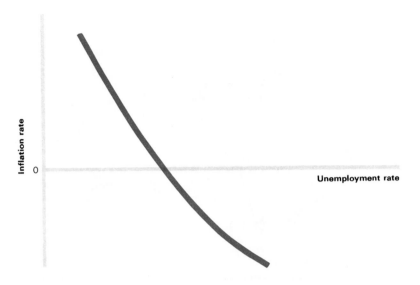

Figure 1-8 *A Phillips Curve*

The Phillips curve suggests a tradeoff between inflation and unemployment: Less unemployment can always be obtained by incurring more inflation — or inflation can be reduced by allowing more unemployment. Recent events, particularly the combination of high inflation *and* high unemployment in years such as 1981 and 1982, have led to skepticism about the Phillips curve. It nonetheless remains useful, as we shall show later.

Nonetheless, there remains a tradeoff between inflation and unemployment which is more sophisticated than a glance at Figure 1-8 would suggest, and which will enable us to make sense of Figure 1-9. In the short run of, say, two years, there is a relation between inflation and unemployment of the type shown in Figure 1-8. The *short-run Phillips curve*, however, does not remain stable. It shifts as expectations of inflation change. In the long run, there is no tradeoff worth speaking about between inflation and unemployment: The unemployment rate is basically independent of the long-run inflation rate.

The short- and long-run tradeoffs between inflation and unemployment are obviously a major concern of policy making and are the basic determinants of the potential success of stabilization policies.

1-3 Aggregate Demand and Supply

The key overall concepts in analyzing output, inflation and growth, and the role of policy are *aggregate demand* and *aggregate supply*. In this section we provide a brief

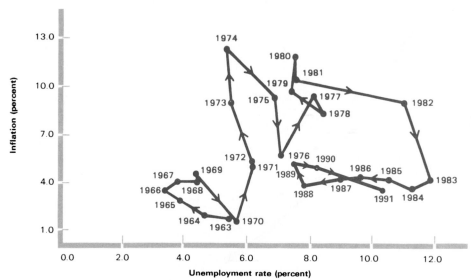

Figure 1-9 *Inflation and Unemployment*

Note: Inflation is the rate of change over the year of the Consumer Price Index.

(*Source:* Adapted from *Bank of Canada Review*)

preview of those concepts and of their interaction, with the aim of showing where we are heading.

The level of output and the price level are determined by the interaction of aggregate demand and aggregate supply. Under some conditions, employment depends only on total spending, or aggregate demand. At other times, supply limitations are an important part of the policy problem and require major attention. From the 1930s to the late 1960s, macroeconomics was very much oriented toward the influence of aggregate demand on employment. Subsequently there was a shift in emphasis to aggregate supply as a result of the slow growth and high inflation experienced by the industrialized countries in the 1970s.

Figure 1-10 shows aggregate demand and supply curves. The vertical axis P is the price level, and the horizontal axis Y is the level of real output or income. Although the curves look like the ordinary supply and demand curves of microeconomics, a full understanding of them will not be reached until Chapters 7 and 8.

Aggregate demand is the total demand for goods and services in the economy. It depends on the aggregate price level, as shown in Figure 1-10. It can be shifted through monetary and fiscal policy. The aggregate supply curve shows the price level associated with each level of output. It can, to some extent, be shifted by fiscal policy.

Aggregate supply and demand interact to determine the price level and output level. In Figure 1-10, P_0 is the equilibrium price level and Y_0 the equilibrium level of output. If the AD curve in the figure shifts up to the right, then the extent to which output and prices, respectively, are changed depends on the steepness of the aggregate supply

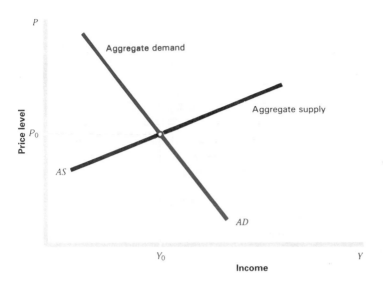

Figure 1-10 *Aggregate Demand and Supply*

The basic tools for analyzing income, inflation, and growth are the aggregate supply and demand curves. Shifts in their aggregate supply or demand will cause the level of output and income to change, thus affecting growth, and will also change the price level, thus affecting inflation. For the first 6 chapters, we concentrate on aggregate demand. Then in the later chapters we introduce the aggregate supply curve, thereby completing the analysis.

curve.[7] If the *AS* curve is very steep, then a given increase in aggregate demand mainly causes prices to rise and has very little effect on the level of output. If the *AS* curve is flat, a given change in aggregate demand will be translated mainly into an increase in output and very little into an increase in the price level.

All these observations are by way of a very important warning. In Chapters 3 through 6 we focus on aggregate demand as the determinant of the level of output. We shall assume that prices are given and constant, and that output is determined by the level of demand — that there are no supply limitations. We are thus talking about the very flat part of the aggregate supply curve, at levels of output below potential.

The suggestion that output rises to meet the level of demand without a rise in prices leads to a very activist conception of policy. Under these circumstances, without any obvious tradeoffs, policy makers would favour very expansionary policies to raise demand and thereby cause the economy to move to a high level of employment and output. There are circumstances where such a policy view is altogether correct. The early 1980s are a case in point. Figure 1-3 shows that in those years output was sub-

---

[7] Experiment with graphs like Figure 1-10 to be sure you understand this fact.

stantially below potential. There were unused resources, and the problem was a deficiency of demand. By contrast, in the 1970s the economy was operating at close to full employment and for most of the decade there was no significant output gap. An attempt to expand output further would run into supply limitations and force up prices rather than the production of goods. In these circumstances, a model that assumes that output is demand-determined and that increased demand raises output and not prices is simply inappropriate.

Should we think that the model with fixed prices and demand-determined output is very restricted and perhaps artificial? The answer is no. There are two reasons for this. First, the circumstances under which the model is appropriate — those of high unemployment — are neither unknown nor unimportant. Unemployment and downward price rigidity are continuing features of the Canadian economy. Second, even when we come to study the interactions of aggregate supply and demand in Chapter 7 and later, we need to know how given policy actions *shift* the aggregate demand curve at a given level of prices. Thus all the material of Chapters 3 through 6 on aggregate demand plays a vital part in the understanding of the effects of monetary and fiscal policy on the price level as well as output in circumstances where the aggregate supply curve is upward-sloping.

What, then, is the warning of this section? It is simply that the very activist spirit of macroeconomic policy under conditions of unemployment must not cause us to overlook the existence of supply limitations and price adjustment when the economy is near full employment.

1-4 Macroeconomic Policy

The aggregate demand and supply framework suggests that under specified conditions there is room for macroeconomic policy to expand demand or to contract it. Policy makers have at their command two broad classes of policies that potentially affect the economy. Monetary policy is controlled by the Bank of Canada. The instruments of monetary policy are changes in the stock of money and some controls over the banking system. *Fiscal policy* is under the control of Parliament and usually is initiated by the government of the day. The instruments of fiscal policy are tax rates and government spending.

One of the central facts of policy is that the effects of monetary and fiscal policy on the economy are not fully predictable in their timing or in the extent to which they affect demand or supply. These two uncertainties are at the heart of the problem of stabilization policy. *Stabilization policies* are monetary and fiscal policies designed to moderate the fluctuations of the economy — in particular, fluctuations in the rates of growth, inflation, and unemployment.

Figure 1-9, which shows large fluctuations of the rates of inflation and unemployment, suggests strongly that stabilization policy has not been fully successful in keeping them within narrow bounds. The failures of stabilization policy are due both to uncertainty about the way it works and to limits on the effects of policy on the economy.

However, questions of political economy are also involved in the way stabilization policy has been operated. The speed at which to proceed in trying to eliminate unemployment, at the risk of increasing inflation, is a matter of judgment about both the economy and the costs of mistakes. Those who regard the costs of unemployment as high relative to the costs of inflation will run greater risks of inflation to reduce unemployment as a relatively minor misfortune.

Political economy affects stabilization policy in more ways than through the costs which policy makers of different political persuasions attach to inflation and unemployment, and the risks they are willing to undertake in trying to improve the economic situation. There may be a *political business cycle* if election results are affected by economic conditions. When the economic situation is improving and the unemployment rate is falling, there is an environment favourable to the government. There is thus the incentive to policy makers running for reelection, or who wish to affect the election results, to use stabilization policy to produce booming economic conditions before elections.

Stabilization policy is also known as *countercyclical* policy, that is, policy to moderate the trade cycle or business cycle. The behaviour, and even the existence, of the trade cycle is substantially affected by the conduct of stabilization policy. Successful stabilization policy smooths out the cycle, while unsuccessful stabilization policy may worsen the fluctuations of the economy. Indeed, one of the tenets of monetarism is that the major fluctuations of the economy are a result of government actions rather than the inherent instability of the economy's private sector.

1-5 Schools of Thought

There have long been two main intellectual traditions in macroeconomics. One school of thought believes that markets work best if left to themselves; another believes that government intervention can significantly improve the operation of the economy. In the 1960s, the debate on these questions involved *monetarists*, led by Milton Friedman, on one side and *Keynesians*, including Franco Modigliani and James Tobin, on the other. In the 1970s, the debate on much the same issues brought to the fore a new group, the *new classical macroeconomists*.

Monetarists and Keynesians

We noted above that there is controversy over the existence of a tradeoff between inflation and unemployment. That controversy arose around 1967–1968 in the context of the debate in macroeconomics between monetarists and nonmonetarists. We have already identified some of the major participants in the debate, but macroeconomists cannot be neatly classified into one camp or the other. Instead, there is a spectrum of views. There are monetarists who make Friedman look like a Keynesian, and Keynesians who make Modigliani look like a monetarist. Not only that; there is no compelling unity in the views that are identified with monetarism, and the eclectic economist is likely to accept some monetarist arguments and reject others. Nor is the debate one in which there is no progress. For example, both theory and empirical evidence have been brought to bear on the issue of the inflation–unemployment tradeoff, and it is no longer central to the monetarist–Keynesian debate.

Another major point of contention is the relation between money and inflation. Monetarists tend to argue that the quantity of money is the prime determinant of the level of prices and economic activity, that excessive monetary growth is responsible for inflation, and that unstable monetary growth is responsible for economic fluctuations. Since they contend that variability in the growth rate of money accounts for the variability in real growth, they are naturally led to argue for a monetary policy of low and constant growth in the money supply, a constant money growth rule. Keynesians, by contrast, point out that there is no close relationship between monetary growth and inflation in the short run and that monetary growth is only one of the factors affecting aggregate demand. Keynesians advocate *activism* and maintain that policy makers are, or at least can be, sufficiently careful and skillful to be able to use monetary and fiscal policy to control the economy effectively.

The skill and care of the policy makers are important because monetarists raise the issue of whether aggregate demand policies might not worsen the performance of the economy. Monetarists point to episodes such as the overexpansionary policies followed by the Bank of Canada in 1971 and argue that policy makers cannot and do not exercise sufficient caution to justify using activist policy. On this issue the activists believe that we can learn from our past mistakes.

A further issue that divides the two camps concerns the proper role of government in the economy. This is not really an issue that can be analyzed using macroeconomic theory, but it is difficult to follow some of the debate without being aware that the issue exists.

Monetarists tend to be conservatives who favour small government and abhor budget deficits and a large public debt. They favour tax cuts during recessions and cuts in public spending during booms, with the net effect of winding up with a smaller share of government in the economy. Activists, by contrast, tend to favour an active role for government and are therefore quite willing to use increased government spending and transfers as tools of stabilization policy. Differences between monetarists and activists must, therefore, be seen in a much broader perspective than their particular disagreements about the exact role of money in the short run.

The New Classical School

The new classical macroeconomics, which developed in the 1970s, remained influential into the 1990s. This school of macroeconomics, which includes among its leaders Robert Lucas, Thomas Sargent, Robert Barro, Edward Prescott, and Neil Wallace, shares many policy views with Friedman. It sees the world as one in which individuals act rationally in their self-interest in markets that adjust rapidly to changing conditions. The government, it is claimed, is likely only to make things worse by intervening. That model is a challenge to traditional macroeconomics, which sees a role for useful government action in an economy that is viewed as reacting sluggishly, with slowly adjusting prices, poor information, and social customs impeding the rapid clearing of markets.

The central working assumptions of the new classical school are three:

- Economic agents *maximize*. Households and firms make *optimal* decisions. This means that they use all available information in reaching decisions and that those decisions are the best possible in the circumstances in which they find themselves.

- Decisions are *rational* and are made using all the relevant information. Expectations are rational when they are statistically the best predictions of the future that can be made using the available information. Indeed, the new classical school is sometimes described as the *rational expectations school*, even though rational expectations is only one part of the theoretical approach of the new classical economists.[8] An implication of rational expectations is that people eventually will come to understand whatever government policy is being used, and thus that it is not possible to fool most of the people all of the time or even most of the time.

- *Markets clear*. There is no reason why firms or workers would not adjust wages or prices if that would make them better off. Accordingly prices and wages adjust in order to equate supply and demand; in other words, markets clear. Market clearing is a powerful assumption, as we shall see presently.

One dramatic implication of these assumptions, which seem so reasonable individually, is that there is no possibility for *involuntary* unemployment. Any unemployed person who really wants a job will offer to cut his or her wage until the wage is low enough to attract an offer from some employer. Similarly, anyone with an excess supply of goods on the shelf will cut prices so as to sell them. Flexible adjustment of wages and prices leaves all individuals in a situation in which they can always work as much as they want at the going wage and firms can produce and sell as much as they want at the going price.

The essence of the rational expectations equilibrium approach is the assumption that markets are continuously in equilibrium. In particular, new classical macroeconomists regard as incomplete or unsatisfactory any theory that leaves open the possibility that private individuals could make themselves better off by trading among themselves. As Lucas put it, "there are no $50 bills lying on the sidewalk," meaning that if there were ways in which individuals could improve their material position, they would do so.

Adherents of the new classical school do not doubt that the great depression did take place, and they recognize that the measured unemployment rate occasionally reaches more than 10 percent. Their explanations for these observations, which are consistent with the view that people are at all times doing what is best for them, will be discussed in Chapter 8.

---

[8] Many economists who are not members of the new classical school also assume that expectations are rational.

The New Keynesians

The new classical group remains highly influential in today's macroeconomics, but a new generation of scholars, the new Keynesians, mostly trained in the Keynesian tradition but moving beyond it, emerged in the 1980s. The group includes among others George Akerlof, Ben Bernanke, Olivier Blanchard, Greg Mankiw, Larry Summers, and Janet Yellen. They do not believe that markets clear all the time but seek to understand and explain exactly why markets can fail.

The new Keynesians argue that markets sometimes do not clear even when individuals are looking out for their own interests. Both information problems and costs of changing prices lead to some price rigidities and, as a result, create a possibility for macroeconomic fluctuations in output and employment. For example, in the labour market, firms that cut wages not only reduce the cost of labour, but are also likely to wind up with a poorer-quality labour force. Thus they will be reluctant to cut wages. If it is costly for firms to change the prices they charge and the wages they pay, the changes will be infrequent; but if all firms adjust prices and wages infrequently, the economy-wide level of wages and prices may not be flexible enough to avoid occasional periods of even high unemployment.

Economic Controversy

This description of the two main strands in macroeconomics may suggest that the field is little more than the battleground between implacably opposed schools of thought. There is no denying that there are conflicts of opinion and even theory between different camps, and because macroeconomics is about the real world, the differences that exist are sure to be highlighted in political and media discussions of economic policy.

It is also the case, though, that there are significant areas of agreement and that the different groups, through discussion and research, continually evolve new areas of consensus and a sharper idea of where precisely the differences lie. For instance, there is now a consensus emerging on the importance of information problems for wage and price setting and economic fluctuations. In this book we do not emphasize the debate, preferring to discuss the substantive matters, but we do indicate alternative views of an issue whenever that is relevant.

1-6 Outline and Preview of the Text

We have sketched the major issues we shall discuss in the book. We now outline our approach to macroeconomics and the order in which the material will be presented. The key overall concepts, as already noted, are aggregate demand and aggregate supply. Aggregate demand is influenced by monetary policy, primarily via interest rates and expectations, and by fiscal policy. Aggregate supply is affected by fiscal policy and also by disturbances such as changes in the supply of oil.

The coverage by chapters starts in Chapter 2 with national income accounting, emphasizing data and relationships that are used repeatedly later in the book. Chapters 3 through 6 are concerned with aggregate demand. Chapters 7, 8, and 9 introduce aggregate supply and show how aggregate supply and demand interact to determine both real income and the price level. Chapters 10 through 15 present material that clarifies and deepens the understanding of aggregate demand and of the ways in which monetary and fiscal policies affect the economy. Chapters 16 through 21 perform a similar service for aggregate supply and the interactions of aggregate supply and demand.

1-7 Prerequisites and Recipes

In concluding this introductory chapter we offer a few words on how to use this book. First, we note that there is no mathematical prerequisite beyond high-school algebra. We do use equations when they appear helpful, but they are not an indispensable part of the exposition. Nevertheless, they can and should be mastered by any serious student of macroeconomics.

The technically harder chapters or sections can be skipped or dipped into. Either we present them as supplementary material, or we provide sufficient nontechnical coverage to help the reader get on without them later in the book. The reason we do present more advanced material or treatment is to afford a complete and up-to-date coverage of the main ideas and techniques in macroeconomics. Even though you may not be able to grasp every point of such sections on first reading — and should not even try to — these sections should certainly be read to get the main message and an intuitive appreciation of the issues that are raised.

The main problem you will encounter will come from trying to comprehend the interaction of several markets and many variables, as the direct and feedback effects in the economy constitute a quite formidable system. How can you be certain to progress efficiently and with some ease? The most important thing is to ask questions. Ask yourself, as you follow the argument: Why should this or that variable affect, say, aggregate demand? What would happen if it did not? What is the critical link?

There is no substitute whatsoever for active learning. Reading sticks at best for 7 weeks. Are there simple rules for active study? The best way to study is to use pencil and paper and work through the argument by drawing diagrams, experimenting with flowcharts, writing out the logic of an argument, working out the problems at the end of each chapter, and underlining key ideas. The study guide to this textbook contains both much useful material and problems that will help in your studies. Another valuable exercise is to take issue with an argument or position, or to spell out the defence for a particular view on policy questions. Beyond that, if you get stuck, read on for half a page. If you are still stuck, go back five pages.

You should also learn to use the index. Several concepts are discussed at different levels in different chapters. If you come across an unfamiliar term or concept, check the index to see whether and where it was defined and discussed earlier in the book.

As a final word, this chapter is designed for reference purposes. You should return to it whenever you want to check where a particular problem fits or to what a particular subject matter is relevant. The best way to see the forest is from Chapter 1.

Key Terms

Monetarists
Keynesians
Supply-side economics
GDP, nominal and real
Inflation
Growth
Unemployment
Business cycle
Potential output
Peak
Trough
Recovery or expansion
Recession

Output gap
Seasonal variation
Balance of payments
Exchange rate, fixed and flexible
Phillips curve
Aggregate demand and supply
Monetary policy
Fiscal policy
Stabilization policies
Activism
New classical macroeconomics
Rational expectations

CHAPTER 2 *National Income Accounting*

Macroeconomics is ultimately concerned with the determination of the economy's total output, the price level, the level of employment, interest rates, exchange rates, and other variables discussed in Chapter 1. A necessary step in understanding how these variables are determined is *national income accounting*.[1]

The national income accounts give us regular estimates of GDP, the basic measure of the performance of the economy in producing goods and services. The first part of the chapter discusses the measurement and meaning of GDP, and the second part describes the relationships between three key macroeconomic variables: output, income, and spending. These relationships are summarized in the circular flow diagram, Figure 2-1.

Figure 2-1 illustrates the interactions of firms and households in a simple economy without government or international trade. Output is produced by firms, and the value of this output is the gross domestic product. GDP includes the value of goods produced, such as automobiles and eggs, along with the value of services, such as haircuts and medical services.

Firms produce the output by employing factors of production, land, labour, and capital, and paying for their use. The payments made by the firms are the incomes earned in the economy. The flow of income is shown in the lower bottom loop of the

---

[1] For a detailed discussion of the concepts and definitions used in Canada's national income accounts, see Statistics Canada, *Guide to the Income and Expenditure Accounts* (Catalogue 13-603E, No. 1, 1990).

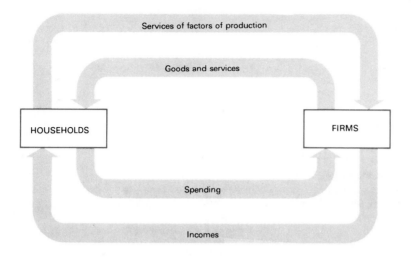

Figure 2-1 *The Circular Flow of Income and Spending*

Production is carried out by firms whose total output is equal to GDP. The output is produced using the services of factors of production, mostly labour, owned by households and paid for by the firms. The payments for the use of factors of production generate the households' income. Household spending out of those incomes, in turn, generates the demand for the goods produced by the firms. Spending on goods is, in the simple case shown here where there is no government and no foreign trade, equal to GDP, and also equal to the income of households. The diagram shows the key relation: Output is equal to income is equal to spending.

circular flow diagram. Thus the value of output is equal to the value of incomes received in the economy.

The goods produced by the firms are sold to households (and to other firms) or are added to inventories. Total *spending* on goods including accumulation of inventories is thus equal to the value of output. The flow of spending is also shown in Figure 2-1.

Looking at the relationships summarized in Figure 2-1, we see that *the value of total output is equal to total income earned in the economy, and is also equal to total spending.* That is the main lesson of this chapter, and the single most important point to remember about national income accounting. There is, however, considerable complexity in the actual national income accounts in relating GDP to incomes and spending. Those complexities arise in large part from the role of the government and from the presence of foreign trade, and we shall have to explain some of them.

We start in Section 2-1 by examining GDP and its measurement, and then move, in Sections 2-2 and 2-3, to the relationships among output, income, and spending summarized in the circular flow diagram. Section 2-4 returns to the distinction between real and nominal GDP, and Section 2-5 discusses various problems with the measurement of GDP.

Section 2-6 paves the way for the economic analysis of the determination of the level of output, which begins in Chapter 3, by systematically setting out the national income relationships studied in this chapter.

2-1 Calculating Gross Domestic Product

GDP is the value of all final goods and services produced in Canada within a given period. It includes the value of such goods produced as houses and whiskey, and the value of services, such as brokers' services and economists' lectures. The output of each of these is valued at its market price, and the values are added together to give GDP.

Table 2-1 shows the calculation of GDP in a simple economy that produces only bananas and oranges. Twenty bananas and sixty oranges are produced. The bananas are valued at $.30 each and oranges at $0.25 each. GDP is equal to $21, the total value of output.

GDP in Canada in 1991 was $674.4 billion. Dividing by population, equal to 27 million in 1991, we obtain GDP per person or per capita of just over $25 000. We can also calculate output per person employed. In 1991 there were on average 12.340 million people employed. Thus GDP per person employed or output per person employed was $54 652.

Final Goods and Value Added

GDP is the value of *final* goods and services produced. The insistence on final goods and services is simply to make sure that we do not double-count. For example, we would not want to include the full price of an automobile in GDP and then also include the value of the tires that were sold to the automobile producer as part of the GDP. The components of the car, sold to the manufacturers, are called *intermediate* goods, and their value is not included in GDP. Similarly, the wheat that goes into bread is an intermediate good, and we do not count the value of the wheat sold to the miller

Table 2-1   *Calculating GDP in a Simple Economy*

	Output	Price per Unit	Value of Output
Bananas	20	$0.30	$ 6.00
Oranges	60	$0.25	$15.00
Total GDP			$21.00

and the value of the flour sold to the baker, as well as the value of the bread, as part of GDP.

In practice, double counting is avoided by working with *value added*. At each stage of the manufacture of a good, only the value added to the good at that stage of manufacture is counted as part of GDP. The value of the wheat produced by the farmer is counted as part of GDP. Then the value of the flour sold by the miller minus

Box 2-1 Value Added and the Goods and Services Tax

The Goods and Services Tax (GST) introduced at the beginning of 1991 is a form of value added tax. It is imposed on the value added at each stage of production. Each firm pays tax on its purchases of intermediate goods and receives a rebate for the tax already paid by its supplier. Table 1 illustrates the process for the case of a loaf of bread assuming a GST of 7 percent.

Table 1 *Value Added at Each Stage and the GST*

Farmer		Baker	
Value of wheat	$0.10	Cost of flour	$0.407
Miller		Less GST rebate	−0.007
Cost of wheat	0.10	Plus GST	0.028
Plus GST	0.007	Value added	0.20
Value added	0.30	Total	$0.628
Total	$0.407	Final consumer	
		Cost of bread	$0.628
		Less GST rebate	−0.028
		Plus GST	0.042
		Final cost	$0.642

The miller pays $.107 for the wheat including the 7 percent GST. Since the flour is sold to another firm, this tax is rebated and the net cost to the baker is $.40 plus GST of $.028. This tax is in turn rebated so that the final cost to the consumer is $.60 before tax. GST is again added so that the consumer's total cost is $.642.

The reason for this system of taxes and rebates is that it ensures that the tax will be paid regardless of whether a good is sold to another firm for further processing or sold to a consumer. For example, the price of flour supplied by a miller is $.40 plus $.028 GST regardless of the identity of the purchaser. If it is bought by a consumer, then there will be no rebate and the total tax paid will be 7 percent of the value of the final good.

the cost of the wheat is the miller's value added. If we follow this process along, we will see that the sum of value added at each stage of processing will be equal to the final value of the bread sold.[2]

Current Output

GDP consists of the value of output currently produced. It thus excludes transactions in existing commodities such as old masters or existing houses. We count the construction of new houses as part of GDP, but we do not add trade in existing houses. We do, however, count the value of realtors' fees in the sale of existing houses as part of GDP. The realtor provides a current service in bringing buyer and seller together, and that is appropriately part of current output.

Market Prices

GDP values goods at market prices. The market price of many goods includes indirect taxes such as the Goods and Services Tax and provincial sales taxes, and thus the market price of goods is not the same as the price the seller of the good receives. The price net of indirect taxes is the factor cost, which is the amount received by the factors of production that manufactured the good. GDP is valued at market prices and not at factor cost. This point becomes important when we relate GDP to the incomes received by the factors of production.

Valuation at market prices is a principle that is not uniformly applied, because there are some components of GDP that are difficult to value. There is no very good way of valuing the services of housepersons, or a self-administered haircut, or, for that matter, the services of the police force or the government bureaucracy. Some of these activities, such as housepersons' services, are simply omitted from currently measured GDP. Government services are valued at cost, so that the wages of government employees are taken to represent their contribution to GDP. There is no unifying principle in the treatment of these awkward cases; a host of conventions is used.

Domestic Product Versus National Product

Statistics Canada provides an alternative measure of output called *gross national product,* or *GNP.* GNP is the value of current output *produced by domestically owned factors of production,* while GDP measures *production within Canada using both Canadian and nonresident factors of production.* Interest and dividends paid by Canadian companies to nonresidents are part of Canadian GDP but not GNP. Since income

---

[2] How about the flour that is directly purchased by households for baking in the home? It is counted as a contribution toward GDP since it represents a final sale.

paid to nonresidents typically exceeds income earned by Canadians from foreign sources, GDP exceeds GNP. As shown in Table 2-2, the difference in 1991 was $22.4 billion.[3]

Table 2-2 *Gross Domestic Product and National Product, 1991*

(billions of dollars)		
Gross domestic product (GDP)		$674.4
Plus: Investment income received from nonresidents	$ 9.7	
Less: Investment income paid to nonresidents	32.1	
Gross national product (GNP)		652.0
Less: Capital consumption allowances	79.2	
Net national product		$572.8

Source: Statistics Canada, 13-001.

Net national product (NNP), as distinct from GNP, deducts from GNP the depreciation of the existing capital stock over the course of the period. Production causes wear and tear; for example, machines wear out as they are used. If resources were not used to maintain or replace the existing capital, GNP could not be kept at the current level. Accordingly, we can use NNP as a measure of the rate of economic activity that could be maintained over long periods, given the existing capital stock and labour force.

Depreciation, or capital consumption allowances, is a measure of the part of GNP that has to be set aside to maintain or replace worn out capital. As shown in Table 2-2, in 1991 capital consumption allowances amounted to $79.2 billion.

2-2 GDP and Income

We now consider the relation between the value of output or GDP and the incomes that are generated in the production process. In this section we show that *income is equal to the value of output* because the receipts from the sale of output must accrue to someone as income. The purchaser of bread is indirectly paying the farmer, the miller, the baker, and the supermarket operator for the labour and capital used in production.

---

[3] Prior to 1986, Canada's national accounts were presented on a national product rather than a domestic product basis. For a brief discussion of the revisions, see Department of Finance, *Quarterly Economic Review*, September 1986.

GDP and Domestic Income

Our statement above, equating the value of output and income, is correct with three qualifications:

1. The first correction arises from depreciation. As already noted, part of GDP has to be set aside to maintain the productive capacity of the economy. Depreciation should not be counted as part of income, since it is a cost of production.

2. The second adjustment arises from indirect taxes — in particular, sales and excise taxes — that introduce a discrepancy between market price and prices received by producers. GDP is valued at market price, but the income accruing to producers does not include the sales and excise taxes that are part of the market price.

3. Finally, there is a statistical discrepancy that represents errors in measurement of the value of output and total incomes.

With these three deductions we can derive *net domestic* income from GDP as shown in Table 2-3. This gives us the value of output at *factor cost* rather than market prices.

Table 2-3 *Gross Domestic Product and Domestic Income, 1991*

(billions of dollars)		
Gross domestic product (GDP)		$674.4
Less: Indirect taxes less subsidies	$81.5	
Capital consumption allowances	79.2	
Statistical discrepancy	1.9	
Net domestic income at factor cost		$511.8

Source: Statistics Canada, 13-001.

Factor Shares in Net Domestic Income

Table 2-4 shows how domestic income is split among different types of income. The most striking fact is that wages and salaries make up nearly 75 percent of the total. The inventory valuation adjustment is made in order to exclude capital gains or losses on inventories that appear as part of profits measured under business accounting procedures but are not related to current production. Rental income includes not only rents received by landlords but also imputed income of owner-occupied housing.[4]

---

[4] GDP includes an estimate of the services homeowners receive by living in their homes. This is estimated by calculating the rent on an equivalent house. Thus the homeowner is treated as if she pays herself rent for living in her house.

↗ + deprec. + indirect taxes = GDP

Table 2-4   *Net Domestic Income and Its Distribution, 1991*

(billions of dollars)

Wages, salaries, and other labour income		383.1	74.9
Corporation profits	31.8		
Less inventory valuation adjustment	−2.1	33.9	6.6
Interest and miscellaneous investment income		54.9	10.7
Net income of unincorporated business			
Farm	3.3		
Nonfarm, including rent	36.6	39.9	7.8
Net domestic income		$511.8	100.0%

Source: Statistics Canada, 13-001.

Net Domestic Income and Personal Income

A considerably more important question from the macroeconomic viewpoint is how much the personal sector (households and unincorporated business) actually receives as income including transfers from government. This is measured by *personal income*. *Transfers* are those payments that do not arise out of current productive activity. Thus, welfare payments and unemployment benefits are examples of transfer payments. The level of personal income is important because it is a prime determinant of household consumption and saving behaviour.

To go from net domestic income to personal income, we have to remove the part of net domestic income that accrues to the corporate sector and add back dividends. As shown in Table 2-5, we also add transfers from government and interest on government debt. These interest payments are part of personal income, but are excluded from GDP because much of the debt has been incurred to finance past government expenditure which does not contribute to current production of goods and services.

Table 2-5   *Net Domestic Income and Personal Income, 1991*

(billions of dollars)

Net domestic income		$511.8
Less: Corporation profits	33.9	
Other adjustments	.8	
Plus: Dividends and interest on government debt	30.1	
Transfers from government	98.4	
Other transfers	1.8	
Personal income		607.4

Source: Statistics Canada, 13-001.

Although we have derived personal income in Table 2-5 by starting with net domestic income and making adjustments, we could also obtain it by adding up the components in a way similar to that shown in Table 2-4. In particular, personal income consists of wages and salaries, plus net income of unincorporated business, plus interest and dividends, plus transfers.

Personal Disposable Income and Its Allocation

Not all personal income is available for spending by households. The amount available for spending, *personal disposable income*, deducts from personal income the personal tax payments and other transfers to government made by the household sector. The other transfers include such items as licence fees and traffic tickets.

Personal disposable income is then available for personal consumption expenditure, other transfers, and saving. By far the largest outlay is for personal consumption, as shown in Table 2-6.

In summary, this section has shown the relation between GDP, which is a measure of productive activity in the economy, and income receipts that accrue to the household sector. The main steps in the long chain we have followed arise from taxes, transfers between sectors, depreciation, and corporation profits.

These intermediate steps remind us that there is an important difference between GDP as the value of output at market prices and the spendable receipts of the household sector. We could have a positive personal disposable income even if GDP were zero, provided there was someone to make the necessary transfer payments. Likewise, GDP could be large and disposable income small if the government sector took in a lot of taxes. The larger is the difference between taxes collected and transfers paid out, the smaller is disposable income relative to GDP.

Table 2-6 *Disposition of Personal Income, 1991*

(billions of dollars)		
Personal income		$607.4
Less: Income taxes	$101.5	
Other transfers to government	38.7	
Personal disposable income		467.2
Less: Personal consumption expenditure	410.4	
Other transfers	8.6	
Personal saving		$ 48.2

Source: Statistics Canada, 13-001.

Summary

We summarize here in a few identities (and in Figure 2-2) the relationships reviewed in Tables 2-3 through 2-6:

GDP − indirect taxes
   − capital consumption allowances — *deprec.*
   = net domestic income (Table 2-3)   (1)

Net domestic income
   = wages and salaries
   + corporation profits
   + interest
   + net income of unincorporated business (Table 2-4)   (2)

Net domestic income
   − corporation profits
   + dividends and interest on government debt
   + transfers
   = personal income (Table 2-5)   (3)

Personal income
   − personal taxes and other transfers to government
   = personal disposable income (Table 2-6)   (4)

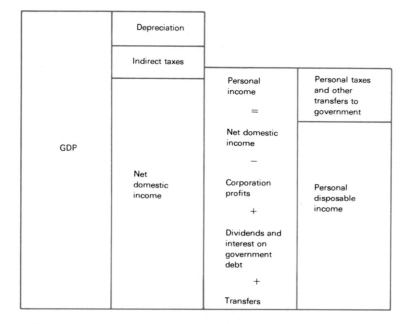

Figure 2-2 *The Relation Between GDP and Personal Disposable Income*

Personal disposable income
>   = personal consumption expenditure
>   + other transfers
>   + personal saving (Table 2-6)   (4a)

2-3 Expenditure Components of GDP

In the previous section, we started with GDP and asked how much of the value of goods and services produced is actually obtained by households. In this section we present a different perspective on GDP by asking who buys the output, rather than who receives the income. More technically, we look at the demand for output and speak of the components of the aggregate demand for goods and services.

   Total demand for domestic output is made up of four components: (1) consumption spending by households; (2) investment spending by businesses; (3) government (federal, provincial and municipal) expenditure on goods and services; and (4) net foreign demand. We shall now look more closely at each of these components.

Consumption

Table 2-7 presents a breakdown of GDP in 1991 by components of demand. The table illustrates that the chief component of demand is consumption spending by the personal sector. This includes anything from food to golf lessons but involves also, as we shall see in discussing investment, consumer spending on durable goods such as automobiles — spending which might be regarded as investment rather than consumption.

Table 2-7   *Gross Domestic Product, Expenditure-Based, 1991*

(billions of dollars)			
Personal consumption expenditure		$410.4	60.9%
Gross business investment		115.3	17.1
Government expenditure on goods and services		157.1	23.3
Net exports of goods and services			
Exports	$165.0		
Less imports	171.5	−6.5	−1.0
Statistical discrepancy		−1.9	−0.3
Gross domestic product		$674.4	100.0%

Source: Statistics Canada, 13-001.

not read

Government

Next in importance we have government expenditure on goods and services. Here we have such items as national defence expenditures, road paving by provincial and municipal governments, and salaries of government employees. It is important to note here that the government component of GDP is expenditure on *goods and services* and excludes transfer payments. For all levels of government in 1991 the transfer component of spending amounted to about $183 billion, so that total budgetary spending was about $340 billion.

Investment

Gross business investment is an item that requires some definitions. First, throughout this book, investment will mean additions to the physical stock of capital. As we use the term, investment does not include buying a bond or purchasing stock in General Motors. In practice, investment includes expenditure on machinery and equipment, nonresidential construction, residential construction, and additions to business inventories of goods. The classification of spending as consumption or investment remains to a significant extent a matter of convention. From the economic point of view, there is little difference between a household building up an inventory of peanut butter and a grocery store doing the same. Nevertheless, in the national income accounts, the individual's purchase is treated as a personal consumption expenditure, whereas the store's purchase is treated as investment in the form of inventory investment. Although these borderline cases clearly exist, we can retain as a simple rule of thumb that investment is associated with the business sector's adding to the physical stock of capital, including inventories.

Similar issues arise in the treatment of household-sector expenditures. For instance, how should we treat purchases of automobiles by households? Since automobiles usually last for several years, it would seem sensible to classify household purchases of automobiles as investment. We would then treat the use of automobiles as providing consumption services. (We could think of imputing a rental income to owner-occupied automobiles.) However, the convention is to treat all household expenditures as consumption spending. This is not quite so bad as it might seem, since the accounts do separate our households' purchases of durable goods such as cars and refrigerators from their other purchases. There is thus information in the accounts on those parts of household spending that, with considerable justification, could be categorized as investment spending. When consumer spending decisions are studied in detail, expenditures on consumer durables are usually treated separately.

The convention that is adopted with respect to the household sector's purchases of houses also deserves comment. The accounts treat the building of a house as investment by the business sector. When the house is sold to a private individual, the transaction is treated as the transfer of an asset, and not then an act of investment. Even if a house is custom-built by the owner, the accounts treat the builder who is employed by the owner as undertaking the act of investment in building the house. The investment is thus attributed to the business sector.

In passing, we note that in Table 2-7, investment is defined as "gross." It is gross in the sense that depreciation is not deducted. Net investment is gross investment minus depreciation.

Net Exports

The item "net exports" appears in Table 2-7 to show the effects of foreign trade on the demand for domestic output. Exports are added in because they represent spending by foreigners on our goods. Imports are subtracted out because they represent the part of domestic spending that is not for domestically produced goods. The practice in the national accounts is to include under consumption, investment and government expenditure all spending by Canadian residents both on domestically produced and foreign goods. To obtain total spending on domestically produced goods (GDP), imports are subtracted out.

The point can be illustrated with an example. Assume that instead of having spent $410 billion, the personal sector had spent $2 billion more. What would GDP have been? If we assume that government and investment spending had been the same as in Table 2-7, we might be tempted to say that GDP would have been $2 billion higher. That is correct if all the additional spending had fallen on our goods. The other extreme, however, is the case where all the additional spending falls on imports. In that event, consumption would be up $2 billion and net exports would be down $2 billion, with no net effect on GDP.

Final Demand

Sometimes it is important to distinguish total spending by domestic residents from the level of output produced. The two can differ because spending can exceed output when imports exceed exports. Domestic demand is thus defined by:

$$\text{Domestic demand} = \text{GDP} + \text{imports} - \text{exports}$$

It is also useful to have a concept of spending that nets out changes in inventories. This is *final domestic demand* and is defined as:

$$\text{Final domestic demand} = \text{domestic demand} - \text{inventory change}$$

In 1991, final domestic demand was $681.5 billion as compared with a GDP of $674.4 billion. The difference reflects the positive value of net exports and negative inventory accumulation.

2-4 Real and Nominal GDP

Nominal GDP measures the value of output in a given period in the prices of that period or, as it is sometimes put, in *current dollars*. Thus 1990 nominal GDP measures the value of the goods produced in 1990 at the market prices that prevailed in 1990, and 1986 GDP measures the value of goods produced in 1986 at the market prices that prevailed in 1986. Nominal GDP changes from year to year for two reasons. The first is that the physical output of goods changes. The second is that market prices change. As an extreme and unrealistic example, one could imagine the economy producing exactly the same output in two years, between which all prices have doubled. Nominal GDP in the second year would be double nominal GDP in the first year, even though the physical output of the economy has not changed at all.

Real GDP measures changes in *physical* output in the economy between different time periods by valuing all goods produced in the two periods *at the same prices*, or in *constant dollars*. Real GDP is now measured in the national income accounts in the prices of 1986. That means that, in calculating real GDP, today's physical output is multiplied by the prices that prevailed in 1986 to obtain a measure of what today's output would have been worth had it been sold at the prices of 1986.

We return to the simple example of Table 2-1 to illustrate the calculation of real GDP. The hypothetical outputs and prices of bananas and oranges in 1986 and 1990 are shown in the first two columns of Table 2-8. Nominal GDP in 1986 was $9, and nominal GDP in 1990 was $21, or an increase in nominal GDP of 133 percent. However, much of the increase in nominal GDP is purely a result of the increase in prices between the two years and does not reflect an increase in physical output. When we calculate real GDP in 1990 by valuing 1990 output in the prices of 1986, we find real GDP equal to $11, which is an increase of 22 percent rather than 133 percent. The 22 percent increase is a better measure of the increase in physical output of the economy than the 133 percent increase.

We see from the table that the output of bananas rose by 33 percent, while the output of oranges increased by 20 percent from 1986 to 1990. We should thus expect

Table 2-8 *Real and Nominal GDP: An Illustration*

1986 Nominal GDP		1990 Nominal GDP		1990 Real GDP[a]	
15 bananas		20 bananas		20 bananas	
at $0.10	$1.50	at $0.30	$ 6.00	at $0.10	$ 2.00
50 oranges		60 oranges		60 oranges	
at $0.15	$7.50	at $0.25	$15.00	at $0.15	$ 9.00
	$9.00		$21.00		$11.00

[a]Measured in 1986 prices.

our measure of the increase in real output to be somewhere between 20 and 33 percent, as it is.[5]

Figure 2-3 shows the behaviour of real and nominal GDP over the past few years. It is particularly noteworthy that nominal GDP rose continuously during the period even while real GDP fell, as it did, for example, during 1982 and 1991. It would clearly be a mistake to regard the increases in nominal GDP as indicating that the performance of the economy was improving during 1982 or 1991 despite the fall in physical output. Real GDP is the better measure of the performance of the economy in pro-

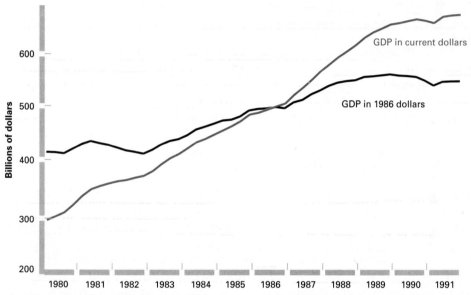

* Quarterly, seasonally adjusted at annual rates.

Figure 2-3 *Real and Nominal GDP**

(*Source:* Adapted from Statistics Canada, 13-001)

---

[5] The increase in real GDP that is calculated depends on the prices that are used in the calculation. If you have a calculator, you might want to compare the increase in real GDP between 1986 and 1990 if the prices of 1990 are used to make the comparison. (Using 1990 prices, real GDP rises 23.5 percent from 1986 to 1990, compared with 22.2 percent using 1986 prices.) The ambiguities that arise in comparisons using different prices to calculate real GDP are an inevitable result of the attempt to use a single number to capture the increase in output of both bananas and oranges when those two components did not increase in the same proportion. However, the ambiguity is not a major concern when there is inflation at any substantial rate, and that is precisely when we most want to use real (rather than nominal) GDP to study the performance of the economy.

ducing goods and services, and it is the measure we use in comparing output in different years.

Price Indexes

The calculation of real GDP gives us a useful measure of inflation known as the *GDP implicit price index*. Returning to the hypothetical example of Table 2-8, we can get a measure of inflation between 1986 and 1990 by comparing the value of 1990 GDP in 1990 prices and 1986 prices. The ratio of nominal to real GDP in 1990 is 1.91 ($= 21/11$). In other words, output is 91 percent higher in 1990 when it is valued using the higher prices of 1990 than when it is valued in the lower prices of 1986. We ascribe the 91 percent increase to price changes, or inflation, over the period 1986–1990.

The GDP implicit price index is the ratio of nominal GDP in a given year to real GDP, and it is a measure of inflation from the period from which the base prices for calculating real GDP are taken, to the current period. Since the GDP implicit price index is based on a calculation involving all the goods produced in the economy, it is a very widely based price index that is frequently used to measure inflation.

The Consumer Price Index

The *consumer price index* (*CPI*) measures the cost of buying a fixed bundle of goods, representative of the purchases of consumers. The GDP implicit price index differs in three main ways from the CPI. First, it measures the prices of a much wider group of goods than the CPI, which is based on the market basket of goods purchased by an average consumer. Second, the CPI measures the cost of a given basket of goods, which is the same from year to year. The basket of goods included in the GDP implicit price index, however, differs from year to year, depending on what is produced in the economy in each year. The goods valued in the implicit price index in a given year are the goods that are produced in the economy in that year. When wheat production is high, wheat receives a relatively large weight in the computation of the GDP implicit price index. By contrast, the CPI measures the cost of a fixed bundle of goods that does not vary over time.[6] Third, the CPI directly includes prices of imports, whereas the implicit price index includes only prices of goods produced in Canada. The movements of the two main indexes used to compute inflation, the GDP implicit price index and the CPI, accordingly differ from time to time.

---

[6]   Price indexes are, however, occasionally revised by changing the weights given to individual goods so as to reflect current expenditure patterns.

Box 2-2   Price Index Formulas

The CPI is a price index which compares the current and base-year cost of a basket of goods of *fixed* composition. If we denote the base-year quantities of the various goods by q_0^i and their base-year prices by p_0^i, the cost of the basket in the base year is $\Sigma p_0^i q_0^i$, where the summation (Σ) is over all the goods in the basket. The cost of a basket of the same quantities but at today's prices is $\Sigma p_t^i q_0^i$, where p_t^i is today's price. The CPI is the ratio of today's cost to the base-year cost, or

$$\text{Consumer price index} = \frac{\Sigma p_t^i q_0^i}{\Sigma p_0^i q_0^i} \times 100$$

This is a so-called *Laspeyres*, or *base-weighted*, price index.

The GDP implicit price index, by contrast, uses the weights of the current period to calculate the price index. Let q_t^i be the quantities of the different goods produced in the current year.

$$\text{GDP implicit price index} = \frac{\text{GDP measured in current prices}}{\text{GDP measured in base-year prices}} \times 100$$

$$= \frac{\Sigma p_t^i q_t^i}{\Sigma p_0^i q_t^i} \times 100$$

This is known as a *Paasche*, or *current-weighted*, price index.

Comparing the two formulas, we see that they differ only in that q_0^i, or the base-year quantities, appears in both numerator and denominator of the CPI formula, whereas q_t^i appears in the formula for the implicit price index. In practice, the CPI and GDP implicit price index differ also because they involve different collections of goods.

Industrial Product Price Index

A third important price index is the industrial product price index. Like the CPI, this is a measure of the cost of a given basket of goods. It differs from the CPI partly in its coverage, which includes, for example, semifinished goods. It differs, too, in that it is designed to measure prices at an early stage of the distribution system. Whereas the CPI measures prices where households actually do their spending, that is at the retail level, the industry selling price index is constructed from prices at the level of the first significant commercial transaction. This difference is important because it makes the latter an index that responds rapidly to changing market conditions and signals changes in prices that are likely to show up at a later time in the CPI.

Table 2-9 *Three Price Indexes (1986 = 100)*

	Consumer Price Index	Industrial Product Price Index	GDP Implicit Price Index
1976	47.5	49.6	53.2
1981	75.5	83.6	80.9
1986	100.0	100.0	100.0
1991	126.2	108.6	121.8
Percent increase, 1976–1991	166%	119%	129%

Source: Statistics Canada, 11-210.

Table 2-9 shows the CPI, the industrial product price index, and the GDP implicit price index for the last 15 years. We note from the table that all three indexes have been increasing throughout the period. This is a reflection of the fact that the average price of goods has been rising, whatever basket we look at. We note, too, that the cumulative increase from 1976 to 1991 differs across indexes. This difference occurs because the indexes represent the prices of different commodity baskets.[7]

2-5 Problems of GDP Measurement

GDP data are, in practice, used not only as a measure of how much is being produced, but also as a measure of the welfare of the residents of a country. Economists and politicians talk as if an increase in real GDP means that people are better off, but GDP data are far from perfect measures of either economic output or welfare.

Most of the difficulties of measuring GDP arise because some outputs do not go through the market. Examples are volunteer activities, housework, and do-it-yourself home improvements. In the case of the government sector, we already noted that production is valued at cost. That is because much of government output is not sold in the market, nor is anything comparable available that would make it possible to estimate the value of government output. How would we measure the value of output of safety from criminals that police expenditures are supposed to produce?

There is also a conceptual problem with much of government output. We include in GDP the value of wages paid for the police and the defence forces. Suppose there was an improvement in public safety and police were taken out of the police force and put to work making candy — at their previous wage. GDP would not change, but the economy's output of useful goods and services certainly would seem to rise.

---

[7] The mechanics of price indexes are briefly described in Box 2-2. Detailed discussion of the consumer price index can be found in Statistics Canada, 62-010.

The problem in this case is that we generally do not deduct negative outputs, or bads, from GDP. We do not attempt to value the decline in public safety that requires increased police forces. Nor do we deduct from GDP the value of pollution produced by factories and cars. These are bads, but they do not show up in the GDP accounts. If we were somehow able to value the amount of public safety provided by society, then a shift of labour out of the police force resulting from an increase in public safety would indeed show up as an increase in GDP. Similarly, improvements in the quality of the environment would show up as having raised output.

2-6 Some Important Identities

In this section we formalize the discussion of the preceding sections by writing down a set of relationships which we use extensively in Chapter 3. We introduce here some notation and conventions that we follow throughout the book. (see p.36)

For analytical work in the following chapters, we simplify our analysis by omitting the distinction between GDP and net domestic income. For the most part we disregard depreciation and thus the difference between gross and net investment. We refer simply to investment spending. We also disregard indirect taxes and nongovernment transfer payments. With these conventions in mind, *we refer to net domestic income and GDP interchangeably as income or output*. These simplifications have no serious consequence and are made only for expositional convenience. Finally, and only for a brief while, we omit both the government and foreign sectors. Thus the assumptions we are making conform to those of the circular flow diagram, Figure 2-1.

A Simple Economy

We denote the value of output in our simple economy, which has neither a government nor foreign trade, by Y. Consumption is denoted by C and investment spending by I. The first key identity we want to establish is that between output produced and spending. Output produced is Y, which can be written in terms of the components of demand as the sum of consumption and investment spending. Accordingly, we can write the identity of output sold and output produced as[8]

$$Y \equiv C + I \tag{5}$$

Now, is Equation (5) really an identity? Is it inevitably true that all output produced is either consumed or invested? After all, do not firms sometimes make goods that

---

[8] Throughout the book we distinguish identities from equations. Identities are statements that are always true because they are directly implied by definitions of variables or accounting relationships. They do not reflect any causality based on economic behaviour but are extremely useful in organizing our thinking. Identities, or definitions, are shown with the sign $\equiv$, and equations with the usual equality sign $=$.

they are unable to sell? The answer to each of the questions is yes. Firms do sometimes make output that they cannot sell, and that accumulates on their shelves. However, *we count the accumulation of inventories as part of investment* (as if the firms sold the goods to themselves to add to their inventories), and therefore all output is either consumed or invested. Note that we are talking here about *actual* investment, which includes investment in inventories that firms might be very unhappy to make. Because of the way investment is defined, output produced is identically equal to output sold.

Identity (5) formalizes the basis of Table 2-7 (we are still assuming away the government and external sectors). The next step is to draw up a corresponding identity for Table 2-6 and Identity (4), which examined the disposition of personal income. For that purpose, it is convenient to ignore the existence of corporations and consolidate or add together the entire private sector. Using this convention, we know that private sector income is Y, since the private sector receives as income the value of goods and services produced. Why? Ask yourself who else would get it. There is no government or external sector yet. Now the private sector receives, as disposable personal income, the whole of income Y. How will that income be allocated? Part will be spent on consumption, and part will be saved. Thus we can write

$$Y \equiv S + C \tag{6}$$

where S denotes private-sector saving. Identity (6) tells us that the whole of income is allocated to either consumption or saving.

Next, Identities (5) and (6) can be combined to read:

$$C + I \equiv Y \equiv C + S \tag{7}$$

The left-hand side of Equation (7) shows the components of demand, and the right-hand side shows the allocation of income. The identity emphasizes that output produced is equal to output sold. The value of output produced is equal to income received, and income received, in turn, is spent on goods or saved.

The identity in Equation (7) can be slightly reformulated to look at the relation between saving and investment. Subtracting consumption from each part of Equation (7), we have

$$I \equiv Y - C \equiv S \tag{8}$$

Identity (8) is an important result. It shows first that in this simple economy, saving is identically equal to income less consumption. This result is not new, since we have already seen it in Equation (6). The new part concerns the identity of the left and right sides: *Investment is identically equal to saving*.

One can think of what lies behind this relationship in a variety of ways. In a very simple economy, the only way the individual can save is by undertaking an act of physical investment — by storing grain or building an irrigation channel. In a slightly more sophisticated economy, one could think of investors financing their investing by borrowing from individuals who save.

However, it is important to recognize that Equation (8) expresses the identity between investment and saving, and that some of the investment might well be undesired inventory investment, occurring as a result of mistakes by producers who expected to sell more than they actually did. The identity is really only a reflection of our definitions — output less consumption is investment, output is income, and income less consumption is saving. Even so, we shall find that Identity (8) plays a key role in Chapter 3.

Reintroducing the Government and Foreign Trade

We can now reintroduce the government sector and the external sector. First, for the government we denote expenditures on goods and services by G and all taxes by TA. Transfers to the private sector (including interest) are denoted by TR. Net exports (exports minus imports) are denoted by NX.

We return to the identity between output produced and sold, taking account now of the additional components of demand G and NX. Accordingly, we restate the content of Table 2-7 by writing

$$Y \equiv C + I + G + NX \tag{9}$$

Once more we emphasize that in Equation (9) we use actual investment in the identity and thus do not rule out the possibility that firms might not all be content with the level of investment. Still, as an accounting identity, Equation (9) must hold.

Next we turn to the derivation of the very important relation between output and disposable income. Now we have to recognize that part of income is spent on taxes, and that the private sector receives net transfers TR in addition to factor income. Disposable income is thus equal to income plus transfers less taxes:

$$YD \equiv Y + TR - TA \tag{10}$$

We have written YD to denote disposable income. Disposable income, in turn, is allocated to consumption and saving, so that we can write

$$YD \equiv C + S \tag{11}$$

Combining Identities (10) and (11) allows us to write consumption as the difference between income, plus transfers minus taxes, and saving:

$$C + S \equiv YD \equiv Y + TR - TA \tag{12}$$

or

$$C \equiv YD - S \equiv Y + TR - TA - S \tag{12a}$$

Identity (12a) states that consumption is disposable income less savings, or alternatively, that consumption is equal to income plus transfers less taxes and saving. Now we use the right-hand side of Equation (12a) to substitute for C in Identity (9). With some rearrangement we obtain

$$S - I \equiv (G + TR - TA) + NX \qquad (13)$$

Saving, Investment, the Government Budget, and Trade

Identity (13) cannot be overemphasized. Its importance arises from the fact that the first set of terms on the right-hand side $(G + TR - TA)$ is the government budget deficit. $(G + TR)$ is equal to government expenditures on goods and services (G) plus government transfer payments (TR), which is total government spending. TA is the amount of taxes received by the government.[9] The difference $(G + TR - TA)$ is the excess of government spending over its receipts, or its budget deficit. The second term on the right-hand side is the excess of exports over imports, or the trade surplus.

Thus Identity (13) states that the excess of savings over investment $(S - I)$ of the private sector is equal to the government budget deficit plus the trade surplus. The identity correctly suggests that there are important relations among the accounts of the private sector, $S - I$, the government budget, $G + TR - TA$, and the external sector. For instance, if, for the private sector, savings is equal to investment, then the government's budget deficit (surplus) is reflected in an equal external deficit (surplus).

Table 2-10 shows the significance of Equation (13). To fix ideas, suppose that private sector saving S is equal to \$30 billion. In the first two rows we assume that exports are equal to imports, so that the trade surplus is zero. In row 1, we assume the government budget is balanced. Investment accordingly has to equal \$30 billion. In the next row we assume the government budget deficit is \$10 billion. Given the level of saving of \$30 billion and a zero trade balance, it has to be true that investment is now lower by \$10 billion. Rows 3 and 4 show how these relationships are affected when there is a trade surplus.

To interpret these relationships, realize that any sector that spends more than it receives in income has to borrow to pay for the excess spending. The private sector has three ways of disposing of its saving. It can make loans to the government, which thereby pays for the excess of its spending over the income it receives from taxes, or it can lend to foreigners, who are buying more from us than we are buying from them. They therefore are earning less from us than they need to pay for the goods they buy from us, and we have to lend to cover the difference. Finally, the private sector can lend to business firms which use the funds for investment.

In Table 2-10 we take saving as fixed at \$30 billion. When the budget and trade are balanced, the private sector has to lend the \$30 billion to firms, which invest that

---

[9] "Government" throughout this chapter means the federal government plus provincial and municipal governments. A breakdown by level of government can be found in Statistics Canada publications.

Table 2-10 *The Budget Deficit, Trade, Saving, and Investment*

S	I	BD (Budget Deficit)	NX (Trade Surplus)
30	30	0	0
30	20	10	0
30	25	0	5
30	15	10	5

amount. Now suppose that the government runs a budget deficit of $10 billion. Then the private sector has to lend $10 billion to government to cover its excess of spending over revenue. Only $20 billion is left to lend to firms for investment. Similarly, if we export more than we import, foreigners need to borrow from us to pay for the excess of what they buy from us over what they sell to us. In rows 3 and 4 we are using $5 billion of our saving to lend to foreigners. Then only $25 billion is left to lend either to firms or to the government.

2-7 Summary

1. As the circular flow diagram shows, output is equal to income and spending.

2. Gross domestic product (GDP) is the value at market prices of all final goods and services produced within a country.

3. Gross national product is the value of output produced by domestically owned factors of production. GDP differs from gross national product in that it includes net payments to nonresident factors of production.

4. Net domestic income is equal to GDP minus depreciation and indirect taxes and represents the value of output at factor cost.

5. Gross domestic product is conveniently divided into consumption, investment, government expenditure on goods and services, and net exports. The division between consumption and investment in the national income accounts is somewhat arbitrary at the edges.

6. Real GDP is the value of the economy's output measured in the prices of some base year. Real GDP comparisons, based on the same set of prices for valuing output, provide a better measure of the change in the economy's physical output than nominal GDP comparisons, which also reflect inflation.

7. The GDP implicit price index is the ratio of nominal to real GDP. It reflects the general rise in prices from the base date by which real GDP is valued. Other

frequently used price indexes are the consumer and industrial product price indexes.

8.   The excess of the private sector's saving over investment is equal to the sum of the budget deficit and the foreign trade surplus.

9.   For the remainder of the book we use a simplified model for expositional convenience. We assume away depreciation, indirect taxes, business transfer payments, and the difference between households and corporations. For this simplified model, Figure 2-4 and Equation (14) review the basic macroeconomic identity.

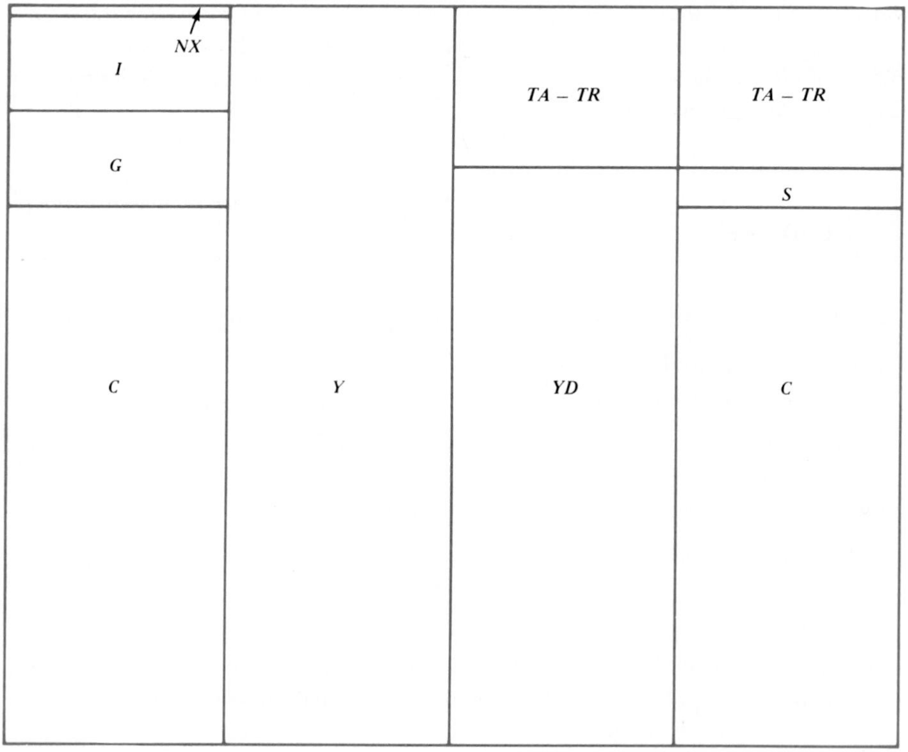

Figure 2-4   *The Basic Macroeconomic Identity*

$$C + G + I + NX \equiv Y \equiv YD + (TA - TR) \equiv C + S + (TA - TR)$$

The left-hand side is the demand for output by components which is identically equal to output supplied. Output supplied is equal to income. Disposable income is equal to income plus transfers less taxes. Disposable income is allocated to saving and consumption.

Key Terms

Gross domestic product (GDP)
Final goods
Value added
Market prices
Factor cost
Gross national product
Depreciation
Net domestic income
Factor shares
Personal income
Transfers

Personal disposable income
Consumption
Government expenditure on goods
   and services
Investment
Net exports
Consumer durables
Real GDP
GDP implicit price index
Consumer price index
Government budget deficit

Problems

1. Show from national income accounting that:
   (a) An increase in taxes (while transfers remain constant) must imply a change in the trade balance, government expenditures, or the saving–investment balance.
   (b) An increase in disposable income must imply an increase in consumption or an increase in saving.
   (c) An increase in both consumption and saving must imply an increase in disposable income.

2. The following is information from the national income accounts for a hypothetical country:

GDP	240
Gross investment	40
Net investment	15
Consumption	150
Government expenditure on goods and services	48
Net domestic income	190
Wages and salaries	146
Net income of unincorporated business	16
Dividends	5
Interest income	13
Government budget surplus	−15
Interest on government debt	7
Government transfer payments	25

   What are:
   (a) Net exports?
   (b) Indirect taxes?

      (c)   Corporate profits?
      (d)   Personal income?
      (e)   Personal disposable income?
      (f)   Personal saving?

3.   What would happen to GDP if the government hired unemployed workers, who had been receiving amount $TR in unemployment benefits, as government employees to do nothing, and now paid them $TR? Explain.

4.   What is the difference in the national income accounts between:
      (a)   A firm's buying an auto for an executive and the firm's paying the executive additional income to buy himself or herself a car?
      (b)   Your hiring your spouse (who takes care of the house) rather than just having him or her do the work without pay?
      (c)   Your deciding to buy a Canadian-made car rather than a German car?

5.   Explain the following terms:
      (a)   Value added
      (b)   Factor cost
      (c)   Inventory investment
      (d)   GDP implicit price index

6.   This question deals with price index numbers. Consider a simple economy where only three items are in the CPI: food, housing, and entertainment (fun). Assume that in the base period, say 1986, the household consumed the following quantities at the then prevailing prices:

	Quantity	**Price per Unit**	**Expenditure**
Food	5	$14	$ 70
Housing	3	10	30
Fun	4	5	20
Total			$120

      (a)   Define the consumer price index.
      (b)   Assume that the basket of goods that defines the CPI is as given in the table. Calculate the CPI for 1990 if the prices prevailing in 1990 are: food, $30 per unit; housing, $20 per unit; and fun, $6 per unit.
      (c)   Show that the change in the CPI relative to the base year is a weighted average of the individual price changes, where the weights are given by the base-year expenditure shares of the various goods.

7.   Refer to Table 2-4 to answer the following.
      (a)   How would a shift by corporations from equity to debt finance affect the distribution of national income?
      (b)   How would the incorporation of a business affect the table?

    (c) What difference would it make if some existing houses were owned by corporations instead of individuals?

8. Assume that GDP is $120, personal disposable income is $100, and the government budget deficit is $7. Consumption is $85 and the trade surplus is $2.
    (a) How large is saving *S*?
    (b) What is the size of investment *I*?
    (c) How large is government spending?

°9. Calculate both Laspeyres and Paasche price indexes for the information in Table 2-8.

° An asterisk denotes a more difficult problem.

CHAPTER 3   *Income and Spending*

(see p.45)

In Chapter 2 we studied the measurement of national income and output. With these fundamental concepts, we are now able to begin our study of the factors that determine the level of national income. Figure 3-1 shows the behaviour of real GDP over the period 1979–1991. Ultimately, we want to know why real GDP sometimes falls (and the rate of unemployment rises), as it did in 1982, and why at other times income rises very rapidly (and unemployment falls), as it did in 1987–1988. This chapter offers a first theory of these fluctuations in real GDP. The cornerstone of this model is the interaction between income and spending: Spending determines output and income, but output and income determine spending.[1]

Before developing this *Keynesian* model of income determination we make some brief comments that place this simple first model in the context of the more comprehensive model of income and price determination that will be developed in later chapters.

A student of microeconomics would have a ready answer to the question: What happens if there is an increase in the demand for a particular good, say shoes? We are likely to get one of three answers:

- Firms will produce more.

- Firms will raise the price.

- Firms will sell from the stock of inventories they hold.

In most cases the adjustment to a demand disturbance will involve all three reactions. The importance of each reaction will depend on a host of factors: Is the increase in

---

[1] Because output is equal to income received in the economy, economists tend to use the terms "income" and "output" interchangeably when discussing the level of economic activity.

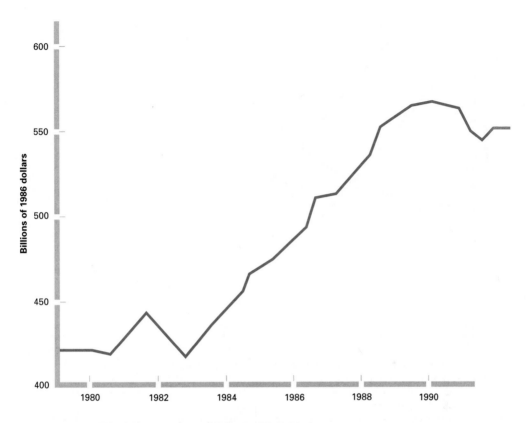

Figure 3-1   *Fluctuations in Real GDP, 1979–1991*

(*Source:* Statistics Canada, 13-001)

demand permanent or only transitory? How easy is it to change the level of production? Are inventories high or low?

We can ask the same question in macroeconomics. What happens if there is an increase in *aggregate demand*, the total amount of goods and services demanded in the economy? The model developed in this chapter provides part of the answer to that question.

In Figure 3-2 we show the economy's aggregate demand curve, introduced in Chapter 1, as well as the aggregate supply schedule. The increase in demand is shown by a rightward shift of the demand schedule, so at each level of prices the quantity demanded is now higher. If the initial market equilibrium was at E, then after the shift in demand the market clears at E', at which point both output and prices have risen.

Many of the questions raised in this book have to do with what we see in Figure 3-2. We highlight two in particular: First, what factors cause the *aggregate* demand or supply curve to shift? Second, given a shift in the aggregate demand or supply curve, is the adjustment made mostly by price changes or mostly by changes in output?

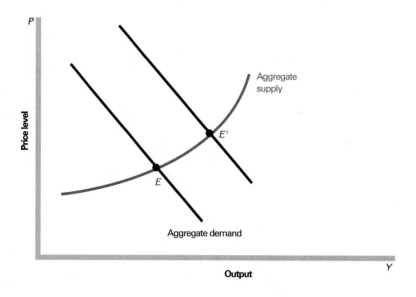

Figure 3-2 *The Effect of a Shift in Aggregate Demand*

In Chapter 1 we introduced aggregate demand and supply schedules. An increase in aggregate demand is shown as a rightward shift of the demand schedule. The effect of increased demand is to raise both output and the price level.

In this chapter we develop a first model of macroeconomic adjustment. The model is extreme in that it assumes that firms are willing to sell *any* amount of output at a given level of prices so that the aggregate supply curve is entirely flat.[2] In this case shifts in aggregate demand affect only output. Of course, this is an extreme case because it assumes prices are fixed, and in later chapters we allow price adjustments. However, the lack of realism pays off. An important point of the model is to show that when output adjusts in response to a change in demand, the increases in output and income have a feedback effect on demand. An increase in demand raises output, but the increases in output and income feed back to demand and cause further rounds of adjustment. We will now study how the equilibrium level of output is determined in this case.

The key concept of *equilibrium output* is introduced immediately, in Section 3-1. We assume initially that the demand for goods is *autonomous* — that is, independent of the level of income.[3] In fact, though, increases in income increase the demand for

---

[2] The assumption that prices are constant is made in order to simplify the exposition of Chapters 3 and 4. In later chapters, starting with Chapter 7, we use the theory of aggregate demand developed here to study the factors that determine the price level and cause it to change over time.

[3] The terms "autonomous" and "induced" are traditionally used to indicate spending that is independent of the level of income and dependent on the level of income, respectively. More generally, autonomous spending is spending that is independent of the other variables explained in a given theory.

consumption goods. In Section 3-2 we therefore extend the basic analysis by introducing the *consumption function*, which relates consumption spending to the level of income. In Sections 3-2 and 3-3 we derive explicit formulas for the equilibrium level of income. Later sections then introduce the government sector and the foreign sector.

3-1 Equilibrium Income

We initially simplify our task by discussing a hypothetical world without a government ($G = TA = TR = 0$) and without foreign trade ($NX = 0$). In such a world, the basic GDP accounting identity of Chapter 2 simplifies to

$$C + I \equiv Y \equiv C + S \tag{1}$$

where Y denotes the *real* value of output and income. Throughout this chapter we refer only to *real* values. For instance, when we speak of change in consumption spending, we mean a change in real consumption spending.

What would determine the level of income if firms could supply any amount of output at the prevailing level of prices? *Demand* must enter the picture. Firms would produce at a level just sufficient to meet demand. To develop this point, we define the concepts of *aggregate demand* and *equilibrium income*.

Aggregate Demand

Aggregate demand is the total amount of goods demanded in the economy. In general, the quantity of goods demanded, or aggregate demand, depends on the level of income in the economy and — as we shall see later — on interest rates, but for now we shall assume that the amount of goods demanded is constant, independent of the level of income.

Aggregate demand is shown in Figure 3-3 by the horizontal line *AD*. In the diagram, aggregate demand is equal to 300 (billion dollars). This means that the total amount of goods demanded in the economy is $300 billion, independent of the level of income.

If the quantity of goods demanded is constant, independent of the level of income, what determines the actual level of income? We have to turn to the concept of equilibrium income.

Equilibrium Income

Income is at its equilibrium level when the quantity of output produced is equal to the quantity demanded. An equilibrium situation is one in which no forces are causing income to change. We now explain why income is at its equilibrium level when it is equal to aggregate demand.

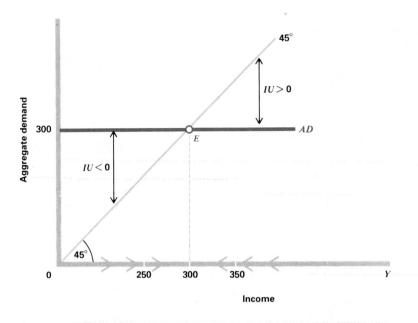

Figure 3-3   *Equilibrium with Constant Aggregate Demand*

Aggregate demand is shown by the *AD* line, and is equal to 300. Income (output) is at its equilibrium level when it is equal to aggregate demand, equal to 300. Thus the equilibrium is shown at point *E*. At any other income level, inventories are changing in a way that causes firms to change their production in a direction that moves income toward the equilibrium level.

In Figure 3-3 we show the level of income on the horizontal axis. The 45° line serves as a reference line that translates any horizontal distance into an equal vertical distance. For any given level of income (*Y*) on the horizontal axis, the 45° line gives the level of aggregate demand on the vertical axis that is equal to that level of income. For instance, at point *E*, both income and aggregate demand are equal to 300.

Point *E* is the point of equilibrium income, at which the quantity of output produced is equal to the quantity demanded. To understand why this should be the equilibrium level of income, suppose that firms were producing some other amount, say 350 units. Then income would exceed demand. Firms would be unable to sell all they produce and would find their warehouses filling with inventories of unsold goods. They would then cut their output. This is shown by the horizontal arrow pointing left from the output level of 350.

Similarly, if output were less than 300, say 250, firms would either run out of goods or be running down their inventories. They would therefore increase output, as shown by the horizontal arrow pointing to the right from the output level of 250.

Thus at point *E*, the equilibrium level of income, firms are selling as much as they produce, people are buying the amount they want to purchase, and there is no tendency for the level of income to change. At any other level of income, the pressure from increasing or declining inventories causes firms to change the level of output.

Equilibrium Income and Unintended Inventory Investment

The adjustment process by which the economy reaches the equilibrium level of income is further illustrated in Table 3-1. Suppose, for example, that firms overestimate demand and decide to produce 350 units of output. Since aggregate demand is only 300, firms will sell 300 units of output and 50 units will be added to their inventories. Thus we will have 50 units of *involuntary, or unintended, inventory investment.* It should be noted that in the national income accounts, additions to inventories count as investment. Of course, this is not intended or desired investment, but it does count as part of investment. Looking at the national income accounts of such an economy, we would see income equal to 350 and consumption plus investment equal to 350, but the equality of income and expenditure does not mean that 350 is the equilibrium level of income, because 50 units of investment were unintended additions to inventories.

Similarly, if firms produce 250 units, demand will exceed income and there will be unintended negative inventory investment — that is, an unintended rundown of inventories. In this case, we would have income equal to 250 units and expenditure equal to 300 − 50 = 250 units. In general, when aggregate demand — the amount people want to buy — is not equal to income, there is unintended inventory investment.[4] We summarize this as

$$IU = Y - AD \tag{2}$$

where IU is unintended additions to inventory.

In Figure 3-3, unintended inventory investment is shown by the vertical arrows. When income exceeds 300, there is unintended inventory investment. When income is less than 300, there are unintended reductions in inventories. In Table 3-1, unintended inventory investment is shown in the last column.

Table 3-1 *Equilibrium Income and Unintended Inventory Change*

Income	Aggregate Demand	Unintended Inventory Change
200	300	− 100
250	300	− 50
300	300	0
350	300	+ 50
400	300	+ 100

[4] We assume that actual and intended consumption are equal, so that all differences between actual and intended aggregate demand are reflected in unintended inventory changes. In practical terms, this means we are not considering situations where firms put "Sold Out" signs in their windows and customers cannot buy what they want.

We can now define equilibrium income more formally, using Equation (2). Income is at its equilibrium level when it is equal to aggregate demand, or when unintended inventory accumulation is zero. That is, income is at its equilibrium level when

$$Y = AD \qquad (3)$$

There are three essential notions in this section:

1. Aggregate demand determines the equilibrium level of income.

2. At equilibrium, unintended changes in inventories are zero.

3. An adjustment process for income based on unintended inventory changes will move income to its equilibrium level.[5]

3-2 The Consumption Function and Aggregate Demand

The preceding section studied the equilibrium level of income (and output) on the assumption that aggregate demand was simply a constant. Now we move to a more realistic specification of aggregate demand and begin to examine the economic varia-bles that determine it.

In our simplified model, which excludes both the government and foreign trade, aggregate demand consists of the demands for consumption and investment. The demand for consumption goods is not in practice autonomous, as we have so far assumed, but rather increases with income — families with higher incomes consume more than families with lower incomes, and countries where income is higher typically have higher levels of total consumption. The relationship between consumption and income is described by the *consumption function*.

The Consumption Function

We assume that consumption demand increases with the level of income.[6]

---

[5] You may have noticed that the adjustment process we describe raises the possibility that output will temporarily exceed its new equilibrium level during the adjustment to an increase in aggregate demand. This is the inventory cycle. Suppose firms desire to hold inventories which are proportional to the level of demand. When demand unexpectedly rises, inventories are depleted. In subsequent periods, the firms have to produce not only to meet the new, higher level of aggregate demand, but also to restore the depleted inventories and raise them to the new higher level. While firms are rebuilding their inventories and also producing to meet the higher level of demand, their total production will exceed the new higher level of aggregate demand.

[6] If the intercept, $\overline{C}$, in Equation (4) is zero, then consumption is proportional to income, implying that at a zero level of income consumption would be zero. In Chapter 10 we show that this special form is supported by the data.

$$C = \overline{C} + cY \qquad 0 < c < 1 \tag{4}$$

This consumption function is shown in Figure 3-4. Along the consumption function, the level of consumption rises with income. The *slope* is c, so that for every \$1 increase in income, consumption rises by \$$c$. For example, if c is 0.90, then for every \$1 increase in income, consumption rises by 90 cents.

The coefficient c is sufficiently important to have a special name, the *marginal propensity to consume*. The marginal propensity to consume is the increase in consumption per unit increase in income. In our case, the marginal propensity to consume is less than 1, which implies that out of a dollar increase in income, only a fraction, c, is spent on consumption.

Consumption and Saving

What happens to the rest, the amount $Y - C$, that is not spent on consumption? If it is not spent, it must be saved. Income is either spent or saved; there are no other uses to which income can be put.

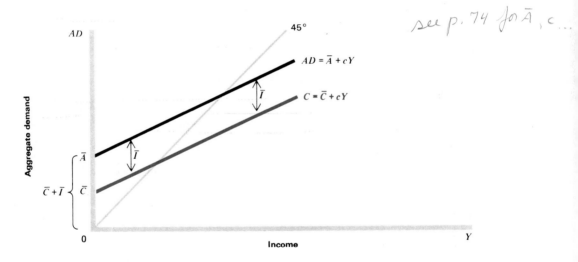

see p. 74 for $\overline{A}, c$ ...

Figure 3-4 *The Consumption Function and Aggregate Demand*

The consumption function shows the level of consumption spending at each level of income. The consumption function is upward-sloping. The slope of the consumption function is the marginal propensity to consume, c. Aggregate demand is the sum of the demands for consumption and investment goods. Investment demand, I, is assumed constant and is added to consumption demand to obtain the level of aggregate demand at each level of income. The line AD shows how aggregate demand increases with income. Its slope is c, the marginal propensity to consume.

More formally, look at Equation (5), which says that income that is not spent on consumption is saved, or

$$S \equiv Y - C \tag{5}$$

Equation (5) tells us that by definition *saving is equal to income minus consumption*. This means that we cannot postulate an independent saving function in addition to the consumption function and still expect consumption and saving to add up to income.

The consumption function in Equation (4) together with Equation (5), which we call the *budget constraint*, implies a saving function. The saving function relates the level of saving to the level of income. Substituting the consumption function in Equation (4) into the budget constraint in Equation (5) yields the saving function

$$S \equiv Y - C = Y - \overline{C} - cY = -\overline{C} + (1 - c)Y \tag{6}$$

From Equation (6), we see that saving is an increasing function of the level of income because the *marginal propensity to save, $s = 1 - c$,* is positive. For instance, suppose the marginal propensity to consume, c, is 0.9, meaning that 90 cents out of each extra dollar of income is consumed. Then the marginal propensity to save, s, is 0.10, meaning that the remaining 10 cents of each extra dollar of income is saved.

Investment Spending and Aggregate Demand

We have now specified one component of aggregate demand, consumption demand. We must also consider the determinants of investment spending, or an *investment function*. We cut short the discussion for the present by simply assuming that investment demand is at a constant level, $\overline{I}$.[7]

Aggregate demand is the sum of consumption and investment demands:

$$\begin{aligned} AD &= C + I \\ &= \overline{C} + cY + \overline{I} \\ &= \overline{A} + cY \end{aligned} \tag{7}$$

The aggregate demand function (7) is shown in Figure 3-4. Part of aggregate demand, $\overline{A}$, is independent of the level of income, or autonomous, but *aggregate demand also depends on the level of income*. It increases with the level of income because consumption demand increases with income. The aggregate demand schedule is obtained by adding (vertically) the level of autonomous investment spending to consumption at each level of income.

---

[7] In later chapters investment spending will become a function of the interest rate and will gain an important place in the transmission of monetary policy.

Equilibrium Income and Output

The next step is to use the aggregate demand function, *AD*, in Figure 3-4 and Equation (7) to determine the equilibrium levels of income and output. We do this in Figure 3-5.

Recall the basic point of this chapter: The equilibrium level of income is such that aggregate demand equals output (which in turn equals income). The 45° line in Figure 3-5 shows points at which income and aggregate demand are equal. The aggregate demand schedule in Figure 3-5 cuts the 45° line at *E*, and it is accordingly at *E* that aggregate demand is equal to income (equals output). Only at *E*, and at the corre-

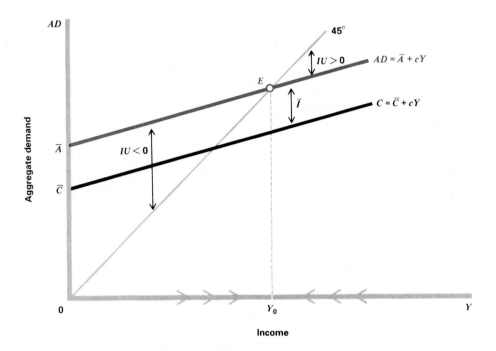

Figure 3-5 *Determination of Equilibrium Income and Output*

Income is at its equilibrium level when aggregate demand is equal to income. This occurs at point *E*, corresponding to the income (and output) level Y_0. At any higher level of income, aggregate demand is below the level of income, firms are unable to sell all they produce, and there is undesired accumulation of inventories. Firms therefore reduce output, as shown by the arrows. Similarly, at any level of income below Y_0, aggregate demand exceeds income, firms run short of goods to sell, and they therefore increase output. Only at the equilibrium income level Y_0 are firms producing the amount that is demanded, and there is no tendency for the level of income to change.

sponding equilibrium levels of income and output (Y_0), does aggregate demand exactly equal income.[8]

The arrows in Figure 3-5 indicate once again how we reach equilibrium. If firms expand production whenever they face unintended decreases in their inventory holdings, then they increase output at any level below Y_0; this is because below Y_0 aggregate demand exceeds income and inventories are declining. Conversely, for income levels above Y_0 firms find inventories piling up and therefore cut production. This process leads to the income level Y_0, at which current production exactly matches aggregate demand and unintended inventory changes are therefore equal to zero. Again, the arrows in Figure 3-5 represent the dynamic process by which the economy moves to the equilibrium level of income Y_0.[9]

The determination of equilibrium output in Figure 3-5 can also be described using Equation (7) and the equilibrium condition in the goods market, which is that income is equal to aggregate demand:

$$Y = AD \tag{8}$$

The level of aggregate demand, AD, is specified in Equation (7). Substituting for AD in Equation (8), we have the equilibrium condition as

$$Y = \overline{A} + cY \tag{9}$$

Since we have Y on both sides of the equilibrium condition in Equation (9), we can collect the terms and solve for the equilibrium level of income and output, denoted by Y_0:

$$Y - cY = \overline{A} \quad \text{or} \quad Y(1 - c) = \overline{A}$$

Thus the equilibrium level of income, at which aggregate demand equals income, is

$$Y_0 = \frac{1}{1 - c} \overline{A} \tag{10}$$

Figure 3-5 sheds light on Equation (10). The position of the aggregate demand schedule is characterized by its slope, c, and intercept, $\overline{A}$. The intercept, $\overline{A}$, is the level of autonomous spending, that is, spending that is independent of the level of income. The other determinant of the equilibrium level of income is the marginal propensity to consume, c, which is the slope of the aggregate demand schedule.

Given the intercept, a steeper aggregate demand function — as would be implied by a higher marginal propensity to consume — implies a higher level of equilibrium income. Similarly, for a given marginal propensity to consume, a higher level of auton-

---

[8] We frequently use the subscript 0 to denote the equilibrium level of a variable.

[9] Do you see that there is once more the possibility of an inventory cycle? Refer to footnote 5.

omous spending — in terms of Figure 3-5, a larger intercept — implies a higher equilibrium level of income. These results, suggested by Figure 3-5, are easily verified using Equation (10), which gives the formula for the equilibrium level of income.

Thus, the larger the marginal propensity to consume, c, and the higher the level of autonomous spending, $\overline{A}$, the higher the equilibrium level of income.

Saving and Investment

There is a useful alternative formulation of the equilibrium condition that aggregate demand is equal to income. In equilibrium, investment demand equals saving. This condition applies only to an economy in which there is no government and no foreign trade.

To understand this relationship, return to Figure 3-5. The vertical distance between the aggregate demand and consumption schedules in that figure is equal to investment demand, $\overline{I}$. Note also that the vertical distance between the consumption schedule and the 45° line measures saving $(S = Y - C)$ at each level of income.

The equilibrium level of income is found where AD crosses the 45° line, at E. Accordingly, at the equilibrium level of income — and only at that level — the two vertical distances are equal. Thus, at the equilibrium level of income, saving equals (intended) investment. By contrast, above the equilibrium level of income, Y_0, saving (the distance between the 45° line and the consumption schedule) exceeds investment demand, while below Y_0, investment demand exceeds saving.

The equality between saving and investment at equilibrium is an essential characteristic of the equilibrium level of income. We can see that by starting with the basic equilibrium condition, Equation (8), $Y = AD$. If we subtract consumption from both Y and AD, we realize that $Y - C$ is saving and $AD - C$ is investment demand. In symbols,

$$Y = AD$$
$$Y - C = AD - C \tag{11}$$
$$S = \overline{I}$$

Thus, the condition $S = \overline{I}$ is merely another way of stating the basic equilibrium condition.[10]

We can also show a diagrammatic derivation of the equilibrium level of income in terms of the balance between saving and investment in Equation (11). In Figure 3-6, we show the saving function. Saving is shown as increasing with the level of income. The slope of the saving function is the marginal propensity to save, $1 - c$. We also have drawn investment demand, indicated by the horizontal line with intercept $\overline{I}$. Equilibrium income is Y_0.

---

[10] In Problem 3 at the end of this chapter, we ask you to derive Equation (10) for Y_0 by starting from $S = \overline{I}$ and substituting for S from Equation (6).

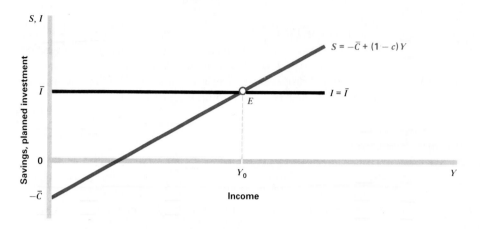

Figure 3-6 *Saving and Investment*

An alternative definition of the equilibrium level of income is that it occurs where saving is equal to (intended) investment. This is shown at point E, with corresponding output level Y_0. At higher levels of income, consumers want to save more than $\bar{I}$. They do not buy all of output, inventories accumulate, and actual investment is made equal to saving because firms undertake undesired inventory investment. They therefore cut output, and the economy moves to income level Y_0.

Figure 3-7 shows a further perspective on the role of saving and investment using the circular flow diagram introduced at the beginning of Chapter 2. Saving is a *leakage* from the circular flow since it is the part of income that is not returned to firms via consumption spending. Investment is an *injection* into the circular flow since it is autonomous and not induced by income. Income and spending are in balance when leakages are equal to injections. This principle continues to hold in the more complicated models introduced below.

3-3 The Multiplier

In this section we develop an answer to the following question: By how much does a $1 increase in autonomous spending raise the equilibrium level of income?[11] There appears to be a simple answer. Since, in equilibrium, income equals aggregate demand, it would seem that a $1 increase in (autonomous) demand or spending should raise equilibrium income by $1. That answer is wrong. Let us now see why.

---

[11] Recall that autonomous spending, A, is spending that is independent of the level of income. Note also that the answer to this question is contained in Equation (10). Can you deduce the answer directly from Equation (10)? This section provides an explanation of that answer.

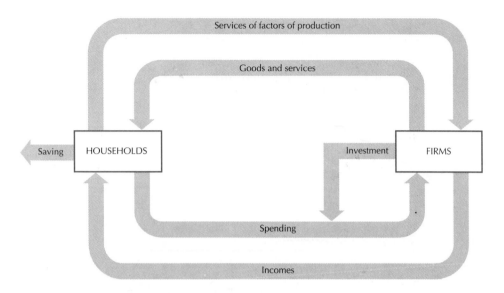

Figure 3-7   *Saving, Investment and the Circular Flow*

Saving is a *leakage* from the circular flow since it is the part of income that is not returned to firms via consumption spending. Investment is an *injection* into the circular flow since it is autonomous and not induced by income. Income and spending are in balance when leakages are equal to injections.

Suppose first that output increased by $1 to match the increased level of autonomous spending. This increase in output and income would in turn give rise to further *induced* spending as consumption rises because the level of income has risen. How much of the initial $1 increase in income would be spent on consumption? Out of an additional dollar of income, a fraction (c) is consumed. Assume then that production increases further to meet this induced expenditure, that is, that output and thus income increase by $1 + c$. That will still leave us with an excess demand, because the expansion in production and income by $1 + c$ will give rise to further induced spending. This story could clearly take a long time to tell. We seem to have arrived at an impasse at which an expansion in output to meet excess demand leads to a further expansion in demand without an obvious end to the process.

It helps to lay out the various steps in this chain more carefully. We do this in Table 3-2. We start off the first round with an increase in autonomous spending, $\Delta\overline{A}$. Next we allow an expansion in production to meet exactly that increase in demand. Production accordingly expands by $\Delta\overline{A}$. This increase in production gives rise to an equal increase in income and, therefore, via the consumption function gives rise in the second round to induced expenditures of size $c(\Delta\overline{A})$. Assume again that production expands to meet the increase in spending. The production adjustment this time is $c\Delta\overline{A}$, and so is the increase in income. This gives rise to a third round of induced spending equal

Table 3-2 *The Multiplier*

Round	Increase in Demand This Round	Increase in Production This Round	Total Increase in Income
1	$\Delta\overline{A}$	$\overline{A}$	$\overline{A}$
2	$c\Delta\overline{A}$	$c\Delta\overline{A}$	$(1 + c)\Delta\overline{A}$
3	$c^2\Delta\overline{A}$	$c^2\Delta\overline{A}$	$(1 + c + c^2)\Delta\overline{A}$
4	$c^3\Delta\overline{A}$	$c^3\Delta\overline{A}$	$(1 + c + c^2 + c^3)\Delta\overline{A}$
.	.	.	.
.	.	.	.
.	.	.	$\dfrac{1}{1 - c}\Delta\overline{A}$
1	1.0	1.0	1.0
2	0.6	0.6	1.6
3	0.36	0.36	1.96
4	0.216	0.216	2.176
5	0.1296	0.1296	2.3056
.	.	.	.
.	.	.	.
.	.	.	2.5

to the marginal propensity to consume times the increase in income $c(c\Delta\overline{A}) = c^2\Delta\overline{A}$. Careful inspection of the last term shows that induced expenditures in the third round are smaller than those in the second round. Since the marginal propensity to consume, c, is less than 1, the term c^2 is less than c. This can be seen also in the lower part of the table, where we assume $c = 0.6$ and show the steps corresponding to those in the upper part of the table.

If we write out the successive rounds of increased spending, starting with the initial increase in autonomous demand, we obtain

$$\Delta AD = \Delta\overline{A} + c\Delta\overline{A} + c^2\Delta\overline{A} + c^3\Delta\overline{A} + \ldots$$
$$= \Delta\overline{A}(1 + c + c^2 + c^3 + \ldots) \tag{12}$$

For a value of $c < 1$, the successive terms in the series become progressively smaller. In fact, we are dealing with a geometric series, so the equation simplifies to

$$\Delta AD = \frac{1}{1 - c}\Delta\overline{A} = \Delta Y_0 \tag{13}$$

From Equation (13), therefore, we find that the cumulative change in aggregate spending is equal to a multiple of the increase in autonomous spending. This could also have been deduced from Equation (10).[12] The multiple $1/(1 - c)$ is called the multiplier. The multiplier is the amount by which equilibrium output changes when autonomous aggregate demand increases by one unit. Because the multiplier exceeds unity, we know that a $1 change in autonomous spending increases equilibrium income and output by more than $1.[13]

The concept of the multiplier is sufficiently important to create new notation. Defining the multiplier as α, we have

$$\alpha = \frac{1}{1 - c} \tag{14}$$

Inspection of the multiplier in Equation (14) shows that the larger the marginal propensity to consume, the larger the multiplier. With a marginal propensity to consume of 0.6, as in Table 3-2, the multiplier is 2.5; for a marginal propensity to consume of 0.8, the multiplier is 5. The reason is simply that a high marginal propensity to consume implies that a large fraction of an additional dollar of income will be consumed, and thereby added to aggregate demand. Accordingly, expenditures induced by an increase in autonomous spending are high and, therefore, so is the expansion in output and income that is needed to restore balance between income and demand (or spending).

Note that the relationship between the marginal propensity to consume, c, and the marginal propensity to save, s, allows us to write Equation (14) in a somewhat different form. Remembering from the budget constraint that saving plus consumption adds up to income, we realize that the fraction of an additional dollar of income consumed plus the fraction saved must add up to a dollar, or $1 \equiv s + c$. Substituting $s \equiv 1 - c$ in Equation (14), we obtain an equivalent formula for the multiplier in terms of the marginal propensity to save: $\alpha = 1/s$.

The Multiplier in Pictures

Figure 3-8 provides a graphical interpretation of the effects of an increase in autonomous spending on the equilibrium level of income. The initial equilibrium is at point E with an income level Y_0. Now autonomous spending increases from $\overline{A}$ to $\overline{A}'$. This is represented by a parallel upward shift of the aggregate demand schedule to AD'. The

---

[12] If you are familiar with the calculus, you will realize that the multiplier is nothing other than the derivative of the equilibrium level of income, Y_0, in Equation (10) with respect to autonomous spending. Use the calculus on Equation (10) and later on Equation (22) to check the statements in the text.

[13] Two warnings: (1) The multiplier is necessarily greater than 1 in this very simplified model of the determination of income, but as we shall see in the discussion of "crowding out" in Chapter 4, there may be circumstances in which it is less than 1; (2) the term "multiplier" is used more generally in economics to mean the effect on some endogenous variable (a variable whose level is explained by the theory being studied) of a unit change in an exogenous variable (a variable whose level is not determined within the theory being examined). For instance, one can talk of the multiplier of a change in the income tax rate on the level of unemployment. However, the classic use of the term is as we are using it here — the effects of a change in autonomous spending on equilibrium output.

upward shift means that now, at each level of income, aggregate demand is higher by an amount $\Delta \bar{A} = \bar{A}' - \bar{A}$.

Aggregate demand now exceeds the initial level of income, Y_0, or output. Consequently, unintended inventory rundown is taking place at a rate equal to the increase in autonomous spending, or to the vertical distance $\Delta \bar{A}$. Firms will respond to that excess demand by expanding production, say to income level Y'. This expansion in production gives rise to induced expenditure, increasing aggregate demand to the level A'. At the same time, the expansion reduces the gap between aggregate demand and output to the vertical distance FG. The gap between demand and output is reduced because the marginal propensity to consume is less than 1.

Thus, a marginal propensity to consume that is positive but less than unity implies that a sufficient expansion in income will restore the balance between aggregate demand and income. In Figure 3-8 the new equilibrium is indicated by point E', and

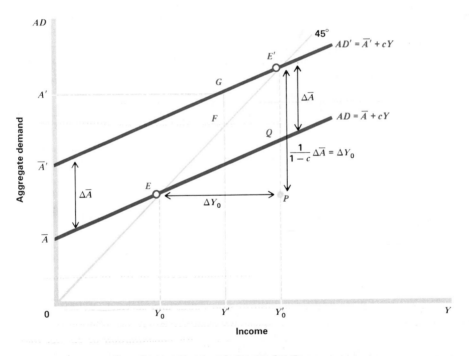

Figure 3-8 *Graphical Derivation of the Multiplier*

When there is an increase in autonomous aggregate demand, the aggregate demand schedule shifts up to AD'. The equilibrium moves from E to E'. The increase in equilibrium income ($Y_0' - Y_0$), equal to distance PE, equal to PE', exceeds the increase in autonomous demand $E'Q$. From the diagram we see that is a result of the AD curve having a positive slope rather than being horizontal. In other words, the multiplier exceeds 1 because consumption demand increases with income — any increase in income produces further increases in demand.

the corresponding level of income is Y_0'. The change in income required is therefore $\Delta Y = Y_0' - Y_0$.

The magnitude of the income change required to restore equilibrium depends on two factors. The larger the increase in autonomous spending, represented in Figure 3-8 by the parallel shift in the aggregate demand schedule, the larger the income change. Furthermore, the larger the marginal propensity to consume — that is, the steeper the aggregate demand schedule — the larger the income change.

As a further check on our results, we verify from Figure 3-8 that the change in equilibrium income exceeds the change in autonomous spending. For that purpose, we use the 45° line to compare the change in income $\Delta Y_0 (= EP = PE')$ with the change in autonomous spending that is equal to the vertical distance between the new and old aggregate demand schedule (QE'). It is clear from Figure 3-8 that the change in income, PE', exceeds the change in autonomous spending, QE'.

Summary

There are three points to remember from this discussion of the multiplier.

1.   An increase in autonomous spending raises the equilibrium level of income.

2.   The increase in income is a multiple of the increase in autonomous spending.

3.   The larger the marginal propensity to consume, the larger the multiplier arising from the relation between consumption and income.

As a check on your understanding of the material of this section, you should develop the same analysis, and the same answers, in terms of Figure 3-6.

3-4 The Government Sector

So far we have ignored the role of the government sector in the determination of equilibrium income. The government affects the level of equilibrium income in two separate ways. First, government expenditures on goods and services, G, are a component of aggregate demand. Second, taxes and transfers affect the relation between income, Y, and *disposable income*, income available for consumption or saving, that accrues to the private sector, YD. In this section, we are concerned with the way in which government expenditures, taxes, and transfers affect the equilibrium level of income.

We start again from the basic national income accounting identities. The introduction of the government restores government expenditures (G) to the expenditure side of Equation (1) of this chapter, and taxes (TA) less transfers (TR) to the allocation of income side. We can accordingly rewrite the identity in Equation (1) as

$$C + I + G \equiv S + (TA - TR) + C \tag{1a}$$

The definition of aggregate demand has to be augmented to include government expenditures on goods and services — the purchases of military equipment and services of bureaucrats, for instance. Thus we have

$$AD = C + I + G \tag{7a}$$

Consumption will no longer depend on income, but rather on disposable income, YD. Disposable income (YD) is the net income available for spending by households after receiving transfers from and paying taxes to the government. It thus consists of income plus transfers less taxes, $Y + TR - TA$. The consumption function is now

$$C = \overline{C} + cYD = \overline{C} + c(Y + TR - TA) \tag{4a}$$

A final step is a specification of fiscal policy. Fiscal policy is the policy of the government with regard to the level of government expenditures, the level of transfers, and the tax structure. We assume that the government purchases a constant amount, $\overline{G}$; that it makes a constant amount of transfers, $\overline{TR}$; and that it collects a fraction, t, of income in the form of taxes:

$$G = \overline{G} \qquad TR = \overline{TR} \qquad TA = tY \tag{19}$$

With this specification of fiscal policy, we can rewrite the consumption function, after substitution from Equation (19) for TR and TA in Equation (4a), as

$$\begin{aligned} C &= \overline{C} + c(Y + \overline{TR} - tY) \\ &= \overline{C} + c\overline{TR} + c(1 - t)Y \end{aligned} \tag{20}$$

Note in Equation (20) that the presence of transfers raises autonomous consumption spending by the marginal propensity to consume out of disposable income, c, times the amount of transfers.[14] The presence of income taxes, by contrast, lowers consumption spending at each level of income. That reduction arises because households' consumption is related to *disposable* income rather than income itself, and income taxes reduce disposable income relative to the level of income.

While the marginal propensity to consume out of disposable income remains c, now the marginal propensity to consume out of income is $c(1 - t)$, where $1 - t$ is the fraction of income left after taxes. For example, if the marginal propensity to consume, c, is 0.8 and the tax rate is 0.25, then the marginal propensity to consume out of income, $c(1 - t)$, is $0.6[= 0.8 \times (1 - 0.25)]$.

Combining Equations (7a), (19), and (20), we have now

---

[14] We are assuming no taxes are paid on transfers from the government. As a matter of fact, taxes are paid on some transfers, such as interest payments on the government debt, and not paid on other transfers, such as welfare benefits.

$$AD = (\overline{C} + \overline{I} + c\overline{TR} + \overline{G}) + c(1 - t)Y$$
$$= \overline{A} + c(1 - t)Y \tag{21}$$

The effects of the introduction of government on the aggregate demand schedule are shown in Figure 3-9. The new aggregate demand schedule, denoted AD' in the figure, starts out higher than the original schedule, AD, but has a flatter slope. The intercept is larger because it now includes both government spending, G, and the part of consumption resulting from transfer payments by the government, $c\overline{TR}$. The slope is flatter because households now have to pay part of every dollar of income in taxes, and are left with only $(1 - t)$ of that dollar. Thus, as Equation (21) shows, the marginal propensity to consume out of income is now $c(1 - t)$ instead of c.

Equilibrium Income

We are now set to study income determination when the government is included. We return to the equilibrium condition for the goods market, $Y = AD$, and using Equation (21), write the equilibrium condition as

$$Y = \overline{A} + c(1 - t)Y$$

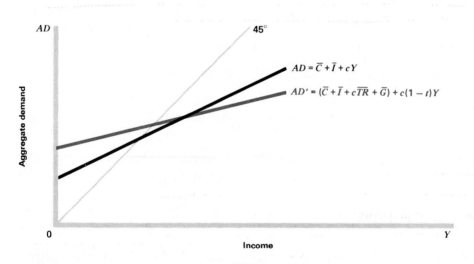

Figure 3-9 *Government and Aggregate Demand*

Government affects aggregate demand through its own expenditures, assumed here to be fixed at the autonomous level $\overline{G}$, through transfers $\overline{TR}$, and through taxes. Taxes are assumed to be a constant proportion, t, of income. Under these assumptions, the introduction of government shifts the intercept of the aggregate demand curve up and flattens the curve.

We can solve this equation for Y_0, the equilibrium level of income, by collecting terms in Y:

$$Y[1 - c(1 - t)] = \overline{A}$$

$$Y_0 = \frac{1}{1 - c(1 - t)}(\overline{C} + \overline{I} + c\overline{TR} + \overline{G}) \tag{22}$$

In comparing Equation (22) with Equation (10), we see that the government sector makes a substantial difference. It raises autonomous spending by the amount of government expenditures, $\overline{G}$, and by the amount of induced spending out of net transfers, $c\overline{TR}$.

Effects of a Change in Government Expenditures

We now consider the effects of changes in fiscal policy on the equilibrium level of income. We distinguish three possible changes in fiscal variables: changes in government expenditures, changes in transfers, and changes in the income tax. The simplest illustration is that of a change in government expenditures. This case is shown in Figure 3-10, where the initial level of income is Y_0.

An increase in government expenditures is a change in autonomous spending and therefore shifts the aggregate demand schedule upward by an amount equal to the increase in government expenditures. At the initial level of income and output, the demand for goods exceeds income, and accordingly, firms expand production until the new equilibrium, at point E', is reached.

By how much does income expand? From Equation (22) we have

$$\Delta Y_0 = \frac{1}{1 - c(1 - t)} \Delta\overline{G} = \overline{\alpha}\Delta\overline{G} \tag{23}$$

where the remaining terms ($\overline{C}$, $\overline{I}$, and $\overline{TR}$) are constant by assumption and we have introduced the notation $\overline{\alpha}$ to denote the multiplier in the presence of income taxes:

multiplier=
$$\overline{\alpha} = \frac{1}{1 - c(1 - t)} \tag{24}$$

Equation (24) shows that *income taxes lower the multiplier*. If the marginal propensity to consume is 0.8 and taxes are zero, the multiplier is 5; with the same marginal propensity to consume and a tax rate of 0.25, the multiplier is cut in half to $1/[1 - 0.8(0.75)] = 2.5$. Income taxes reduce the multiplier because they reduce the induced increase of consumption out of changes in income. This can be seen in Figure 3-9, where the inclusion of taxes flattens the aggregate demand curve, recalling from Figure 3-8 that the larger the multiplier, the steeper is the aggregate demand schedule.

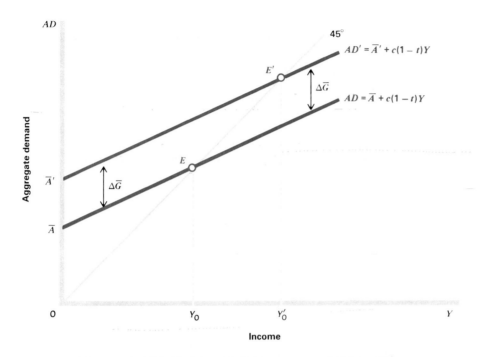

Figure 3-10 *The Effects of an Increase in Government Expenditures*

An increase in government spending shifts the aggregate demand schedule up from *AD* to *AD'*. Income rises from Y_0 to Y_0'. The multiplier is smaller now than it was in Figure 3-8.

Income Taxes as Automatic Stabilizers

We have just seen that a proportional income tax reduces the multiplier. This means that if any component of autonomous demand changes, output will change by less if there is a proportional income tax than in the absence of such taxes. The proportional income tax is one example of the important concept of *automatic stabilizers*. An automatic stabilizer is any mechanism in the economy that reduces the amount by which output changes in response to a change in autonomous demand.

We shall see later that one explanation of the business cycle, the more or less regular movements of real GDP around trend, is that it is caused by shifts in investment demand. It is argued that sometimes investors are optimistic and investment is high, and so therefore is income, while sometimes they are pessimistic, and so both investment and income are low.

Swings in investment demand will have a smaller effect on income when automatic stabilizers are in place. This means that in the presence of automatic stabilizers we should expect income to fluctuate less than it would without them. Higher income tax rates in the post–World War II period are one reason that the business cycle has been less pronounced since 1945 than it was earlier.

The proportional income tax is not the only automatic stabilizer. Unemployment benefits enable the unemployed to continue consuming even if they do not have a job. This means that demand falls less when someone becomes unemployed than it would if there were no benefits. This too makes the multiplier smaller and income more stable. Unemployment benefits and a proportional income tax are two automatic stabilizers that keep the multiplier small, thereby stabilizing the economy by protecting it from responding strongly to every small movement in autonomous demand.

Effects of Increased Transfer Payments

An increase in transfer payments increases autonomous demand, as can be seen in Equation (21), in which autonomous demand includes the term $c\overline{TR}$. A \$1 increase in transfers therefore increases autonomous demand by the amount c. For instance, if the marginal propensity to consume, c, is 0.8, a \$1 increase in transfers increases autonomous demand by \$.80. The increase is less than the full \$1 increase in transfers because part of the transfer, \$.20 in this case, is saved.

Given that a \$1 increase in transfers increases autonomous demand by the amount c, it is clear that the multiplier for an increase in transfers is c times the multiplier for an increase in government spending. For instance, with c equal to 0.8, and a tax rate of 0.25, the government spending multiplier is 2.5. The multiplier for transfers is 0.8 times 2.5, or 2.0.

Effects of an Income Tax Change

The final fiscal policy question is on the effects of a reduction in the income tax rate. This is illustrated in Figure 3-11 by an increase in the slope of the aggregate demand function, because that slope is equal to the marginal propensity to spend out of income, $c(1 - t)$. At the initial level of income, the aggregate demand for goods now exceeds income because the tax reduction causes increased consumption. The new, higher equilibrium level of income is Y_0'.

To calculate the change in equilibrium income, we first obtain the change in spending that arises from the tax cut at the initial level of income. This part is shown as the vertical distance EF in Figure 3-11, and is equal to the marginal propensity to consume out of disposable income times the change in disposable income due to the tax cut, $cY_0\Delta t$. The change in income is then given by this amount times the multiplier evaluated at the new tax rate t'. We can therefore write[15]

$$\Delta Y_0 = \frac{1}{1 - c(1 - t')} cY_0\Delta t \tag{25}$$

---

[15] You should check Equation (26) by using Equation (22) to write out Y_0 corresponding to a tax rate of t, and Y_0' corresponding to t'. Then subtract Y_0 from Y_0' to obtain ΔY_0 as given in Equation (26).

Example: An example clarifies the effects of an income tax cut. Initially the level of income is $Y_0 = 100$, the marginal propensity to consume is $c = 0.8$, and the tax rate $t = 0.2$. Assume now a tax cut that reduces the income tax rate to only 10 percent, or $t' = 0.1$.

At the initial level of income, disposable income rises by $Y_0 \Delta t = 100(t - t') = \$10$. Out of the increase in disposable income of \$10, a fraction $c = 0.8$ is spent on consumption, so that aggregate demand, at the initial level of income, increases by \$8. The increase in income is thus given by

$$\Delta Y_0 = \frac{1}{1 - 0.8(1 - 0.1)} 8 = (3.571) 8 = 28.57 \qquad (26)$$

In our example, a cut in the tax rate such that taxes fall by \$10 at the initial level of income raises equilibrium income by \$28.57. Note, however, that although taxes

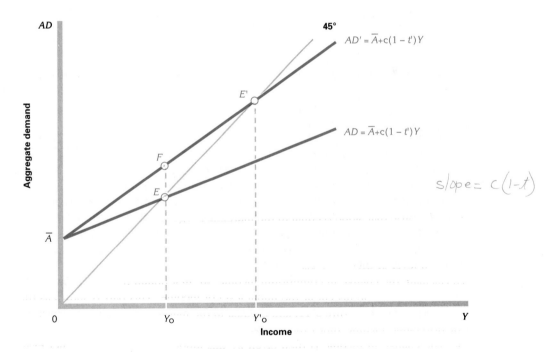

Figure 3-11 *The Effects of a Decrease in the Tax Rate*

A reduction in the income tax rate leaves the consumer with a larger proportion of every dollar of income earned. Accordingly, a larger proportion of every extra dollar of income is consumed. The aggregate demand curve swings upward, from *AD* to *AD'*. It becomes steeper because the income tax cut, in effect, acts like an increase in the propensity to consume. The equilibrium level of income rises from Y_0 to Y_0'.

are initially cut by $10, the government's total taxes received fall by less than $10. Why? The reason is that the government receives 10 percent of the induced increase in income, or $2.857, as taxes. Thus the final reduction in tax receipts by the government is not the initial $10, but rather $7.143.[16]

Summary and Implications

1.   Government expenditures and transfer payments act like increases in autonomous spending in their effects on equilibrium income.

2.   A proportional income tax reduces the proportion of each extra dollar of output that is received as disposable income by consumers, and thus has the same effects on equilibrium income as a reduction in the propensity to consume.[17]

3.   Changes in government spending and taxes affect the level of income. This raises the possibility that fiscal policy can be used to stabilize the economy. When the economy is in a recession, perhaps taxes should be cut or spending increased to get output to rise, and when the economy is booming, perhaps taxes should be increased or government spending cut to get back down to full employment.

4.   Fiscal policy is in practice actively used to try to stabilize the economy. Increases in government spending or a reduction in taxes are used to pull the economy out of a recession. Reduced spending or increased taxes are used to slow a boom.

3-5   The Budget

The budget, and especially the budget deficit, became a major preoccupation of economic policy in the 1980s. By 1985 the federal government budget deficit exceeded $30 billion, or 6 percent of GDP, meaning that the federal government was spending $30 billion more per year than it was receiving in taxes. It had to borrow that $30 billion. The prospect of continuing large deficits loomed unless taxes were raised or government spending cut. There was a strong fear that the economy could not prosper with the threat of large deficits hanging over it.

Why the concern? The fear was that the government's borrowing would make it difficult for private firms to borrow and invest, and thus would slow the economy's growth. Full understanding has to wait until later chapters, but we start now, dealing

---

[16]   We leave it to you to calculate the multiplier relating the change in equilibrium income to the total change in taxes received by the government.

[17]   It might be helpful to note that all the results we have derived can be obtained in a straightforward manner by taking the change in aggregate demand at the initial level of income times the multiplier. (Check this proposition for each of the fiscal policy changes we have considered.) You should consider, too, the effect on equilibrium income of an increase in government expenditures combined with an equal reduction in transfer payments, $\Delta G = -\Delta TR$. (See Problem 11 at the end of this chapter.)

with the government budget, its effects on income, and the effects of income on the budget.

The first important concept is the *budget surplus*, denoted by *BS*. The budget surplus is the excess of the government's revenues, consisting of taxes, over its total expenditure, consisting of expenditures on goods and services and transfer payments.

$$BS = TA - \overline{G} - \overline{TR} \qquad (27)$$

A negative budget surplus, an excess of total expenditure over taxes, is a budget deficit.

Box 3-1   Government in the National Income Accounts

We distinguish three aspects of fiscal policy in the text. *G* is government expenditures on goods and services, *TR* is government transfers, and *TA* is taxes or government receipts. Below we show the data for these variables in 1990, when GDP was \$671.6 billion. We also show the breakdown of the variables among federal, provincial, and municipal governments.

Government Revenue and Expenditure, 1990

	Goods and Services	Transfer Payments Interest on Public Debt	Other	Total Expenditure	Total Revenue
	(billions of dollars)				
Federal	\$ 32.6	\$41.2	\$ 51.3	\$125.1	\$ 99.6
CPP & QPP[a]			13.6	13.6	15.7
Provincial	47.5	18.1	33.0	98.6	97.0
Municipal[b]	68.6	3.8	2.5	74.9	74.5
Total	\$148.7	\$63.1	\$100.4	\$312.2	\$286.8
(% of GDP)	(22.1)	(9.4)	(14.9)	(46.5)	(42.7)
		Total Deficit		\$25.4 (3.8% of GDP)	

[a]Canada Pension Plan and Quebec Pension Plan
[b]Includes hospitals

Source: Department of Finance, *Quarterly Economic Review*, Annual Reference Tables.

Federal and provincial transfer payments are larger than expenditures on goods and services, and interest payments on the public debt are a substantial portion of transfer payments. In 1990, the total deficit of the government sector was \$25.4 billion or 3.8 percent of GDP. Most of this deficit was incurred at the federal level. It should be noted that transfers between levels of government are netted out of these figures. In 1990, the federal government transferred \$26.8 billion to provinces and municipalities.

Substituting in Equation (27) the assumption of a proportional income tax that yields tax revenues $TA = tY$ gives us

$$BS = tY - \overline{G} - \overline{TR} \tag{27a}$$

In Figure 3-12 we plot the budget surplus as a function of the level of income for given $\overline{G}$, $\overline{TR}$, and income tax rate, t. At low levels of income, the budget is in deficit (the surplus is negative) because payments $\overline{G} + \overline{TR}$ exceed income tax collection. For high levels of income, by contrast, the budget shows a surplus, since income tax collection exceeds expenditure.

Figure 3-12 demonstrates that the budget deficit depends not only on the government's policy choices, reflected in the tax rate (t), expenditures ($\overline{G}$), and transfers ($\overline{TR}$), but also on anything else that shifts the level of income. For instance, suppose there is an increase in investment demand that increases the level of output. Then the budget deficit will fall or the surplus will increase because tax revenues have risen even though the government has done nothing that changed the deficit.

We should accordingly not be surprised to see budget deficits in recessions. Those are periods when the government's tax receipts are low. In practice, transfer payments, through unemployment benefits, also increase in recessions, even though we are taking TR as autonomous in our model.

The Effects of Government Expenditures and Tax Changes on the Budget Surplus

Next we show how changes in fiscal policy affect the budget. In particular, we want to find out whether an increase in government expenditures must reduce the budget surplus. At first sight, this appears obvious, because increased government expenditures, from Equation (27), are reflected in a reduced surplus, or increased deficit. On further thought, however, the increased government expenditures will cause an increase (multiplied) in income and, therefore, increased income tax collection. This raises the interesting possibility that tax collection might increase by more than government expenditures.

A brief calculation shows that the first guess is right — increased government expenditures reduce the budget surplus. From Equation (23) the change in income due to increased government expenditures is equal to $\Delta Y_0 = \overline{\alpha}\Delta G$. A fraction of that increase in income is collected in the form of taxes, so that tax revenue increases by $t\overline{\alpha}\Delta G$. The change in the budget surplus, using Equation (24) to substitute for $\overline{\alpha}$, is therefore

$$\begin{aligned}
\Delta BS &= \Delta TA - \Delta \overline{G} \\
&= t\overline{\alpha}\Delta \overline{G} - \Delta \overline{G} \\
&= \left[\frac{t}{1 - c(1 - t)} - 1\right]\Delta \overline{G} \\
&= -\frac{(1 - c)(1 - t)}{1 - c(1 - t)}\Delta \overline{G}
\end{aligned} \tag{28}$$

which is unambiguously negative.

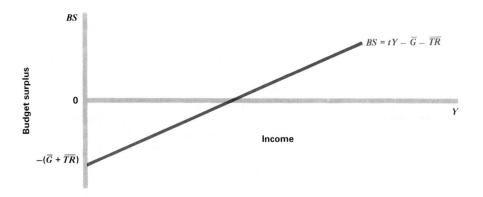

Figure 3-12 *The Budget Surplus*

The budget surplus, or deficit, depends in part on the level of income. Given the tax rate, t, and $\overline{G}$ and $\overline{TR}$, the budget surplus will be high if income is high — because then the government takes in a lot of taxes. If the level of income is low, there will be a budget deficit because government tax receipts are small.

We have, therefore, shown that an increase in government expenditures will reduce the budget surplus, although by considerably less than the increase in spending. For instance, for $c = 0.8$ and $t = 0.25$, a \$1 increase in government purchases will create a \$0.375 reduction in the surplus.[18]

In the same way, we can consider the effects of an increase in the tax rate on the budget surplus. We know that the increase in the tax rate will reduce the level of income. It might thus appear that an increase in the tax rate, keeping the level of government spending constant, could reduce the budget surplus. In fact, an increase in the tax rate increases the budget surplus, despite the reduction in income that it causes, as you are asked to show in Problem 9 at the end of this chapter.[19]

The Full-Employment Budget Surplus

A final topic to be treated here is the concept of the full-employment budget surplus.[20] Recall that increases in taxes add to the surplus and that increases in government expenditure reduce the surplus. Increases in taxes have been shown to reduce the level of income; and increases in government expenditures and transfers, to increase the

---

[18] In this case, $\overline{\alpha} = 1/[1 - 0.8(0.75)] = 2.5$. So $\Delta BS = -2.5(0.2)(0.75) = -0.375$.

[19] The theory that tax rate cuts would increase government revenue (or tax rate increases reduce government revenue) is associated with Arthur Laffer of Pepperdine University. Laffer's argument, however, did not depend on the aggregate demand effects of tax cuts but, rather, on the possibility that a tax cut would lead people to work more. This was a strand in supply-side economics, which we examine in Chapter 15.

[20] The concept of the full-employment surplus was first used by E. Cary Brown, "Fiscal Policy in the Thirties: A Reappraisal," *American Economic Review*, December 1956.

level of income. It thus seems that the budget surplus is a convenient, simple measure of the overall effects of fiscal policy on the economy. For instance, when the budget is in deficit, we would say that fiscal policy is expansionary, tending to increase GDP.

However, the budget surplus by itself suffers from a serious defect as a measure of the direction of fiscal policy. The defect is that the surplus can change because of changes in autonomous private spending, as we have seen. Thus, if the economy moves into a recession, tax revenue automatically declines and the budget deficit increases (or the surplus declines). Conversely, an increase in economic activity causes the budget surplus to increase (or the deficit to decline). These changes in the budget take place automatically for a given tax structure. This implies that we cannot simply look at the budget deficit as a measure of whether government fiscal policy is expansionary or deflationary. A given fiscal policy may imply a deficit if private spending is low and a surplus if private spending is high. Accordingly, an increase in the budget deficit does not necessarily mean that the government has changed its policy in an attempt to increase the level of income.

Since we frequently want to measure the way in which fiscal policy is being used to affect the level of income, we require some measure of policy that is independent of the particular position of the business cycle — boom or recession — in which we may find ourselves. Such a measure is provided by the *full-employment surplus*, which we denote by BS°. The full-employment budget surplus measures the budget not at the actual level of income but, rather, at the full-employment level of income or at potential output. Thus, a given fiscal policy summarized by G, TR, and t is assessed by the level of the surplus, or deficit, that it generates at full employment. Using $Y°$ to denote the full-employment level of income, we can write

$$BS° = tY° - \overline{G} - \overline{TR} \tag{29}$$

Alternative names for the full-employment surplus have been proliferating. Included are the *cyclically adjusted surplus* (or deficit), the *high-employment surplus*, and the *structural surplus*. All these names refer to the same concept. The new names are intended to divert attention from the notion that there is a unique level of full-employment output that the economy has not yet reached. They suggest instead that the concept is merely a convenient measuring rod that fixes a given level of employment as the reference point. Given the difficulty of knowing exactly what is the full-employment level of output, the new names have some justification.

To see the difference between the actual and the full-employment budgets, we subtract the actual budget in Equation (27a) from Equation (29) to obtain

$$BS° - BS = t(Y° - Y) \tag{30}$$

The only difference arises from income tax collection.[21] Specifically, if output is below the full-employment level, the full-employment surplus exceeds the actual surplus.

---

[21] In practice, transfer payments, such as welfare and unemployment benefits, are also affected by the state of the economy, so that *TR* also depends on the level of income. However, the major cause of differences between the actual surplus and the full-employment surplus is taxes.

Conversely, if actual output exceeds full-employment (or potential) output, the full-employment surplus is less than the actual surplus.

Budget Trends

Figure 3-13 shows the actual and cyclically adjusted surplus as a fraction of GDP for the years 1965 to 1990. In periods of rapid growth and relatively low unemployment, such as 1976–1979, the actual surplus rises above the adjusted one, while in recession years such as 1970, 1974, and 1982 the growth of tax revenues slows down and the actual surplus falls below the adjusted one. The emergence of large cyclically adjusted deficits in the period 1975–1978 reflects the expansionary fiscal policy adopted during that period in response to rising unemployment rates. Conversely, the very large actual deficits in 1982–1985 reflect the emergence of very high unemployment rates.

One final word of warning: The high-employment surplus is a better measure of the direction of active fiscal policy than the actual budget surplus, but it is not a perfect measure of the thrust of fiscal policy. The reason is that balanced budget increases in government expenditures are themselves expansionary, so that an increase in government expenditures matched by a tax increase that keeps the surplus constant leads to an increase in the level of income (see appendix). Because fiscal policy involves the

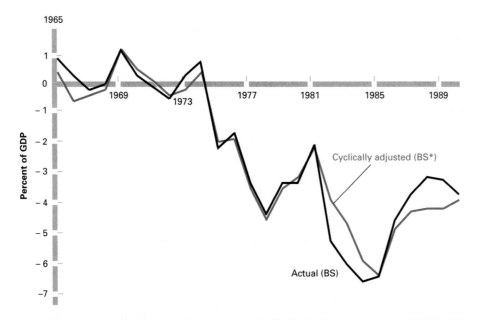

Figure 3-13 *The Actual and Cyclically Adjusted Budget Surplus as a Percent of GDP*

(*Source:* Department of Finance, *Economic Review; The Fiscal Plan,* February 1986)

setting of a number of variables — the tax rate, transfers, and government expenditures — it is difficult to describe the thrust of fiscal policy perfectly in a single number. The high-employment surplus is nevertheless a useful guide to the direction of fiscal policy.

Simultaneous Changes in Taxes and Expenditures

What happens when taxes and government expenditures on goods and services both change? In the previous section we derived in Equation (25) the effect of a cut in taxes as

$$\Delta Y_0 = \bar{\alpha} c Y_0 \Delta t \tag{31}$$

where the multiplier, $\bar{\alpha}$, is evaluated at the new lower tax rate. Suppose there is a simultaneous reduction in government expenditures by the amount of the reduction in tax revenues at the initial level of income. We might expect that such a fiscal policy would have no effect since taxes are being cut by the same amount as expenditures, but Equation (31) shows that is not right. The combined effect of the two actions is actually to lower income.

Why? The reason is that part of the cut in taxes is saved, so that only the fraction c of the tax cut $Y_0\Delta t$ goes to increase aggregate demand. If government expenditures are reduced by the amount $Y_0\Delta t$, aggregate demand is reduced by the entire amount and income is reduced by $\bar{\alpha} Y_0\Delta t$. Thus the net effect of this fiscal policy is a reduction in income.

Returning to the numerical example of the previous section, we saw that, given an initial level of income of $100 and a multiplier $\bar{\alpha} = 3.571$, a reduction of the tax rate from 0.2 to 0.1 would initially reduce tax revenue by $10 and lead to an increase in income of $28.57. A reduction of government expenditures of $10 would have a full multiplier effect and reduce income by $35.71 so that the net decrease in income would be $7.14 (35.71 − 28.57).

Since there is a fall in income, the budget surplus in the end decreases slightly even though at the initial level of income the cuts in taxes and expenditures are equal. The net change in the surplus will be $t'\Delta Y_0 = 0.1(-\$7.14) = -\$0.71$.

Balanced Budget Multiplier

In the example considered above, the combined tax cut and reduction of government expenditures raised the budget deficit. What would happen to the level of income if government expenditures and taxes changed by exactly the same amount, so that the budget surplus remained unchanged between the initial and final level of income? The answer to this question is contained in the famous balanced budget multiplier result. The result is that the balanced budget multiplier is exactly 1. That is, an increase in government expenditures, accompanied by an equal increase in taxes, increases the level of income by exactly the amount of the increase in expenditures. This interesting result is derived in the appendix at the end of this chapter.

3-6 The Foreign Sector

For a country like Canada, which exports about one-quarter of its total output and spends a similar fraction of its income on imports, foreign trade plays an important role in the determination of equilibrium income. When foreign trade is taken into account, we return to the general case represented by the basic accounting identity given in Chapter 2. Aggregate demand becomes

$$AD = C + I + G + NX$$

Denoting exports by X and imports by Q, we have

$$NX = X - Q$$

As in the case of planned investment and government spending, we assume that exports are fixed at a given level (denoted by $\overline{X}$). On the other hand, since imports represent part of domestic demand, they are assumed to depend on income.[22] Using a linear relationship we have

$$Q = \overline{Q} + mY \tag{31}$$

where the slope m is called the *marginal propensity to import*.

To determine the equilibrium level of income, we use the equilibrium condition, $Y = AD$, together with the consumption function (20) and the import function (31)

$$
\begin{aligned}
Y &= (\overline{C} + c\overline{TR}) + c(1 - t)Y + \overline{I} + \overline{G} + \overline{X} - \overline{Q} - mY \\
&= (\overline{C} + c\overline{TR} + \overline{I} + \overline{G} + \overline{X} - \overline{Q}) + [c(1 - t) - m]Y \\
&= \overline{A} + [c(1 - t) - m]Y
\end{aligned}
$$

Solving for the equilibrium level of income Y_0 , we obtain

$$Y_0 = \frac{1}{1 - c(1 - t) + m}\overline{A} \tag{32}$$

Comparing Equation (32) with Equation (22), we see that exports are *injections* into the circular flow and add to autonomous spending. Imports subtract from autonomous spending and are similar to taxes in that they are *withdrawals* from the circular flow and reduce the increases in demand for domestic output induced by increases in income, and thereby lower the multiplier. The higher the marginal propensity to import, the lower the multiplier.

---

[22] We are assuming here that the exchange rate is fixed. The effect of changes in the exchange rate on exports and imports is taken up in Chapter 5.

Interdependence and Repercussion Effects

When we include the foreign sector in our analysis and consider the interaction among countries, we find that income determination in the individual countries of the world economy is interdependent. An increase in income in one country (country A), by increasing country A's imports, affects demand for output abroad and leads, in turn, to a foreign expansion in imports from country A. There is thus a *repercussion effect* that we have so far ignored by assuming that export demand is autonomous.

Table 3-3 provides estimates of the size of repercussion effects and the importance of international linkages. The table, derived from an econometric model of the OECD, shows income multipliers associated with an expansion in one country on that country itself and on other countries.[23] Consider first the case of the United States. An increase of 1 percentage point in U.S. autonomous spending would raise U.S. income by 1.47 percent.

What is the impact on selected other countries? Looking at the top row, we find that German income rises by about 0.25 percent, and the same is true for Japan. Thus, U.S. expansion does affect these countries, although the size of the effect is not overwhelming. The comparison with Canada is of interest here. A U.S. expansion by 1.47 percent raises Canadian income by nearly 0.7 percent. Thus Canada appears considerably affected by U.S. expenditure disturbances. The last entry in the top row of Table 3-3 shows the impact of a U.S. expansion on industrialized countries as a group. The impact here is to increase the group's combined income by three-quarters of a percentage point.

Table 3-3 *The International Transmission of Aggregate Demand Disturbances*

Initiating Country or Group (1 percent increase in autonomous spending)	Affected Country or Group (percentage change in income)				
	United States	Germany	Japan	Canada	OECD
United States	1.47	0.23	0.25	0.68	0.74
Germany	0.05	1.25	0.60	0.60	0.23
Japan	0.04	0.05	1.26	0.06	0.21
Canada	0.06	0.03	0.03	1.27	0.10
OECD	1.81	2.38	1.84	2.32	2.04

Source: OECD Occasional Paper, "The OECD International Linkage Model," January 1979.

[23] The OECD (Organization for Economic Cooperation and Development) is a grouping of 24 industrialized countries, based in Paris, which serves as a framework for international policy discussion. Among the members are the few listed in Table 3-3, plus Italy, the United Kingdom, France, and seventeen others.

Consider for comparison a Canadian expansion. The multiplier for Canadian income of a 1 percent increase in Canadian autonomous spending is 1.27, about the same as the 1.47 multiplier for the United States. The impact on the rest of the world is quite minor, though. The most substantial impact is on the United States (0.06 percent induced income increase) and the impact on Germany or Japan is only 0.03 percent increased income.

What determines the size of the multipliers and spillover effects? Three chief factors should be taken into account in interpreting the multiplier patterns revealed in Table 3-3. First, the size of the country is important. A Canadian expansion, for example, induces only a small percentage increase in U.S. income because a given dollar change in Canadian income and imports will be only a small fraction of U.S. income. By contrast, however, a given increase in U.S. income and imports will be a relatively large fraction of Canadian income.

The second important determinant of multiplier patterns is openness to trade. The spillover effects of an expansion in any one country on the rest of the world will be more substantial the more open the expanding economy.

The third point to note is the extent to which trade patterns are reflected in the multipliers. The United States, for example, benefits relatively more from a Canadian expansion than does Germany. This reflects the fact that Canada has a high marginal propensity to import from the United States in comparison with its propensity to import from Germany.

Table 3-3 allows us to study not only the effects of an individual country's expansion and the induced spillovers but also the effect of a simultaneous joint expansion in all industrialized countries. The last row of the table provides the multipliers for this experiment. Clearly, if all countries expand together — each raising autonomous expenditure by 1 percent — the multiplier effects are much more substantial. Each country benefits not only from its own expansion and its repercussion effects through induced expansion abroad, but also from the autonomous foreign expansion. Accordingly, the multipliers are around 2 in this case, while being in the range of 1.2 to 1.5 for the case of an isolated expansion.

3-7 Summary

1. Income is at its equilibrium level when the aggregate demand for goods is equal to the level of income.

2. Aggregate demand consists of demand by households for consumption, by firms for investment goods, and by government for goods and services. When foreign trade is taken into account, net exports are added.

3. When income is at its equilibrium level, there are no unintended changes in inventories. An adjustment process for the level of income based on the accumulation or decumulation of inventories leads the economy to the equilibrium income level.

4. The level of aggregate demand is itself affected by the level of income because consumption demand depends on the level of income.

5. The consumption function relates consumption spending to income. Income that is not consumed is saved, so that the saving function can be derived from the consumption function.

6. The multiplier is the amount by which a one-dollar change in autonomous spending changes the equilibrium level of income. The greater the propensity to consume, the higher the multiplier.

7. Government expenditures on goods and services and government transfer payments act like increases in autonomous spending in their effects on the equilibrium level of income. An increase in the rate of a proportional income tax has the same effects on the equilibrium level of income as a reduction in the propensity to consume. A proportional income tax thus reduces the multiplier.

8. The budget surplus is the excess of government receipts over its expenditure. When the government is spending more than it receives, the budget is in deficit. The size of the budget surplus (deficit) is affected by the government's fiscal policy variables — government expenditures, transfer payments, and tax rates.

9. The budget surplus is also affected by changes in tax revenue and transfers resulting from changes in the level of income occurring as a result of changes in private autonomous spending. The cyclically adjusted or full-employment (high-employment) budget surplus is accordingly frequently used as a measure of the active use of fiscal policy. The full-employment surplus measures the budget surplus that would exist if income were at the full-employment level.

10. When foreign trade is taken into account, exports add to and imports subtract from autonomous spending. The dependence of imports on income affects the size of the multiplier: the higher the marginal propensity to import, the lower the multiplier.

11. There are repercussion effects by which an increase in foreign income eventually induces an increase in the demand for foreigners' goods through exports. The size of these interdependence and repercussion effects depends on the relative size and openness of the economy. A small economy may be very dependent on a larger one, but a larger economy's level of income does not depend much on the income level in small foreign economies.

Key Terms

Aggregate demand	**Consumption function**
Equilibrium income	**Marginal propensity to consume**
Involuntary (unintended) inventory	**Marginal propensity to save**
investment	**Multiplier**

Automatic stabilizer
Budget surplus
Budget deficit
Balanced budget multiplier

Full-employment or cyclically
   adjusted surplus
Marginal propensity to import
Repercussion effect

Problems

1. Here we investigate a particular example of the model studied in Sections 3-2 and 3-3 with no government. Suppose the consumption function is given by $C = 100 + 0.8Y$, while investment is given by $\bar{I} = 50$.
   - (a) What is the equilibrium level of income in this case?
   - (b) What is the level of saving in equilibrium?
   - (c) If, for some reason, output was at the level of 800, what would the level of involuntary inventory accumulation be?
   - (d) If $\bar{I}$ were to rise to 100 (we discuss what determines I in later chapters), what would the effect be on equilibrium income?
   - (e) What is the multiplier α here?
   - (f) Draw a diagram indicating the equilibria in both 1a and 1d.

2. Suppose consumption behaviour were to change in Problem 1 so that $C = 100 + 0.9Y$, while $\bar{I}$ remained at 50.
   - (a) Would you expect the equilibrium level of income to be higher or lower than in 1a? Calculate the new equilibrium level, Y', to verify this.
   - (b) Now suppose investment increases to $\bar{I} = 100$, just as in 1d. What is the new equilibrium income?
   - (c) Does this change in investment spending have more or less of an effect on Y than in Problem 1? Why?
   - (d) Draw a diagram indicating the change in equilibrium income in this case.

3. We showed in the text that the equilibrium condition $Y = AD$ is equivalent to the $S = I$, or saving = investment, condition. Starting from $S = I$ and the saving function, derive the equilibrium level of income, as in Equation (10).

4. This problem relates to the so-called paradox of thrift. Suppose that $I = \bar{I}$ and that $C = \bar{C} + cY$, where $\bar{C}$ is a constant.
   - (a) What is the saving function, that is, the function that shows how saving is related to income?
   - (b) Suppose individuals want to save more at every level of income. Show, using a figure like Figure 3-6, how the saving function is shifted.
   - (c) What effect does the increased desire to save have on the new equilibrium level of saving? Explain the paradox.

5. Now let us look at a model that is an example of the one presented in Sections 3-4 and 3-5; that is, it includes government expenditures, taxes, and transfers.

It has the same features as the one in Problems 1 and 2 except that it also has a government. Thus, suppose consumption is given by $C = 100 + 0.8YD$ and that $\bar{I} = 50$, while fiscal policy is summarized by $\bar{G} = 200$, $\overline{TR} = 62.5$, and $t = 0.25$.

(a)   What is the equilibrium level of income in this more complete model?

(b)   What is the value of the new multiplier, $\bar{\alpha}$? Why is this less than the multiplier in Problem 1e?

6.   Show that the equilibrium condition in Equation (32) for an economy with a government and foreign sector can be derived using the condition total injections (investment + government spending + exports) equals total withdrawals (saving + taxes + imports).

7.   Using the same model as in Problem 5, determine the following:

(a)   What is the value of the budget surplus, BS, when $\bar{I} = 50$?

(b)   What is BS when $\bar{I}$ increases to 100?

(c)   What accounts for the change in BS between 7b and 7a?

(d)   Assuming that the full-employment level of income, Y°, is 1200, what is the full-employment budget surplus BS° when $\bar{I} = 50$? 100? (Be careful.)

(e)   What is BS° if $\bar{I} = 50$ and $\bar{G} = 250$, with Y° still equal to 1200?

(f)   Explain why we use BS° rather than simply BS to measure the direction of fiscal policy.

8.   Suppose we expand our model to take account of the fact that transfer payments, TR, do depend on the level of income, Y. When income is high, transfer payments such as unemployment benefits will fall. Conversely, when income is low, unemployment is high and so are unemployment benefits. We can incorporate this into our model by writing transfers as $TR = \overline{TR} - bY$, $b > 0$. Remember that equilibrium income is derived as the solution to $Y_0 = C + I + G = cYD + \bar{I} + \bar{G}$, where $YD = Y + TR - TA$ is disposable income.

(a)   Derive the expression for Y_0 in this case, just as Equation (22) was derived in the text.

(b)   What is the new multiplier?

(c)   Why is the new multiplier less than the standard one, $\bar{\alpha}$?

(d)   How does the change in the multiplier relate to the concept of automatic stabilizers?

9.   Now we look at the role taxes play in determining equilibrium income. Suppose we have an economy of the type in Sections 3-4 and 3-5, described by the following functions:

$C = 50 + 0.8YD$
$\bar{I} = 70$
$\bar{G} = 200$
$\overline{TR} = 100$
$t = 0.20$

(a) Calculate the equilibrium level of income and the multiplier in this model.

(b) Calculate also the budget surplus, *BS*.

(c) Suppose that *t* increases to 0.25. What is the new equilibrium income? The new multiplier?

(d) Calculate the change in the budget surplus. Would you expect the change in the surplus to be more or less if $c = 0.9$ rather than 0.8?

(e) Can you explain why the multiplier is 1 when $t = 1$?

10. Suppose the economy is operating at equilibrium, with $Y_0 = 1000$. If the government undertakes a fiscal change so that the tax rate, *t*, increases by 0.05 and government spending increases by 50, will the budget surplus go up or down? Why?

11. Suppose the government decides to reduce transfer payments (such as welfare), but to increase government expenditures on goods and services by an equal amount. That is, it undertakes a change in fiscal policy such that $\Delta \overline{G} = -\Delta \overline{TR}$.

(a) Would you expect equilibrium income to rise or fall as a result of this change? Why? Check out your answer with the following example: Suppose that initially, $c = 0.8$, $t = 0.25$, and $Y_0 = 600$. Now let $\Delta \overline{G} = 10$ and $\Delta \overline{TR} = -10$.

(b) Find the change in equilibrium income, ΔY_0.

(c) What is the change in the budget surplus, *BS*? Why has *BS* changed?

°12. We have seen in Problem 11 that an increase in *G* accompanied by an equal decrease in *TR* does not leave the budget unchanged. What would the effect on equilibrium income be if *TR* and *G* change so as to leave the budget surplus, *BS*, fixed? Hint: Notice that $BS = TA - TR - G$. We want

$$\Delta BS = \Delta TA - \Delta \overline{TR} - \Delta \overline{G} = 0 \tag{P1}$$

so that $\Delta \overline{TR} = \Delta TA - \Delta \overline{G}$. Since *t* is constant,

$$\Delta TA = t \Delta Y_0 \tag{P2}$$

We also know that $Y_0 = \overline{\alpha}(\overline{C} + \overline{I} + \overline{G} + c\overline{TR})$ and

$$\Delta Y_0 = \overline{\alpha}(\Delta \overline{G} + c \Delta \overline{TR}). \tag{P3}$$

Substituting Equations (P1) and (P2) into Equation (P3), derive an expression for ΔY in terms of $\Delta \overline{G}$. Simplify that expression, using the fact that $\overline{\alpha} = 1/[1 - c(1 - t)]$, to obtain the balanced budget result in the case of changes in transfers and government spending. If you have trouble with this problem, check the appendix to this chapter.

°13.   In the preceding problem (see also the appendix) we derived the balanced
       budget multiplier result. It states that if $\Delta G = \Delta TA$ from the initial to final
       equilibrium, then $\Delta Y = \Delta G$. Let us look at an example of this balanced budget
       multiplier in action.
       Consider the economy described by the following functions:

$C = 85 + 0.75\ YD$
$\bar{I} = 50$
$\bar{G} = 150$
$\overline{TR} = 100$
$t = 0.20$

(a)   Derive the multiplier, $\bar{\alpha}$, and the level of autonomous spending, $\bar{A}$.
(b)   From 13a calculate the equilibrium level of income and the budget
       surplus.
(c)   Now suppose $\bar{G}$ rises to 250 while t increases to 0.28. Repeat 13a for the
       new fiscal policy.
(d)   What are ΔTA, $\Delta\bar{G}$, ΔY, and ΔBS?
(e)   In view of this result and that of Problem 11, what do you think the
       effect on income would be if we had a balanced budget change such that
       $\Delta\overline{TR} = \Delta TA$?

°14.   Suppose the aggregate demand function is as in the following figure. Notice
       that at Y_0 the slope of the aggregate demand curve is greater than 1. (This
       would happen if $c > 1$.) Complete this picture as is done in Figure 3-3 to
       include the arrows indicating adjustment when $Y \neq Y_0$ and show what IU is
       for $Y < Y_0$ and $Y > Y_0$. What is happening in this example, and how does it
       differ fundamentally from Figure 3-3?

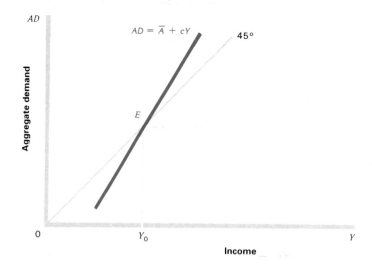

15.   Let us look at the effect of the foreign sector by adding the following equations
       to the model in Problem 9:

$\overline{X} = 150$

$Q = 10 + 0.14Y$

    (a) Calculate the equilibrium level of income and the multiplier in this model.

    (b) Why is the multiplier less than the one obtained in Problem 9?

    °(c) Derive an expression for the trade balance, *NX*, as a function of income and plot it in a diagram with *Y* on the horizontal axis.

    °(d) Show the effect of a change in income on the trade balance, using your diagram. Show also the effect on the trade balance of a change in exports, given income.

    °(e) Calculate the effect on equilibrium income and the trade balance of an increase in exports.

Appendix The Balanced Budget Multiplier

This appendix considers the balanced budget multiplier result mentioned in Section 3-5. The balanced budget multiplier refers to the effects of an increase in government expenditures accompanied by an increase in taxes such that, in the new equilibrium, the budget surplus is exactly the same as in the original equilibrium. The result is that the multiplier of such a policy change, the balanced budget multiplier, is 1.

A multiplier of unity implies that output expands by precisely the amount of the increased government spending with no induced consumption spending. It is apparent that what must be at work is the effect of higher taxes that exactly offset the effect of the income expansion, thus maintaining disposable income, and hence consumption, constant. With no induced consumption spending, output expands simply to match the increased government spending.

We can derive this result formally by noting that the change in aggregate demand ΔAD is equal to the change in government expenditures plus the change in consumption spending. The latter is equal to the marginal propensity to consume out of disposable income, c, times the change in disposable income, ΔYD; that is $\Delta YD = \Delta Y_0 - \Delta TA$, where ΔY_0 is the change in output. Thus,

$$\Delta AD = \Delta \overline{G} + c(\Delta Y_0 - \Delta TA)$$

$$\text{(A1)}$$

Since from one equilibrium to another the change in aggregate demand has to equal the change in output, we have

or

$$\Delta Y_0 = \Delta \overline{G} + c(\Delta Y_0 - \Delta TA)$$

$$\Delta Y_0 = \frac{1}{1 - c}(\Delta \overline{G} - c\Delta TA)$$

$$\text{(A2)}$$

Next we note that by assumption the change in government expenditures between the new equilibrium and the old one is exactly matched by a change in tax collection, so that $G = TA$. It follows from this last equality, after substitution in Equation (A2), that with this particular restriction on fiscal policy we have

$$\Delta Y_0 = \frac{1}{1-c}(\Delta \overline{G} - c\Delta \overline{G}) = \Delta \overline{G} = \Delta TA \qquad \text{(A3)}$$

so that the multiplier is precisely unity.

Another way of deriving the balanced budget multiplier result is by considering the successive rounds of spending changes caused by government policy changes. Suppose each of government expenditures and taxes increase by $1. Let $c(1-t)$, the induced increase in aggregate demand caused by a $1 increase in income in the presence of taxes, be denoted by $\overline{c}$.

Table A3-1 shows the spending induced by the two policy changes. The first column shows the changes in spending resulting from the change in government expenditures and its later repercussions. The second column similarly gives the spending effects in successive rounds of the tax increase. The third column sums the two effects for each spending round, while the final column adds all the changes in spending induced so far. Since $\overline{c}$ is less than 1, $\overline{c}^n$ becomes very small as the number of spending rounds, n, increases, and the final change in aggregate spending caused by the balanced budget increase in governmental spending is just equal to $1.

Table A3-1 *The Balanced Budget Multiplier*

Spending Round	Change in Spending Due To: $\Delta G = 1$	$\Delta TA = 1$	Net This Round	Cumulative Total
1	1	$-\overline{c}$	$1 - \overline{c}$	$1 - \overline{c}$
2	$\overline{c}$	$-\overline{c}^2$	$\overline{c} - \overline{c}^2$	$1 - \overline{c}^2$
3	$\overline{c}^2$	$-\overline{c}^3$	$\overline{c}^2 - \overline{c}^3$	$1 - \overline{c}^3$
4	$\overline{c}^3$	$-\overline{c}^4$	$\overline{c}^3 - \overline{c}^4$	$1 - \overline{c}^4$
.	.	.	.	.
.	.	.	.	.
.	.	.	.	.
n	$\overline{c}^{n-1}$	$-\overline{c}^n$	$\overline{c}^{n-1} - \overline{c}^n$	$1 - \overline{c}^n$

Finally, the balanced budget multiplier can also be thought of from a somewhat different perspective. Consider the goods market equilibrium condition in terms of saving, taxes, transfers, investment, and government expenditures:

$$S + TA - \overline{TR} = \overline{I} + \overline{G} \qquad \text{(A4)}$$

Now, using the definition of the budget surplus,

$$BS = TA - \overline{TR} - \overline{G} = \overline{I} - S \qquad \text{(A5)}$$

If there is no change in the budget deficit or in investment, the equilibrium change in saving is zero. For saving not to change, disposable income must remain unchanged. This says that $\Delta YD = \Delta Y - \Delta TA = 0$, and hence shows once more that the change in income equals the change in taxes. This in turn equals the change in government expenditures.

Hence, the balanced budget multiplier, or more precisely, the multiplier associated with an unchanging budget surplus or deficit, is equal to unity. This perspective on the income determination process is very useful because it emphasizes the fact that a change in the surplus or deficit of one sector is matched by a corresponding change in the deficit or surplus of the remaining sectors. If the government surplus is constrained by fiscal policy to be unchanged, so too must be the private sector's surplus, $S - I$.

CHAPTER 4   *Money, Interest, and Income*

The stock of money, interest rates, and the Bank of Canada seemingly had no place in the model of income determination developed in Chapter 3. Most economists believe that money has an important role to play in the determination of income and employment. Interest rates are frequently mentioned as an important determinant of aggregate spending, and the Bank of Canada and monetary policy receive at least as much public attention as fiscal policy. For instance, the blame for the deep 1980–1982 recession and its extraordinarily high interest rates is often placed on the tight money policy pursued in the U.S. and Canada. This chapter introduces money and monetary policy, and builds an explicit framework of analysis in which the interaction of goods and assets markets can be studied.

This new framework leads to an understanding of the determination of interest rates and of their role in the business cycle. Figure 4-1 shows the interest rate on Treasury bills. This rate represents the payment, per dollar per year, that someone receives who lends to the Government of Canada. Thus an interest rate of 10 percent means that someone who lends $100 to the government for one year will receive 10 percent, or $10, in interest. Figure 4-1 immediately suggests some questions: What factors cause the interest rate to increase, as occurred, for example, in 1988, and what factors cause rates to decline as they did in 1991? Furthermore, when interest rates increase, what are the effects on output and employment?

The model we introduce in this chapter, the *IS-LM model*, is the core of the modern theory of aggregate demand. It maintains the spirit and, indeed, many details of the previous chapter. The model is extended, though, by introducing the interest rate as an additional determinant of aggregate demand and including markets for financial

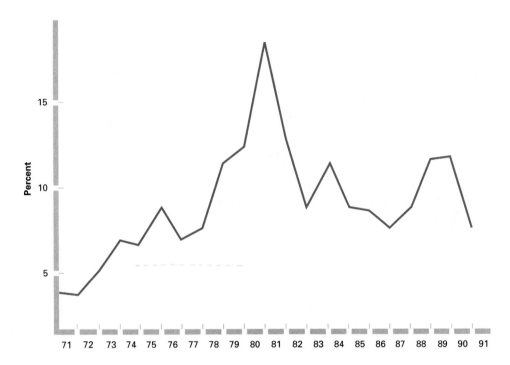

Figure 4-1 *The Interest Rate on Treasury Bills (percent per year)*

(*Source:* Adapted from *Bank of Canada Review*)

assets to determine the interest rate. In other words, the interest rate is now treated, along with income, as an *endogenous* variable. In general, variables whose values are determined by a particular theory are called endogenous, in contrast to *exogenous* variables, whose values are given. In Chapter 3, income, consumption, taxes and imports were treated as endogenous while the interest rate and the components of autonomous spending were considered exogenous. In the model of this chapter, interest rates and income are endogenously determined by equilibrium conditions for the goods and assets markets.

What is the payoff from this complication? The introduction of assets markets and interest rates serves three important purposes:

1. The extension shows how monetary policy works.

2. The analysis qualifies the conclusions of Chapter 3. Consider Figure 4-2, which lays out the logical structure of the model. The inclusion of assets markets in the form of money demand and supply introduces an additional mechanism to the determination of aggregate demand and equilibrium income. An expansionary fiscal policy, for example, would in the first place raise spending and income. That increase in income, though, would affect the assets markets by raising money

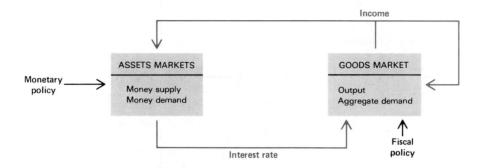

Figure 4-2   *The Structure of the* **IS-LM** *Model*

The *IS-LM* model emphasizes the interaction between goods and assets markets. The model of Chapter 3 looks at income determination by arguing that income affects spending, which in turn determines output and income. Now we add the effects of interest rates on spending and thus income, and the dependence of assets markets on income. Higher income raises money demand and thus interest rates. Higher interest rates lower spending and thus income. Spending, interest rates, and income are determined jointly by equilibrium in goods *and* assets markets.

demand and thereby raising interest rates. The higher interest rates in turn reduce aggregate spending and thus, as we shall show, dampen the expansionary impact of fiscal policy. Indeed, under certain conditions, the increase in interest rates may be sufficiently important to offset *fully* the expansionary effects of fiscal policy. Clearly, such an extreme possibility is an important qualification to our study of fiscal policy in Chapter 3.

3.   Even if the interest rate changes just mentioned only dampen (rather than offset fully) the expansionary effects of fiscal policy, they nevertheless have an important side effect. The *composition* of aggregate demand between investment and consumption spending will depend on the rate of interest. Higher interest rates dampen aggregate demand mainly by reducing investment. Thus, an expansionary fiscal policy would tend to raise consumption through the multiplier, but it would tend to reduce investment through the induced increase in interest rates. The side effects of fiscal expansion on interest rates and investment continue to be a sensitive and important issue in policy making. Because fiscal expansion tends to reduce investment, an influential view is that fiscal policy should not be used as a tool for demand management.

These three reasons justify the more complicated model we study in this chapter. There is the further advantage that the extended model helps us to understand the functioning of financial markets.

Outline of the Chapter

We use Figure 4-2 once more to lay out the structure of this chapter. We start in Section 4-1 with a discussion of the link between interest rates and aggregate demand. Here we use the model of Chapter 3 directly, augmented to include the interest rate as a determinant of aggregate demand. We derive a key relationship — the *IS* curve — that shows combinations of interest rates and levels of income for which the goods markets clear. In this chapter, we restrict the analysis to the case of a closed economy with no foreign trade or capital flows. The open economy case is taken up in Chapters 5 and 6.

In Section 4-2, we turn to assets markets and, in particular, to the money market. We show that the demand for money depends on interest rates and income and that there is a combination of interest rates and income levels, the *LM* curve, for which the money market clears.[1] In Section 4-3, we combine the two schedules to study the joint determination of interest rates and income. Section 4-4 lays out the adjustment process toward equilibrium. Monetary policy is discussed in Section 4-5. Fiscal policy and the important issue of the monetary–fiscal policy mix are considered in Sections 4-6 and 4-7.

4-1 The Goods Market and the *IS* Curve

In this section we derive a goods market equilibrium schedule. The goods market equilibrium schedule, or *IS* schedule, shows combinations of interest rates and levels of output such that aggregate demand equals income. The goods market equilibrium schedule is an extension of income determination with a 45° line diagram. What is new here is that investment is no longer fully exogenous but is also determined by the interest rate. To appreciate the extension of Chapter 3 we briefly review what we found there.

In Chapter 3 we derived an expression for equilibrium income in an economy without foreign trade:

$$Y_0 = \frac{1}{1 - \bar{c}}\bar{A} \qquad \bar{c} = c(1 - t) \tag{1}$$

Equilibrium income in this simple Keynesian model has two determinants: autonomous spending, $\bar{A}$, and the propensity to consume out of income, $\bar{c}$. Autonomous spending

---

[1] The terms *IS* and *LM* are shorthand representations, respectively, of investment equals saving (goods market equilibrium) and money demand (*L*) equals money supply (*M*), or money market equilibrium. The classic article that introduced this model is J.R. Hicks, "Mr. Keynes and the Classics: A Suggested Interpretation," *Econometrica*, 1937, pp. 147–59.

includes government spending, investment spending, and autonomous consumption spending. The propensity to consume out of income, as seen from (1), depends on the propensity to consume out of disposable income, c, and on the fraction of a dollar of income retained after taxes, $(1 - t)$. The higher the level of autonomous spending and the higher the propensity to consume, the higher the equilibrium level of income.

Investment and the Interest Rate

So far, investment spending I has been treated as entirely exogenous — some number such as $70 billion determined altogether outside the model of income determination. Now, as we make our macromodel more complete by introducing interest rates as part of the model, investment spending, too, becomes endogenous. The higher the interest rate, the lower is investment demand.

A simple argument shows why. Investment is spending on additions to the capital stock (machinery, structures, inventories). Such investment is undertaken with the aim of making profits in the future by operating machines and factories. Suppose firms borrow to buy the capital (machines and factories) that they use. Then the higher the interest rate, the more firms have to pay out in interest each year from the earnings they receive from their investment. Thus, the higher the interest rate, the less the profits to the firm after paying interest, and the less it will want to invest. Conversely, a low rate of interest makes investment spending profitable and is, therefore, reflected in a high level of investment demand.

The Investment Demand Schedule

We specify an investment spending function of the form[2]

$$I = \bar{I} - bi \qquad b > 0 \tag{2}$$

where i is the rate of interest and b measures the interest response of investment. $\bar{I}$ now denotes *autonomous* investment spending, that is, investment spending that is independent of both income and the rate of interest.[3] Equation (2) states that the lower the interest rate, the higher is investment demand, with the coefficient b measuring the responsiveness of investment spending to the interest rate.

---

[2] Here and in other places in the book we specify linear (straight-line) versions of behavioural functions. We use the linear specifications to simplify both the algebra and the diagrams. The linearity assumption does not lead to any great difficulties so long as we confine ourselves to talking about small changes in the economy. You should often draw nonlinear versions of our diagrams to be sure you can work with them.

[3] In Chapter 3, investment spending was defined as autonomous with respect to income. Now that the interest rate appears in the model, we have to extend the definition of autonomous to mean independent of both the interest rate and income. To conserve notation, we continue to use $\bar{I}$ to denote autonomous investment, but recognize that the definition is broadened.

Figure 4-3 shows the investment schedule of Equation (2). The schedule shows for each level of the rate of interest the rate at which firms plan to spend on investment. The schedule is negatively sloped to reflect the assumption that a reduction in the rate of interest increases the profitability of additions to the capital stock and therefore to a larger rate of planned investment spending.

The slope of the investment schedule is determined by the coefficient b in Equation (2). If investment is highly responsive to the interest rate, a small decline in interest rates will lead to a large increase in investment, so that the schedule is almost flat. Conversely, if investment responds little to interest rates, the schedule is more nearly vertical. The level of autonomous investment spending, $\bar{I}$, determines the position of the investment schedule. An increase in $\bar{I}$ means that at each level of the interest rate firms plan to invest at a higher rate. This would be shown by a rightward shift of the investment schedule.

The Interest Rate and Aggregate Demand: The *IS* Curve

We now modify the aggregate demand function of Chapter 3 to reflect the new planned investment spending schedule. Aggregate demand still consists of the demand

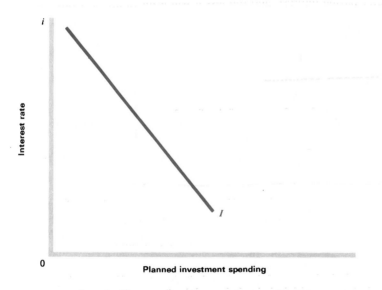

Figure 4-3 *The Investment Schedule*

The investment schedule shows the planned level of investment spending at each rate of interest. Because higher interest rates reduce the profitability of additions to the capital stock, higher interest rates imply lower planned rates of investment spending. Changes in autonomous investment shift the investment schedule.

for consumption, investment, and government spending on goods and services. However, now investment spending depends on the interest rate. We have

$$
\begin{aligned}
AD &= C + I + G \\
&= \overline{C} + c\overline{TR} + c(1 - t)Y + \overline{I} - bi + \overline{G} \\
&= \overline{A} + \overline{c}Y - bi
\end{aligned}
\tag{3}
$$

where

$$
\overline{A} = \overline{C} + c\overline{TR} + \overline{I} + \overline{G}
\tag{4}
$$

From Equation (3) we observe that an increase in the interest rate reduces aggregate demand at a given level of income because an interest rate increase reduces investment spending. Note that the term A, which is the part of aggregate demand unaffected by either the level of income or the interest rate, does include part of investment spending, namely I. As noted earlier, I is the autonomous component of investment spending, which is independent of the interest rate (and income).

At any given level of the interest rate, we can still proceed as in Chapter 3 to determine the equilibrium level of income and output. As the interest rate changes, however, the equilibrium level of income changes. Figure 4-4 is used to derive the *IS* curve.

For a given level of the interest rate, say, i_1, the last term of Equation (3) is a constant (bi_1), and we can in Figure 4-4a draw the aggregate demand function of Chapter 3, this time with an intercept $\overline{A} - bi_1$. The equilibrium level of income obtained in the usual manner is Y_1 at point E_1. Since the equilibrium level of income was derived for a given level of the interest rate i_1, we plot that pair (i_1, Y_1) in the bottom panel as point E_1. We now have one point on the *IS* curve.

Consider next a lower interest rate, i_2. At a lower interest rate, aggregate demand would be higher at each level of income because investment spending is higher. In terms of Figure 4-4a, that implies an upward shift of the aggregate demand schedule. The curve shifts upward because the intercept $\overline{A} - bi$ has been increased. Given the increase in aggregate demand, the equilibrium level of income rises to point E_2, with an associated income level Y_2. At point E_2, in the bottom panel, we record the fact that an interest rate i_2 implies an equilibrium level of income, Y_2 — equilibrium in the sense that the goods market is in equilibrium (or that the goods market *clears*). Point E_2 is another point on the *IS* curve.

We can apply the same procedure to all conceivable levels of the interest rate and thereby generate all the points which make up the *IS* curve. They have in common the property that they are combinations of interest rates and income (output) such that the goods market clears. That is why the *IS* curve is called the *goods market equilibrium schedule*.

Figure 4-4 shows that the *IS* curve is negatively sloped, reflecting the increase in aggregate demand associated with a reduction in the interest rate. We can also derive

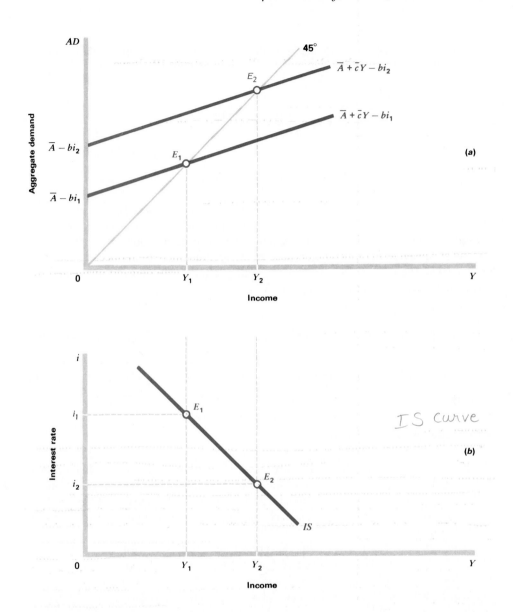

Figure 4-4 *Derivation of the IS Curve*

At an interest rate i_1, equilibrium in the goods market obtains at point E_1 in the upper panel with an income level Y_1. In the lower panel this is recorded as point E_1. A fall in the interest rate to i_2 raises aggregate demand, increasing the level of spending at each income level. The new equilibrium income level is Y_2. In the lower panel, point E_2 records the new equilibrium in the goods market corresponding to an interest rate i_2.

the *IS* curve by using the goods market equilibrium condition, income equals planned spending, or

$$Y = AD$$
$$= \bar{A} + \bar{c}Y - bi \qquad (5)$$

which can be simplified to

$$Y = \bar{\alpha}(\bar{A} - bi) \qquad \bar{\alpha} = 1/(1 - \bar{c}) \qquad (6)$$

where $\bar{\alpha}$ is the multiplier of Chapter 3. Equation (6) should now be compared with (1) at the beginning of this chapter. Note from Equation (6) that a higher interest rate implies a lower level of equilibrium income for a given A, as Figure 4-4 shows.

The construction of the *IS* curve is quite straightforward and may even be deceptively simple. We can gain further understanding of the economics of the *IS* curve by asking and answering the following questions:

- What determines the slope of the *IS* curve?

- What determines the position of the *IS* curve, given its slope, and what causes the curve to shift?

- What happens when the interest rate and income are at levels such that we are not on the *IS* curve?

The Slope of the *IS* Curve

We have already noted that the *IS* curve is negatively sloped because a higher level of the interest rate reduces investment spending, therefore reducing aggregate demand and thus the equilibrium level of income. The steepness of the curve depends on how sensitive investment spending is to a change in the interest rate, and also on the multiplier $\bar{\alpha}$ in Equation (6).

Suppose that investment spending is very sensitive to the interest rate, so that b in Equation (6) is large. Then, in terms of Figure 4-4, a given change in the interest rate produces a large change in aggregate demand, and thus shifts the aggregate demand curve in Figure 4-4a by a large distance. A large shift in the aggregate demand schedule produces a correspondingly large change in the equilibrium level of income. If a given change in the interest rate produces a large change in income, the *IS* curve is very flat. This is the case if investment is very sensitive to the interest rate, that is, if b is large. Correspondingly, with b small and investment spending not very sensitive to the interest rate, the *IS* curve is relatively steep.

The Role of the Multiplier

Consider next the effects of the multiplier $\bar{\alpha}$ on the steepness of the *IS* curve. Figure 4-5 shows aggregate demand curves corresponding to different multipliers. The coef-

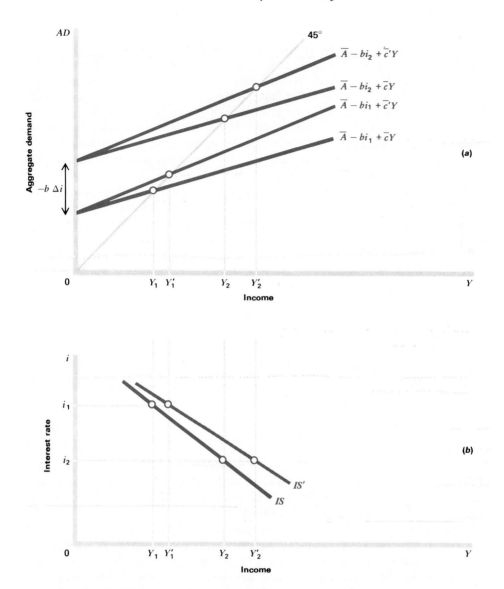

Figure 4-5 *Effects of the Multiplier on the Steepness of the IS Curve*

The diagram shows that corresponding to a higher marginal propensity to spend, and hence a steeper aggregate demand schedule, there is a flatter *IS* schedule.

ficient $\bar{c}$ on the flatter aggregate demand curves is smaller than the corresponding coefficient $\bar{c}'$ on the steeper aggregate demand curves. The multiplier is accordingly larger on the steeper aggregate demand curves. The initial levels of income, Y_1 and Y_1', correspond to the interest rate i_1 on the lower of each of the flatter and steeper aggregate demand curves, respectively.

A given reduction in the interest rate, to i_2, raises the intercept of the aggregate demand curves by the same vertical distance, as shown in the top panel. However, the implied change in income is very different. For the steeper curve, income rises to Y_2', while it rises only to Y_2 on the flatter line. The change in equilibrium income corresponding to a given change in the interest rate is accordingly larger as the aggregate demand curve is steeper; that is, the larger the multiplier, the greater the rise in income. As we see from the lower figure, the larger the multiplier, the flatter the *IS* curve. Equivalently, the larger the multiplier, the larger the change in income produced by a given change in the interest rate.

We have thus seen that the smaller the sensitivity of investment spending to the interest rate and the smaller the multiplier, the steeper the *IS* curve. This conclusion is confirmed using Equation (6). We can turn Equation (6) around to express the interest rate as a function of the level of income:

$$i = \frac{\overline{A}}{b} - \frac{Y}{\overline{\alpha}b}$$
(6a)

Thus, for a given change in Y, the associated change in i will be larger in size as b is smaller and $\overline{\alpha}$ is smaller.

Given that the slope of the *IS* curve depends on the multiplier, fiscal policy can affect that slope. The multiplier is affected by the tax rate: An increase in the tax rate reduces the multiplier. Accordingly, the higher the tax rate, the steeper the *IS* curve.

The Position of the *IS* Curve

Figure 4-6 shows two different *IS* curves, one of which lies to the right and above the other. What might cause the *IS* curve to be at *IS'* rather than at *IS*? The answer is an increase in the level of autonomous spending.

In Figure 4-6*a* we show an initial aggregate demand curve drawn for a level of autonomous spending $\overline{A}$ and for an interest rate i_1. Corresponding to the initial aggregate demand curve is the point E_1 on the *IS* curve in Figure 4-6*b*. Now, at the same interest rate, let the level of autonomous spending increase to $\overline{A}'$. The increase in autonomous spending increases the equilibrium level of income at the interest rate i_1. The point E_2 in Figure 4-6*b* is thus a point on the new goods market equilibrium schedule *IS'*. Since E_1 was an arbitrary point on the initial *IS* curve, we can perform the exercise for all levels of the interest rate and thereby generate the new curve *IS'*. Thus, an increase in autonomous spending shifts the curve out to the right.

By how much does the curve shift? The change in income, as a result of the change in autonomous spending, can be seen from the top panel to be just the multiplier times the change in autonomous spending. That means that the *IS* curve is shifted horizontally by a distance equal to the multiplier times the change in autonomous spending as in the lower panel.

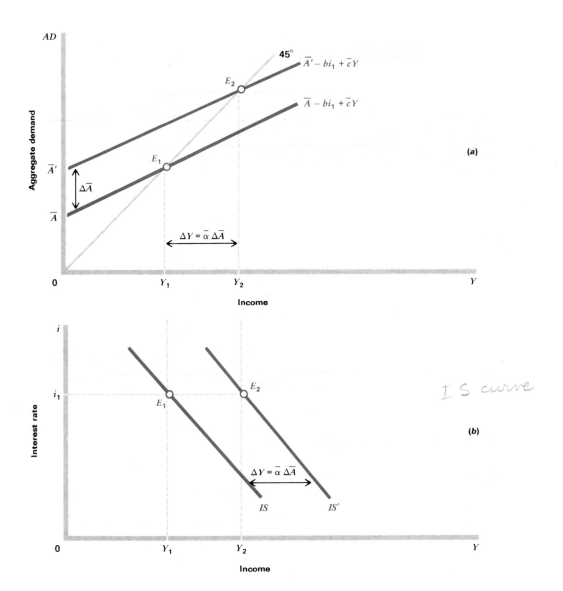

Figure 4-6 *A Shift in the IS Curve Caused by a Change in Autonomous Spending*

An increase in aggregate demand due to higher autonomous spending shifts the aggregate demand curve in (*a*) up, raising the equilibrium level of output at interest rate i_1. The *IS* schedule shifts. At each level of the interest rate, equilibrium income is now higher. The horizontal shift of the *IS* schedule is equal to the multiplier times the increase in autonomous spending.

The level of autonomous spending is, from Equation (4):

$$\overline{A} = \overline{C} + c\overline{TR} + \overline{I} + \overline{G}$$

Accordingly, an increase in government expenditure or transfer payments will shift the *IS* curve out to the right, the extent of the shift depending on the size of the multiplier. A reduction in transfer payments or in government expenditure shifts the *IS* curve to the left.

Positions off the *IS* Curve

We gain understanding of the meaning of the *IS* curve by considering points off the curve. Figure 4-7 reproduces Figure 4-4, along with two additional points — the disequilibrium points E_3 and E_4. Consider first the question of what is true for points off the schedule, points such as E_3 and E_4. In Figure 4-7b at point E_3 we have the same interest rate i_2 as at point E_2, but the level of income is lower than at E_2. Since the interest rate i_2 at E_3 is the same as at E_2, we must have the same aggregate demand function corresponding to the two points. Accordingly, looking now at Figure 4-7a, we find both points are on the same aggregate demand schedule. At E_3 on that schedule, aggregate demand exceeds the level of income. Point E_3 is therefore a point of *excess demand* for goods; the interest rate is too low or income is too low for the goods market to be in equilibrium. Demand for goods exceeds output.

Next, consider point E_4 in Figure 4-7b. Here we have the same rate of interest i_1 as at E_1, but the level of income is higher. Given the interest rate i_1, the corresponding point in Figure 4-7a is at E_4, where we have an *excess supply* of goods since output is larger than aggregate demand — that is, aggregate demand, given the interest rate i_1 and the income level Y_2.

The preceding discussion shows that points above and to the right of the *IS* curve — points like E_4 — are points of excess supply of goods. This is indicated by *ESG* (excess supply of goods) in Figure 4-7b. Points below and to the left of the *IS* curve are points of excess demand for goods (*EDG*). At a point like E_3, the interest rate is too low and aggregate demand is therefore too high, relative to income. *EDG* shows the region of excess demand in Figure 4-7.

Summary

The major points about the *IS* curve are:

1. The *IS* curve is the schedule of combinations of the interest rate and level of income such that the goods market is in equilibrium.

2. The *IS* curve is negatively sloped because an increase in the interest rate reduces planned investment spending and therefore reduces aggregate demand, thus reducing the equilibrium level of income.

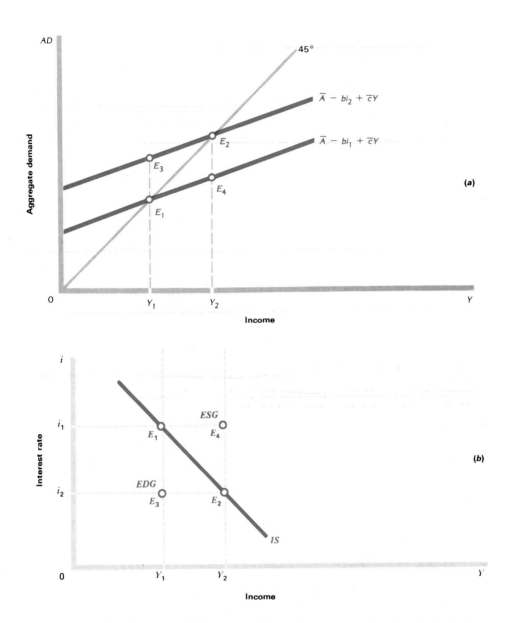

Figure 4-7 *Excess Supply (ESG) and Demand (EDG) in the Goods Market*

Points above and to the right of the *IS* schedule correspond to an excess supply of goods, and points below and to the left to an excess demand for goods. At a point such as E_4, interest rates are higher than at E_2 on the *IS* curve. At the higher interest rates, investment spending is too low, and thus output exceeds planned spending and there is an excess supply of goods.

3. The smaller the multiplier and the less sensitive investment spending is to changes in the interest rate, the steeper the curve.

4. The *IS* curve is shifted by changes in autonomous spending. An increase in autonomous spending, including an increase in government purchases, shifts the *IS* curve out to the right.

5. At points to the left of the curve, there is excess supply in the goods market, and at points to the right of the curve, there is excess demand for goods.

We turn now to examine behaviour in the assets markets.

4-2 The Assets Markets and the *LM* Curve

In the preceding section, we discussed aggregate demand and the goods market. In the present section, we turn to the assets markets. The assets markets are the markets in which money, bonds, stocks, houses, and other forms of wealth are traded. Up to this point in the book, we have ignored the role of those markets in affecting the level of income, and it is now time to remedy the omission.

There is a large variety of assets, and a tremendous volume of trading occurs every day in the assets markets. However, we shall simplify matters by grouping all available financial assets into two groups, *money* and *interest-bearing* assets.[4] We shall frequently refer to the nonmonetary assets simply as *bonds*.

A bond is a promise to pay to its holder certain agreed-upon amounts of money at specified dates in the future. For example, a borrower sells a bond in exchange for a given amount of money today, say $100, and promises to pay a fixed amount, say $6, each year to the person who owns the bond, and to repay the full $100 (the principal) after some fixed period of time, such as three years, or perhaps longer. In this example, the interest rate is 6 percent, for that is the percentage of the amount borrowed that the borrower pays each year.

The Wealth Constraint

At any given time, an individual has to decide how to allocate his or her financial wealth between alternative assets. The more bonds held, the more interest received on total financial wealth. The more money held, the more likely the individual is to

---

[4] We assume in this section that certain assets, such as the capital that firms use in production, are not traded. That too is a simplification. A more complete treatment of the assets markets would allow for the trading of capital and would introduce a relative price for the capital operated by firms. This treatment is usually reserved for advanced courses. For such a treatment of the assets markets, see James Tobin, "A General Equilibrium Approach to Monetary Theory," *Journal of Money, Credit and Banking*, February 1969, pp. 15–29, and by the same author, "Money, Capital, and Other Stores of Value," *American Economic Review*, May 1961, pp. 26–37.

Box 4-I   Assets and Asset Returns

There are four kinds of assets in the economy: money, interest-bearing assets, equities or stocks, and real assets.

Money

The money stock consists of assets that can be immediately used for making payments. It includes currency (notes and coins) and deposits on which cheques can be written. There is no interest paid on currency and most chequable deposits. However, in recent years, interest-bearing chequing accounts have become more common, thus blurring the distinction between money and nonmonetary financial assets. The definition of the stock of money is discussed in more detail in Chapter 11.

Interest-Bearing Assets

These include savings accounts in banks and other financial institutions, mortgages, and bonds. A bond is a promise by a borrower to pay the lender a certain amount (the principal) at a specified date (the maturity of the bond) and in the meantime to pay a given amount of interest per year. Bonds are issued by many types of borrower — the government, municipalities, and corporations. The interest rates on bonds issued by different borrowers reflect the differing risk of default. Default occurs when a borrower is unable to meet the commitment to pay interest or principal.

Equities or Stocks

Equities or stocks are claims to a share of the profits in an enterprise. For example, a share in Alberta Energy entitles the owner to a share of the profits of that corporation. The shareholder or stockholder receives the return on equity in two forms. Most firms pay regular *dividends*, which means that stockholders receive a certain amount of dollars for each share they own. Firms may also retain part of their profits and reinvest them in additional capital equipment. When this occurs, the shares become more valuable and stockholders make *capital gains*. A capital gain is an increase, per period of time, in the price of an asset. Of course, when the outlook for a corporation turns sour, stock prices can fall and stockholders make capital losses.

Real Assets

Real assets, or tangible assets, are the machines, land, and structures owned by corporations, and the consumer durables (washing machines, stereos, etc.) and houses owned by households. These assets carry a return that differs from one asset to another.

Owner-occupied houses provide a return to owners who enjoy living in them and not paying monthly rent; the machines a firm owns contribute to producing output and thus making profits. The assets are called real to distinguish them from financial assets (money, stocks, bonds).

In macroeconomics, to make things manageable, we lump assets into two categories. On one side we have money, with the specific characteristic that it is the only asset that serves as a means of payment. On the other side we have all other assets. Because money offers the convenience of being a means of payment, it carries a lower return than other assets, but that differential depends on the relative supplies of assets. As we see in this chapter, when the Bank of Canada reduces the money stock and increases the supply of other assets (we say "bonds"), the yield on other assets increases.

The appendix to Chapter 11 develops the relationship between interest rates and asset prices or present values. The appendix can be read independently of Chapter 11, and the interested student can study that material now.

---

have money available when he or she wants to make a purchase. The person who has $1000 in financial wealth has to decide whether to hold, say, $900 in bonds and $100 in money, or $500 in each type of asset, or even $1000 in money and none in bonds. Decisions on the form in which to hold assets are *portfolio decisions.*

The example makes it clear that the portfolio decision on how much money to hold and the decision on how many bonds to hold are really the same decision. Given the level of financial wealth, the individual who has decided how many bonds to hold has implicitly also decided how much money to hold. There is thus a *wealth budget constraint* which states that the sum of the individual's demand for money and demand for bonds has to add up to that person's total financial wealth.

An important implication of the wealth budget constraint is that it allows us to discuss asset markets entirely in terms of the money market. Given the supplies of assets and therefore given total wealth, when the money market is in equilibrium, the bond market will turn out also to be in equilibrium. Similarly, when there is excess demand in the money market, there is an excess supply of bonds. We can therefore fully discuss the assets markets by concentrating our attention on the money market.

Real and Nominal Money Demand

At this stage in our analysis, we are assuming that the price level is fixed exogenously. However, to prepare the way for the model of price determination introduced in Chapter 7, we make the crucial distinction between real and nominal variables. The nominal quantity of money is measured in terms of dollars while *real money balances*, *real balances* for short, are the quantity of nominal money divided by the price level. If the nominal quantity of money is $100 and the price level is $2 per good — meaning that the representative basket of goods costs $2 — then the real quantity of money is 50 goods.

To make this distinction clear, we denote the nominal money supply by M and the real money supply by M/P where P is the price level. We continue to assume that all income and expenditure variables are measured in real terms.

The Demand for Money

We now turn to the money market and initially concentrate on the demand for real balances.[5] The demand for money is a demand for real balances because the public holds money for what it will buy. The higher the price level, the more nominal balances a person has to hold to be able to purchase a given quantity of goods. If the price level doubles, then an individual has to hold twice as large a nominal balance in order to be able to buy the same amount of goods.

The demand for real balances depends on the level of real income and the interest rate. It depends on the level of real income because individuals hold money to finance their expenditures, which, in turn, depend on income. The demand for money depends also on the cost of holding money. The cost of holding money is the interest that is forgone by holding money rather than other assets. The higher the interest rate, the more costly it is to hold money rather than other assets and, accordingly, the less cash will be held at each level of income.[6] Individuals can economize on their holdings of cash, when the interest rate rises, by being more careful in managing their money, or by making transfers from money to bonds whenever their money holdings reach any appreciable magnitude. If the interest rate is 1 percent, then there is very little benefit from holding bonds rather than money. However, when the interest rate is 10 percent, one would probably go to some effort not to hold more money than needed to finance day-to-day transactions.

On these simple grounds, then, the demand for real balances increases with the level of real income and decreases with the interest rate. The demand for real balances, denoted by L, is accordingly written[7]

$$L = kY - hi \qquad k > 0 \qquad h > 0 \tag{7}$$

The parameters k and h reflect the sensitivity of the demand for real balances to the level of income and the interest rate, respectively. A $5 increase in real income raises

---

[5] The demand for money is studied in depth in Chapter 12; here we only briefly present the arguments underlying the demand for money.

[6] In recent years, it has become more common to pay interest on some forms of money holdings. Nevertheless there do remain sizable parts of money holdings, including currency, on which no interest is paid. Overall, money earns less interest than other assets, and the analysis of this chapter is still applicable.

[7] Once again, we use a linear equation to describe a relationship. You should experiment with an alternative form, for example, $L = kY + h'/i$, where k and h' are positive. How would the equivalent of Figure 4-8 look for this demand function?

money demand by $5k$ real dollars. An increase in the interest rate by 1 percentage point reduces real money demand by h real dollars.

The demand function for real balances, Equation (10), implies that for a given level of income, the quantity demanded is a decreasing function of the rate of interest. Such a demand curve is shown in Figure 4-8 for a level of income Y_1. The higher the level of income, the larger is the demand for real balances, and therefore the further to the right is the demand curve. The demand curve for a higher level of real income Y_2 is also shown in Figure 4-8.

The Supply of Money, Money Market Equilibrium, and the *LM* Curve

Now we study equilibrium in the money market. For that purpose we have to say how the supply of money is determined. The nominal quantity of money M is controlled by the Bank of Canada, and we take it as given at the level $\overline{M}$. We assume the price level is constant at the level $\overline{P}$, so that the real money supply is at the level $\overline{M}/\overline{P}$.[8]

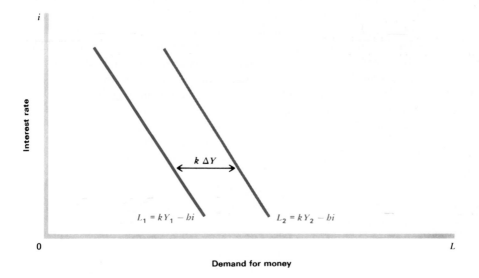

Figure 4-8 *The Demand for Real Balances as a Function of the Interest Rate and Real Income*

The demand for real balances is drawn as a function of the rate of interest. The higher the rate of interest, the lower the quantity of real balances demanded, given the level of income. An increase in income raises the demand for money. This is shown by a rightward shift of the money demand schedule.

---

[8] Since for the present we are holding constant the money supply and price level, we refer to them as exogenous and denote that fact by a bar.

In Figure 4-9, we show combinations of interest rate and income levels such that the demand for real balances exactly matches the available supply. Starting with the level of income Y_1, the corresponding demand curve for real balances, L_1, is shown in Figure 4-9b. It is drawn, as in Figure 4-8, as a decreasing function of the interest rate. The existing supply of real balances M/P is shown by the vertical line, since it is given and therefore is independent of the interest rate. The interest rate i_1 has the property that it clears the money market. At that interest rate, the demand for real balances equals the supply. Therefore, point E_1 is an equilibrium point in the money market. That point is recorded in Figure 4-9a as a point on the *money market equilibrium schedule*, or the *LM* curve.

Consider next the effect of an increase in income to Y_2. In Figure 4-9b the higher level of income causes the demand for real balances to be higher at each level of the interest rate, and so the demand curve for real balances shifts up and to the right, to L_2. The interest rate increases to i_2 to maintain equilibrium in the money market at that higher level of income. Accordingly, the new equilibrium point is E_2. In Figure 4-9a we record point E_2 as a point of equilibrium in the money market. Performing the same exercise for all income levels, we generate a series of points that can be linked to give us the *LM* schedule.

The *LM* schedule, or money market equilibrium schedule, shows all combinations of interest rates and levels of income such that the demand for real balances is equal to the supply. Along the *LM* schedule, the money market is in equilibrium.

The *LM* curve is positively sloped. An increase in the interest rate reduces the demand for real balances. To maintain the demand for real balances equal to the fixed

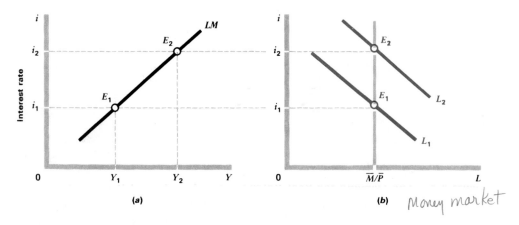

(a)

(b) Money market

Figure 4-9 *Derivation of the **LM** Curve*

The right-hand panel shows the money market. The supply of real balances is the vertical line $\overline{M}/\overline{P}$. The nominal money supply $\overline{M}$ is fixed by the central bank, and the price level $\overline{P}$ is assumed given. Demand for money curves L_1 and L_2 correspond to different levels of income. When the income level is Y_1, L_1 applies, and the equilibrium interest rate is i_1. This gives point E_1 on the *LM* schedule in (a). At income level Y_2, greater than Y_1, the equilibrium interest rate is i_2, yielding point E_2 on the *LM* curve.

supply, the level of income has, therefore, to rise. Accordingly, money market equilibrium implies that an increase in the interest rate is accompanied by an increase in the level of income.

The *LM* curve can be obtained directly by combining the demand curve for real balances, Equation (10), and the fixed supply of real balances. For the money market to be in equilibrium, demand has to equal supply, or

$$\frac{\overline{M}}{P} = kY - hi \tag{8}$$

Solving for the interest rate:

$$i = \frac{1}{h}\left(kY - \frac{\overline{M}}{P}\right) \tag{8a}$$

The relationship (8a) is the *LM* curve.

Next we ask the same questions about the properties of the *LM* schedule that we asked about the *IS* curve.

The Slope of the *LM* Curve

The larger the responsiveness of the demand for money to income, as measured by k, and the lower the responsiveness of the demand for money to the interest rate h, the steeper the *LM* curve will be. This point can be established by experimenting with Figure 4-9. It can also be confirmed by examining Equation (11a), where a given change in income Y has a larger effect on the interest rate i, the larger is k and the smaller is h. If the demand for money is relatively insensitive to the interest rate, so that h is close to zero, the *LM* curve is nearly vertical. If the demand for money is very sensitive to the interest rate, so that h is large, then the *LM* curve is close to horizontal. In that case, a small change in the interest rate is accompanied by a large change in the level of income to maintain money market equilibrium.

The Position of the *LM* Curve

The real money supply is held constant along the *LM* curve. It follows that a change in the money supply will shift the *LM* curve. In Figure 4-10, we show the effect of an increase in the money supply. In Figure 4-10*b*, we draw the demand for real money balances for a level of income Y_1. With the initial real money supply $\overline{M}/\overline{P}$, the equilibrium is at point E_1, with an interest rate i_1. The corresponding point on the *LM* schedule is E_1.

Consider the effect of an increase in the nominal money supply to M' so that the real money supply shifts to $\overline{M'}/\overline{P}$ and the money supply schedule shifts to the right. At the initial level of income and, hence, on the demand schedule L_1, there is now an

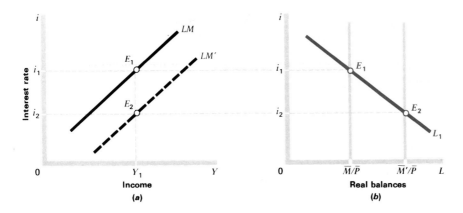

Figure 4-10 *A Shift in the LM Curve Caused by an Increase in the Supply of Money*

An increase in the stock of real balances shifts the supply schedule in the right panel from $\overline{M}/\overline{P}$ to $\overline{M}'/\overline{P}$. At the initial income level Y_1, the equilibrium interest rate in the money market falls to i_2. In the left panel we show point E_2 as one point on the new *LM* schedule, corresponding to the higher money stock. Thus an increase in the real money stock shifts the *LM* schedule down and to the right.

excess supply of real balances. To restore money market equilibrium at the income level Y_1, the interest rate has to decline to i_2. The new equilibrium is, therefore, at point E_2. This implies that in Figure 4-10a, the *LM* schedule shifts to the right and down to *LM'*. At each level of income the equilibrium interest rate has to be lower to induce people to hold the larger real quantity of money. Alternatively, at each level of the interest rate the level of income has to be higher so as to raise the transactions demand for money and thereby absorb the higher real money supply. These points can be noted, too, from inspection of the money market equilibrium condition in Equation (8).

Positions off the *LM* Curve

Next we consider points off the *LM* schedule, to characterize them as points of excess demand or supply of money. For that purpose, look at Figure 4-11, which reproduces Figure 4-9 but adds the disequilibrium points E_3 and E_4. Look first at point E_1, where the money market is in equilibrium. Next assume an increase in the level of income to Y_2. This will raise the demand for real balances and shift the demand curve to L_2. At the initial interest rate, the demand for real balances would be indicated by point E_4 in Figure 4-11b, and we would have an excess demand for money equal to the distance E_1E_4. Accordingly, point E_4 in Figure 4-11a is a point of excess demand for money: The interest rate is too low and/or the level of income too high for the money

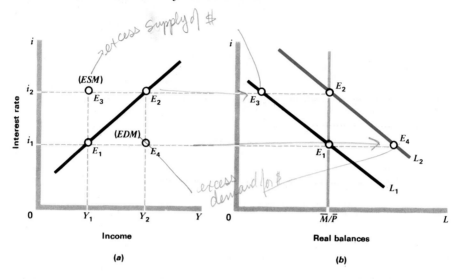

Figure 4-11   *Excess Demand (EDM) and Supply (ESM) of Money*

Points above and to the left of the *LM* schedule correspond to an excess supply of real balances; points below and to the right to an excess demand for real balances. Starting at point E_1 in the left panel, an increase in income takes us to E_4. At E_4 in the right panel, there is an excess demand for money — and thus at E_4 in the left panel there is an excess demand for money. By a similar argument, we can start at E_2 and move to E_3, at which the level of income is lower. This creates an excess supply of money.

market to clear. Consider, next, point E_3 in Figure 4-11*b*. Here we have the initial level of income Y_1, but an interest rate that is too high to yield money market equilibrium. Accordingly, we have an excess supply of money equal to the distance E_3E_2. Point E_3 in Figure 4-11*a* therefore corresponds to an excess supply of money.

More generally, any point to the right and below the *LM* schedule is a point of excess demand for money, and any point to the left and above the *LM* curve is a point of excess supply. This is shown by the *EDM* and *ESM* notations in Figure 4-11*a*.

Summary

The following are the major points about the *LM* curve.

1. The *LM* curve is the schedule of combinations of the interest rate and level of income such that the money market is in equilibrium.

2. When the money market is in equilibrium, so is the bond market. The *LM* curve is, therefore, also the schedule of combinations of the level of income and the interest rate such that the bond market is in equilibrium.

3. The *LM* curve is positively sloped. Given the fixed money supply, an increase in the level of income, which increases the quantity of money demanded, has to be accompanied by an increase in the interest rate. This reduces the quantity of money demanded and thereby maintains money market equilibrium.

4. The *LM* curve is shifted by changes in the money supply. An increase in the money supply shifts the *LM* curve to the right.

5. At points to the right of the *LM* curve, there is an excess demand for money, and at points to its left, there is an excess supply of money.

We are now ready to discuss the joint equilibrium of the goods and assets markets.

4-3 Equilibrium in the Goods and Assets Markets

The conditions that have to be satisfied for the goods and money markets, respectively, to be in equilibrium are summarized by the *IS* and *LM* schedules. The task now is to determine how these markets are brought into *simultaneous* equilibrium. For simultaneous equilibrium, interest rates and income have to be such that both the goods market and the money market are in equilibrium. That condition is satisfied at point *E* in Figure 4-12. The equilibrium interest rate is therefore i_0, and the equilibrium level of income is Y_0, given the exogenous variables — the real money supply and fiscal policy.[9] At point *E*, both the goods market and the assets markets are in equilibrium.

Figure 4-12 summarizes our analysis: The interest rate and the level of output are determined by the interaction of the assets (*LM*) and goods (*IS*) markets.

It is worth stepping back now to review our assumptions and the meaning of the equilibrium at *E*. The major assumption is that the price level is constant and that firms are willing to supply whatever amount of output is demanded at that price level. Thus, we assume the level of output Y_0 in Figure 4-12 will be willingly supplied by firms at the price level $\bar{P}$. We repeat that this assumption is one that is temporarily needed for the development of the analysis; it will be dropped in Chapter 7 when we begin to study the determinants of the price level.

At the point *E*, in Figure 4-12, the economy is in equilibrium, given the price level, because both the goods and money markets are in equilibrium. The demand for goods is equal to the level of income on the *IS* curve, and on the *LM* curve the demand for money is equal to the supply of money. That also means the supply of bonds is equal to the demand for bonds, as the discussion of the wealth budget constraint showed. Accordingly, at point *E*, firms are producing the amount of output that is demanded (there is no unintended inventory accumulation or decumulation), and individuals have the portfolio compositions they desire.

---

[9] Recall that exogenous variables are those whose values are not determined within the system being studied.

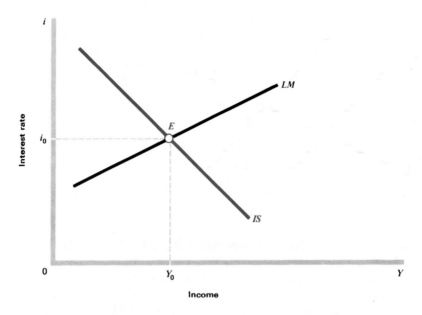

Figure 4-12   *Goods and Assets Market Equilibrium*

Goods and assets markets clear at point *E*. Interest rates and income are such that the public holds the existing stock of money and planned spending equals output.

Changes in the Equilibrium Levels of Income and the Interest Rate

The equilibrium levels of income and the interest rate change when either the *IS* or the *LM* curve shifts. Figure 4-13, for example, shows the effects of an increase in autonomous investment on the equilibrium levels of income and the interest rate. Such an increase raises autonomous spending $\bar{A}$ and therefore shifts the *IS* curve to the right. That results in a rise in the level of income and an increase in the interest rate at point *E'*.

Recall that an increase in autonomous spending $\Delta \bar{I}$ shifts the *IS* curve to the right by the amount $\bar{\alpha}\Delta\bar{I}$, as we show in Figure 4-13. In Chapter 3, where we dealt only with the goods market, we would have argued that $\bar{\alpha}\Delta\bar{I}$ would be the change in the level of income resulting from the change of $\Delta\bar{I}$ in autonomous spending. It can be seen in Figure 4-13 that the change in income here is only ΔY_0, which is clearly less than the shift in the *IS* curve.

What explains the fact that the increase in income is smaller than the increase in autonomous spending *I* times the simple multiplier? Diagrammatically, it is clear that it is the slope of the *LM* curve. If the *LM* curve were horizontal, there would be no difference between the extent of the horizontal shift of the *IS* curve and the change

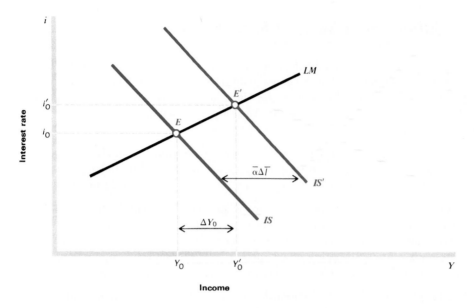

Figure 4-13 *Effects of an Increase in Autonomous Spending on Income and the Interest Rate*

An increase in autonomous spending shifts the *IS* schedule out and to the right. Income increases, and the equilibrium income level rises. The increase in income is less than is given by the simple multiplier $\bar{\alpha}$. This is because interest rates increase and dampen investment spending.

in income. If the *LM* curve were horizontal, then the interest rate would not change when the *IS* curve shifts.

What is the economics of what is happening? The increase in autonomous spending does tend to increase the level of income, but an increase in income increases the demand for money. With the supply of money fixed, the interest rate has to rise to ensure that the demand for money stays equal to the fixed supply. When the interest rate rises, investment spending is reduced because investment is negatively related to the interest rate. Accordingly, the equilibrium change in income is less than the horizontal shift of the *IS* curve $\bar{\alpha}\Delta\bar{I}$.

We have now provided an example of the use of the *IS-LM* apparatus. That apparatus is most useful for studying the effects of monetary and fiscal policy on income and the interest rate, and we so use it in Sections 4-5 and 4-6. Before we do, however, we discuss how the economy moves from one equilibrium, such as *E*, to another, such as *E'*.

4-4 Adjustment Toward Equilibrium

Suppose the economy were initially at a point like E in Figure 4-13, and that one of the curves then shifted, so that the new equilibrium was at a point like E'. How would that new equilibrium actually be reached? The adjustment will involve changes in both the interest rate and the level of income. To study how they move over time, we make two assumptions.

1. Output increases whenever there is an excess demand for goods and contracts whenever there is an excess supply of goods. This assumption reflects the adjustment of firms to undesired decumulation and accumulation of inventories.

2. The interest rate rises whenever there is an excess demand for money and falls whenever there is an excess supply of money. This adjustment occurs because an excess demand for money implies an excess supply of other assets (bonds). In attempting to acquire more money, people sell off bonds and thereby cause their prices to fall or their yields (interest rate) to rise.

A detailed discussion of the relationship between the price of a bond and its yield is presented in the appendix to Chapter 11. Here we give only a brief explanation. For simplicity, consider a bond which promises to pay the holder of the bond $5 per year forever. The $5 is known as the bond *coupon*, and a bond which promises to pay a given amount to the holder of the bond forever is known as a *perpetuity*. If the yield available on other assets is 5 percent, the perpetuity will sell for $100 because at that price it too yields 5 percent (= $5/$100). Now suppose that the yield on other assets rises to 10 percent. Then the price of the perpetuity will drop to $50, because only at that price does the perpetuity yield 10 percent; that is, the $5 per year interest on a bond costing $50 gives its owners a 10 percent yield on their $50. This example makes it clear that the price of a bond and its yield are inversely related, given the coupon.

In point 2 above we assumed that an excess demand for money causes asset holders to attempt to sell off their bonds, thereby causing the bonds' prices to fall and their yields to rise. Conversely, when there is an excess supply of money, people attempt to use their money to buy up other assets, raising the assets' prices and lowering their yields.

In Figure 4-14 we apply the analysis to study the adjustment of the economy. Four regions are represented, and they are characterized in Table 4-1. We know from Figure 4-11 that there is an excess supply of money above the *LM* curve, and hence we show *ESM* in regions I and II in Table 4-1. Similarly, we know from Figure 4-7 that there is an excess demand for goods below the *IS* curve. Hence, we show *EDG* for regions II and III in Table 4-1. You should be able to explain the remaining entries of Table 4-1.

The adjustment directions specified in assumptions 1 and 2 above are represented by arrows in Figure 4-14. Thus, for example, in region IV we have an excess demand for money that causes interest rates to rise as other assets are sold off for money and their prices decline. The rising interest rates are represented by the upward-pointing arrow. There is, too, an excess supply of goods in region IV, and, accordingly, involuntary inventory accumulation to which firms respond by reducing output. Declining output is indicated by the leftward-pointing arrow. The adjustments shown by the arrows will lead ultimately, perhaps in a cyclical manner, to the equilibrium point E. For example, starting at E_1 we show the economy moving to E, with income and the interest rate increasing along the *adjustment path* indicated.

Table 4-1 *Disequilibrium and Adjustment*

| | Goods Market | | Money Market | |
| | Disequilibrium | Income Adjustment | Disequilibrium | Interest Rate Adjustment |
Region				
I	ESG	Falls	ESM	Falls
II	EDG	Rises	ESM	Falls
III	EDG	Rises	EDM	Rises
IV	ESG	Falls	EDM	Rises

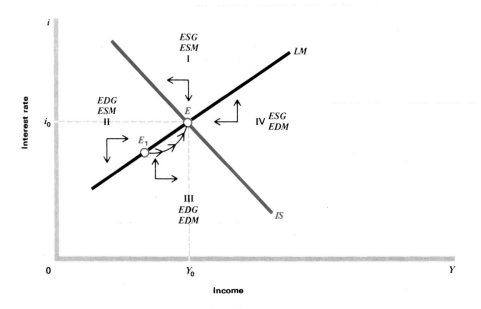

Figure 4-14 *Disequilibrium and Dynamics in the Goods and Money Markets*

Income and interest rates adjust to the disequilibrium in goods markets and assets markets. Specifically, interest rates fall when there is an excess supply of money and rise when there is an excess demand. Income rises when aggregate demand for goods exceeds output and falls when aggregate demand is less than output. The system converges over time to the equilibrium at E.

Rapid Asset Market Adjustment

For many purposes it is useful to restrict the dynamics by the reasonable assumption that the money market adjusts very quickly and the goods market adjusts relatively slowly. Since the money market can adjust merely through the buying and selling of bonds, the interest rate adjusts rapidly and the money market effectively is always in equilibrium. Such an assumption implies that we are always on the *LM* curve: Any departure from the equilibrium in the money market is almost instantaneously eliminated by an appropriate change in the interest rate. In disequilibrium, we therefore move along the *LM* curve, as is shown in Figure 4-15.

The goods market adjusts relatively slowly because firms have to change their production schedules, which takes time. For points below the *IS* curve, we move up along the *LM* schedule with rising income and interest rates, and for points above the *IS* schedule, we move down along the *LM* schedule with falling output and interest rates until point *E* is reached. The adjustment process is stable in that the economy does move to the equilibrium position at *E*.

The adjustment process shown in Figure 4-15 is very similar to that of Chapter 3. To the right of the *IS* curve, there is an excess supply of goods, and firms are therefore accumulating inventories. They cut production in response to their inventory buildup, and the economy moves down the *LM* curve. The difference between the adjustment process here and in Chapter 3 is the following: Here, as the economy moves toward the equilibrium level of income, with a falling interest rate, desired investment spending is actually rising.[10]

Now that we have established that the economy does adjust toward its equilibrium position, we turn to examine the effects of monetary and fiscal policy on the equilibrium interest rate and level of income.

4-5 Monetary Policy

In this section we are concerned with the effect of an increase in the money supply on the interest rate and level of income. We break up that inquiry into two separate questions. First, what is the ultimate effect of the increase in the money supply when the new equilibrium is reached? Second, how is that new equilibrium reached, or what is the transmission mechanism?

Through monetary policy the Bank of Canada affects the quantity of money and thereby the interest rate and income. The chief instrument, studied in more detail in Chapter 13, is *open market operations*. In an open market operation the Bank of Canada purchases bonds in exchange for money, thus increasing the stock of money,

---

[10] In a more detailed analysis, one would want to allow for the possibility that desired investment would be cut back in response to excess inventories. This again raises the possibility of the inventory cycle, referred to in Chapter 3.

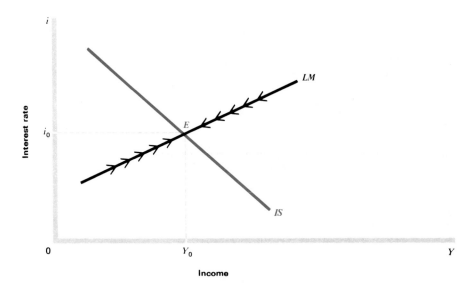

Figure 4-15 *Adjustment to Equilibrium When the Money Market Adjusts Quickly*

If the money market adjusts very rapidly, then the economy is always in monetary equilibrium. In the diagram this corresponds to always being on the *LM* schedule. When there is excess demand for goods, output and interest rates are rising, and when there is excess supply of goods, output and interest rates are falling.

or it sells bonds in exchange for money paid by the purchasers of the bonds, thus reducing the money stock.

We take here the case of an open market purchase of bonds. The purchase is made by the Bank of Canada, which pays for its purchases with money that it can create. One can usefully think of the Bank printing money with which to buy bonds, even though that is not strictly accurate, as we shall see in Chapter 12. The purpose of an open market operation is to change the available *relative* supplies of money and bonds and thereby change the interest rate or yield at which the public is willing to hold this modified composition of assets. When the Bank buys bonds, it reduces the supply of bonds available in the market and thereby tends to increase their price, or lower their yield. Only at a lower interest rate will the public be prepared to hold a larger fraction of their given wealth in the form of money, and a lower fraction in the form of bonds.

In Figure 4-16 we show graphically how the open market purchase works. The initial equilibrium at point E is on the initial LM schedule that corresponds to a real money supply, $\overline{M/P}$. Consider next an open market operation that increases the nominal quantity of money, and given the price level, the real quantity of money. We showed before that, as a consequence, the LM schedule will shift to LM'. Therefore, the new equilibrium will be at point E' with a lower interest rate and a higher level of income.

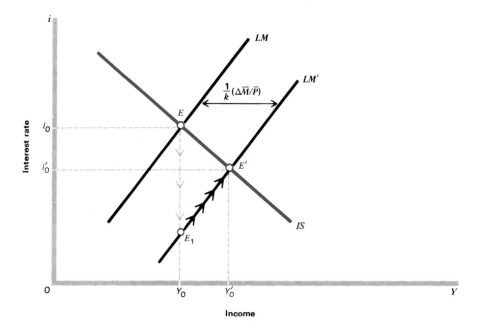

Figure 4-16   *The Adjustment Path of the Economy Following an Increase in the Money Stock*

An increase in the real money stock shifts the *LM* schedule down and to the right. Interest rates immediately decline from E to E_1 and then, through their effect on investment, cause spending and income to rise until a new equilibrium is reached at E'. Once all adjustments have taken place, a rise in the real money stock raises equilibrium income and lowers equilibrium interest rates.

The equilibrium level of income rises because the open market purchase reduces the interest rate and thereby increases investment spending.

By experimenting with Figure 4-16, you will be able to show that the steeper the *LM* schedule, the larger the change in income. If money demand is very sensitive to the interest rate, then a given change in the money stock can be absorbed in the assets markets with only a small change in the interest rate. The effects of an open market purchase on investment spending would then be small. By contrast, if the demand for money is not very sensitive to the interest rate, a given change in the money supply will cause a large change in the interest rate and have a big effect on investment demand.[11] Similarly, if the demand for money is very sensitive to income, a given increase in the money stock can be absorbed with a relatively small change in income.

---

[11] In Problem 3 we ask you to provide a similar explanation of the role of the slope of the *IS* curve, which is determined by the multiplier and the interest sensitivity of investment demand, in determining the effect of monetary policy on income.

Consider next the adjustment process to the monetary expansion. At the initial equilibrium point E, the increase in the money supply creates an excess supply of money to which the public adjusts by attempting to reduce its money holdings by buying other assets. In the process, asset prices increase and yields decline. By our assumption that the assets markets adjust rapidly, we move immediately to point E_1, where the money market clears, and where the public is willing to hold the larger real quantity of money because the interest rate has declined sufficiently. At point E_1, there is an excess demand for goods. The decline in the interest rate, given the initial income level Y_0, has raised aggregate demand and is causing inventories to run down. In response, output expands and we start moving up the LM' schedule. Why does the interest rate rise in the adjustment process? It does so because the increase in income raises the demand for money and that increase has to be checked by higher interest rates.

Thus the increase in the money stock first causes interest rates to fall as the public adjusts its portfolio and then — through lower interest rates — increases aggregate demand.

The Transmission Mechanism

Two steps in the *transmission mechanism* — the process by which changes in monetary policy affect aggregate demand — are essential. The first is that an increase in real balances generates a *portfolio disequilibrium* — at the prevailing interest rate and level of income, people are holding more money than they want. This causes portfolio holders to attempt to reduce their money holdings by buying other assets, thereby changing asset prices and yields. In other words, the change in the money supply changes interest rates. The second stage of the transmission process occurs when the change in interest rates affects aggregate demand.[12]

These two stages of the transmission process are essential in that they appear in almost every analysis of the effects of changes in the money supply on the economy. The details of the analysis will often differ — some analyses will have more than two assets and more than one interest rate; some will include an influence of interest rates on other categories of demand, such as consumption.[13]

Table 4-2 provides a summary of the stages in the transmission mechanism and shows the two critical links between the change in real balances and the ultimate effect on income. We now study these linkages in more detail.

---

[12] We refer to the responsiveness of aggregate demand, rather than investment demand, to the interest rate because consumption demand may also respond to the interest rate. Higher interest rates may lead to more saving and less consumption at a given level of income. Empirically, it has been difficult to isolate such an interest rate effect on consumption.

[13] Some analyses also include a mechanism by which changes in real balances have a direct effect on aggregate demand through the real balance effect. The argument is that wealth affects consumption demand (as we shall see in Chapter 9) and that an increase in real balances increases wealth and therefore consumption demand. This effect would not apply in the case of an open market purchase, which merely exchanges one asset for another (bonds for money) without changing wealth. The real balance effect is not very important empirically because the relevant real balances are only a small part of wealth.

Table 4-2   *The Transmission Mechanism*

(1)	(2)	(3)	(4)
Change in real money supply	Portfolio adjustments lead to a change in asset prices and interest rates	Spending adjusts to the change in interest rates	Output adjusts to the change in aggregate demand

Monetary Policy and the Liquidity Trap

In discussing the effects of monetary policy on the economy, two extreme cases have received much attention. The first is the *liquidity trap*, a situation in which the public is prepared, at a given interest rate, to hold whatever amount of money is supplied. This implies that the *LM* curve is horizontal and that changes in the quantity of money do not shift it. In that case, monetary policy carried out through open market operations[14] has no effect on either the interest rate or the level of income. In the liquidity trap, monetary policy is powerless to affect the interest rate.

There is a liquidity trap at a zero interest rate. At a zero interest rate, the public would not want to hold bonds, since money, which also pays zero interest, has the advantage over bonds of being usable in transactions. Accordingly, if the interest rate ever, for some reason, was zero, increases in the quantity of money could not induce anyone to shift into bonds and thereby reduce the interest rate on bonds even below zero. An increase in the money supply in that case would have no effect on the interest rate and income, and the economy would be in a liquidity trap.

The belief that there was a liquidity trap at a low positive (rather than zero) interest rate was quite prevalent during the forties and fifties. It was a notion associated with the Keynesian followers and developers of the theories of the great English economist John Maynard Keynes — although Keynes himself did state that he was not aware of there ever having been such a situation.[15] The importance of the liquidity trap stems from its presenting a circumstance under which monetary policy has no effect on the interest rate and thus on the level of real income. Belief in the trap, or at least the strong sensitivity of the demand for money to the interest rate, was the basis of the Keynesian belief that monetary policy has no effect on the economy. There is no strong evidence that there ever was a liquidity trap, and there certainly is not one now.

---

[14]   We say "through open market operations" because an increase in the quantity of money carried out simply by giving the money away increases individuals' wealth and, through the real balance effect, has some effect on aggregate demand. An open market purchase, however, increases the quantity of money and reduces the quantity of bonds by the same amount, leaving wealth unchanged.

[15]   J.M. Keynes, *General Theory of Employment, Interest and Money* (New York: Macmillan, 1936), p. 207.

The Classical Case

The polar opposite of the horizontal *LM* curve — which implies that monetary policy cannot affect the level of income — is the vertical *LM* curve. The *LM* curve is vertical when the demand for money is entirely unresponsive to the interest rate. Under those circumstances, any shift in the *LM* curve has a maximal effect on the level of income. Check this by moving a vertical *LM* curve to the right and comparing the resultant change in income with the change produced by a similar horizontal shift of a nonvertical *LM* curve.

The vertical *LM* curve is called the *classical case*. It implies that the demand for money depends only on the level of income and not at all on the interest rate. The classical case is associated with the classical *quantity theory of money*, which argues that the level of nominal income is determined solely by the quantity of money. As we shall see, a vertical *LM* curve implies not only that monetary policy has a maximal effect on the level of income, but also that fiscal policy has no effect on income. The vertical *LM* curve, implying the comparative effectiveness of monetary policy over fiscal policy, is sometimes associated with the view that "only money matters" for the determination of output. Since the *LM* curve is vertical only when the demand for money does not depend on the interest rate, the interest sensitivity of the demand for money turns out to be an important issue in determining the effectiveness of alternative policies.

These two extreme cases, the liquidity trap and the classical case, suggest that the slope of the *LM* curve is a key determinant of the effectiveness of monetary policy in affecting output. The slope of the *LM* curve in turn depends on the interest sensitivity of money demand. The more sensitive to the interest rate is the quantity of money demanded, the flatter is the *LM* curve.

4-6 Fiscal Policy and Crowding Out

Whenever governments run budget deficits, borrowing to pay for the excess of their spending over the tax revenue they receive, the issue of *crowding out* is raised. Crowding out occurs when expansionary fiscal policy causes interest rates to rise, thereby reducing private spending, particularly investment.

When we introduced fiscal policy in Chapter 3, we had not yet included the assets markets in the analysis. Thus we could not discuss the effects of changes in fiscal policy on interest rates. In this section we consider how fiscal policy works when the interdependence of goods and assets markets is taken into account in the *IS-LM* model.

Our aim is to see how explicit consideration of the role of interest rates affects the conclusions we reached in Chapter 3 about fiscal policy. Is it still the case that an increase in government spending raises output and employment? Do tax cuts still increase output, or is it possible that the effects of fiscal policy on interest rates are so important that our previous conclusions about the effects of fiscal policy on the economy are reversed?

Fiscal Policy in the *IS-LM* Model

Figure 4-17 shows how fiscal policy fits into the *IS-LM* model. Fiscal policy affects aggregate demand directly. For instance, an increase in government spending increases aggregate demand, tending to raise output. However, the higher output level raises the interest rate by increasing money demand, and thereby dampens the effects of the fiscal policy on output. The higher interest rates reduce the level of investment spending, or crowd out investment. Thus a fiscal policy that increases output may actually reduce the rate of investment.

Figure 4-18 illustrates the effect of an increase in government spending. At unchanged interest rates, a higher level of government spending will increase aggregate demand and output will rise. At each level of the interest rate, equilibrium income rises by the multiplier times the increase in government spending. For example, if government spending rises by 100 and the multiplier is 2, then equilibrium income must increase at each level of the interest rate by 200. Thus the *IS* schedule shifts to the right by 200.

If the economy is initially in equilibrium at point E and now government spending rises by 100, we would move to point E_1 *if the interest rate stayed constant*. At E_1 the goods market is in equilibrium in that aggregate demand equals income, but the assets market is no longer in equilibrium. Income has increased, and therefore the quantity of money demanded is higher. At interest rate i_0, the demand for real balances now exceeds the given real money supply. Because there is an excess demand for real balances, the interest rate rises, but as interest rates rise, private spending is cut back. Firms' investment demand declines at higher interest rates, and thus aggregate demand falls off.

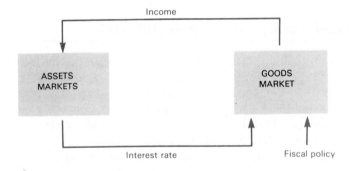

Figure 4-17 *Fiscal Policy in the* IS-LM *Model*

Fiscal policy affects aggregate demand and thus has an impact on output and income. But changes in income affect the demand for money and thereby equilibrium interest rates in assets markets. These interest rate changes feed back to the goods market and dampen the impact of fiscal policy.

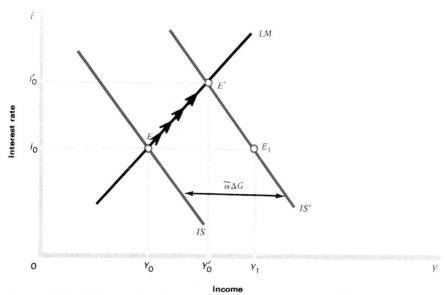

Figure 4-18 *Effects of an Increase in Government Spending*

An increase in government spending raises aggregate demand at each level of the interest rate and thus shifts the *IS* schedule out and to the right to *IS'*. At point *E* there is now an excess demand for goods. Output rises, and with it the interest rate, because the income expansion raises money demand. The new equilibrium is at point *E'*. The increase in income $(Y - Y_0)$ is less than the amount indicated by the simple multiplier $(Y_1 - Y_0)$ because higher interest rates crowd out some investment spending.

What is the complete adjustment, taking into account the expansionary effect of higher government spending and the dampening effects of higher interest rates on private spending? Figure 4-18 shows that only at point *E'* do both the goods and assets markets clear. Only at point *E'* is aggregate demand equal to income and, at the same time, the quantity of real balances demanded is equal to the given real money stock. Point *E'* is therefore the new equilibrium point.

The Dynamics of Adjustment

We continue to assume that the money market clears fast and continuously, while output adjusts only slowly. This implies that as government spending increases, we stay initially at point *E*, since there is no disturbance in the money market. The excess demand for goods, however, leads firms to increase output, and that increase in output and income raises the demand for money. The resulting excess demand for money, in turn, causes interest rates to be bid up, and we proceed up along the *LM* curve with rising output and rising interest rates, until the new equilibrium is reached at point E'.

The Extent of Crowding Out

Comparing E' to the initial equilibrium at E, we have seen that increased government spending raises both income and the interest rate. Another important comparison is between points E' and E_1, the equilibrium in the goods market at unchanged interest rates.

Point E_1 corresponds to the equilibrium we studied in Chapter 3 where we neglected the impact of interest rates on the economy. In comparing E_1 and E' it becomes clear that the adjustment of interest rates and their impact on aggregate demand dampen the expansionary effect of increased government spending. Income, instead of increasing to the level Y_1, rises only to Y_0'. This leads us to the following question: What factors determine the extent to which interest rate adjustments dampen the output expansion induced by increased government spending?

The extent to which a fiscal expansion raises income and the interest rate depends on the slopes of the *IS* and *LM* schedules and on the size of the multiplier. By drawing for yourself different *IS* and *LM* schedules you will be able to show the following:

1. The flatter the *LM* schedule, the more income increases and the less interest rates increase.

2. The flatter the *IS* schedule, the less income increases and the less interest rates increase.

3. The larger the multiplier $\bar{\alpha}$, and thus the larger the horizontal shift of the *IS* schedule, the more income and interest rates increase.

To illustrate these conclusions, we turn to the two extreme cases we discussed in connection with monetary policy, the liquidity trap and the classical case.

The Liquidity Trap

If the economy is in the liquidity trap so that the *LM* curve is horizontal, then an increase in government spending has its full multiplier effect on the equilibrium level of income. There is no change in the interest rate associated with the change in government spending, and thus no investment spending is cut off. There is therefore no dampening of the effects of increased government spending on income.

You should draw your own *IS-LM* diagrams to confirm that if the *LM* curve is horizontal, monetary policy has no impact on the equilibrium of the economy and fiscal policy has a maximal effect on the economy. Less dramatically, if the demand for money is very sensitive to the interest rate, so that the *LM* curve is almost horizontal, fiscal policy changes have a relatively large effect on output, while monetary policy changes have little effect on the equilibrium level of output.

So far, we have taken the money supply to be constant at the level $\overline{M}$. It is possible that the central bank might instead manipulate the money supply so as to keep the interest rate constant. In that case the money supply is responsive to the interest rate: The central bank increases the money supply whenever there are signs of an increase in the interest rate, and reduces the money supply whenever the interest rate seems about to fall. The more responsive the money supply with respect to the interest rate, the flatter will be the LM curve, and fiscal policy will again have large impacts on the level of output.

The Classical Case and Crowding Out

If the LM curve is vertical, then an increase in government spending has no effect on the equilibrium level of income. It only increases the interest rate. This case is shown in Figure 4-19*a*, where an increase in government spending shifts the IS curve to IS' but has no effect on income. If the demand for money is not related to the interest rate, as a vertical LM curve implies, then there is a unique level of income at which the money market is in equilibrium.

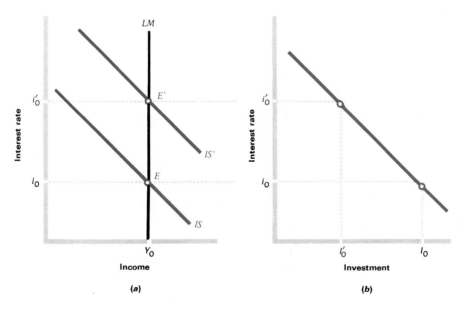

Figure 4-19 *Full Crowding Out*

With a vertical LM schedule, a fiscal expansion, shifting out the IS schedule, raises interest rates, not income. Government spending displaces, or crowds out, private spending, one-for-one.

Thus, with a vertical curve, an increase in government spending cannot change the equilibrium level of income, but only raises the equilibrium interest rate. However, if government spending is higher and output is unchanged, there must be an offsetting reduction in private spending. The increase in interest rates crowds out private investment spending. Crowding out, as defined earlier, is the reduction in private spending (and particularly investment) associated with the increase in interest rates caused by fiscal expansion. There will be full crowding out if the *LM* curve is vertical.[16]

In Figure 4-19 we show the crowding out in panel (*b*), where the investment schedule of Figure 4-3 is drawn. The fiscal expansion raises the equilibrium interest rate from i_0 to i_0' in panel (*a*). In panel (*b*), as a consequence, investment spending declines from the level I_0 to I_0'. Now it is easy to verify that if the *LM* schedule were positively sloped rather than vertical, interest rates would rise less with a fiscal expansion and as a result investment spending would decline less. The extent of crowding out thus depends on the slope of the *LM* curve and therefore on the interest responsiveness of money demand. The less interest-responsive is money demand, the more a fiscal expansion crowds out investment rather than raising output.

The view that increased government spending crowds out private spending, largely or even completely, is held by most monetarists.[17] They believe money determines income or, as we saw above, that money demand does not depend on the interest rate, implying a vertical *LM* schedule. However, there is also another case where crowding out can be complete, as we shall see in Chapter 7. If the economy is at full employment so that output cannot expand, then, of course, increased expenditure on goods by the government must mean that some other sector uses fewer goods and services. Interest rates increase to crowd out private spending by an amount exactly equal to the higher level of government spending.

Is Crowding Out Likely?

How seriously must we take the possibility of crowding out? Here three points must be made. First, in an economy with unemployed resources there will not be full crowding out because the *LM* schedule is not, in fact, vertical. A fiscal expansion will raise interest rates, but income will also rise. Crowding out thus, rather than being full, is a matter of degree. The increase in aggregate demand raises income, and with the rise in income it raises the level of saving. This expansion in saving, in turn, makes it possible to finance a larger budget deficit without completely displacing private borrowing or investment.

We can look at this proposition with the help of Equation (9), which states the equilibrium condition in the goods market already studied in Chapter 3:[18]

---

[16] Note again that, in principle, consumption spending could be reduced by increases in the interest rate, and then both investment and consumption would be crowded out.

[17] We discuss monetarism in Chapter 19.

[18] We have simply rearranged Equation (1a) in Section 3-4 of Chapter 3, cancelling consumption on both sides.

$$S = I + (G + TR - TA) \tag{9}$$

Here the term $G + TR - TA$ is the budget deficit. Now from Equation (9) it is clear that an increase in the deficit, given saving, must lower investment. In simple terms, when the deficit rises, the government has to borrow to pay for its excess spending. That borrowing "uses up" part of saving, leaving less available for firms to borrow to further their investment plans. However, it is equally apparent that if saving rises with a government spending increase, because income rises, then there need not be a one-for-one decline in investment. In an economy with unemployment, crowding out is incomplete because increased demand for goods raises real income and output; savings rise and interest rates do not rise enough (because of interest-responsive money demand) to choke off investment.

The second point is that, with unemployment and thus a possibility for output to expand, interest rates need not rise at all when government spending rises, and there need not be any crowding out. This is because the monetary authorities can *accommodate* the fiscal expansion by an increase in the money supply. Monetary policy is accommodating when, in the course of a fiscal expansion, the money supply is increased so as to prevent interest rates from increasing. Monetary accommodation is also referred to as *monetizing budget deficits*, meaning that the Bank of Canada prints money to buy the bonds with which the government pays for its deficit.[19] When the Bank accommodates a fiscal expansion, both the *IS* and the *LM* schedule shift to the right as in Figure 4-20. Output will clearly increase, but interest rates need not rise. Accordingly, there need not be any adverse effects on investment.

The third comment on crowding out is an important warning. So far we are assuming an economy with given prices and less than full employment. When we talk about fully employed economies in Chapter 7, crowding out becomes a much more realistic possibility, and accommodating monetary policy may turn into an engine of inflation.

4-7 The Composition of Output

We have now seen that both monetary and fiscal policy can be used to expand aggregate demand and thus raise the equilibrium level of output. Since the liquidity trap and the classical case represent, at best, extremes useful for expositional purposes, it is apparent that policy makers can use either monetary or fiscal policy to affect the level of income.

Table 4-3 summarizes the effects of expansionary monetary and fiscal policy on output and the interest rate. These are the effects shown in Figures 4-16 and 4-18.

---

[19] The term "accommodation" is used more generally. For instance, when oil prices increased in the 1970s, there was much discussion of whether central banks should accommodate the higher prices by raising the money stock. This issue, and the meaning of accommodation in that context, are discussed in Chapter 8.

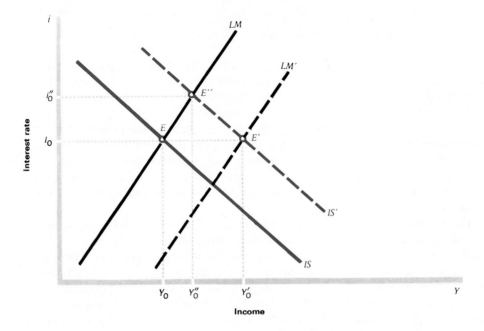

Figure 4-20 *Monetary Accommodation of Fiscal Expansion*

A fiscal expansion shifts the *IS* curve to *IS'*, and moves the equilibrium of the economy from *E* to *E''*. Because the higher level of income has increased the quantity of money demanded, the interest rate rises from i_0 to i_0'', thereby crowding out investment spending. However, the central bank can accommodate the fiscal expansion, creating more money and shifting the *LM* curve to *LM'*, and the equilibrium of the economy to *E'*. The interest rate remains at level i_0, and the level of output rises to Y_0'.

We now examine the policy choices of an economy that is in equilibrium with an income level Y_0, below the full-employment level Y^*. What can be done to raise income? From the preceding analysis and Table 4-3, it is obvious that we could use an expansionary monetary policy. By increasing the money supply, we could shift the *LM* curve down and to the right, lower interest rates, and raise aggregate demand. Alternatively, we can use an expansionary fiscal policy to shift the *IS* curve up and to the right. Finally, we can use a combination of monetary and fiscal policy. What package should we choose?

The choice of monetary and fiscal policy as tools of stabilization policy is an important and controversial topic. In Chapter 14 we address some technical issues that deal with the flexibility and speed with which these policies can be implemented and can take effect. Here we do not discuss speed and flexibility, but rather look at what these policies do to the composition of aggregate demand.

In that respect, there is a sharp difference between monetary and fiscal policy. Monetary policy operates by stimulating interest-responsive components of aggregate

Table 4-3 *Summary: Policy Effects on Income and Interest Rates*

Policy	Equilibrium Income	Equilibrium Interest Rate
Monetary Expansion	+	−
Fiscal Expansion	+	+

demand, primarily investment spending and, in particular, residential construction. There is strong evidence that the earliest and strongest effect of monetary policy is on residential construction.

Fiscal policy, by contrast, operates in a manner that depends on precisely what goods the government buys or what taxes and transfers it changes. Here we might be talking of government expenditures on goods and services such as defence spending, or a reduction in the corporate profits tax, or in sales taxes, or social insurance contributions. Each policy affects the level of aggregate demand and causes an expansion in output, except that the type of output and the beneficiaries of the fiscal measures differ. An investment subsidy, discussed below, increases investment spending. An income tax cut has a direct effect on consumption spending. Given the quantity of money, all expansionary fiscal policies have in common is that they will raise the interest rate.

An Investment Subsidy

Table 4-4 shows examples of the impact of different fiscal policies on key variables. One interesting case is an investment subsidy, shown in Figure 4-21. When the government subsidizes investment, it essentially pays part of the cost of each firm's investment. A subsidy to investment shifts the investment schedule in panel (*a*). At each interest rate, firms now plan to invest more. With investment spending higher, aggregate demand increases.

In panel (*b*), the *IS* schedule shifts by the multiplier times the increase in autonomous investment brought about by the subsidy. The new equilibrium is at point *E'*, where goods and money markets are again in balance. Note, however, that although

Table 4-4 *Alternative Fiscal Policies*

	Interest Rate	Consumption	Investment	Income
Income Tax Cut	+	+	−	+
Government Spending	+	+	−	+
Investment Subsidy	+	+	+	+

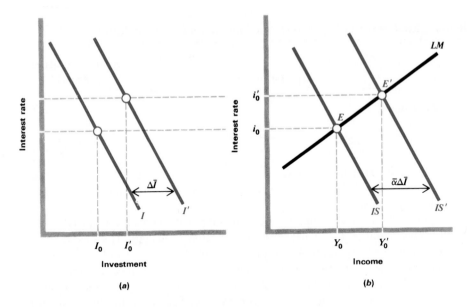

Figure 4-21   *An Investment Subsidy*

An investment subsidy shifts the investment schedule in panel (*a*) at each interest rate out and to the right. The increase in planned investment shows in panel (*b*) as a shift of the *IS* curve. Equilibrium income rises to Y_0', and the interest rate increases to i_0'. At the higher interest rate, investment is still higher, I_0', than it was initially. Thus an investment subsidy raises interest rates, income and investment.

interest rates have risen, we see in panel (*a*) that investment is higher. Investment is at the level I_0', up from I_0. The interest rate increase thus has dampened but not reversed the impact of the investment subsidy. Here is an example where both consumption, induced by higher income, and investment rise as a consequence of fiscal policy.

The Policy Mix

In Figure 4-22 we show the policy problem of reaching full-employment output $Y°$ for an economy that is initially at point E with unemployment. Should we choose a fiscal expansion, moving to point E_1 with higher income and higher interest rates, or should we choose a monetary expansion, leading to full employment with lower interest rates at point E_2? Should we pick a policy mix of fiscal expansion and accommodating monetary policy, leading to an intermediate position?

Once we recognize that all the policies raise income but differ significantly in their impact on different sectors of the economy, we open up a problem of political econ-

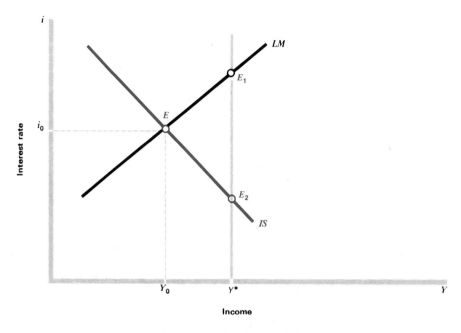

Figure 4-22 *Expansionary Policies and the Composition of Output*

In an economy with output Y_0 below the full-employment level $Y°$, there is a choice of using monetary or fiscal expansion to move to full employment. Monetary expansion would move the *LM* curve to the right, putting the equilibrium at E_2. Fiscal expansion shifts the *IS* curve, putting the new equilibrium at E_1. The expansionary monetary policy reduces the interest rate, while the expansionary fiscal policy raises it. The lower interest rate in the case of monetary policy means that investment is higher at E_2 than it is at E_1.

omy. Given the decision to expand aggregate demand, who should get the primary benefit? Should the expansion take place through a decline in interest rates and increased investment spending, should it take place through a cut in taxes and increased personal spending, or should it take the form of an increase in the size of government?

Questions of speed and predictability of policies apart, the issues raised above have been settled by political preferences. Conservatives (with a small c!) will argue for a tax cut anytime. They will favour stabilization policies that in a recession cut taxes and in a boom cut government spending. Over time, given enough cycles, the government becomes very small, just as a conservative would want it to be. The counterpart view belongs to those who feel that there is much scope for government spending on education, the environment, job training and rehabilitation, and the like, and who, accordingly, favour expansionary policies in the form of increased government spending. Growth-minded people and the construction industry finally argue for expansionary policies that operate through low interest rates.

The recognition that monetary and fiscal policy changes have different effects on the composition of output is important. It suggests that policy makers can choose a *policy mix* that will both get the economy to full employment and also make a contribution to solving some other policy problem. We anticipate here several subsequent discussions in which we point out two other targets of policy which have been taken into account in setting monetary and fiscal policy — growth and balance of payments equilibrium.

4-8 A Formal Treatment of the *IS-LM* Curve

Our exposition so far has been verbal and graphic. We now round off the analysis with a more formal treatment that uses the equations of the *IS* and *LM* schedules to derive and discuss fiscal and monetary policy multipliers.

Equilibrium Income and the Interest Rate

The intersection of the *IS* and *LM* schedules determines equilibrium income and the equilibrium interest rate. We can derive expressions for these equilibrium values by using the equations of the *IS* and *LM* schedules. From Section 4-1 we remember the equation of the *IS* schedule or goods market equilibrium schedule as

$$IS \text{ schedule:} \qquad Y = \overline{\alpha}(\overline{A} - bi) \qquad (10)$$

and the equation describing money market equilibrium as[20]

$$LM \text{ schedule:} \qquad i = \frac{1}{h}\left(kY - \frac{\overline{M}}{\overline{P}}\right) \qquad (11)$$

The intersection of the *IS* and *LM* schedules in the diagrams corresponds to a situation where both the *IS* and *LM* equations hold — the same interest rate and income levels assure equilibrium in both the goods and money market. In terms of the equations, that means we can substitute the interest rate from the *LM* equation (11) into the *IS* equation (10):

$$Y = \overline{\alpha}\left[\overline{A} - \frac{b}{h}\left(kY - \frac{\overline{M}}{\overline{P}}\right)\right] \qquad (12)$$

---

[20] To deal with the case where liquidity preference is not only high but at some rate, say $i°$, perfectly elastic, we could rewrite the *LM* equation as $\overline{M}/\overline{P} = kY - h(i - i°)$, so that real money demand depends on the excess of the interest rate above some floor level $i°$. With this information, Equation (11) becomes $i = i° + (1/h)[kY - \overline{M}/\overline{P}]$. If h is extremely high, the interest rate is $i = i°$ or the *LM* schedule is horizontal at the level $i°$.

Collecting terms and solving for the equilibrium level of income, we obtain

$$Y_0 = \psi h \overline{\alpha} \overline{A} + \psi b \overline{\alpha} \left(\frac{\overline{M}}{P} \right) \tag{12a}$$

where

$$\psi = \frac{1}{h + bk\overline{\alpha}}$$

Equation (12a) shows the equilibrium level of income depending on two exogenous variables: autonomous spending $\overline{A}$, including fiscal policy parameters ($\overline{C}$, $\overline{I}$, $\overline{G}$, t, $\overline{TR}$), and the real money stock $\overline{M}/P$. The higher the level of autonomous spending $\overline{A}$ and the higher the stock of real balances, the higher the equilibrium income.

The equilibrium rate of interest, i_0, is obtained by substituting the equilibrium income level Y_0 from (12a) into the equation of the LM schedule, (11):

$$i_0 = \psi k \overline{\alpha} A - \psi \frac{\overline{M}}{P} \tag{13}$$

Equation (13) shows that the equilibrium interest rate depends on the parameters of fiscal policy captured in the multiplier and the term $\overline{A}$, and on the real money stock. A higher real money stock implies a lower equilibrium interest rate.

For policy questions we are interested in the precise relation between changes in fiscal policy or changes in the real money stock and the resulting changes in equilibrium income. The monetary and fiscal policy multipliers provide the relevant information.

The Fiscal Policy Multiplier

The fiscal policy multiplier tells us how much an increase in government spending changes the equilibrium level of income, holding the real money supply constant. Examine Equation (12a) and consider the effect of an increase in government spending on income. The increase in government spending $\Delta \overline{G}$ is a change in autonomous spending, so that $\Delta \overline{A} = \Delta \overline{G}$. The effect of the change in $\overline{G}$ is given by

$$\frac{\Delta Y_0}{\Delta \overline{G}} = \psi h \overline{\alpha} = \frac{h \overline{\alpha}}{h + bk\overline{\alpha}} \tag{14}$$

We note that the expression in Equation (14) is zero if h is very small and will be equal to $\overline{\alpha}$ if h approaches infinity. This corresponds, respectively, to vertical and horizontal LM schedules. Similarly, a large value of either b or k serves to reduce the effect on income of government spending. Why? A high value of k implies a large increase in money demand as income rises and hence a large increase in interest rates in order to maintain money market equilibrium. In combination with a high b, this implies a large reduction in private aggregate demand. Equation (14) thus presents the algebraic analysis that corresponds to the graphical analysis of Figures 4-18 and 4-19.

The Monetary Policy Multiplier

The monetary policy multiplier tells us by how much an increase in the real money supply increases the equilibrium level of income, keeping fiscal policy unchanged. Using Equation (12a) to examine the effects of an increase in the real money supply on income, we have

$$\frac{\Delta Y_0}{(\overline{M/P})} = \psi b\overline{\alpha} = \frac{b\overline{\alpha}}{h + bk\overline{\alpha}} \tag{15}$$

The smaller h and k and the larger b and $\overline{\alpha}$, the more expansionary the effect of an increase in real balances on the equilibrium level of income. Large b and $\overline{\alpha}$ correspond to a very flat *IS* schedule. Equation (15) thus corresponds to the graphical analysis presented in Figure 4-16.

The Classical Case and the Liquidity Trap

We now turn to two special cases that demonstrate the role of the demand function for real balances in the effectiveness of monetary and fiscal policies. Consider first the possibility that money demand does not depend at all on interest rates and is simply proportional to real income. This happens if the parameter h is zero, so that real money demand is simply

$$L = kY \tag{16}$$

In this case, equating the demand and supply of money leads to[21]

$$Y = (1/k)\frac{\overline{M}}{P} \tag{17}$$

This case is called the *classical* case because classical (that is, nineteenth-century) economists did not give much emphasis to the interest response of money demand. The case is important because it has the following implication: If money demand does

---

[21] The demand for real balances is $L = kY$ and the supply $\overline{M/P}$. Thus, with demand equal to supply, $\overline{M/P} = kY$ or $Y = (1/k)\overline{M/P}$.

not depend on the interest rate but only on the level of income, as in (16), the money supply alone determines income.

In this classical case the level of nominal income, PY, is proportional to the nominal money stock. Changes in the nominal money stock lead to changes in income in the same proportion. Furthermore, while income does respond to money, it is totally unresponsive to fiscal policy. We also can see the point from (12a) by setting $h = 0$.

Interest Rates and Fiscal Policy

How is it possible that fiscal policy should have no effect at all on income? After all, if the government were to spend more, how is it possible that the increased spending should not raise income? The reasoning is as follows. An increase in government spending does lead to an incipient rise in aggregate demand and income, but that immediately raises the demand for money. With the money supply unchanged, interest rates will shoot up to clear the money market. The rise in interest rates causes investment spending to decline. The fall in investment spending compensates exactly for the higher government spending, and the level of income is unchanged.

We can see this by looking at the investment equation (18), obtained by substituting in the equilibrium interest rate from (13):

$$I = \bar{I} - bi_0 = \bar{I} - \psi b k \bar{\alpha} A + \psi b \frac{\overline{M}}{P} \tag{18}$$

From the definition of ψ given in Equation (12a), we see that in the case where $h = 0$, the coefficient multiplying $\overline{A}$ in Equation (18) is -1. This means that a \$1 increase in A, given the real money stock, leads to an equal reduction of investment. That is what we call full crowding out. In general, with h not equal to zero, the coefficient of $\overline{A}$ is a fraction, as shown in Equation (18). The larger is h, the smaller is the fraction of an extra dollar of government spending that is offset by reduced investment spending.

The Liquidity Trap

The other extreme for monetary and fiscal policy is represented by a world where h is infinite. Then money and other assets are effectively perfect substitutes. In such a world, Equation (12a) reduces to

$$Y_0 = \bar{\alpha}\overline{A} \tag{19}$$

This is the "multiplier world" of Chapter 3, where autonomous spending entirely determines the level of real income. It occurs if the economy is in a liquidity trap.

In the liquidity trap, money does not matter for income determination because money demand is so responsive to interest rates. The smallest change in interest rates is sufficient to eliminate imbalances in the money market that might arise from changes in the money supply or in income. Since corrective changes in interest rates are so small, they do not affect aggregate demand. This can be verified from Equation (18) which shows that with h extremely high, investment spending is not influenced by changes in either autonomous spending or the money supply.

4-9   Summary

1.   The *IS-LM* model presented in this chapter incorporates the assets markets as well as the goods market. It lays particular stress on the channels through which monetary and fiscal policy affect the economy.

2.   The *IS* curve shows combinations of the interest rate and level of income such that the goods market is in equilibrium. Increases in the interest rate reduce aggregate demand by reducing the demand for investment goods. Thus, at higher interest rates, the level of income at which the goods market is in equilibrium is lower: The *IS* curve slopes downward.

3.   The demand for money is a demand for real balances. The demand for real balances increases with income and decreases with the interest rate, the cost of holding money rather than other assets. With an exogenously fixed supply of real balances, the *LM* curve, representing money market equilibrium, is upward-sloping. Because of the wealth constraint, equilibrium of the money market implies equilibrium of the remaining assets markets, summarized here under the catch-all "bond market."

4.   The interest rate and level of income are jointly determined by simultaneous equilibrium of the goods and money markets. This occurs at the intersection point of the *IS* and *LM* curves.

5.   Assuming that output is increased when there is an excess demand for goods, and that the interest rate rises when there is an excess demand for money, the economy does move toward the new equilibrium when one of the curves shifts. Typically we think of the assets markets as clearing rapidly, so that in response to a disturbance, the economy tends to move along the *LM* curve to the new equilibrium.

6.   Monetary policy affects the economy in the first instance by affecting the interest rate, and then by affecting aggregate demand. An increase in the money supply reduces the interest rate, increases investment demand and aggregate demand, and thus increases equilibrium income.

7.   Taking into account the effects of fiscal policy on the interest rate modifies the multiplier results of Chapter 3. Fiscal expansion, except in extreme circumstances, still leads to an income expansion. However, the rise in interest rates that comes about through the increase in money demand caused by higher income dampens the expansion.

8. The smaller the induced changes in interest rates, and the smaller the response of investment to these interest rate changes, the more effective is fiscal policy.

9. In the liquidity trap, the interest rate is constant because money demand is completely elastic with respect to the interest rate. Monetary policy has no effect on the economy, whereas fiscal policy has its full multiplier effect on income, and no effect on interest rates.

10. In the classical case, the demand for money is independent of the interest rate. In that case, changes in the money stock change income, but fiscal policy has no effect on income — it affects only the interest rate. In this case there is complete crowding out of private spending by government spending.

11. Neither the liquidity trap nor the classical case applies in practice, but they are useful cases to study in order to show what determines the magnitude of monetary and fiscal policy multipliers.

12. A fiscal expansion, because it leads to higher interest rates, displaces or crowds out some private investment. The extent of crowding out is an important issue in assessing the usefulness and desirability of fiscal policy as a tool of stabilization policy.

13. In an economy that is less than fully employed, crowding out need not occur. The monetary authorities can provide an accommodating monetary policy that avoids the rise in interest rates associated with the income expansion.

14. The question of the monetary–fiscal policy mix arises because expansionary monetary policy reduces the interest rate while expansionary fiscal policy increases the interest rate. Accordingly, expansionary fiscal policy increases income while reducing the level of investment; expansionary monetary policy increases income and the level of investment.

15. Governments have to choose the mix in accordance with their objectives for economic growth, or increasing consumption, or from the viewpoint of their beliefs about the desirable size of the government.

Key Terms

Endogenous variable	**Wealth budget constraint**
Exogenous variable	**Open market operation**
IS curve	**Transmission mechanism**
LM curve	**Liquidity trap**
Bond	**Classical case**
Money	**Crowding out**
Portfolio decisions	**Monetary–fiscal policy mix**
Real balances (real money balances)	**Investment subsidy**

Problems

1. The following equations describe an economy. (Think of C, I, G, etc., as being measured in billions and i as percent; a 5 percent interest rate implies $i = 5$.)

    $C = 0.8(1 - t)Y$ $t = 0.25$
    $I = 900 - 50i$ $G = 800$
    $L = 0.25Y - 62.5i$ $\overline{M/P} = 500$

    (a) What is the equation that describes the *IS* curve?
    (b) What is the general definition of the *IS* curve?
    (c) What is the equation that describes the *LM* curve?
    (d) What is the general definition of the *LM* curve?
    (e) What are the equilibrium levels of income and the interest rate?
    (f) Describe in words the conditions that are satisfied at the intersection of the *IS* and *LM* curves, and why this is an equilibrium.

2. Continue with the same equations.
    (a) What is the value of $\overline{\alpha}$, which corresponds to the simple multiplier (with taxes) of Chapter 3?
    (b) By how much does an increase in government spending of $\Delta\overline{G}$ increase the level of income in this model, which includes the assets markets?
    (c) By how much does a change in government spending of $\Delta\overline{G}$ affect the equilibrium interest rate?
    (d) Explain the difference between your answers to 2a and b.

3. (a) Explain in words how and why the multiplier $\overline{\alpha}$ and the interest sensitivity of aggregate demand affect the slope of the *IS* curve.
    (b) Explain why the slope of the *IS* curve is a factor in determining the working of monetary policy.

4. Explain in words how and why the income and interest sensitivities of the demand for real balances affect the slope of the *LM* curve.

5. (a) Why does a horizontal *LM* curve imply that fiscal policy has the same effects on the economy as we derived in Chapter 3?
    (b) What is happening in this case in terms of Figure 4-2?
    (c) Under what circumstances might the *LM* curve be horizontal?

6. We mentioned in the text the possibility that the interest rate might affect consumption spending. An increase in the interest rate could, in principle, lead to increases in saving and therefore a reduction in consumption, given the level of income. Suppose that consumption were in fact reduced by an increase in the interest rate. How would the *IS* curve be affected?

7. Suppose that the money supply, instead of being constant, increased (slightly) with the interest rate. How would this change affect the construction of the *LM* curve?

8. **(a)** How does an increase in the tax rate affect the *IS* curve?
   (b) How does it affect the equilibrium level of income?
   (c) How does it affect the equilibrium interest rate?

9. Draw a graph of how *i* and *Y* respond over time (that is, use time as the horizontal axis) to an increase in the money supply. You may assume that the money market adjusts much more rapidly than the goods market.

10. **(a)** Show that the less interest-sensitive the demand for money, the larger effect a given change in the money stock has on output.
    (b) How does the response of the interest rate to a change in the money stock depend on the interest sensitivity of money demand?

11. The economy is at full employment. Now the government wants to change the composition of demand toward investment and away from consumption — without allowing aggregate demand to go beyond full employment. What is the required policy mix? Use the *IS-LM* diagram to show your policy proposal.

12. Discuss the role of the parameters $\bar{\alpha}$, h, b, and k in the transmission mechanism linking an increase in government spending to the resulting change in equilibrium income. In developing the analysis, use the following table:

(1)	(2)	(3)
Increase in *G* raises aggregate demand and output	The increase in income raises money demand and hence interest rates	The increase in interest rates reduces investment spending and hence dampens the income expansion

13. Consider an economy where the government has a choice of two alternative programs for contraction. One is the removal of an investment subsidy; the other is a rise in income tax rates. Use the *IS-LM* schedule and the investment schedule, as shown in Figure 4-21, to discuss the impact of these alternative policies on income, interest rates, and investment.

14. Suppose the parameters k and $\bar{\alpha}$ are 0.5 and 2, respectively. Assume there is an increase of $1 billion in government spending. By how much must the real money stock be increased to hold interest rates constant?

CHAPTER 5 *International Trade and Exchange Rates*

Economic influences from other countries have a powerful effect on the Canadian economy. Canada is linked to the rest of the world through two broad channels: *trade* and *finance*. The trade linkage arises from the fact that some of our output is exported to foreign countries, while some purchases are of goods that are produced elsewhere and imported. In 1990, exports amounted to 28 percent of GDP, while imports were 25 percent of GDP.

The international linkages in the area of finance arise from the fact that Canadian residents, whether households, banks, or corporations, can hold assets in foreign countries, and foreigners can choose to hold Canadian assets. Although households are likely to hold mainly domestic assets, portfolio managers for banks and corporations consider the relative attractiveness of lending and borrowing in the U.S., Europe, or Japan as well as in Canada.

We show in this chapter how the *IS-LM* analysis has to be modified to take international trade and exchange rates into account. In the following chapter, we consider the financial linkages and show how these affect income, exchange rates, and the ability of monetary policy to affect interest rates.

5-1 The Balance of Payments and Exchange Rates

The balance of payments is the record of transactions of the residents of a country with the rest of the world. There are two main accounts in the balance of payments: the *current account* and the *capital account*.

The current account records trade in goods and services, as well as transfer payments. Services include freight, royalty payments, and interest payments; transfer payments consist of remittances, gifts, and grants. The current account balance is equal to exports less imports and net transfers to foreigners. Net exports of goods alone is referred to as the *merchandise trade balance*.

The capital account records borrowing and lending as well as purchases and sales of assets such as stocks, bonds, and land. There is a capital account surplus, or a net capital inflow, when our receipts from borrowing and the sale of assets exceed our payments for lending and the purchase of assets.

Surpluses and Deficits

The simple rule for balance of payments accounting is that any private transaction that gives rise to disbursement of foreign currency is recorded as a payment. Thus, imports of goods, foreign travel, purchase of foreign stocks, and lending to foreigners are all payment items. Conversely, any transactions, such as exports and borrowing from foreigners, that give rise to the acquisition of foreign exchange are recorded as receipts.

The overall balance of payments is the sum of the current and capital account balances. An overall deficit in the balance of payments means that Canadian residents make more payments to foreigners than they receive from foreigners. Any such gap must be matched by *net official financing*. This item records foreign currency transactions carried out by the Bank of Canada on behalf of the government of Canada. The foreign exchange held for this purpose is referred to as *official international reserves*.

Table 5-1 shows the details of Canada's balance of payments in 1991, and Figure 5-1 shows the movements in the major categories since 1971. With the exception of 1982–1984, the typical pattern has been a surplus on merchandise trade more than offset by a deficit on services and transfers, leaving a substantial current account deficit. Much of this deficit is attributable to a large outflow of dividend and interest payments associated with accumulated foreign indebtedness and foreign ownership of Canadian businesses.

In 1991 there was a large capital account surplus. This reflected the fact that receipts arising from borrowing from foreigners and sales of Canadian assets to foreigners exceeded payments arising from lending to foreigners and purchases of foreign assets by Canadians.

Fixed Versus Flexible Exchange Rates

We now examine in more detail the way in which central banks, through their official transactions, finance, or provide the means of paying for, balance of payments surpluses and deficits. At this point we distinguish between fixed and floating rate systems.

Under a flexible (or floating) exchange rate, the central bank allows the exchange rate to be determined by the foreign exchange market. In Figure 5-2 we illustrate the supply and demand for foreign exchange in the exchange market. The exchange rate

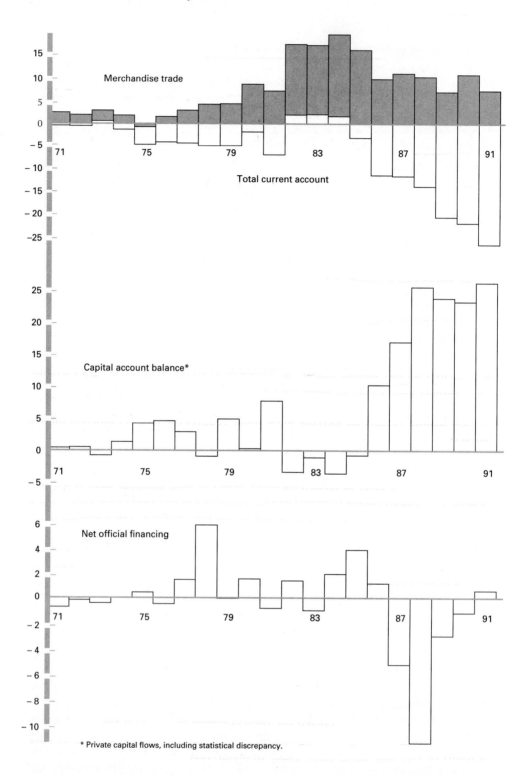

Figure 5-1   *Canada's Balance of International Payments, Billions of Dollars*

(*Source: Bank of Canada Review*)

Table 5-1 *Canadian Balance of International Payments, 1991*

	(billions of dollars)		
	Receipts (+)	Payments (−)	Balance
Current account			
Merchandise trade	$141.7	$134.3	7.4
Travel	7.7	14.8	−7.1
Other services	15.7	19.4	−3.7
Investment income	8.7	31.7	−23.0
Transfers	3.6	4.0	−0.4
Balance on current account			−26.8
Capital account			
Net private capital movements*			26.2
Net official financing			0.6

*Includes statistical discrepancy
Source: *Bank of Canada* Review.

is measured on the vertical axis as the domestic currency price of foreign exchange (for example, 1.25 Canadian dollars per U.S. dollar). The supply of foreign currency offered in exchange for Canadian dollars equals exports and capital inflows. It is upward-sloping because an increase in the price reduces the cost of exports in foreign markets. The demand curve represents imports and capital outflows and is downward-sloping because an increase in the price raises the cost of imports. The equilibrium exchange rate is e_1, determined by the intersection.

A change in the price of foreign exchange under flexible exchange rates is referred to as *currency appreciation* or *depreciation*. A currency depreciates (appreciates) when it becomes less (more) expensive in terms of foreign currency. For example, if the value of the Canadian dollar falls from 90 U.S. cents to 84 U.S. cents (the domestic currency price of U.S. dollars rises from $1/.90 = 1.11$ to $1/.84 = 1.19$), the Canadian dollar depreciates. Conversely, an appreciation means that the value of our currency rises in terms of foreign exchange.

In a fixed rate system, central banks stand ready to buy and sell their currency at a fixed price in terms of foreign exchange. Figure 5-2 illustrates that a fixed exchange rate is like any other price support scheme, such as one in an agricultural market. If the price is fixed below the equilibrium level, say at e_2, the central bank has to meet the excess demand by exchanging foreign currency for Canadian dollars.

A change in the price of foreign exchange under a fixed exchange rate is referred to as *devaluation* or *revaluation*. A devaluation (revaluation) takes place when the value of the currency in terms of foreign exchange is reduced (increased) by official action.

The value of the Canadian dollar has been determined at various times under both fixed and flexible exchange rate regimes. Figure 5-3 shows the fluctuations in its value in terms of the U.S. dollar since 1926. Between 1926 and 1929, Canada and most other countries fixed their rates by maintaining convertibility into gold at a fixed price.

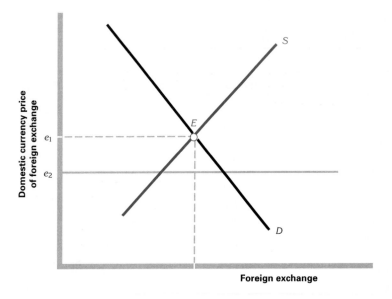

Figure 5-2   *The Foreign Exchange Market*

The exchange rate is measured on the vertical axis as the domestic currency price of foreign exchange. The supply of foreign exchange equals exports and capital inflows and is upward-sloping since an increase in the price reduces the cost of exports. The demand equals imports and capital outflows and is downward-sloping since an increase in the price raises the price of imports. To fix the exchange rate at e_2 below the equilibrium rate e_1, the central bank has to meet the excess demand by selling foreign currency from its reserves.

A floating rate was in effect during the 1930s until the outbreak of World War II, when a fixed rate of 90.5 U.S. cents was established. The Canadian dollar was revalued to 100 U.S. cents in 1946, but this rate was abandoned in 1950 in favour of a floating rate. Under the influence of market forces, our dollar soon rose above 100 U.S. cents and remained there until 1961.

   After a rapid depreciation in 1961 and early 1962, it was decided to return to a fixed rate. A value of 92.5 U.S. cents was established in May 1962. In 1970, the Canadian dollar came under strong upward pressure and a floating rate was again adopted. By 1972, the rate had risen above 100 U.S. cents and was close to 104 cents in 1974. Subsequently, it drifted down and in 1985 reached an all-time low below 70 cents. By 1988 it was back above 80 cents, where it has since remained.

Exchange Market Intervention

In a fixed rate system, the central bank has to buy or sell foreign currency to make up for any excess supply or demand arising from private transactions. Such purchases and

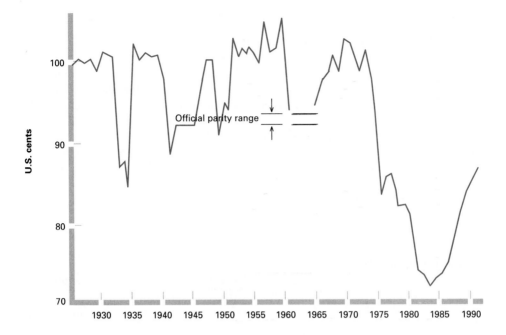

Figure 5-3 *The Canadian Dollar, 1926–1991*

(*Source:* Adapted from *Bank of Canada Review, Federal Reserve Bulletin*)

sales are referred to as exchange market *intervention*. In order to be able to ensure that the rate stays fixed, it is obviously necessary to hold an inventory of foreign exchange that can be sold in exchange for domestic currency. Thus, the Bank of Canada holds reserves of U.S. dollars, and gold that can be sold for U.S. dollars, for the purpose of exchange market intervention.

The ability of a country to maintain the value of its currency depends on its stock of foreign exchange reserves. If it persistently runs deficits in the balance of payments, the central bank eventually will run out of reserves and will be unable to continue intervention. Before that point is reached, the central bank is likely to resort to a devaluation. In 1967, for instance, Britain devalued sterling from $2.80 per pound to $2.40 per pound.

Under flexible exchange rates, intervention is not required. In a system of clean floating, central banks do not intervene in foreign exchange markets and thus allow exchange rates to be freely determined. In practice, the flexible rate system has not been one of clean floating, but rather one of *managed*, or *dirty*, *floating*. Under managed floating, central banks intervene by buying or selling foreign currency and attempt to influence exchange rates. The reasons for this intervention are discussed in the last section of this chapter.

Alternative Measures of the Exchange Rate

Table 5-2 shows several measures of the exchange rate. The first three columns give *bilateral nominal exchange rates*. They are bilateral in the sense that they are exchange rates for one currency against another, and they are nominal because they express the exchange rate as so many dollars per unit of the foreign currency.

Often we want to characterize the movement of the Canadian dollar relative to all other currencies in a single index, just as we use a price index to show how the prices of goods in general have changed. The fourth column of Table 5-2 shows an index of the *multilateral* rate which represents the price of a basket of foreign currencies, each weighted by its importance to Canada in international trade. Thus the U.S. dollar receives the largest weight.

Nominal exchange rates measure the price of foreign currencies but they do not tell us whether domestic goods are becoming relatively cheaper or more expensive than foreign goods. To do this we need an index of the exchange rate that is adjusted for price changes so as to measure the relative price of foreign goods in terms of domestic goods. The *real exchange rate* is given by the ratio of the price of foreign goods, measured in the domestic currency, relative to prices of goods at home. Thus the real exchange rate is:

$$\frac{\text{Real exchange}}{\text{rate}} = \frac{(\text{nominal exchange rate})(\text{foreign price level})}{(\text{domestic price level})}$$

The last column in Table 5-2 shows an index of the Canada–U.S. real exchange rate. Comparing the first and last columns, we see, for example, that between 1971 and 1976, the Canadian inflation rate was above the U.S. rate. This is reflected in the larger decline in the real exchange rate (12.1 percent) compared with the decline in the nominal rate (2.4 percent).

Table 5-2 *Measures of the Exchange Rate*

	Canadian dollars per:			Indexes (1981 = 100)	
	U.S. dollar	British pound	German mark	Multilateral	Real*
1971	1.010	2.469	.290	81.5	94.3
1976	.986	1.781	.392	80.5	82.9
1981	1.200	2.429	.532	100.0	100.0
1986	1.389	2.039	.643	115.9	115.2
1991	1.146	2.028	.693	99.2	94.4

*Calculated using U.S. and Canadian national accounts implicit price indexes.

Source: Bank of Canada Review; U.S. Dept. of Commerce, *Survey of Current Business*.

5-2 Equilibrium Income and the Trade Balance With Fixed Exchange Rates

In this section we fit foreign trade into the *IS-LM* framework. As in Chapters 3 and 4, we assume that the domestic and foreign price levels are given. We ignore the nonmerchandise items in the current account so that the trade balance and the current account balance are the same. Finally, we postpone consideration of capital account transactions to Chapter 6.

A word of warning is in order concerning the following sections. The exposition assumes thorough familiarity with the *IS-LM* analysis and therefore proceeds quite rapidly. However, the material is not more difficult than that of the previous chapters and should be accessible with careful reading.

Domestic Spending and Spending on Domestic Goods

In an open economy, part of domestic output is sold to foreigners (exports), and part of spending by domestic residents falls on foreign goods (imports). Thus it is no longer true that domestic spending determines domestic output. What is true now is that *spending on domestic goods* determines domestic output.

The way in which external transactions affect the demand for domestic output was examined in Section 3-6. Aggregate demand for domestically produced goods is

$$AD = C + I + G + NX \tag{1}$$

where NX is the trade balance (net exports). Assuming that exports are fixed at the level $\overline{X}$ and that imports, Q, depend on income, we have

$$NX = X - Q = \overline{X} - \overline{Q} - mY \tag{2}$$

The relationship expressed in Equation (2) is illustrated in the lower panel of Figure 5-4. Imports are low at low levels of income, so that given the fixed level of exports, there is a trade surplus, $NX > 0$. As income rises, import spending increases until we reach income level Y, where imports match exports, so that trade is balanced. A further increase in income gives rise to a trade deficit.

Goods Market Equilibrium

With these modifications, the equation for the *IS* curve becomes

$$Y = \overline{\overline{\alpha}}(\overline{A} - bi) \tag{3}$$

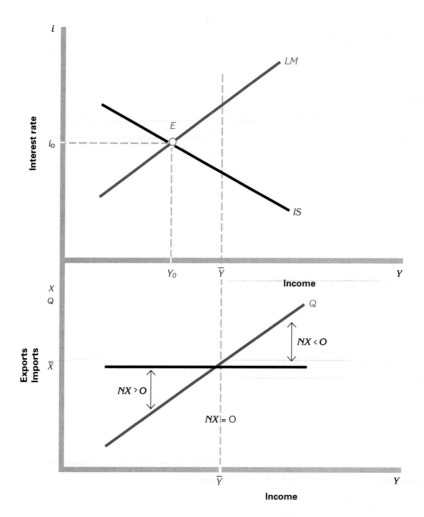

Figure 5-4 *Goods and Money Market Equilibrium*

The *LM* schedule is familiar from the closed economy. The *IS* schedule represents goods market equilibrium but now includes net exports as a component of demand. As shown in the lower panel, imports depend on the level of income so that, given exports, there is a level of income $\bar{Y}$ at which trade is balanced. Equilibrium obtains at point *E*, where goods and money markets clear. At *E* there is a trade surplus.

where autonomous spending now includes exports minus the autonomous component of imports and is thus given by

$$\bar{A} = \bar{C} + c\overline{TR} + \bar{I} + \bar{G} + \bar{X} - \bar{Q} \tag{4}$$

and the open economy multiplier is

$$\bar{\bar{\alpha}} = 1[1 - c(1-t) + m] \qquad (5)$$

Figure 5-4 illustrates the goods market equilibrium condition (3) which is the *IS* curve in an open economy. The schedule slopes down because an increase in output causes an excess supply of goods although the increase in income is only partly spent on domestic goods, the rest going to taxes and saving as well as to imports. To compensate for the excess supply, interest rates have to decline to induce an increase in aggregate demand, and the curve is therefore downward-sloping. We also show in Figure 5-4 the *LM* schedule which is unaffected by the inclusion of international trade.

Equilibrium Income and the Balance of Trade

As in the closed economy case, the equilibrium of the economy in Figure 5-4 is at point *E*, the intersection of the *IS* and *LM* curves. The trade account need not be in balance, since a deficit can be financed by running down foreign exchange reserves, and reserves can be accumulated if there is a surplus. The assumption is that the central bank buys or sells foreign exchange so as to maintain the exchange rate.[1] In the case shown in Figure 5-4, equilibrium income is below the level $\bar{Y}$ at which trade is in balance so that there is a trade surplus and the central bank will be accumulating foreign exchange.

Disturbances

How do internal and external disturbances — shifts in the level or composition of spending or changes in exports — affect equilibrium income and the balance of trade? We can think of three types of disturbances, the effects of which we will briefly analyze in turn: (1) an increase in autonomous domestic spending that falls on our own goods, (2) an increase in exports, and (3) a shift in demand from imports to domestic goods.

Before going through the exercises, we indicate the results we expect to find. First, any autonomous increase (decrease) in spending on our goods should result in an increase (decrease) in equilibrium output and income, but we would expect the trade balance to worsen if domestic income expands because the higher income leads to increased import spending. Second, it is not so clear how an increase in exports affects the trade balance. Say exports increase, and as a consequence domestic income rises. This income increase, in turn, raises import spending, and we are not certain whether

---

[1] We are abstracting here from a complication discussed in Chapter 6. Foreign exchange transactions will have an effect on the domestic money supply unless offsetting action is taken by the central bank. At this point we are assuming that there is no link between the balance of payments and the money supply.

the net effect on the trade balance is an improvement or a worsening. In fact we can show that the net effect is actually an improvement — induced import spending dampens but does not offset the trade balance improvement resulting from an increase in exports. Table 5-3 summarizes those results.

The Effects of an Increase in Autonomous Spending

We now proceed to our analysis. First, consider an autonomous increase in our spending on domestic goods, perhaps because of expansionary fiscal policy. In Figure 5-5, we show the effect to be a shift in the *IS* curve. At the initial equilibrium *E* there is an excess demand for goods, and accordingly, the equilibrium income level increases. The new equilibrium is at point *E'*, where output and interest rates have risen and where we have a reduction in the trade surplus. The expansion in output increases import spending, and thus at *E'* the trade surplus is less than at *E*. The first lesson is, therefore, that expansionary domestic policies or autonomous increases in spending raise income but cause a worsening of the trade balance.

A second point worth making concerns the size of the income expansion induced by an expansionary policy, that is, the size of the multiplier. By comparison with a closed economy, we have less of an expansion in an open economy. Multipliers are smaller because induced spending on domestic goods is less. Part of an increase in income is now spent on imports rather than domestic goods. Imports are a *leakage* from the domestic multiplier process. Indeed, the larger the fraction of an increase in income that is spent on imports, the smaller the multiplier, because there is less induced spending on domestic goods.

The Effects of an Increase in Exports

The next disturbance we consider is an increase in exports. An increase in exports raises the demand for domestic goods and thus shifts the *IS* curve to the right (to *IS'*), as shown in Figure 5-6. At the same time, the increase in exports implies that at each level of income the trade balance is improved. Given the higher exports, trade will now be balanced at a higher level of income.

Table 5-3   *The Effect of Disturbances on Income and the Trade Balance*

	Income	Trade Balance
Autonomous increase in spending on domestic goods	+	—
Autonomous increase in exports	+	+
Shift in demand from imports to domestic goods	+	+

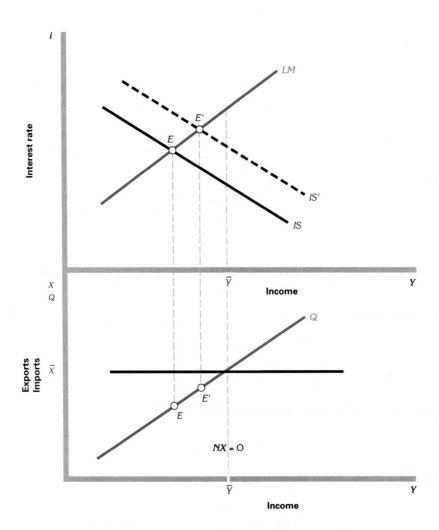

Figure 5-5 *The Effect of an Increase in Domestic Spending*

Starting from equilibrium at E, there is an increase in domestic spending so that the IS schedule shifts to the right to IS' and the new equilibrium is at E'. As shown in the lower panel, the increase in income increases imports and the trade balance worsens.

Starting from a position of balanced trade at point E, we find that the increase in exports raises equilibrium income and improves the balance of trade at point E'. The first part is quite intuitive. Higher demand for our goods leads to an increase in equilibrium output. The trade balance improvement, though, is less intuitive. The increase in exports by itself improves the trade balance, but the increase in income leads to increased import spending, which, it seems, could perhaps offset the direct improvement from the export increase. This is, in fact, not the case, and we leave the demonstration of that result to Problem 1 at the end of this chapter.

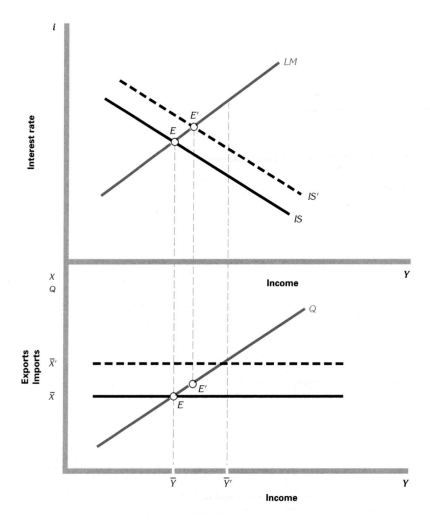

Figure 5-6 *The Effect of an Increase in Exports*

Starting from equilibrium at *E*, there is an increase in exports, the *IS* schedule shifts to *IS'*, and the new equilibrium is at *E'*. In the lower panel, trade is assumed to be in balance at the initial point *E*. As we move up the import schedule to *E'*, imports increase, although by less than the increase in exports, so that the trade balance improves.

A Shift in the Composition of Demand

The last disturbance we consider is a shift in demand from imports to domestic goods. You will recognize that this has the same effects as an increase in exports. It means increased demand for domestic goods and also an improvement in the trade balance.

5-3 Exchange Rates and Equilibrium Income

In the previous section we considered how disturbances affect income and the trade balance given a fixed exchange rate. We now examine how the equilibrium is affected by changes in the exchange rate.

The Exchange Rate and the Goods Market

The exchange rate affects income and the trade balance through its effect on the real exchange rate which we defined in Section 5-1 as the relative price of foreign and domestic goods. In symbols, we have

$$\text{Real exchange rate} = \frac{eP^\circ}{P} \tag{6}$$

where e is the exchange rate, P is the domestic price level, and P° is the foreign price level. Assuming that P and P° are fixed, a devaluation (or depreciation under flexible rates) increases the real exchange rate and thus increases the relative price of imported goods in the home market and lowers the relative price of exports in the foreign market.

Table 5-4 illustrates the effect of a devaluation on relative prices. We assume that Canada produces and exports rye whisky and Britain produces and exports Scotch whisky. Scotch is priced at £6.00 and rye at $10.00. These prices, in terms of the respective producers' currencies, are assumed to remain constant. Now, at an exchange rate of $2.00 per pound, the relative price of Scotch in terms of rye (the real exchange rate) is $12.00/$10.00 = 1.2, meaning that Scotch costs 20 percent more than rye. Next, consider a devaluation of the Canadian dollar by 25 percent. The table shows that the Canadian dollar price of Scotch rises and that the sterling price of rye declines. Both in Canada and in Britain, rye becomes *relatively* cheaper, or Scotch becomes relatively more expensive. The Canadian dollar devaluation lowers the sterling price

Table 5-4   *The Effect of Exchange Rate Changes on Relative Prices*

	Scotch Whisky	Rye Whisky	Real Exchange Rate
Canadian dollar price			
(a) $2.00/pound	$12.00	$10.00	1.2
(b) $2.50/pound	$15.00	$10.00	1.5
Sterling price			
(a) $2.00/pound	£6.00	£5.00	
(b) $2.50/pound	£6.00	£4.00	

of Canadian goods and raises the dollar price of British goods. The real exchange rate now becomes \$15.00/\$10.00 = 1.5, so that Scotch now costs 50 percent more than rye. Clearly, the increase in the relative price of British goods will affect the pattern of demand, increasing both Canadian and British demands for rye at the expense of the demand for Scotch.

This relationship can be summarized in terms of the international competitiveness of the domestic economy. A devaluation or depreciation leads to an improvement in competitiveness and an increase in net exports. Conversely, a revaluation or appreciation leads to a loss of competitiveness and a decrease in net exports. Incorporating this effect into our analysis, Equation (2) for net exports becomes

$$ NX = \bar{X} - \bar{Q} - mY + q\frac{eP^{\circ}}{P} \tag{2a}$$

As we have seen, aggregate demand for domestic goods consists of total spending by residents (including spending on imports) plus net exports. Thus the level of aggregate demand and the position of the *IS* curve depend on the exchange rate. Using Equation (2a), the equation of the *IS* curve becomes

$$ Y = \bar{\bar{\alpha}}\left(\bar{A} - bi + q\frac{eP^{\circ}}{P}\right) \tag{3a}$$

The *IS* schedule corresponding to Equation (3a) is shown in Figure 5-7. It represents goods market equilibrium given the level of the real exchange rate. What happens to the schedule if there is a change in the exchange rate with prices held constant?

A devaluation or depreciation will improve competitiveness and increase the net export component of aggregate demand. Thus, for a given interest rate and income level, there will be excess demand for domestic goods. To restore equilibrium, output must rise or the interest rate must rise. Therefore, as shown in Figure 5-7, the *IS* schedule shifts up and to the right. A revaluation or appreciation would, of course, shift the schedule down and to the left.

Internal and External Balance Under a Fixed Exchange Rate

We now draw on the analysis of income and the trade balance in the previous section to examine policy making under a fixed exchange rate. In particular we consider the circumstances under which a devaluation or revaluation may be desirable, and the effect of such changes in the exchange rate on income and the trade balance.

From a policy perspective we would want to be able to achieve both *internal* and *external balance*. Internal balance means that output is at the full-employment level while external balance occurs when the trade balance is zero. It is clear enough why internal balance should be an aim of policy, but why is external balance desirable? Under a fixed exchange rate, a balance of payments deficit cannot be maintained indef-

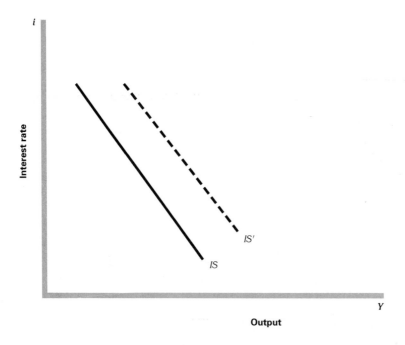

Figure 5-7 *Effect of Depreciation or Devaluation on the IS Curve*

The *IS* curve is drawn for a given exchange rate. A depreciation or devaluation improves competitiveness, increases the demand for domestic goods, and shifts the *IS* curve to the right.

initely, as the financing of the deficit requires the country to use its reserves of foreign currency. Such reserves will run out in the face of continual deficits. Hence, a country on a fixed exchange rate cannot aim to run a balance of payments deficit indefinitely. On the other hand, a country on fixed rates wants to avoid running a permanent surplus, because that causes it to acquire foreign currencies to add to its reserves indefinitely. Since the foreign exchange could be used to buy and consume foreign goods, the country is permanently forgoing some consumption it could otherwise have had, when it chooses to run permanent balance of payments surpluses.

The policy problem is illustrated in Figure 5-8. For a given level of exports we may not be able to achieve *both* internal and external balance. At the level of income $\overline{Y}$, trade is in balance, while full employment is reached at income $Y°$. Since the two levels of income do not coincide, we get three regions. To the left of $\overline{Y}$, we have a trade surplus, and to the right we have a deficit. To the left of $Y°$, we have unemployment, and to the right we have overemployment or a boom.

In region I, there is unemployment and a trade surplus. Here there is no policy conflict: Monetary and/or fiscal policy can take the economy to higher income levels

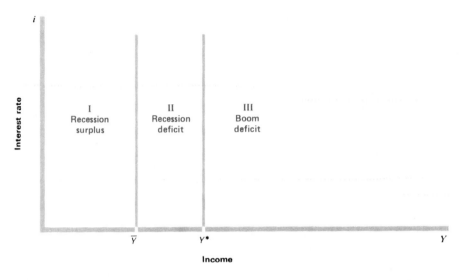

Figure 5-8 *The Policy Conflict Between Internal and External Balance*

At $\overline{Y}$, trade is in balance, but full employment is reached at Y°. A policy conflict arises in region II: External balance requires demand restraint while full employment requires expansion.

without the risk that external constraints will become binding. In region III there is also no conflict since the economy is overemployed and is experiencing a current account deficit. In this situation, demand restraint through tight money or restrictive fiscal policy will help cure the deficit and reduce demand toward full employment.

However, there is a conflict in region II. Here we have to choose whether we want to use tight policies to achieve trade balance or expansionary policies to achieve full employment. Not only are we unable to reach both targets simultaneously by manipulating aggregate demand, but any attempt to reach one target gets us farther away from the other. The problem arises because there are more targets of policy than instruments with which to move the economy toward its targets. In our case we have only one policy instrument — aggregate demand policies. However, we have two independent targets — external and internal balance.

The policy conflict can be solved by finding another policy instrument that will improve the trade balance and thereby increase Y until it coincides with Y°. An obvious solution is a devaluation.

Effect of a Devaluation

The analysis of a devaluation is complicated by the fact that policies that shift spending from imports to domestic goods generally also affect aggregate demand in the goods market. Accordingly, policies to improve the trade balance generally have to be accompanied by policies that adjust aggregate demand.

Figure 5-9 shows a situation in which the equlibrium is initially at point E in region II of Figure 5-8. Suppose that expansionary fiscal policy is used to shift the IS curve to IS' so that the economy moves to E' where income is at the full-employment level. Now suppose there is a devaluation that shifts spending from imports to domestic goods so that trade is in balance at full employment. The devaluation will also affect the demand for domestic goods and the IS curve shifts further out to the right to IS" so that the new equlibrium is at E" where Y is above the full-employment level. Consequently, we have to use a further policy to offset the expansionary effect of the devaluation. We could use either monetary or fiscal policy to shift the economy's equlibrium back to the full-employment level.

The important point is: In general it is necessary to combine both *expenditure switching policies*, which shift demand between domestic and imported goods, and *expenditure reducing* (or *expenditure increasing*) *policies*, to cope with the targets of internal and external balance. The point is of general importance and continues to apply when we take account of capital flows and other factors omitted in this section.

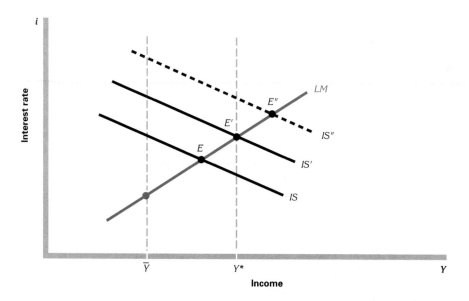

Figure 5-9 *The Policy Conflict and Devaluation*

At the initial equilibrium at E, there is unemployment and a trade deficit. Expansionary fiscal policy could be used to move the economy to full employment at E'. A devaluation would restore external balance but it would also shift the IS curve further to IS". A contractionary policy would then be required to avoid the overemployment at E".

Although it is possible to maintain full employment, we should not conclude that current account adjustment with a devaluation is costless. Current account adjustment involves not only a cut in spending to the level of income, but also, in many instances, an increase in the real exchange rate. Foreign goods become more expensive, thus reducing the purchasing power of the goods we produce. Therefore our standard of living falls.

5-4 Summary

1. The balance of payments accounts are a record of the transactions of the economy with other economies. The capital account describes transactions in assets, while the current account covers transactions in goods and services and transfers.

2. Transactions that give rise to the disbursement of foreign exchange are recorded as payments, while those that give rise to the acquisition of foreign exchange are recorded as receipts. The balance of payments deficit (or surplus) is the sum of the deficits (or surpluses) on current and capital accounts.

3. Under fixed exchange rates, central banks stand ready to meet all demands for foreign currencies arising from balance of payments deficits or surpluses at a fixed price in terms of the domestic currency. They have to offset the excess demands for, or supplies of, foreign currency (that is, the balance of payments deficits or surpluses, respectively), at the pegged (fixed) exchange rate by running down, or adding to, their reserves of foreign currency.

4. Under floating or flexible exchange rates, the exchange rate may change from moment to moment. In a system of clean floating, the exchange rate is determined by supply and demand without central bank intervention to affect the rate. Under dirty floating, the central bank intervenes by buying and selling foreign exchange in an attempt to influence the exchange rate.

5. Bilateral exchange rates express the value of one currency against another while an index of the multilateral rate represents the price of a basket of foreign currencies weighted by their importance in international trade. An index of the real exchange rate measures a country's competitiveness by taking into account changes in price levels.

6. The introduction of trade in goods means that some of the demand for our output comes from abroad and that some spending by our residents is on foreign goods. There is equilibrium in the goods market when the demand for domestically produced goods is equal to the output of those goods.

7. An increase in autonomous demand for domestic goods increases domestic output and worsens the trade balance. An increase in exports increases domestic income and reduces the trade deficit. A shift in demand toward domestically produced goods increases the level of income and reduces the trade deficit, or increases the trade surplus.

8. The real exchange rate affects the trade balance and the level of aggregate demand. Given the domestic and foreign price levels, a devaluation or depreciation improves competitiveness and shifts the *IS* curve to the right.

9. In equilibrium, the trade account may be in deficit, and there may be a policy conflict in that trade balance and full employment cannot be attained using monetary and fiscal policy. An expenditure switching policy, such as devaluation, is needed to change the allocation of spending between imports and domestic goods.

Key Terms

Fixed exchange rates
Flexible exchange rates
Balance of payments
Current account
Capital account
Trade balance
Intervention
Clean floating

Dirty (managed) floating
Revaluation
Appreciation
Depreciation
Multilateral exchange rate
Real exchange rate
Internal and external balance

Problems

1. Consider the model of Section 5-2 in which the *IS* curve is described by Equations (2), (3), and (4). Assume, as a simplification, that the interest rate is given. In terms of Figure 5-4, the central bank holds the interest rate constant at i_0 so that the *LM* curve is effectively horizontal at this level.
   (a) What is the balance of trade?
   (b) What is the equilibrium level of income?
   (c) What is the balance of trade at that equilibrium level of income?
   (d) What is the effect of an increase in exports on the equilibrium level of income? What is the multiplier?
   (e) What is the effect of increased exports on the trade balance?

2. Suppose that, in Problem 1,
   $\bar{A} = 400$ $c(1 - t) = 0.8$ $b = 30$ $i_0 = 5$ (percent) $m = 0.2$
   $\bar{X} = 250$ $\bar{Q} = 0$
   (a) Calculate the equilibrium level of income.
   (b) Calculate the balance of trade.
   (c) Calculate the open economy multiplier, that is, the effect of an increase in $\bar{A}$ on equilibrium output.

(d) Assume there is a reduction in export demand of $\Delta \bar{X} = 1$ (billion). By how much does income change? By how much does the trade balance worsen?

(e) How much does a 1 percentage point increase in the interest rate (from 5 to 6 percent) improve the trade balance? Explain why the trade balance improves when the interest rate rises.

(f) What policies can the country pursue to offset the impact of reduced exports on domestic income and employment as well as on the trade balance?

3. Use a diagram similar to Figure 5-6 to show the effect on income and the trade balance of a shift in demand from imports to domestically produced goods. Assume trade is in balance at the initial equilibrium.

4. Consider a country that is in a position of full employment and balanced trade. Which of the following types of disturbances can be remedied with standard aggregate demand tools of stabilization? Indicate in each case the impact on external and internal balance as well as the appropriate policy response.
    (a) A loss of export markets.
    (b) A reduction in saving and corresponding increase in demand for domestic goods.
    (c) An increase in government spending.
    (d) A shift in demand from imports to domestic goods.
    (e) A reduction in imports with a corresponding increase in saving.

5. (a) Use the formula for the foreign trade multiplier to discuss the impact on the trade balance of an increase in autonomous domestic spending.
    (b) Comment on the proposition that the more open the economy, the smaller the domestic income expansion.

6. Use the data in Table 5-2 to calculate the value for 1991 of a multilateral exchange rate index with a base 1986 = 100. Assume the following country weights:

U.S.	.85
Britain	.05
Germany	.10

CHAPTER 6 *International Capital Flows and Stabilization Policy*

In this chapter we consider the role of the capital account in determining the balance of payments and equilibrium income. It plays an important role because of the high degree of international integration of capital markets. In particular, yields on Canadian assets are closely linked to yields on comparable assets in the United States. If Canadian interest rates fall relative to U.S. rates, there will be a capital outflow from Canada as lenders move their funds out of Canada and borrowers attempt to raise funds in the domestic market rather than abroad.

The relationship between capital flows and interest rates has important implications for stabilization policy. Since monetary and fiscal policy affect interest rates, they have an effect on the balance of payments through the capital account as well as the trade account as discussed in Chapter 5. In a flexible exchange rate regime there will be further effects on the exchange rate and therefore on equilibrium income.

6-1 Capital Flows and Equilibrium Income With Fixed Exchange Rates

In introducing capital flows, we assume that the foreign rate of interest (i°) is given and that the higher the home country's rate of interest, the higher the rate at which capital flows into the home country. In Figure 6-1 we show the rate of capital inflow *CF*, or the capital account surplus, as an increasing function of the rate of interest. When the domestic interest rate equals the foreign rate, the capital flow is zero. If the domestic interest rate is higher, there will be an inflow; conversely, if the domestic rate is lower, there will be an outflow.

Under the assumptions given above, the capital account surplus is given by a relationship of the form:

$$CF = a(i - i^\circ) \tag{1}$$

Combining this with Equation (2a) from Section 5-3 above, we obtain the overall balance of payments surplus *BP* as:

$$BP = \overline{X} - \overline{Q} - mY + q\frac{eP^\circ}{P} + a(i - i^\circ) \tag{2}$$

Equation (2) shows that an increase in income worsens the trade balance and reduces the overall surplus, while an increase in the interest rate increases the capital inflow and increases the overall surplus.

The Balance of Payments (*BP*) Curve

If we set the overall balance of payments surplus equal to zero in Equation (2), we obtain the equation of the *BP curve*. The BP curve shows the combinations of income and the interest rate for which the overall balance of payments is zero. A graphic

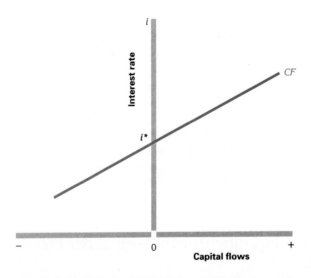

Figure 6-1 *Interest-Responsive Capital Flows*

derivation of this relationship is given in Figure 6-2. In the upper left-hand panel we show the capital account surplus for a given foreign interest rate (i^*) as in Figure 6-1. The trade surplus NX is plotted against income in the lower panel for a given level of the real exchange rate (eP^*/P). It is negatively sloped since an increase in income increases imports and reduces NX. The BP curve is shown in the upper right-hand panel. At point E_1, we have both a zero capital account balance, since $i = i^*$, and a zero current account balance, since $Y = \overline{Y}$. Thus E_1 is a point on the BP curve.

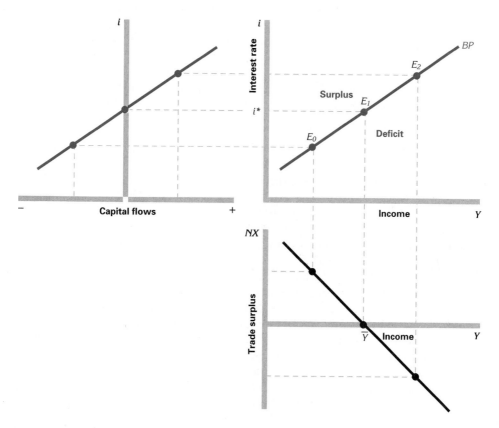

Figure 6-2   *The Balance of Payments Equilibrium Schedule*

In the upper left-hand panel we show the capital account surplus, and in the lower panel we show the trade surplus. At point E_1 in the upper right-hand panel, we have both a zero capital account balance, since $i = i^*$, and a zero current account balance, since $Y = Y$. At E_2, we have a higher interest rate and a higher level of income such that there is a capital account surplus matched by an equal trade deficit. Similarly at E_0, we have a capital account deficit and an equal trade surplus. By joining up these points we obtain a positively sloped BP curve which shows the combinations of income and the interest rate for which the overall balance of payments is zero.

At E_2, we have a higher interest rate and a higher level of income such that there is a capital account surplus matched by an equal trade deficit. Similarly at E_0, we have a capital account deficit and an equal trade surplus.

By joining up these points we obtain a positively sloped *BP* curve. It is drawn for a given real exchange rate (eP°/P) and a given foreign interest rate (i°). To confirm that the slope is positive, start with an income expansion that raises imports and worsens the balance of payments. To restore a zero overall balance of payments, the interest rate must be raised to attract capital inflows and offset the trade deficit. Thus a higher level of income must be matched by a higher interest rate to remain on the *BP* curve.

As shown in Figure 6-2, at points above the *BP* curve we have a balance of payments surplus and at points below the curve we have a deficit. To see why this is so, consider what happens if we hold income constant and vary the domestic interest rate. At the interest rate for which we are on the curve, we have a zero balance. At a higher rate the trade balance will be the same but there will be a higher net capital inflow (or smaller net outflow) and therefore an overall surplus. Conversely, a lower interest rate will reduce the capital account surplus (or increase the deficit) and lead to an overall deficit.

The Steepness of the BP Curve

We have shown that the *BP* curve is positively sloped. What determines the steepness of the curve? The magnitude of the slope depends on the marginal propensity to import (m) and the degree of capital mobility as measured by the effect on capital flows of a change in the domestic interest rate (a). The higher the degree of capital mobility, the flatter is the schedule. If capital flows are highly responsive to interest rates, then a small increase in the interest rate will bring about very large flows and thus allow a large increase in the trade deficit. The larger the marginal propensity to import, the steeper the schedule. An increase in income worsens the trade balance by the increase in income times the marginal propensity to import. Thus a high propensity means that a given increase in income produces a large deficit, and requires a large increase in interest rates to bring about a matching increase in capital inflow. These results can be confirmed by setting $BP = 0$ in Equation (2) and solving for i to obtain the equation for the *BP* curve in the form

$$i = i^\circ + \frac{m}{a}Y - \frac{1}{a}\left(\overline{X} - \overline{Q} + q\,\frac{eP^\circ}{P}\right) \tag{2a}$$

Thus the slope of the *BP* curve is m/a.

Equilibrium Income and the Balance of Payments

Figure 6-3 illustrates the equilibrium of an economy under a *fixed exchange rate* with both trade and capital flows. As was the case in Section 5-2 above, the intersection of the *IS* and *LM* curves determines the equilibrium income and interest rate. Since the overall balance of payments need not be zero, the *BP* curve serves to determine whether there will be a surplus or a deficit. The case illustrated in Figure 6-3 involves a surplus at equilibrium.

Since the *BP* and *LM* curves are both positively sloped, the assumption made as to which is steeper may have an important effect on the conclusions of our analysis. In Figure 6-3, we have made the *BP* curve relatively flat under the assumption that there is a high degree of capital mobility. This is likely to be appropriate for a country like Canada whose financial markets are closely integrated with those in the United States. This assumption is maintained throughout this section and is discussed further in Section 6-4 below.[1]

Monetary and Fiscal Policy

The effect of an expansionary fiscal policy on income and the balance of payments is illustrated in Figure 6-4. For simplicity we assume that we begin with *IS* and *LM*

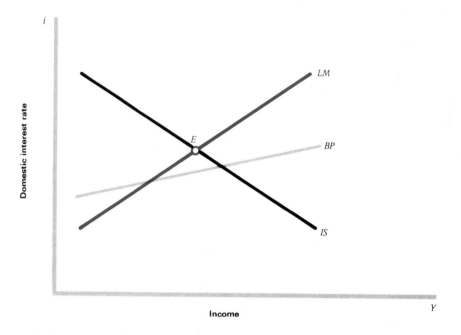

Figure 6-3 *Goods and Money Market Equilibrium With Capital Flows*

Equilibrium income and the interest rate are determined by the intersection of the *IS* and *LM* schedules. The position of the *BP* schedule determines whether there is a surplus or deficit in the balance of payments. At the point *E* there is a surplus.

---

[1] In Problem 3 at the end of this chapter you are asked to consider the opposite case in which the *BP* curve is steeper than the *LM* curve.

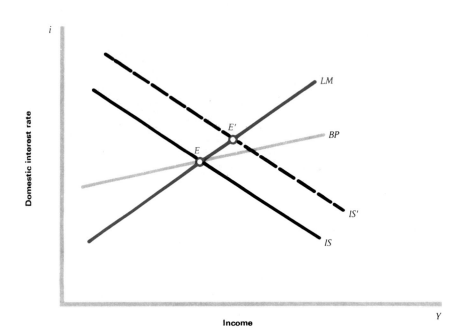

Figure 6-4   *Fiscal Policy and the Balance of Payments*

Expansionary fiscal policy shifts the *IS* curve up and to the right and the economy moves from *E* to *E′* where both income and the interest rate are higher. The trade account worsens since higher income increases imports, while the capital account improves since higher interest rates attract capital inflows. The net effect is an improvement since *E′* is above the *BP* schedule. This reflects the assumption that capital is highly mobile.

curves that intersect at the point *E* which is on the *BP* curve; that is, we assume that we begin at an equilibrium at which we have a zero balance of payments surplus. The *IS* curve shifts to the right and the new equilibrium is at *E′* where income and the interest rate are higher.

What will be the effect of expansionary fiscal policy on the balance of payments? The answer to this question is complicated by the fact that both the trade account and the capital account are affected. As in Section 5-2 above, the trade balance worsens because the higher income increases import spending. On the other hand, the higher interest rate increases the net capital inflow and improves the balance of payments. Since the point *E* in Figure 6-4 is above the *BP* curve, the net effect is an *improvement* in the overall balance of payments. The capital account effect dominates the trade account effect because of our assumption that capital is highly mobile.

Turning to monetary policy, Figure 6-5 shows the effect of an increase in the money supply. The *LM* curve shifts to the right and the equilibrium income rises and the interest rate falls as we move from *E* to *E′*. The new equilibrium point is below the

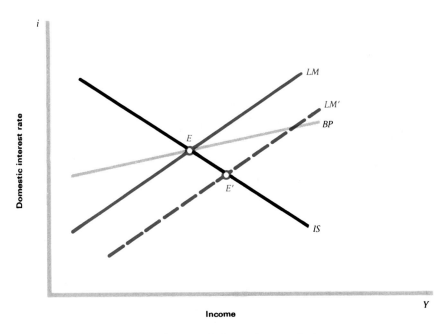

Figure 6-5 *Monetary Policy and the Balance of Payments*

An increase in the money supply shifts the *LM* curve down and to the right so that income rises and the interest rate falls. The balance of payments worsens since the higher income increases imports and the lower interest rate reduces the net capital inflow.

BP curve so that an expansionary monetary policy leads to a balance of payments deficit. In this case, the trade account and capital account effects work in the same direction. The higher level of income causes a worsening of the trade account and the lower interest rate causes a worsening of the capital account.

Internal and External Balance

Figure 6-6 illustrates internal and external balance in an economy with capital flows. The full-employment output is shown as Y° so that at the point E we have both full employment and balance of payments equilibrium. The four quadrants represent the four possible policy problems. For example, if we are at point E_1, we have deficient demand and a balance of payments deficit. The appropriate policy to produce internal and external balance requires a higher level of employment for internal balance and higher interest rates and/or a lower level of income for external balance.

In terms of the earlier analysis, there is a policy dilemma at E_1 because employment considerations suggest income should be raised and balance of payments considerations

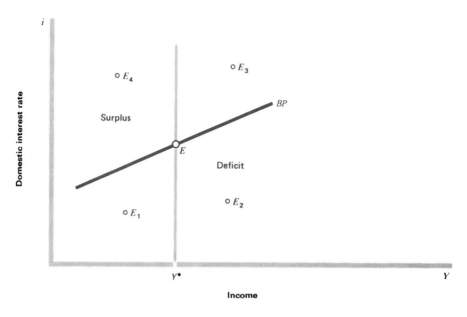

Figure 6-6   *Internal and External Balance*

The internal balance schedule is a vertical line at the full-employment level of income. Along the *BP* schedule, the overall balance of payments is zero. The four quadrants represent the four possible policy problems. An appropriate combination of monetary and fiscal policy can be used to move the economy to the point *E*.

suggest it should be reduced. However, now there is a way out of the dilemma. Suppose we reduce the money supply and thus raise interest rates. To offset the effects of the higher interest rates on income, we could use expansionary fiscal policy. Clearly, we would keep income constant and reach balance of payments equilibrium by getting interest rates high enough. However, we can do better. We can use fiscal policy to get us all the way to full employment and use tight money, in the form of higher interest rates, to achieve balance of payments equilibrium. Thus we can get to point *E* with both internal and external balance.[2]

The lesson we have just derived is that under fixed exchange rates, we should expand income through fiscal policy whenever there is unemployment and use tight money whenever there is a balance of payments deficit. With a situation like point E_4, we want to use the same principle, but the economic conditions are different. Here we have a surplus and unemployment. Accordingly, we need expansionary fiscal policy to achieve full employment and expansionary monetary policy to reduce interest rates.

---

[2]   The idea of the policy mix for internal and external balance was suggested by Robert Mundell in his important paper, "The Appropriate Use of Monetary and Fiscal Policy under Fixed Exchange Rates," *I.M.F. Staff Papers*, March 1962.

Actually there is no dilemma at point E_4, since any form of expansionary policy moves us in the right direction with respect to both targets.

We leave it to you to work through the remaining cases and note here merely the principle: Under fixed exchange rates and with capital mobility, we use monetary policy to achieve external balance and fiscal policy to achieve full employment. What is the experience with such a rule? There is little doubt that tight money, for balance of payments reasons, is the oldest remedy in the policy maker's medicine chest. Since monetary policy is a flexible tool, attainment of external balance in the short run through tight money is relatively easy.

Limitations of the Policy Mix

The argument for a fiscal–monetary policy mix to handle both internal and external balance problems is persuasive, but it overlooks two important limitations. The first problem is that a country will typically not be indifferent to the level of domestic interest rates. Even if fiscal policy were sufficiently flexible to implement the policy mix, it would still be true that the composition of domestic output would depend on the mix. Thus, a country that attempts an expansion in aggregate demand, together with tight money, effectively restricts the construction sector and investment spending in general. The notion of a policy mix with monetary policy devoted to the balance of payments therefore overlooks the fact that the interest rate determines the composition as well as the level of aggregate spending.

The second consideration concerns the composition of the balance of payments. Countries are not indifferent about the makeup of their balance of payments between the current account deficit and the capital account surplus. Even if the overall balance is in equilibrium so that one target is satisfied, there is still the problem that a capital account surplus or capital inflow means net external borrowing. Our country's debts to foreigners are increasing. Those debts will eventually have to be repaid.

Under a system of fixed exchange rates, there are circumstances under which a country, much like an individual, will find it useful to borrow in order to finance, say, a transitory shortfall of export earnings. However, continued large-scale borrowing from abroad is not consistent with a fixed exchange rate over long periods. Large-scale borrowing eventually places the country in a position where the interest payments to foreigners become a major burden. Faced with the prospect of continued foreign borrowing on a large scale in order to maintain its fixed exchange rate, a country would be well advised to implement adjustment policies that improve the current account balance. Such policies would typically be a devaluation accompanied by restrictive monetary and/or fiscal policy to reduce domestic demand.

6-2 The Balance of Payments and the Money Supply

The analysis of the balance of payments presented above has been based on the assumption that there is no link between the domestic money supply and the foreign exchange market intervention that is required to maintain a fixed exchange rate. However, such a link does exist, since intervention involves buying and selling foreign currency in exchange for domestic currency.

Consider, for example, the foreign exchange transactions required when there is a balance of payments deficit. The central bank offsets the excess demand for foreign currency by selling currency out of its reserves. It receives domestic currency in payment and thus withdraws money from circulation.[3] In general, a balance of payments deficit leads to a decline in the domestic money supply and a surplus leads to an increase in the money supply.

It is possible, of course, for the central bank to undertake offsetting open market operations. The process by which the central bank uses open market operations to offset the effects of foreign exchange transactions and insulate the domestic money supply from the balance of payments is called *sterilization*.[4] For example, if the Bank of Canada sells U.S. dollars in exchange for Canadian dollars, it can prevent a reduction in the money supply by simultaneously purchasing an equal Canadian dollar amount of bonds. Thus, we can say that in the analysis so far presented, we have assumed that the central bank breaks the link between the balance of payments and the money supply through sterilization.

The Adjustment Process Without Sterilization

Suppose we assume that the central bank does not carry out sterilization operations and permits the money supply to be determined by the balance of payments surplus or deficit. How will this affect the analysis of monetary and fiscal policy given in Section 6-1?

We consider first the effect of an increase in the money supply as illustrated in Figure 6-5 of the previous section. The *LM* curve shifts to the right and the economy moves from *E* to *E′* where there is a balance of payments deficit. In the absence of sterilization, the money supply will fall and the *LM* curve will shift back until the deficit is eliminated and equilibrium is restored at the starting point *E*. Thus, we conclude that in the absence of sterilization, monetary policy has no effect since the money supply is automatically determined by the balance of payments and cannot be controlled by the central bank.

In the case of fiscal policy, the result is quite different. Suppose we have an expansionary fiscal policy as illustrated in Figure 6-7. As in Figure 6-4, the *IS* curve shifts to the right and the economy moves to *E′* where there is a balance of payments surplus. In the absence of sterilization, the money supply will rise, the *LM* curve will shift to the right, and the economy will move along the adjustment path shown to the new equilibrium at *E″*. In this case the effect of fiscal policy is reinforced by the automatic

---

[3] Strictly speaking, it is the monetary base rather than the total money supply that is affected. The change in the money supply is then determined by the multiplier process discussed in Chapter 13.

[4] Open market operations are purchases and sales of bonds by the central bank. The process by which these transactions affect the money supply is described in detail in Chapter 13.

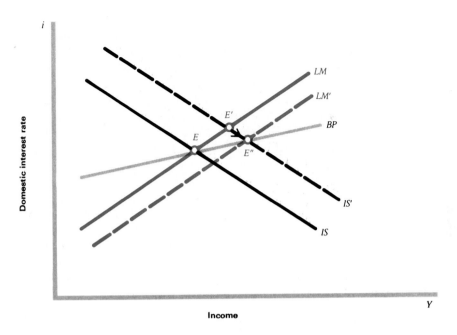

Figure 6-7 *Adjustment to an Expansionary Fiscal Policy Without Sterilization*

An expansionary fiscal policy moves the economy to the point E' where there is a balance of payments surplus. As a result the money supply increases until a new equilibrium is reached at E''.

adjustment of the money supply so that we get a larger increase in income than occurs with sterilization.

In general, if no sterilization operations are undertaken by the central bank, the equilibrium point is determined by the intersection of the IS and BP curves. The LM curve shifts automatically as the money supply changes in response to balance of payments surpluses or deficits. Algebraically, the equilibrium income and interest rate can be obtained by solving the equation for the BP curve, given in Equation (2a) above, together with the equation for the IS curve, as shown in Equation (3a) in Chapter 5. The equation for the LM curve serves to determine the required money supply given the equilibrium values of income and the interest rate.

*6-3 Capital Flows and Equilibrium Income With Flexible Exchange Rates

In this section we apply the model developed above to an economy with a flexible exchange rate. The analysis can be considerably simplified by assuming that capital is perfectly mobile, as is done in the next section. The more general case considered here can be omitted without any loss of continuity.

Figure 6-8 shows the determination of equilibrium income and the interest rate under a flexible exchange rate. As in Section 6-1, we assume the *LM* curve is steeper than the *BP* curve. In the present case, however, all three curves must intersect at the same point, because the overall balance of payments surplus or deficit must be zero in equilibrium. Thus the point *E'* in Figure 6-8 is not an equilibrium, since it lies below the *BP* curve. Because there will be a deficit at *E'*, the currency will depreciate, competitiveness will improve, and the net export component of aggregate demand will increase. As we saw in Section 5-3, this means that the *IS* curve shifts up and to the right as indicated by the arrows.

However, this is not the end of the story. Changes in the exchange rate cause the *BP* curve to shift as well. A depreciation will increase net exports for a given level of income so that a higher level of income will be required to maintain the trade balance at a constant level. Alternatively, the trade balance improvement can be offset by a

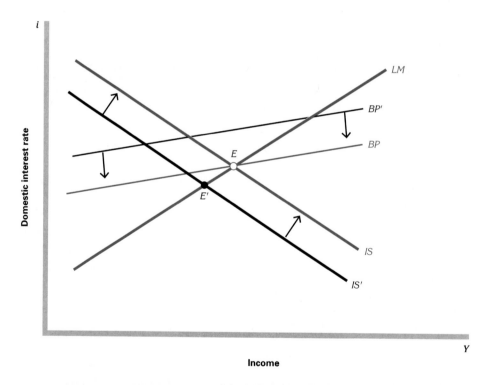

Figure 6-8 *Equilibrium With Flexible Exchange Rates*

The equilibrium is at *E* where all three curves intersect. At *E'*, there is a balance of payments deficit. The currency will depreciate and the *IS* and *BP* curves will shift to the right until the deficit is eliminated at point *E*.

reduction in the interest rate and a deterioration of the capital account. Thus the *BP* curve shifts down and to the right as shown in Figure 6-8.[5]

Monetary and Fiscal Policy

Figure 6-9 shows the effect of an increase in the money supply. The *LM* curve shifts to the right and intersects the *IS* curve at *E'*. At *E'*, there is a balance of payments deficit so that the currency depreciates and the *IS* and *BP* curves shift to the right. The new equilibrium is at *E''* where all three curves intersect. The net effect is an

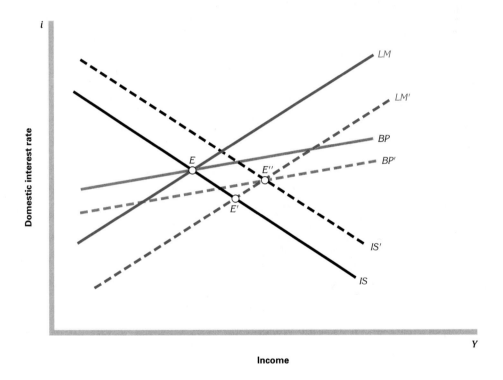

Figure 6-9   *Monetary Policy Under Flexible Exchange Rates*

An increase in the money supply shifts the *LM* curve to the right. At *E'* there is a balance of payments deficit so that the *IS* and *BP* curves shift to the right until the new equilibrium is reached at *E''*.

[5] It can be shown that a given change in the exchange rate will cause the *BP* curve to shift in the horizontal direction by a larger amount than the *IS* curve. The shift in *BP* is given by $\Delta Y = (1/m)(qP^\circ/P)\Delta e$, and the shift in *IS* is given by $\Delta Y = \bar{\bar{\alpha}}(qP^\circ/P)\Delta e$. From inspection of Equation (5) of Chapter 5 which defines $\bar{\bar{\alpha}}$, we see that $1/m > \bar{\bar{\alpha}}$ so that the *BP* shift is larger.

increase in income and a fall in the interest rate. With a lower interest rate, there will be an increased net capital outflow. Since the overall deficit must remain at zero, the current account must improve. It follows that the negative effect of increased imports resulting from the higher income level must be more than offset by the positive effect of the depreciation.

The effect of a fiscal expansion is illustrated in Figure 6-10. The *IS* curve shifts to the right and intersects the *LM* curve at *E'*. At *E'*, there is a surplus so that the currency appreciates and the *IS* curve shifts back to the left. The *BP* curve also shifts to the left and the new equilibrium is at *E"* so that we end up with a higher income and interest rate. With a higher interest rate, there will be an increased net inflow of capital and therefore a deterioration of the current account.

The fall in net exports and the shift in the *IS* curve back to *IS"* in Figure 6-10 represents another example of a crowding out effect that attenuates the impact on income of a fiscal expansion. The extent of crowding out depends crucially on the degree of capital mobility as measured by the interest rate effect on capital flows. If

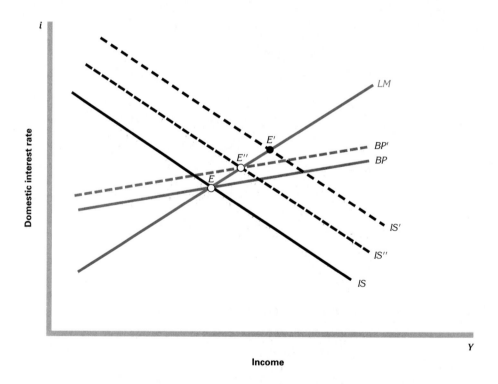

Figure 6-10   *Fiscal Policy Under Flexible Exchange Rates*

A fiscal expansion shifts the *IS* curve to the right. At *E'* there is a balance of payments surplus so that the *IS* and *BP* curves shift to the left until the new equilibrium is reached at *E"*.

capital is highly mobile, then the *BP* curve will be relatively flat and there will be a large crowding out effect. As we shall see in the next section, in the limiting case of perfect capital mobility, there will be complete crowding out and fiscal policy will have no effect.

6-4 Perfect Capital Mobility: The Mundell–Fleming Model

For the remainder of this chapter, we confine our attention to the special case in which international capital is perfectly mobile. The assumption of *perfect capital mobility* means that there will be very large capital flows whenever the domestic interest rate deviates from the the foreign rate, so that we can have balance of payments equilibrium only when the domestic rate is equal to the foreign rate. For many purposes this is a useful approximation to the Canadian case.

The extension of the *IS-LM* model to an open economy with perfect capital mobility is generally referred to as the *Mundell–Fleming model*. Robert Mundell is a Canadian economist, currently a professor at Columbia University, and the late Marcus Fleming was a research economist at the International Monetary Fund.[6] They developed the model in the 1960s but it remains an extremely useful way of understanding how policies work under high capital mobility.

The assumption of perfect capital mobility leads to a considerable simplification of our model. Since the domestic interest rate is constrained to be equal to the foreign rate, Equation (2a) of Section 6-1 that describes the *BP* schedule is replaced by:[7]

$$i = i^* \tag{2b}$$

As illustrated in Figure 6-11, the *BP* curve will be a horizontal line at the interest rate i^*.

---

[6] Mundell's work on international macroeconomics has been extraordinarily important, and the adventurous student should certainly consult his two books: *International Economics* (New York: Macmillan, 1967) and *Monetary Theory* (Pacific Palisades, California: Goodyear, 1971). See also R. Mundell, "Capital Mobility and Stabilization Policy under Fixed and Flexible Exchange Rates," *Canadian Journal of Economics*, November 1963; and Marcus Fleming, "Domestic Financial Policies under Fixed and under Floating Exchange Rates," IMF Staff Papers, November 1962. An up-to-date discussion can be found in Jacob Frenkel and Michael Mussa, "Asset Markets, Exchange Rates and the Balance of Payments," in R.W. Jones and P. Kenen, eds., *Handbook of International Economics*, Vol. 2 (Amsterdam: North-Holland, 1985). Recent econometric model simulations in line with the Mundell–Fleming model can be found in R. Bryant *et al.*, eds., *Empirical Macroeconomics for Interdependent Economies* (Washington, D.C.: Brookings Institution, 1988) and Pete Richardson, "The Structure and Simulation Properties of the OECD's Interlink Model," *OECD Economic Studies*, no. 10, Spring 1988.

[7] Equation (2b) follows directly from (2a) when the coefficient *a* is increased without limit.

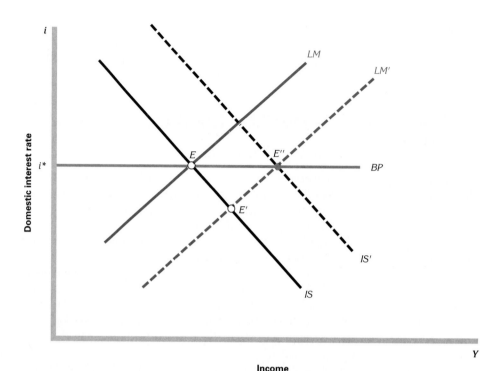

Figure 6-11   *Monetary Policy With Perfect Capital Mobility*

Under perfect capital mobility, the *BP* schedule is horizontal at the foreign interest rate. An increase in the money supply shifts the *LM* curve down and to the right. At *E'*, the interest rate is below the foreign rate so there will be a capital outflow. Under fixed rates, the central bank must decrease the money supply back to its original level and there will be no change in income. With flexible rates, there will be a depreciation, the *IS* curve will shift up and to the right, and the new equilibrium will be at *E''*.

Monetary Policy Under Perfect Capital Mobility

The implications of perfect capital mobility are very strong. Under fixed exchange rates, sterilization is not possible and the central bank has no control over the money supply. This follows from the fact that at any point off the *BP* curve (that is, at any domestic interest rate that deviates from the foreign rate), there will be an indefinitely large capital account surplus or deficit. The central bank is forced to allow the money supply to adjust so as to maintain the domestic interest rate equal to the foreign rate.

The effect of an increase in the money supply is illustrated in Figure 6-11. Beginning at point *E*, the *LM* curve shifts down and to the right to *LM'*. At the point *E'*, goods and money markets are in equilibrium but interest rates are below the foreign level and there will be massive capital outflows. To maintain a fixed exchange rate, the central bank must sell foreign exchange and allow the domestic money supply to return to its original level. Indeed, with perfect capital mobility, the economy could never get to E' since the response of capital flows would force an immediate reversal of any attempt to change the money supply.

In contrast to the fixed exchange rate case, monetary policy is quite effective under flexible exchange rates. If the central bank does not intervene and allows market forces to determine the exchange rate, the capital outflow precipitated by the shift in the LM curve will cause the currency to depreciate. As a result, the IS curve will shift up and to the right, and the depreciation will continue until competitiveness has improved enough to raise demand and output to the level indicated by point E'' where the domestic interest rate again equals the foreign rate.[8]

We thus conclude that, under flexible exchange rates, the central bank can control the money supply, and monetary policy affects the level of income. However, in contrast to the closed economy case of Chapter 4, with perfect capital mobility the link between the money supply and income is not via the interest rate. In the present case, a monetary expansion increases income via a depreciation of the currency and an increase in the net export component of aggregate demand.

It is also worth noting the international implications of this analysis. We have seen that a monetary expansion in the home country leads to depreciation, an increase in net exports, and therefore an increase in output and employment. However, our increased net exports correspond to a deterioration in the trade balance abroad. The domestic depreciation shifts demand from foreign goods toward domestic goods. Abroad, output and employment therefore decline. It is for this reason that the depreciation-induced change in the trade balance has been called a *beggar-thy-neighbour policy* — it is a way of exporting unemployment or of creating domestic employment at the expense of the rest of the world.

The recognition that currency depreciation is mainly a way of shifting demand from one country to another, rather than changing the level of world demand, is important. It implies that exchange rate adjustment can be a useful policy when countries find themselves in different stages of a business cycle — for example, one in a boom and the other in a recession. In that event, a depreciation by the country experiencing a recession would shift world demand in that direction and thus work to reduce divergences from full employment in each country.

By contrast, when countries' business cycles are highly synchronized, such as in the 1930s or in the aftermath of the oil shock in 1973, exchange rate movements will not contribute much toward world full employment. The problem is then one of the level of total world spending being deficient or excessive while exchange rate movements affect only the allocation of a given world demand between countries. Nevertheless, from the point of view of an individual country, currency depreciation works to attract

---

[8] In Problem 4 at the end of this chapter, we ask you to show that the current account improves between E and E'', even though the increased level of income increases imports.

world demand and raise domestic output. If every country tried to depreciate to attract world demand, we would have *competitive depreciation* and a shifting around of world demand rather than an increase in the world level of spending. Coordinated monetary and/or fiscal policies are needed to increase demand and output in each country.

Fiscal Policy and Crowding Out Under Perfect Capital Mobility

Figure 6-12 illustrates the effect of a fiscal expansion that shifts the *IS* curve up and to the right. Again the point *E'* cannot be an equilibrium, since the domestic interest rate is above the foreign rate. Under fixed exchange rates the resulting capital inflow

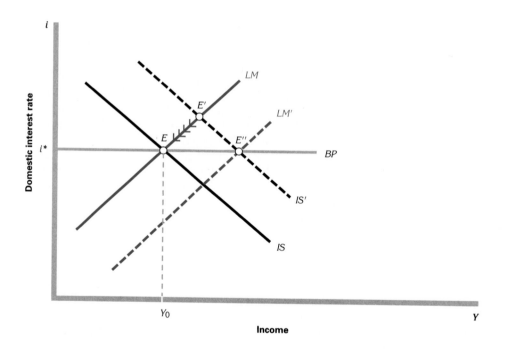

Figure 6-12   *Fiscal Policy With Perfect Capital Mobility*

A fiscal expansion shifts the *IS* curve up and to the right. At *E'*, the interest rate is above the foreign rate so there will be a capital inflow. Under fixed rates, the central bank must allow the money supply to expand so that the *LM* curve shifts out and the new equilibrium is at *E''*. With flexible rates, there will be an appreciation, the *IS* curve will shift back to its original position, and equilibrium will be restored at *E* with complete crowding out.

forces the central bank to purchase foreign currency and allow the money supply to expand. The *LM* curve must shift to the right until it intersects the *IS* curve at *E''*. At this point, income has increased but the interest rate is unchanged from the initial equilibrium level.

Thus we find that under fixed exchange rates and perfect capital mobility, there is no crowding out and fiscal policy changes have a full multiplier effect on income. The effect of an increase in government spending as shown in Figure 6-12 is exactly the same as we obtained in Figure 4-20 of Chapter 4. There we assumed, in the context of a closed economy, that the fiscal expansion was *accommodated* by a discretionary money supply increase so as to maintain a constant interest rate. In the present case, the monetary accommodation is forced on the central bank for balance of payments reasons.

As in the case of monetary policy, our conclusions are reversed if we assume flexible exchange rates. In this case, the capital inflow causes the currency to appreciate. The appreciation continues until the loss of competitiveness has reduced net exports enough to shift the *IS* curve back to its original position where the domestic interest rate again equals the foreign rate. Only when the economy has returned to point *E* in Figure 6-12 will income have reached a level consistent with monetary equilibrium at the foreign rate of interest.

Thus we see that under flexible rates, there is complete crowding out and fiscal policy has no effect on income. The crowding out takes place not as in Chapter 4 because higher interest rates reduce investment, but because the appreciation reduces competitiveness resulting in a decline in net exports.

The analysis of Figure 6-12 can also be applied to other disturbances that shift the *IS* curve. For example, with flexible exchange rates, an increase in the autonomous component of net exports will increase demand and precipitate an appreciation in the same way. In this case the initial increase in net exports will be completely offset and there will be no change in the level or composition of output.

The results of this section for the case of perfect capital mobility are summarized in Table 6-1.

Table 6-1 *The Effects of Monetary and Fiscal Policy Under Perfect Capital Mobility*

	Fixed rates	Flexible rates
Monetary expansion	No income change; reserve losses equal to money increase	Income increases; trade balance improves; currency depreciates
Fiscal expansion	Income increases; trade balance worsens	No income change; net exports fall; currency appreciates

Box 6-1   Canadian Experience With Flexible Exchange Rates in the 1950s

Canada operated under a flexible exchange rate from 1950 to mid-1962. This period, characterized by pronounced cyclical swings, provides an interesting case study of an economy with a flexible exchange rate and a high degree of capital mobility.

The Natural Resource Boom of the Mid-1950s

During the mid-1950s Canada experienced boom conditions fuelled by high world demand for natural resources. Further, the attractive investment opportunities that existed in Canada attracted large capital inflows. As can be seen in Figure 5-3, the effect of the capital account surplus was to push up the value of the Canadian dollar, which remained above 100 U.S. cents and at times rose as high as 105 U.S. cents. This in turn had the effect of reducing exports and increasing imports so that there were deficits in merchandise trade.

During this period, the appreciation of the Canadian dollar acted as a stabilizer and had a desirable dampening effect on aggregate demand. The economy was subject to expansionary disturbances as represented by the outward shift in the IS schedule shown in Figure 6-12. At the point E' we have a balance of payments surplus which causes an appreciation and a movement of the IS back to E.

The question that remains is: Why did the Canadian economy go through a prolonged period of slow growth and high unemployment during the years 1957 to 1961?

The Slow Growth Period, 1957–1961

During 1957 the Canadian economy weakened and the unemployment rate rose, subsequently reaching a peak of 7.9 percent in mid-1958. There was an effort to stimulate the economy in 1958 and 1959 through expansionary fiscal policy, and the cyclically adjusted federal budget balance moved into a deficit position. However, as we have seen, we would not expect fiscal policy to have a lasting effect on income under a flexible exchange rate. An increase in the government deficit leads to a crowding out of private demand in the form of net exports. Clearly, it is necessary for a country with a flexible exchange rate to use monetary policy for stabilization purposes.

How was monetary policy used in this period? During 1958, the money supply was expanded at a rapid rate, but this policy was reversed in 1959 and 1960. During these two years there was virtually no growth in the money supply. As a result, interest rates rose sharply in 1959 and remained relatively high until mid-1961. Thus, the period

1959 to 1961 was characterized by a very restrictive monetary policy, in spite of a clear need for economic stimulus.

A review of statements by the Bank of Canada during this period suggests that the restrictive monetary policy being followed was based on two major concerns. First, rising inflation was seen as an important threat to the Canadian economy even after 1957, when it was clear that a recession had taken hold. Second, the Governor placed great emphasis on what he regarded as the unsatisfactory state of Canada's balance of payments. In his *Annual Report* for 1959 (pp. 7–8) he stated:

> *For some years, as I see it, the Canadian economy has been under the influence of excessive overall spending, which even in periods of relatively high unemployment resulted in a net inflow of imports from other countries. . . . The attempt to accomplish too much too fast has given rise to huge deficits in our international balance of payments on current account, . . . [and] to a large and growing volume of foreign debt, . . . and has gone hand-in-hand with a growing degree of foreign predominance in Canadian business.*

Continuing this theme in his *Annual Report* for 1960 (p. 22), he concluded that:

> *to engage in further large over-all monetary expansion in an attempt to drive down interest rates generally, with or without the motive of thereby reducing the inflow of capital from abroad, is an unsound and dangerous approach. . . .*

It appears that the Bank of Canada's prescription for these supposed ills was to maintain high interest rates so as to reduce imports by curtailing overall aggregate demand, and to reduce the capital inflows by encouraging domestic saving. In retrospect, it is clear that this policy was at odds with the theory of an open economy under a flexible exchange rate. The adoption of restrictive monetary policy induces a capital account surplus and an appreciation of the Canadian dollar. As a result the trade account moves toward a deficit position, income falls, and unemployment rises. This adjustment process is quite consistent with the observed behaviour of the Canadian economy over the period 1959 to 1961.

Thus we conclude that mistakes in monetary policy were a major cause of the stagnation of the Canadian economy in the late fifties and early sixties. There was indeed considerable controversy at the time, and in 1960 a group of academic economists called upon the Minister of Finance to dismiss the Governor of the Bank of Canada. Subsequently, there was an acrimonious confrontation between the Minister and the Governor, and the latter finally resigned in July 1961.*

---

*See H. Scott Gordon, *The Economists Versus the Bank of Canada* (Toronto: Ryerson Press, 1961).

6-5 Exchange Rate Expectations and the Interest Parity Condition

A cornerstone of our theoretical model of exchange rate determination in the previous section was international capital mobility. In particular, we assumed that capital markets were highly integrated so that interest rates would be equalized across countries. How does this assumption stand up to the facts?

In Figure 6-13, we show Canadian and U.S. interest rates on 90-day paper. The two rates follow a similar pattern over time but they are by no means equal. Exchange rate expectations provide the key to squaring this fact with our theory.

Exchange Rate Expectations

The theory that implies international equalization of interest rates is incomplete in a world where exchange rates frequently change, and are expected to change. For example, consider a situation in which the German mark is expected to appreciate by 5 percent over the next year relative to the Canadian dollar. Suppose the interest rate

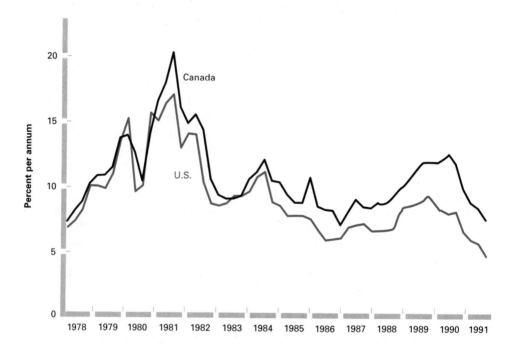

Figure 6-13 *Interest Rates on 90-Day Paper*

(*Source:* Adapted from *Bank of Canada Review*)

in Germany is 6 percent. Then anyone buying German bonds will earn a return in marks of 6 percent. Suppose now that the Canadian interest rate is 10 percent. A German investing in Canada for a year will, at the beginning of the year, exchange his marks for dollars, and then earn 10 percent on his dollars. At the end of the year, he will want to change his dollars back into marks to spend in Germany. However, he expects that by the end of the year, each dollar will be worth 5 percent less in terms of marks, as a result of the expected depreciation. Therefore, in terms of marks, he will expect to earn only 5 percent (10 percent minus 5 percent) by investing in Canadian bonds, whereas he earns 6 percent by investing in German bonds. He will naturally prefer to invest in German bonds.[9]

It is clear, therefore, that we must extend our discussion of interest rate equalization to incorporate expectations of exchange rate changes. Table 6-2 gives some combinations of the domestic interest rate, the foreign interest rate, and exchange rate changes. To find out the return on domestic investments, we just look at our interest rate. For foreign investments, we look at the foreign rate, and at the currency depreciation. Suppose foreign interest rates were 5 percent and exchange rates did not change. In Table 6-2 this is the case of row 1, and the *adjusted* interest differential is 5 percent in favour of the home country. Row 2 considers the case where interest rates abroad are high (15 percent), but where our currency appreciates at the rate of 5 percent or the foreign currency depreciates by that amount. Here the depreciation exactly offsets the higher foreign interest rates, and the adjusted differential is zero — what would be gained in interest is lost through the foreign depreciation. Cases 3 and 4 show circumstances where the foreign depreciation falls short of, and exceeds, the interest differential, respectively. Clearly, in cases 1 and 4, we would want to invest in the home country; in case 2 we are indifferent; and case 3 favours the foreign country.

Table 6-2 *Interest Rates and Currency Depreciation*

	Domestic Interest Rate (1)	Foreign Interest Rate (2)	Depreciation (3)	Adjusted Interest Differential (1) − (2) − (3)
	(in percentages)			
1.	10	5	0	5
2.	10	15	−5	0
3.	10	15	−2	−3
4.	10	15	−10	5

[9] You should confirm that a Canadian who expects the dollar to depreciate by 5 percent would, given the 6 percent and 10 percent interest rates, also prefer to buy German bonds.

The trouble, of course, is that we do not know ahead of time how the exchange rate will move. We know the interest rates on, say, three-month Treasury bills in Canada and the United Kingdom, so that we can compute the interest differential, but we do not know whether the pound will appreciate or depreciate over the next three months. Even if we somehow knew the direction, we would certainly not know the precise amount.

Investors then have to form *expectations* about the behaviour of the exchange rate; that is, in deciding whether to invest at home or abroad, they have to make forecasts of the future behaviour of the exchange rate. Given these forecasts, we would expect that in a world of high capital mobility, the interest differentials, adjusted for expected depreciation, should be negligible. That means that a country that is certain to depreciate will have interest rates above the world level, and conversely, a country that is expected to appreciate will have interest rates below the world level.

The Interest Parity Condition

The introduction of exchange rate expectations modifies our condition for balance of payments equilibrium. We maintain the assumption of perfect capital mobility, but replace the condition that the domestic rate i is equal to the foreign rate i° with

$$i = i^\circ + x \tag{1}$$

where x is the expected rate of depreciation of the domestic currency. This condition is called the *interest parity condition.*

Using this equation to describe the balance of payments equilibrium implies that the *BP* schedule will still be horizontal but its position will depend on exchange rate expectations. This implies that speculative capital flows related to expectations of changes in exchange rates will have macroeconomic consequences. In Figure 6-14, the *BP* schedule is drawn for a given foreign interest rate and a given expected rate of depreciation, say zero. Suppose that we start in equilibrium at point E and that the market develops the expectation that the home currency will appreciate. This implies that even with a lower home interest rate, domestic assets are attractive, and so the *BP* schedule shifts down by the amount of expected appreciation.

Point E is no longer an equilibrium, given the shift of the *BP* schedule to *BP'*, but rather a position of surplus with large-scale capital inflows motivated by the anticipation of appreciation. The surplus causes the exchange rate to start appreciating, and we move in a southwesterly direction, as indicated by the arrow. The speculative attack causes appreciation, a loss in competitiveness, and, consequently, falling output and employment.[10]

---

[10]   The point E' can be a temporary equilibrium only, because the exchange rate is constant but an appreciation is expected. Ultimately the economy must return to E, where the exchange rate is expected to remain constant.

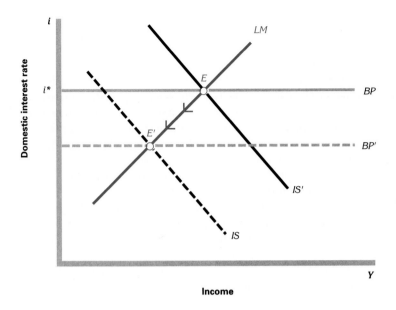

Figure 6-14   *Response to an Expected Appreciation of the Currency*

The initial equilibrium at E is disturbed by the expectation that the home currency will appreciate. The BP schedule shifts down to BP', reflecting the fact that people are willing to hold domestic assets at a reduced interest rate since they are compensated for the differential by anticipated appreciation. At E' there is now a capital inflow that leads to currency appreciation. The IS schedule shifts to IS', and the economy moves into a recession. The capital inflow has brought about a loss of trade competitiveness and thus unemployment at point E'.

This analysis confirms that exchange rate expectations, through their impact on capital flows and thus on actual exchange rates, are a potential source of disturbance to macroeconomic equilibrium.

Exchange Rate Overshooting

The interest parity condition also has important implications for the adjustment process in response to monetary changes. Consider the adjustment to an increase in the money supply in the flexible exchange rate case as shown in Figure 6-11. If we make our usual assumption that the money market adjusts instantaneously, the adjustment path will be along the LM curve from E' to E''. Along this path, the currency is depreciating while the domestic interest rate is below the foreign rate. However, to the extent that this depreciation is anticipated, the interest parity condition is violated since we have $x > 0$ and $i - i^\circ < 0$.

Figures 6-15 and 6-16 illustrate an adjustment process that is consistent with the interest parity condition. Figure 6-16 shows the time paths of the money supply, the exchange rate, and income. Note that the exchange rate is measured by the domestic currency price of foreign exchange so that a depreciation is shown as an increase.

When the money supply is increased at time T_0, there is an immediate depreciation and a fall in the domestic interest rate. As shown in Figure 6-16, this depreciation *overshoots* the final equilibrium value. Thereafter, the domestic currency *appreciates* toward its new equilibrium. Meanwhile, in Figure 6-15, the economy moves initially to E'. At this point, the interest parity condition holds since we have $i - i° < 0$ and $x < 0$ (i.e., investors anticipate an appreciation). As we move toward the new equilibrium, income increases in response to the initial improvement in competitiveness, the currency appreciates, and the interest rate rises back to the level of the foreign rate.

At the new equilibrium, income is higher, the domestic interest rate is unchanged, and the currency has depreciated. However, the exchange rate overshoots the new equilibrium level since, in response to the disturbance, it initially moves beyond the equilibrium it ultimately will reach and then gradually returns to the new equilibrium. Overshooting means that changes in monetary policy produce large changes in exchange rates.

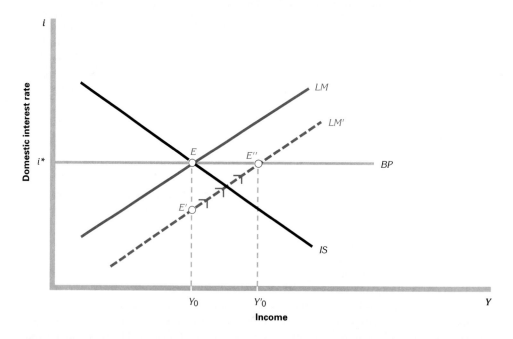

Figure 6-15   *Interest Parity and the Adjustment to an Increase in Money*

When the money supply is increased, the economy initially moves to E' where $i < i°$ and investors anticipate an appreciation of the currency. As we move to E'', income increases, the currency appreciates, and i rises back to the level of $i°$.

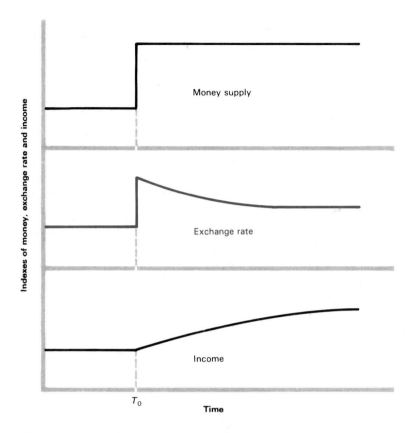

Figure 6-16 *Exchange Rate Overshooting*

The diagram shows indexes of the money supply, exchange rate, and income to illustrate the time paths corresponding to the adjustment process shown in Figure 6-15. An increase in the money stock at time T_0 causes an immediate depreciation. The gain in competitiveness leads to an increase in income over time while the currency appreciates, partially reversing the initial overshooting.

6-6 Summary

1. Capital flows depend on the domestic interest rate relative to foreign rates. The *BP* schedule represents combinations of income and the domestic interest rate for which the overall balance of payments is zero.

2. Under fixed exchange rates an increase in the money supply increases income and causes a deterioration in both the current account and the capital account. An expansionary fiscal policy increases income and improves the capital account but

causes a deterioration in the current account. The capital account effect is larger assuming capital is highly mobile.

3. Internal and external balance can be achieved by combining restrictive monetary policy that improves the capital account with expansionary fiscal policy that increases employment. However, if the balance of payments problem is not temporary, ultimately the imbalance must be dealt with by an alternative policy such as devaluation.

4. The domestic money supply can be insulated from foreign exchange transactions by sterilization operations. If there is no sterilization, then the money supply is automatically determined by the balance of payments and cannot be controlled by the central bank.

5. Under flexible exchange rates, an increase in the money supply causes a depreciation and an increase in income. Expansionary fiscal policy increases income but there is crowding out resulting from an appreciation of the currency.

6. With perfect capital mobility, the domestic interest rate is constrained to be equal to the foreign rate. Under fixed exchange rates fiscal policy has a full multiplier effect on income while monetary policy is completely ineffective. Under flexible rates, on the other hand, fiscal policy is ineffective while monetary policy affects income via the exchange rate.

7. When exchange rate expectations are taken into account, balance of payments equilibrium is described by the interest parity condition that equates the domestic interest rate with the foreign rate plus the expected rate of depreciation. This condition implies that there will be exchange rate overshooting in response to a change in the money supply. An increase in money causes an immediate depreciation beyond the final equilibrium value followed by an appreciation along an adjustment path to the new equilibrium.

Key Terms

BP **curve**
Sterilization
Perfect capital mobility
Beggar-thy-neighbour policy

Competitive depreciation
Interest parity condition
Exchange rate overshooting

Problems

1. Consider an economy with a fixed exchange rate that is initially in internal and external balance. Assume there is an increase in the foreign interest rate.
   (a) Show the effect on the *BP* schedule.
   (b) What policy response would restore internal and external balance?

(c) If the central bank did not undertake sterilization operations, what would be the adjustment process?

2. Under fixed exchange rates, what mix of monetary and fiscal policy should be pursued to offset the following disturbances?
(a) A temporary gain in exports
(b) A permanent gain in exports
(c) A decline in autonomous spending
(d) An increased rate of capital flow (at each level of the domestic interest rate)

3. Suppose we have a limited degree of capital mobility so that the *BP* curve is steeper than the *LM* curve. What would be the effect on the following of an increase in government spending under a fixed exchange rate?
(a) Income and the domestic interest rate
(b) Trade balance
(c) Capital account balance
(d) Overall balance of payments

4. Explain how, with a flexible exchange rate, monetary policy retains its effectiveness when there is perfect capital mobility. How is it that an increase in the money supply leads to an improvement in the current account even though income and therefore imports increase?

5. Consider the effect of an increase in government expenditure in an economy with a flexible exchange rate and perfect capital mobility. Why are the equilibrium levels of income and the interest rate unaffected? What is the effect on the trade account?

6. With perfect capital mobility, what would be the effect on income, the domestic interest rate, and the trade account of an increase in exports? Consider both the fixed and flexible exchange rate cases.

7. Assume you expect the pound to depreciate by 6 percent over the next year. Assume that the Canadian interest rate is 8 percent. What interest rate would be needed on pound securities, such as government bonds, for you to be willing to buy those securities with your dollars today, and then sell them in a year in exchange for dollars?

8. Consider the model of Section 6-3, where we assumed a flexible exchange rate and imperfect capital mobility. Using Equation (2) of Section 6-1, the *BP* curve can be represented by

$$NX = -a(i - i^*)$$

where

$$NX = \bar{X} - \bar{Q} - mY + q\,\frac{eP^*}{P}$$

(a) Assuming no taxes or transfer payments, the goods market equilibrium condition can be written

$$Y = \bar{\bar{A}} + cY - bi + NX$$

where

$$\bar{\bar{A}} = \bar{C} + \bar{I} + \bar{G}$$

Substituting for NX in the goods market equilibrium condition yields

$$Y = \bar{\bar{A}} + cY - bi - a(i - i^*)$$

Show this equation graphically in i,Y space and interpret it.

(b) Also draw an LM schedule in the same space and interpret the intersection point.

(c) Show now the effect of a fiscal expansion on interest rates, income, and the trade account.

(d) Show the effect of a monetary expansion on income, interest rates, and the trade account.

9. This problem draws on the discussion of stabilization policy and beggar-thy-neighbour policy in Section 6-4. Suppose we have two countries with full-employment output levels $\bar{Y}$ and $\bar{Y}^*$ at home and abroad, respectively.

(a) Draw a diagram with actual output levels, Y and Y^*, on the axes. Draw also lines corresponding to potential output levels. Label the resulting four quadrants I, II, III, and IV.

(b) Identify for each of the quadrants the state of demand in each country as boom or recession.

(c) Which policies can be pursued when output exceeds potential in each country? When output exceeds potential in one but falls short of potential in another?

(d) In which quadrants are beggar-thy-neighbour policies particularly dangerous? Where is coordination of policies essential?

PART 2 *Income and the Price Level*

CHAPTER 7

Aggregate Supply and Demand: An Introduction

So far our analysis has assumed that the price level is fixed. We studied the impacts of changes in the money supply, or of taxes, or of government spending, assuming that whatever amount of goods was demanded would be supplied at the *existing price level*.

To put the same point in different words, we have not yet analyzed *inflation*, but of course inflation is one of the major concerns of citizens, policy makers, and macroeconomists. The time therefore has come to bring the price level and inflation rate — the rate of change of the price level — into our analysis of the economy. We have to study the determination of both the level of income — on which we have concentrated so far — and the price level. In this chapter, we confine our discussion to an economy without international trade or capital flows. The open economy case is taken up again in Chapter 9.

Figure 7-1 shows the model of *aggregate demand and supply* that we shall use to study the joint determination of the price level and the level of income. The aggregate demand curve *AD*, which is downward-sloping, is based entirely on the material of the earlier chapters, in particular Chapter 4. We define the aggregate demand curve in this chapter, and show why it slopes downward and what causes it to shift. The aggregate supply curve will be introduced in this chapter and developed further in Chapter 8. The intersection of the *AD* and *AS* schedules at *E* determines the equilibrium level of income, Y_0, and the equilibrium price level, P_0. Shifts in either schedule cause the price level and the level of income to change.

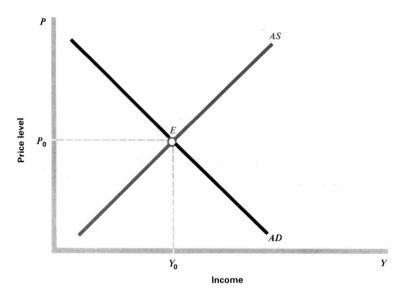

Figure 7-1 *Aggregate Supply and Demand*

The diagram shows the complete model of aggregate demand and supply that is used to explain the joint determination of the levels of income and prices. The aggregate demand curve, AD, is based on the *IS-LM* model studied in earlier chapters. The aggregate supply curve, AS, is developed in this chapter and Chapter 8. Their intersection at point E determines the level of income Y_0 and the price level P_0.

The aggregate demand–supply model is the basic macroeconomic model for studying output and price level determination — just as in microeconomics, demand and supply curves are the essential tools for studying output and price determination in a single market. However, the aggregate demand and supply curves are not as simple as the microeconomic demand and supply curves. There is more going on in the background of the aggregate curves than there is in that of the microeconomic curves.[1]

The aggregate demand–supply model can be used to identify major schools of thought in macroeconomics: strict monetarists, who believe that the quantity of money tightly governs the behaviour of the price level, and old-fashioned Keynesians, who believe that prices do not play a significant role in the short-run analysis of the business cycle. Of course, these are extreme positions or near caricatures, but against these polar extremes we can place in clear perspective the much more subtle and sophisti-

---

[1] The aggregate demand curve is sometimes referred to as the macroeconomic demand curve, both to emphasize that it is different from a regular demand curve in microeconomics and to distinguish it from the aggregate demand schedule in Chapter 3. We stay with the same name, *AD*, here after warning that the present *AD* schedule represents a considerable extension of that in Chapter 3 since it makes interest rates endogenous along the curve.

cated views of modern Keynesians and modern monetarists. These distinctions and their policy implications are the subject of much of macroeconomic discussion, and they will occupy us throughout this book.

7-1   Introducing Aggregate Demand and Supply

Before we go deeply into the factors underlying the aggregate demand and supply curves, we show how the curves will be used. Suppose that the money supply is increased. What effects will that have on the price level and income? In particular, does an increase in the money supply cause the price level to rise, thus producing inflation; or does the level of income rise, as it did in the analysis of earlier chapters; or do both income and the price level rise?

Figure 7-2 shows that an increase in the money supply shifts the aggregate demand curve AD to the right, to AD'.[2] We see later in this chapter why that should be so.

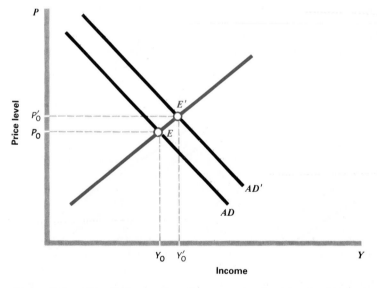

Figure 7-2 *The Effects of an Increase in the Nominal Money Stock*

An increase in the money stock shifts the aggregate demand curve from AD to AD'. The equilibrium moves from E to E', resulting in higher levels of both prices and output. Thus an increase in the money stock in part results in higher prices and not entirely in higher income.

---

[2] The aggregate demand curves are shown here as linear, and shifts in the money supply are represented by parallel shifts. These are approximations, since the AD curve as derived below is not linear in the price level.

The shift of the aggregate demand curve moves the equilibrium of the economy from E to E'. The price level rises from P_0 to P_0', and the level of income from Y_0 to Y_0'. Thus an increase in the money stock causes both the level of income and the price level to rise.

The Slope of the Aggregate Supply Curve

What determines how much the price level rises and how much income increases? Looking at Figure 7-3a we see that if the aggregate supply curve is relatively flat, a shift in the AD curve raises income a lot and prices very little. By contrast, in Figure 7-3b we see that when the aggregate supply curve is nearly vertical, an increase in the money supply mainly causes prices to rise and hardly increases income at all.

If the aggregate supply curve is vertical, or nearly so as in Figure 7-3b, then the analysis of the earlier chapters that showed an increase in the money stock raising income could be very misleading. For example, if the aggregate supply curve is vertical, an increase in the money stock will lead only to higher prices, not to more output. Thus one of the key questions we shall concentrate on is what determines the shape of the aggregate supply curve. When is it vertical, or nearly so as in Figure 7-3b? When is the aggregate supply curve more nearly horizontal as in Figure 7-3a?

We start the analysis here by defining aggregate demand and supply.

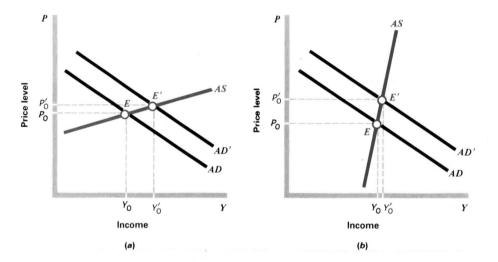

Figure 7-3   *The Interaction of Aggregate Supply and Demand*

The effects of a shift in the aggregate demand curve from AD to AD' depend on the slope of the aggregate supply curve. If the AS curve is relatively flat, as in panel (*a*), the shift in the aggregate demand curve results mainly in an increase in income. By contrast, in panel (*b*), the shift in the aggregate demand curve results almost entirely in an increase in the price level and very little in an increase in income.

Aggregate Demand and Supply Defined

The *aggregate demand curve* shows the combinations of the price level and level of income at which the goods and assets markets are simultaneously in equilibrium. At any point on the aggregate demand curve, for instance point *B* in Figure 7-4, we see that for the given price level, P_B in this case, the level of income at which the goods and assets markets are in equilibrium is Y_B.

We can already give a preliminary explanation of why the aggregate demand curve slopes downward, based on the discussion of monetary policy in Chapter 4. Suppose that the goods and assets markets are in equilibrium at a level of income like Y_B, with a given price level P_B. Now suppose the price level falls. With a given nominal stock of money, a fall in the price level creates an increase in the quantity of real balances. Recall from Chapter 4 that an increase in the quantity of real balances reduces interest rates, increases investment demand, and therefore increases aggregate spending. Accordingly, when the price level falls, the equilibrium level of spending rises; therefore the *AD* curve slopes down. We go into the details in Section 7-3.

We can also see, from the definition of the aggregate demand curve, why the analysis of the previous chapters is not at all wasted. The aggregate demand curve describes

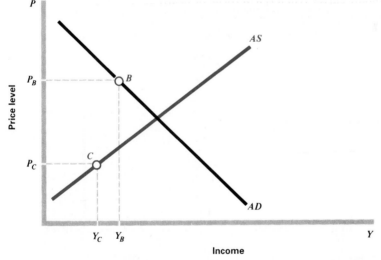

Figure 7-4 *Aggregate Demand and Supply Curves Defined*

At any point on the aggregate demand curve, such as point *B*, both the goods and assets markets are in equilibrium. This is the equilibrium described by the intersection of *IS* and *LM* curves in Chapter 4. For instance, with price level P_B, the level of income at which both goods and assets markets are in equilibrium is Y_B. The aggregate supply curve *AS* describes the relation between the price level and the amount of output firms wish to supply. For instance, at price level P_C, firms want to supply output Y_C.

the joint equilibrium of the goods and assets markets. That is precisely what the *IS-LM* analysis describes. Thus the material we studied in earlier chapters is an essential part of the aggregate demand and supply model we shall use to analyze the simultaneous determination of the levels of income and prices.

The *aggregate supply curve* describes the combinations of income and the price level such that firms are willing, at the given price level, to supply the given quantity of output. For instance, at point *C* in Figure 7-4, with price level P_C, firms are willing to supply output equal to Y_C. The amount of output firms are willing to supply depends on the prices they receive for their goods and the amounts they have to pay for labour and other factors of production. Accordingly, the aggregate supply curve reflects conditions in the factor markets — especially the labour market — as well as the goods markets.

Aggregate Supply: Two Special Cases

In this chapter we concentrate on two special cases in discussing aggregate supply. The first, the *Keynesian case* shown in Figure 7-5*a*, is a horizontal aggregate supply curve. The Keynesian aggregate supply curve is horizontal, indicating that firms will supply whatever amount of goods is demanded at the existing price level.

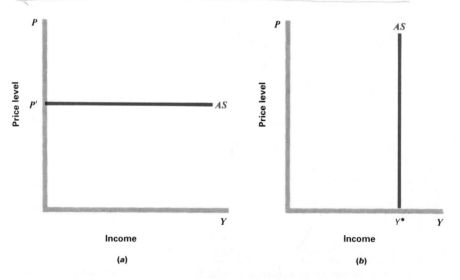

(a)   (b)

Figure 7-5 *Keynesian and Classical Supply Functions*

The Keynesian aggregate supply curve is horizontal, implying that any amount of output will be supplied at the existing price level. This is shown in panel (*a*), where the *AS* curve is horizontal at price level *P'*. The classical supply function is based on the assumption that there is always full employment of labour, and thus that output is always at the level of output corresponding to full employment of labour, *Y*°, and *independent of the price level*. This is shown by the vertical aggregate supply curve in panel (*b*).

The idea underlying the Keynesian aggregate supply curve is that because there is unemployment, firms can obtain as much labour as they want at the current wage. Their average costs of production therefore are assumed not to change as their output levels change.[3] They are accordingly willing to supply as much as is demanded at the existing price level.

Figure 7-5*b* shows the opposite extreme, a vertical supply curve. In the *classical case*, the aggregate supply curve is vertical, indicating that the same amount of goods will be supplied whatever the price level.

The classical supply curve is based on the assumption that the labour market is always in equilibrium with full employment of the labour force. It is vertical at the level of output corresponding to full employment, Y° in Figure 7-5*b*. This level of output and employment is assumed to be maintained by speedy adjustments of wages and prices. For this reason the formal modern version of this theory is sometimes referred to as the *frictionless neoclassical model*. It is described further in the next section and in the appendix to this chapter.

The difference between the classical and Keynesian aggregate supply curves is that the classical supply curve is based on the belief that the labour market works smoothly so as to keep the labour force fully employed. Movements in the wage are the mechanism through which full employment is maintained. The Keynesian aggregate supply curve is instead based on the assumption that the wage does not change much or at all when there is unemployment so that unemployment can continue for some time.

These two cases — the classical with continuous labour market equilibrium, and the Keynesian with little adjustment in wages — are the two extremes. In Chapter 8, we show why the aggregate supply curve is, at least in the short run, positively sloped and lies between the Keynesian and classical cases.

7-2 The Frictionless Neoclassical Model of the Labour Market

In this section, we derive the classical aggregate supply curve starting from microeconomic foundations. As shown in Figure 7-6, there is a downward-sloping demand curve for labour, *ND*. The curve shows that the lower the hourly real wage, the greater the quantity of labour demanded. The real wage is the ratio of the wage rate to the price level, or the amount of goods that can be bought with an hour of work. Also shown is an upward-sloping supply curve of labour, *NS*, indicating that the higher the real wage, the more hours of work workers want to supply.

The full derivation of the demand curve for labour in Figure 7-6 is presented in the appendix to this chapter. The demand curve slopes downward because it is

---

[3] The supply curve described here as Keynesian is not exactly the supply curve implied by Keynes himself in his classic *General Theory*. It is, however, the supply curve that is consistent with the use of the *IS-LM* model (as in Chapter 4), which was often used by Keynesians to describe the determination of output. There is often some difference between the views of Keynes in the *General Theory* and the simpler theories of some succeeding Keynesians. It is almost always the case that original sources are more subtle than the popular versions based on them.

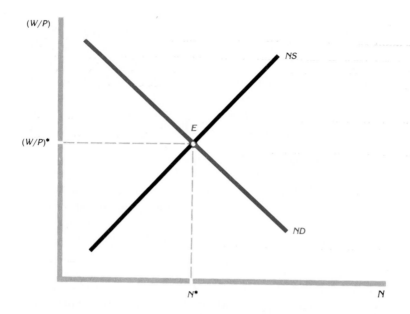

Figure 7-6 *Labour Market Equilibrium and Full Employment*

The labour supply curve *NS* shows the quantity of labour supplied increasing with the real wage. Along *ND* a reduction in the real wage causes an increase in the quantity of labour demanded. The labour market is in equilibrium at point *E*.

assumed that the marginal productivity of labour decreases as more labour is employed. Firms are competitive and are therefore willing to pay a real wage equal to the value of the marginal product of labour. There is a fixed amount of capital. As more labour is added, each new worker has less machinery with which to produce than the previous workers, and therefore the amount the new worker adds to output (the marginal product of labour) is lower than the amount added by previous workers. The marginal productivity of labour is thus declining, and the demand curve slopes downward.

The supply curve of labour is shown as upward-sloping because typically, as the wage rises, more workers come into the labour force seeking work. However, the supply curve could be vertical (or completely inelastic) if the amount of labour supplied is insensitive to the real wage.[4]

---

[4] If you have studied microeconomics, you have probably seen the "backward-bending" labour supply curve, which is negatively sloped at high wages. That occurs because when the wage rises, individuals can both work less and earn more income. They may choose to respond to higher wages by working less. Although the labour supply curve may well slope backward in the long run (we work fewer hours than our grandparents and have much higher wages than they did) the supply curve of labour *for the economy* in the short run of a few years is positively sloped. That is because as the wage rises, people who were not working decide it is worthwhile to take a job rather than work at home, and they enter the labour force. Further, people already on the job may in the short run want to work longer hours when the real wage rises.

The labour supply and demand curves intersect at point E, with a corresponding level of labour input or employment, N^*, and an equilibrium real wage, $(W/P)^*$. N^* is the *full-employment level of employment*. In this idealized, frictionless neoclassical model, everyone is working precisely as much as he or she wants to at the real wage, $(W/P)^*$. In addition, firms are using precisely the amount of labour they want at this real wage.

Corresponding to the full-employment level of employment, N^*, is the full-employment level of output, Y^*. This is the level of output that is produced using the existing amounts of other factors (the capital stock, land, and raw materials) and the amount of labour, N^*.[5]

A Change in the Price Level

In Figure 7-7 we show the labour supply and demand curves with the *nominal wage* on the vertical axis. The price level is assumed to be at a given level, say P_0. With a

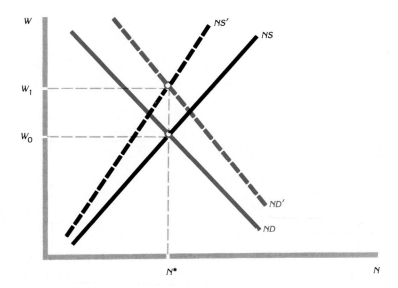

Figure 7-7 *The Effects of a Change in the Price Level on the Labour Market*

Labour supply and demand curves NS and ND are shown for a constant price level. An increase in the price level shifts both curves upward in the same proportion, to NS' and ND', respectively. The equilibrium level of employment N^* is unaffected by the change in the price level.

---

[5] In our description here, technology and the stock of capital are given, but these can change and, as a result, the full-employment level of output will change too. For example, an increase in the capital stock will raise full-employment output, as does an improvement in technology.

constant price level, a change in the nominal wage is also a change in the real wage, and the labour supply and demand curves thus look exactly as they do in Figure 7-6. The equilibrium wage is W_0.

Now suppose there is an increase in the price level. This will cause the labour demand and supply curves in Figure 7-7 to shift up to ND' and NS', respectively. The two curves shift upward by exactly the same amount since, at each level of the nominal wage, the real wage is now lower in the same proportion as the price level has risen. When the two curves shift upward by the same amount, they intersect at the same level of employment, $N°$. Thus the level of employment will remain at $N°$ despite the increase in the price level. The nominal wage rises in Figure 7-7 to the level W_1, but the real wage remains unchanged.

This analysis explains why the aggregate supply curve is vertical in the classical case. An increase in the price level leads to no change in the level of employment and therefore no change in the level of output.

Frictional Unemployment and the Natural Rate of Unemployment

Taken literally, the frictionless neoclassical model implies that there is no unemployment. By including frictions, however, the theory can account for some unemployment of labour. The frictions occur because the labour market is always in a state of flux. Some people are retiring from their jobs, other people are looking for jobs for the first time, some firms are expanding and are hiring new workers, and others have lost business and have to contract, firing workers.

Because it takes time for an individual to find the right new job, there will always be some *frictional unemployment* as people search for jobs. Frictional unemployment is the unemployment that exists as a result of individuals shifting between jobs and looking for new jobs.

There is some amount of frictional employment associated with the full-employment level of employment $N°$ and full-employment level of output $Y°$. That amount of unemployment is called the *natural rate*. The natural rate of unemployment is the rate of unemployment arising from labour market frictions that exists when the labour market is in equilibrium.

We do not go into the determinants and estimates of the natural rate of unemployment here, reserving that for Chapter 17. The important point is that the existence of some unemployment is not necessarily inconsistent with the neoclassical model of the labour market in which the economy is always at the full-employment level of output.

7-3 The Aggregate Demand Schedule

The aggregate demand curve, or schedule, shows, for each price level, the level of income at which the goods and assets markets are simultaneously in equilibrium. At any given price level, we use the *IS-LM* model to determine the level of income at which the goods and assets markets are in equilibrium.

In the top panel of Figure 7-8 we show the *IS-LM* model. The position of the *IS* curve depends on fiscal policy. The *LM* schedule is drawn for a given nominal money stock, M, and a given price level, P_0, and thus for a given real money stock M/P_0. The equilibrium interest rate is i_0, and the equilibrium level of income and spending is Y_0.

A Change in the Price Level

Consider the effect of a fall in the price level from P_0 to P'_0. This reduction in the price level increases the real money stock from $\overline{M}/P_0$ to $\overline{M}/P'_0$. To clear the money market with an increased real money stock, either interest rates must fall, inducing the public to hold more cash balances, or income must rise, thus increasing the transactions demand for money.

Accordingly, the *LM* curve shifts downward and to the right, to *LM'*. The new equilibrium is shown at point E', where once again the money market clears, because we are on the *LM* curve, and the goods market clears, because we are on the *IS* curve. The new equilibrium level of income is Y'_0, corresponding to the lower price level P'_0. Thus a reduction in the price level, *given the nominal quantity of money*, results in an increase in equilibrium income and spending.

The derivation of the *AD* schedule can be seen in the lower panel of Figure 7-8. The economy is initially in equilibrium at points E in both panels. The equilibrium interest rate is i_0, the level of income is Y_0, and the corresponding price level is P_0. Now the price level drops to P'_0. In the upper panel, the equilibrium moves to E' as a result of the shift of the *LM* curve to *LM'*. Corresponding to point E' in the upper panel is point E' in the lower panel, at price level P'_0 and level of income Y'_0.

Thus both E and E' in the lower panel are points on the *AD* schedule. We could now consider all possible price levels and the corresponding levels of real balances. For each level of real balances there is a different *LM* curve in the upper panel. Corresponding to each *LM* curve is an equilibrium level of income, which would be recorded in the lower panel at the price level that results in the *LM* curve in the upper panel. Connecting all these points gives us a downward-sloping aggregate demand curve, *AD*, as shown in Figure 7-8.

The *AD* curve is downward-sloped because there is a definite relation between equilibrium spending and the price level: The higher the price level, the lower are real balances, and hence the lower the equilibrium level of spending and income.

The Slope of the *AD* Schedule

The *AD* schedule shows how the level of real spending changes with the level of prices, given fiscal policy, the quantity of money, and autonomous private spending. The slope of the curve tells us how much real spending changes in response to a change in the level of prices.

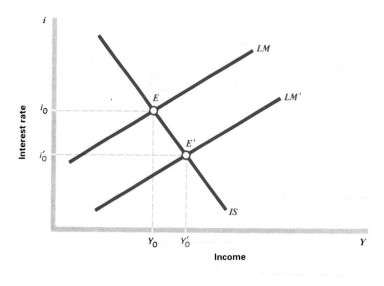

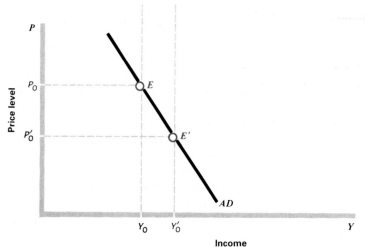

Figure 7-8   *Derivation of the Aggregate Demand Schedule*

The upper panel shows the *IS* schedule and the initial *LM* schedule drawn for the real money stock $\overline{M}/P_0$. Equilibrium is at point *E*. In the lower panel we record that at a price level P_0 the equilibrium level of income and spending is Y_0. This is shown by point *E*. At a lower level of prices, say, P_0', the real money stock is $\overline{M}/P_0'$, and therefore the *LM* schedule shifts to *LM'*. Equilibrium income now is Y_0'. Again in the lower panel we show at point *E'* the combination of the price level P_0' and the corresponding equilibrium level of income and spending Y_0'. Considering different levels of prices and connecting the resulting points such as *E* and *E'*, we derive the aggregate demand schedule *AD*. The schedule shows the equilibrium level of spending at each level of prices, given the nominal money stock and fiscal policy.

In Figure 7-8 we derived the *AD* schedule by considering the effect of changes in the price level, and hence in real balances, on the *LM* schedule and hence on equilibrium income and spending. The slope of the *AD* curve therefore reflects the extent to which a change in real balances changes the equilibrium level of spending, taking both assets and goods markets into account.

However, we have already examined the effects of a change in the stock of real balances on the level of income that equilibrates the goods and assets markets. In Chapter 4 we showed the effect of an increase in the nominal stock of money on equilibrium spending and income, with the price level given. Now we ask what is the effect of a change in real balances due to lower prices, given nominal money.

In discussing monetary policy in Chapter 4 we showed the following results using the *IS-LM* schedules:

- The smaller the interest responsiveness of money demand and the higher the interest responsiveness of investment demand, the larger the increase in equilibrium income and spending caused by an increase in real balances. *= flatter AD*

- The larger the multiplier and the smaller the income response of money demand, the larger the increase in equilibrium income and spending caused by an increase in real balances. *= " "*

Because the slope of the AD curve is determined by the effect of a change in real balances on equilibrium spending and income, the same factors that determine the effects of a change in the stock of money on equilibrium income and spending also determine the slope of the AD curve. If a given change in real balances has a large impact on equilibrium spending, then the *AD* curve will be very flat, because a small change in the price level creates a large change in equilibrium spending. Conversely, if a given change in real balances has a small effect on equilibrium spending and income, then the *AD* curve will be steep: In that case it takes a large change in the price level to create a small change in spending and income.

Accordingly, we see that:

1. (a) The smaller the interest responsiveness of the demand for money, and (b) the larger the interest responsiveness of investment demand, the flatter the *AD* curve.

2. (a) The larger the multiplier, and (b) the smaller the income responsiveness of the demand for money, the flatter the *AD* curve.

To fix ideas further, it is useful to think for a moment about the *AD* schedule in terms of the extreme classical and liquidity trap cases that we learned about in Chapter 4. In the classical case, where money demand is entirely unresponsive to interest rates and the *LM* curve is vertical, changes in real balances have a big effect on income and spending. As illustrated in Figure 7-9, that corresponds to a very flat *AD* schedule, such as *AD'*, as we should expect based on point 1a above. Conversely, in the liquidity trap case, where the public is willing to hold any amount of real balances at unchanged interest rates, a fall in prices and a rise in the real money stock have very little effect

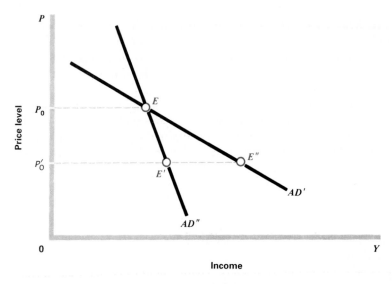

Figure 7-9   *The Slope of the* AD *Schedule*

The diagram shows two possible *AD* schedules. Along *AD″* a change in prices from P_0 to P_0' has a smaller effect on spending than along *AD′*. The former corresponds to the case where changes in real balances have little impact on equilibrium income and spending; the latter to the case where real balance changes exert significant effects.

on income and spending.[6] In Figure 7-9, that would correspond to an almost vertical *AD* curve, as suggested again by point 1a above. A vertical *AD* curve means that aggregate demand is unresponsive to the price level.

You should now experiment with alternative *IS* and *LM* schedules to see how the effects of a change in the price level depend on the slopes of the *IS* and *LM* curves and the factors underlying those slopes. In doing so, you will confirm the points summarized above and implied by the equations in Box 7-1. In Problem 4 at the end of the chapter, we ask you to demonstrate these links.

The Effect of a Fiscal Expansion

We noted above that the same factors that determine the positions of the *IS* and *LM* schedules also determine the position of the *AD* curve. We now show how changes in fiscal and monetary policy shift the *AD* curve, starting with a fiscal expansion.

---

[6]   The reason a reduction in prices increases output in this case is the real balance effect: With lower prices, the value of real balances held is higher, wealth is accordingly higher, and therefore consumption spending and output are higher. The real balance effect is central to monetary theory as developed in the classical treatise by Don Patinkin, *Money, Interest, and Prices* (New York: Harper & Row, 1965).

Box 7-1 A Formal Presentation of Aggregate Demand ~read~

In Chapter 4 we showed that equilibrium income is determined by the intersection of the *IS-LM* curves, given the level of prices and money and formulas for the equilibrium level of income. We demonstrated there that the equilibrium level of income in the *IS-LM* model can be written as

$$Y = \gamma \overline{A} + \beta \frac{\overline{M}}{\overline{P}} \tag{B1}$$

The terms

$$\gamma = \frac{\overline{\alpha} h}{h + k \overline{\alpha} b} \qquad \beta = \gamma \frac{b}{h}$$

are constants that depend on all the parameters. These "multipliers" represent a convenient shorthand notation for all the channels through which the impact of changes in autonomous spending or real balances affect equilibrium income. We remember that γ is interpreted as the government spending multiplier when interest rates are endogenous. The coefficient β is the multiplier for changes in the *real* money stock.

The key point in understanding the *AD* curve is to recognize that it is nothing more than the intersections of *IS-LM* curves for different price levels; this is how we derived it in Figure 7-8. Accordingly, (B1) is the equation that identifies the *AD* schedule. Equation (B1) shows the equilibrium income associated with each level of prices, given exogenous spending, $\overline{A}$, and the *nominal* quantity of money, $\overline{M}$. We can focus more explicitly on the price level by simply solving Equation (B1) for the price level. Rearranging the terms of the resulting equation, we have

$$P = \beta \frac{\overline{M}}{Y - \gamma \overline{A}} \tag{B2}$$

In this convenient form we immediately recognize that the *AD* schedule is drawn for a given level of nominal money and exogenous spending $\overline{A}$. We also note that, given income and exogenous spending, prices are proportional to the money stock. Thus changes in $\overline{M}$ translate into equiproportionate changes in P. We return to this point later in discussing monetarism.

This handy formula for the *AD* schedule makes it easier to consider the factors that determine the position of the *AD* curve.

In Figure 7-10 the initial *LM* and *IS* schedules correspond to a given nominal quantity of money and the price level P_0. Equilibrium obtains at point E, and there is a corresponding point on the *AD* schedule in the lower panel.

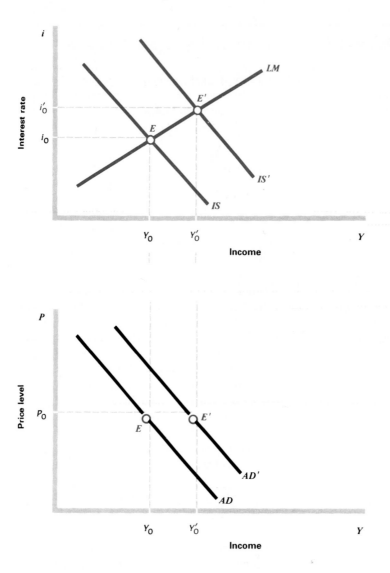

Figure 7-10 *The Effect of a Fiscal Expansion on the AD Schedule*

A fiscal expansion, such as an increase in government spending, shifts the *IS* curve in the upper panel to *IS'*. At any given price level, such as P_0, the equilibrium in the upper panel shifts to *E'*, with higher level of income Y_0' and higher interest rate i_0'. Point *E'* in the lower panel is a point on the new aggregate demand schedule *AD'* corresponding to price level P_0. We could similarly trace the effect of increased government spending on the equilibrium level of income and spending in the lower panel for every price level, and thus show that the *AD* curve shifts out to *AD'* when fiscal policy is expansionary.

Now the government increases the level of spending. As a consequence, the *IS* schedule shifts outward and to the right. At the initial price level there is a new equilibrium at point E' with higher interest rates and a higher level of income and spending. Thus at the initial level of prices, P_0, equilibrium income and spending now are higher. We show this by plotting point E' in the lower panel. Point E' is a point on the new schedule AD' reflecting the effect of higher government spending.

Of course, we could have started with any other point on the original AD curve, and we would then have shown how in the lower panel the rise in government spending leads to a higher equilibrium level of income at each price level. In that way we trace out the entire AD' schedule, which lies to the right of AD.

In fact, we can say more: At each level of prices, and hence of real balances, the AD schedule shifts to the right by an amount indicated by the fiscal policy multiplier developed in Chapter 4. As we saw there, the larger the interest response of money demand, the smaller the interest response of aggregate demand, and the larger the marginal propensity to consume, then the higher is the level of income and spending caused by a fiscal expansion.

Thus if the fiscal policy multiplier derived in Chapter 4 was, for example, 1.5, then a \$1 billion increase in government spending would increase equilibrium income and spending by \$1.5 billion, at the given price level. In response to any change in government spending, the AD schedule would shift to the right by 1.5 times the increase in G.[7]

The Effect of a Monetary Expansion on the *AD* Schedule

An increase in the nominal money stock implies, at each level of prices, a higher real money stock. In the assets markets, interest rates decline to induce the public to hold higher real balances. That decline in interest rates, in turn, stimulates aggregate demand and thus raises the equilibrium level of income and spending. In Figure 7-11 we show that an increase in the nominal money stock shifts the AD schedule up and to the right.

The extent to which an increase in nominal money shifts the AD schedule to the right depends on the monetary policy multiplier. If the monetary policy multiplier is large, say, because money demand is not very interest-elastic and goods demand is, the AD schedule will shift a lot. Conversely, if the LM schedule is nearly flat, in which case monetary policy is ineffective, the AD schedule will shift very little.

We can also ask about the upward shift of the schedule. Here an interesting and important point emerges. Recall that what matters for equilibrium income and spending is the real money supply M/P. If an increase in nominal money is matched by an equiproportionate increase in prices, M/P is unchanged, and hence interest rates,

---

[7]   In Chapter 4 and Box 7-1 we showed that the fiscal policy multiplier is given by the expression $h\bar{\alpha}/(h + kb\bar{\alpha})$, where h is the interest responsiveness of money demand, $\bar{\alpha}$ the simple Keynesian multiplier, k the income response of money demand, and b the interest response of investment demand.

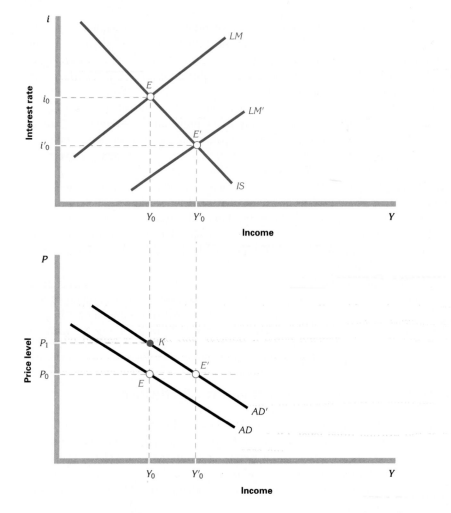

Figure 7-11   *The Effects of an Increase in the Money Stock on the AD Schedule*

An increase in the money stock shifts the *LM* curve to *LM'* in the upper panel. The equilibrium level of income rises from Y_0 to Y_0' at the initial price level P_0. Correspondingly, the *AD* curve moves out to the right, to *AD'*, with point E' in the lower panel corresponding to E' in the upper panel. The *AD* curve shifts up in exactly the same proportion as the money stock increases. For instance, at point K the price level P_1 is higher than P_0 in the same proportion that the money supply has risen. Real balances at K on *AD'* are therefore the same as at E on *AD*.

aggregate demand, and equilibrium income and spending will remain unchanged. This gives us the clue to the vertical shift of the *AD* schedule.

   An increase in the nominal money stock shifts the AD schedule up exactly in proportion to the increase in nominal money. Thus if, starting at point E in the lower panel of Figure 7-11, we have a 10 percent increase in M, real spending will be unchanged only if prices also rise by 10 percent, thus leaving real balances unchanged. Therefore the AD schedule shifts upward by 10 percent. At point K in Figure 7-11, *real* balances are the same as at E, and therefore interest rates and equilibrium income and spending are the same as at E.[8]

We now have completed the derivation of the aggregate demand schedule. The important points to recall are that the AD schedule is shifted to the right both by increases in the money stock and by expansionary fiscal policy. In the remainder of this chapter we show how to use this tool to discuss the effects of monetary and fiscal policy on both the level of income and the price level under alternative assumptions about the supply side.

7-4 Monetary and Fiscal Policy Under Alternative Supply Assumptions

In Figure 7-1 we showed how the aggregate supply and demand curves together determine the equilibrium level of income and prices in the economy. Now that we have shown how the aggregate demand curve is derived, and how it is shifted by policy changes, we use the aggregate demand and supply model to study the effects of monetary and fiscal policy in the two extreme supply cases — Keynesian and classical.

We should expect that the conclusions we reach in the Keynesian supply case are precisely the same as those reached in Chapter 4. In that chapter, in developing the IS-LM model, we assumed that whatever amount of goods was demanded would be supplied at the existing price level. Of course, as Figure 7-5a shows, the Keynesian supply curve implies that this will be the case.

The Keynesian Case

In Figure 7-12 we combine the aggregate demand schedule with the Keynesian aggregate supply schedule. The initial equilibrium is at point E, where AS and AD intersect. At that point, the goods and assets markets are in equilibrium.

Consider now a fiscal expansion. As we have already seen, increased government spending, or a cut in tax rates, shifts the AD schedule out and to the right from AD to AD'. The new equilibrium is at point E', where income has increased. Because firms are willing to supply any amount of output at the level of prices P_0, there is no effect on prices. The only effect of higher government spending in Figure 7-12 is to increase income and employment. In addition, as we know from the IS-LM model that lies behind the AD schedule, the fiscal expansion will raise equilibrium interest rates.

---

[8] We use the algebraic representation of AD to derive this property. Since, as noted in footnote 2 above, we are using linear approximations in graphical representations of AD, a parallel vertical shift can represent a proportional change in P only at one point along the curve such as E.

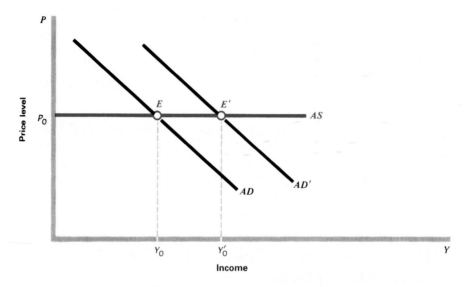

Figure 7-12 *A Fiscal Expansion: The Keynesian Case*

In the Keynesian case, with output in perfectly elastic supply at a given price level, a fiscal expansion increases equilibrium income from Y_0 to Y_0'. This is exactly the result already derived with *IS* and *LM* schedules.

We leave it to you to show that in the Keynesian case an increase in the nominal quantity of money likewise leads to an expansion in equilibrium income. With a horizontal *AS* schedule there is again no impact on prices. The magnitude of the income expansion then depends, in this Keynesian case, only on the monetary policy multiplier that determines the extent of the horizontal shift of the *AD* schedule.

Thus, as we expected, all our conclusions about the effects of policy changes in the Keynesian supply case are those of the simple *IS-LM* model.

The Classical Case: Fiscal Policy

In the classical case, the aggregate supply schedule is vertical at the full-employment level of output. Firms will supply the level of output Y° whatever the price level. Under this supply assumption we obtain results very different from those reached using the Keynesian model. Now the price level is not given, but rather depends on the interaction of supply and demand.

In Figure 7-13 we study the effect of a fiscal expansion under classical supply assumptions. The aggregate supply schedule is *AS*, with equilibrium initially at point

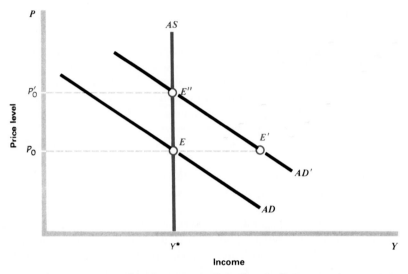

Figure 7-13 *A Fiscal Expansion: The Classical Case*

The supply of output is perfectly inelastic at the full-employment level of output, Y°. A fiscal expansion raises equilibrium spending, at the initial price level P_0, from E to E', but now there is an excess demand because firms are unwilling to supply that much output. Prices increase, and that reduces real balances until we reach point E''. At E'' government spending is higher, but the higher price level means lower real balances, higher interest rates, and hence reduced private spending. At E'' increased government spending has crowded out an equal amount of private spending.

E. Note that at point E there is full employment because, by assumption, firms supply the full-employment level of output at any level of prices.

The fiscal expansion shifts the aggregate demand schedule from AD to AD'. At the initial level of prices, P_0, spending in the economy rises to point E'. At price level P_0 the demand for goods has risen, but firms cannot obtain the labour to produce more output, and supply cannot respond to the increased demand. As firms try to hire more workers, they only bid up wages and their costs of production, and therefore they charge higher prices for their output. The increase in the demand for goods therefore leads only to higher prices, and not to higher income.

The increase in prices reduces the real money stock and leads to an increase in interest rates and a reduction in spending. The economy moves up the AD' schedule until prices have risen enough, and real balances have fallen enough, to raise interest rates and reduce spending to a level consistent with full-employment output. That is the case at a price level P_0'. At point E'' aggregate demand, at the higher level of government spending, is once again equal to aggregate supply.

Crowding Out Again

Note what has happened in Figure 7-13: Output is unchanged at the full-employment level $Y°$, but government spending is higher. That must imply less spending by the private sector. There is thus *full* or *complete crowding out*. Recall that crowding out occurs when an increase in government spending results in less spending by the private sector. Typically, as we showed in Chapter 4, government spending crowds out investment. In the case shown in Figure 7-13, with a classical supply curve, every dollar increase in real government spending is offset by a dollar reduction in private spending, so that crowding out is complete.

We thus reach the following important result: *In the classical case, increased government spending leads to full crowding out*. We now explain the mechanism through which crowding out occurs.

Figure 7-14 shows the *IS-LM* diagram, augmented with the line $Y°$ at the full-employment level of income. The initial equilibrium is at point E, where the money market clears and aggregate demand equals income. The fiscal expansion shifts the *IS* schedule to *IS'*. At an unchanged price level, and assuming firms were to meet the increase in demand by expanding production, we would move to point E'. However, this is not possible under classical supply assumptions. Faced with an excess demand for goods, firms end up raising prices rather than output. The price increase, in turn, reduces real balances and therefore shifts the *LM* schedule up. Prices will increase until the excess demand has been eliminated. That means the *LM* schedule shifts up and to the left until we reach a new equilibrium at point E''.

At E'' the goods market clears at the full-employment level of income. Interest rates have increased compared with the initial equilibrium at E, and that increase in interest rates has reduced private spending to make room for increased government spending. Note that the money market is also in equilibrium. Output and income are the same as at point E. The higher interest rate reduces the quantity of real balances demanded, matching the decline in the real money stock.

Note that we have now seen two mechanisms that produce full crowding out. In Chapter 4, crowding out is complete if the *LM* curve is vertical. In that case, crowding out occurs because money demand is interest-inelastic. In this chapter, full crowding out occurs because aggregate supply limits total output. In brief, in Chapter 4 crowding out is a demand phenomenon; here it is a supply phenomenon.

In Table 7-1 we summarize the effects of a fiscal expansion in the cases of classical and Keynesian supply conditions. In each case we show what happens to income, interest rates, and the price level.

Table 7-1 *The Effects of a Fiscal Expansion*

Aggregate Supply	Income	Interest Rate	Prices
Keynesian	+	+	0
Classical	0	+	+

short-run

long-run

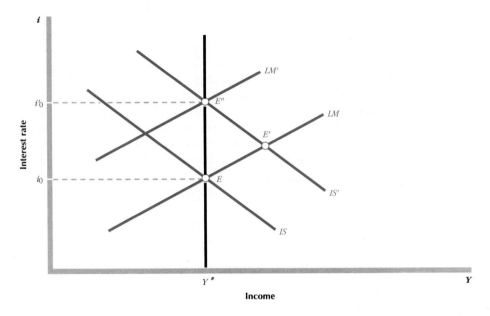

Figure 7-14 *Crowding Out in the Classical Case*

A fiscal expansion in the classical case leads to full crowding out. The fiscal expansion shifts the *IS* schedule to *IS'*. At the initial price level the economy would move to point *E'*, but there is excess demand since firms supply only *Y°*. Prices increase, shifting the *LM* schedule up and to the left until *LM'* is reached. The new equilibrium is at point *E''*, where interest rates have risen enough to displace an amount of private spending equal to the increase in government demand.

The table reinforces our understanding of the two models; in one case only prices adjust; in the other case only income. These models are clearly extremes, and we would expect that often adjustment occurs in both income and prices. That is the adjustment process we study in Chapter 8. We shall see there that the Keynesian case comes close to describing the short-run effects of a fiscal expansion, while the classical case more accurately predicts what happens in the long run after all adjustments have taken place.

Monetary Expansion Under Classical Conditions

We have already seen the impact of monetary policy under Keynesian supply conditions: With prices given, a rise in the nominal money stock is a rise in the real money stock. Equilibrium interest rates decline as a consequence, and income rises. Consider now the adjustments that occur in response to a monetary expansion when the aggregate supply curve is vertical and the price level is no longer fixed.

In Figure 7-15 we study an expansion in the nominal money stock under classical supply conditions. The initial full-employment equilibrium is at point E, where the AD and AS schedules intersect. Now the nominal money stock is increased, and accordingly, the aggregate demand schedule shifts up and to the right to AD'. If prices were fixed, the economy would move to E', the Keynesian equilibrium, but now output is in fixed supply. The increase in aggregate demand leads to an excess demand for goods. Firms that attempt to expand, hiring more workers, bid up wages and costs. Prices increase in response to the excess demand, and that means real balances fall back toward their initial level. In fact prices keep rising until the economy reaches point E'', where AS intersects the new aggregate demand schedule AD'. Only when aggregate demand is again equal to full-employment supply does the goods market clear and the pressure for prices to rise disappear.

Consider now the adjustment that takes place in moving from E to E''. There is no change in income, only a change in the price level. Note, moreover, that prices rise

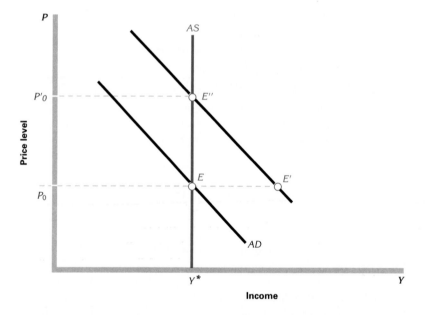

Figure 7-15 *The Effect of a Monetary Expansion Under Classical Supply Assumptions*

Starting from the full-employment equilibrium at point E, an increase in the nominal money stock shifts the aggregate demand schedule to AD'. At the initial price level there is now an excess demand for goods. Prices increase, and thus the real money stock declines toward its initial level. Price increases continue until the economy reaches point E''. Here the *real* money stock has returned to its initial level, and with output unchanged, interest rates are again at their initial level. Thus a monetary expansion affects only prices, not income or interest rates.

in exactly the same proportion as the nominal quantity of money.[9] This we know because we saw earlier that in response to an increase in nominal money the *AD* schedule shifts upward in the same proportion as the increase in money. Thus at point *E″* the real money stock *M/P* is back to its initial level. At *E″* both nominal money and the price level have changed in the same proportion, leaving real money, and hence interest rates and aggregate demand, unchanged. We thus have an important implication of the classical model: *Under classical supply conditions an increase in nominal money raises the price level in the same proportion, but leaves interest rates and real income unchanged.*

In Table 7-2 we summarize the effects of an increase in the nominal money stock under Keynesian and classical supply conditions. Once again we look at the effects on income, prices, and interest rates. In addition we show the effect on real balances *M/P*. The table brings out the fact that under classical supply conditions, none of the real variables, such as income, interest rates, or real balances, are affected by a change in the nominal money stock. Only the price level changes.

Table 7-2   *The Effects of an Increase in the Nominal Money Stock*

Aggregate Supply	Income	Interest Rate	Prices	Real Balances
Keynesian	+	−	0	+
Classical	0	0	+	0

7-5 The Quantity Theory and the Neutrality of Money

The classical model of supply, in combination with the *IS-LM* model describing the demand side of the economy, has extremely strong implications. Because, by assumption, income is maintained at the full-employment level by full wage and price flexibility, monetary and fiscal policy do not affect income. Fiscal policy affects interest rates and the composition of spending between the government and the private sector and between consumption and investment. Monetary policy affects only the price level.

These implications about the effects of monetary policy on income are consistent with the *quantity theory of money*. The quantity theory of money in its strongest form asserts that the price level is proportional to the stock of money. For instance, in the case of the classical supply curve, an increase in the quantity of money produces, in equilibrium, a proportional increase in the price level. In this case, money is *neutral*.

---

[9] In Problem 9 we ask you to use the *IS* and *LM* curves to show how the change in the money supply works. To answer the problem you have to use Figure 7-11, along with the fact that the *LM* schedule shifts as the price level changes.

The Neutrality of Money

Money is neutral when changes in the money stock lead only to changes in the price level, with no real variables (income, employment, and interest rates) changing. For instance, money is neutral in the second row of Table 7-2, where in response to a change in the money stock, only the price level changes, with income, interest rates, and real balances remaining unchanged.

We saw above that the classical supply curve has the powerful and important implication that fiscal policy cannot affect income. The neutrality of money likewise has strong policy implications. For instance, if money were neutral, there would be an easy way to reduce the inflation rate if we ever wanted to do that. All we would have to do would be to reduce the rate at which the money stock is growing.

In practice, it is very difficult to change the inflation rate without producing a recession, as for instance in the period 1979–1983. When a lower growth rate of money leads first to unemployment, and only later to lower inflation, as it did in the recession in 1982, then we know that money is not neutral. Changes in the quantity of money then have real effects; monetary policy affects the level of income. This means that the aggregate supply curve cannot be vertical in the short run. In Chapter 8 we develop the aggregate supply curve, showing why in the short run it is quite flat, whereas over longer periods it is more nearly vertical.

The Modern Quantity Theory: Monetarism

The strict quantity theory asserts that the price level is proportional to the quantity of money. Although the quantity theory is centuries, and perhaps millennia, old, few have believed in the strict quantity theory. That is, few have believed that the price level is strictly proportional to the money stock, or that money is the only factor affecting the price level. Rather, quantity theorists argued and argue that the money stock is, in practice, the single most important factor producing inflation.

Box 7-2 presents quotations from Irving Fisher (1867-1947), widely thought to be the greatest American economist of his time, and from Milton Friedman, the leading exponent of the quantity theory and the importance of money in the modern era. The two differ in emphasis: Fisher comes close to asserting that only changes in the quantity of money affect the price level; Friedman is more clear in arguing that other factors can affect the price level, but that these other factors are of secondary importance.

Friedman is the recognized intellectual leader of an influential group of economists, called *monetarists*, who emphasize the role of money and monetary policy in affecting the behaviour of income and prices. Leading monetarists include the late Karl Brunner of the University of Rochester, Allan Meltzer of Carnegie-Mellon University, William Poole of Brown University, Anna Schwartz of the National Bureau of Economic Research and Hunter College, Robert Barro of Harvard University, David Laidler and Michael Parkin of the University of Western Ontario, and other scholars, both in North America and elsewhere.

Box 7-2 The Quantity Theory of Money

read

Irving Fisher (1867–1947) and Milton Friedman (born 1912) are two of the foremost monetary economists in the United States in this century. Both strongly advocated the quantity theory of money as the right model of price level determination. Fisher wrote in 1920:[a]

> *In recent popular discussions a great variety of reasons have been assigned for the "high cost of living", e.g., "profiteering"; speculation; hoarding; the middleman; the tariff; cold storage; longer hauls on railroads; marketing by telephone; the free delivery system; the individual package; the enforcement of sanitary laws; the tuberculin testing of cattle; the destruction of tainted meat; sanitary milk; the elimination of renovated butter and of "rots" and "spots" in eggs; food adulteration; advertising; unscientific management; extravagance; higher standards of living; the increasing cost of government; the increasing cost of old-age pensions, and of better pauper institutions, hospitals, insane asylums, reformatories, jails and other public institutions; I shall not discuss in detail this list of alleged explanations. While some of them are important factors in raising particular prices, none of them has been important in raising the general scale of prices.*
>
> *The ups and downs of prices roughly correspond with the ups and downs of the money supply. Throughout all history this has been so. For this general broad fact the evidence is sufficient even where we lack the index numbers by which to make accurate measurements. Whenever there have been rapid outpourings from mines, following discoveries of the precious metals used for money, prices have risen with corresponding rapidity. This was observed in the sixteenth century, after great quantities of the precious metals had been brought to Europe from the New World, and again in the nineteenth century, after the Californian and Australian gold mining of the fifties; and, still again, in the same century after the South African, Alaskan, and Cripple Creek mining of the nineties. Likewise when other causes than mining, such as paper money issues, produce violent changes in the quantity or quality of money, violent changes in the price level usually follow.*

Friedman wrote:[b]

> *Since men first began to write systematically about economic matters they have devoted special attention to the wide movements in the general level of prices that have intermittently occurred. Two alternative explanations have usually been offered. One has attributed the changes in prices to changes in the quantity of money. The other has attributed the changes in prices to war or to profiteers or to rises in wages or to some other special circumstance of the particular time and place and has regarded any accompanying change in the quantity of money as a common consequence of the same special circumstance. The first explanation has generally been referred to as the quantity theory of money, although that*

designation conceals the variety of forms the explanation has taken, the different levels of sophistication on which it has been developed, and the wide range of the claims that have been made for its applicability.

In its most rigid and unqualified form the quantity theory asserts strict pro-portionality between the quantity of what is regarded as money and the level of prices. Hardly anyone has held the theory in that form, although statements capable of being so interpreted have often been made in the heat of argument or for expository simplicity. Virtually every quantity theorist has recognized that changes in the quantity of money that correspond to changes in the volume of trade or of output have no tendency to produce changes in prices. Nearly as many have recognized also that changes in the willingness of the community to hold money can occur for a variety of reasons and can introduce disparities between changes in the quantity of money per unit of trade or of output and changes in prices. What quantity theorists have held in common is the belief that these qualifications are of secondary importance for substantial changes in either prices or the quantity of money, so that the one will not in fact occur without the other.

[a] *Irving Fisher,* Stabilizing the Dollar *(New York: Macmillan, 1920), pp. 10–11 and 29.*
[b] *Milton Friedman, "Money: The Quantity Theory," in* The International Encyclopedia of the Social Sciences, *Vol. X, 1968, pp. 432–47.*

Modern quantity theorists differ also from the strict quantity theory in not believing that the supply curve is vertical in the short run. Monetarists such as Friedman argue that a reduction in the money stock does in practice first reduce the level of income, and only later has an effect on prices.

Thus Friedman and other monetarists make an important distinction between the short- and long-run effects of changes in money.[10] They argue that in the long run money is more or less neutral. Changes in the money stock, after they have worked their way through the economy, have no real effects and only change prices: The quantity theory and the neutrality of money are, from this long-run perspective, not just theoretical possibilities, but instead a reasonable description of the way the world works. Nevertheless, in the short run, they argue, monetary policy and changes in the money stock can and do have important real effects.

There is more to monetarism than the argument that money is the most important determinant of macroeconomic performance, but we leave the evidence on this and the other tenets of monetarism for further discussion in Chapters 14 and 19.

---

[10] For a recent statement of the monetarist position, see Milton Friedman, "The Quantity Theory of Money," in *The New Palgrave Dictionary of Economics* (New York: Stockton, 1987), and, by the same author, "Monetary History, Not Dogma," *Wall Street Journal*, February 1987, and "Whither Inflation," *Wall Street Journal*, July 1989. See, too, William Dewald, "Monetarism Is Dead: Long Live the Quantity Theory of Money," *Federal Reserve Bank of St. Louis Review*, July/August 1988. The collection by James Dorn and Anna Schwartz, *The Search for Stable Money* (Chicago: University of Chicago Press, 1987), contains an interesting collection of essays with a monetarist viewpoint. In Irving Fisher's writings, which long precede modern monetarism, he too drew a distinction between the short-run effect of a change in the money stock, which he argued was not neutral, and the long-run effect, which he argued was neutral.

7-6 Summary

1. The aggregate supply and demand model is used to show the determination of the equilibrium levels of both income and prices.

2. The aggregate supply schedule, *AS*, shows at each level of prices the quantity of real output firms are willing to supply.

3. The Keynesian supply schedule is horizontal, implying that firms supply as much goods as are demanded at the existing price level. The classical supply schedule is vertical. It would apply in an economy that has full price and wage flexibility.

4. With wages and prices freely flexible, the equilibrium level of employment is determined in the labour market. The labour market is continuously in equilibrium at the full-employment level of employment. Aggregate supply would therefore be the amount of output produced by that amount of labour. Given that the labour market is always in equilibrium, the aggregate supply curve is vertical at the full-employment level of output.

5. The frictions that exist in real-world labour markets as workers enter the labour market and look for jobs, or shift between jobs, mean that there is always some frictional unemployment. The amount of frictional unemployment that exists at the full-employment level of employment is the natural rate of unemployment.

6. The aggregate demand schedule, *AD*, shows at each price level the level of income at which the goods and assets markets are in equilibrium. This is the quantity of output demanded at each price level. Along the *AD* schedule fiscal policy is given, as is the nominal quantity of money. The *AD* schedule is derived using the *IS-LM* model.

7. Moving down and along the *AD* schedule, lower prices raise the real value of the money stock. Equilibrium interest rates fall, and that increases aggregate demand and equilibrium spending.

8. A fiscal expansion or an increase in the nominal quantity of money shifts the *AD* schedule upward and to the right.

9. Under Keynesian supply conditions, with prices fixed, both monetary and fiscal expansion raise equilibrium income. A monetary expansion lowers interest rates, while a fiscal expansion raises them.

10. Under classical supply conditions, a fiscal expansion has no effect on income, but it raises prices, lowers real balances, and increases equilibrium interest rates. Thus, under classical supply conditions, there is full crowding out and private spending declines by exactly the increase in government spending.

11. A monetary expansion, under classical supply conditions, raises prices in the same proportion as the rise in nominal money. All real variables — specifically, income and interest rates — remain unchanged. When changes in the money stock have no real effects, money is said to be neutral.

12. The strict quantity theory of money states that prices move in proportion to the nominal money stock. Modern quantity theorists or monetarists accept the view that there is no exact link between money and prices, but argue that changes in the money stock are, in practice, the most important single determinant of changes in the price level.

Key Terms

Aggregate supply curve
Aggregate demand curve
Keynesian aggregate supply curve
Classical aggregate supply curve
Frictionless neoclassical model
Frictional unemployment

Natural rate of unemployment
Full crowding out
Quantity theory of money
Neutrality of money
Monetarism

Problems

1. Define the aggregate demand and supply curves.

2. Explain why the classical supply curve is vertical and explain the mechanisms that ensure continued full employment of labour in the classical case.

3. In the frictionless neoclassical model, assume that labour becomes more productive, with the labour demand curve shifting upward and to the right.
    (a) What is the effect of this change on the full-employment levels of employment and output?
    (b) What is the effect on the full-employment real wage?
    (c) How would your answers to (a) and (b) be affected if the labour supply curve were vertical?

4. What is the effect of an increase in the productivity of labour on the equilibrium price level in the frictionless neoclassical model?

5. Discuss, using the *IS-LM* model, what happens to interest rates as prices change along a given *AD* schedule.

6. Show graphically that the larger the interest responsiveness of the demand for money and the smaller the multiplier, the steeper is the *AD* curve.

7. Suppose full-employment output increases from Y° to $Y^{\circ\prime}$. What does the quantity theory predict will happen to the price level?

8. In goods market equilibrium in a closed economy, $S + T = I + G$. Use this equation to explain why, in the classical case, a fiscal expansion must lead to full crowding out.

9. Show, using *IS* and *LM* curves, why money is neutral in the classical supply case. (Refer to footnote 9 for hints.)

10. Suppose the government reduces the personal income tax rate from t to t'.
    (a) What is the effect on the *AD* schedule?
    (b) What is the effect on the equilibrium interest rate?
    (c) What happens to investment?

11. Suppose there is a decline in the demand for money. At each output level and interest rate, the public now wants to hold lower real balances.
    (a) In the Keynesian case, what happens to equilibrium output and to prices?
    (b) In the classical case, what is the effect on output and on prices?

12. Repeat Problem 11, using the quantity theory of money to explain the effect of the money demand shift on prices.

13. Suppose the government undertakes a balanced budget increase in spending. Government spending rises from $\overline{G}$ to $\overline{G}'$, and there is an accompanying increase in tax rates so that at the initial level of output the budget remains balanced.
    (a) Show the effect on the *AD* schedule.
    (b) Discuss the effect of the balanced budget policy on output and interest rates in the Keynesian case.
    (c) Discuss the effect in the classical case.

14. (a) Define the strict quantity theory.
    (b) Define monetarism.
    (c) What type of statistical evidence would you need to collect in order to support or refute the major argument of monetarism presented in this chapter?

Appendix The Neoclassical Model of the Labour Market

The frictionless classical model is an idealized case where wages and prices are fully flexible, where there are no costs either to workers in finding jobs or to firms in increasing or reducing their labour force, and where firms behave competitively and expect to sell all they produce at prevailing prices. That case both serves as a benchmark for the discussion of more realistic cases and also allows us to introduce such useful concepts as the production function and the demand for labour. Throughout, we assume that labour is the only variable factor of production in the short run and that the capital stock is given.

The Production Function

A production function provides a relation between the quantity of factor inputs, such as the amount of labour used, and the maximum quantity of output that can be produced using those inputs. The relation reflects only technical efficiency. In Equation (A1) we write the production function

$$Y = F(N, \dots)$$ (A1)

where Y denotes real output, N is labour input, and the dots denote other cooperating factors (capital, for example) that are in short-run fixed supply. The production function is shown in Figure 7-A1. The production function exhibits *diminishing returns* to labour, which means that the increase in output resulting from the employment of one more unit of labour declines as the amount of labour used increases.

Diminishing returns are shown in the production function by the fact that it is not a straight line through the origin (constant returns) or an upward-curving line (increas-

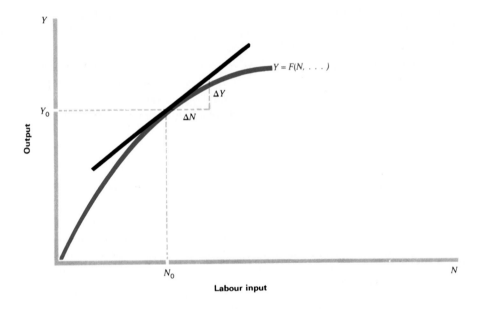

Figure 7-A1   *The Production Function and the Marginal Product of Labour*

The production function links the amount of output produced to the level of labour input, given other factors of production such as capital. The schedule shows diminishing returns. Successive increases in labour yield less and less extra output. The marginal product of labour is shown by the slope of the production function, $\Delta Y/\Delta N$, that is, the increase in output per unit increase in employment. The flattening of the slope shows that the marginal product of labour is declining.

ing returns). Diminishing returns are explained by the fact that as employment increases and other inputs remain constant, each labourer on the job has fewer machines with which to work and therefore becomes less productive. Thus, increases in the amount of labour progressively reduce the addition to output that further employment can bring. An increase in the labour force will always raise output, but progressively less so as employment expands. The marginal contribution of increased employment is indicated by the slope of the production function, $\Delta Y/\Delta N$. It is readily seen that the slope flattens out as we increase employment, thus showing that increasing employment makes a diminishing, but still positive, contribution to output.

Labour Demand

From the production function we proceed to the demand for labour. We are asking how much labour a firm would want to hire. The rule of thumb is to hire additional labour and expand production as long as doing so increases profits. A firm will hire additional workers as long as they will bring in more in revenue than they cost in wages.

The contribution to output of additional labour is called the *marginal product of labour*. It is equal, in Figure 7-A1, to the slope of the production function. The marginal product, as we have seen, is both positive (additional labour is productive) and diminishing, which means that additional employment becomes progressively less productive. *A firm will employ additional labour as long as the marginal product of labour, MPN for short, exceeds the cost of additional labour.* The cost of additional labour is given by the real wage, that is, the nominal wage divided by the price level. The real wage measures the amount of real output the firm has to pay each worker. Since hiring one more worker results in an output increase of *MPN* and a cost to the firm of the real wage, firms will hire additional labour if the *MPN* exceeds the real wage. This point is formalized in Figure 7-A2, which looks at the labour market.

The downward-sloping schedule in Figure 7-A2 is the demand for labour schedule, which is the *MPN* schedule; firms hire labour up to the point at which the *MPN* is equal to the real wage. The *MPN* schedule shows the contribution to output of additional employment. It follows from our reasoning that the *MPN* is positive but that additional employment reduces it, so that the MPN schedule is negatively sloped.

Now consider a firm that currently employs a labour force, N_1, and assume the real wage is $(W/P)_0$, where W is the money wage and P the price of output. At an employment level N_1 in Figure 7-A2, the firm is clearly employing too much labour since the real wage exceeds the *MPN* at that level of employment. What would happen if the firm should reduce employment by one unit? The reduction in employment would decrease output by the *MPN*, and therefore reduce revenue to the firm. On the other side of the calculation, we have the reduction in the wage bill. Per unit reduction in employment, the wage bill would fall at the rate of the real wage $(W/P)_0$. The net benefit of a reduction in the employment level is thus equal to the vertical excess of the real wage over the *MPN* in Figure 7-A2. It is apparent that at the level of employment N_1, the excess is quite sizable, and it pays the firm to reduce the employment

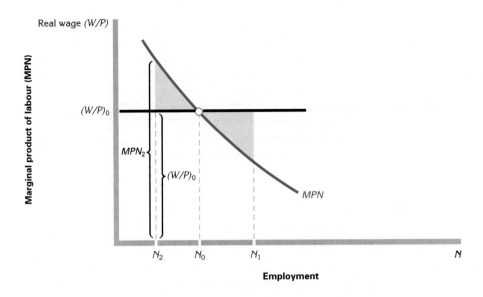

Figure 7-A2 *The Optimal Employment Choice for a Given Real Wage*

The marginal product of labour *MPN* is a declining function of the level of employment because of diminishing returns. Given a real wage $(W/P)_0$, the optimal employment choice is N_0. At N_1 the marginal product of labour is less than the real wage, so that the firm would save by reducing employment. Conversely, at N_2 the marginal product exceeds the real wage, so that the firm would gain by hiring an additional worker.

level. Indeed, it pays to reduce employment until the firm gets to point N_0. Only at that point does the cost of additional labour, the real wage, exactly balance the benefit in the form of increased output.

The same argument applies to the employment level N_2. Here employment is insufficient because the contribution to output of additional employment, MPN_2, exceeds the cost of additional employment, and it therefore pays to expand the level of employment. It is readily seen that with a real wage $(W/P)_0$, the firm's profits are maximized when employment is N_0. In general, given any real wage, the firm's demand for labour is shown by the *MPN* curve.

The firm's optimal employment position is formalized in Equation (A2). At the optimal employment level the marginal product of labour (which is a declining function of employment) $MPN(N)$ is equal to the real wage:

$$MPN(N) = \frac{W}{P} \tag{A2}$$

Equilibrium in the Labour Market

We have now developed the relation between output and employment (the production function) and the optimal employment choice for a given real wage that is implied by the demand for labour. It remains to consider the determination of the real wage as part of labour market equilibrium. This process is illustrated in Figure 7-A3.

We assume that labour supply increases with the real wage (W/P). The labour supply curve, NS, intersects the labour demand curve, MPN, at E. The equilibrium real wage is $(W/P)_0$, and the equilibrium level of employment is N^*.

How would the labour market get to that equilibrium? Suppose that the real wage fell whenever there was an excess supply of labour and that it rose whenever there was an excess demand. In terms of Figure 7-A3 this would mean that the real wage would decline whenever it was above $(W/P)_0$. At $(W/P)_1$, for example, labour demand is only N_1 and thus falls short of the labour supply. This would put downward pressure on the real wage, cause the real wage to fall, and make it profitable to expand employment. Exactly the reverse argument holds for real wages lower than $(W/P)_0$, where there is an excess demand for labour.

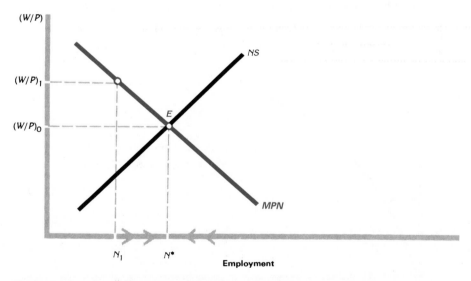

Figure 7-A3   *Equilibrium in the Labour Market*

The labour supply curve is NS. The demand for labour is the marginal product schedule MPN. Labour market equilibrium obtains at a real wage $(W/P)_0$. At that real wage the demand for labour equals the quantity of labour supplied. At a lower real wage there is an excess demand for labour; at a higher real wage there is an excess supply or unemployment.

From Figure 7-A3 we see that adjustment of the real wage would bring the labour market into full-employment equilibrium at a real wage $(W/P)_0$ and an employment level equal to N°. Figure 7-A4 summarizes the complete equilibrium in the labour market and the corresponding level of *full-employment output* Y°, which is the level of output associated with employment equal to the given labour supply.

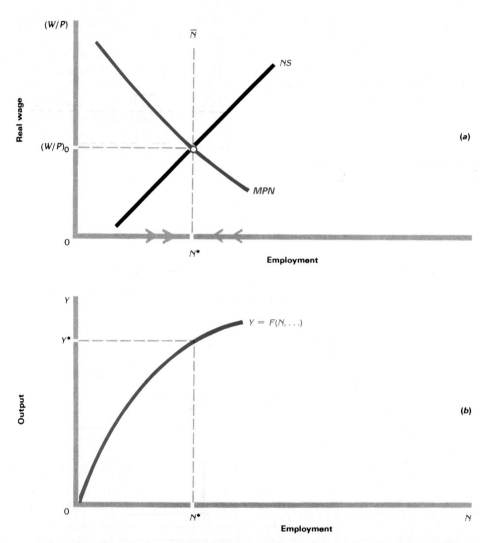

Figure 7-A4   *Equilibrium in the Labour Market and Full-Employment Output*

Part (*a*) of the diagram repeats the labour market equilibrium of Figure 14-A3. Part (*b*) shows the production function. The equilibrium employment level N°, also the full-employment level, leads to an output Y°, which is the full-employment level of output.

CHAPTER 8   *Aggregate Supply in the Short Run*

In Chapter 7, we considered two extreme cases of aggregate supply behaviour — the horizontal Keynesian supply curve and the classical vertical supply curve. We now consider the theory in more detail and show the adjustment process in reponse to disturbances in aggregate demand — monetary or fiscal policy changes or autonomous changes in spending. The development of the supply side of the economy also allows us to study how the economy adjusts to *supply shocks*, such as the increases in oil prices in 1973–1974 and 1979–1980 or the decline in oil prices in 1985–1986.

The supply side of the economy is an essential part of the *dynamics* of prices (inflation) and income, that is, of the adjustment of prices and income over time when the economy is hit by a disturbance. Investing the time needed to study aggregate supply is worthwhile because the theory is essential in understanding inflation and, in particular, the policy dilemma that comes from the existence of a short-run tradeoff between inflation and unemployment.

The theory of aggregate supply is one of the least settled areas in macroeconomics. The difficulty is that from the viewpoint of logic and simplicity, the classical theory of supply is compelling. It states that the labour market clears all the time and that output is always at the full-employment level. After all, if output is below the full-employment level, there are some workers who want to work but cannot find a job. Surely they could find a job by offering to work at a lower real wage. Much of microeconomics suggests that markets are mostly in equilibrium (quantity demanded is equal to quantity supplied) and, if not, are at least moving that way.

Nevertheless, the facts do not support the classical theory of supply.

- Output is not always at the full-employment level. The unemployment rate varies, and is sometimes very high; sometimes there are many people wanting work who cannot find it, and therefore the quantity of labour supplied exceeds the quantity demanded.

- Further, if output is always at the full-employment level, then changes in the money stock affect only prices and not output: Money is neutral. However, changes in monetary policy frequently appear not to be neutral. Sharp reductions in money growth, for instance, when governments try to reduce inflation, almost always cause recessions. Similarly, increases in money growth often appear to cause rapid growth of real output.

Indeed, the broad facts come closer to supporting the Keynesian aggregate supply curve than the classical view. Increases in aggregate demand — caused, for instance, by expansionary fiscal or monetary policy — in the short run raise real output much more than they raise prices.

However, the assumption that prices are completely fixed, which underlies the Keynesian supply function, is bothersome. When prices are fixed and markets do not clear, people can benefit from changing prices. The unemployed would be willing to work at a wage below that earned by the currently employed. Employers should be happy to employ labour at a lower wage. Why do not employers and the unemployed get together, agree on a lower wage, and get rid of unemployment? In other words, why does the labour market not move quickly to equilibrium?

There are two basic answers to this question. One is that wages and prices are sticky in the short run; it takes time for wages and prices to change in response to increases in the quantities of labour and goods demanded. This answer in its extreme form underlies the Keynesian theory of supply, and also underlies more sophisticated new or modern Keynesian theories that will be developed below.

However, we begin this chapter with a discussion of an alternative approach based on the argument that wages and prices are sticky in the short run as a result of *information problems*. Labour and goods markets clear but wages and prices, while fully flexible, adjust only partially because households have only partial information. It simply takes time for households and firms to figure out what exactly is happening in their economic environment, and to recognize that wages and prices should change. Once they do, they adjust fully to the new environment. The intellectual founder of this approach is Robert E. Lucas, Jr., of the University of Chicago, and it has become known as the *rational expectations equilibrium*.[1]

---

[1] See Lucas's famous article, "Some International Evidence on Output–Inflation Tradeoffs," *American Economic Review*, June 1973. For advanced expositions see Steven Sheffrin, *Rational Expectations* (New York: Cambridge University Press, 1983) and Kevin Hoover, *The Classical Macroeconomics* (Oxford: Basil Blackwell, 1988).

8-1 The Market-Clearing Approach: The Lucas Supply Curve

A frequent assumption made in the Lucas approach is that workers and firms know the wage rate and the price of the good being produced in their own industry but do not know the prices of other goods. Thus workers lack information about the aggregate price level and do not know the real wage. Since it is the real wage, not the nominal wage, that determines the supply of labour, workers will have to negotiate on the basis of their expectations concerning the aggregate price level.

In Figure 8-1, which is identical to Figure 7-6, we show labour supply, NS, positively related to the real wage, and a downward-sloping labour demand, ND, which implies that the lower the real wage, the more labour firms demand. If the price level is correctly predicted, then the real wage will adjust to the level $w^\circ = (W/P)^\circ$, at which there is full employment of labour at the level N° and output is at the full-employment level Y°. We call w° the *full-employment real wage*.

Figure 8-2 shows the same equilibrium with the nominal wage, W, on the vertical axis. As in the previous figure, if the price level is correctly predicted, then the equi-

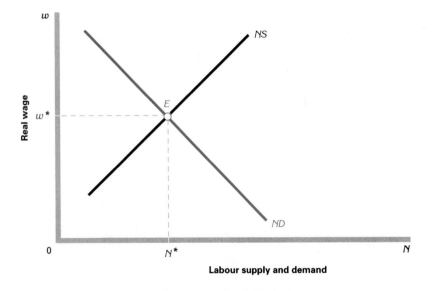

Figure 8-1   *The Full-Employment Real Wage*

The full-employment real wage is determined by the intersection of an upward-sloping supply curve of labour, NS, and a downward-sloping demand curve for labour, ND. At E, the real wage is w° and the quantity of labour is N°. With this level of labour input, output is at the full-employment level Y°.

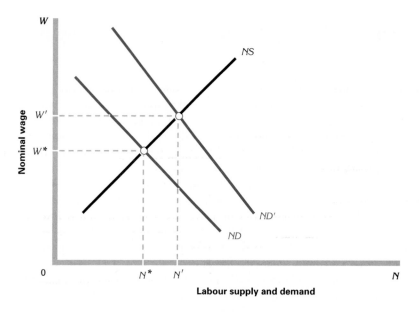

Figure 8-2 *The Effect of Errors in Price Expectations*

The labour supply and demand curves are now shown as functions of the nominal wage. The position of the supply curve depends on the expected price level while the position of the demand curve depends on the actual price level. When the actual and expected are equal, the equilibrium nominal wage is W° and employment is N°. If the actual price level turns out to be higher than expected $(P > P^e)$, the labour demand curve shifts to ND', but the supply curve stays put. The nominal wage and employment rise to W' and N', respectively. Workers supply more labour in the mistaken belief that the real wage is higher. Firms employ more workers in the correct belief that the real wage is lower.

librium will be at full employment. Suppose now that the price level turns out to be higher than anticipated by workers, who continue to supply labour based on the expectation $P^e < P$. At any given nominal wage, workers now supply more labour than they would have if they had correctly predicted the price level to be P. This follows from the fact that at the price level, P^e, and any nominal wage, W, the real wage is higher than it would be at the actual price level P [i.e., with $P^e < P$, $(W/P^e) > (W/P)$].

The demand for labour will, however, shift to the right to ND'. Since firms know the price of their own product, when the demand for labour is aggregated across firms, it will be the actual price level and therefore the actual real wage that will determine demand. It follows that firms will employ the amount of of labour N', which exceeds N°. Thus, *as a result of the underprediction of the price level, the levels of employment and output exceed the full-employment levels.* We could similarly show that if the actual price level is below the predicted level, the labour demand curve would shift to the left, and employment and output would be below the full-employment levels.

We can summarize the above argument in the following aggregate supply equation:

$$Y = Y^\circ + \gamma(P - P^e) \qquad (1)$$

This relationship is called the *Lucas supply curve* because it was advanced in pioneering work by Robert Lucas of the University of Chicago.[2] The Lucas supply curve shows that the amount of output that firms are willing to supply increases as the gap between the actual and expected price level increases.[3]

The key element in the above derivation of the Lucas supply curve is the difference in information between firms and workers. If we begin at full employment and there is an unexpected increase in the price level, workers will not be aware of it. All they can see is that the nominal wage being offered has risen. Because they think the real wage is higher, they will be willing to work more. Thus, at point E' in Figure 8-2, there is a difference of views between firms and workers concerning the real wage. Firms know that at E' the real wage is lower than w° in Figure 8-1; workers, by contrast, believe the real wage is higher than w°. Without this difference in views, an increase in the price level would not increase output.[4]

Table 8-1 shows how the actual real wage, employment, and output are related to $P - P^e$. For example, if the price prediction is too high and the actual price level is lower, the real wage turns out to be too high for full employment, and the level of output will be below the full-employment level. Figure 8-3 shows a graphical representation of the Lucas supply curve. For points such as B, where the actual price level exceeds the prediction, output is above the full-employment level Y°.

Table 8-1 *The Lucas Supply Curve*

Price Level	Real Wage	Output
$P > P^e$	$w < w^*$	$Y > Y^*$
$P = P^e$	$w = w^*$	$Y = Y^*$
$P < P^e$	$w > w^*$	$Y < Y^*$

[2] See the reference in footnote 1.

[3] The particular justification for the Lucas supply function offered in Figure 8-2 was developed by Milton Friedman in "The Role of Monetary Policy," *American Economic Review*, March 1968. Lucas's contribution was to develop the microeconomic foundations for the incomplete information approach and show that they resulted in a supply equation of the form of Equation (1). For the Lucas supply curve to take the form of Equation (1), it is not necessary that firms know the aggregate price level while workers do not. Rather, the assumption is that firms have a more accurate estimate of the price level than workers.

[4] Shouldn't workers refuse to work any more than N° when there is an increase in the demand for their services? After all, they know the firms are better informed than they are, and should suspect they will end up with a lower real wage than w°. This would be true if the demand in a given market were affected only by increases in aggregate demand or the aggregate price level. However, so long as there are also relative shifts in demand, so that a worker in a given market may be facing a relative increase in the demand for her or his services, workers will respond to increases in the wages they are offered on the basis that the increase in demand may be a result of a relative shift in demand. This is worked out in detail in the article by Lucas cited in footnote 1.

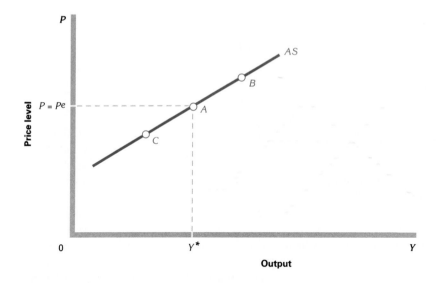

Figure 8-3　*The Lucas Supply Curve*

The AS curve represents Equation (1) and is drawn for a given expected price level, P^e. If the actual price level is equal to the expected price level, that is, $P = P^e$, the amount of output supplied is Y°. If prices are higher, and hence real wages are lower, firms supply more output than Y°; the converse is true if prices are lower.

An Alternative Derivation of the Lucas Supply Curve: The Contracting Approach

The Lucas supply curve can be derived by an alternative approach that assumes that wages are set in advance by negotiating explicit contracts. Suppose that when the wage is fixed, both firms and workers expect the price level to be P^e. As shown in Figure 8-4, the wage rate will be set at W°. If price expectations turn out to be correct, then employment will be at the full-employment level N°.

Now suppose that firms are able to base their employment decisions on the actual price level, even though both firms and workers are committed to the contractually determined nominal wage. If, for example, the actual price level P exceeds P^e, then the demand for labour shifts to the right to ND' while the wage rate remains at the contractually determined level W°. This results in a level of employment N'.

We thus obtain an aggregate supply curve of the same form as shown in Equation (1). In this case, however, firms and workers have the same view of the real wage but errors in expectations cause deviations from full employment because the nominal wage is set in advance.

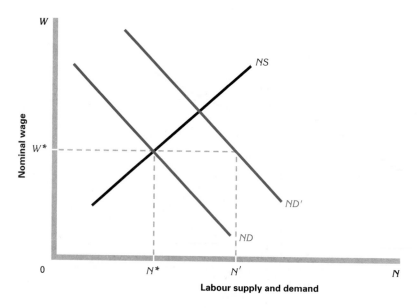

Figure 8-4 *The Contracting Approach*

Given their common expectation of the price level, firms and workers set the wage rate at W°. If price expectations turn out to be correct, employment will be at the full-employment level N°. If the actual price level turns out to be above the expected level, the negotiated wage rate will still apply but firms will employ the amount of labour N'.

Aggregate Supply and Demand With Rational Expectations

As shown above, the Lucas supply curve relates output to the gap between the actual and expected price levels. This leads us to the question of how expectations are formed. The rational expectations approach assumes people use all relevant information in forming expectations of economic variables. In particular, we assume that workers and firms will think through the economic mechanisms underlying the determination of the expected price level. By using all the relevant information, they will not eliminate all forecasting errors, but they will eliminate *systematic* errors. How can they do this?

To begin with, Equation (1) implies that the best prediction that can be made concerning output is that it will be at the full-employment level Y°. Given an aggregate demand schedule and the market clearing condition $AS = AD$, the best prediction of the price level is obtained from the intersection of the AD schedule with a vertical supply curve at the full-employment output. This is illustrated in Figure 8-5. Also shown is the positively sloped Lucas supply curve AS represented by Equation (1). It relates output to the actual price level P, given a value for the expected price level P^e.

In order to make this prediction of the price level, the position of the AD curve must be forecast. This involves predicting the money stock (and the level of autono-

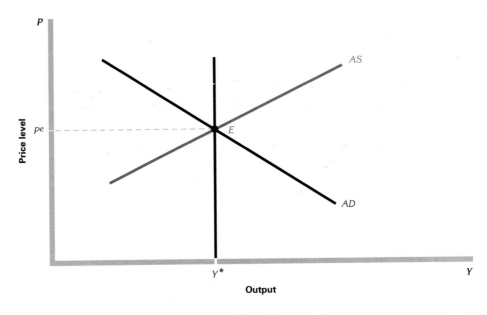

Figure 8-5 *Prediction of Output and the Price Level*

Output will be predicted to be at the full employment level, Y°. The prediction of the price level is obtained at the point E where the aggregate demand schedule, AD, intersects a vertical supply curve at the level of output Y°. The Lucas supply curve, AS, relates output to the price level given the value of the expected price level. It passes through the point E since output will be at the full-employment level if the actual and expected price levels are equal.

mous demand which we shall assume is known). Thus the position of the AD curve in Figure 8-5 depends on the expected money supply.[5]

Anticipated Versus Unanticipated Changes in the Money Supply

We are now ready to see the implications of the Lucas supply curve approach, namely the distinction between anticipated and unanticipated changes in the money supply. The two cases are contrasted in Figure 8-6.

Consider Figure 8-6a. The AS curve is the aggregate supply curve for a given initial expected price level P_o^e. Now suppose the money supply is increased and that the increase was expected. We are thus dealing with an *anticipated* increase in the money stock. The aggregate demand curve certainly shifts up in proportion to the increase in

---

[5] An equation for the expected price level can be obtained by substituting Y° into the AD schedule derived in Box 7-1. Thus we can write $P^e = M^e/(Y^\circ - \gamma\bar{A})$ where M^e is the expected money stock.

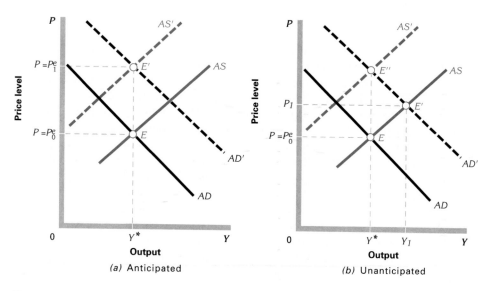

Figure 8-6 *Expected and Unexpected Increases in Money*

(a) An anticipated increase in money is fully reflected in expected prices and hence in the supply curve. With an anticipated increase in money *both* the AS and AD schedules shift upward in the same proportion at output level Y°. Hence, at the new equilibrium, at E', output remains at the level Y°. Thus anticipated money increases have no *real* effects. (b) An unanticipated increase in money is not reflected in expected prices. Therefore initially only the AD schedule shifts. The short-run equilibrium is at E' with output higher. But because prices exceed expected prices, expectations will now be revised upward, the AS schedule will shift, and the economy will move to E''. Unexpected money increases therefore have real effects, but they will be transitory.

the money stock, but at output level Y°, so does the aggregate supply curve since P^e increases in the same proportion as the expected increase in the money stock.

Accordingly, the new equilibrium of the economy is at E', with a price level, P, equal to P_1^e, corresponding to the higher money stock, and unchanged output. Underlying this result are adjustments in the labour market: Both firms and workers knew that the money stock and aggregate demand were going to increase in the proportion P_1^e/P_0^e, and accordingly the nominal wage went up in that same proportion.[6] Thus, with anticipated increases in money there are no *real effects* (just as in the classical case before!); money, nominal wages, and prices, actual and expected, all increase in the same proportion.

---

[6] You may want to use a figure like Figure 8-2 to make sure that you understand why the nominal wage rises in the same proportion as the price level is expected to rise when both firms and workers have the same expectations.

Consider next the case of an *unanticipated* change in the money supply. Now, because there is no change in the price level expected by workers, we have the situation illustrated in Figure 8-6*b*. The increase in the money stock causes the aggregate demand curve to move to *AD'*, as in Figure 8-6*b*, but because the workers did not expect the price level to rise, the aggregate supply curve, *AS*, does not shift. As a result, we move to a new equilibrium at point *E'*. Here actual prices have increased above expected prices, that is, $P > P_0^e$, and as a result output has increased. Thus unanticipated (by the workers) monetary expansion leads to an increase in output.

Under rational expectations, this state of affairs cannot last for long. Prices are above expectations, and forecasts will therefore be revised. For example, if the increase in the money supply is expected to be maintained, price expectations will be revised upward, to P_1^e. Then the *AS* schedule shifts upward to *AS'*. Changes in money matter only while they are unexpected, and an increase in money cannot be unexpected forever. Thus money has only a short-lived influence on activity and is soon *fully* reflected in prices. The central assumptions leading to this result are that expectations are formed rationally and that markets clear.

8-2 Wage Stickiness and the Phillips Curve

In this section we develop the labour market component of a theory of aggregate supply based on sticky wages rather than expectational errors. The assumption that wages are slow to adjust to shifts in demand enables us to derive an aggregate supply curve that produces a gradual adjustment of the economy to disturbances. With gradual adjustment of wages, a monetary or fiscal expansion has an extended effect on output and employment. The key question in the theory of aggregate supply is why the nominal wage adjusts slowly to shifts in demand, or *why wages are sticky*. Wages are sticky, or wage adjustment is sluggish, when wages move slowly over time, rather than being fully and immediately flexible, so as to assure full employment at every point in time.

One obvious reason why wages may be slow to change is that they are fixed in long-term contracts. These contracts may be explicitly negotiated with labour unions or they may be implicit, that is, an unwritten agreement between firm and employee that the wage will remain fixed for a certain period of time. If wages are adjusted at different times for different firms and industries, then the economy-wide average wage will adjust slowly over time to disturbances.

The notion that wages adjust quickly to clear the labour market, as in the neoclassical theory, is clearly at odds with the facts. First, the rate of unemployment fluctuates far more than is consistent with the view that all unemployment is frictional. Figure 8-7 shows the unemployment rate for the period since 1965. It cannot be said that the unemployment rate of nearly 12 percent seen in 1983 is equal to the natural rate. Thus it cannot be that the labour market is always in equilibrium at full employment. Much less can it be believed that the labour market was at full employment in 1933 when the unemployment rate was nearly 20 percent of the labour force.

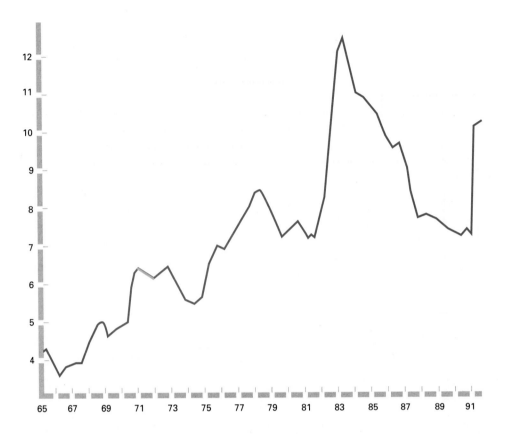

Figure 8-7   *Unemployment Rate, 1965–1991*

(*Source: Bank of Canada Review*)

The Phillips Curve

The second fact that is inconsistent with the neoclassical theory is that there appears to be a systematic relationship between the rate of change of wages and the level of demand. In 1958 A.W. Phillips, then a professor at the London School of Economics, published a comprehensive study of wage behaviour in the United Kingdom for the years 1861–1957.[7] The main finding is summarized in Figure 8-8, reproduced from his article. The Phillips curve is an inverse relationship between the rate of unemployment and the rate of increase in money wages. The higher the rate of unemployment, the

---

[7] A.W. Phillips, "The Relation between Unemployment and the Rate of Change of Money Wages in the United Kingdom, 1861–1957," *Economica*, November 1958.

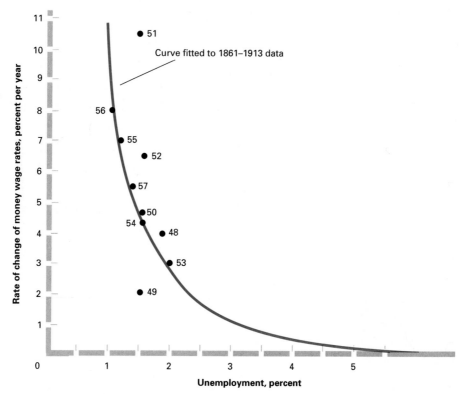

Figure 8-8   *The Original Phillips Curve for the United Kingdom*

(*Source:* A.W. Phillips, "The Relation between Unemployment and the Rate of Change of Money Wages in the United Kingdom, 1861–1957," *Economica*, November 1958)

lower is the rate of wage inflation. In other words, there is a tradeoff between wage inflation and unemployment.

   The Phillips curve shows that the rate of wage inflation decreases as the unemployment rate increases. Letting W be the wage this period, and W_{-1} be the wage last period, the rate of wage inflation, g_w, is defined as

$$g_w = \frac{W - W_{-1}}{W_{-1}} \tag{2}$$

With $u°$ representing the natural rate of unemployment we can write the simple Phillips curve as

$$g_w = -\epsilon(u - u°) \tag{3}$$

where ϵ measures the responsiveness of wages to unemployment. This equation states that wages are falling when the unemployment rate exceeds the natural rate, that is, when $u > u^\circ$, and rising when unemployment is below the natural rate.

The Phillips curve implies that wages and prices adjust slowly to changes in aggregate demand. Why? Suppose the economy is in equilibrium with prices stable and unemployment at the natural rate. Now the money stock increases by, say, 10 percent. Prices and wages both have to rise by 10 percent for the economy to get back to equilibrium, but the Phillips curve shows that for wages to rise by an extra 10 percent, the unemployment rate will have to fall. That will cause the rate of wage increase to go up. Wages will start rising, prices too will rise, and eventually the economy will return to the full-employment level of output and unemployment. In the meantime, the increase in the money stock caused a reduction in unemployment. This point can be readily seen by rewriting Equation (2) (using the definition of the rate of wage inflation) to look at the level of wages today relative to the past level:

$$W = W_{-1}[1 - \epsilon(u - u^\circ)] \tag{3a}$$

For wages to rise above their previous level, unemployment must fall below the natural rate.

Although Phillips's own curve relates the rate of increase of wages or wage inflation to unemployment as in Equation (3) above, the term "Phillips curve" gradually became used to describe either the original Phillips curve or a curve relating the rate of increase of prices — the rate of inflation — to the unemployment rate. Figure 8-9 shows inflation and unemployment data for Canada. The observations for 1963 through 1966 display a Phillips curve tradeoff with the shape of the original Phillips curve of Figure 8-8.

The Policy Tradeoff

The Phillips curve rapidly became a cornerstone of macroeconomic policy analysis. It suggested that policy makers could choose different combinations of unemployment and rates of inflation. For instance, they could have low unemployment as long as they put up with high inflation as in 1966, or they could maintain low inflation by having high unemployment, as in 1963.

However, this simple Phillips curve has not held up well in retrospect. Figure 8-9 shows that the relationship observed in the 1960s clearly does not describe the experience of the 1970s.

The Friedman–Phelps Amendment

Remarkably, the death of the simple Phillips curve was predicted in the late sixties by Professors Milton Friedman, then of the University of Chicago, and Edmund Phelps

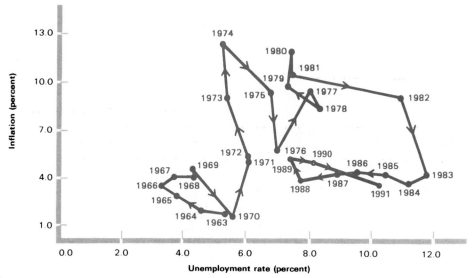

Note: Inflation is the rate of change over the year of the Consumer Price Index.

Figure 8-9 *Inflation and Unemployment*

(*Source: Bank of Canada Review*)

of Columbia.[8] Friedman and Phelps argued that the simple Phillips curve would shift over time as workers and firms became used to and began to expect continuing inflation.

On the basis of economic theory, Friedman and Phelps concluded that the notion of a long-run tradeoff between inflation and unemployment was illusory.[9] The Friedman–Phelps proposition is: *In the long run, the economy will move to the natural rate of unemployment whatever the rate of change of wages and the inflation rate.*

The argument was based on the definition of the natural rate of unemployment as the rate of frictional unemployment consistent with the labour market being in equilibrium. As long as unemployment is above the natural rate, more people are looking for jobs than is consistent with equilibrium in the labour market. This excess unemployment should cause the real wage to fall, so that firms want to hire more workers and fewer want to work, reducing the unemployment rate back to the natural rate. Similarly, when unemployment is below the natural rate, there are too few people available for firms to fill jobs as rapidly as they do normally. The real wage should rise, leading firms to want to employ fewer workers and attracting more people into the

---

[8] Milton Friedman, "The Role of Monetary Policy," *American Economic Review*, March 1968, and Edmund Phelps, *Inflation Policy and Unemployment Theory* (New York: Norton, 1972).

[9] Remember that, at the time they were writing, the facts appeared to support the Phillips curve as a long-run tradeoff; after all, Phillips's own data covered a period of nearly a century.

labour force. The unemployment rate would rise back to the natural level. Thus there is no long-run tradeoff between inflation and unemployment.

Why Are Wages Sticky?

To clarify the assumptions that we make about wage stickiness, we translate the Phillips curve in Equation (3) into a relationship between the rate of change of wages, g_w, and the level of employment. We denote the full-employment level of employment by N^*, and the actual level of employment by N. We then define the unemployment rate as the fraction of the full-employment labour force, N^*, that is not employed.[10]

$$u = \frac{N^* - N}{N^*} \tag{4}$$

Substituting Equation (4) into Equation (3), we obtain the Phillips curve relationship between the level of employment and the rate of change in wages:[11]

$$g_w = \frac{W - W_{-1}}{W_{-1}} = -\epsilon\left(\frac{N^* - N}{N^*}\right) \tag{5}$$

Equation (5) implies that at employment levels above full employment $(N > N^*)$, wages increase, while at employment levels below full employment $(N < N^*)$, wages fall. The extent to which the wage responds to employment depends on the parameter ϵ. If ϵ is large, unemployment has large effects on the wage and the Phillips curve is steep. Equation (5) also implies that there will be a dynamic adjustment in response to a change in aggregate demand and employment. A change in employment this period will have effects on wages in subsequent periods, and the adjustment will take place over time.

The central element in any explanation of wage stickiness is the fact that the labour market involves long-term relations between firms and workers. Most of the labour force expects to continue in its current job for some time. Working conditions, includ-

---

[10] Two related points should be noted: (a) With a positively sloped labour supply curve, the full-employment level of the labour force depends on the real wage. We mean by N^* the equilibrium level of N when the labour market is in the neoclassical equilibrium shown in Figure 8-1, adjusted for frictional unemployment. (b) Equation (4) implies that the unemployment rate is zero at full employment, when $N = N^*$. In fact, there is positive frictional unemployment even when the economy is at full employment. We are implicitly defining the unemployment rate in Equation (4) relative to the natural rate of unemployment. Thus when u in Equation (4) is positive (or negative), the actual rate of unemployment exceeds (or is less than) the natural rate. Actual unemployment can be below the natural rate because people are working overtime.

[11] We note here that the Friedman–Phelps amendment to the Phillips curve adds the expected rate of inflation to the right-hand side of Equation (3). We work with this expectations-augmented Phillips curve in a later chapter, but do not introduce it yet in order to develop the exposition of wage–price and output dynamics step by step.

ing the wage, are renegotiated periodically, but not frequently. That is because it is costly to negotiate frequently if the wage is set by negotiation and costly to obtain information about alternative wages if the wage is supposed to be set by market conditions. Typically, firms and workers reconsider wages and adjust them once a year.[12]

Wages are usually set in nominal terms in economies with low rates of inflation.[13] Thus the agreement is that the firm will pay the worker so many dollars per hour or per month for the next quarter or year. Some formal union labour contracts last two or three years and may fix nominal wages for the period of the contract. Frequently union contracts include separate wage rates for overtime hours, which implies that the more hours worked, the higher the wage rate paid by firms.

At any moment in time, firms and workers will have agreed, explicitly or implicitly, on the wage schedule that is to be paid to currently employed workers. There will be some base wage that corresponds to a given number of hours of work per week and depends on the type of job, with perhaps a higher wage for overtime. The firm then sets the level of employment each period. If demand is high, employment will be high, as will the nominal wage.

Now consider how wages adjust when the demand for labour shifts and firms increase the hours of work. In the short run, wages rise, and with demand up, workers will press for an increase in the base wage at the next labour negotiation. However, it will take some time before all wages are renegotiated. Further, not all wages are negotiated simultaneously. Rather, wage-setting dates are *staggered*, that is, contracts overlap.[14] Assume that wages for half the labour force are set in January and the other half in July. Suppose the money stock went up in September. In the first instance, prices will be slow to adjust because no wage is adjusted until three months after the change in the money stock. Second, when the time comes to renegotiate half the contracts, in January, both the firms and the workers negotiating know that other wages will not change for the next six months.

Workers do not adjust their base wage all the way to the level that will take the economy to the long-run equilibrium because, if they did, their wages would be very high relative to other wages for the next six months. Firms will prefer to employ workers whose wages have not yet risen; there is thus a danger of unemployment to the January wage-setting workers if the renegotiated wages go too high. They are therefore adjusted only part-way toward equilibrium.

Then in July, when the time comes to reset the other half of the wages, those too are not driven all the way to the equilibrium level because the January wages will then

---

[12] The frequency with which wages (and prices) are reset depends on the stability of the level of output and prices in the economy. In extreme conditions, such as hyperinflations, wages might be reset daily or weekly. The need to reset prices and wages frequently is indeed seen as one of the costs of high and unstable rates of inflation.

[13] In economies with high inflation, wages are likely to be *indexed* to the price level, that is, adjusted for changes in prices. Even in Canada some long-term labour contracts contain indexing clauses where the wage is increased to compensate for past price increases. The indexing clauses typically adjust wages once a quarter (or once a year) to compensate for price increases in the past quarter (or year).

[14] The adjustment process we present here is based on John Taylor, "Aggregate Dynamics and Staggered Contracts," *Journal of Political Economy*, February 1980.

be relatively lower. The July wages will then go above the January wages, but still only part-way to the full-employment equilibrium base wage.

This process keeps on going, with the supply curve rising from period to period as wages leapfrog each other, while first one wage and then another is renegotiated. The position of the aggregate supply curve in any period will depend on where it was last period because each unit renegotiating wages has to consider the level of its wage relative to the wages that are not being reset. The level of the wages that are not being reset is reflected in last period's wage rate.

During the adjustment process, firms will also be resetting prices as wages (and thus firms' costs) change. The process of wage and price adjustment continues until the economy is back at the full-employment equilibrium with the same real balances. The real-world adjustment process is more complicated than the January–July example because wages are not reset quite as regularly as that and, also, because not only wage but also price adjustments have to be taken into account.[15] However, the January–July example gives the essence of the adjustment process.

This account of slow wage and price adjustment raises at least two serious questions. The first is why firms and workers do not adjust wages more frequently when clearly understandable disturbances affect the economy. If they did, then perhaps they could adjust wages so as to maintain full employment. Recent research emphasizes that the comparatively small costs of resetting wages and prices can keep adjustment processes from operating fast.[16] Further, the problems of coordinating wage and price adjustments so that wages and prices move back rapidly to equilibrium are formidable in a large economy in which there are many different forces affecting supply and demand in individual markets.

The second question is why firms and unemployed workers do not get together when there is high unemployment, with the firms giving jobs to the unemployed at wages below those their current workers receive. The main reason may be that such practices are bad for the morale and therefore the productivity of those in the labour force who are on the job. There was in fact a limited introduction of such practices in the United States after the 1982 recession, in the so-called *two-tier* wage system. In this system, veterans are on one wage schedule and new employees on a much lower schedule. However, and that is precisely the point of this section, the introduction of the two-tier system did not happen immediately as unemployment developed but, rather, took place slowly over a period of years. That pattern is consistent with the sluggish adjustment of wages.

To summarize, the combination of the assumptions that wages are preset for a period of time and that wage adjustments are staggered generates the type of gradual

---

[15] For an interesting study of the frequency of price adjustments (for newspapers) see Stephen G. Cecchetti, "Staggered Contracts and the Frequency of Price Adjustment," *Quarterly Journal of Economics*, Supplement, 1985.

[16] These theories are at the frontier of research. For the flavour of the argument, see N. Gregory Mankiw, "Small Menu Costs and Large Business Cycles: A Macroeconomic Model of Monopoly," *Quarterly Journal of Economics*, May 1985. A comprehensive but difficult review is presented in Julio Rotemberg, "The New Keynesian Microfoundations," *NBER Macroeconomics Annual*, 1987.

wage and output adjustment we observe in the real world. That accounts for the dynamics. The upward-sloping aggregate supply curve, to which we now turn, is accounted for by overtime wages for some workers and by the fact that wages in those contracts that are renegotiated within the period (such as a quarter) do respond to market conditions.

8-3 The Aggregate Supply Curve

To derive an aggregate supply curve that relates output to the price level we make two additional simplifying assumptions. The first involves the relationship between output and employment and the second involves the relationship between prices and wage costs.

The Production Function

The production function links the level of employment of labour to the level of output. The simplest production function is one in which output is proportional to the input of labour:

$$Y = aN \tag{6}$$

Here Y is the level of output produced, and N is the amount of labour input or employment (measured in hours of work, for example).

The coefficient a is called the input coefficient or *labour productivity*. Labour productivity is the ratio of output to labour input, Y/N, that is, the amount of output produced per unit of labour employed. For instance, if a is equal to 3, then one unit of labour (one hour of work) will produce three units of output.

The assumption in Equation (6) is that the productivity of labour is constant. In fact labour productivity changes over time. It tends to grow over long periods, as workers become better trained, better educated, and equipped with more capital. It also changes systematically during the business cycle. Productivity tends to begin to fall before the start of a recession and then to start recovering either during the recession or at the beginning of the recovery. This productivity behaviour is explained in Box 8-1.

Box 8-1 The Cyclical Behaviour of Productivity

In developing the sticky-wage macroeconomic model, we made a strong assumption about the link between output and employment, namely, $Y = aN$. According to our assumption, labour productivity Y/N is equal to a constant a.

That assumption is readily testable by looking at the cyclical behaviour of labour productivity or output per worker, Y/N. The data given in Table 1 shows that productivity falls as the economy moves into a recession and increases during the recovery. How do we explain these facts, and what implications do they have for our model? Firms maintain a long-term relationship with their labour force. Part of that long-term relationship is that during recessions firms are slow to dismiss personnel, especially highly specialized workers whom the firm does not want to risk losing permanently. This applies also to managers, because even if the firm produces only half the normal level of output, it is difficult to reduce management by half.

Table I   *The Cyclical Behaviour of Productivity*

Recession (Peak to Trough)	Percent Change, Peak to Trough		Percent Change in Four Quarters Following Trough	
	Output	Productivity	Output	Productivity
1974:1–74:3	−0.6	−2.3	1.8	0.3
1979:4–80:2	−1.5	−1.9	5.5	1.9
1981:2–82:4	−7.5	−2.6	7.1	3.7
1990:1–91:1	−2.9	−3.8	1.1	1.7

Source: Department of Finance, *Economic Review* and *Bank of Canada Review.*

Thus employment tends to fluctuate *less* than output or production. During a recession, output falls, but employment falls relatively less. Hence productivity, the ratio of output to employment, falls. Conversely, in a recovery, production rises, but because the firm has kept on or *hoarded* a lot of the work force, employment increases less. Hence productivity rises in a recovery.

The effects we have just described are reinforced by the fact that the firm bases its hiring and firing on expectations about future production. A firm will hire more workers and incur the expense of increasing employment only if there is an expectation that production and output will be higher for some time. Otherwise, paying overtime to the existing labour force would be a cheaper solution. Conversely, firms will lay off or dismiss workers only if they believe the decline in demand will last some time. Here, then, is another source of discrepancy between current employment and current production. Current production may be low but employment high because firms believe demand has declined only transitorily.

By assuming a tight link between output and employment, our model thus simplifies the complex relationships between a firm's production decisions and its employment decisions. For purposes of understanding aggregate supply, the simplification is justifiable, since output and employment do, in practice, move in the same direction, even if not exactly in lockstep.

We simplify by assuming that labour productivity is constant. An important point to notice, though, is that labour productivity is not inversely related to the level of output. The neoclassical demand function for labour shown in Figure 8-1 is built on the assumption that the marginal product of labour decreases as employment increases. If that were so for all levels of output, the average product of labour would also decrease as output increased, but it does not. That is one reason the neoclassical analysis is not an accurate description of the behaviour of wages and prices over the business cycle.[17]

Costs and Prices

The second step in developing the theory of supply is to link firms' prices to their costs. Labour costs are the main component of costs. The guiding principle here is that a firm will supply output at a price that at least covers its costs. Of course, firms would like to charge far more than cost, but competition from existing firms, and firms that might enter the economy to capture some of the profits, prevent prices from getting far out of line with costs.

We assume that firms base price on the labour cost of production. Since each unit of labour produces a units of output, the labour cost of production per unit is W/a. For instance, if the wage is $15 per hour and a is 3, then the labour cost is $5 per unit. The ratio W/a is often called *unit labour cost*.

Firms set price as a *markup*, z, on labour costs:

$$P = \frac{(1 + z)W}{a} \tag{7}$$

The markup over labour costs covers the cost of other factors of production that the firm uses, such as capital and raw materials, and includes an allowance for the firm's normal profits. If competition in the industry is less than perfect, then the markup will also include an element of monopoly profit.[18]

---

[17] A major reason is that the assumption of the neoclassical analysis that capital remains fully employed throughout is not correct. Note from the appendix to Chapter 7 that the diminishing marginal product of labour follows from the assumption that, because the capital stock is fixed in the short run, each succeeding worker has less capital with which to work. However, the use of capital also varies over the cycle, with capital being unemployed in recessions and heavily employed during booms. For instance, factories may run on three shifts a day during booms, using the capital all the time, and only one shift a day during recessions. Data on the use of capital, so-called capacity utilization data, are imperfect but suggest that, if anything, the ratio of capital-in-use to labour may be higher during booms than in recessions. In that case neoclassical theory would not predict that the marginal productivity of labour is lower in booms, as it does in Figure 8-1.

[18] Students who have taken microeconomics will realize that in competitive industries price is assumed to be determined by the market, rather than set by firms. That is quite consistent with Equation (7), for if the industry were competitive, z would cover only the costs of other factors of production and normal profits, and the price would thus be equal to the competitive price. Equation (7) is slightly more general, because it allows also for price setting by firms in industries that are less than fully competitive.

Derivation of the Aggregate Supply Curve

The three components of the aggregate supply curve are the production function (6), the price–cost relation (7), and the Phillips curve (5). By combining these relationships (see the appendix to this chapter for the detailed algebra), we obtain the following equation for the rate of increase of the price level:

$$g_P = \frac{P - P_{-1}}{P_{-1}} = \epsilon \left(\frac{Y - Y^\circ}{Y^\circ} \right) \tag{8}$$

Alternatively, we can rewrite this equation in the form:

$$P = P_{-1} \left[1 + \epsilon \left(\frac{Y - Y^\circ}{Y^\circ} \right) \right] \tag{8a}$$

Finally, defining $\lambda = \epsilon/Y^\circ$, we obtain the *aggregate supply curve*

= employment – wage change linkage

$$P = P_{-1}[1 + \lambda(Y - Y^\circ)] \tag{9}$$

Figure 8-10 shows the aggregate supply curve implied by Equation (9). The supply curve is upward-sloping and shifts over time. If output this period is above the full-employment level, Y°, then next period the AS curve will shift up to AS'. If output this period is below the full-employment level, the AS curve next period will shift down to AS''.

The AS curve is the aggregate supply curve under conditions where wages are less than fully flexible. Prices increase with the level of output because increased output implies increased employment, reduced unemployment, and therefore increased labour costs. The fact that prices rise with output is entirely a reflection of the adjustments in the labour market where higher employment increases wages.[19] Firms pass on these wage increases by raising prices, and for that reason prices rise with the level of output.

---

[19] Note an important implication of markup pricing in Equation (7). Because firms are assumed to maintain a constant markup of price over costs, the real wage does not change with the level of employment in the theory developed in this chapter. Because different theories of aggregate supply have different implications about the cyclical behaviour of real wages, that behaviour has been studied intensively. For instance, some theories suggest that the level of employment is determined by the neoclassical labour demand curve ND in Figure 8-1. In that case the real wage would be high in recessions and low in booms. Empirical evidence shows, however, that wages and employment are essentially independent over the cycle. For a study based on data from twelve countries that reaches this conclusion, see P.T. Geary and J. Kennan, "The Employment–Real Wage Relationship: An International Study," *Journal of Political Economy*, August 1982. It is because the data show no clear pattern that we assume in our theoretical development that the real wage is independent of the level of employment.

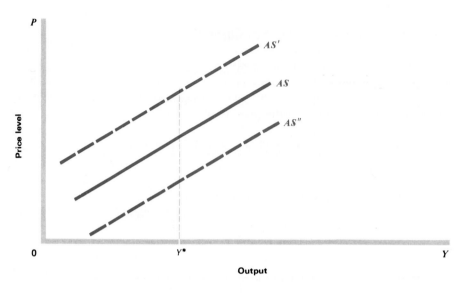

Figure 8-10 *The Aggregate Supply Curve*

The aggregate supply curve *AS* is derived from the Phillips curve, with the added assumptions that output is proportional to employment, and that prices are set as a markup on labour costs. The *AS* curve, too, shifts over time, depending on the level of output. For instance, if output this period is above the full employment level Y^*, the *AS* curve will shift upward to AS' next period.

Properties of the Aggregate Supply Curve

We have now provided a derivation of the aggregate supply schedule, *AS*, used in Chapter 7 and can, with the help of Equation (9), explore its properties more closely. We emphasize three points:

1. The smaller the impact of output and employment changes on current wages, the flatter the aggregate supply schedule. If wages respond very little to changes in unemployment, then the *AS* schedule in Figure 8-10 will be very flat. The coefficient λ in Equation (9) captures this employment–wage change linkage.

2. The position of the aggregate supply schedule depends on the past level of prices. The schedule passes through the full-employment level of output, Y^*, at $P = P_{-1}$. For higher output levels there is overemployment, and hence prices today are higher than those last period. Conversely, when unemployment is high, prices today will be below those last period.

3. The aggregate supply schedule shifts over time. If output is maintained above the full-employment level, Y^*, then over time wages continue to rise and the wage increases are passed on as increased prices.

Rather than discuss these three points in the abstract, in Figure 8-11 we use the aggregate supply curve to examine the effects of a monetary expansion. This will give us a full understanding of both the short-run and long-run implications of the wage–price aggregate supply model.

8-4 The Effects of a Monetary Expansion

In Figure 8-11 we show the economy in full-employment equilibrium at point E. The aggregate supply schedule, AS, is drawn for a given past price level, P_{-1}. It passes through the full-employment output level, Y°, at the price level P_{-1} because when output is at the full-employment level there is no tendency for wages to change, and hence costs and prices are also constant from period to period. The aggregate supply schedule is drawn relatively flat, suggesting a small effect of output and employment changes on wages.

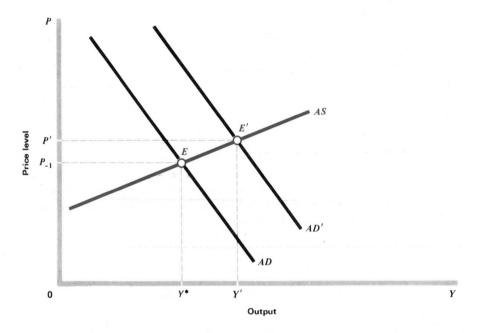

Figure 8-11 *The Short-Run Effect of an Increase in the Money Stock*

The initial equilibrium at E is disturbed by an increase in the money stock that shifts the aggregate demand curve from AD to AD'. Short-run equilibrium is at E' where both the price level and output have increased. Prices are higher because the output expansion has caused an increase in wages, which are passed on into prices. The AS schedule is drawn quite flat, reflecting the assumption that wages are quite sticky.

Short-Run Effects

Suppose now that the nominal money stock is increased. At each price level, real balances are higher, interest rates are lower, and hence the demand for goods rises. The *AD* schedule shifts upward and to the right, to *AD'*. At the initial price level, $P = P_{-1}$, there is now an excess demand for goods. Firms find that their inventories are running down and accordingly hire more labour and raise output until the economy reaches *E'*, the short-run equilibrium point. Note that at *E'* both income and prices have risen. A monetary expansion has led to a short-run increase in income. The rise in prices is due to the increase in labour costs as production and employment rise.

Compare now the short-run result with the Keynesian and classical models of Chapter 7. Our new equilibrium at *E'* has a feature of each: Income is higher, and prices have risen. Whether we are more nearly in the classical or Keynesian situation depends entirely on the slope of the aggregate supply schedule, that is, on the coefficient, λ, that translates employment changes into wage changes.

Medium-Term Adjustment

The short-run equilibrium at point *E'* is not the end of the story. At *E'* output is above normal. Therefore, as Equation (7) indicates, prices will keep on rising. Consider now in Figure 8-12 what happens in the second period. Once we are in the second period, looking back, the price in the preceding period was *P'* at point *E'*. Therefore, the second-period supply curve passes through the full-employment output level at a price equal to *P'*. We show this by shifting the aggregate supply schedule up to *AS'*, reflecting the increase in wages that has taken place since last period in response to the high level of employment.

With the new aggregate supply schedule, *AS'*, and with the aggregate demand schedule unchanged at the higher level *AD'*, the new equilibrium is at *E''*. Comparing *E'* and *E''*, we note that output now has fallen compared with the first period, and prices have risen further. The increase in wages has been passed on by firms as an upward shift of the *AS* schedule, and the resulting price increase reduces real balances, raises interest rates, and lowers equilibrium income and spending. Thus, starting in the second period, we enter a phase of the adjustment process in which the initial expansion begins to be reversed. We continue this process by looking at the long-term adjustment.

Long-Term Adjustment

As long as output is above normal, employment is above normal, and therefore wages are rising. Because wages are rising, firms experience cost increases, and these are passed on, at each output level, as an upward shift of the aggregate supply schedule. As long as the short- and medium-term equilibrium positions of the economy (points *E'*, *E''*, etc.) lie to the right of *Y°*, the *AS* schedule is shifting upward and to the left. As a result, output will be declining toward the full-employment level and prices will keep rising. This adjustment is shown in Figure 8-12.

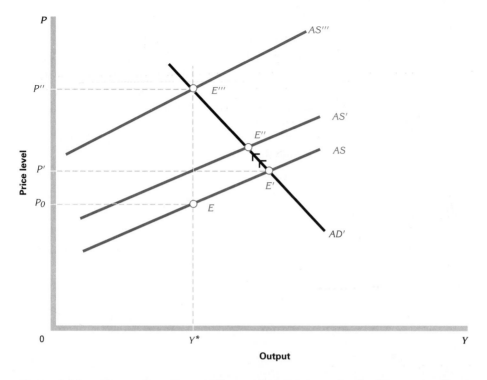

Figure 8-12 *The Longer-Term Effects of an Increase in the Money Stock*

The increase in the money stock led to a short-run equilibrium at E'. But because output is above the full-employment level, wages are rising and the AS curve is shifting upward. In the next period the AS curve shifts to AS', leading to equilibrium in that period at E'', with a higher price level than in the previous period, but lower output. The adjustment from E to E' reflects cost pressures that arise in an overemployed economy. Prices continue to rise and output to fall until the economy reaches equilibrium at E''', with aggregate supply curve AS''', at which point prices have risen in the same proportion as the money stock and output is back at $Y°$.

Figure 8-12 shows that the upward-shifting AS schedule gives us a series of equilibrium positions on the AD schedule, starting with E' and moving up toward E'''. During the entire adjustment process, output is above the full-employment level, and prices are rising. The AS curve keeps shifting up, until the aggregate supply curve, AS''' intersects the aggregate demand curve at E''', at which point the economy has returned to full employment.

At E''', prices have risen in the same proportion as the nominal money stock, and so the real money stock, M/P, is again at the initial level. When real balances and therefore interest rates are again at the initial level, so are aggregate demand, income, and employment. In the long run, once wages and prices have had time to adjust fully, the model has the same predictions as the classical case of Chapter 7. *The difference is only in the adjustment process.* In the classical case a monetary expansion leads immediately to an equiproportionate rise in prices with no real expansion. Here, both income and prices rise in the short and medium term, and only in the long run do we reach the classical case. By assumption, though, the real wage remains constant in the adjustment process. In the short run the predictions of our model more closely resemble the Keynesian case of Chapter 7, and the more slowly that wages adjust to changes in employment, the greater the resemblance.

Because the adjustments of wages and prices are, in fact, slow, the short- and medium-term adjustments are an important aspect of macroeconomics.

8-5 Supply Shocks

From the 1930s to the late 1960s, it was generally assumed that movements in output and prices in the economy were caused by shifts in the aggregate demand curve, by changes in monetary and fiscal policy (including wars as fiscal expansions) and investment demand. However, the macroeconomic story of the 1970s was largely a story of supply shocks.

A supply shock is a disturbance to the economy whose first impact is to shift the aggregate supply curve. The two major supply shocks in the 1970s were the increases in the price of oil in 1973–1974 and 1979–1980. The real price of oil (defined as the world crude oil price in U.S. dollars deflated by the U.S. price level) is shown in Figure 8-13. The first OPEC shock, which produced a quadrupling of the real price of oil during 1973 and 1974, depressed the level of economic activity in the major industrial countries. The second OPEC price increase, which doubled the price of oil, sharply accelerated the inflation rate. The high inflation led to a tough monetary policy in 1980–1982 to fight the inflation, with the result that there was an even deeper recession than in 1973–1975.

These two oil-price-shock-related recessions leave no doubt that supply shocks matter, but the second shock left the oil price so high that some OPEC producers exceeded their production quotas and many new producers came into the market. In mid-1986 and again at the end of 1988, the real price of oil was almost at its end-1973 level. From the point of view of oil consumers that was a favourable oil price shock, but it was bad news for oil-producing regions including western Canada.

The effect of these shocks can be incorporated into our model by taking account of materials prices in the aggregate supply curve. We assume that an increase in the relative price shifts the aggregate supply curve upward. A formal derivation of this relationship is given in the appendix to this chapter.

An Adverse Supply Shock

An *adverse supply shock* is one that shifts the aggregate supply curve up. Figure 8-14 shows the effects of such a shock: The *AS* curve shifts upward to *AS'*, and the equi-

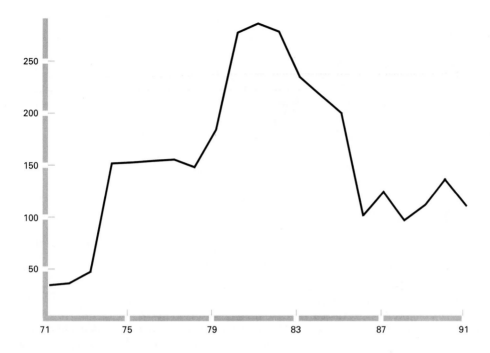

Figure 8-13 *The Real Price of Oil, 1971–1991*

(*Source:* IMF, *International Financial Statistics*)

librium of the economy moves from E to E'. The immediate effect of the supply shock is thus to raise the price level and reduce the level of output. An adverse supply shock is doubly unfortunate: It causes *higher* prices and *lower* output.

There are two points to note about the impact of the supply shock. First, the shock is best thought of as an increase in the price of a raw material used in production. The *AS* curve shifts upward because it now costs firms more to produce each unit of output. Second, we are assuming that the supply shock does not affect the level of potential output, which remains at Y^*.

What happens after the shock has hit? In Figure 8-14, the economy moves, from E' back to E. The unemployment at E' forces wages and thus the price level down. The adjustment is slow because wages are slow to adjust. The adjustment takes place along the *AD* curve, with wages falling until E is reached.

At E the economy is back at full employment, with the price level the same as it was before the shock. However, the nominal wage rate is lower than it was before the shock, because the unemployment in the meantime has forced the wage down. Thus the *real* wage too is lower than it was before the shock: The adverse supply shock reduces the real wage.

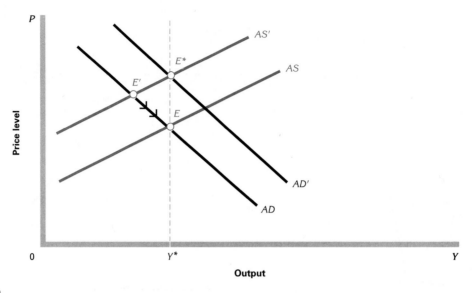

Figure 8-14 *An Adverse Supply Shock*

An increase in the real price of oil shifts the aggregate supply schedule upward and to the left because the cost of production is now higher at each level of output. Because wages do not adjust enough in the short run, the economy moves into an unemployment equilibrium at E'. Prices are higher and output is lower because of the reduction in real balances. Over time, wages decline because of unemployment and the economy returns to the initial equilibrium at E. Accommodating monetary or fiscal policies could shift the AD schedule to AD', reducing the unemployment effects of the supply shock but increasing its inflationary impact.

Accommodation of Supply Shocks

Could the unemployment required to bring down the wage rate be avoided by expansionary monetary and fiscal policy?

To answer that question, we look at Figure 8-14. If, at the time of the oil price increase, aggregate demand could be increased by enough to move the economy to E^* rather than E', prices would rise to the full extent of the upward shift in the aggregate supply curve. Money wages would remain unchanged, and the economy would have stayed at full employment. Of course, the real wage would be lower, but it must fall in any case.

The monetary and fiscal policies that shift the AD curve to AD' in Figure 8-14 are known as *accommodating* policies. There has been a disturbance that requires a fall in the real wage. Policy is adjusted to make possible, or accommodate, that fall in the real wage *at the existing nominal wage*. Accommodation involves a tradeoff between the inflationary impact of a supply shock and its recessionary effects. The more accommodation there is, the greater the inflationary impact and the smaller the unemployment impact.

The Price Level and the Goods and Services Tax

The introduction of the federal Goods and Services Tax (GST) can be viewed as another example of an adverse supply shock since it had a direct effect on the prices paid by consumers.[20] After the introduction of the GST in January 1991, the Bank of Canada indicated that its monetary policy would be designed to accommodate the direct effect on prices of the GST and other increases in indirect taxes such as provincial sales taxes.[21]

The Bank also began providing estimates of the portion of the rate of increase in the consumer price index that can be attributed to increases in indirect taxes. Figure 8-15 shows this decomposition of the quarterly rate of inflation measured by the year-over-year increase in the CPI. The year-over-year increase means the rate of increase from the same quarter of the preceding year (e.g., the figure for the first quarter of 1992 is the rate of increase from the first quarter of 1991 to the first quarter of 1992). Using this measure, the once-for-all effect of the GST on the price level shows up in all the observations of the inflation rate for 1991 and then disappears in 1992. As can be seen from Figure 8-15, it temporarily added 2.4 percent to the inflation rate.

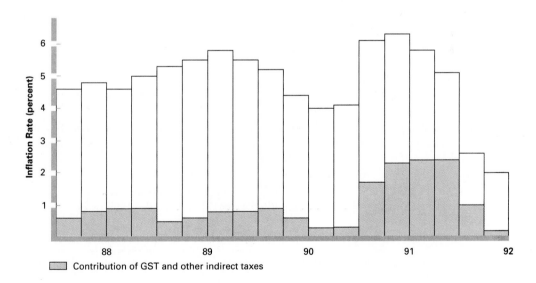

☐ Contribution of GST and other indirect taxes

Figure 8-15   *The Inflation Rate and the GST*

(*Source: Bank of Canada Review*)

[20] For a description of the mechanics of the GST, see Box 2-1 of Chapter 2.
[21] See *Bank of Canada Review*, September 1991, pp. 3–23.

8-6 Expectations, Contracts, and Aggregate Supply

We indicated at the beginning of this chapter that the theory of aggregate supply is as yet unsettled. While there are several competing theories, most have the same aim — to show why the aggregate supply curve slopes up in the short run but is vertical in the long run.[22] Beginning in Section 8-2, we have developed a theory that ascribes the positive slope of the short-run aggregate supply schedule to the slow process of adjustment of wages. Thus we give wage stickiness a fundamental role in our theory.

The rational expectations equilibrium approach, described in Section 8-1, provides an alternative explanation. According to this theory, the positive slope of the aggregate supply curve arises from a lack of complete information about the aggregate price level. This approach implies that unanticipated changes in the money stock (or in fiscal policy) have a positive impact on output and the price level, while anticipated changes affect only the price level. While the early evidence for these propositions was quite favourable, later evidence has been less supportive.[23]

The Cyclical Behaviour of the Real Wage

We saw in Section 8-1 that the Lucas supply curve could be derived on the basis of lack of information on the part of workers concerning the price level, or using a contract approach in which the nominal wage is determined in advance without knowledge of the price level. In either case, the derivation of a positively sloped aggregate supply curve relies on the diminishing productivity of labour. Similarly, both approaches imply that the real wage should decline when expansions in aggregate demand produce an increase in output. This follows from the fact that the increase in output reflects the desire by firms to supply more when the real wage is lower.

The evidence on the cyclical behaviour of the real wage is not very clear, but it certainly does not show that the real wage is consistently lower when output is higher, or, in other words, that the real wage is countercyclical.[24] That is one reason to prefer an approach to aggregate supply that emphasizes sticky wages and assumes the real wage is constant, rather than one that focuses on imperfect information and errors in expectations.[25] However, the Friedman–Phelps amendment to the Phillips curve and

---

[22] The one exception is real business cycle theory (described in Chapter 20), which argues that monetary phenomena are of no importance.

[23] For the early evidence see Robert J. Barro, "Unanticipated Money, Output, and the Price Level in the United States," *Journal of Political Economy*, August 1978; two technically difficult articles that did not support the theory are John Boschen and Herschel Grossman, "Tests of Equilibrium Macroeconomics with Contemporaneous Monetary Data," *Journal of Monetary Economics*, November 1982, and Frederic Mishkin, "Does Anticipated Monetary Policy Matter? An Econometric Investigation," *Journal of Political Economy*, February 1982.

[24] See Robert Barsky and Gary Solon, "Real Wages Over the Business Cycle," NBER Working Paper #2888, March 1989, for evidence that the real wage is basically procyclical.

[25] The contracting approach can be made consistent with the assumption that the real wage is constant, as can be seen, for instance, in the paper by John Taylor referred to in footnote 14.

the rational expectations equilibrium approach both point to the need to embody expectations of inflation in our theory of aggregate supply. This point is taken up when we return to aggregate supply in Chapter 16.

8-7   Summary

1. The rational expectations equilibrium approach to aggregate supply assumes that wages and prices are flexible but that there is a lack of complete information about the aggregate price level. The Lucas supply function then implies that the position of the aggregate supply curve depends on the expected price level. Using this approach, an expected increase in the money stock is fully neutral: The price level rises in proportion to the increase in the money stock and output does not change. However, an anticipated increase in the money supply is not neutral: The price level rises less than proportionately, and real output rises.

2. The labour market does not adjust quickly to disturbances. Rather, the adjustment process takes time. The Phillips curve shows that nominal wages change slowly in accordance with the level of employment. Wages tend to rise when employment is high and fall when employment is low.

3. We assume that the productivity of labour is constant over the business cycle and that prices are based on costs of production. Thus when wages rise because the level of employment is high, prices are increased too.

4. The Phillips curve, together with the assumptions that output is proportional to employment and that price is proportional to costs, implies an upward-sloping aggregate supply curve that shifts over time. A shift in the aggregate demand curve increases the price level and output. The increase in output and employment increases wages somewhat in the current period.

5. The full impact of changes in aggregate demand on prices occurs only over the course of time. High levels of employment generate increases in wages that feed into higher prices. As wages adjust, the aggregate supply curve shifts until the economy returns to equilibrium.

6. The aggregate supply curve is derived from the underlying assumptions that wages (and prices) are not adjusted continuously and that they are not all adjusted together. The positive slope of the aggregate supply curve is a result of some wages being adjusted in response to market conditions and of previously agreed overtime rates coming into effect as employment changes. The slow movement of the supply curve over time is a result of the slow and uncoordinated process by which wages and prices are adjusted.

7. Materials prices, along with wages, are a determinant of costs and prices. Changes in materials prices are passed on as changes in prices and, therefore, as changes in real wages. Materials price changes have been an important source of aggregate supply shocks.

8. Supply shocks, such as a materials price increase or an increase in indirect taxes, pose a difficult problem for macroeconomic policy. They can be accommodated through an expansionary aggregate demand policy, with the effect of increased prices but stable output. Alternatively, they can be offset, so that prices remain stable because of deflationary aggregate demand policy, but then output falls.

9. Both the rational expectations equilibrium approach and the sticky wage theory imply a positively sloped short-run aggregate supply curve. However, the Lucas supply curve derived from the former approach has additional implications that have not been confirmed. These involve the cyclical behaviour of the real wage and the proposition that only unanticipated policy changes affect output.

Key Terms

Market-clearing approach
Lucas supply curve
Rational expectations equilibrium approach
Rational expectations
Phillips curve

Labour productivity
Unit labour cost
Markup
Sticky wages
Supply shock
Accommodation of supply shocks

Problems

1. Using Figures 8-11 and 8-12, analyze the effects of a reduction in the money stock on the price level and on output when the aggregate supply curve is positively sloped and wages adjust slowly over time.

2. In Problem 1, what happens to the level of real balances as a result of the reduction in the nominal money stock?

3. Suppose that the productivity of labour rises, that is, the coefficient a in Equation (6) increases. What are the short- and long-run impacts on prices, output, and the real wage? Compare your answer here with the answers to Problems 3 and 4 in Chapter 7.

4. Discuss the short-run and long-run adjustments to an increase in government spending, using diagrams similar to Figures 8-11 and 8-12.

5. Suppose the economy is in a recession. How can monetary and fiscal policies speed up the recovery? What would happen in the absence of these policies?

6. The government increases income taxes. What are the effects on output, prices, and interest rates (a) in the short run and (b) in the long run?

7. Discuss why wages move only sluggishly.

8. Use the aggregate supply and demand framework to show the effect of a decline in the real price of materials. Show the effects (a) in the short run and (b) in the long run.

9. Suppose a policy could be found to shift the AS curve down.
 (a) What are the effects?
 (b) Why do you think there is great interest in such policies?

10. Suppose that an increase in materials prices is accompanied by a fall in the level of potential output. There is no change in monetary or fiscal policy, and so the AD curve does not shift.
 (a) What is the long-run effect of the disturbance on prices and output? Compare the effect with the case in the text in which potential output does not fall.
 (b) Assume that the upward shift of the AS schedule leads initially to a decline in output below the new potential level. Then show the adjustment process by which output and prices reach the new long-run equilibrium.

11. **(a)** Explain why the short-run aggregate supply curve slopes up in the rational expectations equilibrium approach.
 (b) Explain why anticipated changes in the money stock would have no effect on output in these models.

12. Show the impact on output and the price level of
 (a) A fully anticipated increase in autonomous aggregate demand.
 (b) An increase in autonomous demand that was not anticipated.
 (c) Using diagrams like those in Figures 8-1 and 8-2, explain the economic mechanisms that account for the different answers to parts (a) and (b) of this question.

Appendix   Derivation of the Aggregate Supply Curve

As indicated in the text, the three components of the aggregate supply curve are the production function (6), the price–cost relation (7), and the Phillips curve (5). Since (7) makes the price level proportional to the wage rate, it follows that:

$$\frac{P - P_{-1}}{P_{-1}} = \frac{W - W_{-1}}{W_{-1}}$$

Thus the Phillips curve (5) can be written in the form:

$$\frac{P - P_{-1}}{P_{-1}} = -\epsilon\left(\frac{N^{\circ} - N}{N^{\circ}}\right) \tag{A1}$$

Further, the level of output is proportional to employment (from the production function, Equation (6)). Thus we can replace N and N° in Equation (A1) by Y/a and Y°/a to obtain:

$$\frac{P - P_{-1}}{P_{-1}} = \epsilon\left(\frac{Y - Y^\circ}{Y^\circ}\right)$$

This is Equation (8) given in the text.

Incorporating Materials Prices in the Analysis

We incorporate materials prices in our analysis by modifying the price equation to include not only labour costs and the markup, but also materials prices, which we denote by P_m:

$$P = \frac{W(1 + z)}{a} + \theta P_m \tag{A2}$$

In (A2) the term θ denotes the material requirement per unit of output, and hence θP_m is the component of unit costs that comes from materials inputs.

The wage rate, we recall, increases with the level of output. Hence from Equation (A2) we still get an upward-sloping supply curve. Further, any increase in the price of materials will increase the price level at a given W. Thus an increase in P_m shifts the AS curve upward, as in Figure 8-14.

Alternatively, we can write the price equation in terms of the relative or real price of materials, which we denote by the lower-case p_m. The relative price is given by

$$p_m = \frac{P_m}{P} \tag{A3}$$

Substituting from (A3) into (A2) gives us a modified equation linking wages and prices:

$$P = \frac{1 + z}{1 - \theta p_m}\frac{W}{a} \qquad 1 > \theta p_m \tag{A4}$$

Equation (A4) shows that for given wages, profit margins, and labour productivity, an increase in the real price of materials will increase prices simply because it raises costs. The impact of a change in real materials prices, therefore, is to shift the aggregate supply schedule upward at each level of output, as in Figure 8-14.

CHAPTER 9 *Aggregate Supply and Demand in an Open Economy*

The analysis of income determination and the balance of payments in Chapters 5 and 6 was developed on the assumption that domestic prices were fixed and did not respond to changes in demand. In this chapter, we consider a more realistic model incorporating the aggregate demand and supply analysis of Chapters 7 and 8.

In the first section we modify the derivation of the aggregate demand curve to allow for the effect of changes in the relative price of foreign and domestic goods. We then consider the determination of domestic prices and income in a model with external trade but no international capital flows. In the second section we introduce capital flows and focus on the effect of monetary disturbances under the assumption of perfect capital mobility. The chapter concludes with a discussion of some further issues in the functioning of a flexible exchange rate system.

9-1 The Trade Balance and the Price Level

We begin by adding price level adjustment to the model of Chapter 5, in which we ignore capital flows and treat the trade balance as the total balance of payments. This simplification is of interest for two reasons. First, it enables us to focus on the role of the relative price of foreign and domestic goods in determining equlibrium income and the domestic price level. Second, we eliminate the possibility of achieving external balance with a trade deficit offset by a capital account surplus. As we argued at the end of Section 6-1, this may not be sustainable since it involves a continuing increase in foreign debt which leads to rising interest payments and an increasing current account deficit.

Aggregate Demand in an Open Economy

In the closed economy case considered in Chapters 7 and 8, the process by which the price level affects aggregate demand is as follows. A higher level of prices implies lower real balances, higher interest rates, and lower spending. In an open economy, the relation is slightly more complicated because there is an additional channel through which prices affect demand. An increase in domestic prices now has a direct effect since it leads to a fall in the real exchange rate and a loss of competitiveness. The real exchange rate was defined in Section 5-1 as the relative price of foreign and domestic goods, or

$$\text{Real exchange rate} = \frac{eP^\circ}{P} \tag{1}$$

where e is the exchange rate, P is the domestic price level, and P° is the foreign price level. Assuming that e and P° are fixed, an increase in P reduces the real exchange rate and thus reduces the relative price of imported goods in the home market and increases the relative price of exports in the foreign market. Thus demand shifts from domestic goods to foreign goods.

As we derived in Chapter 5, incorporating this effect into our analysis leads to the following equation for net exports

$$NX = \overline{X} - \overline{Q} - mY + q\frac{eP^\circ}{P} \tag{2}$$

and an equation for the *IS* curve of the form

$$Y = \overline{\overline{\alpha}}\left(\overline{A} - bi + q\frac{eP^\circ}{P}\right) \tag{3}$$

Combining the *IS* curve with the *LM* curve, we obtain an expression for the aggregate demand curve

$$Y = \left(\gamma\overline{A} + \beta\frac{\overline{M}}{P} + \gamma q\frac{eP^\circ}{P}\right) \tag{4}$$

where the parameters γ and β depend on the parameters of the *IS* and *LM* curves.[1]

---

[1] The parameters γ and β and are defined in Section 4-8 of Chapter 4 and again in Box 7-1 of Chapter 7.

The second term on the right-hand side of Equation (4) represents the effect of the price level on demand operating indirectly through real balances, while the third term represents the direct effect operating through the real exchange rate.

In Figure 9-1, we show the downward-sloping demand curve for domestic goods, *AD*, represented by Equation (4). It is drawn for a given level of the nominal money supply and given fiscal policy. In addition, the exchange rate and the foreign price level are given. The short-run aggregate supply curve, *AS*, and the full-employment level of output are also shown in the figure. The economy is shown in equilibrium at the point *E*, where income is at full employment so that we have internal balance.

External Balance and the Adjustment Process Under Fixed Exchange Rates

Also shown in Figure 9-1 is the external balance schedule, *NX*, obtained by setting *NX* equal to zero in Equation (2). It is the set of combinations of income and the domestic

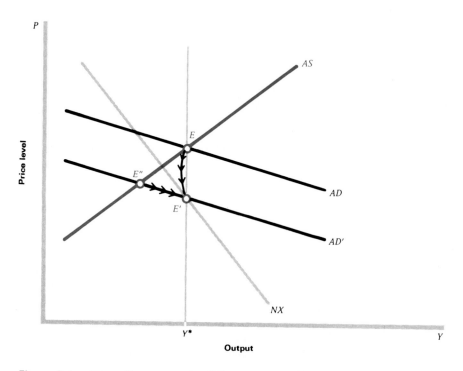

Figure 9-1   *Open Economy Equilibrium With Price Adjustment*

At the point *E*, aggregate demand is equal to aggregate supply but the price level is too high so that we have a trade deficit. External balance can be achieved by contractionary policy that leads to a short-run equilibrium at *E''* and an adjustment path along *AD'* to *E'*. Alternatively, under a fixed exchange rate with no sterilization, the money supply will decline and the economy will move from *E* to *E'* along the path shown.

price level, for which we have a zero balance of trade for given levels of the exchange rate and foreign prices. An increase in domestic income raises imports and worsens the trade balance. To restore external balance, domestic prices must fall so as to improve competitiveness. Thus we show the external balance schedule as downward-sloping. We assume that it is steeper than the aggregate demand schedule.

However, Figure 9-1 represents a situation in which we do not have external balance. The equilibrium point E lies above the NX curve so that the domestic price level is too high in relation to the foreign price level and we have a trade deficit. To achieve external balance, we have to use contractionary policies to shift the aggregate demand curve down to AD' so that it intersects the external balance schedule at E'. The short-run equilibrium will be at E'', where we have unemployment. This puts downward pressure on wages and prices so that the aggregate supply curve shifts to the right and the economy moves along AD' to E'. Thus we are forced to push the economy into a recession to achieve external balance.

This process would occur automatically if the government did not pursue an active stabilization policy and pegged the exchange rate without engaging in sterilization operations. As we saw in Section 6-2, in the absence of offsetting open market operations there will be a link between the balance of payments and the domestic money supply. Indeed, the central bank cannot offset a trade deficit indefinitely through sterilized exchange market intervention, since this would use up its stock of foreign exchange reserves.

Since there is a deficit at point E, pegging the exchange rate without sterilization will lead to a decline in the money supply as the central bank sells foreign currency in exchange for domestic currency. This will cause the aggregate demand curve to shift down, thereby creating excess supply. This will cause the aggregate supply curve to shift down as well, so that the economy will follow the alternative adjustment path shown in Figure 9-1.

Price Level Versus Exchange Rate Adjustment

The adjustment process we have just described is called the *classical adjustment process*. It relies on price adjustments and an adjustment in the money supply based on the trade balance. This process "works" in the sense that it moves the economy to a long-run equilibrium with internal and external balance. However, the mechanism is far from attractive, since it imposes a protracted recession simply to achieve a cut in prices.

An alternative solution is to recognize that external balance can be achieved in either of two ways. To restore competitiveness, domestic prices have to decline relative to foreign prices. As can be seen from the expression given in Equation (1), this can occur either through a decline in domestic prices (P) as in the classical adjustment process, or by a devaluation of the the currency (increase in e) with unchanged domestic prices. An appropriate devaluation will shift the NX schedule up so that it intersects the AS and AD schedules at the point E.

Box 9-1 Relative Prices and the Trade Balance: The J-Curve

In the analysis of this chapter, as well as in Chapters 5 and 6, we assume that an increase in the real exchange rate improves the trade balance. This is consistent with the fact that we consider the trade balance, along with other expenditure components, in real terms. In particular the quantity of imports, Q, is obtained by valuing imports at constant *domestic currency* prices. This is a convenient approximation, but it obscures the fact that a change in the exchange rate has a direct effect on the trade balance since it changes the domestic price of imports. If we denote the quantity of imports valued at constant foreign currency prices by Q^*, the value of imports in terms of domestic currency is eP^*Q^*. The balance of trade in terms of domestic goods is then given by

$$NX = X - Q = X - \frac{eP^*}{P}Q^*$$

From this expression we see that a depreciation (increase in e) may actually lead to a *worsening* of the trade balance because it increases the *value* of imports in terms of domestic goods.

Suppose that we have a depreciation and that domestic and foreign prices remain unchanged. This means that the price of exports remains unchanged while the domestic price of imports rises. This leads to two effects. First, since the relative price of imports has risen, there is a *volume effect* which involves a shift in demand from foreign to domestic goods and an improvement in the trade balance. However, there is also a *price effect* that works in the opposite direction. For any given volume of imports, their value clearly increases because of the higher price, and this tends to worsen the trade balance.

The question, then, is whether the volume effect is strong enough to outweigh the price effect. The empirical evidence on this question is quite strong. It shows that *the volume effects are quite small in the short run, say within a year, and do not outweigh the price effect.*[a] On the other hand, *the long-term volume effect is substantial and leads to the normal response of the trade balance to a relative price change.*

This asymmetry arises from the lags in the adjustment of trade flows to changes in relative prices. In the short run, a depreciation raises the price of imports with very little effect on volumes so that the trade balance worsens. Over time, trade volumes adjust, and eventually the volume effect comes to dominate and the trade balance shows an improvement. This pattern of adjustment is referred to as the *J-curve* because the response of the trade balance over time traces out the letter J.

[a] See Michael C. Deppler and Duncan M. Ripley, "The World Trade Model: Merchandise Trade," *IMF Staff Papers*, March 1978; Duncan M. Ripley, "The World Model of Merchandise Trade: Simulation Applications," *IMF Staff Papers*, June 1980; and "Issues in the Assessment of the Exchange Rates of Industrial Countries," *IMF Occasional Paper No. 29*, July 1984.

The devaluation strategy has the obvious advantage that it does not require a protracted recession to reduce domestic wages and prices. However, it is important to recall the analysis of a devaluation given in Section 5-3. In order to achieve internal and external balance, it is necessary to combine the devaluation with contractionary policies that reduce aggregate demand. If this is not done, the aggregate demand curve will shift up and to the right as a result of the effect of the devaluation on demand for domestic goods. We will then have excess demand for domestic goods and a consequent increase in wages and prices. In the end, the improvement in competitiveness achieved through the devaluation will be offset by an increase in domestic wages and prices.

Box 9-2 Exchange Rates and Relative Price Adjustment

In our model of aggregate supply, we have assumed that wages and prices adjust to achieve full employment. In this box, we consider the possibility that labour attempts to maintain the purchasing power of wages or to keep real wages constant. Suppose that the real wage is fixed in terms of the consumer price index that includes both domestic goods and imports. Assume further that changes in wages are fully passed on in increased domestic prices. Now if we have a depreciation of the domestic currency brought about by some temporary disturbance, import prices rise and this has a direct effect on consumer prices and wages. If money wages increase so as to maintain the real wage and firms increase prices, we get a *wage–price spiral* that ends when domestic wages and prices have risen in proportion to the depreciation so that there is no change in the relative price of foreign and domestic goods.

The effect of this inflation on the level of income and employment will depend on the reaction of the central bank. If the money supply is held constant, then real balances will fall, aggregate demand will be reduced, and there will be unemployment. Further, the economy will remain below full employment as long as there is no downward adjustment of the real wage. On the other hand, if the central bank steps in to prevent unemployment by increasing the money supply, it will do so at the cost of validating the wage and price increases.

To take another example, suppose that there is a permanent fall in export demand because of, say, the introduction of superior technology abroad. To maintain full employment, we must have a depreciation that raises import prices relative to domestic prices and restores competitiveness. However, if domestic wages and prices increase as described above, there will be no change in the relative price, and the consequence will be protracted unemployment.

Thus it may be difficult to change real wages and relative prices through exchange rate changes. The Bank of Canada has indeed argued that this problem is of some importance in Canada. For example, in a speech given in November 1980, the governor stated:[a]

In certain circumstances, for example, a significant decline in the exchange value of the Canadian dollar . . . would not only add almost immediately to the upward pressure on prices and spending but would also, before long, threaten to put increased pressure as well on negotiated wage settlements. . . .

[a] See *Bank of Canada Review*, November 1980, p. 10.

An Increase in the Foreign Price Level

We conclude this section with an analysis of the domestic policy options in the face of an increase in the foreign price level. As discussed in Box 9-3 in Section 9-3 below, this was the situation faced by Canada in the second half of the 1960s when the inflation rate was rising in the U.S.

Consider first the fixed exchange rate case. Figure 9-2 illustrates an initial equilibrium at point E with both internal and external balance. An increase in the foreign price level shifts the NX curve up to NX'. What will be the increase in the domestic price level represented by the vertical shift in this curve? In order to restore trade balance at the same level of income, the domestic price level must increase *in proportion* to the foreign price level so as to restore the initial relative price of foreign and domestic goods.

The improvement in competitiveness also shifts the AD curve up to AD'. The short-run equilibrium is thus at E', where we have excess demand for domestic goods and a trade surplus.

One policy option to restore internal and external balance is to allow the automatic adjustment process to operate. Since there is a trade surplus at E', pegging the exchange rate will cause the money supply to rise and the aggregate demand curve to shift up. Since in addition we have excess demand for goods, the aggregate supply curve will also shift up and the economy will move along an adjustment path like the one shown in Figure 9-2.

The final equilibrium will be at the point E'' where internal and external balance are restored. The relative price of foreign and domestic goods will be unchanged from its initial value since the domestic price level will have risen in proportion to the foreign price level.

In this case, a change in the exchange rate is again a more attractive option. If the domestic currency is *revalued* in proportion to the increase in the foreign price level, the relative price of foreign and domestic goods will remain unchanged and the economy will stay at point E. Thus a revaluation enables the domestic economy to maintain a stable price level and avoid importing foreign inflation.

The important implication of this analysis is that *a country on a fixed exchange rate ties its price level to that of its trading partners and is forced to import foreign inflation.*

In contrast, under a flexible rate, an increase in the foreign price level would lead automatically to a proportional appreciation of the domestic currency so that the domestic price level is *insulated* from the effects of foreign price changes.

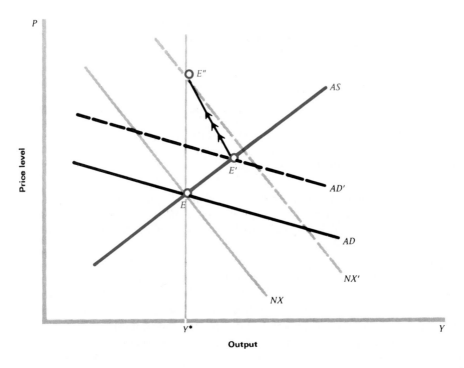

Figure 9-2   *An Increase in the Foreign Price Level*

An increase in foreign prices shifts both the *AD* and the *NX* curves upward and to the right. The short-run equilibrium is at *E'* where we have excess demand for goods and a trade surplus. In the absence of sterilization, the money supply will increase and the *AS* curve will shift up so that the economy moves along an adjustment path to *E"*. At this point internal and external balance are restored with an increase in the domestic price level proportional to that of the foreign price level. Alternatively, if the domestic currency is devalued in proportion to the foreign price increase, the economy will remain in equilibrium at the point *E*.

The Collapse of the Fixed Exchange Rate System

From 1946 to 1973, most countries had exchange rates that were fixed in terms of the U.S. dollar. This was the *Bretton Woods system* that at the end of World War II replaced the unstable exchange rates and restrictive trade policies of the 1930s. Under the Bretton Woods system, countries fixed exchange rates by specifying the rate at which the central bank would buy or sell U.S. dollars in the foreign exchange market.

As we have seen, a system of fixed exchange rates requires that countries pursue very similar policies so that prices of goods in different countries do not get out of line. This was not the case in the late 1960s, when the inflation rate in the United States increased significantly without a similar increase in other countries. Other countries, particularly Germany, were forced to buy up huge amounts of U.S. dollars in an effort to hold down the value of their currencies. In May 1973, the fixed rate system was abandoned and the world economy moved to flexible exchange rates.[2]

9-2 Price Level Determination Under Fixed Exchange Rates and Perfect Capital Mobility

In this section we reintroduce capital flows but restrict the analysis to the case of perfect capital mobility. As we saw in Chapter 6, this involves a considerable simplification and leads to a horizontal *BP* schedule in the form

$$i = i^\circ \qquad (5)$$

How do we incorporate this constraint into an aggregate supply and demand diagram?

Consider first the fixed exchange rate case. We saw in Chapter 6 that with a fixed exchange rate and perfect capital mobility, the money supply becomes an endogenous variable that adjusts automatically to maintain the domestic interest rate equal to the foreign rate. Thus the asset market equilibrium condition, described by the *LM* curve, serves only to determine the required level of the money supply. On the other hand, the condition that the goods market must clear at the given foreign interest rate, i°, determines the set of combinations of income and the price level consistent with the balance of payments constraint for a given level of the exchange rate. An equation for this relationship is obtained by substituting Equation (5) into the *IS* curve given by Equation (3).

$$Y = \overline{\overline{\alpha}}\left(A - bi^\circ + q\frac{ep^\circ}{p}\right) \qquad (6)$$

A graphical derivation of this relationship is shown in Figure 9-3. We begin with a price level P_1 that determines the position of the *IS* curve IS_1 in the top panel. Given the constraint that the domestic interest rate equals the foreign rate, income must be at the level Y_1. If the price level is reduced to P_2, the *IS* curve shifts up and to the right to IS' as a result of the increase in the real exchange rate and the improvement in competitiveness. Thus income rises to Y_2. Tracing out the combinations of P and Y in the lower panel, we obtain the negatively sloped curve labeled $IS_\circ$ that corresponds to Equation (6).[3]

---

[2] As we noted in Chapter 5, Canada had already moved to a flexible rate in 1970.

[3] Comparing Equations (4) and (6), we see that the $IS_\circ$ curve is steeper than the *AD* curve. This reflects the fact that the indirect effect of price level changes on aggregate demand via real balances is absent from the $IS_\circ$ curve.

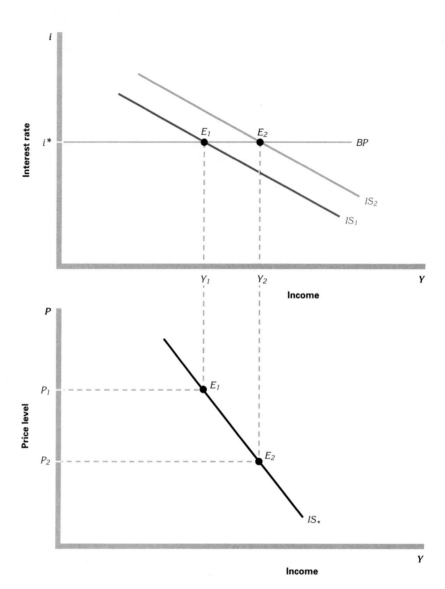

Figure 9-3   *The Balance of Payments Schedule With Perfect Capital Mobility*

Given a price level P_1, the *IS* curve is the schedule IS_1 in the top panel. Since the domestic interest rate equals the foreign rate, income must be at the level Y_1. If the price level is reduced to P_2, the real exchange rate increases, the *IS* curve shifts up and to the right to IS_2, and income increases to Y_2. Tracing out the combinations of P and Y in the lower panel, we obtain the negatively sloped curve labelled IS_*.

Fiscal Policy Under a Fixed Exchange Rate

Figure 9-4 illustrates an economy with perfect capital mobility in equilibrium at the full-employment level of income. The upper panel shows the equilibrium in terms of the *IS* and *LM* curves as was done in Chapter 6, and the lower panel uses the aggregate supply and demand curves together with the balance of payments schedule IS_o derived above.

Suppose now we have an expansionary fiscal policy that shifts the *IS* curve to the right to *IS'*. In the lower panel, the IS_o curve shifts to IS'_o and we have a short-run equilibrium at *E'* with a higher income and a higher price level. The *AD* curve also shifts to the right and the adjustment of the money supply ensures that it also passes through *E'*. The corresponding point in the upper panel is also labelled *E'* and, to be consistent, the *IS* and *LM* curves must shift so as to intersect at this point. How does this come about?

The *IS* curve shifts back to the left because the increase in the price level causes a fall in the real exchange rate and a reduction in competitiveness. The price level increase would also cause the *LM* curve to shift to the left, but this is offset by a more than proportional increase in the money supply. Thus we have a net increase in real balances that shifts the *LM* curve to the right until it passes through *E'*.

Since income is above the full-employment level, we now get an adjustment of wages and prices until we reach the long-run equilibrium at *E"* in the lower panel. In the long run, income returns to the full-employment level, the price level rises, and the real exchange rate falls. Since the interest rate remains unchanged, both the *IS* and *LM* curves must return to their original positions. The *IS* curve shifts back because of the fall in the real exchange rate and competitiveness, while the *LM* curve shifts back because the money supply rises in proportion to the price level so that real balances are unchanged in the long run.

Thus, in the long run, we get complete crowding out of private spending through a reduction in the trade balance. This parallels the short-run result that we obtained in Chapter 6 in the case of a flexible exchange rate. With a flexible rate we get immediate crowding out as a result of an appreciation, while in the present case with a fixed rate we get crowding out in the long run through an increase in the domestic price level.

9-3 Money and Prices Under Flexible Exchange Rates and Perfect Capital Mobility

We saw in Chapter 6 that with a fixed exchange rate and perfect capital mobility, monetary policy has no effect on income. We can therefore confine our attention here to the flexible rate case.

With a flexible exchange rate, the money supply rather than the exchange rate is exogenously determined. The goods market equilibrium condition now serves to deter-

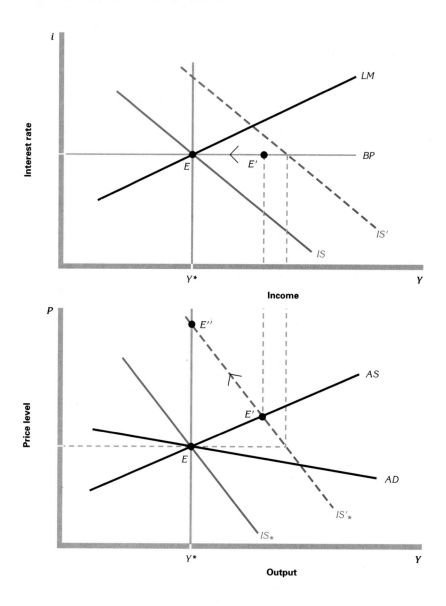

Figure 9-4 *Fiscal Policy Under a Fixed Exchange Rate*

An expansionary fiscal policy shifts the *IS* curve to the right to *IS'*. In the lower panel, the balance of payments schedule *IS₀ curve shifts to IS'₀* and we have a short-run equilibrium at *E'*. The adjustment of the price level and the money supply causes the *AD* curve to shift so that it passes through *E'* (not shown). The *IS* and *LM* curves in the upper panel also shift so as to maintain the domestic interest rate equal to the foreign rate. The long-run equilibrium is at *E''* where we have compete crowding out as a result of a fall in the real exchange rate and loss of competitiveness.

mine the exchange rate and the balance of payments constraint operates via the assets market. The locus of combinations of income and the price level consistent with the balance of payments constraint is obtained from the requirement that the supply and demand for real balances be equal when the domestic interest rate is equal to the foreign rate. Thus we substitute Equation (5) into the *LM* curve to obtain

$$\frac{M}{P} = kY - hi^{\circ} \tag{7}$$

In Figure 9-5, we show an economy in equilibrium with both internal and external balance. Here we use Equation (7) to represent the balance of payments constraint in the lower panel. It is labelled $LM_{\circ}$ and its position depends on the exogenously determined domestic money supply.[4]

The Effect of a Monetary Expansion

As shown in Figure 9-5, a monetary expansion leads to a shift in the *LM* curve to LM' and a shift in the $LM_{\circ}$ curve to $LM'_{\circ}$ and we get a short-run equilibrium at E' with a higher income and price level. The *AD* curve also shifts to the right, and there is a depreciation of the currency that ensures that it passes through E'. The increase in the exchange rate is proportionately greater than the increase in the price level so that, in the short run, we get a net improvement in competitiveness. Thus the *IS* curve also shifts to to the right so that it passes through E' in the upper panel. The increase in the price level shifts the *LM* curve back to the left so that it also passes through E'.

The short-run effect of a monetary expansion is, then, an increase in income and the price level and a depreciation of the currency. With income now above the full-employment level, prices rise and the economy moves along the $LM'_{\circ}$ schedule in the lower panel until it reaches the long-run equilibrium at E''. In the upper panel, the equilibrium is at the original point E. Thus, in the long run, a monetary expansion is entirely neutral and has no effect on real variables. Income returns to its original level, the price level increases in proportion to the money supply increase so that real balances are unchanged, and the currency depreciates proportionately so that the real exchange rate is unchanged. Table 9-1 summarizes these results.

Table 9-1   *The Short- and Long-Run Effects of a Monetary Expansion*

	M/P	*e*	*P*	*ep*/P*	*Y*
Short run	+	+	0	+	+
Long run	0	+	+	0	0

[4] In Problem 5 at the end of the chapter, you are asked to derive the $LM_{\circ}$ schedule using a diagram similar to Figure 9-3.

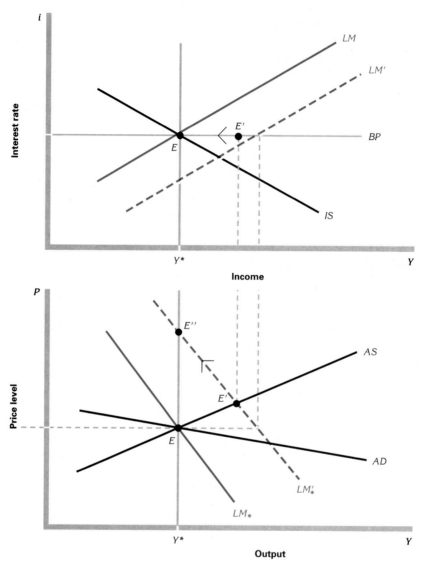

Figure 9-5 *Monetary Expansion Under a Flexible Exchange Rate*

A monetary expansion shifts the *LM* curve to *LM'* and the *LM*₀ *curve to LM'₀,* and we get a short-run equilibrium at *E'*. The depreciation of the currency shifts the *AD* curve so that it also passes through *E'* (not shown). The long-run equilibrium is at *E''* in the lower panel and at the original point *E* in the upper panel, and we have neutrality of money. Income returns to its original level, the price level increases in proportion to the money supply so that real balances are unchanged, and the currency depreciates proportionately so that the real exchange rate is unchanged.

Box 9-3   The Exchange Rate and Monetary Policy in Canada in the Early 1970s

In Chapter 6, we reviewed the Canadian experience under flexible exchange rates in the 1950s when inflation was not a serious problem for policy makers. In this box, we consider the operation of a flexible rate in the early 1970s when inflation became a major preoccupation.

The inflation problem of the 1970s had its origins in the second half of the 1960s when the U.S. economy was experiencing boom conditions largely as a result of expenditures related to the Vietnam war. Demand pressure in the United States spilled over into Canada in the the form of demand for our exports. This process was intensified by the favourable competitive position that Canada enjoyed at the time. The longer-term trends in the Canada–U.S. terms of trade shown in Figure 9-6 suggest that the choice of 92.5 U.S. cents when the Canadian dollar was pegged in 1962 involved a substantial undervaluation of our currency. This is confirmed by the fact that maintenance of this rate required substantial exchange market intervention.

As pressure on the Canadian dollar built up, the Bank of Canada was unwilling or unable to sterilize the effects of exchange market intervention on the money supply. Thus the classical adjustment process discussed in Section 9-1 was brought into play and the rate of growth of the money supply increased. In 1967, the rate of growth of $M1$ was nearly 10 percent compared with an average of about 5 percent between 1960 and 1964. In 1968, the inflationary pressure was intensified by an acceleration of inflation in the United States, and the U.S. inflation rate remained above the Canadian rate until 1973.

The freeing of the Canadian dollar in 1970 provided the Bank of Canada with an opportunity to stem the inflationary pressures. The rate of growth of the money supply was sharply curtailed, and the inflation rate eased thereafter. As would be expected, there was a substantial appreciation of the Canadian dollar. However, shortly after the Bank of Canada had freed itself from the restrictions imposed by a fixed exchange rate and made substantial progress in bringing inflation under control, it appears to have become reluctant to exploit the benefits of a flexible rate.

To begin with, the Bank of Canada attempted to resist the appreciation of the Canadian dollar in 1970 and 1971 by intervening heavily in the foreign exchange market. A substantial appreciation was required to restore the terms of trade to the equilibrium level, and intervention to prevent this from taking place intensified inflationary pressure in Canada.

The second error in policy was the sharp turnaround in monetary policy that occurred in 1971. Subsequent events indicated that the Bank of Canada overreacted to the slowdown in economic activity and rising unemployment experienced in 1970. The rate of growth of $M1$ shot up to a level close to 13 percent in 1971 and rose to 14 percent in 1972. In 1973, there was a sharp increase in the inflation rate, and by 1975 the consumer price index was rising at a rate in excess of 10 percent. There was an increase in the rate of inflation in the United States as well, but the acceleration was more rapid in Canada. As shown in Figure 9-6, the exchange rate was held close to 100 U.S. cents over the period 1972 to 1976, while the difference in inflation rates led to a substantial deterioration in our competitive position.

In retrospect, it appears that Canada missed an opportunity to avoid at least some of the inflation that plagued the world economy in the 1970s. Monetary policy was immobilized in the late 1960s by a commitment to a fixed exchange rate at a time when inflation rates began to rise in other countries. In the early 1970s, the full benefits of a flexible rate were not realized, since the Bank of Canada resisted the appreciation of the Canadian dollar. It appears to have been influenced by a misguided concern for the effect of an appreciation on the competitive position of Canada's export industries. As indicated by our discussion of a money supply increase, the short-run effect is to depreciate the currency and improve competitiveness. However, the longer-run consequence is an increase in prices which restores competitiveness to the equilibrium level.

A second reason for the mismanagement of monetary policy in the early 1970s was the delayed recognition of the importance of controlling the rate of growth of the money supply. As discussed later in Chapter 19, it was not until 1973, when inflationary forces were already entrenched, that the Bank of Canada began to move toward greater emphasis on control of the money supply.

Purchasing Power Parity and the Monetary Theory of the Exchange Rate

The long-run neutrality of money discussed above illustrates the potential role of exchange rates in offsetting the effects of changes in the price level at home or abroad on the real exchange rate. In other words, changes in the exchange rate maintain the *purchasing power* of our goods in terms of foreign goods. The *purchasing power parity* (PPP) theory of exchange rate determination states that exchange rates move primarily as a result of differences in price level behaviour between countries in such a way as to keep the real exchange rate constant.

PPP is a plausible description of the trend behaviour of exchange rates, especially when inflation differentials between countries are large. In particular, we have seen that the PPP relationship does hold in the face of an increase in the money supply, so that if rates of monetary expansion differ between countries, we would expect PPP to hold, at least in the long term.

Another perspective on the relationship between PPP and monetary disturbances is given by the *monetary theory of the exchange rate*, which puts exchange rate determination explicitly in a two-country setting.[5] We assume that PPP holds and that the domestic and foreign interest rates are equal:

---

[5] See J. Bilson, "The Monetary Approach to the Exchange Rate — Some Empirical Evidence," *International Monetary Fund Staff Papers*, March 1978, 48–75; and J. Frenkel, "A Monetary Approach to the Exchange Rate: Doctrinal Aspects and Empirical Evidence," *Scandinavian Journal of Economics*, June 1976, 255–76.

$$\frac{eP^*}{P} = \text{constant} \qquad i = i^*$$

The money demand functions for the domestic and foreign economies can be written as[6]

$$\frac{M}{P} = kY - hi \qquad \frac{M^*}{P^*} = k'Y^* - h'i^*$$

This set of equations implies that the behaviour of the exchange rate over time will depend on the time path of income and the money supply in the two countries. An increase in M relative to M^* will lead to an increase in P relative to P^* and a depreciation of the domestic currency (increase in e). On the other hand, an increase in Y relative to Y^* means an increase in the domestic demand for real balances relative to the foreign demand, a fall in P relative to P^*, and an appreciation of the domestic currency (decrease in e).

Purchasing Power Parity: The Evidence

Figure 9-6 shows the exchange rate (Canadian dollar price of one U.S. dollar) and the real exchange rate in relation to the U.S. The real exchange rate is calculated using the U.S. and Canadian GDP implicit price indexes to measure the price levels.

From 1953 to 1970, similar inflation rates were experienced in the two countries, so the two indexes moved together. Following the floating of the Canadian dollar in 1970, there was a sharp appreciation which dominated the movement of the real exchange rate. From 1972 to 1976, the Canadian inflation rate was substantially above the U.S. rate, and the real exchange rate fell until late 1976 when the Canadian dollar began to depreciate. By 1978, Canada's competitive position had been restored to the level of the early 1970s, but the currency continued to depreciate until 1986. Thereafter there was an appreciation that again brought the real exchange rate back toward its long-term average level.

Figure 9-6 suggests some tendency for the real exchange rate to maintain a constant level in the long run, but there is considerable short-run variation. This reflects two important qualifications to the PPP theory. First, even a monetary disturbance affects the real exchange rate in the short run. Exchange rates tend to move quite rapidly relative to prices, and thus we observe substantial deviations from PPP.

The second qualification concerns the role of nonmonetary disturbances in affecting exchange rates. For example, we saw at the beginning of this section that an expansionary fiscal policy (or any increase in autonomous spending) leads to a fall in the real exchange rate in both the short run and the long run. If we consider an increase in potential output as another example, we will find that the equilibrium real exchange

---

[6] To be consistent, we use asterisks to indicate foreign variables, although we have previously used Y^* to denote full-employment income.

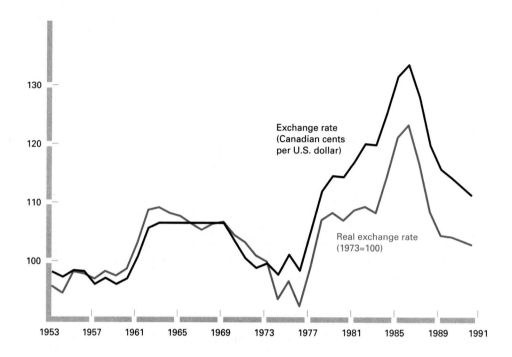

Figure 9-6 *Canada–U.S. Real and Nominal Exchange Rates*

(*Source: Bank of Canada Review* and U.S. Department of Commerce, *Survey of Current Business*)

rate rises and competitiveness improves so as to absorb the increased output. Thus, it is apparent that *real* disturbances will affect the *equilibrium* real exchange rate. In the longer term, exchange rates and prices do not necessarily move together, and the purchasing power parity view of exchange rates does not always hold.

An Increase in the Foreign Interest Rate

In the first half of 1981, the Federal Reserve pushed up interest rates sharply in the U.S. The policy was successful in bringing down the rate of inflation, but it precipitated a severe recession. What options did the Bank of Canada have in the face of this sharp rise in interest rates in the U.S.?

The effects of an increase in the foreign interest rate are illustrated in Figure 9-7. We assume a flexible exchange rate and use a diagram similar to the one in the lower panel of Figure 9-5. The initial equilibrium is at E, and an increase in the foreign interest rate is represented by a shift to the right of the $LM_{\circ}$ schedule. For a given price level and therefore a given supply of real balances, a higher interest rate must be accompanied by a higher level of income to maintain the demand for real balances equal to the supply.

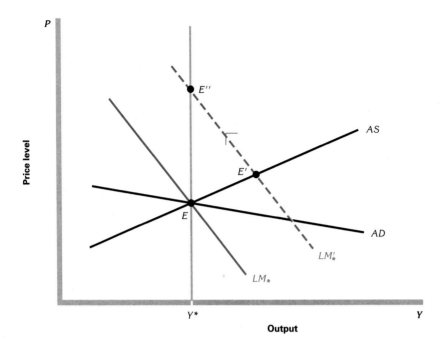

Figure 9-7   *An Increase in the Foreign Interest Rate*

An increase in the foreign interest rate shifts the LM_* *curve to* LM'_*, and we get a short-run equilibrium at E'. The depreciation of the currency shifts the AD curve so that it also passes through E' (not shown). In the long run, the improvement in competitiveness just offsets the negative effect of higher interest rates on demand and the economy moves to E''.

In the absence of a parallel tightening of domestic monetary policy, the immediate effect is a depreciation, causing the AD curve to shift up and to the right so that the short-run equilibrium is at E'. At this point there is excess demand so that the price level rises and we move along the adjustment path to E''. The long-run effect is a fall in the real exchange rate that improves competitiveness and thereby offsets the negative effect of higher interest rates on demand.

We thus conclude that *if the Bank of Canada does not respond by reducing the growth rate of the Canadian money supply, a tightening of monetary policy in the U.S. will cause the Canadian dollar to depreciate and create inflationary pressure in Canada.* For this reason, the Bank of Canada was reluctant to maintain an independent policy strategy and followed the American lead. The result was a sharp decline in the Canadian inflation rate, but at the cost of a drastic increase in the unemployment rate.[7]

---

[7]   For a further discussion of the policy response to a change in foreign interest rates, see G.R. Sparks, "The Theory and Practice of Monetary Policy in Canada: 1945–83," in J. Sargent, ed., *Fiscal and Monetary Policy*, Royal Commission Research Studies, Vol. 21 (Toronto: University of Toronto Press, 1986), pp. 141–43.

The spillover effects of U.S. tight money in this period created problems for other industrialized countries as well. Policy makers were forced to accept higher inflation caused by American policy or to change their own policy. Since most countries did not want to import inflation, they reacted by tightening money. This reduced the effects on exchange rates, but it also meant that American tight money and recession became the world's tight money and a world recession.

Interest Parity and Exchange Rate Overshooting

In Section 6-5 of Chapter 6, we introduced the interest parity condition to explain the empirical observation that Canadian interest rates frequently diverge from U.S. rates. The assumption that domestic and foreign interest rates are equal is replaced with the relationship

$$i = i^* + x \tag{8}$$

where x is the expected rate of depreciation of the domestic currency.

In the context of a model with fixed prices, we saw that the introduction of this relationship modifies the adjustment process in response to an increase in the money supply. In particular, we get an overshooting of the exchange rate in the short run, and this result carries over to the present model that allows for changes in the price level. The adjustment path of income and the price level are the same as that shown in the lower panel of Figure 9-5, but at the short-run equilibrium point E', the domestic interest rate is now below the foreign rate. The movement from E to E' involves an immediate depreciation that overshoots the long-run equilibrium so that along the adjustment path to E'' the currency is appreciating.

Figure 9-8 shows the paths of adjustment following an increase in the money supply at time T_0. In contrast to the fixed price model of Chapter 6, we have long-run neutrality of money. Thus income and real balances return to their initial levels, and the depreciation is matched by an increase in the price level that restores the real exchange rate.

9-4 Exchange Rate Fluctuations and Interdependence

In the 1960s, there was growing dissatisfaction with fixed exchange rates. The Bretton Woods system was called a crisis system because from time to time exchange rates would get out of line and expectations of exchange rate changes would precipitate massive capital flows that often forced the exchange rate changes that speculators expected. Is the flexible rate system put into effect in the 1970s better? Is it less crisis-prone and does it provide a better framework for macroeconomic stability?

At one time it was argued that flexible exchange rates have the advantage of permitting countries to pursue their own national monetary and fiscal policies without having to worry about the balance of payments. This is certainly correct, but it is also misleading. There are important linkages between countries whatever the exchange rate regime.

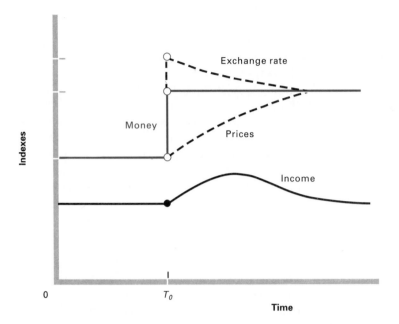

Figure 9-8 *Exchange Rate Overshooting*

A permanent increase in the money supply at time T_0 causes an immediate depreciation that overshoots the long-run equilibrium. In the short run, the real exchange rate rises, competitiveness improves, and there is an expansion of income. As prices adjust and the currency appreciates, income, real balances, and the real exchange rate move back to their original values. Thus, money is neutral in the long run.

Interdependence

Spillover, or *interdependence*, effects have been at the centre of the discussion about flexible exchange rates. As we saw in Section 9-3 above, the effects of the tight U.S. monetary policy in 1981 created problems for all industrialized countries. The reason is clear from our models: As the United States tightens monetary policy, U.S. interest rates rise, and this attracts capital flows. The U.S. dollar appreciates and other currencies depreciate. The U.S. appreciation implies a loss in American competitiveness. World demand shifts from U.S. goods to those produced by other countries. Therefore, American income and employment decline, while income and employment expand in other countries.

There are also spillover effects through prices. When the U.S. dollar appreciates, there is downward pressure on U.S. prices directly through import prices and indirectly through the decline in demand for American goods. However, the opposite occurs in other countries. Their currencies depreciate and their prices increase. Thus there is inflation in other countries, which may welcome an increase in employment as a side effect of U.S. monetary policy but do not welcome the inflation.

In the same way, U.S. fiscal policies exert effects elsewhere. A U.S. fiscal expansion such as occurred during the early 1980s will lead to appreciation of the U.S. dollar and a loss in competitiveness. The direct increase in American spending and the deterioration in U.S. competitiveness are the channels through which American expansion is shared with other countries which experience increased exports.

Policy makers in other countries therefore must decide whether to accept the higher employment–higher inflation effects of U.S. policies or whether they should change their own policies. If the rest of the world does not want *imported inflation*, then their response must be to tighten money. This reponse on the part of Canada and other countries led to a spreading of the 1981–1982 recession throughout the world.

Policy Coordination

The large changes in exchange rates that arise when policies are not fully synchronized between countries pose a major threat to a world of free trade. A substantial appreciation and loss of competitiveness can cause large shifts in demand. Domestic workers become unemployed, and they recognize that foreign workers have gained the jobs they have lost. Thus there will be pressure for protective tariffs or quotas to keep out imports that are "artificially cheap" because of the appreciation.

On the question of independence under flexible exchange rates, the experience of the last 20 years offers a clear answer. Under flexible rates there is as much interdependence as there is under fixed rates, or more. Moreover, because exchange rates react so quickly to policies (good or bad), macroeconomic management does not become easier. To make the system work better than it has in the past clearly requires more coordination of policies.

9-5 Summary

1.   In an open economy, the price level affects aggregate demand directly through the real exchange rate as well as indirectly through real balances and interest rates.

2.   In the short run, a depreciation can lead to a worsening of the trade balance through a rise in the price of imports. Over time, the volume of trade adjusts and we get an improvement in the trade balance. This is called the J-curve effect.

3.   If there is a trade deficit at full employment, contractionary policy is required to reduce the price level so as to achieve external balance. If the central bank pegs the exchange rate without sterilization, then the money supply falls and the price level is reduced through the *classical adjustment process*. Devaluation can also be used to achieve external balance.

4.   Since a depreciation raises the price of imports, it raises the cost of living. If labour is successful in maintaining the real wage constant, the depreciation will

not lead to an adjustment of the real exchange rate, and the result will be protracted unemployment.

5. A country on a fixed exchange rate ties its price level to that of its trading partners. When Canada was on a fixed rate in the second half of the 1960s, it was forced to import U.S. inflation.

6. From 1946 to 1973, most countries had fixed exchange rates. This system collapsed because of divergent policies followed in the major industrial countries.

7. With a fixed exchange rate, expansionary fiscal policy leads to an increase in income and the price level in the short run. In the long run, the price level rises and the real exchange rate falls so that we get complete crowding out through a reduction in the trade balance.

8. With a flexible exchange rate and perfect capital mobility, the short-run effect of expansionary monetary policy is an increase in income and the price level and a depreciation of the currency. In the long run, the initial levels of income and the real exchange rate are restored by proportional increases in the price level and the exchange rate. This neutrality result leads to the purchasing power parity theory of exchange rates. It does not always hold, since the real exchange rate varies in response to nonmonetary disturbances and is affected even by monetary factors in the short run.

9. The floating of the Canadian dollar in 1970 did not stem inflationary pressure, because the Bank of Canada failed to control the rate of growth of the money supply until 1973.

10. The 1981–1982 recession was brought on by tight monetary policy in the U.S. which forced other industrial countries to follow a similar policy to avoid an increase in inflation rates. This was an example of the interdependence among countries that exists even with flexible exchange rates. These interdependence effects make a case for coordination of policies.

11. The interest parity condition leads to a short-run overshooting of the exchange rate in response to an increase in the money supply. Along the adjustment path, the price level rises, the currency appreciates, and income and real balances return to their original levels.

Key Terms

Real exchange rate
The J-curve
Classical adjustment process
Imported inflation
Bretton Woods system

Purchasing power parity
Monetary theory of the exchange rate
Exchange rate overshooting
Interdependence

Problems

1. Consider the model depicted in Figure 9-1. Illustrate the short-run equilibrium of an economy with unemployment and a zero balance of trade. Show the adjustment process assuming (a) sterilization, and (b) no sterilization.

2. With a fixed exchange rate and perfect capital mobility, both the exchange rate and the interest rate are fixed exogenously while the money supply adjusts endogenously. Write down two equations that determine the short-run equilibrium values of income and the price level and indicate how they correspond to the schedules shown in Figure 9-3.

3. Suppose the domestic and foreign price levels and the exchange rate are as follows:

	P	P*	e($/£)
Year 1	100	100	2
Year 2	180	130	

    (a) If there were no real disturbances between year 1 and year 2, what would be the equilibrium exchange rate in year 2?
    (b) If the real exchange rate fell by 50 percent between years 1 and 2, what would the exchange rate be in year 2?

4. Assuming perfect capital mobility, how does the imposition of a tariff affect the exchange rate, output, and the trade balance? (*Hint:* Given the exchange rate, the tariff reduces the demand for imports.)

5. Use a diagram similar to Figure 9-3 to derive the LM_e schedule shown in the lower panel of Figure 9-5. Consider a change in each of the following variables. Which ones would cause the LM_e to shift?
    (a) domestic interest rate   (c) domestic money supply
    (b) foreign interest rate   (d) exchange rate

6. Explain the purchasing power parity theory of the long-run behaviour of the exchange rate. Indicate circumstances under which you would not expect the theory to hold.

7. Figure 9-7 shows the effect of an increase in the foreign interest rate in an aggregate supply and demand diagram. Show the effect in a corresponding *IS-LM* diagram as is done in Figures 9-4 and 9-5.

8. Using both *IS-LM* and aggregate supply and demand diagrams, show the effect of a monetary expansion in a model that includes the interest parity condition. (You may want to refer back to Figure 6-15 of Chapter 6.)

PART 3 *Aggregate Demand and Stabilization Policy*

CHAPTER 10 *Consumption and Saving*

The *IS-LM* model provides a comprehensive framework for understanding the interactions of the main macroeconomic variables that determine aggregate demand. Now we retrace our steps to present a more detailed and sophisticated treatment of the key relationships in the *IS-LM* model. The present chapter deals with the consumption function and with saving; since consumption purchases account for about 60 percent of aggregate demand, this is the natural place to begin. The following three chapters flesh out the behaviour of investment, money demand, and money supply, and thus move us to a more realistic and reliable understanding of the working of the economy.

Our starting point in examining consumption behaviour is the consumption function we have been using in previous chapters. Thus far we have assumed that consumption is a linear function of disposable income:

$$C = \overline{C} + cYD \qquad \overline{C} > 0 \qquad 1 > c > 0 \tag{1}$$

What does the empirical evidence show? Do the data for the postwar period bear out the hypothesis of a consumption function such as Equation (1)? We plot consumption and disposable income (both in 1986 dollars) for each of the years from 1971 through 1991 in Figure 10-1. The diagram clearly reveals a close positive relationship between consumption and disposable income. To find numerical estimates of the intercept ($\overline{C}$) and the marginal propensity to consume (c), we "fit" a regression line to the observations. The regression line is fitted to the data using the method of least squares,

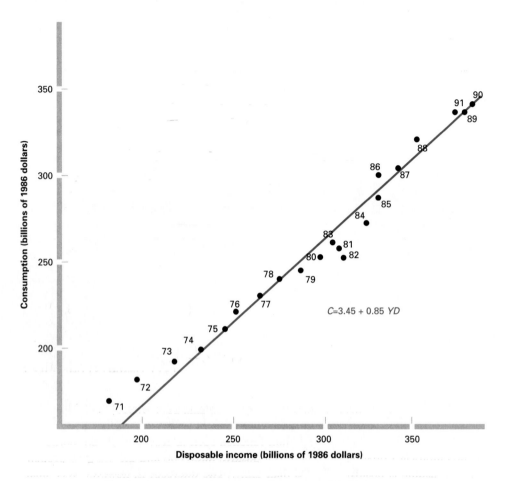

Figure 10-1   *The Consumption–Income Relation, 1971–1991*

which produces the linear equation that best characterizes the relation between consumption and disposable income contained in the data.[1]

The estimated regression line is shown in Figure 10-1 as the solid line and is reported in Equation (2). The estimate of the intercept is 3.45, and the estimate of the marginal propensity to consume is 0.85.

---

[1] It is frequently useful to summarize a relationship, such as that of Figure 10-1, between consumption expenditures and disposable income by writing an equation such as Equation (2), which has specific numerical values in it, rather than the more general form of Equation (1), which does not specify numerical values of the coefficients $\overline{C}$ and c. The line drawn in Figure 10-1 is the line represented by Equation (2). That line is calculated by minimizing the sum of the squares of the vertical distances of the points in Figure 10-1 from the line, and it provides a good description of the general relationship between the two variables. For further details on the fitting of such lines, called least-squares regression lines, see Robert S. Pindyck and Daniel L. Rubinfeld, *Econometric Models and Economic Forecasts*, 3rd ed. (New York: McGraw-Hill, 1991).

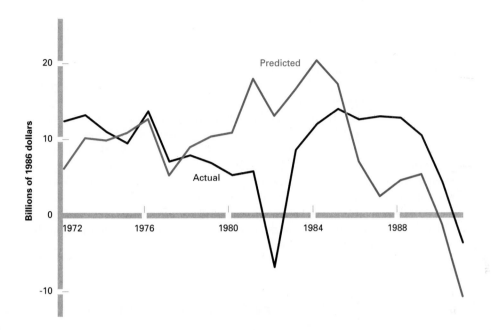

Figure 10-2 *Actual and Predicted Changes in Consumption*

$$C = 3.45 + 0.85YD \qquad \text{(annual data 1971–1991)} \qquad (2)$$

Two characteristics of a consumption function such as Equation (1) are borne out by the empirical Equation (2). There is a positive intercept, and the marginal propensity to consume is positive and less than unity.[2] The intercept is, however, very small relative to disposable income, which is $385.8 billion 1986 dollars, in 1990.[3] If the intercept were actually zero, then we see from Equations (1) and (3) that consumption would be proportional to disposable income, with $C/YD = c$. The marginal and average propensities to consume would be equal. The relationship shown by Figure 10-1 and Equation (2) is essentially one of proportionality, with the average and marginal propensities to consume out of disposable income equal to each other, at about 0.85.

Inspection of the regression line in Figure 10-1 suggests that the estimated equation fits well. There are no points far off the fitted line. As a first approximation, then, Equation (2) provides a reasonable summary of consumption behaviour. However, Figure 10-2 gives a different perspective. It shows the annual changes in consumption

---

[2] You should check the *Canadian Economic Observer* to see how well Equation (2) predicts consumption for 1992. Disposable income in 1986 dollars can be obtained by dividing the current dollar figure by the implicit price index for personal consumption expenditure.

[3] Technically, the intercept is statistically not significantly different from zero. See Pindyck and Rubinfeld, *op. cit.*, for the meaning of tests of significance.

compared with the changes calculated from Equation (2). The errors are quite large, particularly in the 1980s. In addition, the predicted change remains above the actual change from 1978 to 1985 and below the actual change from 1986 to 1991. It appears that the simple consumption function in Equation (2) can be improved upon.

We develop the two basic modern theories of consumption in the remainder of this chapter. They are the *life-cycle* theory, associated primarily with Franco Modigliani[4] of the Massachusetts Institute of Technology, 1986 Nobel Prize winner in economic science, and the *permanent income* theory, associated primarily with Milton Friedman, formerly of the University of Chicago, the 1976 winner of the Nobel Prize in economics. These theories are quite similar. Like much of good macroeconomics, they have in common a careful attention to microeconomic foundations. The life-cycle theory in particular starts from an individual's lifetime consumption planning, and develops from there a macroeconomic theory of consumption and saving.

Box 10-1 describes an empirical puzzle about the simple consumption function that was historically important in leading to the new theories of the consumption function.[5]

10-1 The Life-Cycle Theory of Consumption and Saving

The consumption function (1) is based on the simple notion that individuals' consumption behaviour in a given period is related to their income in that period. The life-cycle hypothesis views individuals, instead, as planning their consumption and saving behaviour over long periods with the intention of allocating their consumption in the best possible way over their entire lifetimes.

The life-cycle hypothesis views savings as resulting mainly from individuals' desires to provide for consumption in old age. As we shall see, the theory points to a number of unexpected factors affecting the saving rate of the economy; for instance, the age structure of the population is, in principle, an important determinant of consumption and saving behaviour.

To anticipate the main results of this section, we state here that we will derive a consumption function of the form

---

[4] Modigliani developed the life-cycle theory together with Richard Brumberg, who died tragically young, and Albert Ando of the University of Pennsylvania. His Nobel Prize lecture, "Life Cycle, Individual Thrift, and the Wealth of Nations," appears in *American Economic Review*, June 1986.

[5] The theories of the consumption function developed hereafter are also useful for explaining another empirical puzzle. In *cross-sectional* studies of the relationship between consumption and income (studies in which the consumption of a sample of families is related to their income), the marginal propensity to consume out of disposable income also appears to be lower than the average propensity to consume, with the average propensity to consume falling as the level of income rises. If you are interested in the reconciliation of this evidence with the long-run evidence of Kuznets, you should look at the ingenious explanation advanced by Milton Friedman through the permanent-income hypothesis. Follow up the reference given in footnote 9.

$$C = aWR + cYL \qquad (3)$$

where WR is real wealth, a is the marginal propensity to consume out of wealth, YL is *labour income*, and c is the marginal propensity to consume out of labour income. Labour income is the income that is earned by labour, as opposed to the income earned by other factors of production, such as the rent earned by land or the profits earned by capital.

In developing the life-cycle hypothesis of saving and consumption, we show what determines the marginal propensities a and c in Equation (3), why wealth should affect consumption, and how the life-cycle hypothesis helps explain the Kuznets puzzle described in Box 10-1.

Consider a person who expects to live for NL years, work and earn income for WL years, and be in retirement for (NL − WL) years. The individual's year 1 is the first

---

Box 10-1 A Historical Consumption Function Puzzle

The puzzle consists of two types of evidence that made their appearance in the late 1940s and that were apparently in conflict. The first type of evidence came from estimates of the standard consumption function, Equation (1), using annual data for the U.S. for the 1929–1941 period. (No earlier data were available then.) The estimated equation (in 1972 dollars) is

$$C = 47.6 + 0.73YD \qquad \text{(annual data, 1929–1941)} \qquad (B1)$$

Using Canadian data for the period 1926–1940, the estimated equation (in 1971 dollars) is

$$C = 3.0 + 0.69YD \qquad \text{(annual data, Canada, 1926–1940)} \qquad (B2)$$

These equations imply that the average propensity to consume falls as the level of income rises. It also shows a low marginal propensity to consume. If we used Equation (2) to predict the 1990 average propensity to consume, the estimate would be 0.71, which is far from the actual ratio of 0.88.

The second piece of evidence was the finding by Nobel Prize winner Simon Kuznets (1901–1985), using averages of data over long periods — 10 and 30 years — that there was near proportionality between consumption and income.[a] The average propensity to consume that he found for three overlapping 30-year periods is shown in Table 1. The Kuznets results suggest, using long-term averages, that there is little variation in the ratio of consumption to income and, in particular, that there is no tendency for the average propensity to decline as disposable income rises. Proportionality, though with a higher average propensity to consume, is found also in the consumption function fitted with post–World War II data.

There is clearly a conflict between the implications of the consumption function in Equation (B1) and Kuznet's findings. The Kuznets results suggest that the average propensity to consume is constant over long periods, whereas Equation (B1) suggests it falls as income rises. It is also clear that the consumption function estimated above on the basis of prewar data is inconsistent with the same function estimated on the basis of postwar data, that is Equation (2).

The puzzle of the discrepancy was well known by the time the alternative theories we outline in this chapter were developed. In resolving the puzzle, both theories draw on the notion that consumption is related to a broader income measure than just current income. The broader measures go under the names of *lifetime income* and *permanent income*. These concepts have in common the recognition that consumption spending is maintained relatively constant in the face of fluctuations of current income. Consumption spending is not geared to what we earn today, but to what we earn on average. The important question, obviously, is what "average" means in this context. This is analyzed in the theories developed in this chapter.

Table I *Kuznets's Estimates of the Average Propensity to Consume*

1869–1898	1884–1913	1904–1933
0.867	0.867	0.879

Source: Kuznets, *op. cit.*, Table 16.

[a] Simon Kuznets, *National Product Since 1869 and National Income, A Summary of Findings* (New York: National Bureau of Economic Research, 1946).

year of work. We shall, in what follows, ignore any uncertainty about either life expectancy or the length of working life. We shall assume, too, that no interest is earned on savings, so that current saving translates dollar for dollar into future consumption possibilities. With these assumptions, we can approach the saving or consumption decision with two questions. First, what are the individual's lifetime consumption possibilities? Second, how will the individual choose to distribute his or her consumption over a lifetime?

Consider now the consumption possibilities. For the moment, we ignore property income (income from assets) and focus attention on labour income, YL. Income, YL, and consumption, C, are measured in real terms. Given WL years of working life, *lifetime income* (from labour) is $(YL \times WL)$, income per working year times the number of working years. Consumption over someone's lifetime cannot exceed this lifetime income unless that person is born with wealth, which we initially assume is not the case. Accordingly, we have determined the first part of the consumer's problem in finding the limit of lifetime consumption.

We assume the individual will want to distribute consumption over his or her lifetime so that he or she has a flat or even flow of consumption. Rather than consume a lot in one period and very little in another, the preferred profile is to consume exactly equal amounts in each period.[6] Clearly, this assumption implies that consumption is geared not to *current* income (zero during retirement), but rather to *lifetime* income.

Lifetime consumption equals lifetime income. This means that the planned level of consumption, C, which is the same in every period, times the number of years of life, NL, equals lifetime income:

$$C \times NL = YL \times WL \qquad (4)$$

Dividing through by NL, we have planned consumption per year, C, which is proportional to labour income:

$$C = \frac{WL}{NL} \times YL \qquad (5)$$

The factor of proportionality in Equation (5) is WL/NL, the fraction of lifetime spent working. Accordingly, Equation (5) states that in each year of working life a fraction of labour income is consumed, where that fraction is equal to the proportion of working life in total life.

Numerical example: Suppose a person starts working at age 20, plans to work till 65, and will die at 80. The working life, WL, is thus 45 years ($=65-20$) and the number of years of life, NL, is 60 years (= 80 − 20). Annual labour income, YL, is $30 000. Then

$$\begin{aligned} \text{Lifetime income} &= YL \times WL \\ &= \$30\,000 \times 45 \\ &= \$1\,350\,000 \end{aligned}$$

This person will receive a total of $1 350 000 over a working lifetime.

The lifetime income, $1 350 000, has to be spread over the 60 years of life. The consumer wants to spread it evenly, so

$$\begin{aligned} C &= \$1\,350\,000/60 = \$22\,500 = (WL/NL) \times YL \\ &= (45/60) \times \$30\,000 \\ &= 0.75 \times \$30\,000 \end{aligned}$$

---

[6] Why? The basic reason is the notion of diminishing marginal utility of consumption. Consider two alternative consumption plans. One involves an equal amount of consumption in each of two periods; the other involves consuming all in one period and none in the other. The principle of diminishing marginal utility of consumption implies that in the latter case, we would be better off by transferring some consumption from the period of plenty toward that of starvation. The loss in utility in the period of plenty is more than compensated for by the gain in utility in the period of scarcity, and there is a gain to be made by transferring consumption so long as there is any difference in consumption between the two periods. The principle of diminishing marginal utility of consumption conforms well with the observation that most people choose stable lifestyles — not, in general, saving furiously in one period to have a big bust in the next but, rather, consuming at about the same level every period.

In this example, 0.75 of labour income is consumed each year the person works. Why is the propensity to consume out of labour income in this example equal to 0.75? Because that is the fraction of lifetime that the person works.

Saving and Dissaving

The counterpart of Equation (5) is the saving function. Remembering that saving is equal to income less consumption, we have

$$S \equiv YL - C = YL \times \frac{NL - WL}{NL} \tag{6}$$

Equation (6) states that saving during the period in which the individual works is equal to a fraction of labour income, with that fraction being equal to the proportion of life spent in retirement.

Figure 10-3 shows the lifetime pattern of consumption, saving, and *dissaving*.[7] Over the whole lifetime, there is an even flow of consumption at the rate of C, amounting in total to $C \times NL$. That consumption spending is financed during working life out of current income. During retirement, the consumption is financed by drawing down the savings that have been accumulated during working life. Therefore the shaded areas $(YL - C) \times WL$ and $C \times (NL - WL)$ are equal; or, equivalently, saving during working years finances dissaving during retirement.

The important idea of the life-cycle theory of consumption is apparent from Figure 10-3. It is that consumption plans are made so as to achieve a smooth or even level of consumption by saving during periods of high income and dissaving during periods of low income. This is, therefore, an important departure from the treatment of consumption as being based on current income. It is an important difference because, in addition to current income, the whole future profile of income enters into the calculation of lifetime consumption. Before developing that aspect further, however, we return to Figure 10-3 to consider the role of assets.

Assets

During the working years, the individual saves to finance consumption during retirement. The saving builds up assets, and we accordingly show in Figure 10-3 how the individual's wealth or assets increase over working life and reach a maximum at retirement age. From that time on, assets decline because the individual sells assets to pay for current consumption.

---

[7] Figure 10-3 was developed by Franco Modigliani in "The Life Cycle Hypothesis of Saving, the Demand for Wealth and the Supply of Capital," *Social Research* 33, no. 2, 1966.

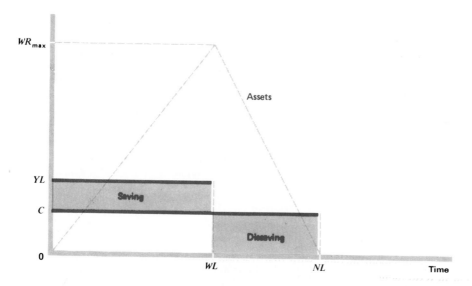

Figure 10-3 *Lifetime Income, Consumption, Savings, and Wealth in the Life-Cycle Model*

During the working life, lasting WL years, the individual saves, building up assets. At the end of the working life, the individual begins to live off these assets, dissaving for the next (NL − WL) years, till the end of life. Consumption is constant at level C throughout the lifetime. All assets have been used up at the end of life.

What is the maximum level that assets reach? Remember that assets are built up to finance consumption during retirement. Total consumption during retirement is equal to $C \times (NL - WL)$. All that consumption is financed out of the assets accumulated by the date of retirement, which is when assets are at their peak.

Denote the maximum level of assets by WR_{max}. Then,

$$WR_{max} = C \times (NL - WL)$$

For instance, in the numerical example above, where C was $22 500 and (NL − WL) was equal to 15, the individual would have $22 500 x 15 = $337 500 saved at the date of retirement. Equivalently, the person has worked for 45 years, saving $7500 each year, thus accumulating $337 500 at age 65.

This simple case gives the spirit of the life-cycle theory of consumption and saving. People do not want to consume over their lifetimes at precisely the same times and in the same amounts as they earn income. Thus they save and dissave so as to consume their lifetime incomes in the pattern they want. Typically, the theory argues, they will save while working, and then use the savings to finance spending in their retirement years.

Saving

The life-cycle theory of consumption is also of course a theory of life-cycle saving. In its simplest version, as in Figure 10-3, the theory implies that individuals save for their retirement while working, but there is a more general theory of saving implied by the life-cycle theory. Namely, individuals aim to have smooth patterns of consumption over their lifetimes. Their income patterns may not be so smooth: They may go to school at one stage, or retire at another, or take a year off to find themselves at the age of 40. *The life-cycle theory of saving predicts that people save a lot when their income is high relative to lifetime average income, and dissave when their income is low relative to the lifetime average.*

Introducing Wealth

The next step is to extend this model by allowing for initial assets, that is, by assuming the individual was born into wealth.[8] We can draw on the previous insight that the consumer will spread any existing resources to achieve an even lifetime consumption profile. The individual who has assets in addition to labour income will plan to use these assets to add to lifetime consumption. A person who is at some point T in life, with a stock of wealth, WR, and with labour income accruing for another $(WL - T)$ years at the rate of YL, and with a life expectancy of $(NL - T)$ years to go, will behave as follows. The person's lifetime consumption possibilities are

$$C \times (NL - T) = WR + (WL - T) \times YL \qquad (7)$$

where we have included wealth, WR, along with lifetime labour income as a source of finance for lifetime consumption. From Equation (7), consumption in each period is equal to

$$C = aWR + cYL \qquad a = \frac{1}{NL - T} \qquad c = \frac{WL - T}{NL - T} \qquad WL > T \qquad (8)$$

where the coefficients a and c are, respectively, the marginal propensities to consume out of wealth and out of labour income.

In the numerical example above, we considered a person starting to work at age 20 who will retire at 65 and die at 80. Thus, $WL = 65 - 20 = 45$; and $NL = (80 - 20) = 60$. We also assumed $YL = 30\ 000$.

Now suppose the person is 40 years old. Accordingly $T = 20$, meaning that the person is in the twentieth year of working life. We can calculate the propensity to

---

[8] The individual may receive wealth early in life through gifts or bequests. In the fully developed life-cycle model, the individual, in calculating lifetime consumption, has also to take account of any bequests he or she may want to leave. We discuss the role of bequests in Box 10-2.

consume out of wealth, a, and the propensity to consume out of income, c, from Equation (8). For this person, at age 40 (i.e., for $T = 20$):

$$a = 1/(NL - T) = 1/(60 - 20) = 0.025$$
$$c = (WL - T)/(NL - T) = (45 - 20)/(60 - 20) = 0.625$$

Suppose now that the individual's wealth is \$200 000. Then from the consumption function, Equation (8), we find:

$$C = (0.025 \times 200\,000) + (0.625 \times 30\,000)$$
$$= 5000 + 18\,750$$
$$= 23\,750$$

Note that the consumption level here is higher than in the previous example. That is because this individual has more wealth at age 40 than he or she would have if all this wealth came from saving out of labour income. (That amount would be \$150 000, since the individual in the previous example saved \$7500 per year and, at $T = 20$, has been working 20 years.) We can conclude that we are dealing here with someone who started out working life with inherited wealth.

Thus, in our model of individual lifetime consumption, we have derived a consumption function like Equation (3), in which both wealth and labour income affect the individual's consumption decisions. It is important to recognize from Equation (8) that the marginal propensities are related to the individual's position in the life cycle. The closer a person is to the end of his or her lifetime, the higher the marginal propensity to consume out of wealth. Thus, someone with two more years of life will consume half his or her remaining wealth in each of the remaining two years. The marginal propensity to consume out of labour income is related both to the remaining number of years during which income will be earned, $WL - T$, and to the number of years over which these earnings are spread, $NL - T$. It is quite clear from Equation (8) that an increase in either wealth or labour income will raise consumption expenditures. It is apparent, too, that lengthening working life relative to retirement will raise consumption because it increases lifetime income and reduces the length of the period of dissaving. The most basic point, however, is that Equation (8) shows both (lifetime) income and wealth as determinants of consumption spending.

To summarize where we have come so far, we note that in this particular form of the life-cycle model:

1. Consumption is constant over the consumer's lifetime.

2. Consumption spending is financed by lifetime income plus initial wealth.

3. During each year a fraction, $1/(NL - T)$, of wealth will be consumed, where $NL - T$ is the individual's life expectancy.

4. Current consumption spending depends on current wealth and lifetime income.

Extensions

The model as outlined makes very strong simplifying assumptions. It can be extended to remove most of the strong assumptions without affecting the underlying result of Equation (8), namely that consumption is related to both labour income and wealth.

First, it is necessary to take account of the possibility that savings earn interest, so that a dollar not consumed today will provide more than a dollar's consumption tomorrow. Second, the analysis has to be extended to allow for the fact that individuals are uncertain of the length of their lifetimes and, also, that they sometimes want to leave bequests to their heirs. In the latter case, they would not plan to consume all their resources over their own lifetimes. Similarly, the model has to be extended to take account of the composition of the family over time, so that some consumption is provided for children before they begin to work. These extensions are important and have interesting implications for the behaviour of consumption, but — as stated above — they do not change the basic result contained in Equation (8).

A final extension is very important. In practice, one never knows exactly what one's lifetime labour income will be, and lifetime consumption plans have to be made on the basis of predictions of future labour income. This, of course, raises the issue of how income is to be predicted. We do not pursue the issue here, but leave it to the next section on permanent income, which is an estimate of lifetime income. However, *expected* lifetime labour income would be related to *current* disposable labour income, leading to a form of the consumption function like Equation (3), perhaps with other variables also included.

Indeed, it is useful to think of the life-cycle and permanent-income theories as being fundamentally the same, with the life-cycle theory developing most carefully the implications of the model for the role of wealth and other variables in the consumption function, and the permanent-income theory concentrating on the best way to predict lifetime income.

Aggregate Consumption and Saving

The theory outlined so far is strictly a microeconomic theory about consumption and saving by individuals over the course of their lifetimes. How does it relate to aggregate consumption, which is, after all, the focus of macroeconomic interest in consumption? Imagine an economy in which population and the GDP were constant through time. Each individual in that economy would go through the life cycle of saving and dissaving outlined in Figure 10-3. The economy as a whole, though, would not be saving. At any one time, the saving of working people would be exactly matched by the dissaving of retired people. However, if the population were growing, there would be more young people than old, thus more saving in total than dissaving, and there would be net saving in the economy. Thus, aggregate consumption depends in part on the age distribution of the population. It also depends on such characteristics of the economy as the average age of retirement and the presence or absence of government pensions. These surprising implications of the theory indicate the richness of the approach.

Implications

We return to Equation (3) to emphasize again the role of wealth. Note from Equation (3) that with an increase in wealth, the ratio of consumption to disposable income would rise. This has a bearing on the puzzle described in Box 10-1. On the basis of Equation (B1), the average propensity to consume seems to decline with income but, on the basis of Kuznets's findings, remain constant over long periods.

If we divide through in Equation (8) by YD, we obtain

$$\frac{C}{YD} = a\frac{WR}{YD} + c\frac{YL}{YD} \tag{9}$$

Now, if the ratio of wealth to disposable income and the ratio of disposable labour income to total disposable income are constant, then Equation (9) shows that the ratio of consumption to disposable income will be constant. However, if the ratio of wealth to disposable income is changing, the average propensity to consume will also be changing.

This suggests, as an explanation of the Kuznets puzzle, the possibility that the ratio of wealth to disposable income is roughly constant over long periods and that it varies considerably in the short run. This also helps explain the fluctuations in consumption shown in Figure 10-2, as resulting from short-run changes in the wealth–income ratio.

The life-cycle hypothesis also provides a channel for the stock market to affect consumption behaviour. The value of stocks held by the public is part of wealth and is included in WR in Equation (8). When the value of stocks is high — when the stock market is booming — WR is high and tends to increase consumption, and the reverse occurs when the stock market is depressed.

We continue now to the permanent-income theory of consumption, bearing in mind that we have not yet discussed the determinants of expected lifetime labour income in Equation (9) in any detail, and recalling that the two theories should be thought of as complementary rather than competing.

Box 10-2 The Life-Cycle Hypothesis, Consumption by the Elderly, and Bequests

Although the life-cycle hypothesis remains the leading microeconomic theory of consumption behaviour, recent empirical evidence raises questions about the particular form of the theory developed in this chapter. In the form of the theory developed by Modigliani, the assumption is that people save mainly for retirement and draw down their savings during that period.

There is some evidence contesting the assumed motive for saving and the implication that people draw down their savings when old. Laurence Kotlikoff and Lawrence

Summers have made calculations suggesting that most saving is done to provide bequests rather than to provide for consumption when old.[a] Of course, the savings are there for the old to use in retirement, but, they argue, the amount of wealth in the economy is far too large for people to have been saving only for their retirement. Rather, they conclude, people are saving mainly to pass wealth on to their descendants.

A detailed examination of the consumption propensities of the elderly by Sheldon Danziger, Jacques van der Gaag, Eugene Smolensky, and Michael Taussig contains the remarkable conclusion that the elderly save a higher proportion of their incomes than the young.[b] This fact is inconsistent with the simple form of the life-cycle hypothesis set out in this chapter.

How might this evidence be reconciled with existing theories? First, the facts are not yet definitive. Franco Modigliani has taken strong issue with the detailed calculations that underlie the Kotlikoff–Summers claim.[c] In Japan, where similar results have been found, the elderly typically move in and pool their wealth with their children.[d] They are thus probably drawing down wealth during their retirement, but their wealth cannot be distinguished from that of the children, who are saving.

If the basic evidence that the elderly who remain on their own accumulate wealth holds up, an explanation will have to take into account their increasing fears of being left alone without financial help from family, and with possibly large medical expenses, as they get older. The need for wealth may increase with age if complete insurance against medical expenses is not available, as it is not in the United States.

Whether people save for their own lifetimes, or also save to pass wealth on to their children, including transfers that take place during the parents' lifetime such as paying for university education, does not affect the fact that wealth belongs in the consumption function, as in Equation (3). However, as Section 10-4 shows, the question of the goals of saving has potentially important implications for the effects of fiscal policy on the economy.

[a] "The Role of Intergenerational Transfers in Aggregate Capital Accumulation," *Journal of Political Economy*, August 1981.

[b] "The Life Cycle Hypothesis and the Consumption Behaviour of the Elderly," *Journal of Post-Keynesian Economics*, Winter 1982–1983.

[c] "The Role of Intergenerational Transfers and Life Cycle Saving in the Accumulation of Wealth," *Journal of Economic Perspectives* 2 (Spring 1988). See also the discussion of this article by Laurence Kotlikoff that follows in the journal.

[d] See Albert Ando and Arthur Kennickell, "How Much (or Little) Life Cycle Saving Is There in Micro Data?" in *Macroeconomics and Finance: Essays in Honor of Franco Modigliani*, edited by Rudiger Dornbusch, Stanley Fischer, and John Bossons (Cambridge, Mass.: MIT Press, 1986).

10-2 Permanent-Income Theory of Consumption

In the long run, the consumption–income ratio is very stable, but in the short run, it fluctuates. The life-cycle approach explains this by pointing out that people want to maintain a smooth profile of consumption even if their lifetime income profile is uneven, and thus emphasizes the role of wealth in the consumption function. Another explanation, which differs in details from but entirely shares the spirit of the life-cycle approach, is the permanent-income theory of consumption.

The theory, which is the work of Milton Friedman,[9] argues that people gear their consumption behaviour to their permanent or long-term consumption opportunities, not to their current level of income. A suggestive example provided by Friedman involves someone who is paid or receives income only once a week, on Fridays. We do not expect that individual to concentrate his or her entire consumption on the one day on which income is received, with zero consumption on all the other days. Again we are persuaded by the argument that individuals prefer a smooth consumption flow rather than plenty today and scarcity tomorrow or yesterday. On that argument, consumption on any one day of the week would be unrelated to income on that particular day but would, rather, be geared to average daily income — that is, income per week divided by the number of days per week. It is clear that in this extreme example, income for a period longer than a day is relevant to the consumption decision. Similarly, Friedman argues, there is nothing special about a period of the length of one quarter or one year that requires the individual to plan consumption within the period solely on the basis of income within the period; rather, consumption is planned in relation to income over a longer period.

The idea of consumption spending that is geared to long-term or average or permanent income is appealing and essentially is the same as the life-cycle theory. It leaves two further questions. The first concerns the precise relationship between current consumption and permanent income. The second question is how to make the concept of permanent income operational, that is, how to measure it.

In its simplest form, the permanent-income hypothesis of consumption behaviour argues that consumption is proportional to permanent income:

$$C = cYP \tag{10}$$

where YP is permanent (disposable) income. From Equation (10), consumption varies in the same proportion as permanent income. A 5 percent increase in permanent income raises consumption by 5 percent. Since permanent income should be related to long-run average income, this feature of the consumption function is clearly in line with the observed long-run constancy of the consumption–income ratio.

Estimating Permanent Income

The next problem is how to think of and measure permanent income. We define permanent income as follows:[10] Permanent income is the steady rate of consumption

---

[9] Milton Friedman, *A Theory of the Consumption Function* (Princeton, N.J.: Princeton University Press, 1957).

[10] There is no standard definition of permanent income in Friedman's exposition of his theory. The definition given above is similar to average lifetime income, but it is not quite the same, because it effectively converts wealth into income in defining permanent income. Those with no labour income and only wealth are defined as having permanent income equal to the amount they could consume each year by using up wealth at a steady rate over the remainder of their lives.

a person could maintain for the rest of his or her life, given the present level of wealth and income earned now and in the future.

To think about the measurement of permanent income, imagine someone trying to figure out what his or her permanent income is. The person has a current level of income and has formed some idea of the level of consumption he or she can maintain for the rest of life. Now income goes up. The person has to decide whether that income increase represents a permanent increase or merely a *transitory* change, one that will not persist. In any particular case, the individual may know whether the increase is permanent or transitory. A government official who is promoted one grade will know that the increase in income is likely to be maintained, and a worker who has exceptionally high overtime in a given year will likely regard that year's increased income as transitory. However, a person is often not so certain about what part of any change in income is likely to be maintained and is therefore permanent, and what part is not likely to be maintained and is therefore transitory. Transitory income is assumed to have no substantial effect on consumption.

The question of how to infer what part of an increase in income is permanent is typically resolved in a pragmatic way by assuming that permanent income is related to the behaviour of current and past incomes. To give a simple example, we might estimate permanent income as being equal to last year's income plus some fraction of the change in income from last year to this year:

$$YP = Y_{-1} + \theta(Y - Y_{-1}) \qquad 0 < \theta < 1 \tag{11}$$
$$= \theta Y + (1 - \theta)Y_{-1}$$

where θ is a fraction and Y_{-1} is last year's income. The second line in Equation (11) shows permanent income as a *weighted average* of current and past income. The second formulation is, of course, equivalent to that in the first line.

To understand Equation (11), assume we had a value of $\theta = 0.6$, that this year's income was $Y = \$25\ 000$, and that last year's income was $Y_{-1} = \$24\ 000$. The value of permanent income would be $YP = \$24\ 600$ ($= 0.6 \times \$25\ 000 + 0.4 \times \$24\ 000$). Thus, permanent income is an average of the two income levels. Whether it is closer to this year's or last year's income depend. on the weight, θ, given to current income. Clearly, in the extreme, with $\theta = 1$, permanent income is equal to current income.

Some special features of Equation (11) deserve comment. First, if $Y = Y_{-1}$, that is, if this year's income is equal to last year's, then permanent income is equal to the income earned this year and last year. This guarantees that an individual who had always earned the same income would expect to earn that income in the future. Second, note that if income rises this year compared with last year, then permanent income rises by less than current income. The reason is that the individual does not know whether the rise in income this year is permanent. Not knowing whether the increase in income will be maintained or not, the individual does not immediately increase the expected or permanent income measure by the full amount of the actual or current increase in income.

Rational Expectations and Permanent Income

An estimate of permanent income that uses only current and last year's income is likely to be an oversimplification. Friedman forms the estimate by looking at incomes in many earlier periods, as well as current income, but with weights that are larger for the more recent, as compared with the more distant, incomes.[11]

The rational expectations approach, discussed in Chapter 8 and in the following section, emphasizes that there is no simple theory that would tell us how expectations are or should be formed without looking at how income changes in practice. If, in practice, changes in income are typically permanent or long-run changes, then consumers who see a given change in their income will believe that it is mostly permanent. Such consumers would have a high θ in Equation (11). Consumers whose income is usually very variable will, however, not pay much attention to current changes in income in forming an estimate of permanent income. Such consumers will have low values of θ.[12]

At the same time, any sensible theory of expectations, including rational expectations, would emphasize that a formula like (11), based on the behaviour of income in the past, cannot include all the factors that influence a person's beliefs about future income. The discovery of a vast amount of oil in a country, for instance, would raise the permanent incomes of the inhabitants of the country as soon as it was announced, even though a (mechanical) formula like Equation (11), based on past levels of income, would not reflect such a change.

Permanent Income and the Dynamics of Consumption

Using Equations (10) and (11), we can now rewrite the consumption function:

$$C = cYP = c\theta Y + c(1 - \theta)Y_{-1} \qquad (12)$$

The marginal propensity to consume out of current income is then just $c\theta$, which is clearly less than the long-run average propensity to consume, c. Hence, the permanent-income hypothesis implies that there is a difference between the short-run marginal propensity to consume and the long-run marginal (equal to the average) propensity to consume.

The reason for the lower short-run marginal propensity to consume is that when current income rises, the individual is not sure that the increase in income will be maintained over the longer period on which consumption plans are based. Accordingly,

---

[11] Friedman also adjusts permanent income by taking into account the growth of income over time.

[12] Recall that although we restricted our measure of permanent income to a two-year average, there is no reason why the average should not be taken over longer periods. If current income is unstable, an appropriate measure of permanent income may well be an average over five or more years, perhaps adjusted for the fact that income is on average growing over time.

the person does not fully adjust consumption spending to the higher level that would be appropriate if the increase in income were permanent. However, if the increase turns out to be permanent, that is, if next period's income is the same as this period's, then the person will (next year) fully adjust consumption spending to the higher level of income. Note, though, that the adjustment here is completed in 2 years only because we have assumed, in Equation (11), that permanent income is an average of 2 years' income. Depending on how expectations of permanent income are formed, the adjustment could be much slower, or, if the consumer knew that this year's increase in income was permanent, he or she would increase consumption more rapidly than indicated by Equation (12).[13]

The argument is illustrated in Figure 10-4. Here we show the long-run consumption function as a straight line through the origin with slope c, which is the constant average and marginal propensity to consume out of permanent income. The lower flat consumption function is a short-run consumption function drawn for a given history of income which is reflected in the intercept $c(1 - \theta)Y_0$. Assume that we start out in long-run equilibrium with actual and permanent income equal to Y_0 and consumption therefore equal to cY_0, as is shown at the intersection, point E, of the long-run and short-run consumption functions. Assume next that income increases to the level Y'. In the short run, which means during the current period, we revise our estimate of permanent income upward by θ times the increase in income and consume a fraction, c, of that increase in permanent income. Accordingly, consumption moves up along the short-run consumption function to point E'.

Note immediately that in the short run the ratio of consumption to income declines as we move from point E to E'. Going one period ahead and assuming that the increase in income persists, so that income remains at Y', we get a shift in the consumption function. The consumption function shifts upward because, as of the given higher level of income, the estimate of permanent income is now revised upward to Y'. Accordingly, consumers want to spend a fraction of c of their new estimate of permanent income, Y'. The new consumption point is E'', at which the ratio of consumption to income is back to the long-run level. The example makes clear that in the short run, an increase in income causes a decline in the average propensity to consume because people do not anticipate that the increase in income will persist or be permanent. Once they observe that the increase in income does persist, however, they fully adjust consumption to match their higher permanent income.

Like the life-cycle hypothesis, the permanent-income hypothesis has some unexpected and interesting implications. For instance, we noted above that an individual whose income is very unstable would have a low value of θ, whereas one whose income is more stable would have a higher value of θ. Looking at Equation (12), this means

---

13   There is another reason consumption may adjust relatively slowly even to changes in permanent income: The consumer may take time to purchase consumer durables. For instance, someone whose permanent income has doubled will at some point end up in a more luxurious house, but will take some time to buy such a house and the furnishings that go with it. Here, as in much of economic life, there are two reasons for slow adjustment to changes: Expectations change slowly, and there are lags in adjusting to changed circumstances.

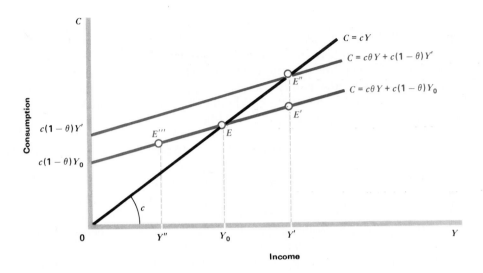

Figure 10-4 *The Effects on Consumption of a Sustained Increase in Income*

The short-run consumption functions, shown in colour, have marginal propensity to consume of $c\theta$. The position of the short-run consumption function depends on the level of income in the previous period. The long-run consumption function is shown by the black line and has average and marginal propensity to consume equal to c. When the level of income rises from Y_0 to Y', consumption rises only to E' in the short run, because consumers are not sure the change in income is permanent. With income remaining at Y', the short-run consumption function shifts up and consumption rises to point E'', as consumers realize their permanent income has changed.

that the short-run marginal propensity to consume of someone whose income is very variable will be relatively low because the short-run marginal propensity to consume is $c\theta$. Friedman showed that this implication is borne out by the facts. Farmers, for instance, have very variable incomes and a low marginal propensity to consume out of current income.

The Life-Cycle and Permanent-Income Hypotheses

To conclude this section, it is worth briefly considering again the relationship between the life-cycle and permanent-income hypotheses. The two hypotheses are not mutually exclusive. The life-cycle hypothesis pays more attention to the motives for saving than the permanent-income hypothesis does, and provides convincing reasons to include wealth as well as income in the consumption function. The permanent-income hypothesis, on the other hand, pays more careful attention to the way in which individuals form expectations about their future incomes than the original life-cycle hypothesis does. Recall that current labour income entered into the life-cycle consumption function to reflect expectations of future income. The more detailed analysis of the determinants of expected future income that is provided by the permanent-income hypothesis can be, and has been, included in the life-cycle consumption function.

Indeed, modern theories of the consumption function combine the expectations formation emphasized by the permanent-income approach with the emphasis on wealth and demographic variables suggested by the life-cycle approach. A simplified version of a modern consumption function would be

$$C = aWR + b\theta YD + b(1 - \theta)YD_{-1} \tag{13}$$

where YD in Equation (13) would be disposable labour income. Equation (13) combines the main features that are emphasized by modern consumption theory.[14] It also shows the role of wealth, which is an important influence on consumption spending.

We end this section by repeating a warning. An equation like (13) performs quite well on average in predicting consumption, but it is always important to remember the underlying theory when using it. Equation (13) embodies the estimate of permanent income implied by Equation (11). If we have knowledge about some particular change in income — for example, that it is transitory — then we should use that knowledge in predicting consumption. For instance, as we shall see, a temporary one-year tax increase that reduced current disposable income would reduce current consumption by much less than a tax increase of the same size that was known to be permanent, even though Equation (13) does not show that.

10-3 Rational Expectations, Excess Sensitivity, and Liquidity Constraints

One of the most fascinating areas of research in modern consumption theory concerns the question of whether consumption responds excessively to changes in current income. Modern research in this area, originating with work by Robert Hall of Stanford University and Marjorie Flavin of the University of Virginia, focuses on the combined implications of rational expectations and the life-cycle–permanent-income theory of consumption.[15]

In the previous section we noted that if expectations are rational, consumers' estimates of their permanent incomes should be consistent with the way income actually

---

[14] To fix these ideas, you should draw a graph of Equation (13) with consumption on the vertical axis and current disposable labour income on the horizontal axis. What is the intercept? How does the diagram differ from Figure 10-4? Show the effects of (1) a transitory increase in income, (2) a sustained increase in income, and (3) an increase in wealth.

[15] See Robert E. Hall, "Stochastic Implications of the Life Cycle–Permanent Income Hypothesis: Theory and Evidence," *Journal of Political Economy* 86, December 1978; and Marjorie Flavin, "The Adjustment of Consumption to Changing Expectations about Future Income," *Journal of Political Economy* 89, October 1981.

changes in the real world. When current income increases, it is usually impossible to be certain whether this increase represents a transitory or a permanent rise in income, but the consumer can use experience to determine what is the expected relationship between changes in current and in permanent income. For example, historically a $1 increase in current income might typically have represented a 25-cent increase in permanent income, with the remaining 75 cents being transitory. Let θ be the fraction of a dollar increase in current income that represents the permanent increase. Then the consumption function in (10) together with this extra information about the current-income–permanent-income relation will yield a propensity to consume out of current income equal to $c\theta$. Thus, if $c = 0.9$ and $\theta = 0.25$, the marginal propensity to consume out of current income should be 0.225, as implied by Equation (12).

The researcher determines the value of θ, the proportion of a current change in income that is permanent, by examining the past behaviour of income.[16] The next step is to see whether consumption reacts to the change in income by the right amount, $c\theta$, implied by the combined rational expectations–permanent-income theory. The striking finding, for instance in Flavin's 1981 paper referred to above, is that consumption *systematically* responds too much to current income, or is excessively sensitive. When income rises, consumption goes up by more than $c\theta$, and when income falls, consumption goes down by more than $c\theta$.[17]

On the assumption, still, that the permanent-income hypothesis serves as a correct framework of consumption behaviour, there are two possible explanations for this overreaction. The first is that households do not correctly understand how changes in income are to be divided between those that are permanent and those that are transitory. This shortcoming is called a failure of the rational expectations hypothesis; it implies that households have not done their homework and are not forecasting in the best possible way and using all available information about how income behaves. For simplicity, we can call this the *myopia hypothesis*, where myopia means shortsightedness. The alternative hypothesis is that while households in fact understand how income changes are divided between those that are permanent and those that are transitory, they fail to adjust to these changes properly because of *liquidity constraints*.

Excess Sensitivity, Liquidity Constraints, and Myopia

A liquidity constraint exists when a consumer cannot borrow to sustain current consumption in the expectation of higher future income. Students in particular should

---

16 Income changes over time in a more complicated way than is implied by Equation (11), but that does not affect the principle that the test figures out how *estimated* permanent income should change with current income, and then sees whether changes in consumption are in accord with that estimate.

17 More recently, Angus Deaton of Princeton University has argued that consumption may be too insensitive to changes in income or, as he puts it, excessively smooth. See, for instance, his paper, "Life-Cycle Models of Consumption: Is the Evidence Consistent With the Theory?" in *Advances in Econometrics, Fifth World Congress*, Vol. 2, edited by Truman Bewley (New York: Cambridge University Press, 1987). The issue turns on the nature of the behaviour of income, with Deaton essentially arguing that changes in income tend to be more permanent than other researchers have believed. The issue is as yet unsettled.

appreciate the possibility that liquidity constraints exist. Most students can look forward to a much higher income in the future than they receive as students. The life-cycle theory says they should be consuming on the basis of their lifetime incomes, which means they should be spending much more than they earn. To do that, they would have to borrow. They can borrow to some extent, through student loan plans, but it is entirely possible that they cannot borrow enough to support consumption at its permanent level.

Such students are liquidity-constrained. When they leave university and take jobs, their incomes will rise, and their consumption will rise, too. According to the life-cycle theory, consumption should not rise much when income rises, so long as the increase was expected. In fact, because of the liquidity constraint, consumption will rise a lot when income rises. Thus consumption will be more closely related to *current* income than is implied by the theory.

Alternatively, consider a household that suffers a decline in current income and that believes the decline is transitory because in the past, on average, falls in income have been mostly transitory. The household would therefore maintain consumption substantially unchanged, dissaving today. If there are no assets to run down to finance the excess of consumption over income, the household would borrow today, repaying the loan when income rises again as expected. Here imperfect capital markets come in. If the household cannot borrow because nobody wants to lend against uncertain (though likely) future income, then it faces liquidity constraints and for that reason is forced to consume according to current rather than permanent income. Consumption will then fall substantially along with current income — an overreaction, in terms of the permanent-income theory, that occurs because of the impossibility of borrowing.

How serious are these liquidity constraints in fact? There is substantial evidence that liquidity constraints help account for the excess sensitivity of consumption to income, and separate evidence that low-income households are indeed liquidity-constrained.[18] When liquidity constraints are present, consumption behaves more like the simple Keynesian consumption function Equation (2) than life-cycle theory implies.

The strength of liquidity constraints will depend on economic conditions. Suppose the government initiates a tax cut. If we are in a period of deep recession during which many households have already run down their assets, the tax cut will translate into a large increase in spending: Liquidity-constrained household members, by definition, are spending less than they would like and hence will spend every extra penny they can lay their hands on. By contrast, a tax cut that occurs in a period of prosperity will have much less of an impact because few households are in a liquidity-constrained position in which they spend, at the margin, all of an extra dollar of income.

The alternative explanation for the sensitivity of consumption to current income, that consumers are myopic, is hard to distinguish in practice from the liquidity con-

---

[18] For instance, Marjorie Flavin, "Excess Sensitivity of Consumption to Current Income: Liquidity Constraints or Myopia?" *Canadian Journal of Economics* 18, February 1985; Fumio Hayashi, "The Effect of Liquidity Constraints on Consumption: A Cross-Sectional Analysis," *Quarterly Journal of Economics* 100, February 1985; and Stephen P. Zeldes, "Consumption and Liquidity Constraints: An Empirical Investigation," *Journal of Political Economy* 97, April 1989.

straints hypothesis. For instance, David Wilcox, an economist with the U.S. Federal Reserve, has shown that the announcement that social security benefits will be increased (which always happens at least six weeks before the change) does not lead to a change in consumption *until the benefit increases are actually paid.*[19] Once the increased benefits are paid, recipients certainly do adjust spending — primarily on durables. This could be either because recipients do not have the assets to enable them to adjust spending before they receive higher payments (liquidity constraints), or because they fail to pay attention to the announcements (myopia), or perhaps because they do not believe the announcements.

10-4 Further Aspects of Consumption Behaviour

In this section we briefly review three topics in consumption, starting with international comparisons of saving behaviour.

International Differences in Saving Rates

The most commonly quoted comparison of saving rates internationally is that which shows household saving rates as a percentage of disposable income (See Box 10-3 for a Canada–U.S. comparison). The data in Table 10-1 are, however, more relevant to the concern over economic growth, which is related to total saving as a share of GNP rather than to household saving as a share of disposable income. Total saving includes the saving of corporations that use part of their profits to reinvest in the business rather than paying the money out to their shareholders.[20]

Government saving increases national saving, and government dissaving (budget deficits) reduces national saving. A good part of the difference among national saving rates is accounted for by differences in government saving rates. Thus for the period 1981–1987 the Japanese government sector saved 6.6 percent of GNP more than the Canadian government sector. The Italian government ran such large budget deficits that it used up a large part of the available (and comparatively large) private sector saving, which was therefore not available to finance investment.

---

[19] David W. Wilcox, "Social Security Benefits, Consumption Expenditure, and the Life Cycle Hypothesis," *Journal of Political Economy* 97, April 1989. For another study that suggests that many consumers essentially consume all their current income, see John Campbell and N. Gregory Mankiw, "Consumption, Income, and Interest Rates: Reinterpreting the Time Series Evidence," *NBER Macroeconomics Annual*, 1989.

[20] A major question that has been examined in the literature is whether households "pierce the corporate veil" when businesses that they own undertake saving, and save correspondingly less themselves. There is some evidence to this effect for the United States, in the fact that the sum of corporate and household savings has been reasonably stable. This is known as Denison's law, after Edward Denison of the Brookings Institution. See Paul David and Jon Scadding, "Private Savings: Ultrarationality, Aggregation, and 'Denison's Law'," *Journal of Political Economy* 82, March/April 1974.

Table 10-1 *International Comparisons of Saving Rates, 1981–1987*

(percent)						
	U.S.	**Japan**	**Germany**	**U.K.**	**Italy**	**Canada**
Net national saving[a]	3.9	20.2	10.7	6.2	7.5	9.4
Gross national saving[b]	16.3	31.1	21.8	17.5	15.6	20.3
Gross private saving[b]	18.7	26.8	20.0	18.4	21.7	22.5
Government saving[b]	−2.4	4.3	1.8	−0.9[c]	−6.0	−2.2

[a]As percentage of NNP.
[b]As percentage of GNP.
[c]Adjusted to account for apparent discrepancy in original data.

Source: OECD, *Historical Statistics.*

The difference between net and gross national saving rates (the first two rows of the table) arises from the depreciation of the capital stock. However, it is widely suspected that data on depreciation are highly unsatisfactory, and economists are therefore generally reluctant to put much weight on net saving rates.

However suspect the data may be, there is no question that there is an enormous difference between the national saving rates (whether gross or net) in Japan and other countries. The United States is among the lowest gross savers in the group and is far and away the lowest net saver. The concern in the United States over this low saving rate is really a concern over the low growth rate of the American economy; the high-saving countries in Table 10-1 are indeed the rapidly growing countries.

While demographic factors appear to account for some of the differences in national saving rates, there has not yet been a satisfactory explanation that accounts for most of the differences. This is a major challenge for consumption theory. Some economists will in the end argue that there may simply be differences in national attitudes toward saving, but most hope to find economic explanations for those underlying attitudes.

Some differences among national saving rates appear to be due to differences in government saving rates, but as we shall see below, there is even a question as to whether the private sector might not systematically offset the impact of changes in government saving.

Consumption, Saving, and Interest Rates

What can be done about a low saving rate? One suggestion is to make saving more worthwhile for the saver. Anyone who saves receives a return in the form of interest or of dividends and capital gains (an increase in the price) on stocks. It seems, then, that the natural way to raise saving is to raise the return available to savers. Think of

Box 10-3   Saving Rates in Canada and the U.S.

As shown in Table 2 below, the private saving rates in Canada have been substantially larger than those in the United States. The analysis of Carroll and Summers[a] suggests that differences in tax structures between the two countries were an important factor in explaining this divergence. The Canadian personal income tax provided greater incentives for saving through deductibility of contributions to Registered Pension Plans and Registered Retirement Savings Plans. In contrast, the U.S. personal income tax provided disincentives to save through the deductibility of interest paid on loans incurred to purchase durable goods and housing.

Table 2   *Saving in Canada and the U.S., 1983–1985*

		(percent of GNP)		
	Corporate	**Personal**	**Government**	**Total**
Canada	3.5	8.9	− 5.3	7.1
U.S.	2.3	3.9	− 3.3	2.9

Source: Carroll and Summers, *op. cit.*

[a]Chris Carroll and Lawrence H. Summers, "Why Have Private Saving Rates in the United States and Canada Diverged?" National Bureau of Economic Research, Working Paper No. 2319, 1987.

someone saving and receiving an interest rate of 5 percent each year for each dollar saved. Surely an increase in the rate to, say, 10 percent would make that person save more.

But should we really expect an increase in the interest rate to increase savings? It is true that when the interest rate rises, saving is made more attractive, but it is also made less necessary. Consider someone who has decided to save an amount that will ensure that $10 000 per year will be available for retirement. Suppose the interest rate is now 5 percent, and the person is saving $1000 per year. Now let the interest rate rise to 10 percent. With such a high interest rate, the individual needs to save less now to provide the given $10 000 per year during retirement. It may be possible to provide the same retirement income by saving only about $650 a year. Thus an increase in the interest rate might reduce saving.

What do the facts show? Does saving rise when the interest rate increases because every dollar of saving generates a higher return, or does saving fall because there is less need to save to provide a given level of future income? The answers from the data are ambiguous. Many researchers have examined this question, but few have found strong positive effects of interest rate increases on saving. Typically, research suggests the effects are small and certainly hard to find.[21]

Tax Cuts, the Barro–Ricardo Hypothesis, and Saving

A proposition that tax cuts will increase saving and have little effect on consumption, originally noted and rejected by David Ricardo in the nineteenth century, was revived and supported in 1974 by Robert Barro of Harvard University.[22] Here is the argument: Suppose the budget is balanced initially, and the government cuts taxes. There will be a budget deficit, financed by borrowing. The debt that is issued today must be retired next year or in some future year, along with the interest that it carries. To repay the debt, the government will have to raise taxes in the future. Thus a tax cut today means a tax increase in the future. Hence permanent income is really unaffected by this intertemporal shifting of tax rates.

However, if permanent income is unaffected by the tax cut, then consumption should be unaffected. When taxes are cut today, households save the tax cut so that they can pay the higher taxes tomorrow. Of course households may not in fact behave in exactly the way prescribed by the Barro–Ricardo hypothesis. They may see themselves as recipients of present tax cuts, but (perhaps rationally) they may not see themselves but rather future generations (in whose well-being they are not especially interested) as paying the future taxes.[23] Liquidity constraints, already noted above, are another possible reason why behaviour may not conform to the Barro–Ricardo hypothesis.[24]

---

[21] The best-known study finding positive interest rate effects is Michael Boskin, "Taxation, Saving, and the Rate of Interest," *Journal of Political Economy*, Part 2, April 1978. For more typical results, see Gerald A. Carlino, "Interest Rate Effects and Intertemporal Consumption," *Journal of Monetary Economics*, March 1982. Campbell and Mankiw, referred to above, also find very little effect of the interest rate on saving.

[22] "Are Government Bonds Net Wealth?" *Journal of Political Economy* 82, November/December 1974. Theory and evidence on this topic are extensively analyzed in Douglas Bernheim, "Richardian Equivalence: An Evaluation of Theory and Evidence," *NBER Macroeconomics Annual*, 1987; and Lawrence Kotlikoff, *What Determines Saving?* (Cambridge, Mass.: MIT Press, 1989).

[23] We noted above that whether individuals save for their children affects fiscal policy. If parents are concerned enough about their children, they will regard future taxes to be paid by their children as equivalent to taxes on themselves, and the Ricardian view then is more likely to be true. Thus the discussion in Box 10-2 of the importance of bequests also has implications for the effectiveness of fiscal policy in affecting aggregate demand.

[24] Evidence on the effects of tax cuts on consumption has been examined by James Poterba, "Are Consumers Forward Looking? Evidence from Fiscal Experiments," *American Economic Review, Papers and Proceedings*, Vol. 78, May 1988. Poterba concludes that tax cuts do increase consumption.

10-5 Consumption and the *IS-LM* Framework

In this section we discuss briefly how the more sophisticated theories of consumption we have developed in this chapter affect the *IS-LM* analysis of Chapter 4. We focus on two implications. The first is that consumption is a function of wealth and not, as we assumed previously, of income only. The second is that the response of consumption to various changes — for instance, in autonomous spending — may take time, as individuals gradually adjust their estimates of permanent income.

Wealth in the Consumption Function

The life-cycle hypothesis and estimated consumption functions of a form like Equation (13) show that the rate of consumption depends on the level of wealth as well as on disposable income. This means that the position of the *IS* curve, representing equilibrium in the goods market, depends on the level of wealth.

Figure 10-5 shows how an increase in the level of wealth affects equilibrium output and the interest rate. The economy is initially in equilibrium at point *E*. There is then an increase in wealth: Perhaps the stock market has gone up because everyone is

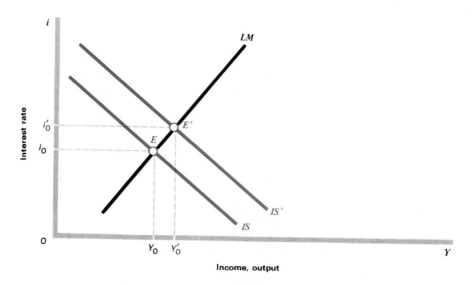

Figure 10-5 *The Effects of a Shift in Wealth*

An increase in wealth shifts the consumption function, raising consumption demand at any level of income. Accordingly, the *IS* curve shifts to *IS'*, the level of output rises from Y_0 to Y_0', and the interest rate rises from i_0 to i_0'.

optimistic that the economy is recovering from a recession. The higher wealth raises consumption spending, and the *IS* curve thus shifts up to *IS'*. The new equilibrium is at *E'*.

At *E'*, the interest rate and level of output are higher than at *E*. Thus an increase in wealth raises equilibrium output. Since the increase in wealth was assumed to result from expectations that the economy was recovering from a recession, we see that the expectation is partly self-fulfilling. A self-fulfilling prophecy is one which, purely as a result of being made, produces the prophesied result.

The Dynamics of Adjustment

In Section 10-3 and Figure 10-4, we examined the dynamic response of consumption spending to a shift in disposable income. Now we want to embody that dynamic adjustment in a full *IS-LM* model. The slow adjustment of consumption to a given change in disposable income will mean that income itself adjusts slowly to any given shift in autonomous spending that is not at first recognized as permanent, as we now show.

We assume here that people do not know whether the shift in autonomous demand is permanent or transitory. Rather, the only way they can figure that out is by seeing whether the change in demand persists or goes away. Figure 10-6 illustrates the effects of a permanent shift in autonomous demand, the nature of which (permanent or transitory) is not known to consumers.

Suppose that the economy is initially in equilibrium at point *E*. Now there is a shift in autonomous investment demand. In the long run, such a shift will move the *IS* curve to *IS'*. The extent of the shift is determined by the *long-run* multiplier $1/(1 - c)$, where c is the long-run propensity to consume. When expectations of income have fully adjusted, the economy will be at position *E'*, with output level Y_0' and interest rate i_0'.

In the short run, however, the marginal propensity to consume is not c, but only $c\theta$. Thus the short-run multiplier is only $1/(1 - c\theta)$. In the short run, the *IS* curve shifts only to *IS''*. Thus the immediate effect of the shift in investment demand is to raise income to Y_0'' and the interest rate to i_0''.

Next period, the *IS* curve shifts again. It does not shift all the way to *IS'*, though. Consumers have adjusted their estimate of permanent income upward, but they have not yet adjusted it all the way to Y_0', because income last period was only Y_0'' and not Y_0'. (To keep the diagram simple, we do not show the *IS* curve for the second or later periods.) Income and the interest rate will rise above Y_0'' and i_0'', but still fall short of Y_0' and i_0'.

This process continues, with the consumption function gradually shifting up over time, as people come to realize that their permanent incomes have risen. A single shock to autonomous demand therefore produces a slow, or *distributed lag*, effect on output. Figure 10-7 shows how income adjusts gradually to its new equilibrium level. The time pattern of changes in income caused by the increase in investment demand is called the *dynamic* multiplier of income with respect to autonomous investment.

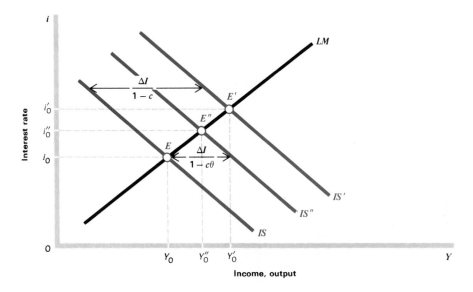

Figure 10-6 *The Dynamics of Adjustment to a Shift in Investment Demand*

Autonomous investment demand rises by amount ΔI, but it is not known whether the shift is permanent or transitory. It is in fact permanent, so that the *IS* curve will eventually be at *IS'*, shifted to the right by an amount $[\Delta I/(1 - c)]$, where $[1/(1 - c)]$ is the long-run multiplier. But in the first period, the *IS* curve shifts only to *IS"*, by amount $[\Delta I/(1 - c\theta)]$, determined by the short-run consumption function and multiplier. Over time, the economy moves gradually from E'' to E', as individuals come to recognize that the shift in investment demand is permanent.

Policy Implications

Suppose we have a permanent decline in investment expenditure. As we have seen, the decline in spending would lead to a fall in output and employment, occurring over a period of time.

Suppose the government wants to offset the reduction in aggregate demand by using tax cuts to keep income at the full-employment level. Since consumption adjusts only gradually to the changes in income resulting from both the initial fall in investment and tax cuts, the policy maker who wants to stabilize output *over time* will have to know about the adjustment pattern of consumption so as not to overreact. The problems may be further complicated by the fact that frequently the policy maker, too, reacts only with a lag to changed circumstances.

In the short run, consumption does not respond fully to changes in income. Therefore, it takes a relatively large tax cut to obtain a given change in consumption with which to offset the decline in investment. Over time, though, consumption adjusts to the change in disposable income, and the tax cut that was initially just sufficient to

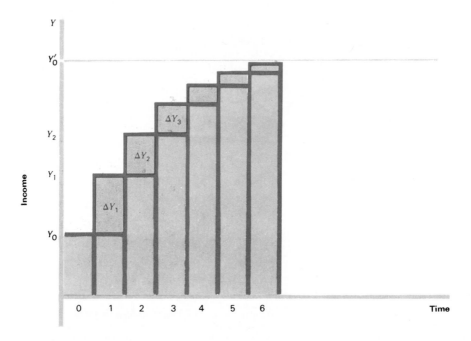

Figure 10-7 *The Income and Adjustment Process*

The figure shows the *dynamic multiplier* of investment spending on income. This is how a given change in autonomous investment spending affects the level of output over time. Income rises in the first period from Y_0 to Y_1. Then in subsequent periods it continues to rise toward its long-run equilibrium level Y_0'.

offset reduced investment now turns out to be too generous. The compensating policy must therefore be one of a tax cut that is *front-loaded* and gradually phased down to the long-run level. The difference between the short-run and long-run tax cuts is determined by the relative size of the short-run and long-run tax multipliers.

Indeed, the observant reader will recall that we assumed consumers had no special knowledge about the nature of the changes in income they experience as a result both of the initial change in investment and of subsequent tax adjustments. Remarkably enough, if consumers knew that the investment shift was permanent, and if they could be persuaded that the change in government policy was permanent, a one-time reduction in taxes, calculated using the long-run multiplier implied by the consumption function, would precisely stabilize income. In that case, the response to the fall in investment would recognize the permanent nature of the change, implying that the long-run multiplier is relevant; and the response to the tax change would also recognize the permanent nature of the change. Consumption would adjust immediately, rather than gradually.

The conclusion of this section is that policy making, and understanding the behaviour of the economy, cannot be successful unless careful attention is paid to expectations formation — bearing in mind that expectations depend in part on how the policy makers are perceived to be acting. This is the message of rational expectations, to which we return in Chapter 20.

10-6 Summary

1. The simple Keynesian consumption function

$$C = 3.45 + .85YD \tag{2}$$

accounts well for observed consumption behaviour. The equation suggests that out of an additional dollar of disposable income, 85 cents is spent on consumption. Since the intercept is small in relation to consumption, the consumption function implies that the ratio of consumption to income, C/YD, is approximately constant and independent of the level of income.

2. Early empirical work on consumption showed that the average propensity to consume declined with the level of income. Postwar studies, by contrast, find a relatively constant average propensity to consume of about 0.9.

3. The evidence is reconciled by a reconsideration of consumption theory. Individuals want to maintain relatively smooth consumption profiles over their lifetime. Their consumption behaviour is geared to their long-term consumption opportunities — permanent income or lifetime income plus wealth. With such a view, current income is only one of the determinants of consumption spending. Wealth and expected income play a role, too. A consumption function that represents this idea is

$$C = aWR + b\theta YD + b(1 - \theta)YD_{-1} \tag{13}$$

which allows for the role of real wealth, WR, current disposable income, YD, and lagged disposable income, YD_{-1}.

4. The life-cycle hypothesis suggests that the propensities of an individual to consume out of disposable income and out of wealth depend on the person's age. It implies that saving is high (low) when income is high (low) relative to lifetime average income. It also suggests that aggregate saving depends on the growth rate of the economy and on such variables as the age distribution of the population.

5. The permanent-income hypothesis emphasizes the formation of expectations of future income. It implies that the propensity to consume out of permanent income is higher than the propensity to consume out of transitory income.

6. Both theories do well, in combination, in explaining aggregate consumption behaviour, but there are still some consumption puzzles, including the excess sensitivity of consumption to current income and the fact that the elderly do not appear to draw down their savings as they age. In addition, differences in national saving rates have not been well explained.

7. The excess sensitivity of consumption to current income may be caused by liquidity constraints that prevent individuals from borrowing enough to maintain smooth consumption patterns. It could also be accounted for by myopia about future income prospects.

8. The rate of consumption, and thus of saving, could in principle be affected by the interest rate, but the evidence for the most part shows little effect of interest rates on saving.

9. The Barro–Ricardo hypothesis implies that cuts in tax rates that produce deficits will not affect consumption. The evidence seems to show that tax cuts do, however, affect consumption.

10. Lagged adjustment of consumption to income results in a gradual adjustment of the level of income in the economy to changes in autonomous spending and other economic changes. An increase in autonomous spending raises income, but the adjustment process is spread out over time because the rising level of income raises consumption only gradually. This adjustment process is described by dynamic multipliers that show by how much income changes in each period following a change in autonomous spending (or other exogenous variables).

Key Terms

Life-cycle hypothesis
Dissaving
Permanent income
Rational expectations
Liquidity constraints

Myopia
Dynamic multiplier
Excess sensitivity
Barro–Ricardo hypothesis

Problems

1. What is the significance of the ratio of consumption to GDP in terms of the level of economic activity? Would you expect it to be higher or lower than normal during a recession (or depression)? Do you think the ratio would be higher in developed or developing countries? Why?

The Life-Cycle Hypothesis

2. The text implies that the ratio of consumption to accumulated savings declines over time until retirement.
   (a) Why? What assumption about consumption behaviour leads to this result?
   (b) What happens to this ratio after retirement?

3. (a) Suppose you earn just as much as your neighbour but are in much better health and expect to live longer than she does. Would you consume more or less than she does? Why? Derive your answer from Equation (5).
   (b) According to the life-cycle hypothesis, what would be the effect of the Canada Pension Plan on your average propensity to consume out of (disposable) income?
   (c) How would Equation (8) be modified for an individual who expects to receive \$X per year of retirement benefits? Verify your result in problem 3(b).

4. Give an intuitive interpretation of the marginal propensity to consume out of wealth and income at time T in the individual's lifetime in Equation (8).

5. In Equation (5), consumption in each year of working life is given by

$$C = \frac{WL}{NL} \times YL \tag{5}$$

   In Equation (8), consumption is given as

$$C = aWR + cYL \qquad a = \frac{1}{NL - T} \qquad c = \frac{WL - T}{NL - T} \tag{8}$$

   Show that Equations (5) and (8) are consistent for an individual who started life with zero wealth and has been saving for T years. (Hint: First calculate the individual's wealth after T years of saving at rate $YL - C$. Then calculate the level of consumption implied by Equation (8) when wealth is at the level you have computed.)

Permanent-Income Hypothesis

6. In terms of the permanent-income hypothesis, would you consume more of your Christmas bonus if (a) you knew there was a bonus every year; (b) this was the only year such bonuses were given out?

7. Suppose that permanent income is calculated as the average of income over the past 5 years; that is,

$$YP = \frac{1}{5}(Y + Y_{-1} + Y_{-2} + Y_{-3} + Y_{-4})$$

Suppose, further, that consumption is given by $C = 0.9YP$.

(a)   If you have earned $10 000 per year for the past 10 years, what is your permanent income?

(b)   Suppose next year (period $t + 1$) you earn $15 000. What is your new YP?

(c)   What is your consumption this year and next year?

(d)   What is your short-run marginal propensity to consume (MPC) and your long-run MPC?

(e)   Assuming you continue to earn $15 000 starting in period $t + 1$, graph the value of your permanent income in each period, using the above equation.

8.   Explain why good gamblers (and thieves) might be expected to live very well even in years when they don't do well at all.

9.   The graph (below) shows the lifetime earnings profile of a person who lives for four periods and earns incomes of $30, $60, and $90 in the first three periods of the life cycle. There are no earnings during retirement. Assume that the interest rate is 0.

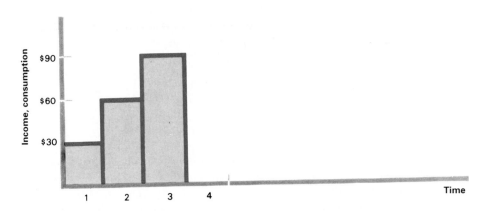

(a)   You are asked to determine the level of consumption, compatible with the budget constraint, for someone who wants an even consumption profile throughout the life cycle. Indicate in which periods the person saves and dissaves and in what amounts.

(b)   Assume now that, contrary to 9a, there is no possibility of borrowing. The credit markets are closed to the individual. Under this assumption, what is the flow of consumption the individual will pick over the life cycle? In providing an answer, continue to assume that, if possible, an even flow of consumption is preferred. (Note: You are assuming here that there are liquidity constraints.)

(c)   Assume next that the person described in 9b receives an increase in wealth, or nonlabour income. The increase in wealth is equal to $13. How will that wealth be allocated over the life cycle with and without access to the credit market? How would your answer differ if the increase in wealth were $23?

(d) Relate your answer to the problem of excess sensitivity of consumption to current income.

10. Consider the consumption function in Equation (13). Assume autonomous investment spending is constant, as is government spending. The economy is close to full employment and the government wishes to maintain aggregate demand precisely constant. In these circumstances, assume there is an increase in real wealth of $10 billion. What change in income taxes will maintain the equilibrium level of income constant in the present period? What change is required to maintain income constant in the long run?

11. Equation (13) shows consumption as a function of wealth and current and lagged disposable income. To reconcile that consumption function with the formation of permanent-income expectations, you are asked to use Equation (11) and the consumption function

$$C = 0.045WR + 0.55YD + 0.17YD_{-1}$$

to determine the magnitude of θ and $(1 - \theta)$ that is implied by Equation (13).

12. (a) Explain why the interest rate might affect saving.
    (b) Why does this relation matter?

Adjustment and Dynamics

13. Here is a challenge to your ability to develop diagrams. You are asked to show short-run and long-run income determination in the 45° diagram of Chapter 3. Assume that investment demand is totally autonomous and does not respond to the interest rate. Thus, you do not need to use the full *IS-LM* model.

    (a) Draw the short-run and long-run consumption functions and the aggregate demand schedule, with $I = \bar{I}$.
    (b) Show the initial full equilibrium.
    (c) Show the short-run and long-run effects of increased investment on equilibrium income.

CHAPTER 11 *Investment Spending*

Consumption spending in Canada is on average about 60 percent of real GDP, and thus accounts for much of aggregate demand. Investment spending is typically about 20 percent of real GDP, but it fluctuates more than consumption. Changes in the components of aggregate demand during the two most recent business cycles are given in Table 11-1. The table shows the percentage changes from peak to trough and for the first year of recovery. In both cases, investment played a major role in the movements of GDP during the recession and the subsequent recovery.

Table 11-1 *Real GDP and Its Components in Recession and Recovery*

	Recession 1981 II to 1982 IV	Recovery 1982 IV to 1983 IV	Recession 1990 I to 1991 I	Recovery 1991 I to 1992 I
	(percent change)			
Consumption	−2.6	5.1	−2.6	1.2
Investment	−17.9	3.2	−10.0	7.1
Government	4.7	−.5	1.8	1.9
Net exports[a]	14.5	−2.5	1.4	−4.8
GDP	−5.2	6.2	−3.1	1.2

[a]Change in net exports as a percentage of exports.

Source: Statistics Canada, 11-010.

The cyclical importance of investment spending, shown in Table 11-1, goes back a long way. For instance, in the great depression, gross investment fell to less than 4 percent of output in 1933. Understanding investment, then, is of prime importance in understanding the business cycle.

In this chapter we continue our in-depth analysis of the components of aggregate demand. We provide a foundation for the essential component of the simple investment function of Chapter 4 — that investment demand is reduced by increases in the interest rate — and also, go beyond that investment function by discussing the roles of output and taxes in determining investment. We also examine how investment spending can be affected by policy. High interest rates, caused by restrictive monetary policy and expansive fiscal policy, reduce investment spending; policies that reduce interest rates and provide tax incentives for investment can increase investment spending.

One simple relationship is vital to the understanding of investment. Investment is spending devoted to increasing or maintaining the stock of capital. The stock of capital consists of the factories, machines, offices, and other durable products used in the process of production. The capital stock also includes residential housing as well as inventories. Investment is spending that adds to these components of capital stock. Recall the distinction drawn in Chapter 2 between *gross* and *net investment*. Gross investment represents total additions to the capital stock. Net investment subtracts depreciation — the reduction in the capital stock that occurs each period through wear and tear and the simple ravages of time — from gross investment. Net investment thus measures the increase in the capital stock in a given period of time.

In this chapter, we disaggregate investment spending into three categories. The first consists of spending by business firms on productive capital in the form of *machinery and equipment* and *nonresidential construction.* The second is residential construction, which consists of spending on houses and apartment buildings. These two categories comprise *fixed investment* as opposed to the third one, *inventory investment*, some aspects of which were discussed in Chapter 3.

Table 11-2 shows investment spending in these categories for 1990, and Figure 11-1 shows the components of investment since 1971. Although inventory investment is

Table 11-2   *Gross Business Investment, 1990*

	(billions of 1986 dollars)
Machinery and equipment	$ 45.9
Nonresidential construction	30.0
Residential construction	35.4
Total fixed investment	111.3
Change in inventories	−2.4
Gross business investment	$108.9

Source: Statistics Canada, 11-010.

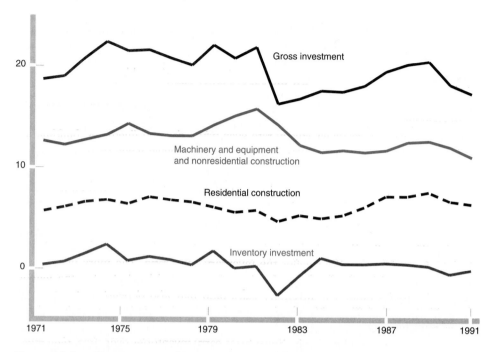

Figure 11-1 *Components of Investment Spending as a Percentage of GDP*

(*Source:* Department of Finance, *Economic Review*)

a small fraction of GDP, it shows wide fluctuations and can be negative as in the recession years 1982 and 1990.

In the remainder of this chapter, we develop theories and discuss evidence about the determinants of the rate of investment in each of the three major categories shown in Table 11-2 and Figure 11-1. We will develop what look like different models to explain each of the categories of investment spending. However, the theories are essentially similar, sharing a common view of the interaction between a desired capital stock and the rate at which the economy adjusts toward that desired stock.

11-1 Inventory Investment

Inventories consist of raw materials, goods in the process of production, and completed goods held by firms in anticipation of their sale. The ratio of inventories to monthly shipments in Canadian manufacturing has generally been in the range of 1.5 to 2.5. Inventories are held for several interrelated reasons.

- Sellers hold inventories to meet future demand for goods because goods cannot be instantly manufactured or obtained from the manufacturer to meet demand.

- Inventories are also held because it is less costly for a firm to order goods less frequently in large quantities than to order small quantities frequently, just as the average householder finds it useful to keep several days' supplies on hand in the house so as not to have to visit the supermarket daily.

- Producers may hold inventories as a way of smoothing their production. It is costly to keep changing the level of output on a production line, and producers therefore may produce at a relatively steady rate even when demand fluctuates, building up inventories when demand is low and drawing them down when demand is high.[1]

- Some inventories are held as an unavoidable part of the production process; there is an inventory of meat and sawdust inside the sausage machine during the manufacture of sausage, for example.

Firms have a desired ratio of inventories to final sales that depends on economic variables. The smaller the cost of ordering new goods and the greater the speed with which such goods arrive, the smaller the inventory–sales ratio. The more uncertainty about the demand for the firm's goods, given the expected level of sales, the higher the inventory–sales ratio. The inventory–sales ratio may also depend on the level of sales, with the ratio falling with sales because there is relatively less uncertainty about sales as sales increase.

Finally, there is the *interest rate*. Since firms carry inventories over time, they must tie up money to buy and hold them. There is an interest cost involved in such inventory holding, and the desired inventory–sales ratio should be expected to fall with increases in the interest rate.

Anticipated Versus Unanticipated Inventory Investment

The most interesting aspect of inventory investment lies in the distinction between anticipated (desired) and unanticipated (undesired) investment. Inventory investment could be high in two circumstances. First, if sales are unexpectedly low, firms would find unsold inventories accumulating on their shelves; this constitutes unanticipated inventory investment. This is the type of inventory investment discussed in Chapter 3. Second, inventory investment could be high because firms plan to restore depleted inventories. The two circumstances obviously have very different implications for the behaviour of aggregate demand. Unanticipated inventory investment is a result of unexpectedly low aggregate demand. On the other hand, planned inventory investment can be a response to recent, unexpectedly high aggregate demand; that is, rapid accumulation of inventories could be associated with either rapidly declining aggregate demand or rapidly increasing aggregate demand.

---

[1] This reason for holding inventories, the so-called *production-smoothing* model of inventory behaviour, has been the focus of much recent research. Although most evidence has been against the production-smoothing model (see, for instance, Jeffrey A. Miron and Stephen P. Zeldes, "Seasonality, Cost Shocks, and the Production Smoothing Model of Inventories," *Econometrica*, July 1988), there is some evidence suggesting that the data, rather than the theory, may be at fault. See Ray C. Fair, "The Production Smoothing Model is Alive and Well," NBER Working Paper 2877, February 1989.

Inventories in the Business Cycle

Inventory investment fluctuates substantially in the business cycle — proportionately more than any other component of aggregate demand. This is well illustrated in the 1990–1991 recession. In Figure 11-2, we show sales by Canadian manufacturing industries as measured by shipments and the ratio of inventories to shipments. As we move into the recession in 1990, sales begin to decline. Initially, however, there is relatively little adjustment in production, so there is an *unintended* buildup of inventories and the inventory–sales ratio increases. As the recession proceeds, production is cut back and the rate of increase in the inventory–sales ratio slows down. As demand picks up again in the second quarter of 1991, increases in production lag behind, allowing inventories to decline. Thus the inventory–sales ratio decreases as the economy moves out of the recession.

Note that this behaviour of inventories reflects the adjustment mechanism for output that we discussed in Chapter 3. When there is a fall in aggregate demand, firms involuntarily accumulate inventories. They cut back production in order to get output back in line with demand. As we noted in the footnotes in Chapter 3, though, in the process of reducing production to cut back inventories, firms may cause a larger reduction in GDP for a while than would have happened had inventories not been unintentionally accumulated. This is known as the *inventory cycle.*

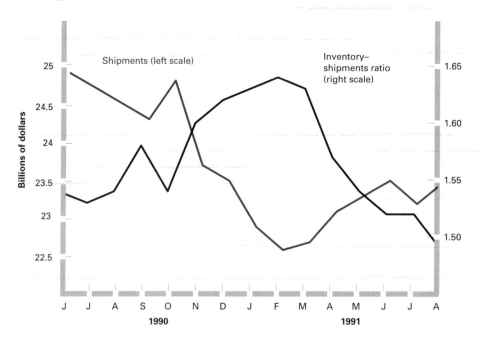

Figure 11-2 *Manufacturing Shipments and Inventory–Shipments Ratio*

(*Source:* Adapted from Statistics Canada 11-010)

To understand the inventory cycle, consider the case of a hypothetical automobile dealer who sells, say, 30 cars per month, and holds an average of one month's sales, namely 30 cars, in inventory. As long as sales stay steady at 30 cars per month, the dealer will be ordering 30 cars per month from the factory. Now suppose sales drop to 25 cars per month, and it takes the dealer two months to respond to the change. During those two months his or her inventory will have climbed to 40 cars. In the future he or she will want an inventory of only 25 cars on hand. Thus, when the dealer does respond to the fall in demand, orders from the factory are cut from 30 to 10 in the third month, to get the inventory back to one month's sales. After the desired inventory–sales ratio has been restored, the dealer will then order 25 cars per month from the factory. We see in this extreme case how the drop in demand of 5 cars, instead of leading to a simple drop in car output of 5 cars per month, causes a drop of output of 20 cars in one month, followed by the longer-run drop in output of 5 cars per month.

11-2 Business Fixed Investment: The Neoclassical Approach

The machinery, equipment, and structures used in the production of goods and services constitute the *stock* of business fixed capital. Our analysis of business fixed investment in this section proceeds in two stages. First, we ask how much capital firms would like to use, given the costs and returns of using capital and the level of output they expect to produce. That is, we ask what determines the *desired capital stock*. The desired capital stock is the capital stock that firms would like to have in the long run, abstracting from the delays they face in adjusting their use of capital. However, because it takes time to order new machines, build factories, and install the machines, firms cannot instantly adjust the stock of capital used in production. Second, therefore, we discuss the rate at which firms adjust from their existing capital stock toward the desired level over the course of time. The rate of adjustment determines how much firms spend on adding to the capital stock in each period; that is, it determines the rate of investment.

The Desired Capital Stock: Overview

Firms use capital, along with labour, to produce goods and services for sale. The firms' goal is, of course, to maximize their profits. In deciding how much capital to use in production, they have to balance the contribution that more capital makes to their revenues against the cost of using more capital. The *marginal product of capital* is the increase in output produced by using one more unit of capital production. The *rental (user) cost of capital* is the cost of using one more unit of capital in production.

To derive the rental cost of capital, we think of the firms as financing the purchase of the capital (whether the firm produces the capital itself or buys it from some other firm) by borrowing, at an interest cost i. In order to obtain the services of an extra unit of capital, in each period the firm must pay the interest cost i for each dollar of capital that it buys. Thus the basic measure of the rental cost of capital is the interest rate.[2] Later we shall go into more detail about the rental cost of capital, but for the time being we shall think of the interest rate as determining the rental cost.

In deciding how much capital they would like to use in production, firms compare the value of the marginal product of capital with the user or rental cost of capital. The value of the marginal product of capital is the increase in the *value* of output obtained by using one more unit of capital. For a competitive firm, it is equal to the price of output times the marginal product of capital. So long as the value of the marginal product of capital is above the rental cost, it pays the firm to add to its capital stock. Thus the firm will keep investing until the value of the output produced by adding one more unit of capital is equal to the cost of using that capital, the rental cost of capital.

The desired capital stock is thus reached when we have

$$\text{Value of marginal product of capital} = \text{rental cost of capital} \qquad (1)$$

The general relationship among the desired capital stock (K°), the rental cost of capital (rc), and the level of output is then given by

$$K^\circ = g(rc, y) \qquad (2)$$

Equation (2) indicates that the desired capital stock depends on the rental cost of capital and the level of output. The lower the rental cost of capital, the larger the desired capital stock; and the greater the level of output, the larger the desired capital stock.[3]

To give content to these relationships, we have to specify what determines the productivity of capital and what determines the user (rental) cost of capital.

The Marginal Productivity of Capital

In understanding the marginal productivity of capital, it is important to note that firms can substitute capital for labour in the production of output. Different combinations of capital and labour can be used to produce a given level of output. If labour is relatively cheap, the firm will want to use relatively more labour, and if capital is relatively cheap, the firm will want to use relatively more capital.

---

[2] Even if the firm finances the investment out of profits it has made in the past — retained earnings — it should still think of the interest rate as the cost of using the new capital, since it could otherwise have lent out those funds and earned interest on them, or paid them out as dividends to shareholders.

[3] In writing Equation (2), we assume that the real wage paid to labour is given and does not change as the rental cost of capital changes. In general, the rental cost of capital *relative to* the real wage determines the desired capital stock, given Y. (See footnote 5 for an example.)

As the firm combines progressively more capital with relatively less labour in the production of a given amount of output, the marginal product of capital declines. This relation is shown in the downward-sloping schedules in Figure 11-3. These schedules show how the marginal product of capital falls as more capital is used in producing a given level of output. The schedule YY_1 is drawn for a level of output Y_1. The schedule YY_2 is drawn for the higher output level Y_2. The marginal product of capital, given the capital stock, say, K_0, is higher on the schedule YY_2 than on YY_1. That is because more labour is being used in combination with the given amount of capital K_0 to produce the level of output Y_2 than to produce Y_1.

Figure 11-3 shows the marginal product of capital in relation to the level of output and the amount of capital being used to produce that output. Figure 11-4 is a similar diagram which shows the desired capital stock as related to the rental cost of capital and the level of output. Given the level of output, say Y_1, the lower the rental cost of capital, the more capital the firm will want to use. In producing a higher level of output, say Y_2, the firm will use both more capital and more labour, given the rental cost of capital.

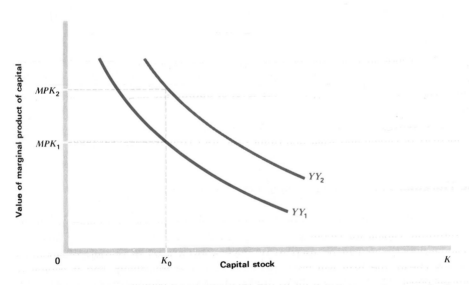

Figure 11-3 *The Marginal Product of Capital in Relation to the Level of Output and the Capital Stock*

The marginal product of capital decreases as relatively more capital is used in producing any given level of output. Thus the schedules YY_1 and YY_2 are downward-sloping. The higher the level of output, for any given capital input, the higher the marginal product of capital. Thus schedule YY_2, with output level Y_2 greater than Y_1, is above schedule YY_1.

The Cobb–Douglas Production Function

While Equation (2) provides the general relationship determining the desired capital stock, a particular form of the equation, based on the *Cobb–Douglas production function*,[4] is frequently used in studies of investment behaviour. The particular equation that is used is[5]

$$K^* = \frac{\gamma Y}{rc} \tag{3}$$

where γ is a constant. In this case, the desired capital stock varies in proportion to output. Given output, the desired capital stock varies with the rental cost of capital.

Expected Output

In determining the desired stock, we have to specify the relevant time period for which the decision on the capital stock applies. In this section, we are discussing the capital stock that the firm desires to hold at some future time. For some investments, the future time at which the output will be produced is a matter of months or only weeks. For other investments — such as power stations — the future time at which the output will be produced is years away.

This suggests that the notion of permanent income (in this case, permanent output) introduced in Chapter 10 is relevant to investment as well as consumption. For longer-lived investments, the firm's capital demand is governed primarily by its views on the

---

[4] The Cobb–Douglas production function is written in the form

$$Y = N^{1-\gamma} K^{\gamma} \qquad 1 > \gamma > 0$$

where N is the amount of labour used. This production function is particularly popular because it is easy to handle, and also because it appears to fit the facts of economic experience reasonably well. The coefficient γ appearing in Equation (3) is the same as the γ of the production function. The reader trained in calculus will want to show that γ is the share of capital in total income, under the assumption that factors are paid their marginal products.

[5] We draw attention here to a subtle point: Equation (3) gives the marginal product of capital (*MPK*) when the input of labour is held fixed, while in Figures 11-3 and 11-4 we work with the *MPK* when labour is being adjusted so that output is kept fixed. The desired capital stock that corresponds to Figures 11-3 and 11-4 is

$$K^* = \left[\frac{\gamma w}{(1-\gamma)rc} \right]^{1-\gamma} Y \tag{3a}$$

where w is the real wage.

Equation (3a), like Equation (3), implies that desired capital is proportional to Y and varies inversely with the rental cost of capital. We use Equation (3) rather than Equation (3a) in the text because it is the form that has been used in empirical studies.

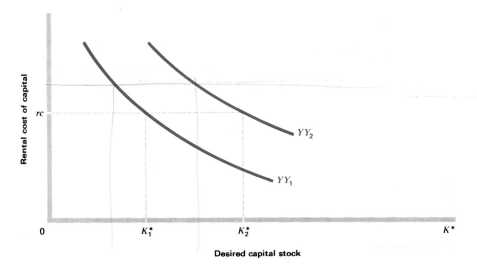

Figure 11-4 *The Desired Capital Stock in Relation to the Level of Output and the Rental Cost of Capital*

Firms' desired capital stock is chosen at the point at which the value of the marginal product of capital is equal to the rental cost of capital. At rental cost rc and output level Y_1, the firm's desired capital stock is K_1°. An increase in the level of output to Y_2 raises the desired capital stock to K_2°. An increase in the rental cost of capital (not shown) would reduce the desired capital stock at each level of output.

level of output it will be producing on average in the future. The firm's long-run demand for business fixed capital, which depends on the normal or permanent level of output, is thus relatively independent of the current level of output, and depends on *expectations* of future output levels. However, it is affected by current output to the extent that current output affects expectations of permanent output.[6]

The Rental Cost of Capital Again

As a first approximation, we identified the rental cost of capital, rc, with the interest rate, on the argument that firms would have to borrow to finance their use of capital. Now we go into more detail on the cost per period of using capital.

To use capital for a single period, say a year, the firm can be thought of as buying the capital with borrowed funds and paying the interest on the borrowing. At the end of the year, the firm will have some of the capital left, but the capital is likely to have

---

[6] The role of permanent income in investment has been emphasized by Robert Eisner. Much of his work is summarized in his book *Factors in Business Investment* (Cambridge, Mass.: Ballinger, 1978).

depreciated over the course of the year. We shall assume that the firm intends to continue using the remaining capital in production in future years and that its depreciation simply represents the using up of the capital in the process of production — physical wear and tear. We now examine the rental cost, taking into account interest costs and depreciation. Later we will show that taxes also affect the rental cost of capital.

Leaving aside taxes, the rental cost of using capital consists of interest and depreciation costs.[7] We assume that the rate of depreciation is a constant, equal to d, implying that a fixed proportion d of the capital is used up per period. The rental cost, or user cost, of capital per dollar's worth of capital, which we denote by rc, is therefore

$$rc = \text{interest rate} + d \tag{4}$$

The Real Rate of Interest

We have now to take a careful look at the interest rate term in Equation (4). The distinction between the *real* and *nominal* interest rates is essential here. The real interest rate is the nominal (stated) rate of interest minus the rate of inflation.

It is the *expected real* rate of interest that should enter the calculation of the rental cost of capital. Why? The firm is borrowing in order to produce goods for sale. On average, across all firms, it is reasonable to believe that the prices of the goods the firms sell will be rising along with the general price level. Thus the value of what the firm will be producing in the future will be rising with the price level, but the nominal amount of interest it has to pay back on account of its borrowings does not rise with the price level. The real value of the debt it has incurred by borrowing will be falling over time, as a result of inflation, and it should take that reduction in the real value of its outstanding debts into account in deciding how much capital to employ.

Accordingly, we can be more precise in the way we write Equation (4) for the rental cost of capital. We write the rental cost of capital, taking account of expected inflation at the rate π^e, as

$$rc = r + d = i - \pi^e + d \tag{5}$$

where r is the real interest rate, i the nominal interest rate, and

$$r = i - \pi^e \tag{6}$$

Equation (6) states that the real rate of interest is the nominal interest rate minus the expected rate of inflation.[8]

---

[7] Why is depreciation considered a cost? The firm continues using the capital and therefore has to devote expenditures to maintaining the productive efficiency of capital, thus offsetting wear and tear. We are assuming that, per dollar of capital, d dollars per period are required to maintain productive efficiency.

[8] Accordingly the real interest rate in Equation (6) is the *expected* real rate. At the end of the period, when the rate of inflation is known, we can also state what the *actual*, or realized, real rate of interest for the period was — namely, the nominal interest rate, i, minus the actual rate of inflation.

To reiterate, it is important to note that the interest rate relevant to the firm's demand for capital is the *real* rate, and not the nominal rate. This makes it clear that the nominal rate of interest is not a good guide to the rental cost of capital. If the rate of inflation is zero and is expected to be zero and the nominal interest rate is 5 percent, then the real interest rate is 5 percent. By contrast, if the nominal interest rate is 10 percent and inflation is at the rate of 10 percent, the real interest rate is zero. Other things equal, the desired capital stock in this example would tend to be higher with the nominal interest rate of 10 percent than with the nominal rate of 5 percent — because those rates correspond to real rates of zero and 5 percent, respectively. As you have no doubt deduced, and as we shall show, investment spending tends to be higher when the rental cost of capital is lower. However, because of the distinction between real and nominal interest rates, that is *not* the same as saying that investment tends to be higher when the nominal rate of interest is lower.

Taxes and the Rental Cost of Capital

The rental cost of capital is affected by tax variables as well as by the interest rate and depreciation. The two main tax variables to consider are the corporate income tax and the investment tax credit. The corporate income tax is an essentially proportional tax on profits, whereby the firm pays a proportion, say, t, of its profits in taxes. The investment tax credit allows firms to deduct from their taxes a certain fraction, say τ, of their investment expenditures in each year. Thus a firm spending $1 million for investment purposes in a given year could deduct 10 percent of the $1 million, or $100 000, from the taxes it would otherwise have to pay the federal government.

We want to know what effects the corporate income tax and the investment tax credit have on the rental cost of capital. The easier case is the investment tax credit. The investment tax credit reduces the price of a capital good to the firm by the ratio τ, since the government returns to the firm a proportion τ of the cost of each capital good. The investment tax credit therefore reduces the rental cost of capital.

To a first approximation, the corporate income tax, surprisingly, has no effect on the desired stock of capital. In the presence of the corporate income tax, the firm will want to equate the *after-tax* value of the marginal product of capital with the *after-tax* rental cost of capital in order to ensure that the marginal contribution of the capital to profits is equal to the marginal cost of using it.

Let us focus on the interest component of the rental cost. The basic point is that interest cost is treated as a deduction from revenues in the calculation of the corporation's taxes. Suppose there were no corporate income tax, no inflation, no depreciation, and an interest rate of 10 percent. The desired capital stock would be that level of the capital stock, say, K_0^*, such that the marginal product of capital was 10 percent. Now suppose that the corporate income tax rises to 35 percent and the interest rate remains constant. At the capital stock K_0^*, the after-tax marginal product of capital is now 6.5 percent (since 35 percent of the profits are paid in taxes). If the interest rate stays at 10 percent and the firm gets to deduct 35 percent of its interest payments from taxes, the after-tax cost of capital will be 6.5 percent too. In this case, the desired capital stock is unaffected by the rate of corporate taxation.

However, there are complexities in the tax laws, which we do not go into here, which make the total effect of the corporate income tax on the desired capital stock ambiguous. The ambiguities arise when the special tax treatment of depreciation,[9] of inflation, and of investment financing other than through borrowing is taken into account.[10]

In summary, the investment tax credit reduces the rental cost of capital and increases the desired stock of capital. The corporate income tax has ambiguous effects on the desired stock of capital.

The Stock Market and the Cost of Capital

We have so far assumed that the firm finances its investment by borrowing, but a firm can also finance investment by selling shares or equity. The people buying the shares expect to earn a return from dividends and/or, if the firm is successful, from the increase in the market value of their shares, that is, *capital gains*.

When the stock market is high, a company can raise a lot of money by selling relatively few shares. When stock prices are low, the firm has to sell more shares to raise a given amount of money. The owners of the firm, existing shareholders, will be more willing for the firm to sell shares to raise new money if they have to sell few shares to do so. If many shares have to be sold, the current shareholders will own a smaller share of the company in the future. Thus we expect corporations to be more willing to sell equity to finance investment when the stock market is high than when it is low.

In estimating the rental cost of capital, economists sometimes assume that the investment project will be financed by a mixture of borrowing and equity. The cost of equity capital is frequently measured by the ratio of the firm's dividends to the price of its stock.[11] Then, obviously, the higher the price of the stock, the lower the cost of equity capital, and the lower the overall cost of capital.[12] That is why a booming stock market is good for investment.

---

[9] For tax purposes, depreciation is counted as a business expense, but these allowances follow complicated rules and are not generally equal to the depreciation that the capital stock actually undergoes.

[10] As we describe below, some investment is financed through the sale of equities. Part of the return to equity holders typically takes the form of dividend payments. However, dividends are not treated as a deduction from profits in the calculation of corporate income taxes. Thus the basic argument presented in the case of interest payments, that the corporate income tax does not affect the desired capital stock, would not apply for equity-financed investment.

[11] An alternative measure is the ratio of the firm's earnings (some of which are not paid out to shareholders) to the price of its stock. However, neither measure is really correct, for the cost of equity capital is the amount the investment is expected to yield in the future to the people who buy it now.

[12] An alternative approach to the firm's investment decision, Tobin's q theory of investment, focuses on the stock market as the primary source of funds. The basic approach is outlined in James Tobin, "A General Equilibrium Approach to Monetary Theory," *Journal of Money, Credit and Banking*, February 1969. For an empirical implementation, see Lawrence H. Summers, "Taxation and Corporate Investment: A q-Theory Approach," *Brookings Papers on Economic Activity*, 1981. In Section 11-4, we outline the q theory in discussing housing investment.

Summary and Effects of Fiscal and Monetary Policy on the Desired Capital Stock

We summarize, using Equation (2), which states that the desired capital stock increases when the expected level of output rises and when the rental cost of capital falls.

The rental cost of capital falls when the real interest rate and the rate of depreciation fall. It likewise falls when the investment tax credit rises. Changes in the rate of corporate taxation have ambiguous effects on the desired capital stock.

The major significance of these results is their implication that monetary and fiscal policy affect the desired capital stock. Fiscal policy exerts an effect through both the corporate tax rate, t, and the investment tax credit, τ. Both these instruments are used to affect capital demand and thus investment spending.

Fiscal policy affects capital demand by its overall effects on the position of the *IS* curve, as discussed in Chapter 4. A high-tax–low-government-spending policy keeps the real interest rate low and encourages the demand for capital. (At this point you want to refer to Figure 4-22.) A high-government-spending–low-tax policy that produces large deficits raises the real interest rate and discourages the demand for capital.

Monetary policy affects capital demand by affecting the market interest rate.[13] A lowering of the nominal interest rate by the Bank of Canada (given the expected inflation rate), as reflected in a downward shift in the *LM* curve, will induce firms to desire more capital. This expansion in capital demand, in turn, will affect investment spending, as we shall now see.

From Desired Capital Stock to Investment

Equation (2) specifies the desired capital stock. The actual capital stock will often differ from the capital stock firms would like to have. At what speed do firms change their capital stocks in order to move toward the desired capital stock? In particular, is there any reason why firms do not attempt to move to their desired capital stocks immediately?

Since it takes time to plan and complete an investment project, and because attempts to invest quickly are likely to be more expensive than gradual adjustment of the capital stock, it is unlikely that firms would attempt to adjust their capital stocks to the long-run desired level instantaneously. Very rapid adjustment of the capital stock would require crash programs by the firm which would distract management from its routine tasks and interfere with ongoing production. Thus, firms generally plan to adjust their capital stocks gradually over a period of time rather than immediately.

---

[13] We should note that the Bank of Canada is able to affect *nominal* interest rates directly by its sales and purchases of bonds. Its ability to control *real* interest rates is more limited.

Capital Stock Adjustment

There are a number of hypotheses about the speed with which firms plan to adjust their capital stock over time; here we single out the *gradual adjustment hypothesis,* or *flexible accelerator model.*[14] The basic notion behind the gradual adjustment hypothesis is that the larger the gap between the existing capital stock and the desired capital stock, the more rapid a firm's rate of investment. The hypothesis is that firms plan to close a fraction, λ, of the gap between the desired and actual capital stocks each period. Denote the capital stock at the end of the last period by K_{-1}. The gap between the desired and actual capital stocks is $K^\circ - K_{-1}$. The firm plans to add to last period's capital stock (K_{-1}), a fraction $(λ)$ of the gap so that the capital stock at the end of current period (K) will be

$$K = K_{-1} + λ(K^\circ - K_{-1}) \tag{7}$$

The amount of net investment implied by Equation (7) is given by

$$I = K - K_{-1} = λ(K^\circ - K_{-1}) \tag{8}$$

This is the gradual adjustment formulation of net investment. Notice that Equation (8) implies that the larger the gap between actual and desired capital stocks, the larger is investment.[15] With a zero gap, net investment is zero.

In Figure 11-5 we show the adjustment process of capital in a circumstance where the initial capital stock is K_1 and the given desired capital stock is K°. The assumed speed of adjustment is $λ = 0.5$. Starting from K_1, one-half the discrepancy between target capital and current actual capital is made up in every period. First-period net investment is therefore $0.5(K^\circ - K_1)$. In the second period, investment will be less because the previous period's investment reduces the gap. Investment continues until the actual capital stock reaches the level of target capital. The speed with which this process allows actual capital to reach target capital is determined by λ. The larger λ is, the faster the gap is reduced.

In Equation (8), we have reached our goal of deriving an investment function that shows current investment spending determined by the desired stock of capital K° and the actual stock of capital K_{-1}. According to Equation (8), any factor that increases the desired stock increases the rate of investment. Therefore an increase in expected output, or a reduction in the real interest rate, or an increase in the investment tax credit will each increase the rate of investment. We thus have derived a quite complete theory of business fixed investment that includes many of the factors we should expect to affect the rate of investment. Further, the theory of investment embodied in Equa-

---

[14] The term "flexible accelerator" is used because the model is a generalized form of the older accelerator model of investment, in which investment is proportional to the change in the level of output. The original accelerator model is examined in Section 11-3.

[15] Gross investment, as opposed to net investment described in Equation (8), includes, in addition, depreciation. Thus, gross investment is $I + dK_{-1}$, where d is again the rate of depreciation.

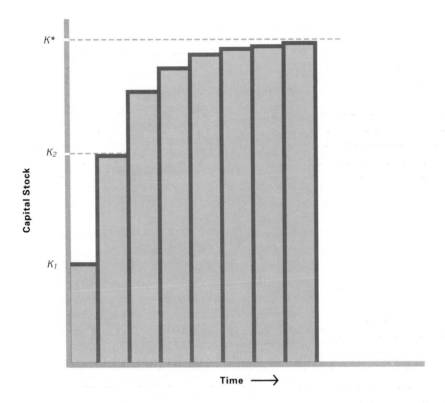

Figure 11-5 *The Gradual Adjustment of the Capital Stock*

The desired capital stock is K°, and the current capital stock is K_1. The firms plan to close half the gap between the actual and the desired capital stock each period ($\lambda = 0.5$). Thus, in period one it moves to K_2, with (net) investment equal to $(K_2 - K_1)$, which in turn is equal to one-half of $(K^\circ - K_1)$. In each subsequent period it closes half the gap between the capital stock at the beginning of the period and the desired capital stock, K°.

tion (8) also contains aspects of *dynamic behaviour*, that is, behaviour that depends on values of economic variables in periods other than the current period.

There are two sources of dynamic behaviour in Equation (8). The first arises from expectations. The K° term depends on the firm's estimate of future or permanent output. To the extent that the firm forms its estimates of permanent output as a weighted average of past output levels, there will be lags in the adjustment of the level of permanent output to the actual level of output. In turn, investment will therefore also adjust slowly to a change in the level of output. The second source of dynamic behaviour arises from adjustment lags. Firms plan to close only a proportion of the gap between the actual and desired capital stocks each period, as shown in Figure 11-5. The adjustment lags produce a lagged response of investment to changes in the variables that affect the desired capital stock.

The Timing of Investment and the Investment Tax Credit

The flexible accelerator model provides a useful summary of the dynamics of investment, but it does not sufficiently emphasize the *timing* of investment. Because investment is undertaken for the long run and often requires several years to complete, there is flexibility in the dates on which the actual investment is undertaken. For example, suppose a firm wanted to have some machinery in place within three years. Suppose that it knew the investment tax credit would be raised substantially a year from now. Then the firm might be wise to delay the investment for a year and to make or acquire the machinery at a faster rate during the next two years, receiving the higher investment tax credit as the reward for waiting the extra year. Similarly, if a firm anticipated that the cost of borrowing next year would be much lower than this year, it might wait a year to undertake its investment project.

The flexibility in the timing of investment leads to an interesting contrast between the effects of the investment tax credit and the income tax on investment and consumption, respectively. We saw in Chapter 10 that a *permanent* change in the income tax has a much larger effect on consumption than a *transitory change*. However, the rate of investment *during the period* that a *temporary* investment tax credit is in effect would be higher than the rate of investment that would occur over the same period during which a *permanent* credit of the same magnitude was in effect. Why? If firms knew the investment tax credit were temporary, they would advance the timing of their planned investments in order to take advantage of the higher credit during the current period. If there were a permanent change in the investment tax credit, then the desired capital stock would rise and there would on that account be more investment, but there would not be a bunching of investment.

It is for this reason that temporary changes in the investment tax credit have been suggested as a highly effective countercyclical policy measure. However, this is not a simple policy tool, as expectations about the timing and duration of the credit might conceivably worsen the instability of investment.

Empirical Results

How well does the neoclassical model summarized in Equation (8) explain the behaviour of investment?

To use Equation (8), it is necessary to substitute some specific equation for $K°$, the desired capital stock. Frequently the Cobb–Douglas form is chosen. Using Equation (3) in Equation (8) yields a (net) investment function of the form

$$I = \lambda\left(\frac{\gamma Y}{rc} - K_{-1}\right) \qquad (9)$$

The rental cost of capital, rc, in Equation (9), is as in Equation (5), but adjusted for taxes.

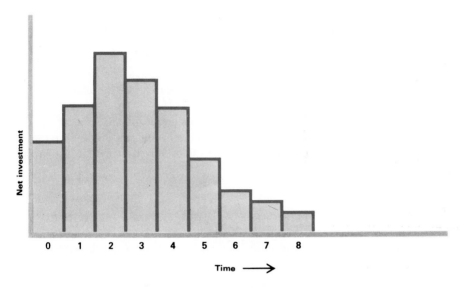

Figure 11-6 *Effects of an Increase in Output in Period Zero on Net Investment in Subsequent Periods (Years)*

Early empirical evidence, in particular that of Dale Jorgenson and his associates,[16] showed that an investment function including the variables in Equation (9) provided a reasonable explanation of the behaviour of business fixed investment. However, the form shown in Equation (9) could be improved upon by allowing more scope for investment to respond slowly to changes in output. The empirical evidence suggests that the adjustment of investment to output takes the bell-shaped form in Figure 11-6. The major impact of a change in output on actual investment occurs with a two-period (year) lag. The impact in the first year is less than the impact two years later.

There are two, not mutually exclusive, explanations for the behaviour shown in Figure 11-6, corresponding to the two sources of dynamic behaviour in Equation (8) that we discussed above. The first possibility is that the lag pattern of Figure 11-6 reflects the way in which expectations about future output, and thus the long-run desired capital stock, are formed. In that view, only a sustained increase in output will persuade firms that the capital stock should be increased in the long run. Figure 11-6 would then imply that it takes about two years for changes in the variables that determine the desired capital stock to have a major impact on expectations.

16 See Dale W. Jorgenson, "Econometric Studies of Investment Behaviour: A Survey," *Journal of Economic Literature*, December 1971. For an application of the theory with Canadian data, see G.O. Gaudet, J.D. May, and D.G. McFetridge, "Optimal Capital Accumulation: The Neoclassical Framework in a Canadian Context," *Review of Economics and Statistics*, August 1976.

The second explanation relies less on expectations and more on the physical delays in the investment process. That interpretation would be that Figure 11-6 reflects the long time it takes for a change in the desired capital stock to be translated into investment spending. In the economy as a whole, the maximum impact on investment of a change in the desired capital stock happens only two years after the change in the desired stock.

For many purposes, it does not matter which explanation of the form of Figure 11-6 is correct, and it is difficult to tell the explanations apart empirically. It is undoubtedly true that both explanations are relevant. The important point is that lags in the determination of the level of business fixed investment are long.

Summary on the Neoclassical Theory of Business Fixed Investment

The main conclusions of the theory of business fixed investment as developed here are as follows:

1. Over time, net investment spending is governed by the discrepancy between actual and desired capital.

2. Desired capital depends on the rental (user) cost of capital and the expected level of output. Capital demand rises with expected output and the investment tax credit, and declines with an increase in real interest rates.

3. Monetary and fiscal policies affect investment via the desired capital stock, although with long lags.

4. The empirical evidence is broadly consistent with the neoclassical theory, but certainly leaves room for improvement.

11-3 Business Fixed Investment: Alternative Approaches

In this section we briefly discuss the way a firm approaches its investment decisions and also describe approaches to business fixed investment other than the neoclassical theory.

The Business Investment Decision: The View from the Trenches

Business people making investment decisions typically use *discounted cash flow analysis*. The principles of discounting are described in the appendix to this chapter. Consider a businessperson deciding whether to build and equip a new factory. The first step is to figure out how much it will cost to get the factory into working order, and how much revenue the factory will bring in each year after it starts operation.

For simplicity we consider a very short-lived project, one that costs $100 in the first year to set up and that then generates $50 in revenue (after paying for labour and raw materials) in the second year and a further $80 in the third year. By the end of the third year the factory has disintegrated.

The manager wants to know whether to undertake such a project. Discounted cash flow analysis says that the revenues received in later years should be *discounted* to the present in order to calculate their present value. As the appendix on discounting shows, if the interest rate is 10 percent, $110 a year from now is worth the same as $100 now. Why? Because if $100 were lent out today at 10 percent, a year from now the lender would end up with $110. Thus, to calculate the value of the investment project, the businessperson calculates its present discounted value at the interest rate at which the business can borrow. If the present value is positive, then the project is undertaken.

Suppose that the relevant interest rate is 12 percent.[17] The calculation of the present discounted value of the investment project is shown in Table 11-3. The $50 received in year 2 is worth only $44.65 today: $1 a year from now is worth $1/1.12 = 0.893 today, and so $50 a year from now is worth $44.65. The present value of the $80 received in year 3 is calculated similarly. The table shows that the present value of the net revenue received from the project is positive ($8.41) and thus that the firm should undertake the project.

Table 11-3   *Discounted Cash Flow Analysis and Present Value*

	Cost or Revenue	Present Value
	($)	
Year 1	− 100	− 100.00
Year 2	50	50 × 1/1.12 = 44.65
Year 3	80	80 × 1/1.222 = 63.76
Net present value		8.41

Note that if the interest rate had been much higher, say 18 percent, the decision would have been *not* to undertake the investment project. We thus see how the interest rate affects the investment decision of the typical firm. The higher the interest rate, the less likely the firm will be to undertake any given investment project.

Each firm has at any time an array of possible investment projects, and estimates of the costs and the revenues from those projects. Depending on the level of the interest rate, it will want to undertake some of the projects and not undertake others. Taking all firms in the economy together and adding their investment demands, we obtain the total demand for investment in the economy at each interest rate.

---

[17] The interest rate here is nominal, because we are calculating the present value of dollars to be received in the future.

This approach to the investment decision, which, of course, can be applied to investment projects of any duration and complexity, seems far from the description of Section 11-2 in terms of a desired capital stock and rate of adjustment. Actually, the two approaches are quite consistent.

First, we should think of the desired capital stock as being the stock of capital that will be in place when the firms have their factories and new equipment in operation. Second, the adjustment speed tells us how rapidly firms on average succeed in installing that capital. We started with the formulation in terms of the desired capital stock because the framework provides a very clear way of including the different factors that affect investment. For instance, it is easy to see how expectations of future output and taxes affect investment.

However, since the two approaches are consistent, the same factors could be included using discounted cash flow analysis. The effects of expectations of future output can be analyzed using the discounted cash flow approach by asking what determines the firms' projections of their future revenues (corresponding to the $50 in year 2 and $80 in year 3 in the example above); expected demand for their goods and their output must be relevant. Similarly, taxes can be embodied by analyzing how taxes affect the amount of revenue the firm has left after taxes in each future year; the investment tax credit reduces the amount the firm has to lay out in the early years when it is actually building the project — because the government provides a refund of part of the cost of the project through taxes.

Finally, the firm makes decisions about the speed of adjustment by considering the cash flows associated with building the project at different speeds. If the project can be built more rapidly, the firm will decide on the speed with which it wants the project brought into operation by considering the present discounted costs and revenues associated with speeding it up.

The Accelerator Model of Investment

The *accelerator model of investment* asserts that the rate of investment is proportional to the *change* in the economy's output. To derive the accelerator model of investment, assume that there is complete adjustment of the capital stock to its desired level within one period (that is, that $\lambda = 1$), so that $K = K^{\circ}$; that there is no depreciation, so that $d = 0$; and that the desired capital–output ratio is a constant, independent of the rental cost of capital:

$$K^{\circ} = vY \tag{10}$$

In Equation (10), v is a constant equal to the desired capital-to-output ratio. Substituting Equation (10) into Equation (8), setting $\lambda = 1$, and noting that $K_{-1} = K^{\circ}_{-1}$ (when $\lambda = 1$), we obtain

$$I = v(Y - Y_{-1}) \tag{11}$$

which is precisely the accelerator model of investment.

The accelerator model creates the potential for investment spending to fluctuate a good deal. If investment spending is proportional to the change in output, then when the economy is in a recovery, investment spending is positive, and when the economy is in a recession, investment will be negative.[18] Thus the accelerator model predicts that investment will fluctuate considerably, as Figure 11-1 shows it does.

The Accelerator Model and Cost of Capital Effects

The neoclassical model of investment assumes that the cost of capital affects the desired stock in just the same way as expected output does. This can be seen in Equation (9), which relates investment to the ratio of output to the rental cost of capital (Y/rc). One issue is whether the rental cost of capital matters in fact as much for investment as the neoclassical model implies.

Some research suggests that the (somewhat expanded) accelerator model of Equation (10), which ignores the cost of capital, does about as good a job of explaining investment behaviour as the neoclassical model.[19] The more general accelerator model is expanded in empirical work to make the rate of investment depend not only on the change in income this period but also on the change in income in earlier periods. In empirical applications this simple accelerator model therefore differs from the neoclassical model mainly in that it omits the cost of capital.

There are also findings that the rental cost of capital does affect investment.[20] It is clear from the conflicting findings that the evidence is not strong enough to decide the precise relative roles of the cost of capital and expectations of future output. No doubt both are major determinants of investment spending. Certainly theory suggests that the rental cost of capital should play an important role in affecting investment.

Why Does Investment Fluctuate?

The facts with which we started this chapter show that investment fluctuates much more than consumption spending. The accelerator model provides one explanation of these fluctuations. There are two other basic explanations: the uncertain basis for expectations and the flexibility of the timing of investment.

Keynes, in the *General Theory*, emphasized the uncertain basis on which investment decisions are made. In his words, "we have to admit that our basis of knowledge for estimating the yield ten years hence of a railway, a copper mine, a textile factory, the

---

[18] The accelerator is not in practice a complete model of investment, for gross investment spending cannot be negative.

[19] Peter K. Clark, "Investment in the 1970's: Theory, Performance and Predictions," *Brookings Papers on Economic Activity*, 1979:1.

[20] For example, Martin Feldstein, "Inflation, Tax Rules and Investment: Some Economic Evidence," *Econometrica*, July 1982, and Ben Bernanke, "The Determinants of Investment: Another Look," *American Economic Review*, Papers and Proceedings, May 1983.

goodwill of a patent medicine . . . amounts to little and sometimes to nothing. . . ."[21] Thus, he argued, investment decisions are very much affected by how optimistic or pessimistic the investors feel.

The term "animal spirits" is sometimes used to describe the optimism or pessimism of investors, suggesting that there may be no good basis for the expectations on which investors base their decisions. If there is no good basis for the expectations, then they could change easily — and the volume of investment along with the expectations.

The second possible reason for fluctuations in investment is that investment decisions can be delayed if the project will take a long time to come into operation. Suppose a firm has an investment project it would like to undertake, but the economy is currently in a recession and the firm is not sure when the recession will end. Further, at the current time it cannot even usefully fully employ all the capital it already has. Such a firm might choose to wait until the prospects for the economy look better — when the recovery gets under way — before deciding to start the investment project.

Either or both of these factors could help account for the substantial fluctuations that are seen in business investment spending. Indeed, they may also explain the success of the accelerator theory of investment, for if firms wait for a recovery to get under way before investing, their investment will be closely related to the change in GDP.

11-4 Residential Construction

We study residential construction separately from other fixed investment both because somewhat different theoretical considerations are relevant[22] and because residential construction is especially sensitive to changes in interest rates.

Figure 11-7 shows residential construction spending in constant (1986) dollars for the period 1971–1991. Residential construction declines in recession periods such as 1975, 1982, and 1990–1991.

Theory

Residential construction consists of the building of single-family and multi-family dwellings which we shall call housing. Housing is distinguished as an asset by its long life. Consequently, investment in housing in any one year tends to be a very small proportion of the existing stock of housing, about 3 percent. The theory of residential

---

[21] J.M. Keynes, *The General Theory of Employment, Interest and Money* (London: Macmillan, 1936), pp. 149–50.

[22] In the concluding section of this chapter, we explain further why slightly different theoretical models are used in explaining business fixed investment and residential construction.

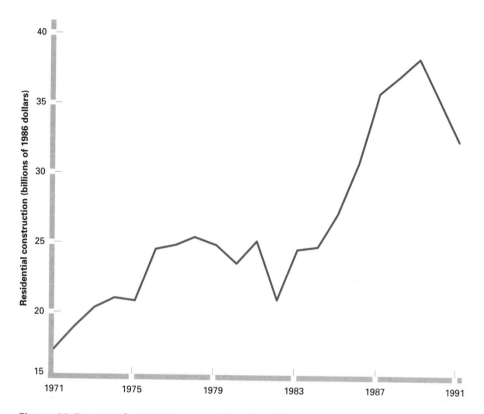

Figure 11-7 *Residential Construction Spending*

(*Source:* Department of Finance, *Economic Review*)

investment starts by considering the demand for the existing stock of housing. Housing is viewed as one among the many assets that a wealth holder can own.

In Figure 11-8*a* we show the demand for the stock of housing in the downward-sloping DD_0 curve. The lower the price of housing (P_H), the greater the quantity demanded. The position of the demand curve itself depends on a number of economic variables. First, the greater wealth is, the greater the demand for housing. The more wealthy individuals are, the more housing they desire to own. Thus an increase in wealth would shift the demand curve from DD_0 to DD_1. Second, the demand for housing as an asset depends on the real return available on other assets. If returns on other forms of holding wealth, such as bonds, are low, then housing looks like a rel-atively attractive form in which to hold wealth. The lower the return on other assets, the greater the demand for housing. A reduction in the return on other assets, such as bonds or common stock, shifts the demand curve from DD_0 to DD_1.

Third, the demand for the housing stock depends on the net real return obtained by owning housing. The gross return, before taking costs into account, consists of rent,

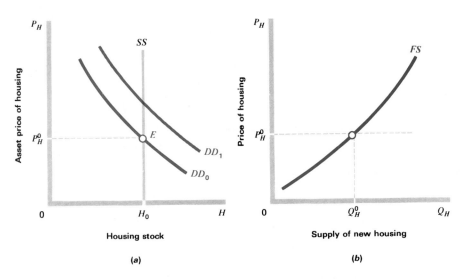

Figure 11-8 *The Housing Market: Determination of the Asset Price of Housing and the Rate of Housing Investment*

The supply and demand for the stock of housing determine the asset price of housing (P_H^0) in panel (a). The rate of housing investment (Q_H^0) is determined by the flow supply of housing at price P_H^0, in panel (b).

if the housing is rented out, or the implicit return that the homeowner receives by living in the home, plus capital gains arising from increases in the value of the housing. In turn, the costs of owning the housing consist of interest costs, typically the mortgage interest rate, plus any real estate taxes, and depreciation. These costs are deducted from the gross return and, after tax adjustments, constitute the net return. An increase in the net return on housing, caused, for example, by a reduction in the mortgage interest rate, makes housing a more attractive form in which to hold wealth and shifts up the demand curve for housing from DD_0 to DD_1.

The price of housing is determined by the interaction of this demand with the stock supply of housing. At any time the stock supply is fixed; there is a given stock of housing that cannot be adjusted quickly in response to price changes. The supply curve of the stock of housing is the SS curve of Figure 11-8a. The equilibrium *asset price of housing*, P_H^0, is determined by the intersection of the supply and demand curves. The asset price of housing is the price of a typical house or apartment. At any one time, the market for the stock of housing determines the asset price of housing.

The Rate of Investment

We now consider the determinants of the rate of investment in housing, and for the purpose turn to Figure 11-8b. The curve FS represents the supply of new housing as a function of the price of housing. This curve is the same as the regular supply curve of any industry. The supply curve shows the amount of a good that suppliers want to sell at each price. In this case, the good being supplied is new housing. The position of the FS curve is affected by the costs of factors of production used in the construction industry and by technological factors affecting the cost of building.

The curve FS is sometimes called the flow supply curve, since it represents the *flow* of new housing into the market in a given time period. In contrast, the *stock* supply curve SS represents the total amount of housing in the market at a moment of time.

Given the price of housing established in the asset market, P_H^0, building contractors supply the amount of new housing, Q_H^0, for sale at that price. The higher the asset price, the greater the supply of new housing. Now the supply of new housing is simply gross investment in housing or total additions to the housing stock. Figure 11-8 thus represents our basic theory of the determinants of housing investment.

Any factor affecting the demand for the existing stock of housing will affect the asset price of housing, P_H, and thus the rate of investment in housing. Similarly, any factor shifting the flow supply curve FS will affect the rate of investment. We have already investigated the major factors shifting the DD demand curve for housing, but will briefly repeat that analysis.

Suppose the interest rate, the rate potential homeowners can obtain by investing elsewhere, rises. Then the asset demand for housing falls and the price of housing falls; that, in turn, induces a decline in the rate of production of new housing, or a decline in residential construction. Alternatively, suppose that the mortgage interest rate rises: Once again there is a fall in the asset price of housing and a reduction in the rate of construction.

Because the existing stock of housing is so large relative to the rate of investment in housing, we can ignore the effects of the current supply of new housing on the price of housing in the short run. However, over time, the new construction shifts the SS curve of panel (*a*) to the right as it increases the housing stock. The long-run equilibrium in the housing industry would be reached, in an economy in which there was no increase in population or wealth over time, when the housing stock was constant. Constancy of the housing stock requires gross investment to be equal to depreciation, or net investment to be equal to zero. The asset price of housing would have to be at the level such that the rate of construction was just equal to the rate of depreciation of the existing stock of housing in long-run equilibrium. If population or income and wealth were growing at a constant rate, the long-run equilibrium would be one in which the rate of construction was just sufficient to cover depreciation and the steadily growing stock demand. In an economy subjected to continual nonsteady changes, that long-run equilibrium is not necessarily ever reached.

Minor qualifications to the basic theoretical structure arise chiefly because new housing cannot be constructed immediately in response to changes in P_H. Rather, it takes a short time for that response to occur. Thus, the supply of new housing responds, not to the actual price of housing today, but to the price expected to prevail when the construction is completed. However, the lags are quite short; it takes less than a year to build a typical house. Another qualification stems from that same construction delay. Since builders have to incur expenses before they sell their output, they need financing over the construction period, and hence the position of the flow supply curve is affected by the interest rate.

The q Theory of Investment

We digress for a moment to note that the model of the housing market which emphasizes the asset market and the rate of addition to the stock can similarly be used to analyze business fixed investment. Indeed, an increasingly popular view of business fixed investment is the q theory that focuses on the stock market (see footnote 12). It can be cast in terms very similar to that of the housing model. At any one moment all the shares in the economy are in inelastic supply, just like the housing stock. Stock market investors place a value on those shares, with the price of shares in the stock market corresponding to P_H in Figure 11-8.

The price of a share in a company is the price of a claim on the capital in the company. The managers of the company can then be thought of as responding to the price of the stock by producing more new capital, that is, investing, when the price of shares is high and producing less new capital or not investing at all when the price of shares is low.

What is q? It is an estimate of the value the stock market places on a firm's assets relative to the cost of producing those assets. When the ratio is high, firms will want to produce more assets, so that investment will be rapid. Similarly, P_H can be thought of as the price of an existing house relative to the cost of building a new one. When that ratio is high, there will be lots of building.

Monetary Policy and Residential Construction

Monetary policy has powerful effects on the housing market. Most of the loans obtained to finance new construction are mortgages provided by financial institutions, particularly life insurance companies, trust companies, mortgage loan companies, and chartered banks. When interest rates rise, the supply of mortgage funds is affected in two ways. First, the interest cost to financial institutions of attracting deposits rises as the return on alternative investments increases. Second, the proportion of their assets channelled into mortgages falls as the yields on other securities rise.

The demand for housing is sensitive to interest rates, and the reason for this can be seen in Table 11-4. It shows the monthly payment that has to be made to repay a $50 000 mortgage with a 25-year amortization period at various interest rates. The monthly payment approximately doubles when the interest rate doubles. Thus an essential component of the cost of owning a house rises almost proportionately with the interest rate. It is therefore not surprising that the demand for housing is very sensitive to the interest rate.

Table 11-4 *Monthly Payments on Mortgages*

Interest rate	5%	10%	15%
Monthly payment	$292	$454	$640

Note: The assumed mortgage is a loan for $50 000, paid back over 25 years with equal monthly payments.

The above statement has to be qualified, since we should be concerned with the real and not the nominal interest cost of owning a house — and certainly much of the rise of the mortgage interest rate is a result of increases in the expected rate of inflation. However, the nominal interest rate also affects the homeowner. This results from the fact that a mortgage contract typically requires that the borrower pay a fixed amount each month over the lifetime of the mortgage. Even if the interest rate rises only because the expected rate of inflation has risen — and thus the real rate is constant — the payments that have to be made today by a borrower go up, but the inflation has not yet happened. Thus the real payments made today by a borrower rise when the nominal interest rate rises, even if the real rate does not rise.[23] Given the higher real monthly payments when the nominal interest rate rises, we should expect the nominal interest rate also to affect housing demand.

11-5 Concluding Remarks

We have presented several different models to explain the different categories of investment behaviour in this chapter. Nonetheless, there is a basic common element in the models, the interaction of the demand for the stock of capital with investment. In each case we started by examining the determinants of the desired stock — capital or housing. The discussion of inventory investment started by examining the determinants of the desired inventory–sales ratio. Then, in each case, we went on to analyze or describe the determinants of the rate per year of that type of investment.

We come now to the question of why there is a difference between the theoretical models used to explain the level of business fixed investment and residential construction. The fundamental difference arises from the degree of standardization of the capital and the associated question of the existence of a good market for the used capital goods. Much of business fixed investment is in capital that is specifically designed for a given firm and is not of much use to other firms. It is, accordingly, difficult to establish a market price for the stock of that type of capital, and the theory used in discussing residential construction would be difficult to apply in that case. Although housing, too, varies a good deal, it is, nonetheless, possible to talk of a price of housing. Further, used housing is a very good substitute for new housing, whereas that is less often true for many capital goods.

To look ahead, note that the emphasis in this chapter has been on investment as a component of aggregate demand. However, the definition of investment as adding to the capital stock suggests that it is also an important determinant of aggregate supply. We turn to the supply-side aspect of investment in Chapter 21.

---

[23] How can the real payments rise if the real interest rate stays the same? The explanation is that today's real payments rise, but the real present value of future payments falls: The repayment stream tilts toward the present.

11-6 Summary

1. Investment constitutes about 20 percent of aggregate demand, but fluctuations in investment account for a large share of business cycle movements in GDP. We analyze investment in three categories: business fixed investment, residential construction, and inventory investment.

2. Investment is spending that adds to the capital stock.

3. Inventory investment fluctuates proportionately more than any other class of investment. Firms have a desired inventory-to-sales ratio. The actual ratio may get out of line if sales are unexpectedly high or low, and then firms change their production levels to adjust inventories. For instance, when aggregate demand falls at the beginning of a recession, inventories build up. Then, when firms cut back production, output falls even more than did aggregate demand. This is the inventory cycle.

4. The neoclassical theory of business fixed investment sees the rate of investment being determined by the speed with which firms adjust their capital stocks toward their desired levels. The more output the firm expects to produce, and the smaller the rental or user cost of capital, the larger the desired capital stock. Since investment is undertaken for future production, it is expected future (permanent) output that determines the desired capital stock.

5. The real interest rate is the nominal (stated) interest rate minus the inflation rate.

6. The higher the real interest rate, the lower the price of the firm's stock, and the higher the rate of depreciation of capital, the higher the rental cost of capital. Taxes also affect the rental cost of capital, in particular through the investment tax credit. The investment tax credit is, in effect, a government subsidy for investment.

7. In practice, firms decide how much to invest using discounted cash flow analysis. This analysis gives answers that are consistent with those of the neoclassical approach.

8. The accelerator model of investment is a special case of the gradual adjustment model of investment. It predicts that investment demand is proportional to the change in output.

9. Empirical results show that business fixed investment responds with long lags to changes in output. The accelerator model, which does not take into account changes in the rental cost of capital, does almost as good a job of explaining investment as the more sophisticated neoclassical model.

10. The theory of housing investment starts from the demand for the stock of housing, affected by wealth, the interest rates available on alternative investments, and the mortgage rate. Increases in wealth increase the stock demand for hous-

ing; increases in either the interest rate on alternative assets or the mortgage rate reduce the stock demand. The price of housing is determined by the interaction of the stock demand and the given stock supply of housing available at any given time. The rate of housing investment is determined by the rate at which builders supply housing at the going price.

11. Housing investment is affected by monetary policy because housing demand is sensitive to the interest rate (real and nominal), and also because it affects the supply of mortgage funds.

12. We now summarize the common elements of the different models. First, aggregate investment is the sum of the different types of investment spending. Thus any variable that affects any of the categories of investment analyzed also affects aggregate investment. Second, monetary and fiscal policy both affect investment, particularly business fixed investment and housing investment. Third, there are substantial lags in the adjustment of investment spending to changes in output and other determinants of investment. This is true particularly for business fixed investment and inventory investment. Such lags are likely to increase fluctuations in GDP.

Key Terms

Business fixed investment	**Cobb–Douglas production function**
Residential construction	**Real interest rate**
Inventory investment	**Gradual adjustment hypothesis**
Inventory cycle	**Discounted cash flow analysis**
Desired capital stock	**Accelerator model of investment**
Marginal product of capital	**Present discounted value**
Rental (user) cost of capital	**q theory**

Problems

1. (a) Explain how final sales and output can differ.
    (b) Point out from Figure 11-2 periods of planned and unplanned inventory investment and decumulation.
    (c) During a period of slow but steady growth, how would you expect final sales and output to be related? Explain. Draw a hypothetical figure like Figure 11-2 for such a period.

2. We have seen in Chapters 10 and 11 that permanent income and output, rather than current income and output, determine consumption and investment.
    (a) How does this affect the *IS-LM* model built in Chapter 4? (Refer to Figure 10-4.)
    (b) What are the policy implications of the use of "permanent" measures?

3. In Chapter 4 it was assumed that investment rises during periods of low interest rates. That, however, was not the case during the 1930s, when investment and interest rates were both very low. Explain how this can occur. What would have been appropriate fiscal policy in such a case?

4. According to the description of business fixed investment in this chapter, how would you expect a firm's investment decisions to be affected by a sudden increase in demand for its product? What factors would determine the speed of its reaction?

5. Describe how a car rental agency would calculate the rate at which it rents cars, and relate your description to Equation (5).

6. It is often suggested that investment spending is dominated by "animal spirits" — the optimism or pessimism of investors. Is this argument at all consistent with the analysis of Sections 11-2 and 11-3?

7. Here are the cash flows for an investment project:

Year 1	Year 2	Year 3
− 200	100	120

   Should this firm undertake the project:
   (a) If the interest rate is 5 percent?
   (b) If the interest rate is 10 percent?

8. Is there any relation between the neoclassical theory of investment and the way firms make their investment decisions in practice?

9. Explain how the two panels of Figure 11-8 react together over time. What would happen if the demand for housing stock (DD) shifted upward and to the right over time?

10. Using Figure 11-8, trace carefully the step-by-step effects on the housing market of an increase in interest rates. Explain each shift and its long-run and short-run effects.

11. Suppose that an explicitly temporary tax credit is enacted. The tax credit is at the rate of 10 percent and lasts only one year.
    (a) What is the effect of this tax measure on investment in the long run (say, after four or five years)?
    (b) What is the effect in the current year and the following year?
    (c) How will your answers under (a) and (b) differ if the tax credit is permanent?

*12. For this question use the Cobb–Douglas production function and the corresponding desired capital stock given by Equation (3). Assume that $\gamma = 0.3$, $Y = \$250$ million and $rc = .15$.
    (a) Calculate the desired capital stock K^*.
    (b) Now suppose that Y is expected to rise to $300 million. What is the corresponding desired capital stock?

(c)   Suppose that the capital stock was at its desired level before the change in income was expected. Suppose further that $\gamma = 0.4$ in the gradual adjustment model of investment. What will the rate of investment be in the first year after expected income changes? In the second year?

(d)   Does your answer in (c) refer to gross or net investment?

Appendix Interest Rates, Present Values, and Discounting

In this appendix we deal with the relationships among bond coupons, interest rates and yields, and the prices of bonds. In doing so, we shall introduce the very useful concept of present discounted value (*PDV*).

Section 1

We start with the case of a perpetual bond, or perpetuity. Such bonds have been issued in a number of countries, including the United Kingdom, where they are called Consols. The Consol is a promise by the British government to pay a fixed amount to the holder of the bond every year and forever. Let us denote the promised payment per Consol by Q_c, the *coupon*.[24]

The *yield* on a bond is the return per dollar that the holder of the bond receives. The yield on a savings account paying 5 percent interest per year is obviously just 5 percent. Someone paying $25 for a Consol that has a coupon of $2.50 obtains a yield of 10 percent [($2.50/25) $\times$ 100%].

The yield on a Consol and its price are related in a simple way. Let us denote the price of the Consol by P_c and the coupons by Q_c. Then, as the above example suggests, the yield i is just

$$i = \frac{Q_c}{P_c} \tag{A1}$$

which says that the yield on a perpetuity is the coupon divided by the price. Alternatively, we can switch Equation (A1) around to

$$P_c = \frac{Q_c}{i} \tag{A2}$$

---

[24] The coupon rate is the coupon divided by the face value of the bond, which is literally the value printed on the face of the bond. Bonds do not necessarily sell for their face value, though customarily the face value is close to the value at which the bonds are sold when they first come on the market.

which says that price is the coupon divided by the yield. Thus, given the coupon and the yield, we can derive the price, or given the coupon and the price, we can derive the yield.

None of this is a theory of the determination of the yield or the price of a perpetuity. It merely points out the relationship between price and yield. Our theory of the determination of the yield on bonds is presented in Chapter 4. The interest rate in Chapter 4 corresponds to the yield on bonds, and we tend to talk interchangeably of interest rates and yields.

We shall return to the Consol at the end of the appendix.

Section 2

Now we move to a short-term bond. Let us consider a bond which was sold by a borrower for $100, on which the borrower promises to pay back $108 after 1 year. This is a 1-year bond. The yield on the bond to the person who bought it for $100 is 8 percent. For every $1 lent, the lender obtains both the $1 principal and 8 cents extra at the end of the year.

Next we ask a slightly different question. How much would a promise to pay $1 at the end of the year be worth? If $108 at the end of the year is worth $100 today, then $1 at the end of the year must be worth $100/108, or 92.6 cents. That is the value today of $1 in 1 year's time. In other words, it is the present discounted value of $1 in 1 year's time. It is the present value because it is what would be paid today for the promise of money in 1 year's time, and it is discounted because the value today is less than the promised payment in a year's time.

Denoting the 1-year yield or interest rate by i, we can write that the present discounted value of a promised payment Q_1, 1 year from now, is

$$PDV = \frac{Q_1}{1 + i} \tag{A3}$$

Let us return to our 1-year bond and suppose that the day after the original borrower obtained the money, the yield on 1-year bonds rises. How much would anyone now be willing to pay for the promise to receive $108 after 1 year? The answer must be given by the general formula (A3). That means that the price of the 1-year bond will fall when the interest rate or yield on such bonds rises. Once again, we see that the price of the bond and the yield are inversely related, given the promised payments to be made on the bond.

As before, we can reverse the formula for the price in order to find the yield on the bond, given its price and the promised payment Q_1. Note that the price P is equal to the present discounted value, so that we can write

$$1 + i = \frac{Q_1}{P} \tag{A4}$$

Section 3

Next we consider a 2-year bond. Such a bond would typically promise to make a payment of interest, which we shall denote Q_1, at the end of the first year, and then a payment of interest and principal (usually the amount borrowed), Q_2, at the end of the second year. Given the yield i on the bond, how do we compute its *PDV*, which will be equal to its price?

We start by asking first what the bond will be worth 1 year from now. At that stage, it will be a 1-year bond, promising to pay the amount Q_2 in 1 year's time, and yielding i. Its value 1 year from now will accordingly be given by Equation (A3), except that Q_1 in Equation (A3) is replaced by Q_2. Let us denote the value of the bond 1 year from now by PDV_1, and note that

$$PDV_1 = \frac{Q_2}{1 + i} \tag{A5}$$

To complete computing the *PDV* of the 2-year bond, we can now treat it as a 1-year bond, which promises to pay Q_1 in interest 1 year from now, and also to pay PDV_1 1 year from now, since it can be sold at that stage for that amount. Hence, the *PDV* of the bond, equal to its price, is

$$PDV = \frac{Q_1}{1 + i} + \frac{PDV_1}{1 + i} \tag{A6}$$

or

$$PDV = \frac{Q_1}{1 + i} + \frac{Q_2}{(1 + i)^2} \tag{A6a}$$

As previously, given the promised payments Q_1 and Q_2, the price of the bond will fall if the yield rises, and vice versa.

It is now less simple to reverse the equation for the price of the bond to find the yield than it was before; that is because from Equation (A6), we obtain a quadratic equation for the yield, which has two solutions.

Section 4

We have now provided the outline of the argument whereby the present discounted value of any promised stream of payments for any number of years can be computed. Suppose that a bond, or any other asset, promises to pay amounts $Q_1, Q_2, Q_3 \ldots, Q_n$ in future years, 1, 2, 3, $\ldots$, n years away. By pursuing the type of argument given in Section 3, it is possible to show that the *PDV* of such a payments stream will be

$$PDV = \frac{Q_1}{1+i} + \frac{Q_2}{(1+i)^2} + \frac{Q_3}{(1+i)^3} + \cdots \frac{Q_n}{(1+i)^n} \tag{A7}$$

As usual, the price of a bond with a specified payments stream will be inversely related to its yield.

Section 5

The formula (A7) is the general formula for calculating the present discounted value of any stream of payments. Indeed, the payments may also be negative. Thus, in calculating the *PDV* of an investment project, we expect the first few payments, for example, Q_1 and Q_2, to be negative. Those are the periods in which the firm is spending to build the factory or buy machinery. Then in later years the Q_i becomes positive as the factory starts generating revenues.

Firms undertaking discounted cash flow analysis are calculating present values using a formula such as (A7).

Section 6

Finally, we return to the Consol. The Consol promises to pay the amount Q_c forever. Applying the formula, we can compute the present value of the Consol by

$$PDV = Q_c \left[\frac{1}{(1+i)} + \frac{1}{(1+i)^2} + \frac{1}{(1+i)^3} + \cdots \frac{1}{(1+i)^n} + \cdots \right] \tag{A8}$$

The terms in the parentheses on the right-hand side constitute an infinite series, the sum of which can be calculated as $1/i$. Thus,

$$PDV = \frac{Q_c}{i} \tag{A9}$$

This section casts a slightly different light on the common-sense discussion of Section 1 of this appendix. Equations (A8) and (A9) show that the Consol's price is equal to the *PDV* of the future coupon payments.

CHAPTER 12 *The Demand for Money*

Money is a means of payment or medium of exchange. Since money is used for purchasing goods, individuals are interested in the purchasing power of their money holdings — the value of their cash balances in terms of the goods the cash will buy. In other words, they are concerned with their *real balances* rather than their *nominal* money holdings. Two implications follow:

1.   *Real* money demand is unchanged when the price level increases, and all real variables, such as the interest rate, real income, and real wealth, remain unchanged.

2.   *Nominal* money demand increases in proportion to the increase in the price level, given the constancy of the real variables just specified.[1]

We have a special name for behaviour that is not affected by changes in the price level, all real variables remaining unchanged. An individual is free from *money illusion* if a change in the level of prices, holding all real variables constant, leaves real behaviour, including real money demand, unchanged. By contrast, an individual whose real behaviour is affected by a change in the price level, all real variables remaining unchanged, is said to suffer from money illusion.

In Chapter 4, we assumed that the demand for money increases with the level of real income and decreases with the nominal interest rate. Recall that the response of the demand for money to interest rates is important in determining the effectiveness of fiscal policy. Changes in fiscal variables, such as tax rates or government spending, affect aggregate demand if the demand for money changes when the interest rate

---

[1]   Be sure you understand that (1) and (2) say the same thing in slightly different ways.

changes — if the demand for money is interest-elastic. If the demand for money does not react at all to changes in the interest rate, increases in government spending totally crowd out private spending and leave the level of income unaffected.

The demand for money has been studied very intensively at both the theoretical and empirical levels. There is by now almost total agreement that the demand should, as a theoretical matter, increase as the level of real income rises and decrease as the nominal interest rate rises. Empirical work bears out these two properties of the demand-for-money function.

12-1 Definition and Functions of Money

The Bank of Canada publishes several *monetary aggregates* that are used as measures of the money supply. The major ones are shown in Table 12-1.[2] The most widely used concept is *M1*, which includes currency and *demand deposits*. Currency consists of notes and coin in circulation outside the banking system, and demand deposits are chequing accounts at the chartered banks. *M2* is a broader measure of the money supply that includes personal savings accounts and nonpersonal *notice deposits*.[3]

Table 12-1 *Components of the Money Stock, June 1991*

(billions of dollars, average of Wednesdays)	
(1) Currency	$ 19.8
(2) Demand deposits	20.6
MI = (1) + (2)	40.4
(3) Personal savings deposits	208.7
(4) Nonpersonal notice deposits	23.4
M2 = MI + (3) + (4)	272.5
(5) Nonpersonal term deposits	42.5
(6) Foreign currency deposits*	7.7
M3 = M2 + (5) + (6)	322.7
(7) M2+ = M2 + deposits at other deposit-taking institutions	463.4

*Deposits of residents booked in Canada.

Source: Bank of Canada Review, Tables C2, E1.

---

[2] For a detailed description of the definitions, see *Bank of Canada Review*, Table E1 and the appended notes. Details concerning recent revisions are available annually, usually in the February issue.

[3] A notice deposit is an account on which the bank reserves the right to require notice before a withdrawal can be made. Personal savings accounts have such a provision, but it is not normally enforced. (Look at the small print in your passbook!)

Table 12-1 also shows the broader definition of the money supply, $M3$. $M3$ includes all Canadian dollar deposits in chartered banks and foreign currency deposits held by residents. The components of $M3$ that are not part of $M1$ or $M2$ are in general less *liquid* in that they cannot immediately and conveniently be used for making payments. However, they are assets that are close to being money in the sense that they are available with only a little difficulty for making payments.

Although $M2$ includes the major assets that serve as a means of payment or can easily be converted into a means of payment, it includes only deposits in the chartered banks. $M2+$ includes deposits in other financial institutions such as trust companies and credit unions.

Historically, there have often been changes in the type of assets which can be used as means of payment, and simultaneous disagreements about what constitutes money in those circumstances. When cheques first began to be widely used in England early in the nineteenth century, there was a disagreement over whether demand deposits should be regarded as part of the money stock. Now that point is not disputed. We can expect there to be continuing changes in the financial structure over the years, with consequent changes in the definitions of the various money supply concepts.

In summary, there is no unique set of assets which will always constitute the money supply. At present, there are arguments for using a broader definition of the money stock than $M1$ and even arguments for using a less broad definition — should $1000 bills be included, for example? Further, over the course of time, the particular assets that serve as a medium of exchange, or means of payment, will certainly change further.

The Functions of Money

Money is so widely used that we rarely step back to think how remarkable a device it is. It is impossible to imagine a modern economy operating without the use of money or something very much like it. In a mythical barter economy in which there is no money, every transaction has to involve an exchange of goods (and/or services) on both sides of the transaction. The examples of the difficulties of barter are endless. The economist wanting a haircut would have to find a barber wanting to listen to a lecture on economics; the actor wanting a suit would have to find a tailor wanting to watch movies; and so on. Without a medium of exchange, modern economies could not operate.

Using money as a medium of exchange eliminates the necessity for a "double coincidence of wants" in exchanges. By the double coincidence, we have in mind the above examples. The wants of two individuals would have to be identically matched for the exchange to take place. For instance, the man selling movie tickets would have to find a buyer whose goods he wanted to buy (the suit), and the woman selling suits would have to find a buyer whose goods she wanted to buy (the movie tickets).

There are four traditional functions of money, of which the *medium of exchange* is the first.[4] The other three are store of value, unit of account, and standard of deferred payment.

---

[4] See W.S. Jevons, *Money and the Mechanism of Exchange* (London: Routledge & Kegan Paul, 1910).

A *store of value* is an asset that maintains value over time. Thus, an individual holding a store of value can use that asset to make purchases at a future date. If an asset were not a store of value, then it would not be used as a medium of exchange. Imagine trying to use ice cream as money in the absence of refrigerators. There would hardly ever be a good reason for anyone to give up goods for money (ice cream) if the money were sure to melt within the next few minutes. If the seller were unwilling to accept the ice cream in exchange for his or her goods, then the ice cream would not be a medium of exchange. However, there are many stores of value other than money — such as bonds, stocks, and houses.

The *unit of account* is the unit in which prices are quoted and books kept. Prices are quoted in dollars and cents, and dollars and cents are the units in which the money stock is measured. Usually, the money unit is also the unit of account, but that is not essential. In the German hyperinflation of 1922–1923, dollars were the unit of account for some firms, whereas the mark was the medium of exchange.

Finally, as a *standard of deferred payment*, money units are used in long-term transactions, such as loans. The amount that has to be paid back in 5 or 10 years is specified in dollars and cents. Dollars and cents are acting as the standard of deferred payment. Once again, though, it is not essential that the standard of deferred payment be the money unit. For example, the final payment of a loan may be related to the behaviour of the price level, rather than being fixed in dollars and cents. This is known as an indexed loan.

The last two of the four functions of money are, accordingly functions which money usually performs, but not functions that it necessarily performs. The store of value function is one that many assets perform.

There are fascinating descriptions of different types of money that have existed in the past that we do not have room to review here,[5] but there is one final point we want to emphasize. *Money is whatever is generally accepted in exchange*. However magnificently a piece of paper may be engraved, it will not be money if it is not accepted in payment. However unusual the material of which it is made, anything that is generally accepted in payment is money. The only reason money is accepted in payment is that the recipient believes that it can be spent at a later time. There is thus an inherent circularity in the acceptance of money. Money is accepted in payment because it is believed that it will also be accepted in payment by others.

The Motives for Holding Money

In the following two sections we review the theories corresponding to Keynes's famous three motives for holding money.[6] In doing so, we will concentrate on the effects of changes in income and the interest rate on money demand. The three motives are:

---

[5] See Paul Einzig, *Primitive Money* (New York: Pergamon Press, 1966).
[6] J.M. Keynes, *The General Theory of Employment, Interest and Money* (London: Macmillan, 1936), Chapter 13.

- The transactions motive, which is the demand for money arising from the use of money in making regular payments.

- The precautionary motive, which is the demand for money to meet unforeseen contingencies.

- The speculative motive, which arises from the uncertainties about the money value of other assets that an individual can hold.

In discussing the transactions and precautionary motives, we are mainly discussing $M1$, whereas the speculative motive refers more to broader aggregates, as we shall see.

Although we examine the demand for money by looking at the three motives for holding it, we cannot separate a particular person's money holdings, say $500, into three neat piles of, say, $200, $200, and $100, each being held for a different motive. Money being held to satisfy one motive is always available for another use. The person holding unusually large balances for speculative reasons also has those balances available to meet an unexpected emergency, so that they serve too as precautionary balances. All three motives influence an individual's holdings of money, and as we shall see, each leads to the prediction that the demand for money should fall as the interest rate on other assets increases.

This final point is worth emphasizing. Money ($M1$, that is, currency and some chequable deposits) generally earns no interest or less interest than other assets. Anyone holding money is giving up interest that could be earned by holding some other asset, such a a savings deposit or a bond. The higher the interest loss from holding a dollar of money, the less money we expect the individual to hold. Thus, the greater the interest rate on money itself if interest is paid on demand deposits, the higher the demand for money; and the higher the interest rate on alternative assets, the lower the demand for money. In practice, we can measure the cost of holding money as the difference between the interest rate paid on money (perhaps zero) and the interest rate paid on the most nearly comparable other asset, such as a savings deposit or, for corporations, a certificate of deposit or commercial paper. The interest rate on money is referred to as the *own* rate of interest, and the *opportunity cost* of holding money is equal to the difference between the yield on other assets and the own rate.

12-2 The Transactions Demand for Money

The transactions demand for money arises from the use of money in making regular payment for goods and services. In the course of each month, an individual makes a variety of payments for such items as rent or mortgage, groceries, the newspaper, and other purchases. In this section we examine how much money an individual would hold for such purchases.

In analyzing the transactions demand, we are concerned with a tradeoff between the amount of interest an individual forgoes by holding money and the costs and inconveniences of holding a small amount of money. To make the problem concrete, consider someone who is paid $1800 each month. Assume the person spends the $1800 evenly over the course of the month, at the rate of $60 per day. At one extreme, the individual could simply leave the $1800 in cash (whether currency or demand deposits) and spend it at the rate of $60 per day. Alternatively, on the first day of the month the individual could take the $60 to spend that day and put the remaining $1740 in a daily-interest savings account. Then every morning the person could go to the bank to withdraw that day's $60 from the savings account. By the end of the month the depositor would have earned interest on the money retained each day in the savings account. This would be the *benefit* of keeping money holdings down as low as $60 at the beginning of each day. The *cost* of keeping money holdings down is simply the cost and inconvenience of the trips to the bank to withdraw the daily $60. To decide on how much money to hold for transactions purposes, the individual has to weigh the costs of holding small balances against the interest advantage of doing so.

We now study the tradeoff in more detail and derive a formula for the demand for money. Suppose the nominal monthly income of the individual is Y_N.[7] We make the simplifying assumption that Y_N is paid into a savings account, rather than a chequing account, each month. The money is spent at a steady rate over the course of the month. To spend it, the individual has to get it out of the savings account and into cash, which may be currency or a chequing account. If left in the savings account, the deposit earns interest at a rate of i per month. It earns zero interest as cash. The cost to the individual of making a transfer between cash and the savings account (which we henceforth call bonds for convenience) is $\$tc$. That cost may be the individual's time, or it may be a cost explicitly paid to someone else to make the transfer. For convenience we refer to it as a broker's fee.

The Inventory Approach

The approach we are describing is known as the *inventory-theoretic approach*.[8] You should think of this theory applying equally well, with small changes in terminology and assumptions, to firms and households.

The individual has to decide how many transactions to make between bonds and cash each month. If just one transaction is made, transferring Y_N into cash at the beginning of the month, the cash balance over the course of the month will be as shown in Figure 12-1a. It starts at Y_N, is spent evenly over the month, and is down to

---

[7] As a reminder, nominal income, Y_N, is defined as real income, Y, times the price level P: $Y_N = PY$.

[8] The approach was originally developed to determine the inventories of goods a firm should have on hand. In that context, the amount Y_N would be the monthly sales of the good, tc the cost of ordering the good, and i the interest rate for carrying the inventory. The analogy between money as an inventory of purchasing power, standing ready to buy goods, and an inventory of goods, standing ready to be bought by customers, is quite close. The inventory-theoretic approach to the demand for money is associated with the names of William Baumol and James Tobin. (William Baumol, "The Transactions Demand for Cash: An Inventory Theoretic Approach," *Quarterly Journal of Economics*, November 1952; and James Tobin, "The Interest Elasticity of Transactions Demand for Cash," *Review of Economics and Statistics*, August 1956.) The most famous result of Baumol's and Tobin's work is the square-root law of the demand for money, which is presented later in Equation (4).

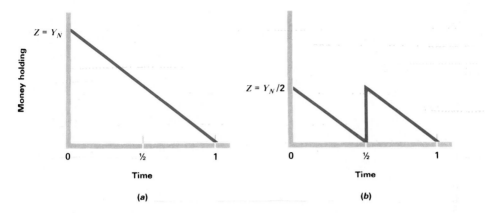

Figure 12-1 *The Amount of Cash Held During the Month Related to the Number of Withdrawals*

Panel (*a*) shows the pattern of money holding during the month when the individual makes just one transaction from the savings account to cash during the month. At the beginning of the month the individual transfers the entire amount to be spent, Y_N, into cash, and then spends it evenly over the month. Panel (*b*) shows the pattern of money holding when there are two transactions, one at the beginning of the month and one in the middle of the month. In panel (*a*) average cash holdings for the month are $Y_N/2$; in panel (*b*) they are $Y_N/4$.

zero by the end of the month, at which time a new payment is received by the individual and transferred into the person's chequing account. If the individual makes two withdrawals from the savings account, $Y_N/2$ is transferred into cash at the beginning of the month, resulting in a cash balance that is run down to zero in the middle of the month. At this point another $Y_N/2$ is transferred into cash and spent evenly over the rest of the month.[9] Figure 12-1b shows the individual's cash holdings in that case.

We shall denote the size of a cash withdrawal from the bond portfolio (savings account) by Z and the number of withdrawals from the bond portfolio by n. Thus, n is the number of times the individual adds to the cash balance during the month. If n equal-sized withdrawals are made during the month, transferring funds from the savings account to the chequing account, then the size of each transfer is Y_N/n, since a total of Y_N has to be transferred from the savings account into cash. For example, if Y_N is $1800, and n, the number of transactions, is 3, then Z, the amount transferred to cash each time, is $600. Accordingly, we can write

$$nZ = Y_N \qquad (1)$$

$$3Z = 1800$$

9 With simple interest being paid on the savings account, the individual's transactions between bonds and cash should be evenly spaced over the month. We leave the proof of that for the case where there are two transactions to Problem 8.

Suppose that the amount Z is transferred from bonds to cash at each withdrawal. What then is the *average* cash balance over the course of the month? We want to find the size of the average cash balance in order to measure the interest that is lost as a result of holding cash; if that amount were not held as cash, it could be held as interest-earning bonds. In Figure 12-1a, the average cash balance held during the month is $Y_N/2 = Z/2$, since the cash balance starts at Y_N and runs down in a straight line to zero.[10] In the case of Figure 12-1b, the average cash balance for the first half of the month is $Y_N/4 = Z/2$, and the average cash balance for the second half of the month is also $Z/2$. Thus, the average cash balance for the entire month is $Y_N/4 = Z/2$. Similarly, if three withdrawals were made, the average cash balance would be $Y_N/6 = Z/2$. In general, the average cash balance is $Z/2$, as you might want to confirm by drawing diagrams similar to Figure 12-1 for $n = 3$ or other values of n.

The interest cost of holding money is the interest rate times the average cash balance, or $iZ/2$. From Equation (1), that means the total interest cost is $iY_N/2n$. The other component of the cost of managing the portfolio is the brokerage cost, or the cost in terms of the individual's time and inconvenience in managing his or her money. That cost is just the number of withdrawals made, n, times the cost of each withdrawal, tc, and is thus equal to $n \times tc$. The total cost of managing the portfolio is the interest cost plus the total brokerage cost:

$$\text{Total cost} = (n \times tc) + \frac{iY_N}{2n} \tag{2}$$

Equation (2) shows formally that the brokerage cost $(n \times tc)$ increases as the number of withdrawals (transactions between bonds and money) rises, and that the interest cost decreases as the number of withdrawals increases. It thus emphasizes the tradeoff faced in managing money, and suggests that there is an optimal number of withdrawals the individual should make to minimize the total cost of holding money to meet transactions requirements for buying goods.

To derive that optimal point, we want to find the point at which the benefit of carrying out another withdrawal is less than, or just equal to, the cost of making another transaction between bonds and money. If the benefit of making another transaction were greater than the cost, then another withdrawal should be made, and the original point could not have been optimal. The cost of making another transaction is always equal to tc. In Figure 12-2, we show the costs of making a further transaction by the marginal cost curve MC, which is horizontal at the level tc. The financial benefit from making another transaction is represented by the MB (marginal benefit) curve in Figure 12-2, which represents the interest *saved* by making another withdrawal and thus having a smaller cash balance on average during the month.

The more transactions between money and bonds an individual makes, the lower is the total interest cost, but the reduction of the interest cost obtained by making more transactions falls off rapidly as the number of withdrawals increases. There is a

---

[10] The average cash balance is the average of the amount of cash the individual holds at each moment during the month. For instance, if $400 is held for 3 days and zero for the rest of the month, the average cash balance would be $40, or one-tenth (3 days divided by 30 days) of the month times $400.

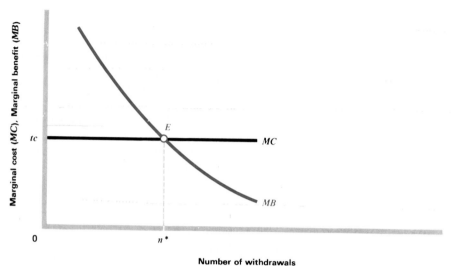

Figure 12-2 *Optimal Cash Management Determining the Optimal Number of Withdrawals*

The marginal cost of making another transaction is the constant amount, *tc*, as shown by the *MC* curve. The marginal benefit of making another transaction is the amount of interest saved by holding smaller money balances. The marginal benefit decreases as the number of withdrawals from the savings account increases. Point *E* is the point at which the cost of managing money holdings is minimized. Corresponding to point *E* is $n°$, the optimal number of transactions to make between the savings account and money.

substantial saving in interest costs by making two withdrawals rather than one, but very little saving in interest costs by making thirty-one transactions rather than thirty. This suggests that the marginal benefit of making more withdrawals decreases as the number of withdrawals becomes large. The *MB* curve in Figure 12-2 is, accordingly, downward-sloping.[11]

In Figure 12-2, the optimal number of transactions is given by $n°$, the number at which the marginal benefit in terms of interest saved is equal to the marginal cost of making a transaction. Given the number of transactions and the individual's income, we also know the average cash balance *M*, using the relationship between average money holdings and the size of each transfer which we derived earlier:

$$M = \frac{Z}{2} = \frac{Y_N}{2n} \tag{3}$$

---

[11] Two points about Figure 12-2: First, note that we have, for convenience, drawn the curves as continuous, even though you will recognize that it is only possible to make an integral number of transactions, and not, for example, 1.6 or 7.24 transactions. Second, if you know the calculus, try to derive the equation of the marginal benefit curve from the component of costs in Equation (2) that is due to interest lost.

Properties of Money Demand

From Figure 12-2 we can see two important results. First, suppose the brokerage cost rises. That shifts the *MC* curve up, decreases the number of withdrawals *n*, and therefore (from Equation (3), where *M* is inversely related to *n*) increases the average holding of money. Second, an increase in the interest rate shifts up the *MB* curve, which therefore increases *n*, and thus (again from Equation (3)) reduces the holding of money: When the interest rate is higher, the individual is willing to make more trips to the bank to earn the higher interest now available. Figure 12-2 thus shows one of the key results we wanted to establish: that the demand for money is inversely related to the interest rate.

In the case of an increase in income, Figure 12-2 is unfortunately less useful. An increase in income shifts up the *MB* curve and increases the number of transactions, but from Equation (3) we see that an increase in the number of transactions accompanying an increase in income does not necessarily imply that the demand for money rises, since it seems that *n* could increase proportionately more than Y_N. However, more complete algebraic analysis of the individual's optimal behaviour will show that the demand for money in this model rises when income rises.

The famous *square-root formula* for money demand, developed by William Baumol and James Tobin,[12] makes the results of the graphical analysis of Figure 12-2 more precise and resolves the ambiguity about the effects of income on the demand for money. The formula gives the demand for money that is obtained as a result of minimizing the total costs in Equation (2) with respect to the number of withdrawals and then using Equation (3) to derive the cash balance.[13] The formula is

$$M^\circ = \sqrt{\frac{tc \times Y_N}{2i}} \tag{4}$$

Equation (4) shows that the transactions demand for money increases with the brokerage fee, or the cost of transacting, and with the level of income. The demand for money decreases with the interest rate.

Money Demand Elasticities

Equation (4) also shows that an increase in income raises the demand for money proportionately less than the increase in income itself. To put the same point somewhat differently, the ratio of income to money, Y_N/M, rises with the level of income. A person with a higher level of income holds proportionately less money. This point is

---

[12] See the references in footnote 8.

[13] If you can handle calculus, try to derive Equation (4) by minimizing total cost in Equation (2).

sometimes put in different words by saying that there are *economies of scale* in cash management.

Yet another way of saying the same thing is that the income elasticity of the demand for money is less than 1. (It is equal to 1/2 in Equation (4).) The income elasticity measures the percentage change in the demand for money due to a 1 percent change in income.[14] Similarly, Equation (4) implies that the elasticity of the demand for money with respect to the brokerage fee is 1/2, and the elasticity with respect to the interest rate is −1/2.

What accounts for the fact that people can somehow manage with less cash per dollar of spending as income increases? The answer is that cash management is more effective at high levels of income because the average cost per dollar of transaction is lower with large-size transactions. In turn, the lower average cost of transactions results from the fixed brokerage fee per transaction; it costs as much to transfer $10 as $10 million, so that the average cost per dollar transferred is lower for large transfers.

However, in the case of households, we should recognize that the "brokerage cost" *tc*, the cost of making withdrawals from a savings account, is in part the cost of time and the nuisance of having to go to the bank. Since the cost of time to individuals is likely to be higher the higher their income, *tc* may rise with Y_N. In that case, an increase in income would result in an increase in the demand for money by more than the income elasticity of 1/2 indicates, because *tc* goes up together with Y_N.

The Demand for Real Balances

We started this chapter by emphasizing that the demand for money is a demand for real balances. It is worth confirming that the inventory theory of the demand for money implies that the demand for real balances does not change when all prices double (or increase in any other proportion). When all prices double, both Y_N and *tc* in Equation (4) double — that is, both nominal income and the nominal brokerage fee double. Accordingly, the demand for nominal balances doubles, so that the demand for real balances is unchanged. The square-root formula does not imply any money illusion in the demand for money. Thus we should be careful when saying the income elasticity of demand for money implied by Equation (4) is 1/2. The elasticity of the demand for *real* balances with respect to *real* income is 1/2. If income rises only because all prices (including *tc*) rise, then the demand for *nominal* balances rises proportionately.

Integer Constraints

So far we have ignored the important constraint that it is possible to make only an integral number of transactions, such as 1, 2, 3, etc., and that it is not possible to make

---

[14] The income elasticity of demand is $\dfrac{\Delta(M/P)}{M/P} \bigg/ \dfrac{\Delta Y}{Y}$. Similarly, the interest elasticity is $\dfrac{\Delta(M/P)}{M/P} \bigg/ \dfrac{\Delta i}{i}$.

1.25 or 3.57 transactions. However, when we take account of this constraint, we shall see that it implies that many people do not make more than the essential one transaction between money and bonds within the period in which they are paid.[15]

Consider our previous example of the person who received $1800 per month. Suppose, realistically, that the interest rate per month on savings deposits is 1/2 percent. The individual cannot avoid making one initial transaction, since income initially arrives in the savings account. The next question is whether it pays to make a second transaction. That is, does it pay to keep half the monthly income for half a month in the savings account and make a second withdrawal after half a month? With an interest rate of 1/2 percent per month, interest for half a month would be 1/4 percent. Half the income would amount to $900, and the interest earnings would, therefore, be $900 × 1/4 percent = $2.25.

Now if the brokerage fee exceeds $2.25, the individual will not bother to make more than one transaction, and $2.25 is not an outrageous cost in terms of the time and nuisance of making a transfer from the savings to the chequing account. Thus, for many individuals whose monthly net pay is below $1800, we do not expect formula (4) to hold exactly. Their cash balance would instead simply be half their income. They would make one transfer into cash at the beginning of the month; Figure 11-1*a* would describe their money holdings. For such individuals, the income elasticity of the demand for money is 1, since their demand for money goes up precisely in proportion with their income. The interest elasticity is zero, so long as they make only one transaction.

The very strong restrictions on the income and interest elasticities of the demand for money of Equation (4) are not valid when the integer constraints are taken into account. Instead, the income elasticity is an average of the elasticities of different people, some of whom make only one transaction from bonds to money, and the elasticity is therefore between 1/2 and 1. Similarly, the interest elasticity is also an average of the elasticities across different individuals, being between −1/2 and zero.[16] Because firms deal with larger amounts of money, they are likely to make a large number of transactions between money and bonds, and their income and interest elasticities of the demand for money are therefore likely to be close to the 1/2 and −1/2 predicted by Equation (4).

The Payment Period

Once the integer constraints are taken into account, it can also be seen that the transactions demand for money depends on the frequency with which individuals are paid (the payment period). If one examines the square-root formula (4), the demand for

---

[15]   If we had assumed that individuals were paid in cash, it would turn out that many people would not make any transactions between money and bonds in managing their transactions balances.

[16]   See Robert J. Barro, "Integer Constraints and Aggregation in an Inventory Model of Money Demand," *Journal of Finance*, March 1976.

money does not seem to depend on how often a person is paid, since an increase in the payments period increases both Y_N and i in the same proportion. Thus the demand for money appears unaffected by the length of the period. However, consider a person who makes only one transaction from bonds to money at the beginning of each month and would therefore have money demand of $Y_N/2$. If such a person were paid weekly, his or her demand for money would be only one-quarter of the demand with monthly payments. Thus we should expect the demand for money to increase with the length of the payment period.

Summary

The inventory-theoretic approach to the demand for money gives a precise formula for the transactions demand for money. The income elasticity of the demand for money is 1/2, and the interest elasticity is $-1/2$. When integer constraints are taken into account, the limits on the income elasticity of demand are between 1/2 and 1, and the limits on the interest elasticity are between $-1/2$ and zero. We have outlined the approach in terms of an individual's demand for money, but a similar approach is relevant for firms.

Some of the assumptions made in deriving the square-root formula are very restrictive. People do not spend their money evenly over the course of the month, and they do not know exactly what their payments will be. Their cheques are not paid into savings accounts, and so on. It turns out, though, that the major results we have derived are not greatly affected by the use of more realistic assumptions. There is thus good reason to expect the demand for money to increase with the level of income and to decrease as the interest rate on other assets (or, generally, the cost of holding money) increases.

12-3   Other Motives for Holding Money

In discussing the transactions demand for money, we focused on transactions costs and ignored uncertainty. In this section, we concentrate on the demand for money that arises from uncertainty about (1) the size and timing of receipts and payments and (2) the money value of other assets.

The Precautionary Motive

We first consider the precautionary motive that arises because a person is uncertain about what amounts will be received and what payments will be required.[17] Such a

---

[17] See Edward H. Whalen, "A Rationalization of the Precautionary Demand for Cash," *Quarterly Journal of Economics*, May 1966.

person might decide to have a hot fudge sundae, or need to take a cab in the rain, or have to pay for a prescription. If the individual did not have money with which to pay, he or she would incur a loss. The loss could be missing a fine meal, or missing an appointment, or having to come back the next day to pay for the prescription. For concreteness, we shall denote the loss incurred as a result of being short of cash by q. The loss clearly varies from situation to situation, but as usual we simplify.

The more money an individual holds, the less likely he or she is to incur the costs of illiquidity (that is, not having money immediately available), but the more money that is held, the more interest that is given up. We are back to a tradeoff situation similar to that examined in relation to the transactions demand. Somewhere between holding so little money for precautionary purposes that it will almost certainly be necessary to forgo some purchase (or to borrow in a hurry) and holding so much money that there is little chance of not being able to make any payment that might be necessary, there must be an optimal amount of precautionary balances to hold. That optimal amount will involve the balancing of interest costs against the advantages of being liquid.

Once more, we write down the total costs of holding an amount of money M.[18] This time we are dealing with expected costs, since it is not certain what the need for money will be. We denote the probability that the individual is illiquid during the month by $p(M, \sigma)$. The function $p(M, \sigma)$ indicates that the probability of the person's being illiquid at some time during the month depends on the level of money balances M being held and the degree of uncertainty, σ, about the net payments that will be made during the month. The higher is M, the lower the probability of illiquidity; and the higher the degree of uncertainty, σ, the higher the probability of illiquidity. The expected cost of illiquidity is $p(M, \sigma)q$ — the probability of illiquidity times the cost of being illiquid. The interest cost associated with holding a cash balance of M is just iM. Thus, we have

$$\text{Expected costs} = iM + p(M, \sigma)q \tag{5}$$

To determine the optimal amount of money to hold, we compare the marginal costs of increasing money holding by \$1 with the expected marginal benefit of doing so. The marginal cost is again the interest forgone, or i. That is shown by the MC curve in Figure 12-3. The marginal benefit of increasing money holding arises from the lower expected costs of illiquidity. Increasing precautionary balances from zero has a large marginal benefit, since that takes care of small, unexpected disbursements that are quite likely. As we increase cash balances further, we continue to reduce the probability of illiquidity, but at a decreasing rate. We start to hold cash to insure against quite unlikely events. Thus, the marginal benefit of additional cash is a decreasing function of the level of cash holdings — more cash on hand is better than less, but at a diminishing rate. The marginal benefit of increasing cash holdings is shown by the MB curve in Figure 12-3.

---

[18] This paragraph contains technical material that is optional and can easily be skipped.

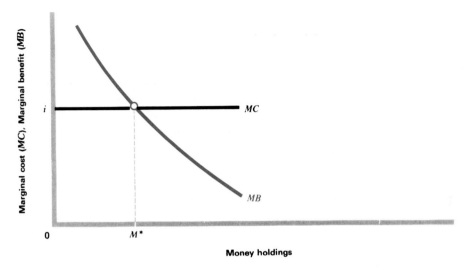

Figure 12-3 *The Precautionary Demand for Money*

The *MC* schedule shows the marginal cost of holding an extra dollar of money; holding an extra dollar means losing interest, and so the *MC* curve is horizontal at a level equal to the interest rate (or, more generally, the difference between the interest rate on money and alternative assets). The marginal benefit (*MB*) of holding an extra dollar is that the consumer is less likely to be short of money when it is needed. The marginal benefit declines with the amount of money held. The optimal amount of money to hold is shown by *M°*, where marginal cost is equal to marginal benefit.

The optimal level of the precautionary demand for money is reached where the two curves intersect. That level of money is shown as *M°* in Figure 12-3. Now we can use Figure 12-3 to examine the determinants of the optimal level of the precautionary demand. It is apparent that precautionary balances will be larger when the interest rate is lower. A reduction in the interest rate shifts the *MC* curve down and increases *M°*. The lower cost of holding money makes it profitable to insure more heavily against the costs of illiquidity. An increase in uncertainty leads to increased money holdings because it shifts up the *MB* curve. With more uncertainty about the flow of spending, there is more scope for unforeseen payments and thus a greater danger of illiquidity. It therefore pays to insure more heavily by holding larger cash balances. Finally, the lower the costs of illiquidity *q*, the lower the money demand. A reduction in *q* moves the *MB* curve down. Indeed, if there were no cost to illiquidity, no one would bother to hold money. There would be no penalty for not having it, while, at the same time, holding it would mean a loss of interest.

The model of precautionary demand can be applied to goods other than money. It is a broad theory that applies to any commodity inventory that is held as insurance against contingencies. For instance, cars carry spare tires. You can work out circumstances under which one would want to have more than one spare tire in a car, and even circumstances in which zero would be the optimal number. The idea of the precautionary demand for money or for goods is quite general. So, too, are the determinants of the precautionary demand: the alternative cost in terms of interest forgone, the cost of illiquidity, and the degree of uncertainty that determines the probability of illiquidity.

The Speculative Demand for Money

The transactions demand and the precautionary demand for money emphasize the medium of exchange function of money, for each refers to the need to have money on hand to make payments. Each theory is more relevant to the M1 definition of money than any other, though the precautionary demand could certainly explain part of the holding of savings accounts and other relatively liquid assets which are part of M2. Now we move over to the store of value function of money and concentrate on the role of money in the investment portfolio of an individual.

An individual who has wealth has to hold that wealth in specific assets. Those assets make up a *portfolio*. One would think an investor would want to hold the asset which provides the highest returns. However, given that the return on most assets is uncertain, it is unwise to hold the entire portfolio in a single *risky asset*. You may have the hottest tip that a certain stock will surely double within the next two years, but you would be wise to recognize that hot tips are far from infallible, and that you could lose a lot of money in that stock as well as make money. A prudent, risk-averse investor does not put all his or her eggs in one basket. Uncertainty about the returns on risky assets leads to a diversified portfolio strategy.

As part of that diversified portfolio, the typical investor will want to hold some amount of a safe asset as insurance against capital losses on assets whose prices change in an uncertain manner. The safe asset would be held precisely because it is safe, even though it pays a lower expected return than risky assets. Money is a safe asset in that its nominal value is known with certainty.[19] In a famous article, James Tobin argued that money would be held as the safe asset in the portfolios of investors.[20] The title of the article, "Liquidity Preference as Behaviour towards Risk," explains the essential notion. In this framework the demand for money, the safest asset, depends on the expected yields, as well as on the riskiness of the yields, on other assets. The riskiness of the return on other assets is measured by the variability of the return. Using reasonable assumptions, Tobin shows that an increase in the expected return on other assets — an increase in the opportunity cost of holding money (that is, the return lost

---

[19] Of course, when the rate of inflation is uncertain, the real value of money is also uncertain, and money is no longer a safe asset. Even so, the uncertainties about the values of equity are so much larger than the uncertainties about the rate of inflation that money can be treated as a relatively safe asset.

[20] James Tobin, "Liquidity Preference as Behaviour towards Risk," *Review of Economic Studies*, February 1958.

by holding money) — lowers money demand. By contrast, an increase in the riskiness of the returns on other assets increases money demand.

An investor's aversion to risk certainly generates a demand for a safe asset. The question we want to consider is whether that safe asset is money. That is, we want to ask whether considerations of portfolio behaviour do generate a demand for money. The relevant considerations in the portfolio are the returns and the risks on assets. From the viewpoint of the yield and risks of holding money, it is clear that savings or term deposits have the same risks as currency or chequable deposits, but they generally pay a higher yield. The risks in both cases are the risks arising from uncertainty about inflation. Given that the risks are the same, and with the yields on savings and term deposits higher than on currency and demand deposits, portfolio diversification explains the demand for assets such as savings and term deposits better than the demand for $M1$. We therefore regard the speculative demand as applying primarily to $M2$ or $M3$.

The implications of the speculative, or risk-diversifying, demand for money are similar to those of the transactions and precautionary demands. An increase in the interest rate on nonmoney assets, such as long-term bond yields or equity yields, will reduce the demand for $M2$. An increase in the rate paid on savings accounts will increase the demand for savings accounts, perhaps even at the cost of the demand for $M1$, as people take advantage of the higher yields they can earn on their investment portfolios to increase the size of those portfolios.

One final point on the speculative demand. Many individuals with relatively small amounts of wealth will indeed hold part of that wealth in savings accounts in order to diversify their portfolios. However, bigger investors are sometimes able to purchase other securities, such as Treasury bills, that pay higher interest and also have fixed (that is, risk-free) nominal values. For such individuals or firms, the demand for a safe asset is not a demand for money.

12-4 Empirical Evidence

This section examines the empirical evidence — the studies made using actual data — on the demand for money. We know that the interest elasticity of the demand for money plays an important role in determining the effectiveness of monetary and fiscal policies. We showed in Section 12-3 that there are good theoretical reasons for believing the demand for real balances should depend on the interest rate. The empirical evidence supports that view very strongly. Empirical studies have established that the demand for money is responsive to the interest rate. An increase in the interest rate reduces the demand for money.

The theory of money demand also predicts that the demand for money should depend on the level of income. The response of the demand for money to the level of income, as measured by the income elasticity of money demand, is also important from a policy viewpoint. The income elasticity of money demand provides a guide to the Bank of Canada as to how fast to increase the money supply to support a given rate of growth of GDP without changing the interest rate.

Suppose that the aim is for GDP growth of 10 percent: 6 percent real growth and 4 percent inflation. If the Bank of Canada wants to provide a sufficient growth rate of money to prevent interest rates from rising, it has to know the income elasticity of the demand for real balances. Suppose the real income elasticity is 1/2. Then we would require monetary growth of 7 percent to prevent an increase in interest rates. Why? First, the demand for nominal money increases in proportion to the price level, since money demand is a demand for real balances. Thus 4 percent growth in money is needed to meet the increased demand from the 4 percent increase in the price level. The 6 percent growth in real income would increase the demand for real balances by 3 percent (= 6 percent × 1/2), given the real income elasticity of 1/2. Hence the needed 7 percent (=4 + 3) growth in the nominal money supply to meet the increased demand arising from the increase in income.

Lagged Adjustment

The empirical work on the demand for money has introduced one complication that we did not study in the theoretical section: that the demand for money adjusts to changes in income and interest rates with a lag. When the level of income or the interest rate changes, there is first only a small change in the demand for money. Then, over the course of time, the change in the demand for money increases, slowly building up to its full long-run change. Reasons for this lag are not yet certain. The two usual possibilities exist in this case too. The lags may arise because there are costs of adjusting money holdings, or they may arise because money holders' expectations are slow to adjust. If people believe that a given change in the interest rate is temporary, they may be unwilling to make a major change in their money holdings. As time passes and it becomes clearer that the change is not transitory, they are more willing to make a larger adjustment.

Empirical Results

There are several published studies of the demand for money in Canada using postwar data.[21] Table 12-2 shows the results for the demand for $M1$ reported in one of these. The table shows the elasticities of the demand for real balances with respect to real income and the interest rate on corporate paper. This interest rate is relevant to the demand for money because corporate paper is an asset which is very liquid for investors that hold it instead of money for short periods of time.

---

[21] See, for example, K. Clinton, "The Demand for Money in Canada, 1955–70," *Canadian Journal of Economics*, February 1973; N. Cameron, "The Stability of Canadian Demand for Money Functions," *Canadian Journal of Economics*, May 1979; S. Poloz, "Simultaneity and the Demand for Money in Canada," *Canadian Journal of Economics*, August 1980.

Table 12-2   *Elasticities of Demand for M1*

	Income	Interest Rate
Short run	0.22	−0.054
Long run	0.73	−0.18

Source: S. Poloz, "Simultaneity and the Demand for Money in Canada," *Canadian Journal of Economics,* August 1980, p. 413.

In the short run (one quarter), the elasticity of demand with respect to real income is 0.22. This means that a 1 percent increase in real income raises money demand by 0.22 percent, which is considerably less than proportionately. The table shows that the interest elasticity of money demand with respect to interest rates is negative: An increase in interest rates reduces money demand. The short-run interest elasticity is quite small. An increase from 8 percent to 10 percent — that is, a 25 percent increase (10/8 = 1.25) — reduces the demand for money by only 1.35 percent (= 0.054 x 25 percent).

The long-run elasticities exceed the short-run elasticities by a factor of more than 3, as Table 12-2 shows. The long-run real income elasticity is 0.73, meaning that in the long run the increase in real money demand occurring as a result of a given increase in real income is only 73 percent as large as the increase in real income. Real money demand thus rises less than proportionately to the rise in real income. The long-run interest elasticity is −0.18, meaning that an increase in i from 8 to 10 percent would reduce the demand for money by 4.5 percent.

How long is the long run? That is, how long does it take the demand for money to adjust from the short-run to the long-run elasticities shown in Table 12-2? The answer is given in Table 12-3, which shows the elasticities of the demand for real balances in response to changes in the level of income and interest rates after one, two, three, four, and eight quarters. Three-fourths of the adjustment is complete within the first year, and more than 90 percent of the adjustment is complete within the first two years.

Table 12-3   *Dynamic Patterns of Elasticities of Money Demand with Respect to Real Income and Interest Rates*

Quarters Elapsed	Income	Interest Rate
1	0.22	−0.054
2	0.37	−0.092
3	0.48	−0.119
4	0.55	−0.138
8	0.69	−0.172
Long run	0.73	−0.182

Source: Calculated using the elasticities shown in Table 12-2 and reported by Poloz, *op.cit.*

Table 12-4 shows the long-run elasticities obtained in a recent study of the demand for M2.[22] Compared with the value shown in Table 12-2, the income elasicity is lower (0.50 compared with 0.73), as would be expected because M2 includes assets that cannot be used directly as a means of payment. In addition to the corporate paper rate, which represents the return on alternative assets, the rate on 90-day fixed-term deposits is included. Since it represents an own rate of return, its elasticity has a positive sign. Further, the differential between this own rate and a comparable rate offered by trust and mortgage loan companies is included to take account of the competition from nonbank institutions whose deposits are not included in M2. Taking all the interest rate elasticities into account, a one-percentage-point increase in all rates would result in a reduction in demand for M2 of -0.16 ($1.18 - 1.34$).[23]

Table 12-4 *Long-Run Elasticities of Demand for M2*

Income	Interest Rates		
	90-day paper	Chartered bank term deposits	Term deposit differential*
0.50	-1.34	1.18	3.56

*90-day term deposits at chartered banks versus trust and mortgage loan companies.

Source: F. Caramazza, "Technical Note: The Demand for M2 and M2+ in Canada," *Bank of Canada Review,* December 1989, Table 1.

In summary, we have so far described three essential properties of money demand:

1. The demand for real money balances responds negatively to the rate of interest. An increase in interest rates reduces the demand for money.

2. The demand for money increases with the level of real income. However, because the income elasticity of money demand is less than 1, money demand increases less than proportionately with income.

3. The short-run responsiveness of money demand to changes in interest rates and income is considerably less than the long-run response.

There is one other important question to be considered: How does money respond to an increase in the level of prices? Here a number of researchers have found strong evidence that an increase in prices raises nominal money demand in the same proportion. We can add, therefore, a fourth conclusion:[24]

---

[22] F. Caramazza, "Technical Note: The Demand for M2 and M2+ in Canada," *Bank of Canada Review,* December 1989, pp. 3–19.

[23] The elasticity for the term deposit differential does not enter this calculation, since this variable would be unaffected by an equal increase in all rates.

[24] The study of the demand for M2 discussed above assumes a unitary elasticity in the long run, but allows for deviations from 1 in the short run.

4. The demand for nominal money balances is proportional to the price level. There is no money illusion; in other words, the demand for money is a demand for real balances.

Financial Innovation and Money Demand

Over the past fifteen years there have been a number of innovations in Canadian financial markets that have affected the demand for money.[25] Some of these have affected individual depositors; others have affected the banking arrangements of businesses.

For individual depositors, the major change has been the introduction of daily-interest accounts. Prior to 1979, the standard savings account in a chartered bank paid interest on the minimum balance held over each calendar month. Most individuals were unable to earn interest on funds available for periods of less than a month and thus were likely to keep funds received from salary payments in chequing accounts. The introduction of savings accounts which pay interest on daily balances provided a new option which reduced the demand for $M1$.

In 1981, banks and other financial institutions began offering daily-interest chequing accounts. A few years later, they began paying higher interest rates on balances above some minimum such as $2000 and a much lower rate on balances below the minimum. Daily-interest savings accounts with graduated interest rates were also introduced, with rates on large balances closely tied to rates on nonmonetary assets such as Treasury bills. Similarly, businesses were induced to shift from noninterest-bearing chequing accounts to nonpersonal term deposits.

Another innovation affecting business depositors has been the provision of more cash management services that enable the banks' customers to reduce their holdings of transactions balances and earn more interest. For example, there are arrangements under which surplus funds are automatically shifted at the end of each day to higher-interest accounts. Such practices further reduce the demand for $M1$.

12-5 The Income Velocity of Money and the Quantity Theory

The *income velocity of money* is the number of times the stock of money is turned over per year in financing the annual flow of income. It is equal to the ratio of GDP to the money stock. Thus in 1990 GDP was $671.6 billion, the money stock ($M1$) averaged 38.6 billion, and velocity was therefore about 17. The average dollar of money balances financed $17 of spending on final goods and services; that is, the public held on average just under $0.06 of $M1$ per dollar of income. Although we usually calculate

---

[25] See C. Freedman, "Financial Innovation in Canada: Causes and Consequences," *American Economic Review*, May 1983, and *Bank of Canada Review*, February 1991, pp. 3–14.

velocity for the economy as a whole, we can also calculate it for an individual. For instance, for someone earning $20 000 per year, who has average money balances during the year of $2000, the income velocity of money holdings is 10.[26]

Income velocity (from now on we shall refer to velocity rather than income velocity) is defined as

$$V = \frac{Y_N}{M} \tag{6}$$

which is the ratio of nominal income to nominal money stock. An alternative way of writing Equation (6) recognizes that Y_N is equal to the price level, P, times real income Y. Thus

$$M \times V = P \times Y \tag{7}$$

The Quantity Theory

Equation (7) is the famous *quantity equation*, linking the product of the price level and the level of output to the money stock. The quantity equation became the (classical) *quantity theory of money* when it was argued that both V, the income velocity of money, and Y, the level of output, were fixed. Real output was taken to be fixed because the economy was at full employment, and velocity was assumed not to change much. Neither of these assumptions holds in fact, but it is, nonetheless, interesting to see where they lead. *If both V and Y are fixed, then it follows that the price level is proportional to the money stock.* Thus the classical quantity theory was a theory of inflation. The classical quantity theory is the proposition that the price level is proportional to the money stock:

$$P = \frac{V}{Y}M \tag{7a}$$

The classical quantity theory applies in the *classical case* supply function examined in Chapter 7. Recall that in that case, with a vertical aggregate supply function, changes in the quantity of money result in changes in the price level, with the level of output remaining at its full-employment level. When the aggregate supply function is not

---

[26] Why do we say "income velocity" and not simply "velocity"? There is another concept, *transactions velocity* — that is, the ratio of total transactions to money balances. Total transactions far exceed GDP for two reasons. First, there are many transactions involving the sale and purchase of assets that do not contribute to GDP. Second, a particular item in final output typically generates total spending on it that exceeds the contribution of that item to GDP. For instance, one dollar's worth of wheat generates transactions as it leaves the farm, as it is sold by the miller, as it leaves the baker for the supermarket, and then as it is sold to the household. One dollar's worth of wheat may involve several dollars of transactions before it is sold for the last time. Transactions velocity is thus higher than income velocity.

vertical, increases in the quantity of money increase both the price level and output, and the price level is therefore not proportional to the quantity of money. Of course, if velocity is constant, nominal GDP (the price level times output) is proportional to the money stock.

Velocity and Policy

Velocity is a useful concept in economic policy making. We see how to use it by rewriting (6) as

$$Y_N = V \times M \tag{6a}$$

Given the nominal money stock and velocity, we know the level of nominal GDP. Thus, if we can predict the level of velocity, we can predict the level of nominal income, given the money stock.

Further, *if* velocity were constant, changing the money supply would result in proportionate changes in nominal income. Any policies, including fiscal policies, that did not affect the money stock would not affect the level of income. You will probably now recognize that we have previously discussed a case of constant velocity. In Chapter 4, we discussed the effectiveness of fiscal policy when the demand for money is not a function of the interest rate and the *LM* curve is therefore vertical. The vertical *LM* curve is the same as the assumption of constant velocity.

Velocity and the Demand for Money

The discussion of constant velocity is closely related to the behaviour of the demand for money. Indeed, the notion of velocity is important because it is a convenient way of talking about money demand.

We now examine the relationship between velocity and the demand for money. Let the demand for real balances be written $L(i,Y)$, consistent with Chapter 4. Recall that Y is real income. When the supply of money is equal to the demand for money, we have

$$\frac{M}{P} = L(i,Y) \tag{8}$$

or $M = P \times L(i,Y)$. Now we can substitute for the nominal money supply into Equation (6) to obtain

$$V = \frac{Y_N}{P \times L(i,Y)} = \frac{Y}{L(i,Y)} \tag{6b}$$

where we have recognized that $Y_N/P = Y$ is the level of real income. Income velocity is the ratio of the level of real income to the demand for real balances.

Box 12-1   Money Demand and High Inflation

The demand for real balances depends on the alternative cost of holding money. That cost is normally measured by the yield on alternative assets, say Treasury bills, commercial paper, or term deposits, but there is another margin of substitution. Rather than holding their wealth in financial assets, households or firms can also hold real assets: stocks of food, or houses, or machinery. This margin of substitution is particularly important in countries where inflation is very high and capital markets do not function well. In that case it is quite possible that the return on holding goods can even be higher than that on financial assets.

Consider a household deciding whether to hold $100 in currency or a demand deposit or else to hold it in the form of groceries on the shelf. The advantage of holding groceries is that, unlike money, they maintain their real value. Rather than having the purchasing power of money balances eroded by inflation, the household gets rid of money, buying goods and thus avoiding a loss.

This "flight out of money" occurs systematically when inflation rates become high. In a famous study of hyperinflations (defined in the study as inflation rates of more than 50 percent per month), Phillip Cagan of Columbia University found large changes in velocity taking place as inflation increased.[a] In the most famous hyperinflation, that in Germany in 1922–1923, the quantity of real balances at the height of the hyperinflation had fallen to one-twentieth of its preinflation level. The increased cost of holding money leads to a reduction in real money demand and with it to changes in the public's payments habits as everybody tries to pass on money like a hot potato. We shall see more on this in Chapter 18, in which we study money and inflation.

In well-developed capital markets, interest rates will reflect expectations of inflation and hence it will not make much difference whether we measure the alternative cost of holding money by interest rates or inflation rates. However, when capital markets are not free because interest rates are regulated or have ceilings, it is often appropriate to use inflation, not interest rates, as the measure of the alternative cost. Franco Modigliani has offered the following rule of thumb: The right measure of the opportunity cost of holding money is the higher of the two, interest rates or inflation.

[a] Phillip Cagan, "The Monetary Dynamics of Hyperinflation," in *Studies in the Quantity Theory of Money*, edited by Milton Friedman (Chicago: University of Chicago Press, 1956).

From Equation (6b) we note that velocity is a function of real income and the interest rate. An increase in the interest rate reduces the demand for real balances and therefore increases velocity: When the cost of holding money increases, money holders make their money do more work and thus turn it over more often.

The way in which changes in real income affect velocity depends on the income elasticity of the demand for money. If the income elasticity of the demand for real balances were 1, then the demand for real balances would change in the same proportion as income. In that case, changes in real income would not affect velocity. Suppose that real income increased by 10 percent. The numerator, *Y*, in Equation (6b) would increase by 10 percent, as would the denominator, and velocity would be unchanged. However, we have seen that the income elasticity of the demand for money is less than 1. That means that velocity increases with increases in real income. For example, suppose that real income rose 10 percent, and the demand for real balances increased only by 7.3 percent (= 0.73 × 10 percent), as Poloz's results suggest. Then the numerator of Equation (6b) would increase by more than the denominator, and velocity would rise.

The empirical work reviewed in Section 12-4 makes it clear that the demand for money and, therefore, also velocity do react systematically to changes in interest rates and the level of real income. The empirical evidence therefore decisively refutes the view that velocity is unaffected by changes in interest rates and that fiscal policy is, accordingly, incapable of affecting the level of nominal income. In terms of Equation (6b), and using the analysis of Chapter 4, expansionary fiscal policy can be thought of as working by increasing interest rates, thereby increasing velocity, and thus making it possible for a given stock of money to support a higher level of nominal GDP.

Velocity in Practice

The empirical evidence we reviewed in Section 12-4 is useful in interpreting the behaviour of velocity. Figure 12-4 shows a striking and steady increase in velocity. The velocity of *M*1 has increased from under 8 in the early 1960s to 17 in 1990. The average dollar finances twice the income flow now that it did in the early 1960s. This increase in velocity can of course be explained by the same factors that explain the demand for money. Velocity has risen because income has risen (since the income elasticity of demand is less than 1) and because interest rates have risen.

12-6 Summary

1. The demand for money is a demand for real balances. It is the purchasing power, not the number, of their dollar bills that matters to holders of money.

2. The money supply (*M*1) is made up of currency and demand deposits. *M*2 and *M*3 are broader measures that include savings accounts and term and notice deposits.

3. The chief characteristic of money is that it serves as a means of payment.

4. There are two broad reasons why people hold money and thus forgo interest that they could earn by holding alternative assets. These reasons are transactions costs and uncertainty.

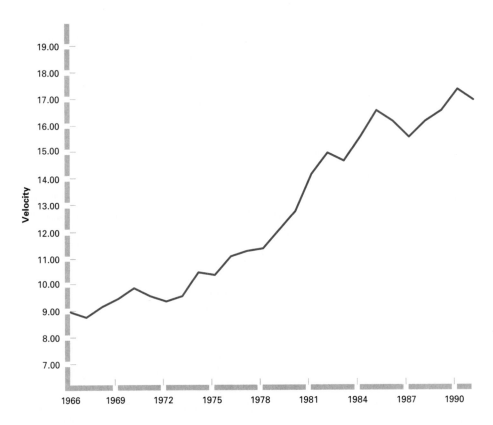

Figure 12-4   *The Income Velocity of Money (M1)*

(*Source:* Adapted from *Bank of Canada Review*)

5. Transactions costs are an essential aspect of money demand. If it were costless to move (instantaneously) in and out of interest-bearing assets, nobody would hold money. Optimal cash management would involve transfers from other assets (bonds or saving deposits) just before outlays, and it would involve immediate conversion into interest-bearing form of any cash receipts. The existence of transactions costs — brokerage costs, fees, and time costs — makes it optimal to hold some money.

6. The inventory-theoretic approach shows that an individual will hold a stock of real balances that varies inversely with the interest rate but increases with the level of real income and the cost of transactions. The income elasticity of money demand is less than unity, implying that there are economies of scale.

7. Transactions costs, in combination with uncertainty about payments and receipts, give rise to a precautionary demand for money. Money holdings provide insur-

ance against illiquidity. The higher the variability of net disbursements and the higher the cost of illiquidity, the higher are optimal money holdings. Since holding money implies forgoing interest, optimal money holdings will vary inversely with the rate of interest.

8. Portfolio diversification involves the tradeoff between risk and return. Savings accounts form part of an optimal portfolio because they are not risky — their nominal value is constant. Savings accounts dominate currency or demand deposits, which are also safe nominal assets, because they bear interest. Thus the speculative portfolio demand for money is a demand for savings or term deposits.

9. The empirical evidence provides strong support for a negative interest elasticity of money demand and a positive income elasticity. Because of lags, short-run elasticities are much smaller than long-run elasticities.

10. Over the past twenty years the demand for money (*M*1) has declined as a result of both the introduction of new assets and improvements in cash management methods.

11. The income velocity of money is defined as the ratio of income to money or the rate of turnover of money. Since the 1960s, velocity has increased to a level of about 17.

12. The empirical evidence implies that an increase in real income raises velocity, as does an increase in the rate of interest. At higher levels of income or at higher interest rates, there is a lower demand for money in relation to income. Higher interest rates lead people to economize on cash balances.

13. Inflation implies that money loses purchasing power, and inflation thus creates a cost of holding money. The higher the rate of inflation, the lower the amount of real balances that will be held. Hyperinflations provide striking support for this prediction. Under conditions of very high expected inflation, money demand falls dramatically relative to income. Velocity rises as people use less money in relation to income.

Key Terms

Real balances	Transactions demand
Money illusion	Inventory-theoretic approach
*M*1	Square-root formula
*M*2, *M*3	Precautionary demand
Liquidity	Speculative demand
Medium of exchange	Income velocity of money
Store of value	Quantity equation
Unit of account	Quantity theory of money
Standard of deferred payments	Hyperinflation

Problems

1. To what extent would it be possible to design a society in which there was no money? What would the problems be? Could currency at least be eliminated? How? (Lest all this seems too unworldly, you should know that some people are beginning to talk of a "cashless economy" in the next century.)

2. Evaluate the effects of the following changes on the demand for $M1$ and $M2$. Which of the functions of money do they relate to?
   (a) Automatic teller machines which allow 24-hour withdrawals from savings accounts at banks.
   (b) The employment of more tellers at your bank.
   (c) An increase in inflationary expectations.
   (d) Widespread acceptance of credit cards.
   (e) Fear of an imminent collapse of the government.
   (f) A rise in the interest rate on nonchequable savings deposits.

3. (a) Determine the optimal strategy for cash management for the person who earns $1600 per month, can earn 0.5 percent interest per month in a savings account, and has a transaction cost of $1.
   (b) What is the individual's average cash balance?
   (c) Suppose income rises to $1800. By what percentage does the person's demand for money rise? (Pay attention to the integer constraints.)

4. Discuss the various factors that go into an individual's decision regarding how many traveller's cheques to take on a vacation.

5. In the text, we said that the transactions demand for money model can also be applied to firms. Suppose a firm sells steadily during the month and has to pay its workers at the end of the month. Explain how it would determine its money holdings.

6. This chapter emphasized that the demand for money is a demand for real balances. Thus the demand for nominal balances rises with the price level. At the same time, inflation causes the real demand to fall. Explain how these two assertions can both be correct.

7. "Muggers favour deflation." Comment.

*8. The assumption was made in the text that, in the transactions demand for cash model, it is optimal to space transactions evenly throughout the month. Prove this as follows in the case where $n = 2$. Since one transaction must be made immediately, the only question is when to make the second one. For simplicity, call the beginning of the month $t = 0$ and the end of the month $t = 1$. Then consider a transaction strategy which performs the second transaction at the time t. If income is Y_N, then this will require moving tY_N into cash now and $(1 - t)Y_N$ at time t. Calculate the total cost incurred under this strategy, and try various values of t to see which is optimal. (If you are familiar with calculus, prove that $t = 1/2$ minimizes total cost.)

*9. For those students familiar with calculus, derive Equation (4) from Equation (2) by minimizing total costs with respect to n.

.

CHAPTER 13 *The Money Supply Process*

We have so far taken the money supply to be given and determined by the Bank of Canada. By and large, the Bank is indeed able to determine the money supply quite closely, but it does not set it directly. In this chapter we study the ways in which the actions of the Bank of Canada, the chartered banks, and the public interact in determining the stock of money. In addition, we shall examine in some detail the way in which the Bank of Canada operates monetary policy.

We noted in Chapter 12 that the money supply measure $M1$ is the sum of demand deposits, DD, and currency held by the public, CU.

$$M1 = DD + CU \qquad (1)$$

A broader measure of the money supply is $M2$, which includes personal savings and nonpersonal notice deposits, SD.

$$M2 = M1 + SD \qquad (2)$$

Table 13-1 summarizes the data in Table 12-1 and shows the components of the money stock in June 1991. $M1$ was \$40.4 billion, of which about one-half was currency. $M2$ was nearly seven times as large, with personal savings deposits making up the major portion of the difference between $M1$ and $M2$. Since these deposits have been growing more rapidly than $M1$, $M2$ has been growing more rapidly than $M1$. This can be seen in Figure 13-1, which shows the behaviour of these aggregates since 1968.

Table 13-1 *Components of the Money Stock, June 1991*

(billions of dollars, average of Wednesdays)				
(1)	**(2)**	**(3)**	**(4)**	**(5)**
Currency	Demand deposits	MI = (1) + (2)	Savings deposits*	M2 = (3) + (4)
19.8	20.6	40.4	232.1	272.5

*Personal savings and nonpersonal notice deposits.
Source: Bank of Canada Review.

For the remainder of this chapter we shall ignore the distinction between demand and savings deposits and consider the money supply process as if there were only a uniform class of deposits D. Using that simplification, we define money as deposits plus currency:

$$M = CU + D \tag{3}$$

13-1 The Money Supply and the Banking System

Starting from Equation (3), we now begin to demonstrate how the process of money stock determination is related to the balance sheets of the nonbank public, the chartered banks, and the Bank of Canada. The money supply is an asset of the nonbank public, and the deposit component is a liability of the banks — that is, a debt the banks owe their customers. As we shall see below, the Bank of Canada influences the money supply by changing the composition of its own balance sheet.

Balance Sheets and the Money Supply

Table 13-2 shows simplified balance sheets of the three sectors that play a role in determining the money supply. Money in the form of currency or deposits is an asset of the nonbank public. In addition, we show holdings of government securities (Treasury bills or government bonds) as an asset, and loans from chartered banks as a liability of this sector. These loans appear as an asset of the chartered banks, and deposits appear as a liability of the bank sector.

The other assets in the balance sheet of the chartered banks are government securities and *cash reserves*. Cash reserves are held by the chartered banks to meet (1) the demands of their customers for currency and (2) payments their customers make by cheques which are deposited in other banks. Cash reserves consist of currency held

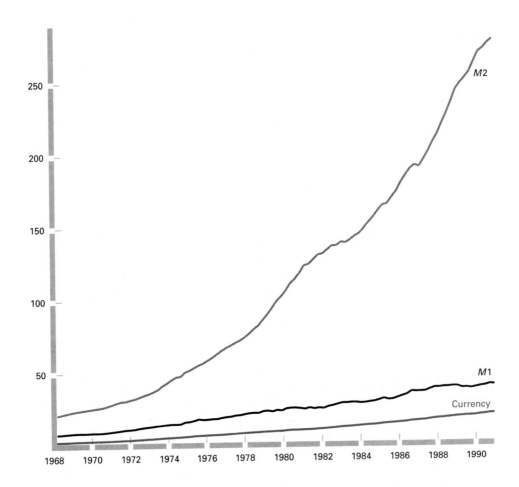

Figure 13-1 *Monetary Aggregates*

(*Source:* Adapted from *Bank of Canada Review*)

by the chartered banks (*till money*) and also of deposits held by the chartered banks at the Bank of Canada. A detailed balance sheet for the chartered banks is shown in Table 13-3.

Cash reserves appear as a liability in the balance sheet of the Bank of Canada. The chartered banks use their accounts at the Bank of Canada to make payments among themselves. Thus, when my bank has to make a payment to your bank because I paid you with a cheque drawn on my bank account, it makes the payment by transferring money from its account to your bank's account at the Bank of Canada. The process by which the net amounts owing among the banks are settled at the end of each day is referred to as as the *clearing system*. Chartered banks and other financial institutions

Table 13-2 *Balance Sheets*

Nonbank Public		Chartered Banks	
Assets	**Liabilities**	**Assets**	**Liabilities**
Money:	Bank loans	Cash reserves	Deposits
Currency		Bank loans	
outside banks		Government	
Deposits		securities	
Government			
securities			

Bank of Canada	
Assets	**Liabilities**
Government	Monetary base:
securities	Currency in circulation*
	Deposits of chartered banks

*This item includes both the currency held by the nonbank public (currency outside banks) and the till money included in the cash reserves of the chartered banks.

Table 13-3 *Balance Sheet of the Chartered Banks, June 1991*

(billions of dollars)

Assets		Liabilities	
Bank of Canada notes		Demand deposits	22.5
and deposits	5.5	Personal savings deposits	208.7
Loans and investments		Nonpersonal term and	
Government of Canada		notice deposits	65.7
securities	28.6	Government of Canada	
Loans	302.6	deposits	.8
Other securities	14.8	Other liabilities, net	53.8
Total Canadian dollar			
major assets	351.5		351.5

Source: Bank of Canada Review, Tables C1, C2.

that are members of the *Canadian Payments Association* and participate in the clearing are required to hold deposits at the Bank of Canada.

    The other items shown in the simplified balance sheet of the Bank of Canada are government securities on the asset side and *currency in circulation* on the liability side (see Table 13-4 for a detailed balance sheet). The sum of currency in circulation and

Table 13-4   *Balance Sheet of the Bank of Canada, June 1991*

(millions of dollars)

Assets		Liabilities	
Government of Canada		Notes in circulation	
securities	21 626	Held by chartered banks	3 947
Advances	62	Other	17 682
Net foreign currency		Deposits	
assets	144	Chartered banks	1 529
Other assets, net	16	Other Canadian Payments	
		Association members	57
		Government of Canada	11
Total assets	23 226	Total liabilities	23 226

Source: *Bank of Canada Review*, Table B2.

deposits of the chartered banks at the Bank of Canada is called the *monetary base*. Part of the currency is held by the nonbank public (*currency outside banks*), and the remainder is held by the chartered banks as till money.

Open Market Operations

The Bank of Canada does not have direct control over the volume of bank deposits, but it can control the money supply indirectly through the monetary base which appears on the liability side of its balance sheet. An important means by which the Bank of Canada changes the monetary base is *open market operations*. Open market operations are purchases or sales of government securities by the central bank.

We examine the mechanics of an open market *purchase*, in which the Bank of Canada buys, say, $1 million of government bonds from individuals or businesses that make up the nonbank public. The accounting for the open market purchase is shown in Table 13-5. The Bank of Canada's holdings of government securities rise by $1 million, and the nonbank public's holdings fall by the same amount. How does the Bank of Canada pay for the bonds? It writes a cheque on itself, and the seller deposits the proceeds in a chartered bank which in turns sends the cheque to the Bank of Canada. Thus chartered bank reserves increase by $1 million and the monetary base has been increased by the amount of the open market purchase.

If the seller of the bond chooses to hold some part of the proceeds in the form of currency rather than bank deposits, then the increase in bank reserves and deposits will be correspondingly reduced by the *currency drain*. Table 13-6 shows the case in which 5 cents out of each dollar is held in the form of currency. Bank reserves and deposits will increase by $0.95 million, and if we assume that the chartered bank obtains the required currency from the Bank of Canada, then the liability side of the

Table 13-5 *An Open Market Purchase From the Nonbank Public*

Nonbank Public

Assets		Liabilities	
Government securities	− 1		
Deposits	+ 1		

Chartered Banks

Assets		Liabilities	
Cash reserves	+ 1	Deposits	+ 1

Bank of Canada

Assets		Liabilities	
Government securities	+ 1	Chartered bank deposits	+ 1

Table 13-6 *An Open Market Purchase With Currency Drain*

Nonbank Public

Assets		Liabilities	
Government securities	− 1		
Currency	+ .05		
Deposits	+ .95		

Chartered Banks

Assets		Liabilities	
Cash reserves	+ .95	Deposits	+ .95

Bank of Canada

Assets		Liabilities	
Government securities	+ 1	Chartered bank deposits	+ .95
		Currency	+ .05

Bank of Canada's balance sheet will show an increase of $0.95 million of chartered bank deposits and $0.05 million of currency. However, the increase in the monetary base, the sum of currency and deposits at the Bank of Canada, will still be $1 million, the amount of the open market purchase. In general, an open market operation affects the monetary base by the amount of the purchase or sale *regardless of the way in which changes in the money supply are split between currency and bank deposits.* The composition of the base is affected by this split, and it is for this reason that we view the central bank as controlling the monetary base as a whole rather than either of its components.

We have assumed so far that the open market purchase is made from the nonbank public. What will happen if the seller is a chartered bank? This case is illustrated in Table 13-7. The chartered bank receives a cheque from the Bank of Canada and exchanges it for a deposit. Thus the monetary base is increased as in the previous case, but the transaction has no direct effect on the nonbank public.

Table 13-7   *An Open Market Purchase From a Chartered Bank*

	Chartered Banks		
Assets		**Liabilities**	
Government securities	− I		
Cash reserves	+ I		
	Bank of Canada		
Assets		**Liabilities**	
Government securities	+ I	Chartered bank deposits	+ I

Government Deposits and the Base

The detailed balance sheets of the chartered banks and the Bank of Canada shown in Tables 13-3 and 13-4 show Government of Canada deposits on the liability side. The account maintained at the Bank of Canada is used by the federal government for receipts and payments. In the absence of offsetting transactions, fluctuations in government revenues and expenditures would thus be reflected in fluctuations in the monetary base. For example, in a period in which the government receives more than it spends, there would be a transfer of deposits from the accounts of the public at the chartered banks to the government's account at the Bank of Canada so that cash reserves would be reduced.

To avoid these effects, the Government of Canada maintains deposits with the chartered banks as well as with the Bank of Canada. Transfers of these deposits between the chartered banks and the Bank of Canada can then be used to offset the effects of government transactions. In addition, these transfers provide an alternative to open market operations as a means of changing the monetary base. The effect of a transfer from the Bank of Canada to the chartered banks is illustrated in Table 13-8. In this case the base is increased by the amount of the transfer.

Table 13-8   *A Transfer of Government Deposits From the Bank of Canada to the Chartered Banks*

	Chartered Banks		
Assets		**Liabilities**	
Cash reserves	+ I	Government deposits	+ I
	Bank of Canada		
Assets		**Liabilities**	
		Chartered bank deposits	+ I
		Government deposits	− I

The Money Supply and the Monetary Base

As described above, the Bank of Canada's control over the money supply operates through its control of the monetary base. It does not have direct control over the volume of bank deposits held by the nonbank public, but it can control the monetary base since it appears on the liability side of the Bank of Canada's balance sheet.

A relationship between the monetary base and the money supply can be derived as follows. The money supply was defined in Equation (3) as the sum of currency (CU) and deposits (D). The monetary base (B) is:

$$B = CU + R \tag{4}$$

where R denotes cash reserves. Ignoring other items in the balance sheet of the chartered banks and denoting bank loans by L, we have

$$R + L = D \tag{5}$$

Thus the money supply can be decomposed as follows

$$M = CU + D = CU + R + L = B + L \tag{6}$$

Here we see that the money supply is composed of the base, which is a liability of the Bank of Canada, and a component equal to the volume of loans made by the chartered banks. Thus the money supply can be increased either by changes in the base initiated by the Bank of Canada or by the extending of credit by the chartered banks. The making of loans by the banks involves the creation of money, since the banks simply create deposits which show up on the liability side of their balance sheet to match the increase in loans on the asset side. We pursue this point further in the discussion of the deposit expansion process in the next section.

13-2 The Money Multiplier

In the previous section, we showed that the chartered banks can increase the money supply by making loans. If this is so, what limits the size of the money supply given the size of the monetary base as determined by the Bank of Canada? The money multiplier provides an answer to this question. The *money multiplier* is defined as the ratio of the money supply to the monetary base.

The potential expansion of bank credit and the money supply is essentially limited by two factors. First, it depends on the proportion of the money supply that the nonbank public chooses to hold in the form of currency rather than deposits. Second, it depends on the amount of cash reserves that the chartered banks choose to hold in order to meet their customers' demands for currency and to meet any indebtedness to other banks arising from the clearing of cheques.

Using Equations (3) and (4), the ratio of the money supply to the monetary base can be written

$$\frac{M}{B} = \frac{CU + D}{CU + R} = \frac{CU/D + 1}{CU/D + R/D}$$

Denoting the public's desired ratio of currency to deposits by $cu = CU/D$, and the bank's desired ratio of reserves to deposits by $re = R/D$, we can write the money multiplier as

$$\frac{M}{B} = \frac{cu + 1}{cu + re} \tag{7}$$

It is clear from Equation (7) that the money multiplier is greater than 1. For this reason, the monetary base is sometimes referred to as *high-powered money*. It is also clear that the smaller the reserve ratio, re, and the smaller the currency deposit ratio, cu, the larger is the money multiplier. The smaller is cu, the smaller is the proportion of the "high-powered money" that is being used as currency (which translates high-powered money only one for one into money) and the larger the proportion that is available as cash reserves (which translate more than one for one into money).

The Value of the Multiplier

We can calculate the money multiplier as given by Equation (7) using the actual values of the components that existed in June 1991 as shown in Tables 13-1 and 13-3. For $M2$, we have $cu = 19.8/252.7 = .078$, and $re = 5.5/252.7 = .022$, so that

$$\frac{M}{B} = \frac{1.078}{.100} = 10.8$$

The same result can be obtained by taking the ratio of the $M2$ money stock ($272.5 billion) to the sum of currency ($19.8 billion) and reserves ($5.5 billion).

What determines the values of the two ratios that enter into the money multiplier? The currency–deposit ratio is determined primarily by payment habits. It has a strong seasonal pattern and is highest around Christmas. The cash reserve ratio reflects two distinct components of the banks' demand for reserves. The first is the level of the *minimum required cash reserve ratio* prescribed under the Bank Act. From 1985 to 1991, the required ratios were 10 percent for demand deposits, 2 percent for the first $500 million of notice deposits at each bank, and 3 percent for additional notice deposits. In November 1991, the Bank of Canada announced that the required minimum ratios were to be reduced to zero.

The second factor affecting the reserve–deposit ratio is the amount of cash reserves held by the chartered banks to meet the demands on them for currency or for payments to other banks through the clearing system. In a system with minimum reserve requirements, only *excess cash reserves* held beyond the level of *required reserves* are available for this purpose. With the abolition of reserve requirements, total holdings of cash reserves are available to the banks. The way in which the money supply is determined under a system of zero reserve requirements is discussed in the next section.

The behaviour of the money multipliers over the period 1968 to 1991 is shown in Figure 13-2. A glance at this figure shows that they are far from constant. This reflects a number of factors, including a downward trend in the ratio of currency to demand deposits, changes in the required minimum reserve ratios, and changes in the proportions of demand and notice deposits.

The Deposit Expansion Process

As we noted in the previous section, the process of bank lending plays an important role in the operation of the money multiplier and the determination of the money supply. When banks make loans or purchase securities, they pay for the assets they acquire by creating deposits. A bank that makes a loan to a customer does not give the customer currency, but rather gives the loan in the form of a deposit at the bank and allows the customer to draw on the deposit either by taking out currency or writing a cheque on the account.

For purposes of illustration we assume a currency–deposit ratio of 0.25 and a cash reserve ratio of 0.15. Suppose the monetary base has been increased by one dollar by an open market purchase. We start by considering the individual who sold the bond to the Bank of Canada. That person is paid with a cheque which he or she takes to the bank. Since this person, like all asset holders, has a currency–deposit ratio of cu, he or she will keep a fraction $cu/(1 + cu)$ as currency and deposit the balance. With $cu = 0.25$, 20 cents ($= 0.25/1.25$) is kept as currency and 80 cents is deposited.

At this stage the money stock has increased by only one dollar as a result of the increase in the monetary base. The effect of the deposit on the bank's balance sheet is shown in Table 13-9*a*. The bank has increased its cash reserves by 80 cents as a result of depositing at the Bank of Canada the cheque received from its customer and then paying out 20 cents in currency.

Figure 13-2   *The Money Multipliers, 1968–1991*

(*Source:* Adapted from *Bank of Canada Review*)

Now comes the crucial stage. The bank does not want to hold the entire extra 80 cents as cash reserves. The bank's reserve ratio is only *re*, so that it will hold only *re* of an extra dollar of deposits it receives in the form of cash reserves and lend out the rest to earn interest. Given *re* = 0.15, it will lend out 68 cents (= 0.85 × 80 cents).

This loan is shown in Table 13-9*b*. For simplicity, we assume the borrower receives the loan of 68 cents in the form of currency. It is at this stage that the bank's lending activities have increased the money supply by more than the increase in the monetary base. The person who sold the bond to the Bank of Canada has 1 more dollar of money, but the person who borrowed from the bank also has more money holdings — the 68 cents lent by the bank. The money supply has increased by $1.68.

Table 13-9 *Effects of Lending on Bank Balance Sheets* °

(a)		(b)	
Assets	**Liabilities**	**Assets**	**Liabilities**
Cash reserves 80	Deposits 80	Cash reserves 12	Deposits 80
		Loans 68	

*In (a), reserves and deposits both increase by 1/(1 + *cu*). In (b), the bank lends out the fraction 1 − *re* of the reserves. The values of *cu* and *re* are 0.25 and 0.15 respectively.

The person receiving the 68 cents will now want to hold a fraction $cu/(1 + cu)$ as bank deposits, but when this amount is deposited in a bank, the bank will want to lend out a fraction $1 - re$.

Clearly this process can keep going through many stages. As we show in the appendix to this chapter, when we add up the increases in currency and deposits, we get the multiplier expression given in Equation (7). In our numerical example, the increases in the money stock add up to:

$$\frac{0.25 + 1}{0.25 + 0.15} = 3.125$$

The process described above is known as the *multiple expansion of bank deposits*. It shows how an increase in deposits leads to further deposits, and therefore shows how the money multiplier works. There is one further interesting aspect of the multiplier. It is possible to say that the banking system creates money in the sense that if there were not a banking system, a one-dollar increase in the monetary base would increase the money stock by only one dollar. With the banking system, the one-dollar increase in the base leads to more than a one-dollar increase in M.

The interesting point is that, at each stage of the process, no one bank believes it is, or can be said to be, creating money. At each stage, each bank in the process is only lending out money that has been deposited with it. Each bank manager would rightly, and no doubt vehemently, deny that the bank is creating money. The system as a whole, though, is creating money through the successive rounds of loans and subsequent further bank deposits.

13-3 Short-Run Control of the Money Supply

The discussion of the money multiplier and bank credit expansion given above is useful for determining the upper limit of the money supply given the monetary base and the two ratios that represent the behaviour of the public and the chartered banks. However, it is of limited relevance to the way in which the Bank of Canada controls the money supply in the short run. To see why this is so, we have to examine in detail the rules governing reserve requirements under the Bank Act.[1]

Reserve Averaging Period

An individual bank is subject to erratic day-to-day fluctuations in its cash position as cheques are cleared and deposits are transferred from one bank to another. In view of this, the reserve requirements have not been applied to each day's holdings of cash reserves, but to the average level over some specified period. From 1969 to 1991, this reserve averaging period was two weeks. Thus, banks did not need to adjust to changes in their cash reserves on a particular day unless they were approaching the end of a two-week period with an average level of reserves below the minimum requirement.

Furthermore, the level of required cash reserves in effect at any time was not based on the current volume of deposits, but rather on the average volume of deposits during the preceding month. Thus, an expansion of loans and deposits would not affect total excess reserves during the current month, but would increase the level of required reserves that would have to be held in the following month. Of course, to the extent that the banks were not all expanding their loans at the same rate, deposits and cash would be redistributed, so that the faster-growing banks would tend to lose reserves to the slower-growing ones.

Chartered bank holdings of Bank of Canada notes that could be counted toward reserve requirements were also calculated as an average over the preceding month. This means that changes in the public's demand for currency had no effect on a bank's reserve position in the current month unless they induced the bank to reduce or replenish its till money by respectively increasing or running down its deposits at the Bank of Canada.

These institutional arrangements had the following important implication for the implementation of monetary policy: *The Bank of Canada could control not only the total base, but also the reserve component of the base. Further, since required cash reserves were determined by deposits in the preceding month, effective control could be exercised over the excess cash reserves of the chartered banks.* This principle carries over into the new system with zero reserve requirements.

The Zero Reserve Requirement System

Beginning in November 1991, new rules were put in place that eliminated cash reserve requirements.[2] Under the argument given above, required reserves were seen to be

---

[1] For a detailed description of the requirements under the Bank Act, see *Bank of Canada Review*, notes to Table C10.

[2] The details of the new system are described in a series of papers prepared by the Bank of Canada. See "The Implementation of Monetary Policy in a System with Zero Reserve Requirements," *Bank of Canada Review*, May 1991, pp. 23–34.

unnecessary for purposes of central bank control of the money supply. Furthermore, they put the chartered banks at a disadvantage compared with other financial institutions such as trust companies that offered banking services and had access to the clearing system but were not subject to minimum cash reserve requirements.

The new rules apply to chartered banks and other members of the Canadian Payments Association that participate in the clearing system and settle through the Bank of Canada. These institutions are required to maintain a zero or positive balance each day in their accounts at the Bank of Canada. In addition, they must maintain an average balance over each month that equals or exceeds zero.[3]

The Process of Monetary Policy Implementation

The process by which the Bank of Canada implements monetary policy on a day-to-day basis focuses on the supply of Bank of Canada deposits available to chartered banks and other financial institutions for settlement of payments.[4] These deposits are referred to as *settlement balances*, and the determination of the supply is referred to as the daily *cash setting*. The details of the process are as follows:

1. At the close of each day, deposits at the Bank of Canada are transferred among institutions to settle obligations arising from the clearing of cheques and other money transfers.

2. The Bank of Canada makes an estimate of the effects on total settlement balances of items such as government receipts and payments.

3. A transfer of government deposits between the chartered banks and the Bank of Canada is made to neutralize the effects of the above items and to achieve the desired cash setting.

The objective of the cash setting is to induce the desired change in short-term interest rates and the money supply by causing the actual level of settlement balances to diverge from the level which the banks find it desirable to maintain. Suppose that the Bank of Canada wishes to bring about a contraction of the money supply. By setting the level of settlement balances below the level regarded by the banks as a minimum acceptable one, it will induce the banks to sell assets in an attempt to increase their balances.[5] However, the banking system as a whole will be frustrated in this attempt, since the assets it sells will be paid for by cheques drawn on the banks; assets and deposits will fall but the volume of settlement balances will remain the same. In addition, interest rates will rise since the banks will have to offer increased yields to induce

---

[3] The monthly requirement applies to the sum of all daily positive settlement balances less the sum of all daily overdraft loans taken to avoid a negative daily position. See the reference in footnote 2.

[4] See "Bank of Canada Cash Management: The Main Technique for Implementing Monetary Policy," *Bank of Canada Review*, January 1991, pp. 3–25.

[5] The assets used by the chartered banks to adjust their settlement balances are typically short-term loans such as day-to-day loans and call loans.

nonbank investors to increase their holdings of securities at the expense of their holdings of bank deposits. As long as the supply of settlement balances is kept below the level desired by the banks, the money supply will continue to fall and interest rates will continue to rise.[6]

Table 13-10 illustrates the case in which a particular bank (Bank A) reduces loans or sells securities in an amount $100 million in response to a shortage of settlement balances. If the individual or firm on the other side of the transaction pays with a cheque drawn on another bank (Bank B), then Bank B's deposits will fall and it will lose balances in favour of Bank A when the cheque is cleared. However, the total supply of settlement balances remains unaffected.

Table 13-10   *Response to a Shortage of Settlement Balances*

	Bank A	Bank B	Total
Assets			
Settlement balances	+ 100	− 100	0
Loans and securities	− 100		− 100
Liabilities			
Deposits		− 100	− 100

Thus, if the Bank of Canada wishes to reduce the money supply by some target amount, it keeps the banks in a tight cash position until the target is achieved, and then restores the supply of settlement balances to the level desired by the banks. Similarly, an increase in the money supply is brought about by injecting additional cash into the banking system and inducing the banks to bid for additional assets. In practice, this control of the money supply through the cash setting by the Bank of Canada is a process of successive approximation, because the level of settlement balances desired by the banks varies and cannot easily be predicted. By testing the reaction of the banks to a particular supply of balances, the Bank of Canada can estimate the target levels that the banks are attempting to achieve and adjust the supply accordingly.

The Role of the Bank Rate

The *Bank Rate* is the rate of interest at which the Bank of Canada makes advances to chartered banks and other members of the Canadian Payments Association. These advances must be taken by a bank that fails to meet the requirement that it maintain a nonzero settlement balance. Since the cheque clearing takes place at the close of the business day, a bank may be left with insufficient balances to meet its obligations.

---

[6] Why should the banks continue to sell assets if they know there is a limited supply of settlement balances? Each individual bank is forced to do so to maintain its *share* of the supply. A bank that did not sell assets would lose balances to the other banks, as illustrated in Table 13-10.

If this happens the bank is required to make up the deficiency by taking an overdraft loan. Similarly, if a bank fails to meet the requirement of a nonzero average balance, it must take an advance from the Bank of Canada.

The Bank Rate is set each week at 1/4 of 1 percent above the rate of interest on 91-day Treasury bills. This system automatically maintains a penalty cost to a bank that makes use of Bank of Canada advances to maintain its cash position rather than selling Treasury bills or other short-term assets.

Control of the Money Stock and Control of the Interest Rate

We end this section with a simple but important point: The Bank of Canada cannot simultaneously set both the interest rate and the stock of money at any given target levels that it may choose. If the Bank of Canada wants to achieve a given interest rate target, it has to supply the amount of money that is demanded at that interest rate. If it wants to set the money supply at a given level it has to allow the interest rate to adjust to equate the demand for money to that supply of money.

Figure 13-3 illustrates the point. Suppose that the price level is $P = \bar{P}$ and that the Bank of Canada wants to set the interest rate at a level i° and the money stock at the

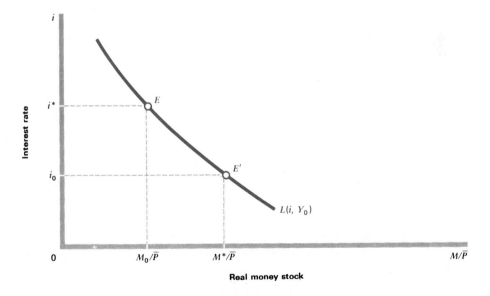

Figure 13-3   *Controlling the Money Stock and Interest Rates*

The Bank of Canada cannot simultaneously set both the interest rate and the money stock levels it wants. Suppose it wanted the interest rate to be i° and the money stock to be M°. These two levels are inconsistent with the demand for money. If the Bank insists on the interest rate level i°, it will have to accept a money stock equal to M_0. If instead the Bank wants to set the money stock at M°, it will end up with an interest rate equal to i_0.

level M^*. However, if the demand for money function is $L(i, Y_0)$, the Bank has to accept that it can set only the combinations of the interest rate and the money supply that lie along the money demand function. At the interest rate i^*, it can have the supply of real balances $M_0/\overline{P}$. At the target money supply M^*, it can have the interest rate i_0. It cannot have both $M^*/\overline{P}$ and i^*.

The point is sometimes put more dramatically as follows. When the Bank of Canada decides to set the interest rate at some given level and keep it fixed, a policy known as *pegging* the interest rate, it loses control over the money supply. It has to to supply whatever amount of money is demanded at that interest rate. If the money demand curve were to shift, because of income growth, say, the Bank would have to allow the money supply to increase.

13-4 Summary

1. The supply of money is controlled by the Bank of Canada through its control of the monetary base, which appears on the liability side of its balance sheet. The monetary base is the sum of currency in circulation and deposits of the chartered banks at the Bank of Canada. The money supply can be expressed as the sum of the base and the volume of bank credit.

2. Chartered banks and other members of the Canadian Payments Association maintain deposits at the Bank of Canada in order to participate in the clearing system. This involves the settlement of the net amounts owing among the banks as a result of the clearing of cheques and other payments.

3. The Bank of Canada controls the money supply primarily through shifts in government deposits between the chartered banks and the Bank of Canada. It can also use open market operations — that is, purchases and sales of government securities.

4. The money multiplier is the ratio of the money supply to the monetary base. It shows how, given the base, the size of the money supply is limited by the currency–deposit ratio and the cash reserve ratio.

5. The adjustment to a change in the monetary base takes place in stages as banks lend out the excess reserves which arise from deposit creation in the previous stage.

6. In late 1991, the requirement that chartered banks hold a minimum ratio of cash reserves to deposits was eliminated. Under the present system, the Bank of Canada determines interest rates and the money supply through the daily cash setting. This refers to the setting of the supply of deposits at the Bank of Canada that are available to chartered banks and other financial institutions for the settlement of payments (settlement balances).

7. The Bank Rate is the rate of interest payable by chartered banks on advances from the Bank of Canada. A bank is required to take these advances if its clearing balance falls below zero. The Bank Rate is automatically set each week at 1/4 of 1 percent above the Treasury bill rate.

Key Terms

Cash reserves
Clearing system
Canadian Payments Association
Monetary base
Open market operation
Money multiplier
Required cash reserve ratio

Excess cash reserves
Multiple expansion of bank deposits
Zero reserve requirements
Settlement balances
Cash setting
Bank Rate

Problems

1. Show the effects on the balance sheets of the nonbank public, the individual banks, and the Bank of Canada of the following transactions:
   (a) Bank A makes a loan of $1000 to a customer who initially holds the proceeds in Bank A.
   (b) The borrower writes a cheque for $1000 to someone who deposits it in Bank B.
   (c) Bank A sells a $1000 Treasury bill to an individual who makes payment with a cheque drawn on Bank B.
   (d) What is the net effect on the balance sheets of all of the above transactions?

2. Table 13-6 shows the effect of an open market purchase with currency drain. If the reserve ratio is 0.10, what would be the amount of bank lending in the next round of expansion? What would be the total expansion of the money supply arising from the money multiplier process? (Note: the currency–deposit ratio is $0.05/0.95 = 0.0526$.)

3. A scheme for "100 percent banking," involving a reserve–deposit ratio of unity, has been proposed to enhance control over the money supply.
   (a) Why would such a scheme improve money supply control?
   (b) What would bank balance sheets look like?
   (c) How would banking remain profitable?

4. Discuss the impact of credit cards and automated teller machines on the money multiplier.

5. The Canada Deposit Insurance Corporation insures deposits in chartered banks and other financial institutions against bank default. Discuss the implications for the money multiplier.

6. This problem extends the money multiplier by distinguishing between $M1$ and $M2$. Assume $CU/DD = c$, $DD/SD = d$, where $M1 = CU + DD$ and $M2 = M1 + SD$. Suppose further that the banks have reserve ratios r_d and r_s for demand and savings deposits respectively. Assume $r_s < r_d$.
    (a) Derive an expression for the $M1$ money multiplier.
    (b) Derive an expression for the $M2$ money multiplier.
    (c) What would be the effect of a decrease in d on $M1$, $M2$, and bank loans?

Appendix   Multiple Expansion of Bank Deposits

In Section 13-2, the money multiplier was expressed in Equation (7) as

$$\frac{M}{B} = \frac{cu + 1}{cu + re} \tag{A1}$$

Table A13-1 shows the successive steps by which the money multiplier builds up following an increase in the monetary base of \$1. Round 1 is the process described in Table 13-9, ending with the bank making a loan. Round 2 starts when the borrower spends the loan, and the person receiving the proceeds holds some of that amount as currency and deposits the rest in a bank. Round 2 ends once again with a bank loan, and so forth.

We can now add up the increases in currency, deposits, reserves, and bank credit occurring over all the rounds together — that is, during the entire process. As in the case of the expenditure multiplier in Chapter 3, we have the sum of an infinite series, denoted here as *SUM* and given by[7]

$$
\begin{aligned}
SUM &= 1 + \left(\frac{1 - re}{1 + cu}\right) + \left(\frac{1 - re}{1 + cu}\right)^2 + \left(\frac{1 - re}{1 + cu}\right)^3 + \ldots \\
&= \frac{cu + 1}{cu + re}
\end{aligned}
\tag{A2}
$$

---

[7] Technical note: The formula for the sum of a geometric series, which can in general be written

$$SUM = 1 + a + a^2 + \ldots .$$

where a is a number between minus and plus 1, is

$$SUM = \frac{1}{1 - a}$$

This is the same formula used to obtain the expenditure multiplier in Chapter 3.

Table A13-1 *Multiple Expansion of Bank Deposits, Bank Loans, and the Money Multiplier*

Increase in H	Increase in currency	Increase in deposits	Increase in reserves	Increase in bank loans	Stage
1	$\dfrac{cu}{1+cu}$	$\dfrac{1}{1+cu}$	$\dfrac{re}{1+cu}$	$\dfrac{1-re}{1+cu}$	Round 1
	$\dfrac{cu}{1+cu}\left(\dfrac{1-re}{1+cu}\right)$	$\dfrac{1}{1+cu}\left(\dfrac{1-re}{1+cu}\right)$	$\dfrac{re}{1+cu}\left(\dfrac{1-re}{1+cu}\right)$	$\dfrac{1-re}{1+cu}\left(\dfrac{1-re}{1+cu}\right)$	Round 2
	$\dfrac{cu}{1+cu}\left(\dfrac{1-re}{1+cu}\right)^2$	$\dfrac{1}{1+cu}\left(\dfrac{1-re}{1+cu}\right)^2$	$\dfrac{re}{1+cu}\left(\dfrac{1-re}{1+cu}\right)^2$	$\dfrac{1-re}{1+cu}\left(\dfrac{1-re}{1+cu}\right)^2$	Round 3
	$\dfrac{cu}{1+cu}\left(\dfrac{1-re}{1+cu}\right)^n$	$\dfrac{1}{1+cu}\left(\dfrac{1-re}{1+cu}\right)^n$	$\dfrac{re}{1+cu}\left(\dfrac{1-re}{1+cu}\right)^n$	$\dfrac{1-re}{1+cu}\left(\dfrac{1-re}{1+cu}\right)^n$	Round $n+1$
	$\dfrac{cu}{1+cu}\,SUM$	$\dfrac{1}{1+cu}\,SUM$	$\dfrac{re}{1+cu}\,SUM$	$\dfrac{1-re}{1+cu}\,SUM$	Total
	$\dfrac{cu}{cu+re}$	$\dfrac{1}{cu+re}$	$\dfrac{re}{cu+re}$	$\dfrac{1-re}{cu+re}$	After substituting for *SUM* from Equation (A2)

We use Equation (A2) in arriving at the bottom row of Table A13-1, which shows that currency increases by the fraction $[cu/(cu+re)]$ of \$1 following the increase in B of \$1, that deposits increase by $[1/(cu+re)]$, that reserves increase by $[re/(cu+re)]$, and, finally, that bank credit increases by $[(1-re)/(cu+re)]$.

Adding the increases in currency and deposits, we discover that the two together have risen by the amount $[(cu+1)/(cu+re)]$, which is the money multiplier. Table A13-1 thus provides another way of thinking about the money multiplier. The table also shows how, and by how much, the banking system creates loans (or buys securities) when the central bank increases the monetary base.

In the numerical example given in the text, currency increases by \$0.625 $[cu/(cu+re)]$, deposits by \$2.50 $[1/(cu+re)]$, reserves by \$0.375 $[re/(cu+re)]$, and bank loans by \$2.125 $[(1-re)(cu+re)]$. The money stock increases by \$3.125, or 3.125 times the increase in the monetary base. This is the value that can be obtained directly from the sum of the infinite series shown in Equation (A2).

CHAPTER 14 *Problems of Stabilization Policy*

Figure 14-1, which shows the unemployment rate over the period 1931–1991, gives the clear impression that stabilization policy has left something to be desired. Standing out is the disaster of the great depression decade of the 1930s, when the unemployment rate reached nearly 20 percent of the labour force. Unemployment has also at times been high in the post–World War II period, as in the recessions of 1982–1983 and 1990–1991.

The historical record forcefully raises the question of why the economy has not done better. The preceding chapters have laid out a clear body of theory that seems to show exactly the measures that can be used to maintain full employment. High unemployment, or a large GDP gap, can be reduced by expansionary monetary or fiscal policy. Similarly, a boom and inflation can be contained by restrictive monetary or fiscal policies.

The policies needed to prevent the fluctuations in unemployment seen in Figure 14-1 accordingly appear to be simple. The policy maker knows the full-employment level of output. If there is unemployment, a model such as the one we have developed in the preceding chapters can be used to calculate the level of government spending or taxes needed to get income to the full-employment level. If it is all so simple, how did the fluctuations in Figure 14-1 occur?

The answer must be that policy making is far from simple. Part of the difficulty arises from the possible *conflict between the maintenance of full employment and the target of low inflation.* That important issue is discussed in Chapters 16 and 17. Other difficulties are described in this chapter.

We begin by discussing the types of disturbance that cause the economy to move away from the full-employment level of output in the first place. Then we briefly

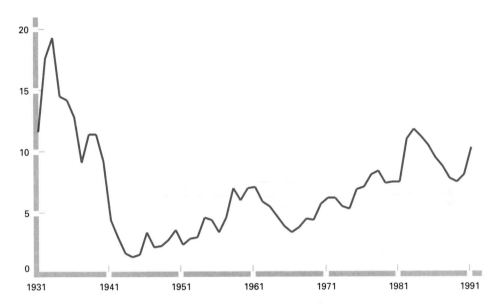

Figure 14-1 *Unemployment Rate in Canada, 1931–1987*

(*Source:* Adapted from Statistics Canada, 11-505, 11-210)

describe *econometric models*, models of the economy with specific numerical values for parameters and multipliers, that can be used to assist policy making. The bulk of the chapter is taken up by a discussion of three factors that in large measure account for the frequent failure of policy to achieve its targets. The three *handicaps of policy making* are

1. lags in the effects of policy;

2. the role of expectations in determining private sector responses to policy;

3. uncertainty about the effects of policy.

In a nutshell, we are going to argue that a policy maker who (1) observes a disturbance, (2) does not know whether it is permanent or not, (3) takes time to develop a policy which (4) takes still more time to affect behaviour and (5) has uncertain effects on aggregate demand is very poorly equipped to do a perfect job of stabilizing the economy.

14-1 Economic Disturbances

Before identifying in detail the obstacles in the way of successful policy making, we discuss economic disturbances in terms of their sources, persistence, and importance for policy. Disturbances are shifts in aggregate demand or aggregate supply that cause output, interest rates, or prices to diverge from their target paths.

We return to the aggregate supply and demand model as the framework for the discussion of economic disturbances in this chapter. In Figure 14-2 we show the *AS* and *AD* schedules and the full-employment level of output, $Y°$. The economy is initially at full employment at point *E*. What disturbances might cause the economy to move away from full employment? Obviously, anything that shifts the *IS* and/or *LM* curves would shift the *AD* curve and move the economy away from *E*.

In terms of overall economic impact, the major disturbances to the economy that have affected aggregate demand have typically been wars. The effects of the increases

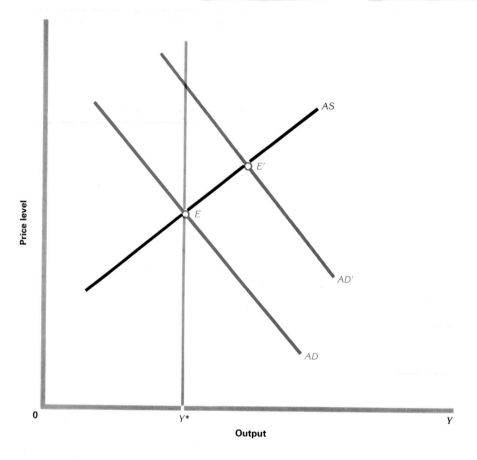

Figure 14-2 *An Aggregate Demand Disturbance*

The economy is initially in equilibrium at point *E*, with level of output $Y°$. An increase in government spending shifts the *AD* curve to *AD'*. This disturbance tends to raise the level of output above the full-employment level. Monetary and/or fiscal policy, or even rationing, may be used to keep the level of demand in check, shifting the *AD'* curve back to *AD*.

in government spending associated with World War II and the Korean War can be seen in Figure 14-1 in the very low unemployment rates in those periods. Of these, World War II had the largest impact on the economy. At the height of the war, in 1944, federal government spending exceeded 40 percent of income.

As shown in Figure 14-2, the increase in government spending would shift the *AD* schedule upward so that both output and prices increase. To free resources needed for war, the government can both raise taxes and perhaps run a tight monetary policy, but this is not usually enough to prevent wartime inflations.[1]

Changes in government spending or tax policies not connected with wars may also constitute economic disturbances. Government spending or taxes may be increased or reduced for reasons which have to do with the government's view of desirable social policies. Those changes too may affect the level of aggregate demand if not accompanied by appropriate monetary and fiscal policies. In a country like Canada that is heavily dependent on foreign trade, changes in foreign demand for our exports may be an important source of disturbances.

Other economic disturbances that lead to changes in aggregate demand, which originate in the private sector, are shifts in the consumption or investment function. If consumers decide to consume more out of their disposable income at any given level of income, the *AD* curve of Figure 14-2 shifts upward, tending to increase the level of income. If there is no economic explanation for the shift in the consumption function, then it is attributed to a change in the tastes of consumers between consumption and saving. In such a case, we describe the shift as a disturbance.

Similarly, if investment spending increases for no apparent economic reason, then we attribute the increase to an unexplained change in the optimism of investors about the returns from investment. Again, we regard that change in investment behaviour as a disturbance to the system. Changes in the optimism of investors are sometimes described as changes in their *animal spirits*, a term that suggests that there may be little rational basis for those spirits.[2] Some shifts in the investment function are caused by new inventions that require large amounts of investment for their successful marketing, such as the development of the railways in the nineteenth century and the spread of the automobile in the 1920s.

Shifts in the demand for money may affect the interest rate, and thus indirectly affect the rate of investment. Another source of disturbances is changes in supply conditions, such as the oil price shocks discussed in Chapter 8. In addition, the behaviour of wages may constitute a source of economic disturbances.

---

[1] Often *rationing* is used to limit private demand in wartime. For instance, in World War II, a system was set up under which investment projects had to be approved. That system served to reduce the overall rate of private investment and also to direct investment toward areas helpful for the war effort. There was also some rationing of consumption goods, which reduced consumption expenditure as some of the rationed demand spilled over into increased saving rather than being diverted toward the purchase of goods. Thus, the aggregate level of consumption spending was reduced by using rationing to reduce the consumption of various goods essential for the war effort (gasoline, tires, meat, shoes, etc.).

[2] Keynes, in particular, argued that shifts in the investment function were a major cause of fluctuations in the economy. See J.M. Keynes, *The General Theory of Employment, Interest and Money* (London: Macmillan, 1936), Chapter 22.

Finally, disturbances may be caused by the policy makers themselves. There are two different arguments concerning this possibility. First, since policy making is difficult, it is entirely possible that the attempts of policy makers to stabilize the economy could be counterproductive. Indeed, a forcefully stated and influential view of the causes of the great depression argues that an inept monetary policy in the United States was chiefly responsible for the severity of the depression.[3] The argument of Friedman and Schwartz is basically that the officials in charge of the American central bank in the early 1930s did not understand the workings of monetary policy and therefore carried out a policy that made the depression worse rather than better.

The second argument, that policy makers themselves may be responsible for economic disturbances, arises from the relationship between election results and economic conditions in the period before the election. If it appears that incumbents tend to be reelected when economic conditions, primarily the unemployment rate, are improving in the year before the election, it is tempting for them to try to *improve* economic conditions in the period before the election; their efforts may involve tax reductions or increases in government spending. It is now quite common to talk of the *political business cycle*. The political business cycle consists of economic fluctuations produced by economic policies designed to help win elections.

While some evidence supports the notion of a political business cycle, the argument should be regarded as tentative because the link between economic conditions and election results is not yet firmly established.

We proceed next to discuss economic models and the three factors that make the task of policy makers far more difficult than an overliteral interpretation of the simple aggregate supply and demand model in Figure 14-2 might suggest.

14-2   Econometric Models for Policy Making and Forecasting

Consider a government faced with a recession. It has to decide whether to react, and if so, what policies to change. It could cut taxes or raise government spending and/or it could use expansionary monetary policy, but it has to know not only what policies to change — what medicines to use — but also the right doses. If government spending should be increased by $5 billion, it will not do much good to increase it by $1 billion. On the other hand, if it should be increased by only $1 billion, an increase in government spending of $5 billion will push the economy well beyond the point of full employment and create inflationary pressures.

In other words, policy makers have to know the *multipliers* associated with monetary and fiscal policy. To calculate these multipliers, they typically rely on *econometric models*. An econometric model is an equation or a set of equations with numerical

---

[3] See Milton Friedman and Anna J. Schwartz, *The Great Contraction* (Princeton, N.J.: Princeton University Press, 1965). We review the argument in Chapter 15.

values for parameters, based on the past behaviour of the economy, describing the behaviour of some specific sectors of the economy or the economy as a whole.

Econometric Models of Canada

A considerable number of econometric models of the Canadian economy have been constructed and are used regularly for forecasting and policy analysis. Within the federal government, there are models at the Bank of Canada and the Department of Finance. Models are also maintained by John Helliwell at the University of British Columbia and the Institute of Policy Analysis at the University of Toronto. Models are operated as private commercial enterprises by the WEFA group, DRI (Canada) and Informetrica.

These models describe aggregate demand using an extended *IS-LM* framework. Equations are estimated for the components of aggregate demand using theories similar to those described in Chapters 10–12. The consumption function, for instance, would be similar to the sophisticated function we discussed in Chapter 10, although in most cases it would be disaggregated into several components.

To be useful, the models must also include equations to predict the rate of inflation as well as output. For this purpose the models have aggregate supply sectors along the lines described in Chapter 8.

Fiscal and monetary policy multipliers for two of the Canadian models are shown in Table 14-1. CANDIDE is a model formerly maintained by the Economic Council of Canada model, and RDXF is one of the models at the Bank of Canada. The table shows *dynamic multiplier* effects which take place in stages over time and reflect the various lags built into models. For fiscal policy, the CANDIDE model shows a larger effect on real income in the third year compared with the initial year, while the RDXF model shows declining multiplier effects. In both cases we see crowding out occurring, so that by the tenth year the changes in output are much smaller.

Table 14-1   *Real Income Multipliers From Two Econometric Models*

Policy Change		Year			
		1	3	5	10
Fiscal policy: increase					
in government spending	CANDIDE	1.98	2.25	1.85	0.77
(multiplier effect)	RDXF	1.09	0.58	0.34	0.06
Monetary policy: 1 percent					
decrease in money supply	CANDIDE	0	−0.17	−0.33	−0.21
(percent change in output)	RDXF	−0.22	−0.13	−0.06	−0.06

Source: B. O'Reilly, G. Paulin, and P. Smith, *Responses of Various Econometric Models to Selected Policy Shocks*, Bank of Canada Technical Report 38, July 1983.

For policy changes, the multiplier effects are quite different in magnitude and lag pattern between the two models. This reflects differences in size and degree of disaggregation between the two models as well as differences in the theoretical assumptions used in constructing the equations. At present, there is clearly no consensus on the exact structure of the economy, and thus there is considerable variation among the models.

14-3 Lags in the Effects of Policy

Suppose that the economy is at full employment and has been affected by an aggregate demand disturbance that reduces the equilibrium level of income below full employment. Suppose further that there was no advance warning of this disturbance and that, consequently, no policy actions were taken in anticipation of its occurrence. Policy makers now have to decide *whether to respond at all* and *how* to respond to the disturbance.

The first concern, and the first difficulty, should be over the permanence of the disturbance and its subsequent effects. Suppose the disturbance is only transitory, such as a one-period reduction in consumption spending. When the disturbance is transitory so that consumption rapidly reverts to its initial level, the best policy may be to do nothing at all. Provided suppliers or producers do not mistakenly interpret the increase in demand as permanent but, rather, perceive it as transitory, they will absorb it by production and inventory changes rather than capacity adjustments. The disturbance will affect income in this period but will have very little permanent effect. Policy actions generally do not affect the economy immediately. Any policy actions taken to offset the disturbance this period — for example, a tax reduction — will have their impact on spending and income only over time. In later periods, however, the effects of the initial fall in demand on the level of income will be very small, and without the policy action the economy would tend to be very close to full employment. The effects of a tax cut, therefore, would be to raise income in later periods and move it away from the full-employment level. Thus, if the disturbance is temporary and it has no long-lived effects and policy operates with a lag, then the best policy is to do nothing.

Figure 14-3 illustrates the main issue. Assume an aggregate demand disturbance reduces output below potential, starting at time t_0. Without active policy intervention, output declines for a while but then recovers and reaches the full-employment level again at time t_2. Consider next the path of GDP under an active stabilization policy, but one that works with the disadvantage of lags. Thus, expansionary policy might be initiated at time t_1 and start taking effect some time after. Output now tends to recover faster as a consequence of the expansion and, because of poor dosage and/or timing, actually overshoots the full-employment level. By time t_3, restrictive policy is initiated, and some time after, output starts turning down toward full employment and may well continue cycling for a while. If this is an accurate description of the potency or scope of stabilization policy, then a serious question must arise: Is it worth trying to stabilize output, or is the effect of stabilization policy, in fact, to make things worse? Stabilization policy may actually *destabilize* the economy.

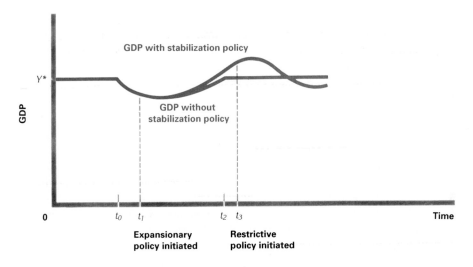

Figure 14-3 *Lags and Destabilizing Policy*

A disturbance at time t_0 reduces output below the full-employment level. It takes until t_1 before policy responds, and there is a further lag until the policy starts working. By the time the full effects of the policy are evident, output would already have returned to the full-employment level even without policy. However, because a policy action has been taken, output now rises *above* the full-employment level and then fluctuates around Y°. The lags in policy thus have made policy a source of fluctuations in output that would not otherwise have happened.

One of the main difficulties of policy making is in establishing whether or not a disturbance is temporary. It was clear enough in the case of World War II that a high level of defence expenditures would be required for some years. However, in the case of the Arab oil embargo of 1973–1974, it was not clear at all how long the embargo would last or whether the high prices for oil that were established in late 1973 would persist. At the time, there were many who argued that the oil cartel would not survive and that oil prices would soon fall — that is, the disturbance was temporary. "Soon" turned out to be 12 years. Let us suppose, however, that it is known that the disturbance will have effects that will last for several quarters, and that the level of income will, without policy, be below the full-employment level for some time. What lags do policy makers encounter?

We now consider the steps required before a policy action can be taken after a disturbance has occurred, and then the process by which that policy action affects the economy. There are delays, or lags, at every stage. It is customary and useful to divide the lags into an *inside* lag, which is the time period it takes to undertake a policy action — such as a tax cut, or an increase in the money supply — and an *outside* lag, which describes the timing of the effects of the policy action on the economy. The inside lag, in turn, is divided into recognition, decision, and action lags.

The Inside Lag

The Recognition Lag

The *recognition lag* is the period that elapses between the time a disturbance occurs and the time the policy makers recognize that action is required. This lag could in principle be *negative* if the disturbance could be predicted and appropriate policy actions considered *before* it even occurs. For example, we know that seasonal factors affect behaviour. Thus it is known that at Christmas the demand for currency is high. Rather than allow this to exert a restrictive effect on the money supply, the Bank of Canada will accommodate this seasonal demand by an expansion in the monetary base. In other cases, the recognition lag has been positive, so that some time has elapsed between the disturbance and recognition that active policy was required.

The major reason that there is any recognition lag at all, apart from the delay in collecting statistical data, is that it is never certain what the consequences of a disturbance will be. That uncertainty in turn is a result of economists' lack of knowledge of the workings of the economy (which was discussed above) as well as political uncertainties.

The Decision and Action Lags

The recognition lag is the same for monetary and fiscal policy. The Bank of Canada and the Department of Finance are in constant contact with one another and share their predictions about the future course of the economy. By contrast, for the *decision lag* — the delay between the recognition of the need for action and the policy decision — there is a difference between monetary and fiscal policy. Once the need for a policy action has been recognized by the Bank of Canada, the decision lag for monetary policy is short. Further, the *action lag*, the lag between the policy decision and its implementation, for monetary policy is also short.

However, fiscal policy actions are less rapid. Once the need for fiscal policy action has been recognized, the government has to prepare legislation for that action. Next, the legislation has to be considered and approved by Parliament before the policy change can be made. Even after the legislation has been approved, the policy change has still to be put into effect. If the fiscal policy takes the form of a change in tax rates, it may be some time before the changes in tax rates begin to be reflected in paycheques, that is, there may be an action lag.

Built-In Stabilizers

The existence of the inside lag of policy making focuses attention on the built-in or automatic stabilizers that we discussed in Chapter 3. One of the major benefits of automatic stabilizers is that their inside lag is zero. Recall from Chapter 3 that the most important automatic stabilizer is the income tax. It stabilizes the economy by reducing the multiplier effects of any disturbance to aggregate demand. The multiplier for the effects of changes in autonomous spending on GDP is inversely related to the income tax rate. The higher the tax rate, the smaller the effects of any given change in autonomous demand on GDP. Similarly, unemployment compensation is another automatic stabilizer. When workers become unemployed and reduce their consumption, that reduction in consumption demand tends to have multiplier effects on output. Those multiplier effects are reduced when a worker receives unemployment compensation because disposable income is reduced by less than the loss in earnings.

Although built-in stabilizers have desirable effects, they cannot be carried too far without also affecting the overall performance of the economy. The multiplier could be reduced to 1 by increasing the tax rate to 100 percent, and that would appear to be a stabilizing influence on the economy. However, with 100 percent marginal tax rates, the desire to work, and consequently the level of GDP, would be reduced. Thus there are limits on the extent to which automatic stabilizers are desirable. Nonetheless, automatic stabilizers play an important role in the economy; it has been argued that the absence of significant unemployment compensation in the 1930s was one of the major factors making the great depression so severe, and that the existence of the stabilizers alone makes the recurrence of such a deep depression unlikely.

The Outside Lag

The inside lag of policy is a *discrete* lag in which policy can have no effect on the economy until it is implemented. The outside lag is generally a *distributed* lag: Once the policy action has been taken, its effects on the economy are spread over time. There is usually a small immediate effect of a policy action, but other effects occur later.

The idea that policy operates on aggregate demand and income with a distributed lag is shown in Figure 14-4. The process illustrated is the same as that represented by the numerical results from the econometric models shown in Table 14-1.

Suppose that we are considering a once-for-all increase in the monetary base in period 1, as shown in the lower panel of Figure 14-4. This increase in the base, by affecting interest rates and therefore aggregate spending, changes the level of income in subsequent periods by the amounts indicated in the upper panel of Figure 14-4. The height of the bars shows the amount by which GDP exceeds the level that it would have had in the absence of the policy change. The main point to be made is that monetary or fiscal actions taken now affect the economy over time.

If we measure time in quarters, the impact in the initial period is likely to be relatively small, with most of the effect coming later in the adjustment period as illustrated in Figure 14-4. Thus, if it were necessary to increase the level of employment rapidly to offset a demand disturbance, a large policy change would be necessary. However, in later quarters large effects on GDP would be built up, so that there would probably be an overcorrection of the unemployment leading to inflationary pressures. It would then be necessary to reverse policy and undertake contractionary actions to avoid the inflationary consequences of the initial expansionary policy.

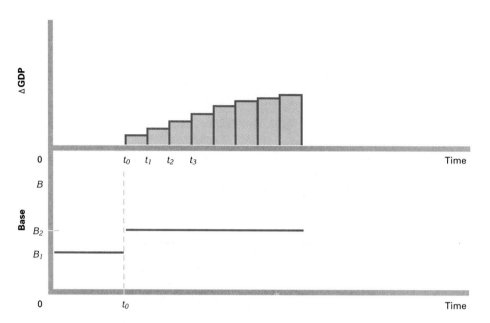

Figure 14-4 *Dynamic Multipliers for the Effects of a Change in the Monetary Base on GDP*

An increase in the monetary base causes GDP to increase by successively larger amounts as we move through time. The height of the bars shows the amount by which GDP exceeds the level that it would have reached in the absence of the policy change.

It should thus be clear that when policy acts slowly, with the impacts of policy building up over time, considerable skill is required of policy makers if their own attempts to correct an initially undesirable situation are not to lead to problems that themselves need correcting. Recall also that we have been talking here about the *outside* lag, and that the policy action we are considering would be taken only six months after the initial disturbance if the inside lag is six months long.

Why are there such long outside lags? We have already discussed some of the reasons for these lags in Chapter 10 on the consumption function, where current consumption depends on lagged income, and also in Chapter 11 on investment, where the accelerator models imply that investment depends on lagged and current income. Similar lags are also present in the financial sector of the economy, where the demand for money depends on lagged income. Each of these sources of lags creates an outside lag, and their interaction generally produces longer lags than each of the underlying lags.

Because the point is so important, let us describe in more detail how the lags of monetary policy arise. Suppose the Bank of Canada conducts an expansionary monetary policy. Because aggregate demand depends heavily on lagged values of income, interest rates, and other economic variables, the policy initially has effects mainly on short-term interest rates and not on income. Short-term interest rates, such as the Treasury bill rate, affect long-term interest rates with a lag. The long-term interest rates in turn affect investment with a lag, and also affect consumption by affecting the value of wealth.[4] Then, when aggregate demand is affected, the increase in aggregate demand itself produces lagged effects on subsequent aggregate demand through the fact that both consumption and investment depend on past values of income. So the effects of the expansionary policy will be spread through time, as in Figure 14-4.

Monetary Versus Fiscal Policy Lags

The discussion in the previous paragraph suggests that fiscal policy and certainly changes in government spending, which act directly on aggregate demand, may affect income more rapidly than monetary policy. This is indeed the case. However, the fact that fiscal policy acts faster on aggregate demand than monetary policy must not lead us to overlook the fact that fiscal policy has a considerably longer inside lag. Moreover, the inside lag for government spending is longer than that for taxes because, when the government purchases goods and services, it has to decide what goods to buy, have bids for the sale of those goods submitted by the private sector, and then award the contracts. In summary, therefore, fiscal policy is attractive because of the short outside lag, but that advantage is more than offset by a potentially long inside lag.

Our analysis of lags indicates clearly one difficulty in undertaking stabilizing short-term policy actions: It takes time to set the policies in action, and then the policies themselves take time to affect the economy. However, that is not the only difficulty. Further difficulties considered in Sections 14-4 and 14-5 arise from uncertainty about the exact timing and magnitude of the effects of policy.

14-4 The Role of Expectations

We have discussed the two basic sources of lags in economic behaviour in earlier chapters. The first source is the costs of rapid adjustment. For example, in Chapter 11 we showed how the costs of adjusting the actual capital stock to the desired capital stock led to lags in the investment function. The second source of lags is expectations. In this section we focus on expectations, their formation, and the effects they have on policy and its effectiveness.

While it is undoubtedly true that the past behaviour of a variable influences expectations about its future behaviour, it is also true that consumers and investors will

---

[4] Recall that in Chapter 10 we discussed the life-cycle model of consumption demand, in which consumption is affected by the level of wealth. Part of wealth is the value of stock market assets; the value of stock market assets rises when the long-term interest rate falls. Thus, interest rates affect consumption through a wealth effect.

sometimes use more information than is contained in the past behaviour of a variable when trying to predict its future behaviour.

Consider, for example, forecasts of permanent income or long-run average income. In Chapter 10, as in Friedman's original work on the consumption function, permanent income is estimated as an average of income in the recent past. Suppose, however, that you were a resident of a small country that had just discovered vast gold deposits. You would then take the information about the gold discovery into account in forming an estimate of your permanent income. You would *immediately* estimate a permanent income substantially higher than your historical average income. Alternatively, suppose that you have been estimating the expected rate of inflation as an average of past rates of inflation, at a time when the inflation rate is high and a new government is elected on a strictly anti-inflationary platform. Then you would lower your estimate of the inflation rate; that is, you would use more information in predicting it than is contained solely in its past behaviour.

It is, in general, very difficult to incorporate all relevant information that is used by economic agents within a simple econometric model. That means that there will inevitably be errors in what the models predict for the consequences of various policy actions, meaning, in turn, that it is difficult to control the economy precisely.

Expectations and Policy

It is particularly important to consider the effects of a given policy action itself on expectations, since it is possible that a new type of policy will affect the way in which expectations are formed.[5] Suppose that the Bank of Canada announced a new monetary policy designed to stabilize the average level of income and avoid booms and recessions. The new policy would be to reduce the money supply whenever the income level rose and to increase the money supply whenever the income level fell. Such a countercyclical rule has implications for expectations. Clearly, it would be inappropriate in the presence of such monetary policy to use an expectations mechanism that implies that an increase in income will persist. The monetary policy rule implies that the money supply should be reduced following an increase in income, and one expects the reduction in money to exert at least a dampening effect on income.

While correct expectations mechanisms must therefore use information about policy responses to disturbances, such care is difficult to apply in practice. Most expectations mechanisms embodied in econometric models of the economy and used for the assessment of policies assume that expectations affecting consumption and investment spending are based entirely on past values.

---

[5] The interactions of policy and expectations have been the focus of the rational expectations approach to macroeconomics, introduced in Chapter 8, and to be pursued in greater detail in Chapter 20. For an early statement, see Thomas J. Sargent and Neil Wallace, "Rational Expectations and the Theory of Economic Policy," *Journal of Monetary Economics*, April 1976.

Econometric Policy Evaluation

The preceding discussion of the effects of a change in policy on expectations is part of a wider *econometric policy evaluation critique* formulated by Robert E. Lucas of the University of Chicago, intellectual leader of the rational expectations approach to macroeconomics.[6] Lucas argues that existing macroeconometric models cannot be used to study the effects of policy changes *because the way private agents (firms and consumers) respond to changes in income and prices depends on the types of policy being followed.*

Lucas argues that problems of this sort are pervasive in macroeconometric models. He does not argue that it will never be possible to use econometric models to study policy, only that existing models cannot be used for the purpose. Accordingly, the Lucas critique is not one that rules out the use of econometric models. It suggests rather that very careful modelling of the responses of consumers and firms to changes in income and prices is necessary.

14-5 Uncertainty and Economic Policy

So far in this chapter we have described the disturbances that affect the economy, econometric models that are used in policy making, the difficulties of making policy when there are long lags in the effects of policy, and the problem of modelling expectations. We can summarize most of the implied problems for policy making by saying that is is impossible to predict the effects of any given policy action exactly.

How should a policy maker react in the face of these uncertainties? We want to distinguish here between uncertainty about the correct model of the economy and uncertainty about the precise values of the parameters of coefficients within a given model of the economy, even though the distinction is not watertight.

First, there is considerable disagreement and therefore uncertainty about the correct model of the economy, as shown by the large number of macroeconometric models. Reasonable economists can and do differ about what theory and empirical evidence suggest are the correct behavioural functions of the economy. Generally, each economist will have reasons for favouring one particular form and will use that form, but, being reasonable, the economist will recognize that the particular formulation being used may not be the correct one, and will thus regard its predictions as subject to a margin of error. In turn, policy makers will know that there are different predictions about the effects of a given policy, and will want to consider the range of predictions that are being made in deciding on policy.

Second, as we noted in Section 14-2, even within the context of a given model there is uncertainty about the values of parameters and multipliers. The statistical evidence

---

[6] See "Econometric Policy Evaluation: A Critique," in R.E. Lucas, Jr., *Studies in Business Cycle Theory* (Cambridge, Mass.: MIT Press, 1981).

does allow us to say something about the likely range of parameters or multipliers,[7] so that at least we can get some idea of the type of errors that could result from a particular policy action.

Uncertainty about the size of the effects that will result from any particular policy action is known as *multiplier uncertainty*. For instance, our best estimate of the multiplier of an increase in government spending might be 1.2. If GDP has to be increased by $6 billion, we would increase government spending by $5 billion, but the statistical evidence might be better interpreted as saying only that we can be quite confident the multiplier is between 0.9 and 1.5. In that case, when we increase government spending by $5 billion, we expect GDP to rise by some amount between $4.5 and $7.5 billion.

What is optimal behaviour in the face of such multiplier uncertainty? The more precisely policy makers are informed about the relevant parameters, the more activist the policy can afford to be. Conversely, if there is a considerable range of error in the estimate of the relevant parameters — in our example, the multiplier — then policy should be more modest. With poor information, very active policy runs a large danger of introducing unnecessary fluctuations in the economy.

14-6 Activist Policy

We started this chapter asking why there are any fluctuations in the economy when the policy measures needed to iron out those fluctuations seen to be so simple. The list of difficulties in the way of successful policy making that we have outlined may have raised a different question: Why should one believe that policy can do anything to reduce fluctuations in the economy?

Indeed, considerations of the sort spelled out in the previous four sections have led Milton Friedman and others to argue that there should be no use of active counter-cyclical monetary policy, and that monetary policy should be confined to making the money supply grow at a constant rate. The precise value of the constant rate of growth of money, Friedman suggests, is less important than that monetary growth be constant and that policy not respond to disturbances. At various times, he has suggested growth rates for money of 2 percent or 4 percent or 5 percent. As Friedman has expressed it, "By setting itself a steady course and keeping to it, the monetary authority could make a major contribution to promoting economic stability. By making that course one of steady but moderate growth in the quantity of money, it would make a major contribution to avoidance of either inflation or deflation of prices."[8] Friedman thus advocates a simple monetary rule in which the central bank does not respond to the

---

[7] We are discussing here *confidence intervals* about estimates of parameters; see Robert S. Pindyck and Daniel L. Rubinfeld, *Econometric Models and Economic Forecasts* (New York: McGraw-Hill, 1991), for further discussion.

[8] Milton Friedman, "The Role of Monetary Policy," *American Economic Review*, March 1968. See also his book, *A Program for Monetary Stability* (New York: Fordham University Press, 1959).

condition of the economy. Policies that respond to the current or predicted state of the economy are called *activist policies*.

In discussing the desirability of active monetary and fiscal policy, we want to distinguish between policy actions taken in response to major disturbances to the economy and *fine tuning* in which policy variables are continually adjusted in response to small disturbances to the economy. We see no case for arguing that monetary and fiscal policy should not be used actively in the face of major disturbances to the economy. Most of the considerations of the previous sections of this chapter indicate some uncertainty about the effects of policy, but there are still clearly definable circumstances in which there can be no doubt that the appropriate policy is expansionary or contractionary. A government coming to power in 1933 should not have worried about the uncertainties associated with expansionary policy that we have outlined. The economy does not move from 20 percent unemployment to full employment in a short time (precisely because of those same lags that make policy difficult). Thus, expansionary measures, such as a rapid growth of the money supply, or increased government expenditures, or tax reductions, or all three, would have been appropriate policy since there was no chance they would have an impact only after the economy was at full employment. Similarly, contractionary policies for private demand are called for in wartime. In early 1982, with unemployment of more than 10 percent and rising rapidly and forecasts of very high unemployment for the next two years, policies designed to reduce unemployment were appropriate.[9] In the event of large disturbances in the future, active monetary and/or fiscal policy should once again be used.[10]

Fine tuning presents more complicated issues. In the case of fiscal policy, the long inside lags make discretionary fine tuning virtually impossible, though automatic stabilizers are in fact fine tuning all the time. On the other hand, with monetary policy decisions being made frequently, fine tuning of monetary policy is indeed possible. The question, then, is whether a small increase in the unemployment rate should lead to a small increase in the growth rate of money, or whether policy should not respond until the increase in unemployment becomes large, say more than 1.0 percent.

The problem is that the disturbance that caused the increase in unemployment may be either transitory or permanent. If transitory, nothing should be done. If permanent, policy should react to a small disturbance in a small way. Given uncertainty over the nature of the disturbance, the technically correct response is a small one, between the zero that is appropriate for a transitory shock and the full response that would be appropriate for a permanent disturbance. Accordingly, we believe that fine tuning is appropriate provided that policy responses are always kept small in response to small disturbances.

However, we should emphasize that the argument for fine tuning is a controversial one. The major argument against it is that in practice policy makers cannot behave as

---

[9] Because the inflation rate was high in 1982, policy making then required some judgment about the costs of inflation compared with those of unemployment, a topic discussed in Chapter 17. Policy making in 1982 was thus more difficult than policy making in 1933.

[10] Interestingly, in the article cited in footnote 8, Friedman argues for the use of active policy in the face of major disturbances.

suggested — making only small adjustments to small disturbances. Rather, it is argued, they tend to try to do too much, if allowed to do anything. Instead of merely trying to offset disturbances, they attempt to keep the economy always at full employment and therefore undertake inappropriate large policy actions in response to small disturbances.

The major lesson of the previous sections is not that policy is impossible, but that policy that is too ambitious in trying to keep the economy always at full employment (with zero inflation) is impossible. The lesson is to proceed with extreme caution, always bearing in mind the possibility that policy itself may be destabilizing. We see no reason why the Bank of Canada should try to keep the money supply always growing at the same rate; we believe, on the contrary, that the stability of the economy would be improved by its following a careful countercyclical policy. Similarly, if fiscal policy were not subject to a long inside lag, we would believe it possible for cautiously used active fiscal policy to be stabilizing.

Rules Versus Discretion

Finally, in this chapter, we want to discuss the issue of "rules versus discretion." The issue is whether the monetary authority and also the fiscal authority should conduct policy in accordance with a preannounced rule that describes precisely how their policy variables will be determined in all future situations, or whether they should be allowed to use their discretion in determining the values of the policy variables at different times.

One example is the constant growth rate rule, say, at 4 percent, for monetary policy. The rule is that no matter what happens, the money supply will be kept growing at 4 percent. Another example would be a rule stating that the money supply growth rate will be increased by 2 percent per year for every 1 percent unemployment in excess of, say, 5 percent. Algebraically, such a rule would be expressed as

$$\frac{\Delta M}{M} = 4.0 + 2(u - 5.0) \tag{1}$$

where the growth rate of money $\Delta M/M$ is at an annual percentage rate, and u is the percentage unemployment rate.

The activist monetary rule of Equation (1) is shown in Figure 14-5. On the horizontal axis, we show the unemployment rate, and on the vertical axis, the growth rate of the money stock. At 5 percent unemployment, monetary growth is 4 percent. If unemployment rises above 5 percent, monetary growth is *automatically* increased. Thus, with 7 percent unemployment, monetary growth would be 8 percent. Conversely, if unemployment dropped below 5 percent, monetary growth would be lowered below 4 percent. The rule therefore gears the amount of monetary stimulus to an indicator of the business cycle. By linking monetary growth to the unemployment rate, an activist, anticyclical monetary policy is achieved, but this is done without any discretion.

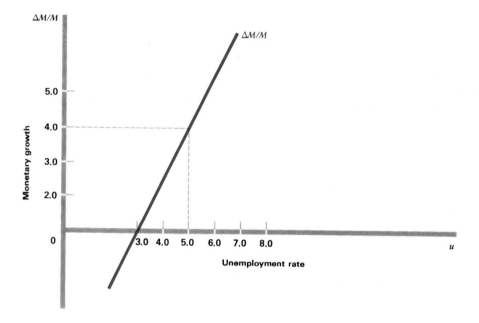

Figure 14-5 *An Activist Monetary Rule*

The figure describes an activist monetary rule. The growth rate of money is high when the unemployment rate is high and is low when unemployment is low. That way monetary policy is expansionary at times of recession and contractionary in a boom.

The issue of rules versus discretion has been clouded by the fact that most proponents of rules have been nonactivists, whose preferred monetary rule is a constant growth rate rule. Consequently, the argument has tended to centre on whether activist policy is desirable or not. The fundamental point to recognize is that we can design *activist rules*. We can design rules that have countercyclical features without at the same time leaving any discretion in their actions to policy makers. The point is made by Equation (1), which is an activist rule because it expands money when unemployment is high and reduces it when unemployment is low. It leaves no room for policy discretion and in this respect is a rule.

Given that the economy and our knowledge of it are both changing over time, there is no case for stating permanent policy rules that would tie the hands of the monetary and fiscal authorities permanently. The practical issue in rules versus discretion then becomes whether the policy makers should announce in advance what policies they will be following for the foreseeable future. This would seem to be a desirable development in that it would aid private individuals in forecasting the future course of the economy.

Box 14-1 Dynamic Inconsistency and Rules Versus Discretion

In the last decade, economists have developed an intriguing argument in favour of rules rather than discretion. The argument is that policy makers who have discretion will in the end not act consistently, even though it would be better for the economy in the long run if they were consistent.[a]

How can that be? Here is a noneconomic example. By threatening to punish their children, parents can generally make the children behave better. So long as the children behave well, all is well, but when a child misbehaves, the parent has a problem, since punishing the child is unpleasant for both parent and child. One solution is not to punish but to threaten to punish next time. However, if there was no punishment this time, there is unlikely to be punishment next time either, and the threat loses its beneficial effect. The dynamically consistent parent should use punishment each time the child misbehaves, thereby producing better behaviour in the long run despite its short-run cost.

What does this have to do with economics? Suppose the inflation rate has risen because of a supply shock. The central bank is considering whether to accommodate it by expanding the money supply or not. If it accommodates, prices will rise more now, but there will be less unemployment, so that seems like a good thing to do. This is the equivalent of not punishing the misbehaving child. However, those in favour of rules who worry about dynamic consistency warn that if the central bank accommodates every inflationary pressure because it fears unemployment, people will soon come to expect it to do that, and they will build an allowance for expected inflation into the wages they set. The central bank will lose whatever reputation it had as an inflation fighter, and the economy will develop an inflationary bias with the inflation rate creeping up over time.

Much better, says the dynamic consistency approach, that the central bank should have a rule that prevents it from making responses that are right from the short-run viewpoint but wrong from the long-run perspective. Those who nonetheless favour discretion for the central bank emphasize the importance of preserving flexibility for monetary policy. To the dynamic inconsistency argument, they counter that as long as the central bank is aware that having a good reputation helps it keep the inflation rate low, it will take any loss of reputation into account when it decides how to respond to particular shocks, and thus will not be dynamically inconsistent.

[a]The basic reference is Finn Kydland and Edward Prescott, "Rules Rather than Discretion: The Inconsistency of Optimal Plans," *Journal of Political Economy*, June 1977. This is very difficult reading. See also V.V. Chari, "Time Consistency and Optimal Policy Design," Federal Reserve Bank of Minneapolis *Quarterly Review*, Fall 1988.

14-7 Targets and Instruments of Monetary Policy

We conclude this chapter with a discussion of some operational problems in the implementation of monetary policy that arise from the existence of uncertainty. We begin with the issue of money supply targets.

Interest Rate Versus Money Supply Targets

Prior to the early 1970s, the Bank of Canada's monetary policy was formulated primarily in terms of target levels of interest rates and other measures of the cost and availability of credit. By 1973, the Bank had become dissatisfied with this approach and was beginning to move toward greater emphasis on control of the money supply. In his Annual Report for 1973 (page 7), Governor Gerald Bouey commented as follows:

> *Looking back on the experience of Canada and other countries over a longer period, . . . there have been more substantial and persisting departures from reasonable steady monetary growth than would appear in retrospect to have been desirable. Since the lags associated with monetary policy are rather long, the full effects of such departures do not become apparent until well after the event. . . . In the light of these considerations, I have a certain amount of sympathy with the case that is often made for more stable monetary growth over time. . . . The Bank of Canada certainly has no intention of basing its operations on any mechanistic formula, but . . . it has been giving considerable weight to underlying rates of monetary growth.*

Although the governor had rejected the idea of a "mechanistic formula" for monetary growth in 1973, two years later the Bank of Canada announced that it would henceforth follow the practice of establishing target ranges for the rate of growth of the narrowly defined money supply ($M1$). The initial target was established in late 1975 at 10 to 15 percent a year. As can be seen in Table 14-2, the target was subsequently reduced in stages to the range of 4 to 8 percent which was announced in February 1981. The practice of announcing target ranges was discontinued in 1982.[11]

Table 14-2 *Bank of Canada Target Growth Rates of M1, 1975–1981*

Base Period	Target Band	Base Period	Target Band
2nd Qtr. 1975	10–15%	June 1978	6–10%
Feb.–Apr. 1976	8–12	2nd Qtr. 1979	5–9
June 1977	7–11	Aug.–Oct. 1980	4–8

---

[11] The targets were abandoned because of instability in the demand for money associated with the financial innovations discussed in Chapter 12. See Bank of Canada *Annual Report* for 1982, pp. 25–29.

Targets in the IS-LM Framework

Let us assume that the Bank of Canada's policy objective is to maintain a particular level of output. The question is whether it can do that more accurately by targeting the money stock or by fixing interest rates.[12] We should think of the analysis as applying to a time horizon of three to six months over which the Bank of Canada could achieve money supply targets with a small margin of error.

Figure 14-6a starts with the *IS* and *LM* curves. Recall that the *LM* curve shows combinations of the interest rate and output at which the money market is in equilibrium. The *LM* curve labelled *LM(M)* is the *LM* curve that exists when the Bank of Canada fixes the money stock. The *LM* curve labelled *LM(i)* describes money market equilibrium when the Bank fixes the interest rate. It is horizontal at the chosen level of the interest rate $i°$.

The problem for policy is that the *IS* and *LM* curves shift as a result of disturbances that cannot be predicted. When they shift, output ends up at a level different from the target level. In Figure 14-6a we show two alternative positions for the *IS* curve, IS_1 and IS_2. We assume that the Bank does not know in advance which *IS* curve will obtain; the position depends, for instance, on investment demand, which is difficult to predict. The Bank's aim is to have income come out as close as possible to the level $Y°$.

In Figure 14-6a we see that the level of output stays closer to $Y°$ if the *LM* curve is *LM(M)*. In that case the level of output will be Y_1 if the *IS* curve is IS_1 and Y_2 if the *IS* curve is IS_2. If policy had kept the interest rate constant, we would in each case have a level of income that is further from $Y°$: Y_1' instead of Y_1, and Y_2' instead of Y_2.

Thus we have our first conclusion: If output deviates from its equilibrium level mainly because the *IS* curve shifts about, then output is stabilized by keeping the money stock constant. The central bank should, in this case, have monetary targets.

We can see from Figure 14-6a why it is more stabilizing to keep *M* than *i* constant. When the *IS* curve shifts to the right and the *LM(M)* curve applies, the interest rate rises, thereby reducing investment demand and moderating the effect of the shift. On the other hand, if the *LM(i)* curve applies, there is no resistance from monetary policy to the effects of the *IS* shift. Monetary policy is thus automatically stabilizing in Figure 14-6a when the *IS* curve shifts, and the money stock is held constant.

In Figure 14-6b we assume that the *IS* curve is stable. Now the uncertainty about the effects of monetary policy results from shifts in the *LM* curve. Assuming that the Bank of Canada can fix the money stock, the *LM* curve shifts because the money demand function shifts. The Bank does not know when it sets the money stock what the interest rate will be. The *LM* curve could end up being either LM_1 or LM_2. Alternatively the Bank could simply fix the interest rate at level $i°$. That would ensure that the level of output is $Y°$.

If the Bank were to fix the money stock, output could be either Y_1 or Y_2. If it fixes the interest rate, output will be $Y°$. Thus we have our second conclusion: If output deviates from its equilibrium level mainly because the demand-for-money function

---

[12] The analysis presented here is based on William Poole, "Optimal Choice of Monetary Policy Instruments in a Simple Stochastic Macro Model," *Quarterly Journal of Economics*, May 1970.

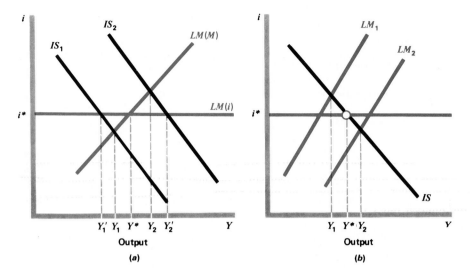

Figure 14-6 *Money and Interest Rate Targets*

In panel (*a*), the *IS* curve shifts. If the Bank of Canada targets the money stock, the *LM* curve is shown by *LM*(*M*). *LM*(*i*) is the *LM* curve when the interest rate is held constant. The aim of policy is to hit output level Y°. If the *LM* curve is *LM*(*M*), the output levels will be either Y_1 or Y_2, depending on where the *IS* curve turns out to be. In the case of an interest rate target, the corresponding levels of output are Y_1' and Y_2', both further from the desired level of output Y°. Thus monetary targeting leads to more stable output behaviour. In panel (*b*) it is the *LM* curve that is shifting, because of shifts in the demand for money. With *LM* shifting and the *IS* curve stable, output will be at the target level Y° if the interest rate is held constant at i°, but will be at either Y_1 or Y_2 if the money stock is held constant. Therefore the Bank should target the interest rate if the demand-for-money function is unstable.

shifts about, then the central bank should operate monetary policy by fixing the interest rate. That way it automatically neutralizes the effects of the shifts in money demand. In this case the central bank should have interest rate targets.

Implications for Bank of Canada Policy

The above analysis indicates that the shift to money supply targeting by the Bank of Canada was appropriate if the main source of disturbances is thought to be the goods market rather than the money market.[13] However, the argument depends on the exis-

---

[13] Another argument for money targeting arises from the distinction between real and nominal interest rates. The nominal interest rate can rise because inflation is expected. If the Bank fights this increase in the nominal rate by increasing the money stock, it is only feeding the inflation. We examine this argument in more detail in Chapter 18.

tence of a stable demand for money. During the late 1970s and early 1980s, the financial innovations discussed in Chapter 12 caused a breakdown in the stability of this relationship and ultimately led to the abandonment of monetary targeting by the Bank of Canada.

The Instrument Problem

The above analysis focuses on a three- to six-month time horizon over which the Bank of Canada can achieve money supply targets. As we argued in Chapter 13, the Bank cannot control the money supply in the short run. The variables over which the Bank of Canada does have direct control are called policy instruments, and the choice of the appropriate variable to control in the face of unpredictable disturbances is known as the instrument problem.

The short-run operating problem can be described as follows. Having chosen its money supply target, should the Bank of Canada implement its policy by setting the level of the interest rate or the monetary base? The analysis of Figure 14-6 can be applied in this context by assuming that the upward-sloping *LM* curve in Figure 14-6*a* is drawn for a given level of the monetary base, rather than the money supply. The shifts in the *LM* curve shown in Figure 14-6*b* then reflect shifts in the money multiplier as well as the demand for money.

The conclusions from the analysis become:

1.   If the demand for money and the money multiplier are stable, then the Bank of Canada should use the base as the instrument and allow interest rates to fluctuate in response to shifts in the *IS* curve.

2.   If the *IS* curve is stable, then the Bank should use the interest rate as the instrument and allow the base to fluctuate in response to shifts in the demand for money and the money multiplier.

The Bank of Canada's Operating Procedure

During the period 1975 to 1982 when the Bank of Canada was setting targets for the money supply, its operating procedure was as follows. Once the money target was set, a projection was made for income and the price level, and a money demand function was used to infer the appropriate setting for the interest rate.[14] Thus the Bank used the interest rate as the instrument.[15]

---

[14]   In algebraic terms the value for the interest rate was obtained using an *LM* equation of the form shown in Equation 11 of Chapter 4.

[15]   For a further discussion of the issues discussed in this section, see G.R. Sparks, "The Theory and Practice of Monetary Policy in Canada: 1945–83," and J.M. Dufour and D. Racette, "Monetary Controls in Canada," in *Fiscal and Monetary Policy*, Research Studies of the Royal Commission on the Economic Union and Development Prospects for Canada, Vol. 21, edited by J. Sargent (Toronto: University of Toronto Press, 1986).

The rationale for this procedure is that, in the short run, the goods market is relatively predictable and the money demand function is relatively stable, but the money supply is not. As we argued in Chapter 13, the money multiplier is likely to be unstable in the short run.

14-8 Summary

1. Despite the apparent simplicity of policies needed to maintain continuous full employment, the historical record of the behaviour of unemployment, shown in Figure 14-1, implies that successful stabilization policy is difficult to carry out.

2. Many of the complications in the execution of stabilization policy are a result of the tradeoff between inflation and unemployment in the short run. This important topic is deferred to Chapter 16. The present chapter concentrates on other sources of difficulty of stabilization policy.

3. The potential need for stabilizing policy action arises from economic disturbances. Some of these disturbances, such as changes in money demand, consumption spending, or investment demand, arise from within the private sector. Others, such as wars, may arise for noneconomic reasons.

4. Inappropriate economic policy may also tend to move the economy away from full employment. Policy may be inappropriate because policy makers make mistakes or because policy is manipulated for political reasons, leading to the political business cycle.

5. Policy makers work with econometric models in predicting the effects of their policy actions. Econometric models are typically statistical descriptions of the types of model we have worked with in earlier chapters and also include an aggregate supply sector. Existing econometric models vary considerably in structure and thus imply widely varying numerical values for policy multipliers.

6. The first difficulty of carrying out successful stabilization policy is that policy works with lags. The inside lag — divided into recognition, decision, and action lags — is the period between when an action becomes necessary and when it is taken. The outside lag is the period between when a policy action is taken and when it affects the economy. The outside lag is generally a distributed lag: The effects of a policy action build up over the course of time.

7. The behaviour of expectations is a further source of difficulty for policy making. First, it is difficult to know exactly what determines expectations and to capture those factors in a simple formula. Second, policy actions themselves are likely to affect expectations.

8. More generally, there is always uncertainty about the effects of a given policy action on the economy. Economists are not agreed on the "correct" model of

the economy, and evidence is not likely to be at hand soon to decisively settle disagreements over some behavioural functions — such as the consumption function. Even if we did know the form of the behavioural functions, the statistical evidence would be insufficient to pinpoint the values of the relevant parameters.

9. There are clearly occasions on which active monetary and fiscal policy actions should be taken to stabilize the economy. These are situations in which the economy has been affected by major disturbances.

10. Fine tuning — continuous attempts to stabilize the economy in the face of small disturbances — is more controversial. If fine tuning is undertaken, it calls for small policy responses in an attempt to moderate the economy's fluctuations, rather than to remove them entirely. A very active policy in response to a small disturbance is likely to destabilize the economy.

11. The real issue in rules versus discretion is whether policy actions should be announced as far in advance as possible. Such announcements are desirable in that they aid private individuals in forecasting the future behaviour of the economy.

12. During the period 1975 to 1981, the Bank of Canada operated monetary policy using target rates of growth of the money supply. This is an appropriate strategy if the money market is stable and the goods market is subject to substantial disturbances.

Key Terms

Economic disturbances	Multiplier uncertainty
Political business cycle	Activist policy
Econometric models	Policy rule
Inside lag	Fine tuning
Recognition lag	Rules versus discretion
Decision lag	Dynamic consistency
Action lag	Targets and instruments of
Outside lag	monetary policy

Problems

1. Suppose the GDP is $4 billion below its potential level. It is expected that next period GDP will be $2 billion below potential, and two periods from now it will be back at its potential level. You are told that the multiplier for government spending is 2, and that the effects of the increased government spending are immediate. What policy actions can be taken to put GDP back on target each period?

2. The basic facts about the path of GDP are as above, but there is now a one-period outside lag for government spending. Decisions to spend today are translated into actual spending only tomorrow. The multiplier for government spending is still 2 in the period that the spending takes place.
   (a) What is the best that can be done to keep GDP as close to target as possible each period?
   (b) Compare the path of GDP in this question with the path in Problem 1, after policy actions have been taken.

3. Life has become more complicated. Government spending works with a distributed lag. Now when $1 billion is spent today, GDP increases by $1 billion this period and 1.5 billion next period.
   (a) What happens to the path of GDP if government spending rises enough this period to put GDP back to its potential level this period?
   (b) Suppose fiscal policy actions are taken to put GDP at its potential level this period. What fiscal policy will be needed to put GDP on target next period?
   (c) Explain why the government has to be so active in keeping GDP on target in this case.

4. Suppose that you knew that the multiplier for government spending was between 1 and 2.5, but that its effects were all over in the period that spending was increased. How would you run fiscal policy if GDP would, without policy, behave as in Problem 1?

5. Explain why monetary policy works with a distributed lag, as in Figure 14-4.

6. Evaluate the argument that monetary policy should be determined by a rule rather than discretion. How about fiscal policy?

7. Evaluate the arguments for a constant growth rate rule for money.

8. (a) What is the unemployment rate at the time you are reading this?
   (b) Should either fiscal or monetary policy be changed to enable the economy to return more rapidly to full employment?

9. Use Figure 14-6 to analyze the short-run problem of instrument choice. What conclusions can you draw for the validity of the Bank of Canada's strategy of using the interest rate as the instrument?

CHAPTER 15 *Fiscal Policy and Public Finance*

This chapter is intended to serve two purposes. The first is to review the experience of the 1930s and the postwar period. The great depression is worth studying for purely historical interest but of equal importance is the fact that the 1930s and the war that followed moulded many of the institutions and views of the modern economy. The role of government expanded markedly, and it was the experience of the 1930s that led to the view, now taken for granted in practice, that the government has primary responsibility for satisfactory economic performance.

The second purpose of the chapter is to discuss a number of questions connected with the budget, government spending, and taxes. These issues are taken up in the last two sections. We begin by describing the financing of the federal government budget deficit, that is, how the government pays for the excess of its spending over its income from taxes. The issue of the burden of the debt is taken up at the conclusion of the chapter.

15-1 The Great Depression

In this section we describe the experience of the 1930s and review the controversy over the causes of the depression. Data describing the performance of the Canadian economy are shown in Figure 15-1 and Table 15-1. As can be seen from the figure, between 1929 and 1933, real income fell by 30 percent and the price level fell by 20 percent. Investment collapsed; indeed, *net* investment was negative from 1932 to 1936.

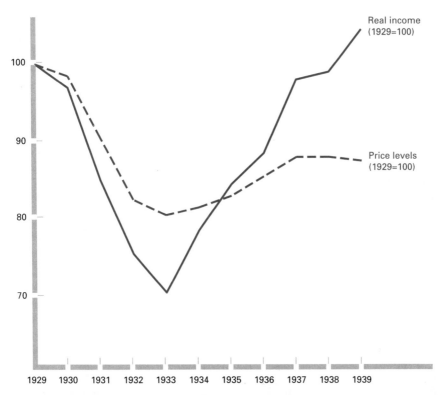

Figure 15-1 *Output and Prices in the Great Depression*

(*Source:* Adapted from Statistics Canada, 11-505)

The unemployment rate rose to nearly 20 percent in 1933 and remained above 11 percent through the 1930s, with the exception of 1937 when it dipped close to 9 percent. By 1933 the stock market had fallen almost to one-third of its 1929 value.

Events in Canada closely mirrored those in the United States, and the economic collapse in the U.S. was a major cause of the decline in Canada. The sharp fall in our exports, shown in Table 15-1, resulted from the fall in income in the U.S. and other countries, and the psychological impact was an important factor in the collapse of investment. In view of this it is necessary to examine events in the U.S. in order to obtain clues as to the causes of the depression.

American Experience in the 1930s

The depression and the stock market crash of October 1929 are popularly thought of as almost the same thing. In fact, the U.S. economy started turning down before the

Table 15-1   *The Great Depression in Canada*

	GNP	Gov't Exp.	Exports	GNE Deflator	Gross Investment	Budget Surplus	Unem- ployment Rate	Stock Market Index
	(billions of 1961 dollars)			(1961 = 100)	(% of GNP)		(%)	(1961 = 100)
1929	12.24	1.70	3.10	50.2	22.2	0.2		49.0
1930	11.71	1.93	2.70	48.8	18.9	−3.9		35.0
1931	10.23	1.94	2.41	45.9	15.5	−6.6	11.6	21.9
1932	9.17	1.79	2.24	41.6	8.8	−7.3	17.6	14.2
1933	8.56	1.47	2.26	40.8	6.8	−5.0	19.3	17.6
1934	9.59	1.58	2.55	41.4	7.7	−4.7	14.5	22.1
1935	10.34	1.68	2.81	41.6	8.6	−4.0	14.2	23.6
1936	10.80	1.67	3.38	42.9	10.0	−0.7	12.8	30.7
1937	11.89	1.79	3.46	44.1	11.8	−0.6	9.1	32.6
1938	11.98	1.93	3.12	44.0	11.3	−2.8	11.4	26.8
1939	12.87	2.02	3.44	43.7	10.3	−0.8	11.4	25.8

Source: Statistics Canada, 11-505.

stock market crash. The peak of the business cycle is estimated to have been in August 1929, and the stock market itself peaked in September 1929. Using September 1929 as the base period, Standard & Poor's composite stock price index fell from 100 in September to 66 in November. It rose again through March 1930, but then the collapse continued until the index fell to 15 in June 1932.

By early 1931, the U.S. economy was suffering from a very severe depression, but not one that was out of the range of the experience of the previous century.[1] It was in the period from early 1931 until Franklin Roosevelt became President in March 1933 that the depression became "great."

American Economic Policy

What was economic policy during this period? The money stock fell from 1929 to 1930, and then fell rapidly in 1931 and 1932 and continued falling through April 1933. At the same time, the composition of the money stock changed. In March 1931 the currency–demand deposit ratio was 18.5 percent; two years later, it was 40.7 percent.

---

[1]   Milton Friedman and Anna J. Schwartz, in *A Monetary History of the United States 1867–1960* (Princeton, N.J.: Princeton University Press, 1963), give a very detailed account of the great depression, comparing it with other recessions and emphasizing the role of the Fed. For a more general economic history of the period see Robert A. Gordon, *Economic Instability: The American Record* (New York: Harper & Row, 1974), Chapter 3.

The fall in the money stock was the result of large-scale bank failures. Banks failed because they did not have the reserves with which to meet customers' cash withdrawals, and in failing they destroyed deposits and hence reduced the money stock. The failures went even further in reducing the money stock, because they led to a loss of confidence on the part of depositors and hence to an even higher desired currency–deposit ratio. Furthermore, banks that had not yet failed adjusted to the possibility of a run by holding increased reserves relative to deposits. The rise in the currency–deposit ratio and the reserve–deposit ratio reduced the money multiplier and hence sharply contracted the money stock.

The American central bank, commonly referred to as the Fed (Federal Reserve System), took very few steps to offset the fall in the money supply; for a few months in 1932 it did undertake a program of open market purchases, but otherwise seemed to acquiesce in bank closings and certainly failed to understand that the central bank should act vigorously in a crisis to prevent the collapse of the financial system.[2]

Canadian experience was similar but for quite different reasons. There was little scope for monetary policy in Canada during the early years of the depression, as there was no central bank. (The Bank of Canada began operations in 1935.) As in the U.S., the money supply fell sharply after the 1929 crash, but there were no bank failures. However, the monetary base fell as a result of the institutional arrangements at the time, under which the volume of bank reserves was determined primarily at the initiative of the chartered banks through a form of borrowing.[3] With the onset of the depression, the demand for loans by credit-worthy borrowers collapsed, and the chartered banks responded by contracting their operations.

Fiscal policy in the U.S. was also not very vigorous. The natural impulse of politicians then was to balance the budget in times of trouble, and much rhetoric was devoted to that proposition. The presidential candidates in 1932 campaigned on balanced budget platforms. In fact, the federal government ran enormous deficits, particularly for that time, averaging 2.6 percent of GNP from 1931 to 1933, and even more later. The belief in budget balancing was more than rhetoric, however, for state and local governments raised taxes to match their expenditures, as did the federal government, particularly in 1932 and 1933. President Roosevelt tried seriously to balance the budget — he was no Keynesian. The full-employment surplus shows fiscal policy (combined state, local, and federal) as most expansionary in 1931, and moving to a more contractionary level from 1932 to 1934. In fact, the full-employment surplus was positive in 1933 and 1934, despite the actual deficits. Of course, the full-employment surplus concept had not been invented in the 1930s.

Economic activity recovered in the period from 1933 to 1937, with fiscal policy becoming more expansionary and the money stock growing rapidly. The growth of the money stock was based on an inflow of gold from Europe which provided an increase in the monetary base. This period also saw a program of legislative action to aid recovery known as the *New Deal*.

---

[2] Friedman and Schwartz speculate on the reasons for the Fed's inaction; the whodunit or "who didn't do it" on pp. 407 to 419 of their book (cited in footnote 1) is fascinating.

[3] See T.J. Courchene, "An Analysis of the Canadian Money Supply: 1925–1934," *Journal of Political Economy*, May/June 1969.

International Aspects

Another important aspect of the depression deserves mention: It was virtually worldwide. To some extent, this was the result of the collapse of the international financial system.[4] It resulted too from the mutual adoption of high tariff policies by many countries, keeping out foreign goods to protect domestic producers. Of course, if each country keeps out foreign goods, the volume of world trade declines, providing a contractionary influence on the world economy.

The experience of the 1930s varied internationally. Sweden suffered its depression in the 1920s and benefited from expansionary policies in the 1930s. Britain's economy too suffered more in the 1920s than in the 1930s. Germany grew rapidly after Hitler came to power and expanded government spending. China escaped the recession until after 1931, essentially because it had a floating exchange rate. As always, there is much to be learned from the exceptions.

15-2   The Great Depression: The Issues and Ideas

What caused the great depression, could it have been avoided, and could it happen again? The question of what caused the depression seems purely academic, but it is much more than that. The depression was the greatest economic crisis the Western world had experienced.

The classical economics of the time had no well-developed theory that would explain persistent unemployment, nor any policy prescriptions to solve the problem. Many economists of the time did, in fact, recommend government spending as a way of reducing unemployment, but they had no macroeconomic theory by which to justify their recommendations.

Keynes wrote his greatest work, *The General Theory of Employment, Interest and Money*, in the 1930s, after Britain had suffered during the 1920s from a decade of double-digit unemployment and while the United States was in the depths of its depression. He was fully aware of the seriousness of the issues. As Don Patinkin of the Hebrew University put it:

> [T]he period was one of fear and darkness as the Western world struggled with the greatest depression that it had known. . . . [T]here was a definite feeling that by attempting to achieve a scientific understanding of the phenomenon of mass unemployment, one was not only making an intellectual contribution, but was also dealing with a critical problem that endangered the very existence of Western civilization.[5]

---

[4] This aspect of the depression is emphasized by Charles Kindleberger, *The World in Depression, 1929–1939* (Berkeley: University of California Press, 1973); and Gottfried Haberler, *The World Economy, Money and the Great Depression* (Washington, D.C.: American Enterprise Institute, 1976).

[5] In "The Process of Writing *The General Theory*: A Critical Survey," in Don Patinkin and J. Clark Leith, eds., *Keynes, Cambridge and the General Theory* (Toronto: University of Toronto Press, 1978), p. 3. For a short biography of Keynes, see D.E. Moggridge, *John Maynard Keynes* (New York: Penguin, 1976).

Keynesian theory explained what had happened, what could have been done to prevent the depression, and what could be done to prevent future depressions. The explanation soon became accepted by most macroeconomists, in the process described as the Keynesian revolution.

The Keynesian Explanation

The essence of the Keynesian explanation of the great depression is based on the simple aggregate demand model developed in Chapter 3. Growth in the 1920s, in this view, was based on the mass production of the automobile and radio and was fuelled by a housing boom. The collapse of growth in the 1930s resulted from the drying up of investment opportunities and a downward shift in investment demand. Some researchers also believe there was a downward shift in the consumption function in 1930.[6] Poor fiscal policy, as reflected in the perverse behaviour of the full-employment surplus from 1931 to 1933, shares the blame, particularly for making the depression worse.

What does this view have to say about the monetary collapse? The Fed argued in the 1930s that there was little it could have done to prevent the depression, because interest rates were already as low as they could possibly go. A variety of sayings of the type "You can lead a horse to water but you can't make it drink" were used to explain that further reductions in interest rates would have had no effect if there was no demand for investment. Investment demand was thought to be very unresponsive to the rate of interest — implying a very steep *IS* curve. At the same time, the *LM* curve was believed to be quite flat, though not necessarily reaching the extreme of a liquidity trap. In this situation, as we saw in Chapter 4, monetary expansion would be relatively ineffective in stimulating demand and output.

It was also widely believed that the experience of the depression showed that the private economy was inherently unstable in that it could self-depress with no difficulty if left alone. The experience of the 1930s, implicitly or explicitly, was the basis for the belief that an active stabilization policy was needed to maintain good economic performance.

The Keynesian model not only offered an explanation of what had happened, but also suggested policy measures that could have been taken to prevent the depression, and that could be used to prevent future depressions. Vigorous use of countercyclical fiscal policy was the preferred method for reducing cyclical fluctuations. If a recession ever showed signs of deteriorating into a depression, the cure would be to cut taxes and increase government spending. Those policies would, too, have prevented the depression from being as deep as it was.

There is nothing in the *IS-LM* model developed in Chapter 4 that suggests fiscal policy is more useful than monetary policy for stabilization of the economy. Nonetheless, it is true that until the 1950s Keynesians tended to give more emphasis to fiscal than to monetary policy.

---

[6] Peter Temin, *Did Monetary Forces Cause the Great Depression?* (New York: Norton, 1976).

The Monetarist Challenge

The Keynesian emphasis on fiscal policy, and its downplaying of the role of money, was increasingly challenged by Milton Friedman and his co-workers[7] during the 1950s. During this period Friedman was developing much of the analysis and evidence that provided the basis for monetarism, which we describe in detail in Chapter 19. The main thrust was a heavy emphasis on the role of monetary policy in determining the behaviour of both output and prices.

If monetary policy was to be given an important role, though, it was necessary to dispose of the view that monetary policy had been tried in the great depression and had failed. In other words, the view that "You can lead a horse to water, etc." had to be challenged.

The view that monetary policy in the 1930s had been impotent was attacked in 1963 by Friedman and Schwartz in their *Monetary History*. They argued that the depression, far from showing that money does not matter, "is in fact a tragic testimonial to the importance of monetary factors."[8] They argued, with skill and style, that the failure of the Fed to prevent bank failures and the decline of the money stock from the end of 1930 to 1933 was largely responsible for the recession being as serious as it was. This monetary view, in turn, came close to being accepted as the orthodox explanation of the depression.[9]

Synthesis

Both the Keynesian and the monetarist explanations of the great depression fit the facts, and both provide answers to the question of why it happened, and how to prevent it from happening again. Inept fiscal and monetary policies both made the great depression severe. If there had been prompt, strong, expansive monetary and fiscal policy, the economy would have suffered a recession but not the trauma it did.

On the question of whether it could happen again, there is agreement that it could not, except, of course, in the event of truly perverse policies. These are less likely now than they were then. For one thing, we have history to help us avoid its repetition. Taxes would not again be raised in the middle of a depression, nor would attempts be made to balance the budget. The Bank of Canada would seek actively to keep the money supply from falling. In addition, the government now has a much larger role in the economy than it did then. The higher level of government spending, which is relatively slow to change, and automatic stabilizers, including income tax,[10] unemploy-

---

[7] See, in particular, Milton Friedman, ed., *Studies in the Quantity Theory of Money* (Chicago: University of Chicago Press, 1956).

[8] Friedman and Schwartz, *op. cit.*, p. 300.

[9] Ben Bernanke, in "Nonmonetary Effects of the Financial Crisis in the Propagation of the Great Depression," *American Economic Review*, June 1983, takes issue with the monetary view, arguing instead that the destruction of the financial system made it difficult for borrowers to obtain funds needed for investment.

[10] Recall from Chapter 3 that a proportional income tax reduces the multiplier.

ment insurance, and social insurance, give the economy more stability than it had then.[11]

There is no inherent conflict between the Keynesian and monetarist explanations of the great depression. The *IS-LM* model, augmented by the supply-side analysis of wage and price adjustment, discussed in Chapter 8, easily combines both explanations. Why, then, has there been controversy over the cause of the great depression? The reason is that the 1930s are seen as the period that set the stage for massive government intervention in the economy. Those opposed to an active role for government have to explain away the debacle of the economy in the 1930s. If the depression occurred because of, and not despite, the government, the case for an active government role in economic stabilization is weakened. Further, the 1930s are a period in which the economy behaved in such an extreme way that competing theories have to be subjected to the test of whether they can explain that period. Those are the main reasons the dispute over the causes of the great depression continues more than 50 years after it began.

15-3 Fiscal Policy in the Postwar Period

The experience of the great depression and World War II resulted in a fundamental change in the role of government expenditures and taxes as instruments of government policy. The 1945 White Paper on Employment and Income established the principle that the federal government had a responsibility to maintain high and stable levels of employment and income. Since then, consideration of the desired degree of fiscal stimulus or restraint has become an important element in the budgets presented to Parliament.

Both the achievements and failures of economic policy in the postwar period can be seen in Figure 15-2. In comparison with earlier eras, the 1950s and 1960s were years of prosperity and steady growth. The first prolonged slump occurred during the years 1958 to 1961 when the unemployment rate reached a peak of 7.1 percent. By 1965, the economy was operating at or near potential, but in retrospect it appears that policy makers misjudged the situation. As can be seen in Figure 15-3, rising income had moved government budgets into a surplus position, but some of the restraining effects of the built-in stabilizers were offset by tax cuts introduced in the federal budget of April 1965. As a result, the cyclically adjusted federal budget moved to a deficit position. Tax increases and some expenditure cuts were imposed in the years 1966–1968, but fiscal restraint came too late to prevent the entrenchment of inflationary forces. The rate of inflation had crept up steadily during the 1960s and by 1969 had reached 4.6 percent.

Perspectives on economic policy in the 1960s appear to differ widely. It was a period in which faith in the efficacy of activist fiscal policy reached a peak. Although the

---

[11] See Martin Baily, "Stabilization Policy and Private Economic Behavior," *Brookings Papers on Economic Activity*, 1978:1 (Washington, D.C.: Brookings Institution, 1978).

Figure 15-2 *Inflation and Unemployment, 1953–1991*

(*Source:* Adapted from Statistics Canada, 11-505, 11-210)

analytical approach consisted basically of the Keynesian tools we have outlined in previous chapters, fiscal activism became known as the "New Economics" in the United States.[12] In one view, the period was one of high employment and prosperity, thanks to the activist stance of policy. An alternative view is that overexpansionist policies in that period were responsible for the inflation that was to prove to be the economic policy problem of the 1970s. Actually, both views are correct. Policy in the early 1960s was indeed successful, and economic policy in the second half of the period was overexpansionary — or, equivalently, not sufficiently contractionary — in the face of increases in spending to a large extent related to the Vietnam war. Government spending in the U.S. rose rapidly, and rising income in the U.S. stimulated demand for Canadian exports, thereby contributing to inflationary pressure in Canada.

The decade of the 1970s began with the federal government in a surplus position, but there was a shift to an expansionary policy in view of the steep rise in unemploy-

---

[12] See the history of the New Economics in W.W. Heller, *New Dimensions of Political Economy* (New York: Norton, 1967). Walter Heller was one of the chief architects of the economic policies of the Kennedy–Johnson administration. With him, as members of the Council of Economic Advisers or staff economists, were highly distinguished economists: James Tobin, Kenneth Arrow, Robert Solow, the late Otto Eckstein, Gardner Ackley, and the late Arthur Okun.

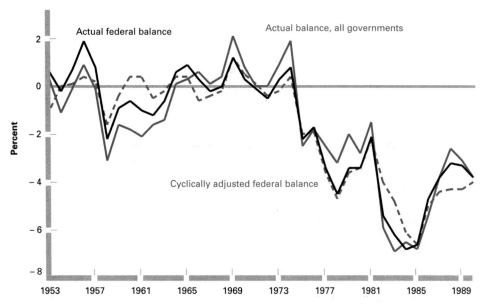

Figure 15-3 *Actual and Cyclically Adjusted Budget Balance as a Percentage of GDP*

(*Source:* Department of Finance, *Economic Review; The Fiscal Plan*, February 1986)

ment that had occurred. With an unemployment rate in excess of 6 percent during most of 1971 and 1972, the federal budget was maintained in a deficit position. In 1975 the emphasis shifted to moderating the inflationary pressures that were building up. At mid-year the unemployment rate was down around 5 percent and the consumer price index was rising at a rate in excess of 10 percent. However, toward the end of the year there was a significant worsening of the outlook. Slower growth and rising unemployment occurred in Canada, while the United States experienced a substantial *decline* in real output. In view of these conditions, an expansionary budget was brought down late in the year which provided for a reduction in personal income taxes of about $1.5 billion in 1975.

As can be seen from Figure 15-3, the federal budget moved to a substantial deficit position in 1975 and 1976. This resulted from both the automatic response of tax revenues and unemployment insurance benefits to relatively low levels of economic activity, and the effects of discretionary policy as reflected in the cyclically adjusted federal balance. Further tax cuts were introduced in 1977 and 1978 in response to rising unemployment rates, but policy decisions were complicated by the emergence of two major dilemmas.

First, although the unemployment rate rose above 8 percent in 1977 for the first time since the 1930s, the rate of inflation continued at an unacceptably high level. By 1981, the consumer price index was rising at a 12 percent rate and more than 7 percent of the labour force was still unemployed. In the third quarter of 1981, Canada plunged into the worst recession of the postwar period, and the inflation rate finally eased as the unemployment rate reached 12 percent at the trough. For the rest of the 1980s, the unemployment rate drifted down. The inflation rate also fell, but at the end of the decade the unemployment rate was still above 7 percent and the inflation rate was still above 4 percent. The 1990–1991 recession brought the inflation rate down below 2 percent but again at the cost of very high unemployment.

The second dilemma that arose in the late 1970s was the rapid growth of the government deficit. This growth was accelerated by the 1981–1982 recession, but, as can be seen in Figure 15-3, much of it was a cyclically adjusted or *structural deficit* arising from an imbalance between tax rates and expenditure programs. By 1985, the structural deficit of the federal government had risen to 6.6 percent of GDP, as compared with an average of less than 0.1 percent over the period 1953 to 1974. Policies to restrain expenditures and increase tax revenues resulted in a decline in the structural deficit to 4 percent of GDP in 1990. The introduction of the Goods and Services Tax (GST) at the beginning of 1991 provided a further boost to revenues, but the government faced a difficult conflict of policy objectives when the 1990–1991 recession pushed the unemployment rate back up above 10 percent and subtantially increased the deficit. The issue of large deficits and a rising national debt are taken up in Section 15-4 below. We conclude this section with a look at government revenue and expenditure.[13]

Government Revenue and Expenditure

Table 15-2 shows the pattern of federal government revenues and expenditures over the period 1970 to 1990. Revenues grew faster than GDP from 1970 to 1975, but grew more slowly in the second half of the 1970s as a result of a slowing down of income growth and the introduction of various tax reductions. As estimated by the Department of Finance, the cumulative effect of the tax changes made in the budgets over the period 1972 to 1981 was a reduction of revenue in the 1982–1983 fiscal year of nearly $25 billion.[14] During the 1980s, there was a large increase in personal income taxes, and revenue growth again exceeded GDP growth.

On the expenditure side, the most rapid growth has been in interest on the public debt and transfer payments. Between 1980 and 1985, total expenditure more than doubled, and the size of the federal deficit tripled. A substantial slowdown in the growth of expenditures was achieved after 1985, and the deficit declined.

---

[13] For a more detailed discussion of fiscal policy, see D. Purvis and C. Smith, "Fiscal Policy in Canada: 1963–84," in J. Sargent, ed., *Fiscal and Monetary Policy*, Research Studies of the Royal Commission on the Economic Union and Development Prospects for Canada, Vol. 21 (Toronto: University of Toronto Press, 1986).

[14] See Department of Finance, *The Federal Deficit in Perspective*, 1983, Annex D. About three-fifths of this revenue loss was attributable to indexation of the personal income tax. Indexation is discussed in Chapter 17.

Table 15-2   *Federal Government Revenue and Expenditure*

		(billions of dollars)			
Revenue	**1970**	**1975**	**1980**	**1985**	**1990**
Personal income and other direct taxes	7.4	15.2	23.5	42.7	73.2
Corporation taxes	2.6	5.8	9.4	12.7	12.6
Indirect taxes	4.0	8.0	12.3	18.9	26.5
Other revenue	1.5	2.8	5.5	8.9	14.0
Total revenue	15.5	31.8	50.7	83.2	126.3
(percent of GDP)	(17.4)	(18.5)	(16.3)	(17.4)	(18.8)
Expenditure					
Goods and services	5.0	9.4	14.9	25.6	32.6
Transfers to persons	4.0	10.6	16.5	31.7	42.2
Transfers to provinces and municipalities	3.4	7.7	12.8	21.8	26.8
Interest on the public debt	1.9	3.7	9.9	24.6	41.2
Other transfers	1.0	4.2	7.2	11.0	9.0
Total expenditure	15.3	35.6	61.3	114.7	151.8
(percent of GDP)	(17.2)	(20.8)	(19.8)	(24.0)	(22.6)
Surplus or Deficit (−)	0.2	−3.8	−10.6	−31.5	−25.5

Source: Department of Finance, *Quarterly Economic Review*, Annual Reference Tables.

Provincial and Municipal Governments

Table 15-3 shows the budgetary position of the provincial and municipal governments. Their expenditures grew at about the same rate as federal outlays during the 1970s, but their revenues grew at a faster rate, and as a result their budget deficit showed little change over the decade.

One of the principal contributions to the growth of revenues during the 1970s was natural resource royalties. By 1980, these accounted for more than 7 percent of total revenues, as compared with less than 2 percent in 1970. Almost all of this revenue goes to Alberta, Saskatchewan, and British Columbia, and the small deficit for provincial and municipal governments in 1980 arose from the net effect of a substantial surplus in these three provinces and a substantial deficit in the remainder.

As in the case of the federal government, the low level of economic activity in the early 1980s led to a marked deterioration in the financial position of the provinces and municipalities. However, during the second half of the decade, they were able to

Table 15-3   *Provincial and Municipal Revenue and Expenditure*

			(billions of dollars)		
Revenue	**1970**	**1975**	**1980**	**1985**	**1990**
Own sources	15.1	29.7	60.3	98.5	145.6
Federal cash transfers	3.3	7.6	12.6	21.3	26.0
Total revenue	18.4	37.3	72.9	119.8	171.6
(percent of GDP)	(20.6)	(21.7)	(23.5)	(25.1)	(25.6)
Expenditures					
Goods and services	14.6	30.1	52.6	82.6	116.0
Transfers to persons	2.8	5.7	11.4	19.7	28.0
Interest on the public debt	1.4	2.8	6.9	15.6	21.9
Other transfers	0.3	1.1	2.9	6.0	7.5
Total expenditure	19.1	39.7	73.8	123.9	173.4
(percent of GDP)	(21.4)	(23.1)	(23.8)	(25.9)	(25.8)
Surplus or Deficit (−)	−0.7	−2.4	−0.9	−4.1	−1.8

Source: Department of Finance, *Quarterly Economic Review*, Annual Reference Tables.

achieve substantial deficit reduction. In 1990, the deficit of provincial and municipal governments as a percentage of GDP was well under 1 percent and less than it had been in 1970. In contrast, the federal deficit was 3.8 percent of GDP. Subsequently, the recession of 1990–1991 pushed all levels of government further into the red.

15-4   Government Deficits and the National Debt

As we indicated in the preceding section, the mounting structural deficit was a major problem in the early 1980s. Beginning with the budget of November 1984, the Minister of Finance adopted a strategy of gradual reduction of the deficit, primarily through a slowdown in the growth of expenditures. The objective was to halt the growth of the debt–income ratio by the end of the decade.

A similar problem existed in the U.S. as a result of substantial tax cuts introduced in 1981 as part of the "supply-side" program of the Reagan administration (see Box 15-1). Many economists on both sides of the border were expressing concern about the implications for the future. There was a fear that continued massive government borrowing would cause interest rates to rise and crowd out private investment. An alternative danger was that rising interest rates would induce the central banks to intervene to hold them down. This would involve increasing the money supply and creating inflationary pressure.

The emergence of unprecedented deficits raises a number of questions that we have not yet considered. We begin this section by examining the relationship between the federal government's deficit and changes in the stocks of money and government debt.

Box 15-1   The Laffer Curve

Arthur Laffer, of Pepperdine University, is among the best known of the supply-side economists. Figure 1 shows the *Laffer curve*, relating tax revenues to the tax rate. The curve shows total tax revenue first increasing as the tax rate rises and then eventually decreasing.

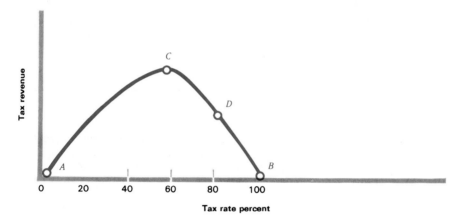

Figure 1   *The Laffer Curve*

The argument supporting the shape of the curve is as follows. Assume that we are discussing the income tax rate. When the tax rate is zero, government tax revenue is certainly zero. Hence we have point *A* on the curve. Further, suppose the tax rate were 100 percent. Then the government would be taking all the income that people earn. There would be no point in working if the government took all earnings, and so income in that case too would be zero. Then tax revenue would be zero. Accordingly, point *B* is also a point on the Laffer curve.

Between *A* and *B*, though, the government certainly takes in some revenue from taxes. Thus we expect the curve to start to rise from point *A* as the tax rate is increased from zero to some very small rate, such as 3 percent. Eventually, though, the curve has to come back down to *B*. Thus at some point it will turn around — perhaps at a tax rate of 60 percent, as shown in Figure 1. Point C is the dividing line: At tax rates below 60 percent, any increase in the tax rate *raises* total tax revenue. At tax rates above 60 percent, any increase in the tax rate *reduces* total revenue. Looking at the same relationship in the opposite direction, we find that, at any tax rate above 60 percent, a *cut* in the tax will *increase* total tax revenue.

Supply-siders were thus arguing in 1981 that the American economy was to the right of the point where the Laffer curve turns down — say, at some point such as *D*. There was no evidence to support this assertion, and it does not appear to have been right, although it is a theoretical possibility.

Supply-siders made a similar claim about the effects of cuts in taxes on saving. When tax rates on saving are cut, the after-tax rate of return rises. For instance, suppose someone is earning 9 percent before tax on savings. The tax rate is 25 percent, implying an after-tax rate of return on savings of 6.75 percent (= 0.75 × 9 percent). Now suppose the tax rate is cut to 20 percent. The after-tax rate of return rises to 7.2 (= 0.8 × 9 percent). Surely, supply-siders argued, such a person will save more.[a] Then there will be more investment, a larger capital stock, and high output. With output higher, total tax revenue could be higher despite the cut in the tax rate.

Whatever the theoretical possibilities, the 1981 tax cuts did not lead to an increase in government revenue in the U.S. This excessively optimistic element in supply-side economics was never believed by any but a small minority of economists, and is now totally dismissed.[b] The emphasis on the role of incentives, though, is a valuable component of supply-side analysis and is discussed further in Chapter 21.

---

[a] There are conflicting income and substitution effects at work in this case, too, and the theoretical effect of the cut in the tax rate on saving is uncertain.

[b] On the supply side, see Jude Wanniski, *The Way the World Works* (New York: Touchstone, 1978); Paul Craig Roberts, *The Supply-Side Revolution* (Cambridge: Harvard University Press, 1984); and Richard H. Fink, ed., *Supply-Side Economics* (Frederick, Md.: University Publications of America, 1982). For a critical view, see Robert Lekachman, *Greed Is Not Enough: Reaganomics* (New York: Pantheon, 1982).

The Mechanics of Financing the Deficit

How does the government pay for its spending? Directly, it pays for most of its spending with cheques, drawn on the Bank of Canada. Aside from the fact that the cheque is drawn on a bank in which private individuals do not have accounts, a payment made by the government looks much like a cheque payment made by anyone else. Like an individual, the federal government must have funds in the account on which it writes cheques. So the question of how the federal government finances its spending is the same as the question of how it makes sure that it has funds in the bank account (at the Bank of Canada) on which it writes its cheques.

The federal government receives the bulk of its revenues from taxes, and in years when taxes are less than expenditures it runs a budget deficit. Total government expenditures consist of expenditures on goods and services, *G*, and transfers, *TR*. Denoting taxes by *TA* and the deficit by *BD*, we know that

$$BD = (G + TR) - TA = -BS \qquad (1)$$

Equation (1) reminds us that the deficit, BD, is just the negative of the surplus, BS.

Now, how does the government make payments when its tax receipts are insufficient to cover its expenditures? The answer is that it has to borrow either from the public or from the Bank of Canada. When the government finances its deficit by borrowing from the private sector, it is engaged in debt financing. It sells securities or debt to the private sector and, in return, receives cheques from individuals and firms (including banks) in exchange for the securities it sells them. The cheques are deposited in government accounts at the chartered banks or at the Bank of Canada, and can then be spent in the same way as tax receipts.

Alternatively, the government can borrow from the Bank of Canada by selling securities to the Bank. However, there is a major difference between government borrowing from the public and from the Bank of Canada. When the Bank of Canada lends to the government by buying securities, it pays for them by giving the government a cheque on the Bank of Canada. When the government spends the deposit it has received at the Bank of Canada in exchange for its debt, it increases the monetary base and the money supply. By contrast, when the government borrows from the public and spends the proceeds, it leaves the monetary base unchanged. Since the monetary base is an important macroeconomic variable, the distinction between selling debt to the public and selling it to the Bank of Canada is essential.

When the government borrows from the central bank to finance its deficit, it is engaged in money financing. Alternatively, the sale of securities to the Bank of Canada is referred to as *monetizing the debt*, meaning that the Bank creates money to finance the debt purchase.

The Government Budget Constraint

We have seen that the government deficit can be financed in two ways: by sales of securities to the private sector and by borrowing from the Bank of Canada. Let ΔD_p and ΔD_b be the change in the value of government bonds held by the private sector and the Bank of Canada, respectively. Writing B for the monetary base, we have

$$BD = \Delta D_b + \Delta D_p = \Delta B + \Delta D_p \qquad (2)$$

Equation (2) is called the government budget constraint. It states that the budget deficit is financed by borrowing either from the Bank of Canada or from the private sector. The change in Bank of Canada holdings of debt causes a corresponding change in the monetary base (ΔB), so that we can say that the budget deficit is financed either by selling debt to the public or by increasing the monetary base. It is in this sense that the Bank of Canada "monetizes" the debt.[15]

---

[15] Note that the government budget constraint (2) also shows that for a given value of the deficit, changes in the monetary base are matched by offsetting changes in the public's holdings of government debt. A positive ΔB matched by a negative ΔD_p is nothing other than an open market purchase.

The view that the deficit is financed either by selling debt to the public or by increasing the monetary base looks at the government sector as a whole, including or "consolidating" the Bank of Canada along with the government in the government sector. When one thinks of the government sector as a whole, relative to the private sector, the transactions in which the Bank of Canada buys debt from or lends to the government are seen as mere bookkeeping entries within the government sector.

Although this consolidation is useful for some purposes, it is important to recognize that the institutional arrangements provide for a clear division of responsibility under which the Bank of Canada determines the division of the total deficit *BD*, in Equation (2), between the change in the base and the change in government debt held by the private sector. There is no *necessary* association between the size of the government deficit in Canada and increases in the base. If the Bank of Canada does not purchase securities when the government is borrowing, the monetary base is not affected by the deficit. On the other hand, there will be a more or less automatic association between Bank of Canada purchases of securities and government borrowing if the Bank of Canada commits itself to maintaining interest rates on government bonds at a constant level. As we saw in Chapter 4, an increase in the government deficit tends to increase the interest rate. If the Bank of Canada wishes to prevent this, it must intervene in the market and purchase securities.

Prior to 1975, the Bank of Canada's policy focused primarily on target interest rates, which could change from time to time, so that there was a link between deficits and Bank of Canada purchases of securities. Between 1975 and 1982 the Bank operated a policy which concentrated on the behaviour of the money supply. A commitment to bring about a given money stock breaks the link between government deficits and increases in the monetary base. If the Bank of Canada increases the base at a rate that should result in the money supply growing at the target rate, the change in the monetary base is not directly associated with the size of the government deficit.

Deficits and the National Debt

It follows from Equation (2) that when the budget is not balanced, the government changes the net amount of claims on it held by the private sector and the Bank of Canada. Those claims are the securities sold to the private sector and the Bank of Canada, and they represent claims for future interest payments. The total stock of government bonds (or claims on the government) outstanding constitutes the national, or public, debt. When the budget is in deficit, the national debt increases — the stock of claims against the government increases. When the budget is in surplus, the national debt decreases. The government takes in more than it pays out, and can use the excess to retire (or buy back) previously issued debt.

The government sells securities more or less continuously. There is, for instance, a weekly Treasury bill auction, at which prospective buyers of Treasury bills (lenders to the federal government) submit sealed bids specifying how much they are prepared to lend at different interest rates. The government sells the amount of Treasury bills it has offered at the auction to the bidders who offer the highest prices, or the lowest interest rates.[16] Longer-term debt issues are less frequent. Issues of government debt are not all made for the purpose of financing the budget deficit. Most debt issues are made to refinance parts of the national debt that are maturing. For example, the government has to pay the amount it borrowed to a Treasury bill holder when the Treasury bill matures. Six months after a 180-day Treasury bill is issued, the government has to pay the face amount of the Treasury bill to the holder. Typically, the government obtains the funds to make those payments by further borrowing. The process by which the government (with the help and advice of the Bank of Canada) finances and refinances the national debt is known as *debt management*. Only a part of debt management is concerned with financing the current budget deficit. Most of it is concerned with the consequences of past budget deficits.

Interest Payments and Deficits

It is useful to distinguish between two components of the budget deficit: The *primary* or *noninterest deficit* and interest payments on the public debt.

$$\text{Total deficit} = \text{primary deficit} + \text{interest payments} \qquad (3)$$

The primary deficit represents all government spending, except interest payments, less government revenue.

$$\text{Primary deficit} = \text{noninterest expenditure} - \text{total revenue} \qquad (4)$$

The distinction between the two components highlights the role of the public debt in the budget. Interest has to be paid when there is debt outstanding. The overall budget will be in deficit unless the interest payments on the debt are matched by a primary surplus. Table 15-4 shows the total federal deficit and the two components.

Consider first the year 1970. Interest payments were $1.9 billion, but there was an overall surplus of $0.2 billion. The primary surplus of $2.1 billion was enough to cover the interest payments and allow some reduction in the stock of debt. By contrast, in 1980 interest payments were five times as large and there was a primary deficit. In 1985, the primary deficit reached 1.4 percent of GDP, and the total deficit was 6.6 percent of GDP. As a result of the subsequent fiscal restraint, in 1990 there was a primary surplus but it was not large enough to cover the burgeoning interest payments.

Table 15-4 draws attention to a key problem in deficit financing. *If there is a primary deficit, then the total deficit will keep growing as the debt grows because of the deficit, and interest payments rise because the debt is growing.* The problem is exactly the

---

[16] Technically, there is no interest paid on Treasury bills. Instead, a Treasury bill is a promise to pay a given amount on a given date, say $100 on June 30. Before June 30, the Treasury bill sells for a *discount* at less than $100, with the discount implying a rate of interest. For instance, if the Treasury bill just described sold for $97.50 on January 1, the holder of the bill for six months would earn a little more than 5 percent per annum, or 2.5 percent for six months.

Table 15-4 *Interest on the Federal Debt and the Primary Deficit*

		(billions of dollars)		
	Primary Deficit	**Interest on Public Debt**	**Total Deficit**	**Primary Deficit (percent of GDP)**
1970	− 2.1	1.9	− 0.2	− 2.4
1975	0.1	3.7	3.8	.06
1980	0.7	9.9	10.6	0.2
1985	6.9	24.6	31.5	1.4
1990	− 15.7	41.2	25.5	− 2.3

Source: Department of Finance, *Quarterly Economic Review*, Annual Reference Tables.

same for an individual as for a country: Someone who is spending more than he or she earns, and borrowing to cover the difference, will find a need to borrow more and more each year just because the interest on past borrowing keeps rising.

Deficits in a Growing Economy

The impossibility of running a permanent debt-financed primary deficit is a dramatic conclusion that certainly seems to justify concern over the massive deficits the Canadian economy faces for the next decade. However, the problem is less serious in a growing economy.

As can be seen in Figure 15-4, the national debt in Canada has risen for most of the past 30 years. Does this mean the government budget is bound to get out of control, with interest payments rising so high that taxes have to keep rising until eventually something terrible happens? The answer is no, because the economy has continued growing. Figure 15-5 shows that the ratio of the debt to GDP declined until 1975 because GDP grew more rapidly than the debt.

Why is it useful to look at the ratio of debt to income rather than at the absolute value of the debt? The reason is that GDP is a measure of the size of the economy, and the debt–GDP ratio is thus a measure of the magnitude of the debt relative to the size of the economy.

We can formalize this discussion by writing the equation for the debt–income ratio and considering explicitly how it changes over time. We define the following symbols:

r = real or inflation-adjusted interest rate
x = primary deficit as a fraction of nominal income
y = growth rate of real income
d = debt-to-income ratio

In the appendix we show that the debt–income ratio rises over time if

$$d(r - y) + x > 0$$

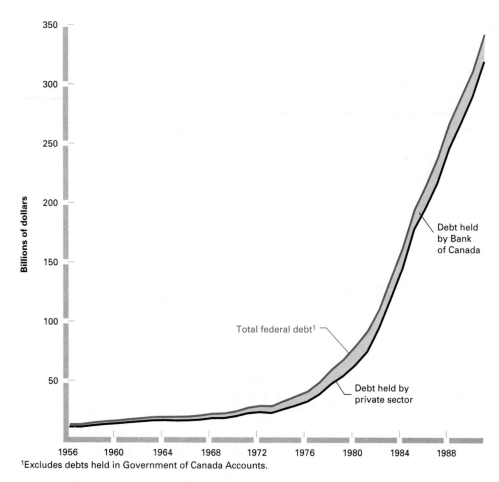

Figure 15-4   *The National Debt*

(*Source:* Adapted from *Bank of Canada Review*)

The evolution of the debt–income ratio depends on the relationship between the real interest rate and the growth rate of output, and the noninterest budget surplus. The higher the interest rate and the lower the growth rate of output, the more likely the debt–income ratio is to be rising. A large noninterest surplus tends to make the debt–income ratio fall.

The above relationship brings out why, over the early 1970s, the debt–income ratio was falling. The real interest rate was practically zero, output grew steadily, and the noninterest budget was in surplus or near balance. In these circumstances debt grows less rapidly than nominal income, and hence the debt–income ratio fell. By contrast, in the 1980s the opposite was the case. Real interest rates were very high, growth was

Figure 15-5 *The National Debt as a Percentage of GDP*

(*Source:* Department of Finance, *Quarterly Economic Review,* Annual Reference Tables)

sluggish, and the noninterest budget was in deficit. As a result the debt–income ratio was rising. In a period of slow growth and high real interest rates, deficits translate into a rapidly rising debt–income ratio.

What would happen if the deficit were too large, so that debt grows relative to income seemingly without bounds? Such a process can really not go on forever. Ultimately the public debt totally overshadows and displaces other assets, and crowding out becomes so pervasive that the public comes to expect *some* action to balance the budget. This might involve inflation,[17] special taxes, or cuts in government spending to balance the budget.

How does inflation help solve the deficit problem? It does so because a large *unanticipated* inflation will reduce the real value of the outstanding stock of government debt. The national debt in most countries is *nominal*, meaning that the government is obliged to pay only a certain number of dollars to the holders of the debt. A policy that raises the price level thus reduces the real value of the payments the government is obliged to make. The debt can therefore virtually be wiped out by a large enough unanticipated inflation — so long as the debt is a nominal debt.

---

[17] See T. Sargent and N. Wallace, "Some Unpleasant Monetarist Arithmetic," Federal Reserve Bank of Minnesota, *Quarterly Review*, Fall 1981. As the title suggests, the treatment is technical. The main point the authors make is that debt problems ultimately become inflation problems. We return to this issue in Chapter 18.

It is important to have some perspective on the relevance of these extreme conditions to the world today. Canada in the mid-1980s was not close to facing a massive debt crisis in which the national debt was so large as to overshadow other macroeconomic problems and in which the government could not finance its deficit by borrowing from the public. However, it did face the prospect of a rapid rise in the ratio of debt to income. By achieving a primary surplus at the end of the decade, the government was able to substantially reduce the growth of the debt-to-income ratio.[18]

There are, though, a number of countries even today where many years of deficits have cumulated into a large public debt that ultimately becomes unmanageable. Often that outcome is clearly visible ahead of time, but on occasion a sharp increase in real interest rates together with a major loss in tax revenues, perhaps because of a world recession, can suddenly make the debt problem much more immediate. In particular, that problem faced many developing countries that had borrowed abroad during the 1970s and in 1980–1981, when the real interest rate was still low. When the real interest rate rose, their heavy indebtedness meant that they had to make large interest payments to foreigners, which for many of the countries was extremely difficult to do. The result was the world debt crisis of 1982–1986.

The Burden of the Debt

To what extent is the national debt a burden? It must be recognized, of course, that corresponding to the liability that we all have as our share of the national debt, there are assets in the form of government securities held by Canadians. With the exception of debt held by foreigners, we owe the national debt to ourselves. Each individual shares in the public debt, but many individuals own claims on the government that are the other side of the national debt. If there is a debt for individuals taken together, it arises from prospective taxes to pay off the debt. The taxes that different individuals would pay to retire the debt would also vary among the population. One could think of the liability that the debt represents cancelling out the asset that the debt represents to the individuals who hold claims on the government. The question at issue, then, is whether the debt is counted as part of wealth for the population as a whole.

Are Bonds Wealth? The Barro–Ricardo Problem

It is possible that individuals in the economy calculate their wealth by taking into account the tax payments they will have to make in the future. Suppose that everyone believed that the national debt would eventually be paid off. Then everyone would know that at some point in the future the federal government would have to run a surplus. Individuals might think the federal government would at some future date

---

[18] For a discussion of deficits and the national debt, see N. Bruce and D. Purvis, "Consequences of Government Budget Deficits"; J. Bossons, "Issues in the Analysis of Government Deficits"; and R. Boadway and S. Clark, "The Government Budget, the Accumulation of Capital, and Long-run Welfare," in J. Sargent, ed., *Fiscal and Monetary Policy*, Research Studies of the Royal Commission on the Economic Union and Development Prospects for Canada, Vol. 21 (Toronto: University of Toronto Press, 1986).

have to raise taxes in order to pay off the debt. In this case an increase in the debt would increase their wealth and at the same time suggest to them that their taxes would be higher in the future. The net effect on aggregate demand might then be zero. The issue raised by this argument is sometimes posed by the question: Are government bonds wealth?

The question whether government bonds are net wealth goes back at least to the classical English economist David Ricardo. It has been given prominence in the work of the new classical economists, in particular Robert Barro.[19] Hence it is known as the *Barro–Ricardo equivalence proposition*. The proposition is that debt finance by bond issue merely postpones taxation, and therefore in many instances is strictly equivalent to current taxation.

The strict Barro–Ricardo proposition that government bonds are not net wealth turns on the argument that people realize their bonds will have to be paid off with future increases in taxes. (Incidentally, after raising this as a theoretical possibility, Ricardo rejected its practical significance.) If so, an increase in the budget deficit unaccompanied by cuts in government spending should lead to an increase in saving that precisely matches the deficit.

When the government reduces taxes to run a deficit, the public recognizes its taxes will be higher in the future. The public's permanent income is thus unaffected by the government's switch from taxes today to taxes tomorrow. Its consumption is accordingly also unchanged. Since the tax cut increased disposable income, but consumption has not risen, saving must rise. The Barro–Ricardo proposition thus implies that a cut in current taxes that carries with it an implied increase in future taxes should lead to an increase in saving.

Empirical research continues in an attempt to settle the issue of whether the debt is wealth.[20] The issue is not yet closed. The theoretical arguments are not conclusive, and it is difficult to isolate the effects of changes in debt on consumption demand in empirical studies. We believe the evidence to date is on balance unfavourable to the Barro–Ricardo proposition, but recognize that the issue has not yet been decisively settled.

Intergenerational Fairness

To the extent that debt does involve some burden, a government that runs a deficit and creates a larger debt shifts the cost of financing current spending to future generations. There are two reasons to suppose that this may happen.

---

[19] See Robert Barro, "Are Government Bonds Net Wealth?" *Journal of Political Economy*, December 1974. A recent theoretical challenge to the Barro–Ricardo view is Oliver Blanchard's "Debt, Deficits and Finite Horizons," *Journal of Political Economy*, April 1985.

[20] Intensive empirical work on this issue is taking place. For examples and reviews, see David Aschauer, "Fiscal Policy and Aggregate Demand," *American Economic Review*, March 1985; Roger Kormendi, "Government Debt, Government Spending and Private Sector Behavior," *American Economic Review*, December 1983; James Barth, George Iden, and Frank Russek, "Do Federal Deficits Really Matter?" *Contemporary Policy Issues*, Fall 1984; John Tatom, "Two Views of the Effects of Government Deficit in the 1980s," *Federal Reserve Bank of St. Louis, Review*, October 1985.

Box 15-2 Optimal Deficits and Intertemporal Tax Distortions

Until recently the typical pattern has been that the debt–income ratio increases in wartime and declines in peacetime. This seems to be a sensible way to proceed, although, under the Barro–Ricardo hypothesis, because current and future taxation have the same effects, it does not matter how the deficit is financed. If the hypothesis does not hold, then debt finance represents a means of giving future generations a share in the economic burden of the war.

An alternative theory of optimal deficits, developed by Finn Kydland of Carnegie-Mellon University and Edward Prescott of the University of Minnesota,[a] focuses on tax distortions, or *tax wedges*. These distortions occur because taxes create a difference between the market price of commodities and their value to consumers and producers. For instance, the income tax means that workers, who take home only an after-tax wage, place a lower value on their work than the employer, who has to pay a pretax wage.

In order to minimize these distortions over time, Kydland and Prescott show that tax *rates* should be kept constant. To see why, suppose that on the contrary taxes were high during war and low during peace. Then, according to this theory, which is a supply-side theory, individuals would work less during the war and more during peace. Rather than have labour supply moving perversely in that way, Kydland and Prescott show that under their assumptions tax rates should be kept constant.

The government budget constraint says that the present value of government spending has to be equal to the present value of taxes. If tax rates are constant, deficits will be high when government spending is *temporarily* high and surpluses will occur when government spending is temporarily low. The reason is that on average the budget has to be balanced. If tax rates are kept constant, then revenues will change relatively little. Government spending can fluctuate more, and when it is high there will be a deficit.

This tax-smoothing argument indeed suggests that the typical pattern of large war-time deficits is the correct one.

---

[a] "A Competitive Theory of Fluctuations and the Feasibility and Desirability of Stabilization Policy," in Stanley Fischer, ed., *Rational Expectations and Economic Policy* (Chicago: University of Chicago Press, 1980).

First, even if Barro–Ricardo equivalence does hold, we have to take into account that part of the debt is owned by foreigners. In that case, for the Canadian economy as a whole, part of the asset represented by the debt is held by foreigners, while the future tax liability accrues entirely to residents. Thus the part of the debt held by foreigners represents a burden on the future.

Second, if Barro–Ricardo equivalence does not hold, then it can be argued that the national debt creates a burden on future generations by reducing their capital stock.

Since debt financing increases the interest rate and reduces investment, the capital stock would be lower with debt financing than otherwise. If individuals regard the debt as part of their wealth, they increase their consumption at a given level of income and this results in a smaller proportion of GDP being invested.

15-5 Summary

1. The great depression shaped both macroeconomics and many of the economy's institutions. The extremely high unemployment and the length of the depression led to the view that the private economy was unstable and that government intervention was needed to maintain high employment levels.

2. Keynesian economics succeeded because it seemed to explain the causes of the great depression — a collapse of investment demand — and because it pointed to expansionary fiscal policy as a means of preventing future depressions.

3. Federal government spending is financed through taxes and through borrowing, which is necessary when the budget is in deficit.

4. Borrowing may be from the private sector or from the Bank of Canada. Lending to the government by the Bank of Canada changes the monetary base, whereas lending by the private sector to the government to finance the deficit does not affect the base.

5. The stock of claims held by the Bank of Canada and the private sector against the government — the national debt — changes with the budget deficit. The national debt increases when there is a budget deficit and decreases when there is a budget surplus.

6. Because the deficit can be financed in two ways, there is no *necessary* connection between the budget deficit and changes in the monetary base. Equation (2), the government budget constraint, says only that the *sum* of changes in the stock of debt and changes in the base is equal to the budget deficit.

7. The debt–income ratio rises if the growth rate of debt — determined by interest payments and the primary deficit — exceeds the growth rate of nominal income.

8. Debt financing of a permanent increase in government spending is not viable if the economy is not growing. The interest payments on the debt would continually increase, making for a rising deficit that has to be funded by ever-increasing borrowing. In a growing economy, small deficits can be run permanently without causing the debt–GDP ratio to rise.

9. The Barro–Ricardo equivalence proposition notes that debt represents future taxes. Accordingly it asserts that debt-financed tax cuts will not have any effect on aggregate demand.

10. With the exception of debt held by foreigners, the national debt is not a burden since we owe it to ourselves. However, the debt may be a burden in the long run because it leads to a decline in the capital stock.

Key Terms

Structural deficit	**National debt**
Laffer curve	**Primary deficit**
Debt finance	**Debt–income ratio**
Money finance	**Barro–Ricardo equivalence**
Monetizing the debt	**Burden of the debt**
Government budget constraint	

Problems

1. Using *IS-LM* curves, describe the competing "autonomous spending" and "monetary" explanations for the great depression.

2. Explain why many people believe the inflationary problems of the 1970s have their roots in the 1960s. How can this be so? What would be the cause? What could have been done to avoid such "heating up" of the economy, in this view?

3. Government budget deficits are often a source of public concern. What would be the implications for stabilization policy of a commitment to a balanced budget every year?

4. Discuss the notion of the monetary–fiscal policy mix. What determines the mix that is chosen? Illustrate, using an *IS-LM* diagram, how the effects of the mixes of 1971 and 1981 differ, given the information below. (Ignore changes in the level of income.)

	1971	1981
Cyclically adjusted federal deficit (% of GNP)	0	1.7
Increase in the Treasury bill rate (percent)	−2.5	5.0

5. What effect does a federal government surplus have on the stock of money and the stock of debt? Explain in detail the mechanics of how the stocks of money and bonds are affected.

6. Suppose the government issues $1 billion in Treasury bills which are bought by the public. Then the Bank of Canada conducts open market purchases of $300 million. Effectively, how has the debt been financed?

7. Under what circumstances are fiscal and monetary policy related rather than existing as two completely independent instruments in the hands of the government?

8. Some people say that a huge government debt is a burden, while others point out that a large debt means individuals own large amounts of government securities and thus are wealthier. Who is right?

9. Suppose the real interest rate is 3 percent, output growth is 7 percent, the debt–income ratio is 50 percent, and the primary deficit is 7 percent of GDP. Will the debt–income ratio rise or fall?

10. Explain in words why a high growth rate of output will tend, other things being equal, to reduce the debt–income ratio. How does your answer help explain Figure 15-5?

11. "Canada faces a fiscal crisis because mounting deficits are driving the debt–income ratio far beyond the range that this country has experienced. From these high debt levels there is no return except by years of high taxes to pay off the debt." Comment on this statement.

Appendix   The Potential Instability of Debt Finance

In this appendix we develop a framework to assess the instability problem associated with debt finance. We focus on the debt–income ratio and ask under what conditions the debt–income ratio will rise over time. Instability arises if the debt–income ratio rises year after year without limits.[21]

The derivation uses definitions, addition, and subtraction and avoids calculus. Its main purpose is for you to see where the formula in the text comes from.

D = nominal stock of debt outstanding
i = nominal interest rate
r = real interest rate
P = price level
Y = level of real output
x = noninterest or primary budget deficit (relative to income)
d = debt–income ratio
y = growth rate of output

The debt–income ratio is defined as the ratio of debt outstanding relative to nominal income.

$$\text{Debt-to-income ratio} = d = \frac{D}{PY} \tag{A1}$$

The increase in debt from one year to the next is the result of the budget deficit.

---

[21] The discussion of debt–income ratios draws on James Tobin, "Budget Deficits, Federal Debt and Inflation in the Short and Long Run," in The Conference Board, *Toward a Reconstruction of Federal Budgeting*, 1982; Robert Eisner and Paul Pieper, "A New View of the Federal Debt and Budget Deficits," *American Economic Review*, March 1984; Willem Buiter, "A Guide to Public Sector Debt and Deficits," *Economic Policy*, November 1985; and Congressional Budget Office, *The Economic Outlook*, February 1984.

It therefore is equal to interest payments, which are equal to the debt outstanding, times the interest rate, iD, plus the noninterest deficit, xPY:

$$D_{t+1} - D_t = \Delta D = iD_t + xP_tY_t \qquad (A2)$$

Over time the debt–income ratio changes by Δd. From Equation (A1) the change over time can be calculated as

$$\Delta d = \frac{D_{t+1}}{P_{t+1}Y_{t+1}} - \frac{D_t}{P_tY_t} = \frac{D_t + \Delta D}{P_tY_t(1+y)(1+\pi)} - d_t \qquad (A3)$$

where we have simply used the definitions of the growth rate $Y_{t+1} = Y_t(1+y)$ and inflation rate $P_{t+1} = P_t(1+\pi)$ and (A1). Note that the growth rate of nominal income appears in (A3) as the term $(1+y)(1+\pi)$. To simplify notation we use the definition $q = 1/(1+y)(1+\pi)$ to denote the reciprocal of the growth rate of nominal income.

Equation (A3) can be simplified to the following form:

$$\Delta d = d\left[\frac{1 + \Delta D/D}{(1+y)(1+\pi)} - 1\right] = qd\left[\left(1 + \frac{\Delta D}{D}\right) - (1+y)(1+\pi)\right] \qquad (A3a)$$

which states that if the growth rate of debt $(1 + \Delta D/D)$ exceeds the growth rate of nominal income $(1+y)(1+\pi)$ then the debt–income ratio must increase.

Our next task is to relate the change in the debt–income ratio to interest rates and the primary deficit. Substituting the expression for the change in nominal debt from (A2) into (A3a) yields

$$\Delta d = qd[(1+i) - (1+y)(1+\pi)] + qx \qquad (A4)$$

Using the approximation $(1+y)(1+\pi) \simeq 1 + y + \pi$ and the definition of the real interest rate, $r = i - \pi$, we get the final form of the equation:[22]

$$\Delta d = q[(r-y)d + x] \qquad (A5)$$

This equation states that the debt–income ratio will be rising if the expression in square brackets is positive. The expression *must* be positive if the real interest rate exceeds the growth rate *and* there is a noninterest deficit $(x > 0)$. It must be falling if the real interest rate is less than the growth rate *and* there is a noninterest surplus. In between there are different possibilities. The important point to recognize is that a shift in the economy toward high real interest rates and low growth rates, combined with a noninterest deficit, cannot but cause the debt–income ratio to be rising.

---

[22] The approximation $(1+y)(1+\pi) \simeq 1 + y + \pi$ neglects the term $y\pi$. If both the growth rate of output and the inflation rate are small fractions, say 0.05 and 0.11, the product is only a small quantity and can be ignored. If on the other hand, inflation is large, say 500 percent, the interaction term $y\pi$ cannot be neglected.

PART 4 *Unemploy-ment, Inflation, and Growth*

CHAPTER 16 *The Rate of Inflation in the Short and Long Run*

From the mid-1960s through the end of the 1970s, the inflation rate exhibited a rising trend in both Canada and the United States. In late 1979, there was a sharp change in monetary policy in the U.S. designed to reverse this trend. The Bank of Canada followed suit, and there was a sharp rise in interest rates in both countries. Although the inflation rate declined sharply in response to this tightening, it remained above 4 percent for most of the 1980s, and monetary policy was again tightened by the Bank of Canada in 1990.

These decisions were dramatic because there was little disagreement among economists of widely different macroeconomic persuasions that moving toward tight money would cause a recession along with a reduction in the inflation rate. There was indeed a sharp contraction in 1981 and 1982, with the unemployment rate in Canada rising above 12 percent. At the beginning of the 1990s, unemployment rose above 10 percent and there was a further decline in inflation. It was hoped that the inflationary bias of the 1960s and 1970s had finally been broken.

In this chapter we address the problem of inflation and unemployment, extending the analysis of Chapter 8 that focused on the determinants of the price level, to examine the inflation rate. We develop the short- and long-run aggregate supply curves, emphasizing the role of inflationary expectations in shifting the supply curve, and we extend the aggregate demand curve to take account of ongoing inflation.

A key question is: Why is it apparently inevitable that inflation stabilization should bring about unemployment and recession? The distinction between the short- and long-run aggregate supply curves is essential here. In the short run, inflation cannot be reduced without creating a recession; in the long run, though, there is no tradeoff between inflation and unemployment.

We develop the analysis of the determination of output and inflation in Sections 16-1 to 16-6. This material includes the analysis of adjustments to changes in money growth and to fiscal policy changes. The chapter concludes with an important application of the dynamic model, the examination of alternative strategies for reducing inflation.

16-1 Inflation, Expectations, and the Aggregate Supply

In Chapter 8, we derived the aggregate supply curve which shows the price level at which firms are willing to produce and sell different levels of output. The aggregate supply curve is

$$P = P_{-1}[1 + \lambda(Y - Y^\circ)] \tag{1}$$

where P is the price level, Y the level of output, and Y° the full-employment level of output.

Recall now that the aggregate supply curve builds on three foundations:

- The Phillips curve, which shows that the lower the level of unemployment, the more rapidly wages increase.

- The relationship between the unemployment rate and the level of output: The lower the unemployment rate, the higher the output.

- The assumption of *markup pricing*, which is that firms' prices are based on labour costs: The higher the wage, the higher the prices.

The Phillips curve in turn is the result of market pressure on wages. When the unemployment rate is low, firms find it difficult to obtain the labour they demand and, accordingly, offer higher wages to attract workers. Thus wages rise more rapidly when unemployment is low. When the unemployment rate is high, jobs are difficult to find and firms can fill any vacancies they might have without raising wages — indeed, wages may even be falling as workers compete for scarce jobs.

In this chapter we develop the aggregate supply curve in two directions. First, we modify it to include *expected inflation*: Firms and workers take account of expected increases in the price level when they are fixing wages. Second, we transform the aggregate supply curve into a relationship between output and the *inflation rate* rather than the price level. That way we can use the aggregate supply curve to model ongoing inflation — that is, continuing changes in the price level.

Wage Setting and Expected Inflation

In setting wages, firms and workers react to conditions in the labour market. Thus, when output and employment are high, wages tend to rise fast. When output and employment are low, wages do not rise fast and may even fall. The Phillips curve introduced in Chapter 8 summarizes the link between wage inflation and the output gap. With the notation $g_w = (W - W_{-1})/W_{-1}$ for the rate of wage inflation, the Phillips curve is

$$g_w = \lambda(Y - Y^\circ) \tag{2}$$

which states that the higher the level of output, the larger the rate of wage increase.

Friedman and Phelps pointed out[1] one major flaw in the Phillips curve as described in Equation (2): It ignores the effects of expected inflation on wage setting. Workers are interested in *real* wages (the amount of goods they can buy with their wages), not *nominal* wages (the dollar value of wages).

It is clear that workers, who are concerned with the real wage they receive, will want the nominal wage to fully reflect the inflation they expect during the period between the time the wage is fixed and the time the wage is actually paid. In other words, quite independent of the effects of the level of employment on wage bargaining, workers will want compensation for expected inflation.

What about the other side? Why do firms agree to raise wages more rapidly when they expect higher prices? The reason is that they can afford to pay higher nominal wages if they will be able to sell their goods at higher prices. If all prices are rising, each firm can expect to be able to sell its output for a higher price because the prices of competing goods are increasing. Indeed, when wages and prices are rising at the same rate, both firms and workers are in essentially the same position as they would be if there were no inflation and the real wage were constant.

When expected inflation is taken into account, the Phillips curve becomes

$$g_w = \pi^e + \lambda(Y - Y^\circ) \tag{3}$$

Here π^e is the expected inflation rate. Equation (3) is called the *expectations-augmented* Phillips curve; that is, it is the original Phillips curve augmented or adjusted to take account of expected inflation. At any given level of output, the higher the expected rate of inflation, the more wages rise: Indeed, the assumption is that nominal wages rise 1 percent faster for each extra 1 percent of expected inflation.

The Aggregate Supply Curve

The next step is to transform the expectations-augmented Phillips curve into a relationship between the inflation rate and the level of output, which depends on the

---

[1] See footnote 8 in Chapter 8. In addition, we continue for the most part to omit from the aggregate supply curve changes in the prices of factors of production other than labour, such as raw materials.

expected rate of inflation. Once again we assume that firms maintain a constant markup of prices over wages, but this implies that the rate of increase of prices will be equal to the rate of increase in wages. Denote the rate of increase of prices or the rate of inflation as $\pi = (P - P_{-1})/P_{-1}$. With this notation, the statement that inflation is equal to the rate of wage increase becomes

$$\pi = g_w \tag{4}$$

Substituting the rate of wage increase (Equation (3)) into (4) yields the *dynamic aggregate supply curve*:

$$\pi = \pi^e + \lambda(Y - Y^\circ) \tag{5}$$

Equation (5) is one of the two building blocks of a model of the inflation process. It is the *expectations-augmented aggregate supply curve*, which we use in the remainder of this chapter to study the behaviour of output and inflation. The fundamental difference between that curve (Equation (5)) and the aggregate supply curve of Equation (9) in Chapter 8 is the inclusion of the expected inflation rate. In addition, because Equation (5) deals with the inflation rate rather than the price level, it is a convenient form of the supply curve for studying ongoing inflation.

16-2   Short- and Long-Run Aggregate Supply Curves

Expectations-augmented short-run aggregate supply curves are shown in Figure 16-1. There is an aggregate supply curve corresponding to each expected rate of inflation. For example, on *SAS* the expected inflation rate is 5 percent, as can be seen from the fact that when $Y = Y^\circ$, at point A on *SAS*, the inflation rate on the vertical axis is 5 percent. (Note from Equation (5) that when $Y = Y^\circ$, $\pi = \pi^e$.) The short-run aggregate supply curve shows the relationship between the inflation rate and the level of output when the expected rate of inflation is held constant. The curves are called short-run because it is assumed that the expected rate of inflation is constant (or at least does not change much) in the short run of a few months or as much as a year.

Given the expected inflation rate, the short-run aggregate supply curve shows the inflation rate rising with the level of output: The higher the level of output, the higher the rate of inflation. This is a reflection of the effect of higher output levels on the rate of increase of wages and, through higher wages, on the rate of increase of prices.

The higher the expected inflation rate, the higher the aggregate supply curve. Thus on *SAS'*, the expected inflation rate is 10 percent. Similarly, for any expected inflation rate, there is a corresponding short-run aggregate supply curve, parallel to *SAS* and *SAS'*, with the vertical distance between any two short-run supply curves equal to the difference in expected inflation rates between them.

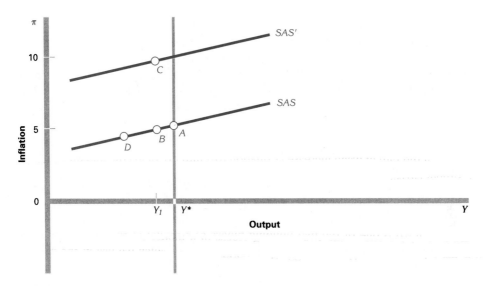

Figure 16-1 *The Short-Run Aggregate Supply Curve*

The expected inflation rate is constant on a short-run aggregate supply curve: It is 5 percent on *SAS*, 10 percent on *SAS'*. Each short-run aggregate supply curve is shown quite flat, reflecting the fact that, in the short run, it takes a large change in output to generate a given change in inflation.

On each short-run aggregate supply curve, there is a tradeoff between inflation and output. To reduce the inflation rate, it is necessary to reduce the level of output, producing a recession, forcing the rate of wage increase down through unemployment, and thus achieving a lower inflation rate.

We show the short-run aggregate supply curves in Figure 16-1 as quite flat, reflecting the evidence that in the short run — up to a year or even two — it takes a large recession to bring about a substantial reduction in the inflation rate. That was the choice made, for example, in 1982–1983 and again in 1991 when the inflation rate was reduced.

Changes in the Expected Inflation Rate

Each aggregate supply curve is drawn for a given expected rate of inflation. As the expected rate of inflation changes, the economy moves from one short-run aggregate supply curve to another. That means that the combination of the level of output and inflation rate that occurs depends on the expected inflation rate. For instance, the level of output of Y_1 in Figure 16-1 would be consistent with a low inflation rate at point *B* on *SAS* and a higher inflation rate at point *C* on *SAS'*.

Changes in the expected rate of inflation help explain why the simple Phillips curve relationship seen in Figure 8-9 for 1963–1966 seemed to break down later. Through the end of the 1960s, there was relatively little awareness of inflation, and the economy was basically moving along an *SAS* curve. When, at the end of the 1960s, people began to expect inflation to continue, the short-run aggregate supply curve began to shift, generating higher inflation at each given output level. The Friedman–Phelps analysis thus can explain why the simple Phillips curve of the 1960s seemed to break down in the 1970s — and their analysis was made before the Phillips curve began to shift.

The conclusion of this section is the most important practical lesson macroeconomists and economic policy makers learned in the last 20 years. *The short-run aggregate supply curve shifts with the expected rate of inflation. The inflation rate corresponding to any given level of output therefore changes over time as the expected inflation rate changes. The higher the expected inflation rate, the higher the inflation rate corresponding to a given level of output.* That is why it is possible for the inflation rate and the unemployment rate to increase together, or for the inflation rate to rise while the level of output falls.

The Vertical Long-Run Aggregate Supply Curve

On each short-run aggregate supply curve, the expected inflation rate is constant and, except at points such as *A*, at which $Y = Y^*$, will turn out to be different from the actual inflation rate. For instance, at point *D* on *SAS* in Figure 16-1 the expected inflation rate is 5 percent, but the actual inflation rate is only 4 percent.

If the inflation rate remains constant for any long period, firms and workers will expect that rate to continue, and the expected inflation rate will become equal to the actual rate. The assumption that $\pi = \pi^e$ is what distinguishes the *long-run* from the short-run aggregate supply curve. The long-run aggregate supply curve describes the relationship between inflation and output when actual and expected inflation are equal.

With the actual and expected inflation rates equal (that is, $\pi = \pi^e$), the aggregate supply curve (5) shows that

$$Y = Y^* \tag{6}$$

The long-run aggregate supply curve, *LAS*, in Figure 16-2 is a vertical line joining points on short-run aggregate supply curves at which the actual and expected inflation rates are equal.

The meaning of the vertical long-run aggregate supply curve is that *in the long run the level of output is independent of the inflation rate.* Note the important contrast between the short and the long run: In the short run, with a given expected rate of inflation, higher inflation rates are accompanied by higher output; in the long run, with the expected rate of inflation equal to the actual rate, the level of output is independent of the inflation rate.

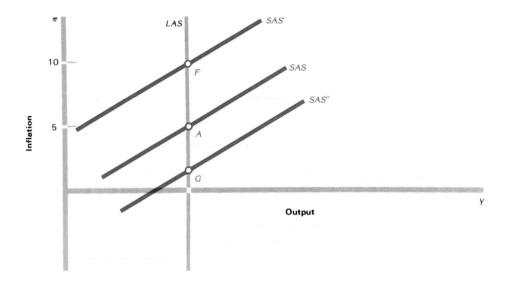

Figure 16-2 *Short- and Long-Run Aggregate Supply Curves*

The long-run aggregate supply curve joins points on short-run aggregate supply curves at which expected inflation is equal to actual inflation. It is thus the vertical line *LAS*, at the level of output Y^*.

16-3 The Role of Expected Inflation

Many of the controversies in macroeconomics are connected with the inclusion of expected inflation in the aggregate supply function. We therefore expand the discussion of the expectations-augmented Phillips curve in this section. There are three key questions. First, what exactly is the process by which expected inflation comes to be reflected in wages? Second, is it clearly *expected* inflation rather than compensation for *past* inflation that shifts the short-run aggregate supply curve? Third, what determines expected inflation?

Wage Adjustment

Wages are generally set before the work is done. Further, these are typically nominal, or dollar, wages. In some cases, wages are adjusted once a year in an annual salary review.

It is in the adjustment of these wages that expected inflation makes its way into the wage. Wages will adjust both because prices are higher at the time the contract is negotiated than they were last time the wage was set and because inflation is expected between the time the wage is negotiated and the time it will actually be paid. Thus, as the process of inflation gets under way, wages fixed in each successive period are higher than they would otherwise have been.

Because some wages are preset for one or two years or even more, it takes time for expectations of inflation to work their way into wage adjustments. For instance, if a new policy that will produce lower inflation comes into effect in 1991, it may take until 1994 before all the wages that will eventually be affected by that new policy are fully adjusted. Indeed, as we saw in Chapter 8, if all wages are not adjusted at the same time, it may take much longer for all wages to come into line with a higher inflation rate, because the wage that is set in one firm or union or industry depends on the wages set elsewhere in the economy, not all of which are adjusting to the new conditions simultaneously.

Compensation for Past Inflation or Expected Inflation

We have described the adjustment for inflation in the expectations-augmented Phillips curve or aggregate supply curve as being for expected inflation. Another interpretation is that wage agreements compensate workers not only for expected inflation but also to some extent for past inflation.

The argument here is that when the inflation rate rises, workers who lost out because their real wages were low want compensation for the losses. Note that this argument implies that compensation would be for unexpected inflation only, that is, for inflation not taken into account when the previous contracts were negotiated.

In practice, at low inflation rates, an adjustment for expected inflation is very hard to distinguish from compensation for past inflation. If prices went up 10 percent last year, the firm is quite likely to raise wages this year. That may be compensation just for last year's inflation, or it may be compensation paid in advance for the inflation expected to take place during the coming year. Thus, it is very difficult to determine whether it is expected inflation or recent inflation that is represented by the π^e term in the expectations-augmented aggregate supply curve.

The confusion between whether it is compensation for past inflation or for expected inflation is illustrated by those contracts that contain formal *index* clauses, which adjust wages for inflation. These are called COLA, or cost-of-living adjustments, which are contained in many union contracts.[2] The typical COLA clause adjusts the wage once a year, or once every three months, by an amount that depends on the rate of inflation since the last adjustment. For instance, if the inflation rate in the last year was 8 percent, the wage rate may go up by 6 percent.

Now, is this compensation for past inflation or for future inflation? Because it is based on the past inflation rate, it looks like compensation for past inflation, but the wage that is to be paid is that for the *coming* year. Thus it may be compensation in advance for inflation in the coming year.

---

[2] See W.C. Riddell, *Dealing with Inflation and Unemployment in Canada*, Royal Commission Research Studies, Vol. 25 (Toronto: University of Toronto Press, 1986), pp. 133–35.

Why does it matter whether wage adjustments to inflation respond to yesterday's actual inflation or tomorrow's expected inflation? The difference is very important because the explanation has different implications for how long it takes for the inflation rate to change. If wages for next year reflect last year's inflation and prices are based on wages, as they are, then inflation today will reflect yesterday's inflation, and inflation rates will change only gradually. If it is only expected inflation that matters for wage setting, then perhaps a radical change in policy that changes expectations can also change the inflation rate quickly.

Adaptive Versus Rational Expectations

The question of whether it is compensation for past inflation or future inflation that affects wages is further complicated when we consider how people form their expectations of inflation.

One hypothesis that was used in the 1950s and 1960s, and that still commands some support, is that expectations are *adaptive*; that is, they are based on the past behaviour of inflation. Thus, under adaptive expectations, the rate of inflation expected for next year might be the rate of inflation last year. Under this simplest adaptive expectations assumption, we would have

$$\pi^e = \pi_{-1} \qquad (7)$$

Of course, the adaptive expectations assumption could be more complicated, for instance, if the expected inflation rate is the average of the last three years' inflation.

Note that, if expectations are adaptive, it becomes virtually impossible to tell whether the π^e term in the aggregate supply curve represents expected inflation or compensation for past inflation. If $\pi^e = \pi_{-1}$, there is no difference between past inflation and expected inflation.

The rational expectations view was introduced in Chapter 8. The rational expectations hypothesis is the assumption that people base their expectations of inflation (or any other economic variable) on all the information economically available about the future behaviour of that variable.

The rational expectations approach to macroeconomics, associated primarily with the names of Robert Lucas of the University of Chicago and Thomas Sargent of the University of Minnesota, has been extremely influential. As we have seen in Chapter 8 and shall see in Chapter 20, the approach developed by Lucas, Sargent, and others involves much more than just a theory of expectations. For now, though, we concentrate on the expectations part of the theory.

The rational expectations hypothesis implies that people do not make systematic mistakes in forming their expectations. Systematic mistakes — for instance, always underpredicting inflation — are easily spotted. According to the rational expectations hypothesis, people correct such mistakes and change the way they form expectations accordingly. On average, according to the rational expectations hypothesis, expectations are correct because people understand the environment in which they operate. Of course people make mistakes from time to time, but they do not make *systematic mistakes*.

For much of this chapter we work with the simple adaptive expectations assumption (6) that the expected inflation rate is equal to the lagged inflation rate. The aggregate supply curve is thus[3]

$$\pi = \pi_{-1} + \lambda(Y - Y^*) \tag{8}$$

We use the aggregate supply curve (8), together with an aggregate demand curve to be introduced in the next section, to study the dynamic adjustment of the economy to changes in policy. By way of contrast, we also use the rational expectations assumption and show just how radical are its implications.

16-4 Dynamic Aggregate Demand

The aggregate demand curve introduced in Chapter 7 represents combinations of the *price level* and level of output at which the goods and assets markets are simultaneously in equilibrium. In this chapter, where we are studying continuing inflation, we work with an aggregate demand curve that shows the relationship between the level of output and the *inflation rate*. The dynamic aggregate demand curve shows the relationship between the rate of inflation and the rate of change of aggregate demand.

The dynamic aggregate demand curve used in this chapter, and which is derived in the appendix,[4] is

$$Y = Y_{-1} + \phi(m - \pi) + \sigma f \tag{9}$$

In Equation (9), m is the growth rate of the nominal money stock. Thus $(m - \pi)$ is the rate of change of real balances; When m exceeds π, the money stock is increasing faster than prices, and so real balances (M/P) are increasing. The other term, σf, denotes the impact on demand of a fiscal expansion.

The curve is most simply understood as saying that the *change* in aggregate demand $(Y - Y_{-1})$ is determined by the growth rate of real balances and by fiscal expansion. The higher the level of real balances, the lower the interest rate and the higher the level of aggregate demand; therefore, the more rapidly real balances are growing, the more rapidly the interest rate is falling and the more rapidly aggregate demand is increasing. By the same line of argument, an *increase* in government spending or a *cut* in taxes means an expansionary fiscal policy and hence an increase in demand over the previous period's level.

---

[3] Recall that with the assumption $\pi^e = \pi_{-1}$ in (8) we cannot distinguish the view that the π^e term represents expected inflation from the alternative view that it represents compensation for past inflation.

[4] The parameters ϕ and σ are the money and fiscal multipliers familiar from the *IS-LM* model of Chapter 4.

In the appendix to this chapter we show that the aggregate demand curve (9) is a simplified version of the aggregate demand curve obtained by using the full *IS-LM* model. The simplification is that we omit the expected rate of inflation that affects aggregate demand.[5] To start, we concentrate on presenting the aggregate demand schedule diagrammatically. For simplicity, we therefore suppress the term relating to fiscal policy changes. We return to fiscal policy changes later in the chapter.

In Figure 16-3 we plot the dynamic aggregate demand schedule (9), or *DAD*. The shape of that schedule is most clearly seen by rewriting Equation (9) as[6]

$$\pi = m - \frac{1}{\phi}(Y - Y_{-1}) \tag{10}$$

The schedule is drawn for a given growth rate of money and is downward-sloping. Given the growth rate of money, a lower rate of inflation implies that real balances

$(m - \pi) = \Delta$ of real bal.

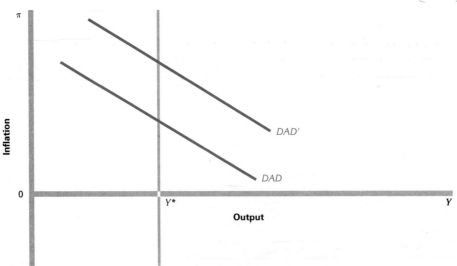

Figure 16-3   *The Dynamic Aggregate Demand Schedule*

The dynamic aggregate demand curve (*DAD*) is downward-sloping and drawn for a given rate of growth of money and lagged output level. The growth rate of money is higher on *DAD'* than on *DAD*.

---

[5] The expected rate of inflation enters because investment is affected by the *real* interest rate, whereas the demand for money is affected by the *nominal* interest rate. Thus when we say above that increases in real balances reduce interest rates, we should, to be more precise, say that while they reduce the nominal interest rate, whether they also reduce the real interest rate depends on how the expected inflation rate is changing.

[6] As noted above, we are now assuming $f = 0$, so that there is no fiscal policy change in the current period.

are higher and thus that the interest rate is lower and aggregate demand is higher. The negative slope results from this connection between lower inflation — implying higher growth in real balances — and higher spending.

The position of the aggregate demand curve depends on the level of output last period. The higher the level of output last period, the higher the inflation rate corresponding to any given level of current output on the aggregate demand curve. A change in the growth rate of money will shift the aggregate demand curve. As we see from Equation (10), a change in the growth rate of money shifts the *DAD* curve vertically by precisely the same amount as changes in the growth rate of money. Thus the dynamic aggregate demand curve, *DAD'* in Figure 16-3, lies above *DAD* by the same distance as the growth rate of money has increased between *DAD* and *DAD'*.

shift AD

16-5 Determining the Inflation Rate and Level of Output

The inflation rate and level of output are determined by aggregate demand and supply. Figure 16-4 shows the intersection of the upward-sloping aggregate supply curve and the downward-sloping aggregate demand curve at point *E*. The inflation rate this period is π_0, and the level of output is Y_0.

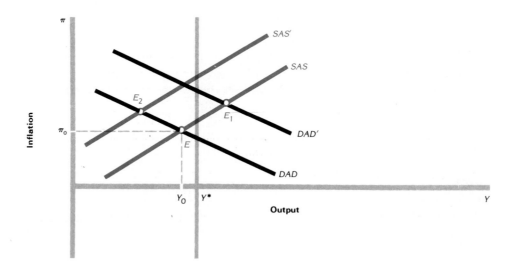

Figure 16-4   *Inflation and Output in the Short Run*

In the short run inflation and output are determined by the intersection of the aggregate supply and demand curves at point *E*. An upward shift of the aggregate demand curve raises both output and inflation. An upward shift of the aggregate supply curve increases the inflation rate while reducing the level of output.

The current rate of inflation and the level of output clearly depend on the positions of the aggregate supply and demand curves. Thus changes in any of the variables that shift the aggregate supply and demand curves will affect the current levels of inflation and output.

The Inflation Rate and Output in the Short Run

Any upward shift in the aggregate demand curve causes an increase in both the rate of inflation and the level of output, as can be seen in the shift from E to E_1 when the *DAD* curve shifts upward to *DAD'*. Such a shift would be caused by an increase in the growth rate of money. It could also be caused by an increase in government spending or a reduction in taxes, though we do not explicitly include those variables in the aggregate demand curve (9).[7] In addition, the position of the aggregate demand curve depends on the level of output last period. The higher the level of output last period (Y_{-1}), the higher the aggregate demand curve.

Given that an increase in the growth rate of money shifts the aggregate demand curve up by exactly the same amount as the rise in the growth rate of money, we see in Figure 16-4 that an increase in the growth rate of money causes both output and inflation to rise but that the increase in inflation is less than the increase in the growth rate of money. Thus, in the short run, a 1 percent increase in money growth produces a less than 1 percent increase in inflation because some of the effects of the increase in money stock show up in higher output. This is exactly the same conclusion that we reached in Chapter 8, when we showed that in the short run an increase in the money stock causes both the price level and the level of output to increase.

Shifts in the aggregate supply curve also affect the rate of inflation and the level of output. An upward shift of the aggregate supply curve, such as the shift from *SAS* to *SAS'*, moves the equilibrium from E to E_2, raising the inflation rate and reducing the level of output. An increase in the expected rate of inflation would cause an upward shift such as that from *SAS* to *SAS'*. The reason is that the higher expected rate of inflation produces more rapid rises in wages that cause more rapid inflation.

Summarizing, we see that in the short run:

- An increase in the growth rate of money causes higher inflation and higher output, but inflation rises less than the growth rate of money.

- An increase in the expected rate of inflation causes higher inflation and lower output.

We also note, and leave to you to show, that the factors we have omitted here from the aggregate supply and demand curves change the inflation rate and output in the short run:

- A supply shock that shifts the aggregate supply curve upward causes higher inflation and lower output.

---

[7] Recall also that changes in expected inflation will shift the aggregate demand curve.

- An increase in expected inflation shifts the aggregate demand curve upward and to the right.[8] To understand this point note from the appendix that the analysis in the text has omitted changes in inflationary expectations as another determinant of dynamic aggregate demand.

The Inflation Rate and Output in the Long Run

From the short run, we move to the hypothetical longest run, in which the growth rate of money is and will continue to be constant, in which expectations have adjusted to actual inflation, and in which output and inflation are constant. Such a situation is called a *steady state*, obviously because nothing is changing. Returning to the aggregate demand equation,

$$\pi = m - \frac{1}{\phi}(Y - Y_{-1}) \tag{10}$$

we recognize that with output constant ($Y = Y_{-1}$), the inflation rate is equal to the growth rate of money. Thus, *in the steady state, the inflation rate is determined solely by the growth rate of money.*

On the aggregate supply side,

$$\pi = \pi^e + \lambda(Y - Y^*) \tag{5}$$

We set $\pi = \pi^e$ and recognize that output is at its potential level Y^*. Thus *in the steady state, output is at its full-employment level.*

In the steady state, then, we have very simple relationships: The growth rate of money determines the inflation rate, and output is at its potential level.

We want now to consider the real-world importance of these steady-state relationships. The first thing to notice is that the economy never reaches a steady state. There are always disturbances affecting aggregate supply and demand: changes in expectations, or in the labour force, or in the prices of other factors of production, or in methods of production on the aggregate supply side; changes in fiscal policy, or in consumer tastes, or in monetary policy on the aggregate demand side. Thus, in practice, the economy will not ever reach a steady state: As it starts on the route toward a steady state, some shock or disturbance will come along to bump it off that route onto another path.

---

[8] When we include inflation in the aggregate demand curve, an increase in expected inflation causes both the aggregate supply and aggregate demand curves to rise, certainly increasing the inflation rate, but producing an uncertain effect on output. The net effect on output depends on whether the aggregate demand or aggregate supply curve moves up more. Typically the aggregate supply curve would shift up more, implying higher inflation and lower output — which corresponds to the conclusion reached above when we omitted expected inflation from the aggregate demand curve.

Steady-state relationships are useful, though, in indicating the long-run behaviour of the economy. Over long periods, we can expect the economy on average to behave as if the steady-state relationships hold. On average, we expect output to be at its potential level,[9] and on average, we expect the inflation rate to be determined by the growth rate of money. We take up the long-run relationship between inflation and output in more detail in the next chapter.

16-6 Dynamic Adjustment of Output and Inflation

Many factors drive the inflation rate and the level of output in the short run, whereas in the steady state, output is at its full-employment level and inflation is determined by the growth rate of money. In this section we ask how the economy moves toward the long-run equilibrium when a shock or disturbance affects aggregate supply or demand. To be specific, we examine the dynamic effects — that is, the effects that take place over time — of a change in the growth rate of money. We summarize here our two building blocks:

$$\text{Dynamic aggregate supply: } \pi = \pi_{-1} + \lambda(Y - Y^\circ) \tag{8}$$

$$\text{Dynamic aggregate demand: } \pi = m - \frac{1}{\phi}(Y - Y_{-1}) \tag{10}$$

Note that we have made the adaptive expectations assumption that expected inflation is equal to last period's inflation rate.

In Figure 16-5, the economy is initially at point E, with output at its potential level, Y°, and with inflation equal to the growth rate of money, m_0, implying an initial inflation rate $\pi_0 = m_0$. Now suppose the growth rate of money increases to a new, higher level, m_1. Let the period in which the growth rate of money changes be period 1.

The immediate short-run effect is a shift in aggregate demand from DAD_0 to DAD_1 so that the inflation rate and output both rise, to π_1 and Y_1, respectively. These changes in turn set off further adjustments. On the aggregate supply side, the increase in inflation causes expected inflation to increase, with the curve shifting to SAS_2. The new aggregate supply curve intersects the Y° line at precisely the same rate of inflation as occurred in period 1, that is, at π_1. The aggregate demand curve also shifts upward, because the level of output was higher last period.

The period 2 equilibrium is at point E_2. Because both the aggregate supply and aggregate demand curves have shifted upward, the inflation rate in period 2, π_2, is certainly higher than π_1. However, it is not clear whether the level of output in period

---

[9] Indeed, some economists define the natural rate of unemployment as the long-run average rate of unemployment. In that case, by definition the unemployment rate is on average over long periods equal to the natural rate, to which the level of potential output corresponds.

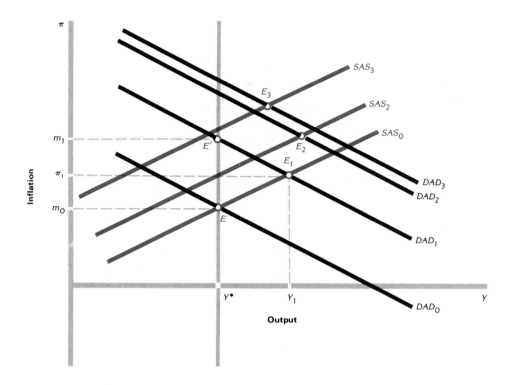

Figure 16-5 *Adjustment to a Change in the Growth Rate of Money*

The increased growth rate of money shifts the aggregate demand curve up, from DAD_0 to DAD_1, raising the inflation rate and output. These changes in turn cause both the supply and demand curves to shift upward in the next period, raising the inflation rate. The process continues until the economy reaches the new steady state.

2, Y_2, is higher or lower than Y_1. That depends on whether it was the aggregate demand or the aggregate supply curve that shifted more from period 1 to period 2.[10]

In Figure 16-5 we show output higher in period 2 than in period 1. The process now continues, with the aggregate supply and demand curves moving yet further upward. We show the third-period equilibrium, E_3, with a higher inflation rate and lower level of output than in the previous period.

It is not worth following the shifts of the aggregate supply and demand curves during the adjustment process in much further detail. Figure 16-6 shows the pattern of adjustment as the economy moves from E_1, the first-period equilibrium, to the eventual steady-state equilibrium at E'. So as to keep the diagram clear, we do not include the shifting supply and demand curves that underlie the pattern of adjustment

---

[10] If $\lambda\phi < 1$, then output rises in period 2 relative to period 1. If ϕ is small, the aggregate demand curve moves up a great deal, thereby tending to cause output in period 2 to be higher than Y_1.

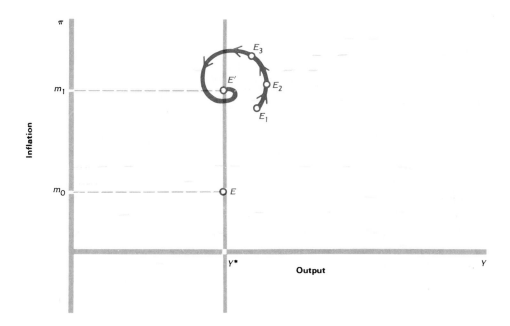

Figure 16-6   *The Full Adjustment Path*

The full adjustment path moves from E_1 to E', but with fluctuations. During the adjustment process there are periods in which output is falling while inflation is rising.

shown, and we have, for convenience, smoothed the time path of adjustment. The first few points that we traced in Figure 16-5, E_1, E_2, and E_3, are also shown in Figure 16-6.

Stagflation

Two special features of the adjustment process can be seen in Figure 16-6. First, there are times when output decreases while the inflation rate increases. For instance, between E_2 and E_3 in Figures 16-5 and 16-6, the inflation rate increases while output decreases. This inverse relationship between the rate of inflation and output is a result of the shifts of the aggregate supply curve caused by changes in expected inflation.

The inverse relationship between the rate of inflation and output is important, for it often occurs in practice and is widely believed not to be consistent with accepted macroeconomics. This is *stagflation*. Stagflation occurs when inflation rises while output is falling, or at least not rising.

If one ignores the role of expected inflation in the Phillips curve, it is easy to conclude that periods in which output and inflation move in opposite directions — equivalently, periods in which both inflation and unemployment increase at the same time — are impossible. Indeed, it is not only changes in expectations, but any supply shock, such as an increase in oil prices, that shifts the aggregate supply curve that can produce stagflation.

Overshooting

The most striking feature of Figure 16-6 is that the economy does not move directly to a new, higher inflation rate following the increase in the growth rate of money. Rather, given the adaptive expectations assumption we are making, the level of output at some stage falls below Y^*. Similarly, the inflation rate is sometimes above its long-run level, m_1. In Figure 16-6, the economy fluctuates around the new long-run equilibrium at E'.

There is one more major lesson from this section. It is that the details of the adjustment process depend on the formation of expectations. Since the shifts in the supply curve are determined by shifting expectations, that point is easy to see in a general way. We make the point more specifically now, though, by replacing the adaptive expectations assumption by rational expectations.

Perfect Foresight Expectations

When there is no uncertainty, the rational expectations assumption is equivalent to the assumption of perfect foresight, namely, that firms and individuals correctly predict what will happen when policy changes. In that case we write

$$\pi^e = \pi \qquad (11)$$

Under rational expectations, and without uncertainty, we assume that people understand how the economy works and have enough information to figure out what the inflation rate will be.

Substituting the perfect foresight assumption into aggregate supply curve (5), we obtain

$$Y = Y^* \qquad (12)$$

This is a radical result, for it means that, under perfect foresight, the economy is always at potential output. It is as if under rational expectations the long-run results take place in the short run.

How can this be? The underlying assumption of the Phillips curve mechanism that includes expected inflation is that firms and workers are trying to set wages at a level such that there will be full employment. In the Friedman–Phelps version of the Phillips curve, the only reason full employment might not be achieved is errors in expectations. If, by assumption, we remove errors in expectations, the economy will always be at full employment.

Expected and Unexpected Changes in Monetary Policy

The timing of policy actions and the formation of expectations become very important under rational expectations. The Friedman–Phelps Phillips curve assumes that wages are set before the period begins. That would mean that wages cannot react to changes in the growth rate of money that are made after wages are set. Thus the rational expectations assumption would leave open the possibility that an *unexpected* change in monetary policy could affect output.

The logic of rational expectations implies that people base their expectations of inflation on the policies they believe the government is following. Suppose the growth rate of money has been m_0 for a long time. Then we will have under rational expectations $\pi^e = m_0$, as long as m_0 is the expected growth rate of money.

Then if the central bank unexpectedly changes the growth rate of money to m_1, the initial impact will be exactly as in Figure 16-5, with the economy moving to point E_1, because the terms of wage contracts have not yet been changed. However, one period later the adjustment under rational expectations will be very different from that in Figure 16-5. Namely, if everyone believes the central bank has indeed changed the growth rate of money, then the aggregate supply curve will move up by just the amount necessary for the economy to go back immediately to full employment, at Y°.[11] One period later, the economy will be in the steady state, with output equal to Y° and inflation equal to m_1. Thus, as noted in Chapter 8, the rational expectations assumption implies that monetary policy will not have real effects unless changes in monetary policy are unexpected.

Inflationary Inertia

At this point we should note that the issue of how π^e gets into the aggregate supply function is clearly crucial. If, instead of expected inflation, the π^e term reflects compensation for past inflation, or if it takes a period of years for changed inflation rates to be reflected in labour contracts, then the adjustment pattern seen in Figures 16-5 and 16-6 is more representative of what will happen than is the rapid adjustment that takes place under rational expectations.

The adjustment pattern in Figures 16-5 and 16-6 displays *inflationary inertia*. Inflationary inertia occurs when the inflation rate reacts slowly to changes in policy (particularly monetary policy) that reduce the steady-state inflation rate.

The key question for policy makers seeking to reduce the inflation rate is whether the economy displays inflationary inertia (as it does if the π^e term in the aggregate supply curve reflects compensation for past inflation, or slow adjustment of wage set-

---

[11] Using the aggregate supply and demand equations, it can be shown that the period 1 inflation rate under the perfect foresight assumption is given by the expression

$$\pi_1 = \frac{m_0 + \lambda\phi m_1}{1 + \lambda\phi}$$

ting because of long-term contracts) or does not (as it would not if there were rational expectations *and* very quick readjustment of wages and prices).

Summary

1.   If inflationary expectations are based on last period's inflation rate — or in general are adaptive, that is, based on past inflation — an increase in the growth rate of money increases both the inflation rate and the level of output in the short run. Both the inflation rate and the level of output continue to fluctuate thereafter, tending eventually to move to the long-run equilibrium of the economy.

2.   In the process of adjustment to a change in the growth rate of money, there are stages at which inflation and output move in opposite directions. This is because the aggregate supply curve is shifting. Stagflation occurs when output is falling while inflation stays high or rises.

3.   Adjustment patterns are radically different under rational expectations. A fully expected change in the growth rate of money does not affect the level of output at all, and affects only inflation. Even if the change in money growth was not expected, output is affected only until expectations adjust to the new growth rate of money. The question of how expectations translate into wages is thus crucial to the dynamics. If it takes time for changed expectations to affect wages, then even with rational expectations the process of adjustment to a change in the growth rate of money will be lengthy, and the economy is said to display inflationary inertia.

16-7 The Adjustment to a Fiscal Expansion

In this section we consider how inflation and output respond to a permanent fiscal expansion. We saw in Chapter 8 that a sustained fiscal expansion leads to a cumulative increase in prices and a decline in the real money stock that raises interest rates until crowding out returns the economy to the initial equilibrium. We now establish exactly the same result in the dynamic framework.

Since we now focus on a fiscal expansion, we return to (9) above and rewrite the equation, moving the inflation rate to the left-hand side:

$$\pi = m - \frac{1}{\phi}(Y - Y_{-1}) + \frac{\sigma}{\phi}f \tag{10a}$$

This equation differs from (10) only in that it includes the current fiscal expansion as an extra term on the right-hand side of the equation. Given output and given the growth rate of money, a fiscal expansion ($f > 0$) will increase the rate of inflation or shift the aggregate demand schedule upward and to the right. Conversely, a current fiscal contraction ($f < 0$) shifts the aggregate demand schedule downward and to the left.

Suppose now that we have a given growth rate of money, m_0, and that the economy is in an initial steady state such that $Y = Y^*$ and $\pi = \pi^e = m$. Now a permanent fiscal expansion takes place, meaning that in the current period, f in (10a) is positive and for every period after, f is zero because government spending now remains constant at the higher level. In Figure 16-7 we show the fiscal expansion as the rightward shift of the aggregate demand schedule from DAD to DAD_1. In the short run, the economy moves to point E_1. Output unambiguously expands and inflation rises.

The subsequent adjustment process can be understood from (10a). Note that in the second period $f = 0$. Hence the aggregate demand schedule will shift downward to DAD_2. Because Y exceeds Y^*, DAD_2 lies above DAD. On the supply side, using (8) the aggregate supply curve shifts upward to SAS_2. The new equilibrium, in period 2,

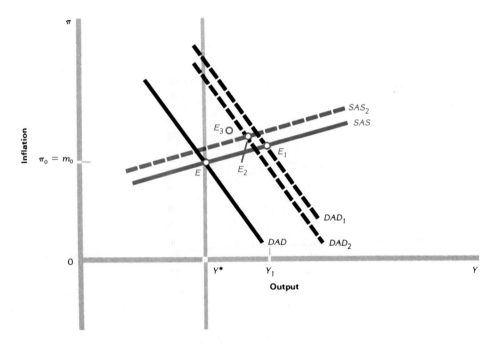

Figure 16-7   *Adjustment to a Sustained Fiscal Expansion*

Starting from the steady state at E, a fiscal expansion shifts aggregate demand to DAD_1 so that in the short run the economy moves to E_1. In the subsequent adjustment the aggregate demand schedule shifts back while the aggregate supply schedule shifts up and to the left as inflationary expectations increase. The economy thus suffers stagflation along a path shown by points E_2 and E_3.

already involves a return of output toward full employment. Inflation may be higher or lower than in period 1, depending on the relative shifts of the two schedules. This process continues over time, with the demand curve shifting inward and the aggregate supply curve shifting upward and to the left. The economy returns to full employment and then overshoots, as in Figure 16-6.

However, there is an important difference. In this case the growth rate of money is not changed and hence, in the long run, we return to the initial rate of inflation, $\pi = m_0$. The typical path of the adjustment to a sustained fiscal expansion would then look like that shown in Figure 16-8. In the transition period inflation will have been higher than the growth rate of money and, as a result, real balances decline, interest rates rise, and real spending declines. The fact that the economy returns to full-employment output, with government spending higher, means that private demand has been crowded out. Once again we note the stagflation syndrome. After the initial expansion, at point E_1 output is falling, but inflation is increasing. Thus fiscal expansion cannot *permanently* raise output above normal, just as increased monetary growth cannot. Of course, output will be above normal for a time, and that may be enough of a motive, at the right time, for a government to implement a fiscal expansion.

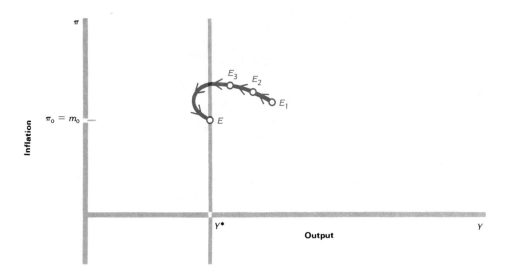

Figure 16-8   *The Smoothed Adjustment Path for a Sustained Fiscal Expansion*

The smoothed adjustment path shows that following an initial expansion to point E_1 inflation rises further, but output falls. In the long run, following a period of unemployment, output returns to full employment, Y°, and inflation to the level determined by the rate of money growth, m_0.

16-8 Alternative Strategies to Reduce Inflation

Suppose the inflation rate in the economy is 10 percent, and the government decides to fight high inflation, intending to try to get the economy down to inflation rates of around 2 to 3 percent. The key question for any government contemplating disinflation is how to disinflate as cheaply as possible — that is, with as small a recession as possible. In this section, we consider alternative strategies for disinflation. The basic method of disinflation should be clear from the previous section: It is to reduce the growth rate of aggregate demand, shifting the *DAD* curve downward. In the model we are using, that can be done by cutting back on money growth and, in the short run, by using fiscal policy. In this section we consider only monetary policy.

Gradualism

Figure 16-9 shows the choices. In panel (*a*), a policy of gradualism attempts a slow and steady return to low inflation. The gradualist policy in Figure 16-9*a* begins with a small reduction in the money growth rate that shifts the aggregate demand curve down from *DAD* to *DAD'*, moving the economy a little way along the short-run aggregate supply curve, *SAS*, from *E* to E_1. In response to the lower inflation at E_1, the short-run aggregate supply curve shifts downward to *SAS'*. A further small cut in the money

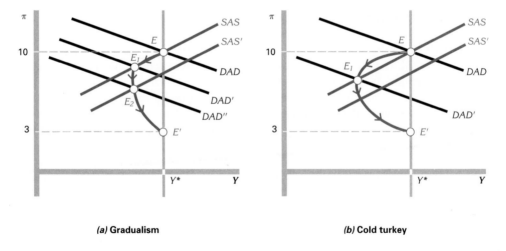

(a) Gradualism   **(b) Cold turkey**

Figure 16-9   *Alternative Disinflation Strategies*

In panel (*a*) policy reduces the inflation rate gradually from 10 to 3 percent, seeking to keep output from falling much below the potential level. In panel (*b*), by contrast, the decision is made to try to end the inflation rapidly, by starting with a large cut in the growth rate of money that produces much lower inflation, at the cost of a large recession.

growth moves the economy to E_2, the aggregate supply curve shifts down again, and the process continues.

Eventually output returns to its potential level, at point E', at a lower inflation rate. There is no massive recession during the adjustment process, although unemployment is above normal throughout.

Cold Turkey

Panel (*b*) of Figure 16-9 shows the alternative. *The cold turkey strategy tries to cut the inflation rate quickly.* The strategy starts with an immediate sharp cutback in money growth, shifting the aggregate demand curve from DAD to DAD' and moving the economy from E to E_1. There is a large recession, but because the aggregate supply curve is relatively flat, the reduction in inflation is small to begin with.

By creating a larger fall in the inflation rate than when gradualism is used, the cold turkey strategy causes the short-run supply curve to move down faster than it does in Figure 16-9*a*. The cold turkey strategy keeps up the pressure by holding the rate of money growth low. Eventually the rate of inflation falls enough that output and employment begin to grow again. The economy returns to point E' with full employment and a lower rate of inflation.

Gradualism Versus Cold Turkey

Figure 16-10 presents the gradualist and cold turkey strategies in an alternative form. In the gradualist strategy the growth rate of money is initially reduced only slightly, and the economy never strays very far from the natural rate of unemployment, but the inflation rate comes down only slowly. The cold turkey strategy, by contrast, starts with a massive cut in the growth rate of money and a large recession. The recession is much worse than it ever is in the gradualist strategy, but the reduction in inflation is more rapid.

Which strategy should be chosen? Is moderate unemployment with higher inflation preferable to high unemployment with lower inflation? We cannot answer that before discussing the costs of inflation and unemployment in Chapter 17. In 1981–1982 a policy closer to cold turkey than to gradualism was chosen.

Credibility

The cold turkey strategy has one major point in its favour. It is clear in the case of cold turkey that a decisive policy change has been made and that the policy has the firm aim of driving down the inflation rate. The gradualist strategy, which takes a long time to be implemented, is more likely to be abandoned if it seems to be producing more unemployment than expected, or if the policy-making team changes.

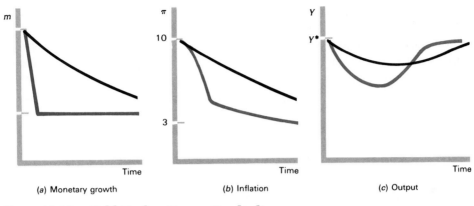

(a) Monetary growth   (b) Inflation   (c) Output

Figure 16-10 *Cold Turkey Versus Gradualism*

This is an alternative way of comparing the two strategies. Cold turkey (coloured curves) cuts the growth rate of money sharply, producing a massive but shorter recession. The gradualist strategy (black curves) produces much less unemployment, but also a much less rapid reduction in the inflation rate.

Thus people forming their expectations rationally will be more likely to believe policy has changed under the cold turkey strategy than under gradualism. A belief that policy has changed will by itself drive down the expected rate of inflation and for that reason cause the short-run Phillips curve to shift down. A credible policy is one that the public believes will be kept up and will succeed. The cold turkey policy gets a *credibility bonus* that gradualism does not.

Credibility and Rapid Deflation

Throughout the period of disinflation, starting with the U.S. change in policy in October 1979, there was strong emphasis on the credibility of policy. Some proponents of rational expectations even believed that if policy could only be made credible, it would be possible to disinflate practically without causing any recession at all.

The argument went like this. The expectations-augmented aggregate supply curve, Equation (5), is

$$\pi = \pi^e + \lambda(Y - Y^\circ) \tag{5}$$

If the policy is credible, people immediately adjust their expectations of inflation to the new policy, with its lower rate of growth of money. Thus the short-run aggregate supply curve will move down immediately when the new policy is announced. Accordingly, it is possible to move immediately from point E in Figure 16-9 to E'. In brief, the argument is that if policy is credible and if expectations are rational, the economy can move to a new long-run equilibrium immediately when there is a change in policy.

The experience of the United States and Canada in the early 1980s, and even more the experience of Britain in the same period when the Thatcher government was pursuing a resolute anti-inflationary policy that led to a 13 percent unemployment rate, casts doubt on this optimistic scenario. The reason the extreme credibility–rational expectations argument does not work is that it is not enough for people to believe a new policy will reduce the inflation rate. The expectations must also be incorporated into wage and other long-term contracts. The economy has, at any time, an overhang of past contracts embodying past expectations, as the contract renegotiations take time. Thus, because of inflationary inertia, a rapid return to lower inflation in economies experiencing inflation rates in the 10 to 20 percent range is unlikely.

It is easiest to change the inflation rate when there are no long-term contracts in the economy. There will be few contracts of that kind if inflation is high and variable, for instance in a hyperinflation. Under such conditions no one will want to sign agreements in nominal terms because they will be gambling too much on the future behaviour of the price level. Long-term contracts disappear, and wages and prices are frequently reset. A credible policy will have rapid effects, but such rapid success cannot be expected in an economy where the structure of contracts has not yet been destroyed by extreme inflation.

It remains true, though, that whatever the structure of contracts, the more credible a policy that aims to disinflate the economy is, the more successful that policy will be.[12]

16-9 Summary

1. The aggregate supply and demand curves introduced in this chapter differ from those of Chapter 8 by showing the relationship between output and the inflation rate rather than output and the price level.

2. The aggregate supply curve is modified further to include expected inflation. Wages increase more rapidly when inflation is expected, thus shifting the aggregate supply curve upward. Expected inflation enters prices which are changed as new wage terms are set. Thus the process through which a change in the expected inflation rate works its way into the aggregate supply curve may be quite slow. For this reason, the inflation process is often said to display inflationary inertia.

3. The short-run aggregate supply curve with a constant expected rate of inflation has a small, positive slope — in fact, the curve is nearly flat — because in the short run changes in output do not cause large changes in prices. In the short run there is a tradeoff between inflation and output. The long-run aggregate sup-

---

[12] The credibility issue is treated in several interesting papers in "Anti-inflation Policies and the Problem of Credibility," *American Economic Review*, Papers and Proceedings, May 1982.

ply curve, with the actual and expected inflation rates equal, is vertical: There is no long-run tradeoff between inflation and output.

4. Under adaptive expectations, expected inflation is based on the recent behaviour of the inflation rate. For most of the chapter we make the particular adaptive expectations assumption that the expected inflation rate is equal to last period's inflation rate. Under rational expectations, there is no simple formula for determining expectations. Rather, people are assumed to form expectations using all the information that is available about the determinants of the inflation rate. Under adaptive expectations, a change in policy would not affect expectations until the actual inflation rate is affected; under rational expectations, people, knowing that policy will change, will adjust their expectations immediately.

5. The dynamic aggregate demand curve is a negatively sloped relationship between the inflation rate and the level of output. Its position is determined by the growth rate of money and by last period's level of output. The basic relationship follows from the link between aggregate demand and real balances: The more rapidly real balances are growing, the more rapidly aggregate demand is increasing. The dynamic aggregate demand curve is also shifted by changes in the aggregate demand curve and by fiscal policy changes.

6. The inflation rate and level of output are determined by the intersection of the aggregate supply and demand curves. In the short run, changes in the growth rate of money affect both output and inflation. In the long run, a change in the growth rate of money affects only the inflation rate.

7. During the process of adjustment to a change in the growth rate of money, assuming adaptive expectations, there are periods of stagflation during which inflation increases while output falls. Typically, there is also overshooting of the new inflation rate; that is, on average, during the adjustment process, the increase in the inflation rate exceeds the increase in the growth rate of money.

8. The adjustment pattern is much more rapid under rational expectations. If the change in the growth rate of money is anticipated, then only the inflation rate changes when the money growth rate changes. If the change in monetary policy is unexpected, it does affect both the level of output and the inflation rate in the short run, but output returns to its potential level as soon as the new policy is understood.

9. There are two basic strategies to reduce the inflation rate. The gradualist strategy aims to bring the inflation rate down slowly, thereby avoiding any large recession. The cold turkey strategy cuts the growth rate of money by a large amount up front, thereby trying to reduce inflation quickly at the cost of a larger recession. The cold turkey strategy may gain from a credibility bonus in that the government reduces expected inflation more rapidly by demonstrating its willingness to pay the price of disinflation.

Key Terms

Expectations-augmented aggregate supply curve
Short-run aggregate supply curve
Long-run aggregate supply curve
Adaptive expectations
Rational expectations
Dynamic aggregate demand curve

Stagflation
Overshooting
Inflationary inertia
Gradualism
Cold turkey
Credibility

Problems

1. Explain why the expected rate of inflation affects the position of the expectations-augmented aggregate supply curve.

2. **(a)** Define the long-run aggregate supply curve.
    (b) Explain why the expectations-augmented long-run supply curve is vertical.
    (c) Does the economy ever reach the long run?

3. **(a)** In Figures 16-5 and 16-6 we show how the economy reaches a higher rate of inflation. Starting at a steady state with 10 percent inflation, show how inflation would shift back to 4 percent if the growth rate of money were reduced immediately to 4 percent.
    (b) Comment on whether inflation displays inertia during this adjustment process.

4. Consider the adjustment to a *transitory* fiscal expansion. For one period only, government spending increases. In the next period, it falls back to the initial level. Use Equations (8) and (10a) to trace the adjustment path of inflation and of output. (*Note:* This is different from the analysis of Section 16-7. Here we have $f > 0$ in period 1 and $f < 0$ in period 2.)

5. Using the assumptions $\pi^e = \pi_{-1}$, $\lambda = 0.4$, and $\phi = 0.5$, and starting from a steady state with money growth equal to the inflation rate equal to 4 percent, calculate the inflation rate and output in the first three periods following an increase in the growth rate of money to 8 percent.

6. Suppose that in Problem 5, expectations are rational instead of adaptive.
    (a) Suppose the change in money growth is announced before it happens, and everyone believes it will take place. What happens to inflation and output?
    (b) Suppose that money growth is unexpectedly increased from 4 percent to 8 percent in period 1, but that people believe from period 2 on that money growth will be 8 percent. Calculate the inflation rate in period 1 and in subsequent periods.

7. Consider an economy that experiences an adverse supply shock. We can model this by introducing into Equation (8) a one-time shock, which we denote by x:

$$\pi = \pi_{-1} + \lambda(Y - Y^*) + x$$

The term x is positive during the supply shock. Show the adjustment process to such a disturbance.

8. The economy finds itself in a recession as a result of an adverse supply shock. Show that either a fiscal expansion or increased monetary growth can speed the return of the economy to full employment.

9. Suppose that a new policy mix of fiscal expansion and a permanent reduction in money growth goes into effect.
    (a) What are the long-run effects on output and inflation?
    (b) How does the fiscal expansion affect the adjustment relative to the one you discussed in answering Problem 3?

Appendix   Dynamic Aggregate Demand

In the text we use the simplified dynamic aggregate demand curve

$$Y = Y_{-1} + \phi(m - \pi) + \sigma f \tag{A1}$$

In (A1), m is the growth rate of the nominal money stock. In this appendix we derive the dynamic aggregate demand curve carefully from the *IS-LM* model of aggregate demand and show exactly where (A1) simplifies matters.

To derive the aggregate demand curve, we return to the goods market equilibrium condition

$$Y = \overline{\alpha}(\overline{A} - br) \tag{A2}$$

where $\overline{A}$ denotes autonomous spending, $\overline{\alpha}$ is the multiplier, and r denotes the *real* rate of interest. Recall that investment demand is determined by the *real* and not the nominal interest rate.

Recognizing that the real interest rate is equal to the nominal interest rate, i, minus the expected rate of inflation, we rewrite (A2) as

$$Y = \overline{\alpha}(\overline{A} - bi + b\pi^e) \tag{A3}$$

In this form we recognize that the goods market equilibrium depends on both the nominal interest rate *and* the expected inflation rate. Given the nominal interest rate, an increase in the expected rate of inflation increases aggregate demand — because the increase implies a lower real interest rate and larger investment demand.

Now we bring in the asset markets by rewriting the condition that the supply of real balances is equal to the demand. Putting the interest rate on the left-hand side, as we did in Equation (11) of Chapter 4, we obtain

$$i = \frac{1}{h}\left(kY - \frac{M}{P}\right) \tag{A4}$$

Substituting (A4) into (A3), we find that the level of output at which both the goods and assets markets are in equilibrium can be written as

$$Y = \bar{\alpha}\left[\bar{A} - \frac{b}{h}\left(kY - \frac{M}{P}\right) + b\pi^e\right] \qquad \text{or}$$

$$Y = \gamma\left(\bar{A} + \frac{b}{h}\frac{M}{P} + b\pi^e\right) \tag{A5}$$

where $\gamma = \bar{\alpha}/[1 + (\bar{\alpha}bk/h)]$.

The aggregate demand curve (A5) shows that the *level* of aggregate demand is determined by autonomous demand (including fiscal policy), real balances, and the expected inflation rate. An increase in any of these three factors will increase the level of aggregate demand. Note that the only difference between the aggregate demand curve here and in the previous chapters is that we are now including the expected inflation rate — and that it enters because, given the nominal interest rate, a higher expected rate of inflation means a lower real interest rate.

It follows that the *change* in aggregate demand is determined by *changes* in autonomous demand, real balances, and the expected inflation rate. Assuming that the only change in autonomous demand comes from fiscal policy, we write

$$\Delta Y = \sigma f + \phi(m - \pi) + \eta(\Delta\pi^e) \tag{A6}$$

where Δ indicates the change in a variable and f is the *change* in fiscal policy.

As described in the text, the term $(m - \pi)$ is the change in real balances, the difference between the growth rate of money and the rate of inflation: When money is growing faster than prices, real balances are increasing, and when money is growing more slowly than prices, real balances are decreasing.

Rewriting (A6) by recognizing that $\Delta Y = Y - Y_{-1}$,

$$Y = Y_{-1} + \sigma f + \phi(m - \pi) + \eta(\Delta\pi^e) \tag{A7}$$

Equation (A7) is the complete aggregate demand relationship between the level of output and the inflation rate. Given last period's income, expectations, the change in fiscal policy, and the growth rate of money, higher inflation rates imply lower aggregate demand.

In the text, we simplify by omitting the change in expected inflation, $\Delta\pi^e$.

CHAPTER 17 *Inflation and Unemployment*

During the recessions of 1981–1982 and 1990–1991, the Canadian economy experienced the highest unemployment rate since the great depression. More than one person in ten in the labour force was unemployed. At the same time there were sharp declines in the rate of inflation, and these episodes provided a clear example of the short-run tradeoff between inflation and unemployment. In this chapter we discuss this tradeoff and the cost–benefit analysis that policy makers must bear in mind when designing stabilization policy.

We start with a discussion of unemployment and develop the concept of the natural rate of unemployment. We then consider the costs of unemployment and inflation and conclude the chapter with a discussion of alternative polices for reducing the inflation rate.

17-1 The Anatomy of Unemployment

An unemployed person is defined as one who is out of work and who (1) has actively looked for work during the previous four weeks, or (2) is waiting to be recalled to a job after having been laid off, or (3) is waiting to report to a new job within four weeks.[1]

---

[1] For a detailed description of the definitions used and the data collection procedures, see notes at the end of Statistics Canada, 71-001.

Table 17-1 shows a breakdown by age and sex of unemployment for two relatively prosperous years when the overall rate was below 8 percent and two recession years when the rate exceeded 10 percent. Table 17-2 and Figure 17-1 show a breakdown by region.

The tables reveal large differences in unemployment rates among groups. For instance, unemployment for the age group 15–24 is consistently higher and rises more sharply in the recessions. The Atlantic provinces have the highest regional rate, while the lowest rates have been experienced in the prairie provinces and Ontario.

For a year such as 1979, when unemployment was at a cyclical low point, the unemployment rate can be interpreted roughly as a measure of *structural unemployment*.[2] Structural unemployment is the unemployment that exists when the economy is at full employment. Structural unemployment corresponds to the *natural rate of unemployment*. Structural unemployment results from the structure of the labour market — that is, from the nature of jobs in the economy and from the labour-force participation patterns of workers. We discuss the determinants of structural unemployment in more detail below when we examine the natural rate of unemployment.

Table 17-1   *Unemployment Rates by Age and Sex*

	1979	1983	1989	1991
Age 15–24	12.9	19.8	11.3	16.5
Men, 25 and over	4.5	9.2	6.1	9.0
Women, 25 and over	7.0	9.6	7.3	9.0
Total	7.4	11.8	7.5	10.5

Source: Bank of Canada Review.

Table 17-2   *Unemployment Rates by Region*

	1979	1983	1989	1991
Atlantic provinces	11.6	15.1	12.3	14.0
Quebec	9.6	13.9	9.3	12.0
Ontario	6.5	10.3	5.1	9.5
Prairie provinces	4.3	9.6	7.3	8.0
British Columbia	7.6	13.8	9.1	10.0

Source: Bank of Canada Review.

[2] In 1979, the prairie provinces, particularly Alberta, were still in the midst of an oil and gas boom and thus had the lowest unemployment rates. By 1984, with the softening of resource markets, Ontario replaced the prairie provinces as the region with the lowest unemployment rate. Thus there was a shift in the regional distribution of structural unemployment.

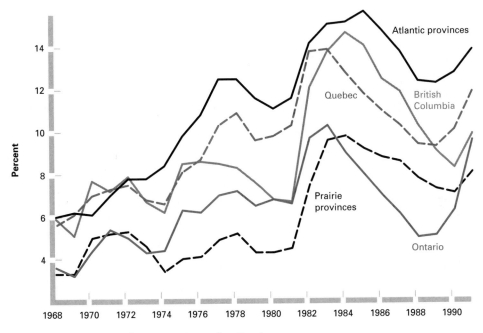

Figure 17-1 *Unemployment Rates by Region*

(*Source:* Adapted from *Bank of Canada Review*)

Cyclical unemployment is unemployment in excess of structural unemployment; it occurs when output is below its full-employment level.

Characteristics of Canadian Unemployment[3]

The anatomy of unemployment is built around three central facts of unemployment behaviour:

1. There are substantial flows of individuals in and out of unemployment each month, and most people who become unemployed in any given month remain unemployed for only a short time.

---

[3] For a detailed discussion of the labour market in Canada, see Surendra Gera, ed., *Canadian Unemployment: Lessons from the 80s and Challenges for the 90s* (Ottawa: Economic Council of Canada, 1991); and W.C. Riddell, *Work and Pay: The Canadian Labour Market*, Research Study No. 17, Royal Commission on the Economic Union and Development Prospects for Canada (Toronto: University of Toronto Press, 1985).

2. Much of the unemployment is accounted for by people who will be unemployed for quite a long time.

3. There is considerable variation of unemployment rates across different regions and groups in the labour force.

The first and second facts may seem contradictory. A numerical example should make it clear that there is no necessary contradiction. Suppose that the labour force consists of 100 people, and that five people become unemployed each month. Suppose that four of those people are unemployed for precisely one month, and one person will be unemployed for six months. Suppose also that the economy is in a steady state, so that this situation has repeated itself every month for years.

We ask first how many people are unemployed at any one time, say September 30. There will be five people who became unemployed September 1, one person who became unemployed August 1 (and who has been unemployed for two months), and so on, back to the person who became unemployed April 1, and whose six months of unemployment will end the next day, on October 1. In total, there will be ten people unemployed. So the unemployment rate is 10 percent. Of the ten, six will suffer a six-month spell of unemployment before they again become employed. This is consistent with the second fact, but remember that we started with five people becoming unemployed each month, four of whom remain unemployed for only a month. That is consistent with the first fact, that most people who become unemployed within a given month remain so for only a short time. We shall return to this example later in this section.

The third fact, variation of unemployment rates across different groups or regions in the labour force, can be examined using the relationship between the overall unemployment rate, u, and the unemployment rates, u_i, of groups within the labour force. The overall rate is a weighted average of the unemployment rates of the groups:

$$u = w_1 u_1 + w_2 u_2 + \ldots w_n u_n \tag{1}$$

The weights, w_i, are the fraction of the labour force that falls within the specific group, say, teenagers.

Equation (1) makes it clear that the overall unemployment rate may conceal the dramatic differences in unemployment rates among regions or groups alluded to in Fact 3. For instance, in 1991, the aggregate unemployment rate was 10.5 percent. For the age group 15–24 the rate was 16.5 percent, while for the group aged 25 and over it was 9.0 percent. In terms of Equation (1), we have

$$10.5\% = (.2)\ 16.5\% + (.8)\ 9.0\%$$

where the shares of the two groups in the labour force are 20 percent and 80 percent respectively.

We now turn to a more detailed examination of the three central facts about the anatomy of unemployment.

Flows In and Out of Unemployment

Figure 17-2 shows how people enter and leave the *unemployment pool*. A person may become unemployed for one of four reasons:

1. The person may be a new entrant into the labour force (looking for work for the first time) or a reentrant (returning to the labour force after not having looked for work for more than four weeks).

2. A person may leave a job in order to look for other employment and be counted as unemployed while searching.

3. The person may be laid off. A *layoff* means that the worker was not fired but will return to the old job if demand for the firm's product recovers. A firm will typically adjust to a decline in product demand by laying off some labour. A firm may also rotate layoffs among its labour force so that the individual laid-off worker may expect a recall even before product demand has fully recovered.

4. A worker may lose a job to which there is no chance of returning, either because the worker was fired or because the firm closed down.

These sources of inflow into the pool of unemployment have a counterpart in the outflow from the unemployment pool. There are essentially three ways of moving out of the pool of unemployment:

1. A person may be hired into a new job.

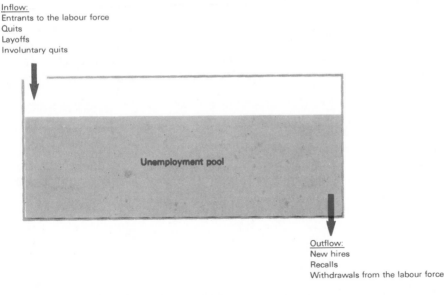

Inflow:
Entrants to the labour force
Quits
Layoffs
Involuntary quits

Unemployment pool

Outflow:
New hires
Recalls
Withdrawals from the labour force

Figure 17-2 *Flows In and Out of the Unemployment Pool*

2.   Someone laid off may be recalled.

3.   An unemployed person may stop looking for a job and thus, by definition, leave the labour force. Such a person may plan to look for a job again soon.

Table 17-3 shows the breakdown of the average flow into unemployment. Notice that a substantial fraction is accounted for by reentrants into the labour force. There is also a substantial flow from the unemployment pool out of the labour force. In June 1988, there were about 550,000 persons not in the labour force who had lost their jobs or had been laid off. This suggests that the distinction between being unemployed and being out of the labour force is not a very sharp one, and that individuals move quite easily in both directions — between being unemployed (meaning essentially that they looked for a job in the last four weeks) and not employed (out of the labour force).

Consideration of the *duration* of spells of unemployment provides an alternative way of looking at flows in and out of unemployment. The duration of unemployment is the length of time a person remains unemployed. Given the unemployment rate, the shorter the average duration of unemployment, the larger the flows. For instance, in the example at the beginning of this section we had a 10 percent unemployment rate with five people becoming becoming unemployed each month. We could also have a 10 percent unemployment rate if ten people became unemployed each month and each one remained unemployed for exactly one month. In the earlier example, the average duration is longer than a month, since four out of five spells end in a month, but one out of five lasts six months. (The average duration is thus two months.) The shorter the average duration, the larger the flows of labour through the unemployment pool, given the overall unemployment rate.

Table 17-4 shows the distribution of unemployment by duration in 1989 and 1991. In the recession year of 1991, about half of those surveyed had been unemployed for less than 14 weeks, but one-quarter had been unemployed for more than six months. Even in the relatively prosperous year 1989, one-sixth had been unemployed for more than six months. These data establish that despite the substantial flows in and out of

Table 17-3   *Flows Into Unemployment*

	1982–1983	1988–1989
	(percent of labour force)	
Job losers	6.8	4.0
Job leavers	1.6	1.6
New entrants	.5	.3
Reentrants	2.5	1.9
	11.4	7.8

Source: Surendra Gera and Kathryn McMullen, "Unemployment in Canada: Issues, Findings, and Implications," in Surendra Gera, *op. cit.*, p. 9.

Table 17-4   *Duration of Unemployment*

| | Number (thousands) | |
Number of weeks	1989	1991
1–4	306	341
5–13	333	415
14–26	174	271
27–52	110	212
53 and over	61	129
Total	984	1368
Average duration	16.4	20.4

Note: Duration here refers to duration up to the end of the week of the survey rather than completed spells of unemployment. Data are for the month of December.

Source: Statistics Canada, 71-001.

unemployment, much of aggregate unemployment is accounted for by people who remain unemployed for a substantial time. Thus, if one believes that unemployment is a more serious problem when it affects only a few people intensely, rather than many people a little, these data suggest that unemployment is a more severe problem than the aggregate unemployment rate indicates.

17-2 The Natural Rate of Unemployment

In this section, we discuss the determinants of the natural rate of unemployment and then examine estimates of changes in the natural rate since the 1960s.

Figure 17-2 points to the factors causing the unemployment rate to change. Increases in the rate of entry to the labour force, quits, layoffs, or other job losses cause the unemployment rate to rise. Increases in hiring, recalls, or withdrawals from the labour force cause the unemployment rate to fall. Each of these factors is in part determined by economic variables, such as the level of aggregate demand and the actual and expected real wage rate. When aggregate demand rises (at a given real wage), firms increase their hiring. When aggregate demand falls, firms lay off workers. Thus there is an immediate link between the factors emphasized in Figure 17-2 and aggregate demand. However, it should be noted that the relationship between aggregate demand and the variables affecting the rate of unemployment is not unambiguous. For instance, an increase in the demand for labour increases quits at the same time as it reduces layoffs. A person thinking of leaving one job to search for another would be more likely to quit when the job market is good and demand is high than when there is heavy unemployment and the prospects of finding a good job quickly are low.

When the unemployment rate is constant, flows in and out of unemployment just balance each other. These flows can match at any level of unemployment. The *natural rate of unemployment*, however, is that rate of unemployment at which flows in and out of unemployment just balance,[4] *and* at which expectations of firms and workers as to the behaviour of prices and wages are correct. As we saw in Chapter 16, at rates of unemployment below this equilibrium level, the rate of inflation increases and for this reason, the natural rate of unemployment is sometimes referred to as the *non-accelerating inflation rate of unemployment (NAIRU)*.

The determinants of the natural rate of unemployment can be thought of in terms of the duration and frequency of unemployment. The *duration* of unemployment is the average length of time a person remains unemployed. The duration depends on (1) the organization of the labour market, in regard to the presence or absence of employment agencies, youth employment services, etc.; (2) the demographic makeup of the labour force; (3) the ability and desire of the unemployed to keep looking for better jobs; and (4) the availability and types of jobs. If all jobs are the same, an unemployed person will take the first one offered. If some jobs are better than others, it is worthwhile searching and waiting for a good one. If it is very expensive to remain unemployed — say, because there are no unemployment benefits — an unemployed person is more likely to accept a job offer than to continue looking for a better job. If unemployment benefits are high, then it may be worthwhile for the unemployed person to continue looking for a better job rather than to accept a poor job when one is offered.

The behaviour of workers who have been laid off is also important when considering the duration of unemployment. Typically, a worker who has been laid off returns to the original job and does not search for another job. The reason is quite simple: Once a worker has been with a firm for a long time, he or she has special expertise in the way that firm works which makes the worker valuable to that firm but is not of great benefit to another employer. In addition, he or she may have built up seniority rights, including a pension. That means that such an individual could not expect to find as good a job if he or she searched for a new one. The best course of action may be to wait to be recalled.

Frequency of Unemployment

The *frequency of unemployment* is the average number of times, per period, that workers become unemployed. There are two basic determinants of the frequency of unemployment. The first is the variability of the demand for labour across different firms in the economy. The second is the rate at which new workers enter the labour

---

[4] We should recognize that when the labour force is growing and the unemployment rate is constant, the pool of unemployed grows over time. For example, with a labour force of 8 million and 5 percent unemployment, total unemployment is 400 000 people. With a labour force of 10 million and 4.5 percent unemployment, there are 450 000 unemployed, and the unemployment pool has grown by 50 000 people.

force: The more rapidly new workers enter the labour force, the faster the growth rate of the labour force and the higher the natural rate of unemployment. Even when aggregate demand is constant, some firms are growing and some are shrinking. The shrinking firms lose labour and the growing firms hire more labour. The greater this variability of the demand for labour across different firms, the higher the unemployment rate. Further, the variability of aggregate demand itself will affect the variability of the demand for labour.

The four factors affecting duration and the two factors affecting frequency of unemployment are the basic determinants of the natural rate of unemployment.

You should note that the factors determining the level of the natural rate of unemployment are not immutable. The structure of the labour market and the labour force can change. The willingness of workers to remain unemployed while looking for, or waiting for, a new job can change. The variability of the demand for labour by different firms can shift. As Edmund Phelps has noted, the natural rate is not "an intertemporal constant, something like the speed of light, independent of everything under the sun."[5] Indeed, the natural rate is difficult to measure, and estimates of it have changed over the last few years from below 5 percent in the 1960s to above 7 percent in the early 1980s.

Estimates of the Natural Rate of Unemployment

Estimates of the natural rate of unemployment typically try to adjust for changes in the composition of the labour force, and perhaps for changes in the natural rate of unemployment of the various groups in the labour force. We can write an equation very similar to Equation (1) for the natural rate, u:

$$\bar{u} = w_1\bar{u}_1 + w_2\bar{u}_2 + \ldots + w_n\bar{u}_n \tag{2}$$

Equation (2) says that the natural rate is the weighted average of the natural rates of unemployment of the subgroups in the labour force.

Table 17-5 shows the composition of the labour force by age and sex, and column (2) of Table 17-6 shows an estimate of the natural rate of unemployment based on the assumption that the natural rates for each group are constant and equal to the observed average unemployment rates for the period 1971–1975.[6] The behaviour of this estimate of the natural rate is dominated by the proportion of younger persons in the labour force. This group has consistently experienced higher unemployment, and, as a result, the estimated natural rate of unemployment rises from 1966 to 1975. Similarly, the reduction in the proportion of younger persons in the 1980s is reflected in a fall in the natural rate.

---

[5] See E. Phelps, "Economic Policy and Unemployment in the Sixties," *Public Interest*, Winter 1974.

[6] It is not unreasonable to suppose that the Canadian economy was on average at full employment over this period, in contrast to the late 1960s when there was excess demand.

Table 17-5 *The Changing Structure of the Labour Force and Unemployment, 1966–1990*

| | Age Group 25 and Over | | Age Group | |
	Males	Females	15–24	Total
Proportion of Labour Force				
1966	55.0	20.8	24.2	100.0
1970	52.2	22.4	25.4	100.0
1975	48.2	24.7	27.1	100.0
1980	45.7	27.8	26.5	100.0
1985	45.5	31.9	22.6	100.0
1990	45.4	35.7	18.9	100.0
Participation Rates				
1966	84.9	31.2	56.3	57.3
1970	83.3	34.5	55.9	57.8
1975	81.9	40.0	62.9	61.1
1980	80.7	46.4	67.2	64.1
1985	78.5	51.8	67.4	65.3
1990	77.1	56.7	68.9	67.0
Average Unemployment Rate				
1966–70	3.3	3.4	7.4	4.3
1971–75	3.9	5.5	10.5	6.0
1976–80	4.7	7.0	13.6	7.7
1981–85	7.9	8.8	17.3	10.4
1986–90	6.7	7.8	13.0	8.3

Source: Statistics Canada, 71-201.

The proportion of women in the labour force has grown steadily over the past 25 years as a result of growth in the female *participation rate* (the fraction of women who are in the labour force). Since the unemployment rate for females was higher than the rate for males during the 1970s and 1980s, the increase in the participation rate for this group has increased the overall natural rate.

A comparison of the estimated natural rate in column (2) of Table 17-6 with the actual rate in column (1) suggests that changes in age and sex alone cannot account for the behaviour over time of the natural rate. The actual unemployment rate shows an upward trend over the period 1966–1990, while the natural rate varies over a narrow range. At times there is a very large gap between the two. Column (3) shows an

Table 17-6 *The Actual and Estimated Natural Rates of Unemployment,*
1966–1990

| | Actual | Estimated Natural Rates | |
	(1)	(2)	(3)
1966	3.4	5.8	5.8
1970	5.7	5.9	6.6
1975	6.9	6.1	7.5
1980	7.5	6.1	7.7
1985	10.5	5.9	6.4
1990	8.1	5.7	

Sources: (1) Statistics Canada, 71-201. (2) Adjusted for age and sex using data in Table 17-5. (3) Pierre Fortin, "How 'Natural' Is Canada's High Unemployment Rate?" *European Economic Review*, 1989.

alternative measure prepared by Pierre Fortin of the University of Quebec at Montreal. It takes account of additional factors and consequently shows more variation over time.[7]

Unemployment Benefits

An important variable taken into account in Fortin's estimate of the natural rate of unemployment is the scope of unemployment insurance benefits. The effect of such programs on the *measured* rate of unemployment depends on the replacement ratio — that is, the ratio of after-tax income while unemployed to after-tax income while employed. There are three channels of influence.

First, the presence of unemployment benefits allows longer job search. The higher the replacement ratio, the less urgent the need to take a job. Second, the measured unemployment rate may reflect *reporting effects*. To collect unemployment benefits people have to be "in the labour force," looking for work even if they do not really want a job. They therefore get counted as unemployed. In the absence of unemployment benefits, some people might not be in the labour force, and hence participation and unemployment rates would be lower.

The third channel is *employment stability*. With unemployment insurance, the consequences of being in and out of jobs are less severe, and accordingly, workers and firms do not find it as much in their interest to create highly stable employment. Further, there is an incentive favouring seasonal jobs for which layoffs in the off-season are not a risk but a virtual certainty, so that the unemployment insurance system becomes a subsidy to seasonal industries.

---

[7] Other attempts to measure the natural rate are given in Robert Ford and David Rose, "Estimates of the NAIRU Using an Extended Okun's Law," Bank of Canada Working Paper, 1989; and Andrew Burns, "The Natural Rate of Unemployment: Canada and the Provinces," in Surendra Gera, *op. cit.*

The substantial liberalization of the benefits payable to the unemployed under Canada's *Unemployment Insurance Act* in the early 1970s provides an interesting case study of these effects. In general there is substantial evidence that the participation rate and the average duration of unemployment were increased.[8] Thus there seems to be little doubt that unemployment compensation does add to the natural rate of unemployment. This does not imply, though, that unemployment compensation should be abolished. Individuals need time to do some searching if the economy is to allocate people efficiently among jobs. It would not make sense to put a skilled worker in an unskilled job the moment she loses her previous job, just because the worker cannot afford to search. Thus, even from the viewpoint of economic efficiency, zero is not the ideal level of unemployment benefits. Beyond that, society may be willing to give up some efficiency so that the unemployed can maintain a minimal standard of living. What is appropriate is a scheme that will create less incentive for firms to lay off labour while at the same time ensuring that the unemployed are not exposed to economic distress. This is obviously difficult to carry off.

17-3 The Costs of Unemployment

The costs of unemployment are so obvious that this section might seem superfluous. Society on the whole loses from unemployment because total output is below its potential level. The unemployed suffer as individuals, both from their income loss while unemployed and from the low level of self-esteem that long periods of unemployment cause.[9] Nevertheless, it is worthwhile looking more closely at the issues connected with the costs of unemployment and the potential benefits from reducing unemployment. We distinguish between cyclical unemployment, associated with short-run deviations of the unemployment rate from the natural rate, and "permanent" or structural unemployment that exists at the natural rate.

Cyclical Unemployment

The fundamental cost of cyclical unemployment is the short-run loss of output.[10] Are there any other costs of unemployment — or, for that matter, offsetting benefits? It

---

[8] See Jean-Michel Cousineau, "Unemployment Insurance and Labour Market Adjustments," in F. Vaillancourt, *Income Distribution and Economic Security in Canada*, Research Study No. 1, Royal Commission on the Economic Union and Development Prospects for Canada (Toronto: University of Toronto Press, 1985).

[9] See Robert J. Gordon, "The Welfare Cost of Higher Unemployment," *Brookings Papers on Economic Activity* 1 (Washington, D.C.: The Brookings Institution, 1973).

[10] This loss will be compounded if current cyclical unemployment has hysteresis effects — that is, if it causes a permanent increase in the natural rate of unemployment. See Pierre Fortin, "Innis Lecture: The Phillips Curve, Macroeconomic Policy, and the Welfare of Canadians," *Canadian Journal of Economics*, November 1991. See also Barry Cozier and Gordon Wilkinson, "Some Evidence on Hysteresis and the Costs of Disinflation in Canada," Bank of Canada Technical Report No. 55, 1991.

is possible to imagine offsetting benefits. We do not discuss here the benefit arising from a temporary reduction in the inflation rate accompanying a temporary increase in unemployment but, rather, focus on the costs of unemployment taken by itself. A possible offsetting benefit occurs because the unemployed are not working and have more leisure. However, the value that can be placed on that leisure is small. In the first place, much of it is unwanted leisure.

Second, there is a fairly subtle issue that we shall have to explore. If a person were free to set his or her hours of work, he or she would work up to the point at which the individual judged the marginal value of leisure to be equal to the marginal return from working an extra hour. We would then be able to conclude that if the work day were slightly reduced, the overall loss would be extremely small. The person acquires extra leisure from working less, at the cost of having less income, but he or she was previously at the point where the marginal value of leisure was equal to the after-tax marginal wage. Thus the benefit of the increased leisure almost exactly offsets the private loss of income. However, the net marginal wage is less than the value of the marginal product of an employed person to the economy. The major reason is that society taxes the income of the employed person, so that society as a whole takes a share of the marginal product of the employed person. When the employed person in our example stops working, he or she loses only the *net*-of-tax wage he or she has been receiving, but society also loses the taxes this person has been paying. The unemployed person values leisure at the net of tax wage, and that value is smaller than the value of his or her marginal product for society as a whole. Therefore, the value of the increased leisure provides only a partial offset to the cost of cyclical unemployment.

Note that we do not count both the individual's personal loss of income and the forgone output as part of the cost of unemployment. The reason is that the forgone output implicitly includes the individual's own loss of income — it estimates the total loss of output to the economy as a whole as a result of the reduction of employment. That loss could in principle be distributed across different people in the economy in many different ways. For instance, one could imagine that the unemployed person continues to receive benefit payments totalling close to his or her previous income while employed, with the benefit payments financed through taxes on working individuals. In that case, the unemployed person would not suffer an income loss from being unemployed, but society would still lose from the reduction in total output available.

However, the effects of an increase in unemployment are, in fact, borne heavily by the unemployed themselves. There is thus an extra cost to society of unemployment that is very difficult to quantify. The cost arises from the uneven distribution of the burden of unemployment across the population. Unemployment tends to be concentrated among the poor, and that makes the distributional aspect of unemployment a serious matter. It is not one that we can easily quantify, but it should not be overlooked. Further, there are many reports of the adverse psychic effects of unemployment that, again, are not easy to quantify but should not be ignored.[11]

---

[11] For a detailed discussion of the issues raised here, see R.G. Lipsey, ed., *Zero Inflation: The Goal of Price Stability* (Toronto: C.D. Howe Institute, 1990).

"Structural" Unemployment

The benefits of reducing the natural rate of unemployment are more difficult to estimate than the costs of cyclical unemployment. We cannot use the short-run output–
employment relationship since the increase in output associated with cyclical changes
in unemployment results in part from the fact that the labour put back to work in the
short run is able to use capital that had not been fully utilized when unemployment
was high. However, in the long run, which is relevant when considering a reduction
in the natural rate of unemployment, it would be necessary to invest to provide for
the capital with which the newly employed would work.

The available estimates of the social benefits of a reduction in long-run unemployment cannot be narrowed down to very solid numbers. Even more difficult is the
estimate of an "optimal" long-run unemployment rate. Here we ask the question
whether any — and, if so, how much — unemployment is desirable in the long run.
A first guess at the answer to that question is that all unemployment is wasteful, since
the unemployed labour could usefully be employed. However, that answer is not right.
Those people who are unemployed in order to look for a better job are performing a
valuable service not only for themselves. They are also performing a service for society
by attempting to put themselves into a position in which they earn the most and are
the most valuable.

Because the composition of demand shifts over time, we can expect always to have
some firms expanding and some contracting. This is true even with a stable level of
aggregate demand. Those who lose their jobs will be unemployed, and they benefit
both society and themselves by not taking the very first job that comes along, but
rather searching for the optimal employment. Accordingly, we can conclude that some
unemployment is a good thing in an economy in which the composition of demand
changes over time. It is one thing to recognize this and quite another to pin down the
optimal rate of unemployment numerically.

17-4 The Costs of Inflation

The costs of inflation are much less obvious than those of unemployment. There is no
direct loss of output from inflation, as there is from unemployment. In studying the
costs of inflation, we again want to distinguish the short run from the long run. In the
case of inflation, though, the relevant distinction is between inflation that is *perfectly
anticipated* and taken into account in economic transactions, and *imperfectly anticipated, or unexpected, inflation*. We start with perfectly anticipated inflation because
that case provides a useful benchmark against which to judge unanticipated inflation.[12]

---

[12] See William J. Fellner, introductory essay in William J. Fellner, ed., *Contemporary Economic Problems*
(Washington, D.C.: American Enterprise Institute, 1973).

Perfectly Anticipated Inflation

Suppose that an economy has been experiencing a given rate of inflation, say 5 percent, for a long time, and that it is correctly anticipated that the rate of inflation will continue to be 5 percent. In such an economy, all contracts would build in the expected 5 percent inflation. Borrowers and lenders will both know and agree that the dollars in which a loan will be repaid will be worth less than the dollars which are given up by the lender when making the loan. Nominal interest rates would be 5 percent higher than they would be in the absence of inflation. Long-term wage contracts will increase wages at 5 percent per year to take account of the inflation, and then build in whatever changes in real wages are agreed to. Long-term leases will take account of the inflation. In brief, any contracts in which the passage of time is involved will take the inflation into account. Inflation has no real costs in such an economy, except for a minor qualification.

That qualification arises because the interest rate that is paid on money might not adjust to the inflation rate. No interest is paid on currency — that is, notes and coin — throughout the the world, and no interest is paid on demand deposits in many countries. It is very difficult to pay interest on currency, so that it is likely that the interest rate on currency will continue to be zero, independent of the perfectly anticipated inflation rate. Interest can be, and in some cases is already, paid on demand deposits. Thus it is reasonable to expect that in a fully anticipated inflation, interest would be paid on demand deposits, and the interest rate paid on demand deposits would adjust to the inflation rate. If so, the only cost of perfectly anticipated inflation is that the inflation makes it more costly to hold currency.

The cost to the individual of holding currency is the interest forgone by not holding an interest-bearing asset. When the inflation rate rises, the nominal interest rate rises, the interest lost by holding currency increases, and the cost of holding currency therefore increases. Accordingly, the demand for for currency falls. In practice, this means that individuals economize on the use of currency by carrying less in their wallets and making more trips to the bank to cash smaller cheques than they did before. The costs of these trips to the bank are often described as the "shoe-leather" costs of inflation. They are related to the amount by which the demand for currency is reduced by an increase in the anticipated inflation rate, and they are small.

We should add that, throughout this discussion, we are assuming inflation rates that are not too high to effectively disrupt the payments system. This disruption has been a real problem in some instances of hyperinflation, but it need not concern us here. We are abstracting, too, from the cost of "menu change." This cost arises simply from the fact that with inflation, as opposed to price stability, people have to devote real resources to marking up prices and changing pay telephones and vending machines as well as cash registers. These costs are there, but, on balance, the costs of fully anticipated inflation are small.

The notion that the costs of fully anticipated inflation are trivial does not square well with the strong aversion to inflation reflected in policy making and politics. The most important reason for that aversion is probably that inflations in Canada have not been steady, and that our inflationary experience is one of imperfectly anticipated inflation, the costs of which are substantially different from those discussed in this section.

There is a further line of argument that explains the public aversion to inflation, even of the fully anticipated, steady kind we are discussing here. The argument is that such a state is not likely to exist, that it is a mirage to believe that policy makers could and would maintain a steady inflation rate at any level other than zero. The argument is that policy makers are reluctant to use restrictive policy to compensate for transitory increases in the inflation rate. Rather than maintain a constant rate of inflation in the face of inflation shocks, the authorities would accommodate these shocks and therefore validate them. Any inflationary shock would add to the inflation rate rather than being compensated for by restrictive policy. In this manner inflation, far from being constant, would in fact be rising as policy makers validate any and every disturbance rather than use policy to rigidly enforce the inflation target. Zero inflation, it is argued, is the only target that can be defended without this risk.[13]

Although there are many examples of countries with long inflationary histories, there does not appear to be any tendency for the inflation rates of those countries to increase over time. The argument thus seems weak. It is true, however, that the inflation rate has been more stable in countries with low rates of inflation than in countries with inflation rates that are on average higher, perhaps providing a germ of validity to the notion.

Imperfectly Anticipated Inflation

The idyllic scene of full adjustment to inflation painted here does not describe economies that we actually know. Modern economies include a variety of institutional features representing different degrees of adjustment to inflation. Economies with long inflationary histories, such as those of Brazil and Israel, have made substantial adjustments to inflation through the use of indexing. Others in which inflation has been episodic, such as the Canadian economy, have made only small adjustments for inflation.

One of the important effects of inflation is to change the real value of assets fixed in nominal terms. A doubling of the price level, such as Canada experienced over the decade of the 1980s, cuts in half the purchasing power of all claims or assets fixed in money terms. Thus, someone who bought a 10-year government bond in 1980 and expected to receive a principal of, say, $100 in constant purchasing power at the 1990 maturity date, actually winds up with a $100 principal that has purchasing power of $50 in 1980 dollars. The doubling of the price level has effectively reduced the real value of the asset by one-half. It has transferred wealth from creditors, who hold bonds, to debtors. This effect operates with respect to all assets fixed in nominal terms — in

---

[13] See Charles R. Nelson, "Inflation and Rates of Return on Common Stocks," *Journal of Finance*, May 1976. See also Franco Modigliani and Richard Cohn, "Inflation, Rational Valuation and the Market," *Financial Analysts Journal*, March–April 1979, for a controversial view of the reasons why inflation affects the stock market.

particular, money, bonds, savings accounts, insurance contracts, and some pensions. Obviously, it is an extremely important effect since it can certainly wipe out the purchasing power of a lifetime's saving that was supposed to finance retirement consumption.

These facts by themselves seem to explain the public concern over inflation. There appears to be a lot riding on each percentage-point change in the price level. That impression is slightly misleading. Many individuals are both debtors and creditors in nominal assets. Almost everyone has some money, and is thus a creditor in nominal terms. Many own housing, financed through mortgages whose value is fixed in nominal terms. Such individuals benefit from inflation because it reduces the real value of their mortgage. Other individuals have borrowed in nominal terms to buy consumer durables, such as cars, and to that extent have their real indebtedness reduced by inflation.

In addition to the redistribution among individuals, inflation brings about transfers among the household, corporate, and government sectors. However, the gains and losses from these wealth transfers basically cancel out over the economy as a whole. When the government gains from inflation, the private sector may have to pay lower taxes later. When the corporate sector gains from inflation, owners of corporations benefit at the expense of others. If we really did not care about the distribution of wealth among individuals, the costs of unanticipated inflation would be negligible. Included in the individuals of the previous sentence are those belonging to different generations, since the current owners of the national debt might be harmed by inflation, to the benefit of future taxpayers.

Inflation redistributes wealth between debtors and creditors because changes in the price level change the purchasing power of assets fixed in money terms. There is room, too, for inflation to affect income positions by changing the distribution of income. A popular line of argument has always been that inflation benefits capitalists or recipients of profit income at the expense of wage earners. Unanticipated inflation, it is argued, means that prices rise faster than wages and therefore allows profits to expand. For Canada in the postwar period, there is no persuasive evidence to this effect. There is evidence that the real return on common stocks, that is the real value of dividends and capital gains on equity, is reduced by unanticipated inflation. Thus, equity holders appear to be adversely affected by unanticipated inflation.[14]

The fact that unanticipated inflation acts mainly to redistribute wealth, the net effects of which redistribution should be close to zero, has led to some questioning of the reasons for public concern over inflation. The gainers, it seems, do not shout as loudly as the losers. Since some of the gainers (future taxpayers) have yet to be born, this is hardly surprising. There is also a notion that the average wage earner is subject to an illusion when both the nominal wage and the price level increase. Wage earners are thought to attribute increases in nominal wages to their own merit rather than to

---

[14] For a discussion of indexation see P. Howitt, "Indexation and the Adjustment to Inflation in Canada," in J. Sargent, *Postwar Macroeconomic Developments*, Research Study No. 20, Royal Commission on the Economic Union and Development Prospects for Canada (Toronto: University of Toronto Press, 1986).

inflation, while the general inflation of prices is seen as causing an unwarranted reduction in the real wage they would otherwise have received. It is hard to know how to test the validity of this argument. Nonetheless, it does appear that the redistributive effects of unanticipated inflation are large, and that, accordingly, some parts of the population could be seriously affected by it.

17-5 Strategies to Deal With Inflation

We have seen the costs of unemployment and the problems that arise from inflation. In this section we consider strategies to deal with inflation without incurring unacceptable costs in terms of unemployment. We begin with a discussion of wage indexation and then consider wage and price controls.

Indexation of Wages

In Chapter 16 we discussed the role of automatic cost of living adjustment (COLA) provisions in wage contracts. COLA provisions link increases in money wages to increases in the price level. The adjustment may be complete — 100 percent indexation — or only partial. Partial indexation takes one of two forms. There may be *a threshold* or *a cap*. A threshold specifies a minimum increase in the price level before indexation comes into play. This implies that small price increases are not compensated for, while larger ones are. A cap puts a limit on the extent to which price increases are compensated for — say 10 percent per year. COLA clauses are designed to allow workers to recover purchasing power lost through price increases.

Why Indexation?

Indexation in some form is a quite common feature of labour markets in many countries. Indexation strikes a balance between the advantages of long-term wage contracts and the interests of workers and firms in not having *real* wages get too far out of line. Bargaining for wages is costly because workers (unions) and the firm have to devote time and effort to arrive at a settlement and often work is disrupted through strikes. It is therefore in the common interest of workers and firms to hold to a minimum the number of times these negotiations take place.

Thus wages are negotiated not once a week or once a month, but rather in the form of two- or three-year contracts. Over the term of these contracts, however, the evolution of prices — consumer prices and the prices at which firms sell their output — is not known with certainty. Therefore real wages paid by firms or received by workers are not known, even if money wages are. To remedy this uncertainty, some provision is made to adjust wages for inflation. Broadly, there are two possibilities. One is to index wages to the CPI and in periodic reviews — say, quarterly — increase wages by the increase in prices over the period. The other is to schedule periodic, preannounced wage increases based on the expected rate of price increase. If inflation were known with certainty, the two methods would come to the same thing, but since inflation can differ from expectations, there will be discrepancies. Prefixed wage increases may turn out to be high or low relative to actual inflation. On that account, indexation on the basis of actual inflation offers greater assurance of stable real wages for workers than do scheduled increases.

Supply Shocks and Indexation

Suppose real material prices increase, and firms pass these cost increases on into higher prices of final goods. Consumer prices will rise, and, under a system of 100 percent indexation, wages would rise. This leads to further price and material costs, and wage increases. Indexation here leads to an inflation spiral that would be avoided under a system of prefixed wage increases because then real wages could fall as a consequence of higher material prices.

The example makes it clear that we must distinguish two possibilities in considering the effects of wage indexing: monetary disturbances and real disturbances. In the case of a monetary disturbance (a shift in the *LM* schedule), there is a "pure" inflation disturbance, and firms can afford to pay the same real wages and therefore would not mind 100 percent indexation. In the case of adverse real disturbances, however, real wages must fall, and full indexation is entirely the wrong system because it stands in the way of downward real wage flexibility.

From the two cases it is apparent that neither completely prefixed wage increases nor complete indexation is likely to be optimal. The best arrangement will depend on the relative importance of monetary and real shocks. Countries that had practised 100 percent indexation — for example, Italy and Brazil in the 1970s — found that it is difficult to adjust to real shocks and that the indexation leads to a wage–price spiral that pushes up inflation with great speed.

Incomes Policy (or Wage and Price Controls)

In Chapter 16, we considered alternative strategies for bringing down the rate of inflation and concluded that the treatments for the inflation disease were painful. Inflation reduction takes time and involves unemployment because that is what is needed to get the rate of wage change down fast, either by law (wage–price controls) or by persuasion. *Incomes policies* are policies that attempt to reduce the rate of wage and price increases by direct action. Either wages and prices are controlled, or the government tries to persuade labour leaders and business to raise wages and prices more slowly than they otherwise would. Income policies, if successful, shift the short-run aggregate supply curve down.[15]

---

[15] For a discussion of incomes policies and other approaches to dealing with inflation, see W.C. Riddell, *Dealing with Inflation and Unemployment in Canada*, Research Study No. 25, Royal Commission on the Economic Union and Development Prospects for Canada (Toronto: University of Toronto Press, 1986).

A wage–price freeze certainly brings the inflation rate down, so why not get rid of inflation that way? The reason is that wages and prices have to change if resources are to be allocated efficiently in the economy. Anti-inflationary policy has to try to reduce the average rate of price increase without interfering with the role of prices in allocating resources. Over a short period, misallocations of resources from frozen wages and prices will be small and not costly, but if wages and prices are kept fixed for a long time, shortages of labour and particular goods will develop. The problem then is to find a way out of controls that does not reignite inflation.

One reason incomes policies have rarely been successful is that they are not combined with appropriate aggregate demand policies. Incomes policies, or wage and price controls, aim to move the aggregate supply curve down, thereby reducing the inflation rate. So long as the aggregate demand curve moves down at the same time, the inflation rate will fall and can stay low. However, if there is no accompanying change in the aggregate demand curve, the wage and price controls will only build up inflationary pressures that will eventually explode.

An interesting recent development is the use of wage and price controls as part of a complete package of economic policy measures taken to end extremely high inflation episodes. In 1985 in Argentina and Israel, and in 1986 in Brazil, policy packages were put into effect to reduce the inflation rate from several hundred percent per year to low double-digit per annum figures. In each case the policy measures involved cuts in the budget deficit and measures to control monetary growth. They also involved as central parts of the package controls on wages and prices. All three programs showed early signs of success. Whether they will ultimately succeed remains to be seen, but their initial success does suggest an important potential role for wage and price controls in rapidly ending inflation, *provided, of course, that the accompanying aggregate demand reduction measures are taken.*

In Chapter 19, we look at the policy choices that have been made by the policy authorities in Canada and consider the consequences for the Canadian economy.

17-6   Summary

1.   The anatomy of unemployment for Canada reveals frequent and short spells of unemployment. Nonetheless, a substantial fraction of unemployment is accounted for by those who are unemployed for quite a long time.

2.   There is considerable variation of unemployment rates across different regions and groups in the labour force.

3.   The concept of the natural rate of unemployment singles out that part of unemployment which would exist even at full employment. The unemployment arises in part because of a high frequency of job changes. The natural rate of unemployment is hard to conceptualize and even harder to measure. It has been estimated to have been above 7 percent in the 1980s compared with a level below 5 percent in the 1960s.

4. The cost of unemployment is the psychic and financial distress of the unemployed as well as the loss of output. The loss of output is not compensated by the unemployed enjoying leisure. For one thing, a larger part of unemployment is involuntary. For another, the social product of labour exceeds the wage rate because of income taxes.

5. The economy can adjust to perfectly anticipated inflation by moving to a system of indexed contracts and to nominal interest rates that reflect the expected rate of inflation. Thus there are no important costs to perfectly anticipated inflation. The only costs are those of changing price tags periodically and the cost of suboptimal holdings of currency.

6. Imperfectly anticipated inflation has important redistributive effects among sectors. Unanticipated inflation benefits monetary debtors and hurts monetary creditors. The government gains real tax revenue, and the real value of government debt declines.

7. Wage indexation links increases in money wages to increases in the price level. It prevents changes in real wages that would otherwise come about if the actual inflation rate differs from what was anticipated.

8. Incomes policies (wage–price controls) attempt to control inflation through direct controls or persuasion. The major disadvantage of this approach is interference with the role of prices in allocating resources.

Key Terms

Structural unemployment
Duration of unemployment
Natural rate of unemployment
Non-accelerating inflation rate of unemployment (NAIRU)

Participation rate
Perfectly anticipated inflation
Wage indexation
Incomes policy

Problems

1. Discuss strategies whereby the government could reduce unemployment in or among:
   (a) Depressed industries
   (b) Unskilled workers
   (c) Depressed geographical regions
   (d) Teenagers.

   Include comments on the *type* of unemployment you would expect in these various groups (that is, relative durations of unemployment spells).

2. Discuss how the following changes would affect the natural or structural rate of unemployment. Comment also on the side effects of these changes.
   (a) Elimination of unions
   (b) Increased participation of women in the labour market
   (c) Larger fluctuations in the *level* of aggregate demand
   (d) An increase in unemployment benefits
   (e) Elimination of minimum wages
   (f) Larger fluctuations in the *composition* of aggregate demand.

3. Discuss the differences in unemployment between adults and youths. What does this imply about the types of jobs (on average) the different groups are getting?

4. Some people say that inflation can be reduced in the long run without an increase in unemployment, and so we should reduce inflation to zero. Others say a steady rate of inflation at, say, 6 percent is not so bad, and that should be our goal. Evaluate these two arguments and describe what, in your opinion, are good long-run goals for inflation and unemployment. How would these be achieved?

5. The following information is to be used for calculations of the unemployment rate. There are two major groups, adults and youths. Youths account for 25 percent of the labour force and adults for 75 percent. Adults are divided into men and women. Women account for 40 percent of the adult labour force. The following table shows the unemployment rates for the groups.

Group	Unemployment Rate
Youths	15%
Adults:	
Men	7%
Women	8.5%

   (a) How do the numbers in this table compare (roughly) with the numbers for the Canadian economy?
   (b) Calculate the aggregate unemployment rate.
   (c) Assume the unemployment rate for youths rises from 15 to 20 percent. What is the effect on female unemployment? (Assume 50 percent of the youths are men.) What is the effect on the aggregate unemployment rate?
   (d) Assume the share of women in the adult labour force increases to 45 percent. What is the effect on the unemployment rate? What is the effect on the aggregate unemployment rate?
   (e) Relate your answers to methods of estimating the natural rate of unemployment.

6. Use the data in Table 17-5 to calculate what unemployment would have been in 1990 if each group had the average unemployment rate of the group over the period 1966–1970. How does your answer differ from the figure shown in column (2) of Table 17-6 and what accounts for the difference?

7. **(a)** What are the economic costs of inflation? Distinguish between anticipated and unanticipated inflation.

   (b) Do you think anything is missing from the list of costs of inflation that economists present? If so, what?

CHAPTER 18 *Money, Deficits, and Inflation*

In this chapter we concentrate on the role of money growth in generating inflation and influencing interest rates and income. We take up four main topics. First, we examine the monetarist proposition that inflation is a monetary phenomenon, which means that inflation is entirely, or at least primarily, due to excessive money growth. Second, we study the linkages among interest rates, inflation, and money growth. The question is whether increased money growth raises or lowers interest rates. Third, we look at the links between budget deficits and money growth, and show how inflation can be viewed as a form of taxation. Finally, we briefly describe hyperinflations and the role of money growth in them.

We establish a few important, basic results in this chapter. The most important is that really high inflation is indeed primarily a monetary phenomenon in the sense that inflation could not continue without continued money growth; but typically in conditions of high inflation there are also high budget deficits underlying the rapid money growth. Such was the case, for instance, in the hyperinflations in 1984–1985 in Israel and Bolivia and in the continuing hyperinflations in Argentina, Brazil, Nicaragua, and Peru. Similarly, in conditions of high inflation nominal interest rates become very high, as expected inflation becomes incorporated into nominal rates.

The real-world application and significance of these results is quite striking and can be seen in many high-inflation countries around the world. However, when inflation rates are lower, in the single-digit or low-double-digit range, real disturbances like supply shocks may well be playing a relatively larger role, and the simple results isolating the role of money become less dominant. Similarly, the role of the deficit in causing money growth becomes less definite; for instance, there was no acceleration in money growth in Canada in the early 1980s despite growing budget deficits.

We start out in Section 18-1 with the linkages between money growth and inflation. Then, in Section 18-2, we discuss evidence on the links between money and inflation, and between inflation and interest rates. In Section 18-3 we analyze the relationship between budget deficits and money growth. We conclude with a discussion of hyperinflation.

18-1 Money and Inflation

In this section we develop Chapter 16's analysis of the dynamics of inflation to show exactly the role played by money growth. Our task is to make sense of the monetarist claim that inflation is always and everywhere a monetary phenomenon.

To obtain a firm understanding of these points, we must keep in mind two distinctions. The first is that between the short run and the long run. The second is that between monetary and other disturbances (for example, fiscal disturbances or oil shocks) to the economy.

Monetarists tend to concentrate on the long run and on economies where changes in money growth are the primary disturbances. Not surprisingly, they tend to be right, *for this special case*, when they argue that money explains most of what is happening to inflation. But as one moves away from the long run and from monetary disturbances, toward short-run inflation determination and alternative shocks, one must become much more eclectic. In the short run, disturbances other than changes in the money stock affect inflation and, conversely, changes in the money stock do have real effects. Even if the disturbances are purely monetary, it will still generally take a while before they are fully reflected in inflation and only in inflation.

A key point in the distinction between the short run and the long run and in determining the dynamics of inflation is the role of expectations. Increased money growth will have real effects as long as inflationary expectations have not fully adapted. Milton Friedman has put this point as follows:

Monetarist analysis goes on to say that any changes in the nominal quantity of money that are anticipated in advance will be fully embedded in inflationary and other expectations, but that unanticipated changes in the quantity of money will not be. An unanticipated increase or decrease in the quantity of money tends to affect total nominal spending some six to nine months later in countries like the United States, Japan or Great Britain. The initial effect is primarily on output rather than on prices. Prices tend to be affected only some 18 months to two years later. This does not mean that there is no further effect on real quantities. On the contrary, the delayed impact on prices means an overshooting of output — up or down depending on the initial stimulus — which will then require an overshooting in the opposite direction to allow the price level to reach its appro-

priate level. As a result the cyclical reaction pattern in both output and prices tend to last for a considerable period — years, not months. . . .[1]

We formalize these ideas by drawing on the model of Chapter 16. While using exactly the same model, we shift the exposition a little to focus on dynamics. Our task is to highlight a number of relationships involving money, interest rates, and inflation.

The Model

The starting point is the aggregate demand equation derived in Chapter 16. Aggregate demand and (real) income will rise whenever real balances are increasing. Conversely, when real balances are falling, so, too, are aggregate demand and income.[2] We write this relation in Equation (1) using the notation $\Delta Y = Y - Y_{-1}$, m = growth rate of money, π = inflation rate:

$$\Delta Y = f(m - \pi) \tag{1}$$

Assume now a given growth rate of money, m_0. In Figure 18-1a we show the schedule $\pi = m_0$, along which output is neither rising nor falling. Now we consider how income is changing at different points in Figure 18-1a. For points above the $\pi = m_0$ schedule, inflation exceeds the given growth rate of money. Hence real balances are falling and so, according to Equation (1), is income. This is indicated by the arrow showing falling income. Conversely, below the schedule inflation is less than money growth, and hence real balances are increasing, interest rates are falling, and demand and income are growing.

The second relationship is the aggregate supply curve

$$\pi = \pi^e + \lambda(Y - Y^\circ) \tag{2a}$$

In Equation (2a) Y° is the full-employment level of income, assumed in this section to be constant. For most of this section we make the simplest adaptive expectations assumption, that inflation expectations are given by last period's inflation rate, substituting $\pi^e = \pi_{-1}$.[3] Making that substitution in Equation (2a), the change in inflation

---

[1] See Milton Friedman, "Monetarism in Rhetoric and Practice," Bank of Japan *Monetary and Economic Studies*, October 1983, p. 2.

[2] In the appendix to Chapter 16 we developed the aggregate demand curve taking account of the role of inflationary expectations in determining the real interest rate. In that case there is an additional term in the aggregate demand relationship equation (1). Under the assumption to be made for much of this section that $\pi^e = \pi_{-1}$, i.e., that the expected inflation rate is equal to last period's inflation rate, current aggregate demand increases with the lagged inflation rate. In order to simplify, we do not include this term on the aggregate demand side in this section. The omission does not affect the general results obtained, except possibly if the expectations effect on aggregate demand was very large.

[3] We discuss behaviour under rational expectations of inflation later in this section.

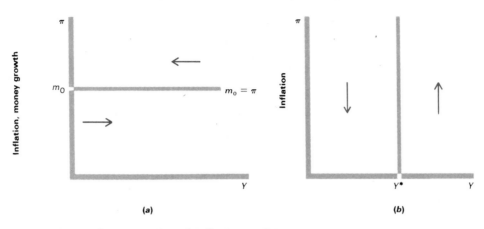

Figure 18-1 *The Dynamics of Inflation and Income*

The panel (*a*) shows the reponse of income to real balances. When inflation exceeds the growth rate of money, real balances are falling and hence demand and income are declining. Conversely, when inflation falls short of money growth, income is rising. The panel (*b*) shows that at income levels above Y° inflation rises and at income levels below Y° inflation declines.

over time, denoted by $\Delta\pi = \pi - \pi_{-1}$, becomes a function of the output gap and is given by

$$\Delta\pi = \lambda(Y - Y^\circ) \tag{2}$$

Focusing again on dynamics, in Figure 18-1*b* we show the arrows that indicate the direction in which inflation is moving. When income is below the full-employment level, inflation is falling, and when income is above the full-employment level, inflation is rising.

Table 18-1 and Figure 18-2 combine the information in the two parts of Figure 18-1. The table shows the direction in which income and inflation are moving in each of the four regions in Figure 18-2. We use the arrows to show the combined movement or the path of inflation and income at each point.

Suppose the economy is at point *A* in region I. Because income is above the full-employment level, inflation is rising, but inflation is below money growth. Therefore real balances are increasing, and hence demand and income are rising. Thus at point *A* income is rising, as is inflation, so that the economy moves in a northeastward direction. We can establish the direction of movement at points *B*, *C*, and *D* in a similar fashion. Note that point *E* is the only point in the diagram where *both* income and inflation are constant. This is the long-run equilibrium to which the economy ultimately converges.

In Figure 18-2 we complete the model by bringing in the *IS* schedule. In the lower diagram, we show on the vertical axis the *real* or *inflation-adjusted* interest rate. Real

Table 18-1 *The Determinants of Income and Inflation*

	$\pi < m$	$\pi > m$
$Y > Y^*$	I Y is ↑ π is ↑	II Y is ↓ π is ↑
$Y < Y^*$	IV Y is ↑ π is ↓	III Y is ↓ π is ↓

aggregate demand, as we saw in the previous chapters, depends on the real interest rate. A higher real interest rate lowers aggregate demand and hence reduces equilibrium income, as shown by the *IS* schedule. The lower part of Figure 18-2 helps us track the real interest rate in the adjustment process. For each level of income in the upper part, we can find the corresponding equilibrium real interest rate on the *IS* schedule. Thus we can follow income, inflation, and the real interest rate all at the same time.

In Figure 18-2 we show a typical adjustment path starting at point *A*. The corresponding point is also labelled *A* in the lower part of Figure 18-2. At *A*, inflation is rising because of overemployment. But because inflation is low relative to money growth, real balances are rising and hence demand and income are growing. The economy thus moves in a northeasterly direction. The driving force is the increasing level of real balances, which reduces interest rates and pushes up demand and income. Over time, as the economy cycles back to point *E*, the real interest rate first declines and then, as the economy enters region II, starts rising. The interest rate overshoots the long-run equilibrium level r° (several times) before it ultimately settles at r°.

An Increase in Money Growth

We now use this framework to examine once more the effects of a sustained increase in money growth. The conclusions are, of course, the same as those in Chapter 16. We start in long-run equilibrium at point *E* in Figure 18-3, where money growth is initially m_0. The inflation rate is equal to the growth rate of money, and income is at its full-employment level. Now the growth rate of money is permanently raised to m'. The new $\pi = m'$ schedule lies above the previous one (which, to avoid cluttering up the diagram, is not drawn). The arrows in each region show the direction in which inflation and income are moving. The path starting at *E* shows the evolution of the economy.

At point *E* the growth rate of money m' now exceeds the initial inflation rate $\pi = m_0$. As a result, the real money stock is increasing. Interest rates are pushed down, and thus aggregate demand and income will be rising. At the very beginning of the

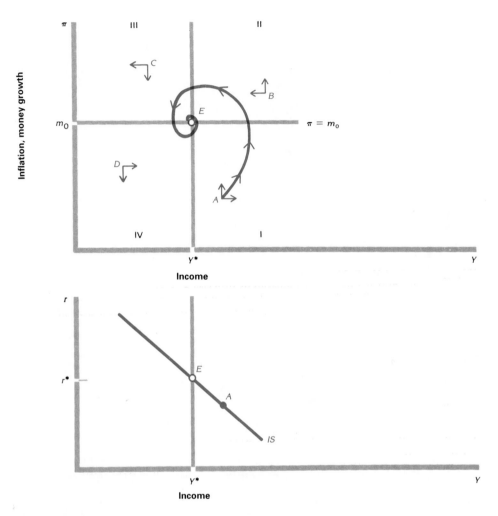

Figure 18-2 *The Adjustment Process*

The upper panel combines the information in Figure 18-1 to show how income and inflation evolve over time. The long-run equilibrium is at point E where inflation equals money growth and income is at the full-employment level. The lower panel shows the real rate of interest corresponding to each level of income along the IS curve. For example, if the economy is at point A in the upper panel, point A on the IS curve gives the corresponding real interest rate. The long-run equilibrium real interest rate is r°.

adjustment process the economy therefore moves horizontally to the right with income rising, but the moment income starts exceeding the full-employment level, inflation increases. Now the path starts pointing in a northeasterly direction with rising income, because inflation remains low relative to money growth, and with inflation rising.

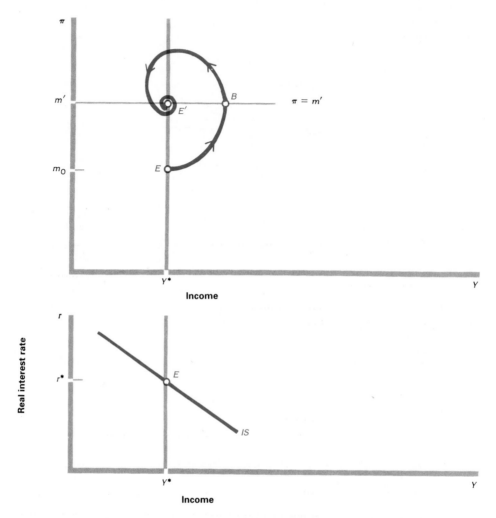

Figure 18-3 *The Adjustment to an Increase in Money Growth*

A sustained increase in money growth from m_0 to m' leads the economy along a path from E to E'. Income first expands, and inflation gradually builds up. In the long run, inflation rises to equal the growth rate of money. The economy returns to full employment at the real interest rate r°.

Over time the economy moves to point B. Here real balances are constant because now inflation has risen to the level of money growth, but income is above the full-employment level. Therefore inflation is still increasing, and the economy is thus pushed into region II. We do not describe the whole path, but it is apparent that the economy will cycle its way gradually to point E'.

Rational Expectations

The exact details of the adjustment path shown in Figure 18-3 depend on the assumptions about expectations. However, the general pattern — that increased monetary growth first raises income and ultimately is fully reflected in higher inflation — is valid for (almost) any assumption about expectations.

Only in a world of complete flexibility of wages and prices combined with rational expectations would the adjustment occur instantly without any dynamics whatsoever. In that case, if a change in the growth rate of money is expected, π^e in Equation (2a) will be equal to m' at the time the growth rate of money changes, and income will remain at its full-employment level throughout.[4]

Once we move away from that extreme case — which requires both rational expectations and full flexibility of prices and wages — the pattern of adjustment is that shown in Figure 18-3. Alternative assumptions about expectations and the adjustment of wages and prices will primarily influence the speed of adjustment and the movement of nominal interest rates, but it will generally imply a slow adjustment pattern of the type seen in Figure 18-3.

Before going further we want to summarize the main results so far. There are four characteristics of the adjustment process and the new long-run equilibrium that are important to retain:

- A sustained increase in the growth rate of money will, in the long run when all adjustments have taken place, lead to an equal increase in the rate of inflation. If money growth rises by 5 percent, so, too, ultimately will the inflation rate.

- A sustained change in money growth will have no long-run effects on the level of income. Thus there is no long-run tradeoff between inflation and income.

- In the short run, during the adjustment process, increased monetary growth will affect the real interest rate, aggregate demand, and income. Specifically, in the initial stages there will be an expansion in income while inflation builds up.

- In the short run, increased money growth will reduce the real interest rate, but in the long run, after all adjustments have taken place, the real interest rate will return to its initial level.

We ask you in Problem 1 at the end of the chapter to demonstrate the corresponding results for a sustained reduction in the growth rate of money. To complete our analysis, we now turn to the behaviour of real balances and the nominal interest rate.

---

[4] Remarkably, in this case the inflation rate would generally start to rise before the growth rate of money increases. That is because if people expect there to be inflation in the future, the quantity of real balances demanded is reduced and the price level therefore starts moving up.

The Fisher Equation

We have noted at various points in this book the relationship between nominal interest rates, real rates, and the expected rate of inflation. The (expected) real rate of interest is the nominal rate less the expected rate of inflation:

$$r^e = i - \pi^e \tag{3}$$

Equation (3) is the Fisher equation, so named after Irving Fisher (1867–1947), the most famous American economist of the first third of this century, who drew attention to the inflation–interest rate linkage.[5]

The Fisher equation immediately draws attention to a very important finding about money growth, inflation, and interest rates. We saw above that in the long run the real interest rate returns to the full-employment level r°, and that actual and expected inflation converge. Using these two facts ($r^e = r^\circ$, $\pi^e = \pi$) we write the long-run relationship as

$$i = r^\circ + \pi \tag{4}$$

With r° constant, Equation (4) implies a central result: *In the long run when all adjustments have occurred, an increase in inflation is reflected fully in nominal interest rates*. Nominal interest rates rise one-for-one with the increase in inflation. The reason we have such a strong inflation–nominal interest rate link is that in the long run the real interest rate is unaffected by purely monetary disturbances.

Of course, we have already seen in Figure 18-3 that the constancy of the real interest rate holds only in long-run equilibrium. During the adjustment process, the real interest rates does change, and hence changes in the nominal interest rate reflect both changes in real rates and changes in inflationary expectations. The path of adjustment depends on the way in which expectations of inflation are formed.

Figure 18-4 shows a possible pattern, which has received considerable attention in empirical work. In response to increased growth in nominal money, at time T_0 the real money stock grows and initially pushes down the nominal interest rate. Then, as income rises and with it inflation, the nominal interest rate is pushed up until, ultimately, after some cycling it has increased by the full increase in money growth and inflation.

The declining phase of the nominal interest rate path is called the *liquidity effect* to denote the impact of increased real balances (liquidity) on the interest rate. The phase of increasing nominal interest rates just after the bottom is reached is called the

---

[5] See Irving Fisher, *The Rate of Interest* (New York, 1907). Fisher taught at Yale and was an effective and sophisticated developer of the quantity theory of money. He had other interests too; he was the inventor of the card index file still used for keeping addresses, and was a health-food enthusiast who wrote several books on the subject. Fisher was an early, if long forgotten, discoverer of the Phillips curve. See the reprinted version of his 1926 article "A Statistical Relation between Unemployment and Price Changes," under the heading "Lost and Found," *Journal of Political Economy*, March/April 1973, pp. 496–502.

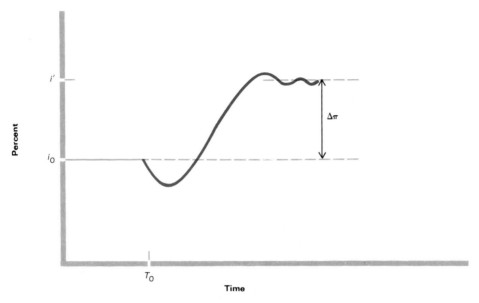

Figure 18-4 *The Fisher Effect*

A sustained increase in money growth leads first to a reduction in nominal interest rates. Then, as income and inflation both increase, the interest rate gradually rises. In the long run it increases by the same amount as money growth and inflation.

income effect. In this phase increasing nominal income pushes up interest rates by increasing the quantity of real balances demanded. The long-run effect is called the *Fisher effect*, or *expectations effect*, to represent the impact of an increase in inflationary expectations, at a constant real interest rate, on the nominal interest rate. These names are suggestive of the three phases of adjustment as the economy is initially surprised by increased money growth and gradually adjusts to it.[6]

Real Balances and Inflation

In Figure 18-5 we present the demand for real balances as a function of the nominal interest rate. We now study the effect of a sustained change in the growth rate of money on the long-run equilibrium level of real balances.

For that purpose we simply combine two of our results. We saw that a sustained change in monetary growth changes, in the long run, the rate of inflation and the nominal interest rate in the same direction and by the same amount. A three-per-

---

[6] For an extensive discussion, see Milton Friedman and Anna Schwartz, *Monetary Trends in the United States and the United Kingdom* (Chicago: University of Chicago Press, 1982), Chapter 10.

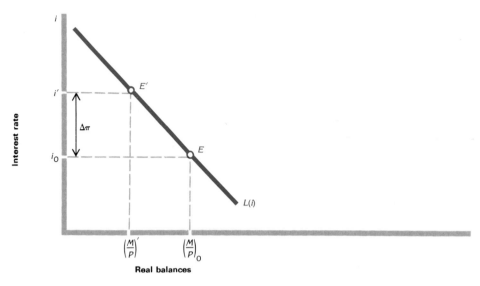

Figure 18-5   *The Demand for Real Balances*

An increase in inflation and accordingly in the nominal interest rate will reduce the equilibrium stock of real balances. As the interest rate increases in long-run equilibrium from i_0 to i', real balances decline from E to E'.

centage-point increase in money growth raises the nominal interest rate by three percentage points in the long run. We therefore conclude from Figure 18-5 that *a sustained increase in money growth and in inflation ultimately leads to a reduction in the real money stock.*

This is a very important result that might seem a bit puzzling: Increased *nominal* money growth reduces the long-run *real* money stock. Conversely, reduced nominal money growth raises the long-run real money stock. The reason is that higher inflation raises the nominal interest rate and hence raises the opportunity cost of holding money. Hence money holders will reduce the amount of real balances they choose to hold. This reduction in real balances is an important part of the adjustment process to an increase in money growth. It means that, *on average, in the adjustment period to an increase in money growth, prices must rise faster than money.*

Figure 18-6, which shows the time paths of inflation and money growth, helps explain the adjustment of real balances. At time T_0 money growth rises from m_0 to m'. At the very beginning, as we saw in Figure 18-3, nothing happens to inflation. Inflation builds up gradually until, with overshooting and cycling, it settles down at the higher level m'. In the phase up to time T_1, money growth exceeds inflation and real balances rise. In the following phase, real balances are falling as the inflation rate exceeds money growth. The diagram is drawn to show that in the phase of decline, real balances fall more than they rise in the initial phase. This is the phase in which the economy adjusts

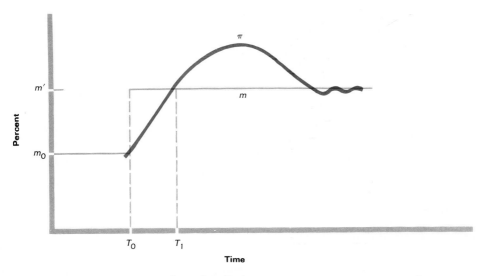

Figure 18-6 *Money Growth and Inflation*

An increase in money growth from m_0 to m' only gradually translates into increased inflation. In the adjustment process prices rise cumulatively more than money as shown by the overshooting of inflation. This implies that real balances will be reduced in the long run.

in a major way to increased money growth as rising income and expectations push up the rate of inflation.

Alternative Expectations Assumptions

Once again, the long-run reduction in real balances in response to higher money growth is a general result. A sustained increase in money growth *must*, in the long run, reduce the equilibrium level of real balances. The particulars of how expectations are formed determines the particular details of the path.

In the extreme case of full wage–price flexibility and rational expectations, there would be an instant adjustment. The announcement of increased money growth would lead to an instant recognition that the opportunity cost of holding money is increased. The public would try to shift out of money because money is now expected to be more expensive to hold, but, of course, the economy in the aggregate cannot get rid of the existing nominal money stock. People trying to spend quickly to get rid of their real balances would cause prices to jump, thereby reducing real balances to the lower desired level. Following the jump, prices and money would start rising at the long-run equilibrium rate m', and the nominal interest rate would have increased to i'. All adjustments would occur literally in no time.

This case of full wage–price flexibility and rational expectations may sound implausible, but it serves as a useful benchmark for comparison. On one side there is a world with only gradual adjustment of inflation and inflationary expectations. In that world, described by Friedman earlier, increased money growth takes time to find itself translated fully into inflation and interest rates. In the other world, all adjustments are instant.

How exactly the real-world adjustment takes place depends in good part on people's experience with inflation. In economies where inflation is the number-one issue — because of a hyperinflation — it takes very little time for adjustment to occur, as we will see later in this chapter. However, in the Canadian economy, where inflation never became a complete way of life, the path of Figure 18-3 is a lot more likely.

18-2 Empirical Evidence

We now turn to evidence on the links between money growth and inflation and between money growth and interest rates.

The Money–Inflation Link

To start, we note the often-made statement that inflation is a monetary phenomenon. The claim that inflation is a monetary phenomenon means that sustained high rates of money growth produce high inflation and that low rates of money growth will eventually produce low rates of inflation. Further, the statement that inflation is a monetary phenomenon means that high rates of inflation cannot long continue without high rates of money growth. The view that inflation is a monetary phenomenon is the implication of the quantity theory of money and is the backbone of monetarist macroeconomics.

Figure 18-7 presents evidence from Canada over the period since 1961, showing that the inflation rate and the growth rate of money have more or less moved together. Although the relationship is clearly positive, it is also obvious that the link between money growth and inflation is not precise.

We expect to find a link between inflation and money growth because we showed earlier that in the steady state the inflation rate is determined by money growth. The aggregate demand curve was

$$\pi = m - \frac{1}{\phi}(Y - Y_{-1}) \tag{5}$$

With $Y = Y_{-1} = Y^\circ$ — that is, with constant income — the inflation rate is equal to the growth rate of money. That is the basis for the view that inflation is, in the long run, a monetary phenomenon. We now want to expand the model slightly to recognize the growth of full-employment income over time. Suppose that income, instead of being constant, grows in the long run at the growth rate of potential income, g°. In

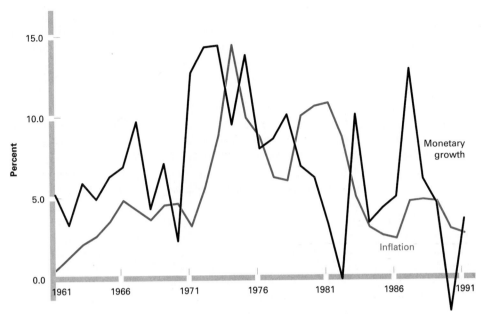

Note: Inflation and monetary growth are annual rates of the GDP implicit price index and of *M*1.

Figure 18-7 *Inflation and Monetary Growth in Canada*

(*Source:* Adapted from *Bank of Canada Review*)

Canada *g*° has been about 4 percent per annum. Some money growth is needed just to meet the increasing demand for real balances arising from growing income. Accordingly, the money growth rate will exceed the inflation rate in the long run.

The difference between money growth and inflation arises from the amount of money growth needed to meet the demand increases resulting from steadily rising income. How much money growth is that? Suppose the income elasticity of money demand is 0.7. Then for every 1 percent that income rises, the demand for real balances rises 0.7 percent. The 4 percent growth in potential income thus increases the demand for real balances by 2.8 percent a year.

If real money demand is rising — say, at the rate of 2.8 percent per year — as a result of income growth, then monetary equilibrium requires that the real money supply increase at the same rate. The growth rate of the real money stock is just the difference between the growth rate of the nominal money stock and the rate of inflation. For instance, if the nominal money stock is increasing at 10 percent and the rate of inflation is 7.9 percent, the real money stock is increasing at 2.1 percent per year.

If the real money supply has to be growing at 2.8 percent per year to maintain monetary equilibrium, then the rate of inflation has to be 2.8 percent less than the rate of money growth, or, in symbols, $\pi = m - 2.8$.

More generally, with $g°$ as the growth rate of potential output and η as the income elasticity of the demand for real balances, the long-run relationship among the inflation rate, the growth rate of money, and the growth rate of output is

$$\pi = m - \eta g° \tag{6}$$

Table 18-2 applies Equation (6) to the data for Canada over the period 1968 to 1990. Column (5) shows the predicted inflation rate using an income elasticity of money demand of unity, and column (6) uses the income elasticities from the empirical studies discussed in Chapter 12. Using either definition of money, the predictions involve considerable error. Using $M1$, predicted inflation is below the actual rate, and using $M2$, the prediction is too high.

In conclusion, the answer to the question "Is inflation a monetary phenomenon in the long run?" is yes. No major inflation can take place without rapid money growth, and rapid money growth will cause rapid inflation. Further, any policy that determinedly keeps the growth rate of money low will lead eventually to a low rate of inflation.

At the same time, the long-run link between money growth and inflation is not precise, as the data of Table 18-2 show. There are two reasons for that. First, increases in income increase the demand for real balances and reduce the inflation rate corresponding to a given rate of money growth. Second, financial institutions change, the definition of money changes, and the demand for money may shift over time.

Inflation and Interest Rates

The Fisher equation asserts a positive link between nominal interest rates and inflation. With the real interest rate approximately constant in the long run, and with expectations of inflation adjusting to actual inflation, the nominal interest rate adjusts to the prevailing rate of inflation.

Figure 18-8 shows quarterly averages of the nominal interest rate on three-month Treasury bills and the rate of inflation. The *realized* real interest rate then is the

Table 18-2 *Money Growth and Inflation, 1968–1990*

Monetary Aggregate	(1) Money (m)	(2) Real GDP (g*)	(3) Income Elasticity (η)	(4) Inflation Rate (π)	(5) (m − g)	(6) (m − ηg*)
	Growth Rates				**Predicted Inflation Rate**	
MI	7.3	3.8	.7	6.7	3.5	4.6
M2	11.7	3.8	.5	6.7	7.9	9.8

difference between the nominal interest rate and the actual rate of inflation or, in symbols,

$$r = i - \pi \qquad (7)$$

We do not have data on expected inflation and hence can reliably report only realized actual rates rather than expected real rates of interest. In the short term, however, with inflation quite predictable, there are no big discrepancies between expected and actual real rates.

Note from Figure 18-8 that in the 1970s there were several episodes of negative real rates, particularly in 1974–1975 when inflation increased sharply and exceeded the interest rate by a significant margin. By contrast, in the period since 1978 the real rate of interest has been *persistently* positive.

Table 18-3 shows international evidence on the interest rate–inflation link. The table conveys clearly the notion of a positive relationship between the *nominal* interest rate

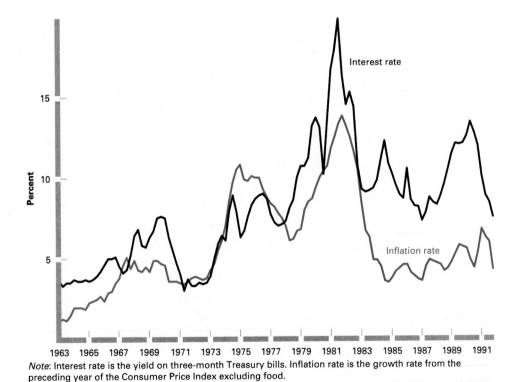

Note: Interest rate is the yield on three-month Treasury bills. Inflation rate is the growth rate from the preceding year of the Consumer Price Index excluding food.

Figure 18-8 *Interest Rates and Inflation*

(*Source:* Adapted from *Bank of Canada Review*)

Table 18-3   *Interest Rates and Inflation, 1988*

Country	Interest Rate (% per annum)	Inflation Rate
Australia	11.9	7.7
Canada	9.4	4.0
France	7.5	3.1
Germany	4.0	1.6
Mexico	66.3	51.7
Italy	11.3	4.8
Switzerland	2.2	2.0
United Kingdom	10.3	6.8
United States	7.6	4.4

Note: Interest rates are short-term market rates. The inflation rate is the average from December to December.

Source: International Financial Statistics, various issues.

and inflation. The link is especially clear for a country like Mexico which had both an exceptionally high inflation rate and an extremely high interest rate. If that had not been the case, real interest rates would have been spectacularly negative.

The evidence we have seen does tend to show that inflation and interest rates move together, within a country over time and across countries, but the evidence does not support a very strict Fisher equation. Year-to-year changes in inflation are not reflected one for one in nominal interest rates. The real rate does move, and hence the Fisher equation is primarily a guide to interest rates when inflationary disturbances are large relative to all other factors determining interest rates.

The Fisher Equation and International Capital Mobility

The data in Table 18-3 show large variation across countries in nominal interest rates. How can we reconcile this with the models of international capital mobility given in Chapters 6 and 9?

The key to reconciling capital mobility with interest rate differentials is provided by the interest parity condition that states that the domestic *nominal* interest rate (i) is equal to the foreign rate (i^*) plus the expected rate of depreciation of the domestic currency (x):

$$i = i^* + x \tag{8}$$

As we saw in Chapter 9, in the longer run we would expect differences in inflation rates between countries to be the major factor in the trend movements in exchange rates. Thus, in long-run equilibrium, a country with a relatively high inflation rate would have a relatively high nominal interest rate (because of the Fisher equation) and a depreciating currency. The rate of depreciation would match the inflation differential in order to maintain the real exchange rate at a constant equilibrium level.

Denoting the domestic and foreign inflation rates by π and π° respectively, and substituting $\pi - \pi^\circ$ for x in Equation (8), we obtain

$$i = i^\circ + \pi - \pi^\circ$$

or

$$i - \pi = i^\circ - \pi^\circ \tag{9}$$

Thus, in long-run equilibrium, the interest parity condition states that *real* interest rates are equalized across countries. Nominal rates will differ according to the differences in inflation rates.

18-3 Money Growth and the Inflation Tax

We have seen that a sustained increase in money growth ultimately translates into increased inflation. In this section, we consider money creation as an alternative to explicit taxation for the purpose of financing government spending. Governments can — and some do — obtain significant amounts of resources year after year by printing money. This source of revenue is sometimes known as seigniorage, which means the government's ability to raise revenue through its right to create money.

When the government finances a deficit by creating money, it in effect keeps printing money, period after period, which it uses to pay for the goods and services it buys. This money is absorbed by the public; but why would the public choose to increase its holdings of nominal money balances period after period?

The only reason, real income growth aside, that the public would be adding to its holdings of nominal money balances is to offset the effects of inflation. Assuming there is no real income growth, in the long run the public will hold a constant level of *real* balances. However, if prices are rising, the purchasing power of a given stock of *nominal balances* is falling. To maintain the real value of its money balances constant, the public has to be adding to its stock of nominal balances, exactly at the rate that will offset the effects of inflation.

When the public is adding to its stock of nominal balances in order to offset the effects of inflation on holdings of real balances, it is using part of its income to increase holdings of nominal money. For instance, suppose someone has an income of $20 000 (nominal) this year. Over the course of the year, inflation reduces the value of that person's real balances. He or she therefore has to add money (say, $300) to a bank account just to maintain the real value of his or her money holdings constant. That $300 is not available for spending. The person seems to be saving $300 in the form of money holdings, but in fact in real terms is not increasing his or her wealth by adding the $300 to nominal balances. All that person is doing is preventing his or her wealth from falling as a result of inflation.

Inflation acts just like a tax because people are forced to spend less than their income and pay the difference to the government in exchange for extra money.[7] The government thus can spend more resources and the public less, just as if the government had raised taxes to finance extra spending. When the government finances its deficit by issuing money, which the public adds to its holdings of nominal balances to maintain the real value of money balances constant, we say the government is financing itself through the inflation tax.[8]

How much revenue can the government collect through the inflation tax? Table 18-4 shows data for Latin American countries in the 1983–1988 period. Clearly the amounts are very significant. The amount of revenue produced is the product of the tax rate (the inflation rate) and the object of taxation (the real monetary base). When real income is constant, inflation tax revenue is given by

$$\text{Inflation tax revenue} = \text{inflation rate} \times \text{real money base} \qquad (10)$$

Table 18-4 *Inflation and Inflation Tax, 1983–1988*

	(percent)		
Country	**Average Tax/GDP***	**Average Inflation**	**Peak-Year Tax/GDP**
Argentina	3.7	359	5.2
Bolivia	3.5	1797	7.2
Brazil	3.5	341	4.3
Chile	0.9	21	1.1
Colombia	1.9	22	2.0
Mexico	2.6	87	3.5
Peru	4.7	382	4.5

* Inflation tax.

Source: M. Selowsky, "Preconditions Necessary for the Recovery of Latin America's Growth," The World Bank, June 1989 (mimeographed).

---

[7] There is one complication in this analysis. The amount that is received by the government is the increase in the *monetary base*. However, the public is increasing its holdings of both bank deposits and currency, and thus part of the increase in the public's holdings of money does not go to the government to finance the deficit. This complication in no way changes the essence of the analysis.

[8] Inflation is often referred to as the "cruellest tax." This does not refer to the above analysis of the inflation tax, but rather to the redistributions of wealth and income associated with unanticipated inflation, discussed in Chapter 17.

The amount of revenue the government can raise through the inflation tax is shown by the curve *AA* in Figure 18-9. When the inflation rate is zero, the government gets no revenue from inflation.[9] As the inflation rate rises, the amount of inflation tax received by the government increases, but of course, as the inflation rate rises, people reduce their holdings of real balances, because it is becoming increasingly costly to hold money. Eventually the quantity of real balances falls so much that the total amount of inflation tax revenue received by the government falls. That happens starting at point *C*. This means there is a maximum amount of revenue the government can raise through the inflation tax: It is shown as amount IR° in Figure 18-9. There is a corresponding inflation rate, denoted π°, the steady-state inflation rate at which the inflation tax is at its maximum.

We can look back to Figure 18-3 to study the long-run effects of money-financed deficits. We start at point *E*. Now the government cuts taxes and finances the deficit by printing money. We assume that the deficit is equal to amount IR' in Figure 18-9, and thus it can be financed entirely through the inflation tax. Now money growth has been permanently increased, and inflation will in the long run move to the rate π', corresponding to the inflation tax revenue IR'.

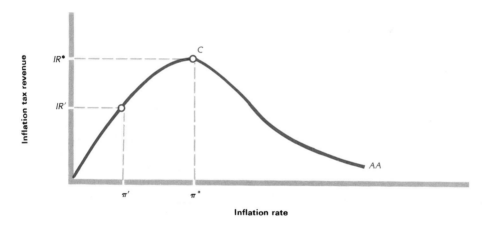

Figure 18-9 *The Inflation Tax*

At a zero inflation rate, the inflation tax revenue is zero. As the inflation rate rises, the government receives more revenue from inflation, up to point *C*, where the tax revenue reaches its maximum of IR°. The corresponding inflation rate is π°. Beyond point *C* the demand for real balances is falling so much as the inflation rate increases that total tax revenues decline.

---

[9] When the economy is growing, the government obtains some revenue from seigniorage even if there is no inflation. That is because when the demand for real monetary base is growing, the government can create some base without producing inflation.

In the long run the economy reaches point E'. In that equilibrium, expectations have fully adjusted to the inflation, and income is at the full-employment level. Inflation equals the growth rate of money,[10] and the inflation rate depends on the deficit size. The larger the deficit, the higher the inflation rate. Figure 18-9 raises the question of what happens if the government tries to finance a deficit larger than $IR°$ by printing money. That cannot be done. We take up that issue in the following section, on hyperinflations.

Inflation Tax Revenue

How much revenue can governments in practice obtain from the printing of money? The amount is quite small in developed economies in which the money base is small relative to the size of the economy. For instance, in Canada the base is about 4 percent of GDP, so that with a 10 percent inflation rate the government would, from Equation (10), be collecting about 0.4 percent of GDP in inflation tax revenue. That is not a trivial amount, but it is not a major source of government revenue either. It is hard to believe that the inflation rate in Canada is set with the revenue aspects of inflation as the main criterion. Rather, the government chooses policies to influence the inflation rate on the basis of an analysis of the costs and benefits of inflation along the lines of Chapter 17.

In countries where the banking system is less developed and where people therefore hold large amounts of currency, the government obtains more revenue from inflation and is more likely to give high weight to the revenue aspects of inflation in setting policy. There have been cases where the government obtains as much as 10 percent of GDP in revenue from the creation of the money base. Further, as we see in the next section, in conditions of high inflation where the conventional tax system breaks down, the inflation tax revenue may be the government's last resort to keep paying its bills.

Unpleasant Monetarist Arithmetic

In a well-known article, Thomas Sargent and Neil Wallace of the University of Minnesota have pointed to an important implication of the government budget constraint.[11] Specifically, *debt financing of a deficit may in the long run be more inflationary than money financing.*

The argument turns on the fact that when a government finances a current deficit through debt, it incurs the obligation to pay interest on that debt in the future. In Chapter 15, the government budget constraint was defined as:

$$\text{Deficit} = \text{bond sales} + \text{increase in monetary base} \qquad (11)$$

---

[10]   Except for an adjustment that takes account of growth in real income.

[11]   "Some Unpleasant Monetarist Arithmetic," Federal Reserve Bank of Minneapolis, *Quarterly Review*, Fall 1981.

We also introduced a distinction between the primary deficit and the total deficit:

$$\text{Total deficit} = \text{primary deficit} + \text{interest payments} \tag{12}$$

Combining (11) and (12), we obtain:

$$\text{Bond sales} + \text{increase in monetary base} = \text{primary deficit} \\ + \text{interest payments} \tag{13}$$

Consider now the choice between debt financing (bond sales) and money financing of a given deficit. If money financing is used, interest payments will be no larger in the future than they are now, but if the government turns to debt financing, it will have a larger deficit in the future. That in turn will have to be financed, either through money finance or debt finance.

Now imagine the following circumstances. The government has a given national debt today. The primary deficits today and in the future are, by assumption, given at some constant level, for example, the primary deficit may be zero. The government is considering whether to finance its current deficit by borrowing or by printing money. If it finances by borrowing, it intends to stop borrowing and switch to money financing in five years.

Under which alternative will the inflation rate ultimately be higher? The answer can be worked out from the following considerations. If the government starts money financing today, it will have to create money at a rate that finances the interest payments on the *existing* national debt. If it waits five years to start money financing, it will have to create money at a rate that finances the interest payments on the national debt that will exist five years from now. Because interest on the debt will have accumulated in the meantime, the debt will be larger five years from now, and therefore so will the inflation rate.

This example shows that, because of the accumulation of interest, short-run debt financing that ends in money financing will generally ultimately be more inflationary than immediate money financing of a given deficit. The arithmetic is unpleasant for monetarists because it suggests that budget deficits may have more to do with the eventual inflation rate than with the current growth rate of money.

The main question raised by this example is whether the government is eventually forced into money financing of a given deficit or whether it can continue debt financing forever. That depends on the relationship between the growth rate of income and the real interest rate. As we saw in Chapter 15, if the real interest rate is above the growth rate of income, and given a zero primary deficit, debt financing cannot continue forever, because the debt becomes a larger and larger part of GDP and interest payments keep mounting up. At some point, in that case, the government will have to turn to money financing. The turn to money financing will provide some revenue, and, if the debt is nominal, may perhaps reduce the value of the outstanding debt through unanticipated inflation.

If the real interest rate is below the growth rate of income, with a zero primary deficit, then the government can continue debt financing without the debt–GDP ratio rising. In that case, debt finance is viable for the long term, and the hard choice posed by the Sargent–Wallace example can be avoided. Note also, though, that the tight link examined by Sargent and Wallace takes future primary deficits as given. If the government is willing to raise taxes at some future date to pay higher interest bills, there is no necessary link between current deficits and future money growth.

The Sargent–Wallace analysis does make clear why permanent deficits cause concern. If the national debt is growing relative to GDP, then ultimately the government will have to raise taxes or raise the inflation rate to meet its debt obligations. That is the long-run threat that leads people to worry about deficits. Of course, in this case the long run may be decades away.

There is a further important point. The Sargent–Wallace concern is about *primary* deficits: If the total deficit is constant as a percentage of GDP, then ultimately the debt–GDP ratio will stabilize provided the economy is growing at all. For instance, a statement that the deficit in Canada would be 5 percent of GDP forever would not mean that the debt would explode as a percentage of GDP. Rather, if the deficit were financed through debt, the debt–GDP ratio would eventually reach a steady state.[12] The explanation is that when the deficit is measured to *include* interest payments, a statement that the deficit will be constant forever means that behind the scenes the primary deficit or surplus is being adjusted to ensure that interest payments are being made without the debt–GDP ratio exploding.

Nominal Interest and the Budget Deficit

Nominal interest rates rise with the inflation rate and increase the measured budget deficit. To make this point we repeat Equation (12):

$$\text{Total deficit} = \text{primary deficit} + \text{interest payments} \qquad (12)$$

Suppose now that the government debt is at the relatively low level of just 20 percent of GDP. With an interest rate of, say, 10 percent, total interest payments are 2 percent of GDP (10 percent interest rate $\times$ 20 percent of GDP debt). Let the inflation rate rise by 90 percent, with the real interest rate remaining unchanged, so that the nominal interest rate goes up to 100 percent. Then total interest payments amount to 20 percent of GDP (100 percent interest rate $\times$ 20 percent of GDP debt), and the budget deficit measured as in (10) rises by no less than 18 percent of GDP. The data in this example are essentially those of Mexico in 1986, where the budget deficit during the inflation looked very large, despite the noninterest part of the budget being in surplus.

---

[12] This is a fairly technical but important point. If the total deficit is kept at a constant ratio to GDP, say 5 percent, that means that behind the scenes increasing interest payments are being met by higher taxes or lower government spending. Suppose that the debt–GDP ratio is denoted d, that GDP is growing at a real rate g, and that the total budget deficit as a percentage of GDP is denoted b. In steady state, debt is being issued at just the rate that keeps the debt–GDP ratio constant. That means that in steady state $b = gd$. Then the steady-state debt–GDP ratio is just equal to b/g. For instance, if the deficit is 5 percent of GDP forever, and the growth rate of GDP is 4 percent, then the debt–GDP ratio will be 1.25, or 125 percent in steady state. At that point, interest payments are a constant proportion of GDP.

The problem here is that the conventional way of measuring the deficit includes *nominal* interest on the debt. This can give a distorted impression of the size of the deficit, because in fact the government is paying the high interest to offset the effect of inflation in reducing the value of its outstanding debt. We should recognize that at the same time as the government has to pay high interest, it also receives revenue from the decline in the value of its outstanding debt, owing to inflation. In the 1970s many economists began to calculate inflation-corrected budget deficits that took account of the government's gain from inflation because the value of its debt fell. The inflation-corrected budget deficit is calculated taking into account the effect of inflation in reducing the outstanding value of the government's debt.

We return to the previous example for an illustrative calculation. Suppose the real interest rate is 5 percent and the primary deficit is zero. Then, with a debt–GDP ratio of 20 percent, the budget deficit at a zero inflation rate is only 1 percent of GDP. When the inflation rate hits 95 percent, with a nominal interest rate of 100 percent, the calculated nominal deficit becomes 20 percent of GDP. But the inflation-corrected deficit is still only 1 percent of GDP, as long as the real interest rate remains at 5 percent.

Although the principle of the calculation of inflation-corrected deficits is clear, there is some controversy about whether they should be used. The question that should be asked is whether the private sector wants to maintain the value of the debt-to-GDP ratio. If so, it will willingly finance the apparently increased nominal deficit by purchases of bonds. People need to step up bond purchases precisely because the real value of their existing bonds is being reduced through inflation. If, on the other hand, the inflation rate is high as a result of unexpectedly high printing of money, then the inflation-corrected deficit does not give a good measure of the extent to which people are willing to continue financing the existing deficit at the existing real interest rate by purchasing bonds.

18-4 Hyperinflation

Large budget deficits are inevitably part of the extreme inflations of 50 to 100 or even 500 percent per year that took place in the mid-1980s in Latin America and Israel. They are also part of the even more extreme cases of *hyperinflation*. Although there is no precise definition of the rate of inflation that deserves the star ranking of hyper rather than high inflation, a working definition takes 1000 percent per annum as the rate that marks a hyperinflation. Table 18-5 shows recent extreme inflation experiences.

In a hyperinflationary economy, inflation is so pervasive and such a problem that it completely dominates daily economic life. People spend significant amounts of resources minimizing the inflationary damage: They have to shop often, to get to the stores before the prices go up; their main concern in saving or investing is how to protect themselves against inflation; they reduce holdings of real balances to a remarkable extent to avoid the inflation tax, but have to compensate by going to the bank more often — daily or hourly instead of weekly, for example — to get currency.

Table 18-5 *Recent High-Inflation Experiences*

	1984	1985	1986	1987	1988	1989
(percent per year)						
Argentina	627	672	90	131	343	1 470
Bolivia	1 231	11 750	276	15	16	15
Brazil	65	58	86	132	682	820
Israel	374	305	48	20	16	19
Mexico	68	58	86	132	114	18
Nicaragua	35	220	681	911	10 205	23 710
Peru	110	163	78	86	825	3 564

The classic hyperinflations have taken place in the aftermath of wars. The most famous of all — though not the most rapid — was the German hyperinflation of 1922–1923. The average inflation rate during the hyperinflation was 322 percent *per month*. The highest rate of inflation was in October 1923, just before the end of the hyperinflation, when prices rose by more than 29 000 percent.[13] In dollars, that means that something that cost $1 at the beginning of the month would have cost $290 at the end of the month. The most rapid hyperinflation was that in Hungary at the end of World War II: The *average* rate of inflation from August 1945 to July 1946 was 19 800 percent per month, and the maximum monthly rate was 41.9 quadrillion percent.[14]

Keynes, in a masterful description of the hyperinflation process in Austria after World War I, tells of how people would order two beers at a time because they grew stale at a rate slower than the price was rising.[15] This and similar stories appear in all hyperinflations. They include the woman who carried her (almost worthless) currency in a basket and found that when she set it down for a moment, the basket was stolen but the money left behind. It was said that it was cheaper to take a taxi than a bus because in the taxi you pay at the end of the ride and in the bus at the beginning.

Hyperinflationary economies are typically marked by widespread indexing, more to the foreign exchange rate than to the price level. That is because it becomes difficult to keep measuring prices on a current basis when they change so fast. Thus prices might be specified in terms of dollars, and the actual amount of the local currency

---

[13] Data based on C.L. Holtferich, *Die Deutsche Inflation, 1914–1923* (New York: Walter de Gruyter, 1980).

[14] At least, so we think. The price level rose 41.9×10^{15} percent in July 1946. Data are from Phillip Cagan, "The Monetary Dynamics of Hyperinflation," in Milton Friedman, ed., *Studies in the Quantity Theory of Money* (Chicago: University of Chicago Press, 1956). This classic paper contains data on seven hyperinflations.

[15] John Maynard Keynes, *A Tract on Monetary Reform* (London: Macmillan, 1923). This remains one of the most readable accounts of inflation. See also Thomas William Guttmann and Patricia Meehan, *The Great Inflation* (London: Gordon and Cremonesi, 1975); and Leland Yeager et al., *Experiences with Stopping Inflation* (Washington, D.C.: American Enterprise Institute, 1981).

(marks in the German case) that has to be paid in each transaction is calculated from the dollar price and the exchange rate. Wages are paid very often at the end of hyper-inflation — in the German case, several times a day.

Deficits and Hyperinflation

The hyperinflationary economies all suffered from large budget deficits and from rapid money printing. In several cases the origin of the budget deficit was wartime spending, which generated large national debts and also destroyed the tax-gathering apparatus of the country.

There is, however, a two-way interaction between budget deficits and inflation. Large budget deficits can lead to rapid inflation by causing governments to print money to finance the deficit. In turn, high inflation increases the measured deficit. As we have seen, inflation increases budget deficits through increases in nominal interest rates. A second link between inflation and deficits arises from the tax-collection system.

As the inflation rate rises, the real revenue raised from taxation falls. The reason is that there are lags in both the calculation and payment of taxes. Suppose, to take an extreme example, that people pay taxes on April 30 on the income they earned the previous year. Consider someone who earned $50 000 last year, who has a tax bill of $10 000 due on April 30. If prices have in the meantime gone up by a factor of 10, as they might in a hyperinflation, the real value of the taxes is only one-tenth of what it should be. The budget deficit can rapidly get out of hand.

In principle the tax system can be indexed to adjust for the inflation, but that is difficult, especially for business taxation, and in any event even indexing lags behind. For example, if the monthly rate of inflation is 20 percent (equivalent to an annual rate of nearly 800 percent), then even if the amount that has to be paid is fixed according to the most recent price index, and if it takes a month to collect taxes, inflation causes the government to lose 20 percent of the value of its taxes.

The Inflation Tax and Accelerating Hyperinflation

Rates of money growth are also very high during hyperinflations, of the same order of magnitude as the inflation rate.[16] The high rates of money growth originate in attempts to finance government spending.

However, as the inflations progress, and the tax collection system breaks down, the government reaches a point where it tries to raise more through money printing than the maximum amount IR^* that it can in Figure 18-9. It can succeed in raising more than IR^* *temporarily*, by printing money even faster than people expected. That increased money growth causes the inflation rate to increase and, as the government

---

[16] On average, though, the growth rate of money is below the inflation rate. That is because people are reducing their holdings of real balances during hyperinflation; if M/P is falling, then P has on average to be growing faster than M.

continues to try to spend more than IR°, it continues driving up the inflation rate. The amount of real money balances that people hold becomes smaller and smaller, as they try to flee the inflation tax, and the government prints money even more rapidly to try to finance its expenditure. In the end the process will break down.

Stopping Hyperinflations

All hyperinflations come to an end. The dislocation of the economy becomes too great for the public to bear, and the government finds a way of reforming its budget process. Often a new money is introduced, and the tax system is reformed. Typically, too, the exchange rate of the new money is pegged to that of a foreign currency, to provide an anchor for prices and expectations. Frequently there are unsuccessful attempts at stabilization before the final success.

The presence of so many destabilizing factors in inflation, particularly the collapse of the tax system as the inflation proceeds, together with an economy that is extremely dislocated by inflation, raises a fascinating possibility. A coordinated attack on inflation may stop the inflation with relatively little unemployment cost. This approach was used in Argentina and Israel in 1985, and Brazil in 1986, when the governments froze wages and prices. That stopped the inflation at a single blow. They also fixed their exchange rates, and there were significant changes in fiscal policy, to put the budget closer to long-run balance. In each case there was little increase in unemployment. Despite the early encouraging signs, the ultimate success of these stabilization programs remains to be established.

One more important feature of the stabilizations should be brought out. *Money growth rates following stabilization are very high.* Why? Because as people expect less inflation, nominal interest rates decline, and the demand for real balances rises. With the demand for real balances increasing, the government can create more money without creating inflation. Thus, at the beginning of a successful stabilization there may be a bonus for the government: It can temporarily finance part of the deficit through the printing of money, without renewing inflation. But it certainly cannot do so for very long periods without reigniting inflation.

18-5 Summary

1. A sustained monetary expansion typically expands income in the short run. In the long run, higher money growth is translated fully into inflation. Real interest rates and income return to the full-employment level. Only under rational expectations and with full wage and price flexibility does a monetary expansion translate instantly into a more rapid rate of inflation with no impact on income.

2. A sustained change in money growth ultimately raises the nominal interest rate by the same amount. This positive association between inflation and nominal interest rates is called the Fisher effect.

Box 18-1 Bolivian Hyperinflation and Stabilization

In the 1920s, Europe experienced hyperinflation, and the experience is reviewed in an important paper by Sargent.[a] Latin America followed in the 1980s. In 1985 Bolivia experienced a full-fledged hyperinflation, as can be seen in Figure 1. At the peak, in

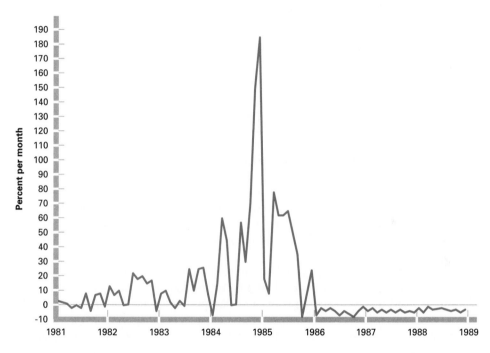

Figure I *Bolivian Hyperinflation, 1981–1988*

(*Source:* Banco Central de Bolivia)

mid-1985, inflation was, at an annual rate, 35 000 percent! There were three main reasons for the hyperinflation. First, like other Latin American countries, Bolivia had overborrowed in the 1970s. When, in the early 1980s, interest rates increased in world markets, debts could no longer be serviced by taking out new loans for the purpose of paying the interest on the old loans. The country was not in a position to service easily the very large external debt. The attempt to do so strained the budget and led to high rates of money creation. Second, commodity prices, especially of tin, fell sharply. For Bolivia, this meant a large fall in real income and in revenues for the government. Third, the substantial political instability led to capital flight. The combination of factors set off an inflationary spiral that forced increasing depreciation of the currency and opened an ever wider gap between government outlays and revenues. Tax collection dropped sharply by more than half, as can be seen in Table 1.

Table I *The Bolivian Hyperinflation*

	1980–1983	1984	1985	1986
Budget deficit[a]	11.9	26.5	10.8	3.0
Tax collection[a]	6.7	2.3	3.1	6.6
Inflation[b]	123	1 282	11 750	276

[a]Percent of GDP.
[b]Percent per year.
Source: World Bank and Banco Central de Bolivia.

By 1984–1985 the government was attempting to finance nearly 25 percent of GDP with money creation, but, of course, by this time the demand for real balances had fallen to negligible levels because of the hyperinflation. It took ever larger rates of inflation to finance the ever-growing deficit.

In August–September 1985 a new government came into power and, in a short time, imposed a drastic stabilization plan. By stopping external debt service and raising taxes, the government brought the drain in the budget under control, reduced money creation from the extreme rates of the past years, and stabilized the exchange rate. Within half a year, the inflation rate had come down to less than 50 percent. Moreover, because the decrease in budget deficit was maintained and reinforced, the gain in disinflation continued. By 1989, inflation rates had fallen to less than 10 percent per year.

The Bolivian stabilization is a good example of how a sharp turn toward fiscal deficit can stop a major inflation, but there should be no illusion about the costs.[b] As a result of austerity (and of poor export prices) Bolivian per capita income in 1989 was 35 percent less than it had been at its peak 10 years earlier. Inflation had been brought under control, but confidence was not sufficient to bring back growth on a significant scale.

While Bolivia succeeded in controlling inflation, in several other Latin American countries inflation was exploding. An important question for these countries was whether wage–price controls (called *heterodox* programs) would be a helpful supplement to the *orthodox* medicine of fiscal austerity. The stabilization attempts, demonstrated several times in 1985–1989 in Argentina and Brazil, were long on the former and short on the latter.[c]

[a] See Thomas Sargent, "The End of Four Big Inflations," in R. Hall, ed., *Inflation* (Chicago: University of Chicago Press, 1982).

[b] See Juan A. Morales, "Inflation Stabilization in Bolivia," in M. Bruno et al., eds., *Inflation Stabilization* (Cambridge, Mass.: MIT Press, 1988); and J. Sachs, "The Bolivian Hyperinflation and Stabilization," *American Economic Review*, May 1987.

[c] See E. Helpman and L. Leiderman, "Stabilization in High Inflation Countries: Analytical Foundations of Recent Experience," *Carnegie Rochester Conference Series on Public Policy*, no. 28 (1988); M. Kiguel and N. Liviatan, "Inflationary Rigidities and Orthodox Stabilization Policies: Lessons from Latin America," *The World Bank Economic Review*, no. 3 (1988); M. Blejer and N. Liviatan, "Fighting Hyperinflation," *IMF Staff Papers*, September 1987; as well as Bruno et al., eds., *Inflation Stabilization*.

3. In the short run, increased money growth will lead to lower nominal interest rates if expectations adjust slowly. This is called the liquidity effect.

4. A sustained monetary expansion ultimately raises nominal interest rates and hence reduces the demand for real balances. That means that prices must on average rise faster than money in the transition to the new long-run equilibrium.

5. Inflation is a tax on real balances. To keep constant the purchasing power of holdings of money in the face of rising prices, a person has to add to nominal balances. In this fashion, resources are transferred from money holders to money issuers, specifically the government.

6. A decision to finance a deficit through bond sales today may mean a higher inflation rate in the future if the government eventually has to finance the deficit through money printing. That is because the interest payments on the debt accumulate to increase future deficits, given a fixed primary deficit. This tradeoff exists when the interest rate exceeds the growth rate of income.

7. Hyperinflations have generally taken place in the aftermaths of wars. Large deficits are typical in hyperinflations. Governments can use the inflation tax to finance deficits to a limited extent, but if too large a deficit has to be financed, inflation explodes.

8. There is a two-way interaction between inflation and budget deficits. Higher inflation rates raise the deficit by reducing the real value of tax collection. Higher nominal interest rates raise the measured deficit by increasing the value of nominal interest payments in the budget. The inflation-corrected deficit adjusts for this latter effect.

9. Money growth rates are very high following a successful inflation stabilization, as people increase their holdings of real balances.

Key Terms

Fisher effect   **Inflation tax**
Liquidity effect   **Seigniorage**
Expectations effect   **Inflation-corrected deficit**
Hyperinflation

Problems

1. **(a)** Show graphically the effects of a reduction in the growth rate of money on income and inflation.

    (b) Show also how the real interest rate adjusts over time. Be specific about the expectations assumption you are using.

2. In the above example, show how the nominal interest rate adjusts to lower inflation.

3. We stated in the text that under rational expectations and with full price and wage flexibility, the inflation rate rises immediately to its new steady-state level when the growth rate of money increases. We also stated that real balance holdings decline when the expected inflation rate rises. How can the level of real balances fall under rational expectations if the inflation rate is equal to the growth rate of money? (*Hint*: With prices fully flexible, they can change all at once when new information becomes available.)

4. **(a)** Explain the Fisher equation that describes the relationship between the nominal interest rate and expected inflation.
   (b) Use Figure 18-8 to show that the real interest rate was very high in 1981.

5. Suppose the ratio of money base to GDP is 10 percent. The government is considering raising the inflation rate from the current 0 to 10 percent per annum and believes it will obtain an increase in government revenue of 1 percent of GDP by doing so. Explain why that calculation overestimates the inflation tax the government will receive at a 10 percent inflation rate.

6. During 1981–1986, the government of Canada added massively to the national debt.
   (a) Explain why you might worry that this is inflationary.
   (b) Explain whether you actually worry that the high deficits of the early 1980s will lead to high inflation later.

7. At the height of the German hyperinflation, the government was covering only 1 percent of its spending with taxes.
   (a) What happened to the rest?
   (b) How could the German government possibly finance the remaining 99 percent of its spending? Refer to Figure 18-9.

8. **(a)** If the debt–GDP ratio is 30 percent, the nominal interest rate is 12 percent, the inflation rate is 7 percent, and the total budget deficit is 4 percent of GDP, calculate the inflation-adjusted deficit.
   (b) Suppose you were to discover in an inflationary economy that the inflation-corrected budget was in surplus. Explain why in that case the government might be able to sustain a low inflation rate if it could only find a way of getting the rate down to start with.

9. Explain how, following the end of hyperinflation, it was possible for the nominal money stock in Germany to increase by a factor of nearly 20 without restarting the inflation.

10. Why do budget deficits create such alarm? Distinguish the short from the long run in developing your answer.

CHAPTER 19 *Monetarism and the Fight Against Inflation in Canada*

The monetarist challenge to mainstream Keynesian discretionary policy first gathered strength during the 1960s and exerted a strong influence on monetary policy in Canada and other industrial countries during the 1970s. Support for monetarism subsequently waned as it failed to deliver on its promise to deal with inflation. In the latter part of the decade, a more sophisticated critique of discretionary policy, known as the *new classical macroeconomics*, or the *rational expectations* approach, gained influence. A detailed discussion of this theory is given in the next chapter.

We begin this chapter with a description of monetarism and its influence on Bank of Canada policy. This is followed by a discussion of anti-inflationary policy in Canada from the mid-1970s to the early 1990s.

19-1 Monetarism

Milton Friedman and monetarism are almost synonymous. Monetarism appears, however, in many shades and covers quite a spectrum from a hard monetarism, beyond the Friedman variety, to eclectic Keynesianism. In that spectrum one would include

Allan Meltzer of Carnegie-Mellon, Thomas Mayer of the University of California at Davis, Phillip Cagan of Columbia University, David Laidler and Michael Parkin of the University of Western Ontario, and William Poole of Brown University, to name only some of the most prominent. But monetarism is not confined to academic economists. Indeed, the Federal Reserve Bank of St. Louis has long been a haven for the monetarist perspective on macroeconomics. If monetarism admits of some diversity, it nevertheless comes down to the proposition that money is extremely important for macroeconomics, that money is more important than other things such as fiscal policy, and, in some variants, that money is virtually all that matters.

We define monetarism by describing Friedman's views, but we should warn you that in so doing we overemphasize Friedman's role in developing and sustaining monetarism. Friedman's views on macroeconomics have been laid out in a series of scholarly articles, books, and popular writing.[1] Outstanding among his publications is *A Monetary History of the United States, 1867–1960*, a book written jointly with Anna J. Schwartz of the National Bureau of Economic Research. Despite its length, the *Monetary History* is an absorbing book that skillfully relates the behaviour of the economy to the behaviour of the stock of money. The book generally attributes changes in the level of prices and in economic activity, including the great depression, to movements in the stock of money.

What are the main features of monetarism?[2]

Emphasis on the Stock of Money

Monetarism emphasized the importance of the behaviour of the money stock in determining (1) the rate of inflation in the long run and (2) the behaviour of real GDP in the short run. Friedman has said:[3]

> *I regard the description of our position as "money is all that matters for changes in* nominal *income and for* short-run *changes in real income" as an exaggeration but one that gives the right flavour of our conclusions.*

The view that the behaviour of the money stock is crucial for determining the rate of inflation in the long run is consistent with the analysis of Chapter 18, as we noted there. The view that the behaviour of the money stock — by which Friedman usually means the *growth rate* of the money stock — is of primary importance in determining the behaviour of nominal and real GDP in the short run is not one we have accepted,

---

[1] Some of Friedman's major articles are reprinted in *The Optimum Quantity of Money* (Chicago: Aldine, 1969). See also his book *A Program for Monetary Stability* (New York: Fordham University Press, 1959), and Milton Friedman and Anna J. Schwartz, *A Monetary History of the United States, 1867–1960* (Princeton, N.J.: Princeton University Press, 1963).

[2] For recent contributions, see James Dorn and Anna J. Schwartz, eds., *The Search for Stable Money* (Chicago: University of Chicago Press, 1988).

[3] "A Theoretical Framework for Monetary Analysis," *Journal of Political Economy*, March/April 1970, p. 217.

nor one to which the evidence of the 1980s has been kind. Our treatment has given emphasis to *both* monetary and fiscal variables in determining the short-run behaviour of nominal and real GDP, but there is no doubt that monetary variables play an important role in determining nominal and real GDP in the short run.

Friedman's view of the primary importance of money is based in part on careful historical studies, in which he and Anna Schwartz were able to relate the booms and recessions of U.S. economic history to the behaviour of the money stock. In general, it appeared that increases in the growth rate of money produced booms and inflations, and decreases in money stock produced recessions and sometimes deflations.[4]

Long and Variable Lags

Monetarism has emphasized that the effects of changes in the growth rate of money on the subsequent behaviour of GDP occur with long and variable lags. On average, it takes a long time for a change in the growth rate of money to affect GDP, and so the lag is long. In addition, the time it takes for this change to affect GDP varies from one historical episode to another — the lags are variable. These arguments are based on empirical and not theoretical evidence. Friedman estimates the lags may be as short as six months and as long as two years.

The Monetary Rule

Combining the preceding arguments, Friedman argues against the use of active monetary policy. He suggests that because the behaviour of the money stock is of critical importance for the behaviour of real and nominal GDP, and because money operates with a long and variable lag, monetary policy should not be used to "fine tune" the economy. The active use of monetary policy might actually destabilize the economy, because an action taken in 1993, say, might affect the economy at any of various future dates, such as in 1994 or 1995. By 1995, the action taken in 1993 might be inappropriate for the stabilization of GDP. Besides, there is no certainty that the policy will take effect in 1995 rather than 1994.[5]

Thus monetarists argue that, although monetary policy has powerful effects on GDP, it should not be actively used lest it destabilize the economy. Accordingly, their view is that the money supply should be kept growing at a constant rate, to minimize the potential damage that inappropriate policy can cause.[6]

---

[4] Strong supporting evidence from the post–World War II period for the view that money matters is provided by Christina Romer and David Romer, "Does Monetary Policy Matter? A New Test in the Spirit of Friedman and Schwartz," *NBER Macroeconomics Annual*, 1989.

[5] For a concise statement, see Milton Friedman, "The Case for a Monetary Rule," *Newsweek*, February 7, 1972, reprinted in *Bright Promises, Dismal Performance*, pp. 225–27. See, too, his article, "The Role of Monetary Policy," *American Economic Review*, March 1968.

[6] In Chapter 14 we discussed the case for a monetary rule that arises from the problem of dynamic inconsistency. This argument was not typically made by monetarists; rather, it is a later argument more associated with the rational expectations equilibrium approach to macroeconomics.

Interest Rates Versus Monetary Targets

In the *IS-LM* model, changes in the money stock affect the economy primarily by changing interest rates, which, in turn, affect aggregate demand and thus GDP. Since the central bank can control the level of interest rates, and since interest rates provide a guide to the effects of monetary policy on the economy, it seems perfectly sensible for it to carry out monetary policy by controlling interest rates. Through the 1950s and most of the 1960s, central banks did carry out monetary policy by attempting to set the level of interest rates.

Friedman and monetarism brought two serious criticisms of the procedure of attempting to set interest rates as the basis for the conduct of monetary policy. The first is that the behaviour of nominal interest rates is not a good guide to the direction, whether expansionary or contractionary, of monetary policy. The *real* interest rate, the nominal interest rate minus the expected rate of inflation, is the rate relevant to determining the level of investment. A high nominal interest rate, together with a high expected rate of inflation, means a low real rate of interest. Thus, monetary policy might be quite expansionary in its effects on investment spending, even when nominal interest rates are high. Consequently, Friedman and other monetarists argued, the central bank should not concentrate on the behaviour of nominal interest rates in the conduct of monetary policy.

The second criticism is that attempts to control nominal interest rates might be destabilizing. Suppose that the central bank desired that monetary policy should be expansionary and that the interest rate should be lowered. To achieve these goals it buys bonds in the open market, increasing the money supply. The expansionary monetary policy itself tends to raise the inflation rate. It thus tends to raise the nominal interest rate as investors adjust their expectation of inflation in response to the behaviour of the actual inflation rate. However, then the central bank would have to engage in a further open market purchase in an attempt to keep the nominal interest rate low, and that would lead to further inflation, further increases in nominal interest rates, and further open market purchases. The end result is that an attempt to keep nominal interest rates low may lead to increasing inflation. Therefore, Friedman argues, the central bank should not pay attention to the behaviour of nominal interest rates in the conduct of monetary policy, and should, rather, keep the money supply growing at a constant rate.

Each of these arguments on the dangers of conducting monetary policy by reference to nominal interest rates is important. It is indeed correct that real, and not nominal, interest rates provide the appropriate measure of the effects of monetary policy on aggregate demand. It is also true that the central bank could, by attempting to keep nominal interest rates low forever, destabilize the economy. However, once the latter danger has been pointed out, the probability that it will destabilize the economy by operating with reference to interest rates is reduced. The use of interest rates as a guide to the direction of monetary policy does not mean that the central bank has to attempt to keep the interest rate fixed forever at some level. Instead, it may aim each month or quarter for an interest rate target that it regards as appropriate for the current and predicted economic situation.

The monetarist case for concentrating on the behaviour of the money stock in the conduct of monetary policy is a strong, but not conclusive, one. The major weakness in the argument is that the demand for real balances may change over time. Indeed, as we indicate in the next section, instability in the demand for money was a major factor in the abandonment of monetary targets by the Bank of Canada in 1982.

Because of shifts in the demand for money, the behaviour of the money stock is not a perfect guide to the conduct of monetary policy. Neither is the behaviour of nominal interest rates. However, the behaviour of the nominal money stock and the behaviour of nominal interest rates both provide some information about the direction in which monetary policy is pushing the economy, imperfect as each measure is. Accordingly, the central bank should pay attention to the behaviour of both interest rates and the supply of money in the conduct of its monetary policy.[7]

The Importance of Fiscal Policy

Friedman has frequently said, if tongue in cheek, that fiscal policy is very important. Although we noted earlier that he argues fiscal policy itself is not important for the behaviour of GDP, he does contend that it is of vital importance in setting the size of government and the role of government in the economy. Friedman is an opponent of big government. He has made the interesting argument that government spending increases to match the revenues available. The government will spend the full tax collection — and some more. Accordingly, he is in favour of tax cuts as a way of reducing government spending.

Friedman stands out in arguing that fiscal policy does not have strong effects on the economy except to the extent that it affects the behaviour of money. Thus he has remarked:

> To have a significant impact on the economy, a tax increase must somehow affect monetary policy — the quantity of money and its rate of growth. . . .
>
> The level of taxes is important — because it affects how much of our resources we use through the government and how much we use as individuals. It is not important as a sensitive and powerful device to control the short-run course of income and prices.[8]

The Inherent Stability of the Private Sector

The final aspect of monetarism we consider here is the monetarist view that the economy, left to itself, is more stable than when the government manages it with discre-

---

[7] The argument is worked out in Benjamin M. Friedman, "Targets, Instruments, and Indicators of Monetary Policy," *Journal of Monetary Economics*, October 1975.

[8] Milton Friedman, "Higher Taxes? No," *Newsweek*, January 23, 1967. Reprinted in "There's No Such Thing as a Free Lunch" (La Salle, Ill.: Open Court Publications, 1975), p. 89.

tionary policy, and that the major cause of economic fluctuations lies in inappropriate government actions. This view is quite fundamental in that it underlies many other monetarist positions, and it may be the litmus test for distinguishing monetarists from other macroeconomists. It is because this point is so fundamental that a major stage in the acceptance of monetarism occurred when Friedman and Schwartz published their *Monetary History of the United States*. In it they provided evidence for the view that the great depression was the result of bad monetary policy rather than private sector instability, arising, say, from autonomous shifts in consumption or investment demand.

Summary: We Are Almost All Partly Monetarists

From the viewpoint of the conduct of economic policy, the major monetarist themes are (1) an emphasis on the growth rate of the money stock, (2) arguments against fine tuning in favour of a monetary rule, and (3) a greater weight that monetarists, as compared for example with Keynesians, place on the costs of inflation relative to those of unemployment.

Although we describe these as the major monetarist propositions relating to policy, it is not true that macroeconomists can be neatly divided into two groups, some subscribing to the monetarist religion and others to a less fundamentalist faith called neo-Keynesianism. Most of the arguments advanced by Friedman and his associates are technical and susceptible to economic analysis and the application of empirical evidence. Many of those propositions are now widely accepted and are no longer particularly associated with monetarism. As Franco Modigliani has remarked, "We are all monetarists now." He adds that we are monetarists in the sense that all (or most) macroeconomists believe in the importance of money.

Slow Adjustment of Wages and Prices

Keynesians and monetarists agree on one fundamental issue: that the economy adjusts only slowly to changes in policy, and that policy changes usually affect output first and inflation later. Accordingly, monetarists, like Keynesians, argued that an inflation could not be reduced without producing a recession. Although both monetarists and Keynesians relied on much the same analysis to explain why disinflation could not come cheaply (the aggregate supply–demand analysis of Chapter 16), that explanation left many economists dissatisfied. They worried that the slow adjustment of wages and prices assumed in those models lacked a firm theoretical basis. Early in the 1970s, a radical new development in macroeconomics seemed to promise improved understanding of the effects of policy measures on the economy. This was the rational expectations equilibrium approach. We discuss this theory in detail in Chapter 20 below.

19-2 Monetarism and the Bank of Canada

As we saw in Chapter 14, in the early 1970s the Bank of Canada moved toward greater emphasis on the control of the money supply in implementing monetary policy. In 1975 it began the practice of announcing target ranges for the rate of growth of the money supply.

In his *Annual Report* for 1975, the governor stressed the importance of bringing down the rate of inflation and addressed the question of how this should be accomplished:

> *One answer sometimes given to this question is that the Bank of Canada should do the job through a sharp and immediate reduction of the growth rate of the money supply to a rate approximately in line with the sustainable real growth of the economy. If that were to happen, it is asserted, inflation would readily come to an end.*
>
> *The trouble with this prescription is not with the medicine but with the dosage, which would be so great that the patient would suffer excessively while it was working. It would sharply curtail the growth of spending on goods and services in the face of continuing large increases in production costs already built into the economy, and this would almost certainly result in extremely weak markets, widespread bankruptcies and soaring unemployment. It must be recognized that the annual rate of increase in average Canadian money incomes that is consistent with price stability is no higher than the trend rate of increase in national productivity, which is usually put at around 2 per cent per year, and we are a long way from that situation. All sorts of existing arrangements, including virtually all wage contracts, are based on the assumption of some continuing inflation. The attempt to force as rapid a transition to price and cost stability as this prescription involves would be too disruptive in economic and social terms to be sensible or tolerable.*[9]

Thus the Bank of Canada clearly rejected a cold turkey policy and opted for gradualism. This strategy was subsequently implemented by successive reductions in the target to the range of 4 to 8 percent established in February 1981. As can be seen in Figure 19-1, the Bank generally kept monetary growth within the target range until the second half of 1981.[10] As discussed in the next section, the Bank abandoned gradualism at that time in response to a severe tightening of monetary policy in the U.S.

After the adoption by the Bank of Canada of a monetarist strategy, the governor enunciated on a number of occasions the philosophy and principles underlying it. In a statement before the House of Commons Standing Committee on Finance, Trade

---

[9] Bank of Canada, *Annual Report*, 1975, p. 10.

[10] The exceptions have been periods in which the payments system was disrupted by postal strikes, as indicated in the chart.

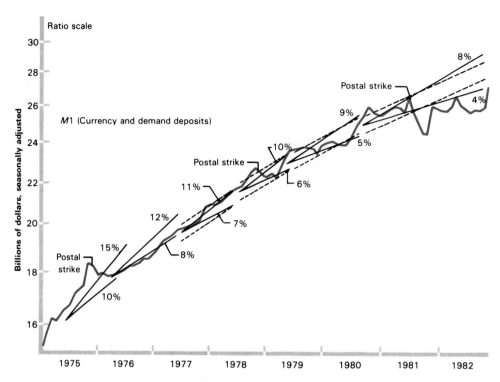

Figure 19-1 *Actual and Target Growth Ranges for M1, 1975–1982*

(*Source:* Adapted from Bank of Canada, *Annual Report*, 1982)

and Economic Affairs, the governor put forward three basic propositions. The first reaffirmed the overriding importance of bringing down the rate of inflation:

> *For quite a few years now the nature of the major threat to the future economic welfare of the country has been unusually clear. That threat is inflation. The idea that some inflation is on balance helpful to the performance of an economy, that inflation is benign — an idea that was never more than superficially plausible but was nevertheless quite popular — is now thoroughly discredited. What has discredited it so effectively is not economic theory but economic experience. The experience of the world economy and the widely varying experience of its national members have shown beyond reasonable question that inflation is malignant. The matter is no longer seriously debated.*

As to the role of monetary policy in fighting inflation, the governor stated:

> *There is one proposition that must never be forgotten, and that is that in a free society no strategy for dealing with inflation will succeed unless it is well sup-*

*ported by firm and continuing control of the rate of monetary expansion in the
society. That proposition is, I assure you, as reliable as any general proposition
in the whole field of economics. Every central banker in the world knows it to
be true, and I doubt that any serious and experienced student of financial affairs
would question it. It is a very firm proposition indeed, and anyone who wants
to participate responsibly in the debate on how to deal with inflation would be
well advised to keep it uppermost in his mind.*

In his third proposition, the governor put forward the distinction between real and
nominal interest rates:

*The basic reason why interest rates are so high is because current and expected
rates of inflation are so high. If you make allowance for the current rate of
inflation, interest rates are not in fact unusually high. They are not so high as to
provide savers with a large real return before taxes or in many cases with a real
return at all after taxes. They are not so high as to discourage borrowers who
expect continued high rates of inflation.*[11]

Thus the Bank of Canada made a clear commitment to an anti-inflation policy based
on monetary gradualism. In doing so, it recognized the consequences not only for the
levels of output and employment, but also for the behaviour of nominal interest rates.
In his *Annual Report* for 1978, the governor stated:

*Whatever their object, however, central bank actions that have the effect of speed-
ing up or slowing down the trend over time in the rate of growth of the money
supply have longer run effects on the level of interest rates that can be quite the
opposite of the effects produced in the short run. A stepped-up rate of monetary
expansion that temporarily lowers interest rates will, if it is sustained, lead eventually to a higher rate of price increase than would otherwise have occurred.
With money losing its value more rapidly, borrowers will be less reluctant to
incur debt since they can repay in dollars of lesser value, while savers and lenders
will for the same reason be more reluctant to provide loans. The consequence of
rising inflation will thus be a growing excess demand for credit in relation to the
supply which will put increasing upward pressure on interest rates. Thus the
eventual result of letting the money supply grow too rapidly is not low interest
rates but high interest rates.*

*If a country wants to have and maintain low interest rates, there is no secret
about how to achieve that. Monetary growth must be reduced until it is only just
sufficient to finance the expansion in production that the economy is capable of
achieving over the longer run without putting pressure on the over-all level of*

---

[11] Reprinted in the *Bank of Canada Review*, November 1980, pp. 13–19. The earliest statement was given
in an address to the Canadian Chamber of Commerce in Saskatoon in September 1975. This speech has
been dubbed the "Saskatoon monetary manifesto" by Thomas Courchene. See T.J. Courchene, *Monetarism and Controls: The Inflation Fighters* (Toronto: C.D. Howe Research Institute, 1976).

prices, and it must be kept there. The immediate effect of this policy will be to raise interest rates but the longer term effect will be to lower them. The low interest rate countries of the world are the ones that have had the greatest success over the years in resisting the temptation to allow inflationary pressures to be underwritten by excessive monetary expansion. The countries that have experienced less success in controlling the process of domestic monetary expansion have higher rates of inflation and higher interest rates.[12]

19-3 The Fight Against Inflation

As discussed in the previous section, the Bank of Canada instituted a policy in late 1975 of gradually reducing the rate of growth of the money supply. At the same time, the government announced a program of wage and price controls to be administered by an Anti-Inflation Board (AIB). The board was given statutory power to control wages and profit margins of private firms with 500 or more employees. Provincial and municipal government wage setting was brought into the program through agreements with the provinces to apply the guidelines established by the federal board. The controls remained in effect until they were phased out beginning in April 1978. Let us examine the performance of the Canadian economy in response to these two policy initiatives.

Wage Settlements and the AIB

The top panel of Figure 19-2 shows the average annual percentage increases in base rates of pay negotiated in wage contracts over the period 1974 to 1983. Prior to the formation of the AIB, wage settlements had risen to nearly 19 percent per year, but during 1976 and 1977 there was a substantial moderation in the rate of increase. However, as shown in the second panel of Figure 19-2, during the same period the seasonally adjusted unemployment rate rose from 6.8 percent to 8.4 percent. To measure the effect of the controls, it is necessary to estimate on the basis of historical experience what wage increases would have occurred in the absence of controls given the actual economic conditions experienced.

In a study undertaken for the Economic Council of Canada, Cousineau and Lacroix estimated that the average annual wage increase in major collective agreements would have been 1.7 percentage points higher in the private sector and 4.3 percentage points higher in the public sector had the anti-inflation guidelines not been in force.[13] In another study, Auld, Christofides, Swidinsky and Wilton concluded that "in the period of AIB wage controls, union wage settlements in the private and public sectors have been between 2 1/2 and 3 1/2 percentage points per annum lower than the pre-AIB wage structure would predict; by 1977 the cumulative wage affect of the AIB was on

---

[12] Bank of Canada, *Annual Report*, 1978, p. 14.
[13] See Economic Council of Canada, *Fourteenth Annual Review* (1977), p. 20.

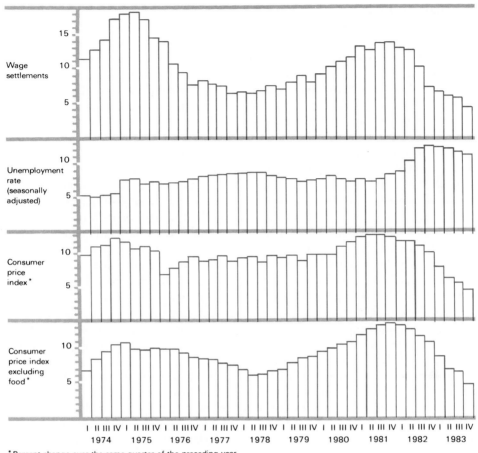

Figure 19-2   *Inflation and Unemployment, 1974–1983*

(*Source:* Adapted from *Bank of Canada Review*)

the order of 3.2 percent in the private and 4.6 percent in the public sectors."[14] Thus it would appear that controls had an impact particularly on public sector wages, but that they were responsible for a limited part of the moderation in negotiated wage increases that occurred.[15]

---

[14] D. Auld, L. Christofides, R. Swidinsky, and D. Wilton, "The Impact of the Anti-Inflation Board on Negotiated Wage Settlements," *Canadian Journal of Economics*, May 1979, p. 209.

[15] For a review of empirical studies on the effect of the AIB, see W.C. Riddell, *Dealing with Inflation and Unemployment in Canada*, Research Studies of the Royal Commission on the Economic Union and Development Prospects for Canada, Vol. 25 (Toronto: University of Toronto Press, 1986), pp. 78–84.

The Rate of Inflation

The third panel of Figure 19-2 shows the rate of inflation as measured by the percentage change in the Consumer Price Index over the same quarter of the preceding year. During 1976 the rate fell dramatically from the level above 10 percent recorded in 1975 to 5.9 percent. However, a closer look at the components of the CPI shows that very little of this decline in the rate of inflation can be attributed to the AIB controls. A major contributing factor was the sharp decline in the rate of increase of food prices which were not subject to controls.

Since food prices typically exhibit wide variations from year to year, it is common to use the CPI excluding food as a measure of the underlying trend in the rate of inflation.[16] As can be seen in the bottom panel of Figure 19-2, this index shows a slow but steady decline from the fourth quarter of 1975 to the second quarter of 1978, when it fell to 6 percent. Unfortunately, in the third quarter of 1978 the downward trend in the underlying rate of inflation was reversed, and by the third quarter of 1981 the CPI excluding food was increasing at a rate above 13 percent, in spite of the fact that the unemployment rate had remained above 7 percent since mid-1976.

In June 1982, the federal government introduced a limited program of wage controls known as the "6 and 5" program that limited wage increases to 6 percent in the first year and 5 percent in the second. The restrictions applied only to the federal public service and Crown corporations. Federal agencies which regulate prices such as telephone rates were asked to adhere to the guidelines, and most provincial governments introduced similar restraint programs.

Concern about the rising rate of inflation also led to a severe tightening of monetary policy. During the first half of 1981, the Federal Reserve pushed up interest rates sharply in the U.S., and the Bank of Canada followed suit. By the middle of the year, short-term interest rates in Canada had risen above 20 percent. As can be seen in Figure 19-2, the rate of inflation subsequently declined sharply, but this was achieved by exploiting the short-run Phillips curve tradeoff and allowing a drastic increase in the unemployment rate.

Was Monetarism a Failure?

The performance of the Canadian economy over the period 1975 to 1983 led to considerable controversy over the monetarist strategy of the Bank of Canada.[17] The success of the Bank's policy was hindered by the impact of supply shocks, difficulties in using

---

[16]   More recently the Bank of Canada has been using the CPI excluding both food and energy to measure the underlying rate.

[17]   See, for example, the following two studies sponsored by the Canadian Institute for Economic Policy: A.W. Donner and D.D. Peters, *The Monetarist Counter-Revolution: A Critique of Canadian Monetary Policy 1975–1979*; and C.L. Barber and J.C.P. McCallum, *Unemployment and Inflation: The Canadian Experience*.

money supply measures as targets of policy, and problems with the implementation of gradualism.

First, with regard to supply shocks, one can accept the monetarist view that control of the money supply is an essential part of any anti-inflationary policy, while at the same time recognizing that other factors influence short-run movements in the price level. In particular, the sharp increases in world prices of oil and other commodities that occurred in 1973–1974 and 1978–1979 led to increases in both the rate of inflation and the unemployment rate.

Second, the Bank of Canada's Annual Reports for 1981 and 1982 both contained detailed discussions of the Bank's experience with the use of $M1$ as a target of monetary policy. It is argued that the usefulness of this measure of the money supply has been impaired by innovations in banking practice such as daily interest savings accounts and expanded cash management services for businesses. Initially the Bank attempted to adjust for these influences on the demand for money, but in November 1982 it announced that it would no longer establish $M1$ targets.

As we saw in Chapter 14, the use of money supply targets is appropriate when the demand for money is stable and the main source of disturbances is the goods market. The breakdown in the stability of the money demand thus forced the Bank to abandon money supply targets.

Lastly, the Bank of Canada has argued on a number of occasions that the failure of its anti-inflation policy over the period 1975–1980 was in part caused by excessive gradualism. For example, in a statement before the House of Commons Standing Committee on Finance, Trade and Economic Affairs, Governor Bouey stated:

> *The experience of the past few years appears to have led some observers to conclude that the Bank's approach to reducing inflation has failed. If they mean that progress in reducing inflation is less than the Bank hoped, I agree with them. But if they mean, as I think some of them do, that the Bank's approach was misconceived, then they have misread the history of the period. What they should conclude is that given the economic and financial developments over that period, many of which were unpredictable, it would have been better if the slowing of monetary growth had been less gradual so that it would have had more impact on inflation. That is the moral that should be drawn. In this connection I would point out that the rate of monetary expansion today is very much lower than it was five years ago and although we have arrived at this position through a very gradual process, the impact on total spending can be expected to be much firmer from now on than it was when we started on this path.*[18]

This view was supported by the experience of the period 1981–1983 when the Bank of Canada abandoned gradualism. Following the lead of the Federal Reserve in the United States and Prime Minister Thatcher's government in Britain, the bank brought down the inflation rate by a severe tightening of monetary policy. Experience in all

---

[18] See *Bank of Canada Review*, November 1980, p. 1.

three countries showed that controlling monetary growth can indeed bring down the rate of inflation, but, because of the long lags, the process is very slow unless the economy is pushed into a very deep recession.

Recovery From the 1981–1982 Recession

As we noted above, the 1981–1982 recession was brought on by a severe tightening of monetary policy that led to a reduction of the inflation rate at the expense of a sharp increase in unemployment. Figure 19-3 shows the pattern of the recovery which lasted until the first quarter of 1990. As shown in the top panel, the unemployment rate remained above 10 percent through the end of 1985, but then fell steadily to a level of about 7.5 percent.

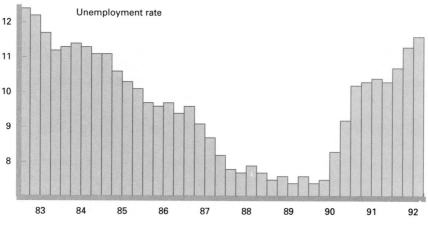

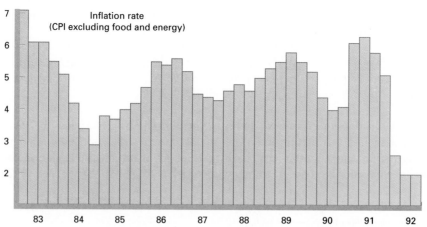

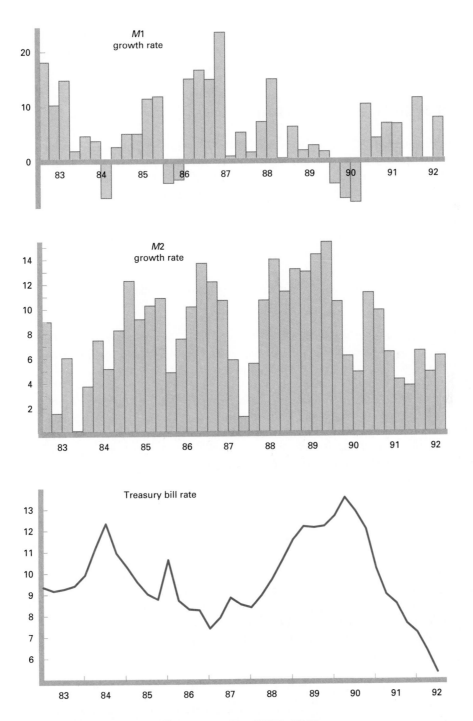

Figure 19-3   *The Canadian Economy, 1983–1992*

The second panel shows the inflation rate as measured by the year-to-year change in the CPI excluding food and energy. It fell below 4 percent in 1984 but then crept up and remained in the range of 4–5 percent from 1986 through 1988.

Renewal of the Fight Against Inflation

At the beginning of 1987, John Crow assumed the position of governor of the Bank of Canada. In a lecture given at the University of Alberta a year later, he clearly set out the Bank's strategy in a renewed fight against inflation.[19] First, he reaffirmed a commitment to price stability as the primary goal of monetary policy:

> *Monetary policy should be conducted so as to achieve a pace of monetary expansion that promotes stability in the value of money. This means pursuing a policy aimed at achieving and maintaining stable prices.*

Second, he argued that the Bank should view a positive rate of inflation as unacceptable even if it were stable and therefore predictable:

> *It is sometimes argued that the necessary ingredient from the monetary side for good economic performance is not a stable general price level but just predictability in the general rate of inflation. In my view, the notion of a high, yet stable rate of inflation is simply unrealistic.*
>
> *The crux of the matter is that success in what is in effect an attempt to mimic price stability by achieving a stable inflation rate depends on strong public confidence that the authorities would not accept a further acceleration in the rate of inflation. However, if the authorities were unwilling to act to get the rate of inflation down from, for example, 4 percent, why should anyone believe they would be any more willing to get back to 4 percent if for one reason or another upward pressures on prices led the inflation rate to rise to 5 percent? And so on. This is why a commitment to a steady rate is ultimately not credible.*

Lastly, he stated that the Bank did not have any plans to return to formal targeting of any monetary aggregate. However, he indicated that broader aggregates such as $M2$ were viewed as the most useful "indicative policy guides."

A further element in this policy strategy was announced jointly by the Governor and the Minister of Finance in early 1991. Monetary policy was to be directed toward achieving declining *target rates of inflation* as measured by the year-over-year rate of increase in the consumer price index excluding food and energy. The targets were specified as:[20]

---

[19] See *Bank of Canada Review*, February 1988, pp. 4–5.
[20] See "Background Note on the Targets," *Bank of Canada Review*, March 1991, and "Targets for Reducing Inflation: Further Operational and Measurement Considerations," *Bank of Canada Review*, September 1991.

- 3 percent by the end of 1992

- 2.5 percent by the middle of 1994

- 2 percent by the end of 1995

Returning to Figure 19-3, we see that monetary policy as reflected in the growth rates of monetary aggregates was tightened in response to an increase in the inflation rate in 1989. In 1990 there was a marked slowdown in the growth of M2, a *decline* in M1, and a sharp rise in interest rates. Beginning in the second quarter of 1990 the economy moved into recession, and by the beginning of 1991 the unemployment rate was above 10 percent.

The short-run tradeoff between unemployment and inflation again asserted itself and, after allowing for the effects of the GST,[21] the inflation rate fell below 3 percent in 1991. In early 1992 the Bank of Canada's target of 2 percent by the end of 1995 had already been reached!

As in the earlier period of anti-inflation monetary policy, the recession of 1990–1991 provoked considerable controversy. Many economists argued that the tightening in 1990 was excessive and exacerbated the downturn. Monetary policy was blamed for causing an appreciation of the Canadian dollar during 1989–1991 that was harmful to our competitive position and led to a loss of jobs. On the other hand, the Bank and its supporters argue that the groundwork has been laid for a return to real income growth without inflation that has not been seen since the early 1960s.

19-4 Summary

1. Monetarism lays heavy stress on the money stock as determining the level of output in the short run and the inflation rate in the long run.

2. Monetarists generally view the money supply as having powerful, but not easily predictable, effects on the economy. Money works with long and variable lags, and for that reason monetarists favour a monetary rule. They argue that interest rates are a poor guide to the direction of monetary policy, and they also believe that the private sector of the economy is inherently stable.

3. Monetarism's influence on monetary policy in Canada was reflected in the adoption of money supply targets in 1975. This practice was abandoned in 1982 because of instability in the demand for money. Targets for the rate of inflation were introduced in 1991.

---

[21] The effect of the GST as estimated by the Bank of Canada was about 2.4 percent. The major impact occurred in the first quarter of 1991 but it appears in the rate of inflation for all four quarters because inflation is measured as the rate of increase of prices over the same quarter of the preceding year.

Key Terms

Monetarism
Anti-Inflation Board (AIB)

Monetary rule

Problems

1. Figure 19-3 shows the growth rate of money for the 1983–1991 period. To what extent do those data justify the view that inflation is caused by money growth? (Explain your answer.)

2. Using the *IS-LM* model, examine the effects of a combination of tight money and easy fiscal policy on the real interest rate. To what extent is that analysis supported by the data in Figure 19-3 and the data on fiscal policy given in Chapter 15?

3. Discuss the problem of measuring the effect on the rate of inflation of a wage and price controls program such as the Anti-Inflation Board. Use the dynamic aggregate supply curve of Chapter 16 as a framework for your answer.

4. Compare and evaluate the anti-inflation strategies followed by the Bank of Canada during the 1970s and the early 1990s.

CHAPTER 20 *Current Issues in Macroeconomic Policy*

The ideas of economists and political philosophers, both when they are right and when they are wrong, are more powerful than is commonly understood. Indeed, the world is ruled by little else.
John Maynard Keynes, 1936

As an advice-giving profession we are in way over our heads.
Robert E. Lucas, Jr., 1980[1]

In this chapter we describe the major currents of thought in macroeconomics since the latter part of the 1970s when a sophisticated critique of discretionary policy, known as the *new classical macroeconomics*, or the *rational expectations* approach, gained influence.

Any student may wonder about a field where opinions and policy prescriptions change so often, and you may worry too about the difference of views among macroeconomists at a given time. For instance, what should you conclude when one economist says that the budget deficit is the biggest problem facing the economy in the early 1990s, and another says that it is better to maintain the current level of government spending and taxes by borrowing to finance the deficit?

---

[1] The quotes are from J.M. Keynes, *The General Theory of Employment, Interest and Money* (London: Macmillan, 1936), p. 383; and Robert E. Lucas, "Rules, Discretion, and the Role of the Economic Adviser," in his book *Studies in Business Cycle Theory* (Cambridge, Mass.: MIT Press, 1981).

There certainly are disagreements among economists, but it is also true that those disagreements, and the distinguishing features of different points of view, are systematically exaggerated by the media. Macroeconomic controversies are always in the newspapers because macroeconomics concerns some of the most important issues of daily life — whether jobs are hard or easy to find, whether prices are rising slowly or fast, whether living standards will rise fast or hardly at all. The disagreements are systematically exaggerated because disagreements are news.

Behind the rapidly changing macroeconomics fashions of the media is a more balanced macroeconomic analysis that addresses current economic problems while at the same time weighing carefully evidence that leads to changes — mostly small, but sometimes large — in macroeconomic theories.

We begin the chapter with a detailed description of the new classical macroeconomics. This approach is then contrasted with the new Keynesian approach. Some of this material has appeared earlier in the book, but this chapter can be viewed as primarily drawing together and explaining the origins of competing theories that are now part of a balanced approach to modern macroeconomics.

20-1   The New Classical Macroeconomics

The failure to reduce inflation in the 1970s and the apparent inability of macro policy to achieve its goals led to a reconsideration of the premises of modern macroeconomics. The reconstruction, called the *new classical macroeconomics* or the *rational expectations equilibrium approach*, emphasizes central three elements:

- the need to model explicitly the microeconomic motives and incentives that underlie the actions and responses of individuals

- the role of expectations and the adjustment to new information

- the limited scope for discretionary stabilization policies

These are among the hallmarks of the rational expectations equilibrium approach to macroeconomics, which we have discussed in earlier chapters, but to which we now give systematic consideration.

Among the leading members of the school are Robert Lucas of the University of Chicago, Thomas Sargent of the Hoover Institution, Edward Prescott and Neil Wallace of the University of Minnesota, and Robert Barro of Harvard.[2]

The rational expectations approach acquired that name because the assumption of rational expectations in conjunction with the expectations-augmented aggregate supply

---

[2] For an introduction, see Robert E. Lucas, "Understanding Business Cycles," in Robert E. Lucas, ed., *Studies in Business Cycle Theory*; Steven Sheffrin, *Rational Expectations* (Cambridge: Cambridge University Press, 1983); David Begg, *The Rational Expectations Revolution in Macroeconomics* (Baltimore: Johns Hopkins University Press, 1983); Kevin Hoover, *The New Classical Macroeconomics* (Oxford: Basil Blackwell, 1988); and Robert J. Barro, ed., *Modern Business Cycle Theory* (Cambridge, Mass.: Harvard University Press, 1989).

curve has such striking implications. In this context the supply curve is generally referred to as the *Lucas supply curve* that we defined in Chapter 8. Recall that in Chapters 8 and 16, we defined the rational expectations hypothesis as assuming that *individuals form expectations using information efficiently and do not make systematic mistakes in expectations.*

We saw in Chapter 8 that under rational expectations, only unexpected changes in monetary policy would have real effects. In Chapter 16, we noted further that this approach implies that an expected reduction in the growth rate of money will reduce the inflation rate without causing a recession. We also noted the important role of credibility of policy in determining its effectiveness.

However, the group known as the rational expectations school has a broader aim. The rational expectations equilibrium approach attempts to build all of macroeconomics on explicit microeconomic foundations, that is, on the assumption that individuals maximize utility, firms maximize profits, and markets are in equilibrium. *The emphasis on markets being in equilibrium is far more fundamental than just the rational expectations assumption.* It is for this reason that we add "equilibrium" in referring to the approach as the rational expectations equilibrium approach.

Rational Expectations as a Theory of Expectations

The assumption that expectations are rational, that they are based on the efficient use of information, and that they are not systematically incorrect is made on occasion by almost all macroeconomists. Use of the assumption does not automatically qualify the user as a member of the rational expectations equilibrium school.

The question of whether individuals make systematic mistakes in expectations is an empirical one. Indeed, there is some evidence that individuals do make systematic mistakes.[3] At the level of the individual firm forecasting sales, some firms seem to be perpetual optimists, others perpetual pessimists. It has to be recognized that firms or individuals may make mistakes in forecasts for long periods. In normal times, they may use simple rules of thumb for forecasting. Nonetheless, the rational expectations approach suggests that if forecast errors are expensive to the forecaster, any systematic errors will eventually be corrected by the people making them.

Beyond that, rational expectations as a theory of expectations implies that policy cannot rely for its effectiveness on systematic misunderstandings by the public. For instance, if at first the public does not understand that countercyclical tax changes are transitory, those changes will have powerful effects on the economy. However, as people begin to realize that tax changes are reversed as the economy reaches full employment, such a policy comes to have less powerful effects because the tax changes are understood to be transitory. The expectations part of rational expectations suggests that it is best, in formulating policy, to assume that the public will soon understand

---

[3] See Michael C. Lovell, "Tests of the Rational Expectations Hypothesis," *American Economic Review*, March 1986. See, too, the challenging paper by Amos Tversky and Daniel Kahneman, "Judgment Under Uncertainty: Heuristics and Biases," *Science* (1984), pp. 1124–31.

how a particular policy is working. It also implies that any policy that works for some time only because the public does not correctly anticipate its effects is doomed to eventual failure.

Money and Business Cycles

The early work in this area was done by Robert Lucas. Lucas saw the Phillips curve, the tradeoff between inflation and unemployment, as the central empirical fact that had to be explained. He aimed to explain it in a model in which prices can move to make supply equal to demand.[4]

Why is the Phillips curve a central problem for an equilibrium approach to macroeconomics? In the first place, there is evidence, provided by Friedman and Schwartz, and by many others, that changes in monetary policy affect the real economy. Thus, any serious theory would have to try to account for that fact. However, we showed in Chapter 7 that when prices are flexible, an increase in the money stock is fully neutral, raising prices but not output. If prices are not assumed to be sticky — and the essence of the equilibrium approach is to assume that prices are free to move so as to clear markets — it is necessary to explain why an increase in the money stock that raises prices appears to be accompanied by higher output. Equivalently, it has to be explained why reducing the inflation rate without creating a recession appears to be impossible.

In Chapter 8, we showed that the basic assumption behind the Lucas supply curve is the lack of complete information. We considered two approaches which centred on the labour market. One, which we called the contracting approach, assumes that wages are set in advance by negotiating contracts before prices are known, while the level of employment is determined by the demand for labour by firms that do know prices. Another approach is based on the assumption that workers and firms know the wage rate and the price of the good being produced in their own industry but do not know the prices of other goods. Thus workers lack information about the aggregate price level and the real wage. In either case, output and employment deviate from the full-employment level whenever the actual price level differs from the level that was anticipated.

The second approach outlined above can be put in a more general framework that focuses on goods markets in the way that Lucas did when he originally built up his supply curve from microeconomic foundations. The explanation assumes that individuals have imperfect information about the current price level and thus mistake movements in *absolute* prices for *relative* price changes.

The model starts from the quantity supplied of a particular good which increases with the *relative* price of that good. This is simple microeconomics. The aggregate price level (P_t) is not known at the time suppliers have to decide how much to produce and sell. Instead, suppliers base their output decisions on the estimated, or expected,

---

[4]   The most influential single article is Robert E. Lucas, "Some International Evidence on Output–Inflation Tradeoffs," *American Economic Review*, September 1973.

aggregate price level, P_t^e. Denoting the price and quantity of the particular good, i, by P_{it} and Y_{it} respectively, the supply curve of good i is

$$Y_{it} = \delta \frac{P_{it}}{P_t^e} \qquad (1)$$

In a competitive market each supplier knows the price in his or her market, but because information is imperfect, suppliers know only P_{it} in their individual market, not any other prices or the aggregate price level. On the basis of P_{it} and the price level they expect, P_t^e, they have to make a best estimate of the actual relative price of good i, that is, P_{it}/P_t.

Individuals know that there are two types of shocks in the economy. Some shocks are *relative*, or specific to individual markets. These relative shocks sum to zero across the markets, some markets having higher than average demand, others having less than the average. There are also *aggregate* shocks, which raise quantity demanded at a given price in every market. An unexpected increase in the money stock is one such shock.

Consider the supplier who has some initial expectation of the aggregate price level, P_t^e, and who observes the price P_{it} in the market. Suppose the relative price, P_{it}/P_t^e, is high. The supplier has to decide whether that is because there has been an increase in demand in all markets, raising the aggregate price level, or just in his or her market, raising the relative price. If the high price in market i is a result of a shock to the money stock that affects all markets, the relative price will be unchanged and the supplier will not want to raise output. If the shock is specific to market i, the relative price will be higher and the supplier will want to raise output.

The key result that Lucas establishes is this: The rational calculation is to assume that when the price in market i is high, that is partly because the aggregate price level is high and partly because there has been a relative shock in market i. The statistically best guess that individuals in the market can make assigns responsibility for the high price between its two possible sources. When seeing a price that seems high relative to the expected aggregate price level, suppliers will react to the higher price by producing more, though the reaction is less than if the suppliers were certain the relative price in their market was high.

The next step is to look at all markets together. If there has been no shock to the money supply, the relative shocks will cancel out in their total effects on output. Output will be higher than average in some markets and lower than average in others. However, if there has been an unexpected increase in the money stock, output will on average be higher than normal because everyone partly mistakes the increase in aggregate demand for a shift in relative demand and produces more than average. The sum of output across markets, that is, total production, will be higher when the money stock has unexpectedly increased. Similarly prices will on average be higher because demand in each market is greater.

Lucas thus succeeded in producing a Phillips curve type of tradeoff in which a higher average price level would be accompanied by higher output. The Lucas demonstration of a possible Phillips curve based on incomplete information attracted much attention, particularly the demonstration that with regard to monetary policy, only unexpected changes in the stock of money affect the price level. Under these circumstances, there appears to be no role for monetary policy to systematically affect output or unemployment.[5] Any systematic policy, such as increased monetary expansion in a recession (remember that recessions are possible as a result of surprises), would be predicted by market participants, and wages and prices would be set accordingly. Unless the central bank had better information, or shorter reaction lags than the market, it could not, according to this theory, have a systematic *real* effect.

20-2 The Rational Expectations Equilibrium Approach to Policy

The rational expectations approach has led to a sophisticated view of policy making, in at least two respects. First, there is the sophisticated treatment of expectations. The rational expectations approach emphasizes that economic agents do not react mechanically to every policy change. Rather, they try to figure out what the policy change means for the behaviour of the economy and for future changes in policy, and they behave accordingly. For instance, as we noted in Chapter 10, economic agents adjust their consumption more in response to a permanent income tax cut than to a transitory tax cut of the same size. Second, by attempting to build macroeconomics on microeconomic foundations, the rational expectations equilibrium approach has brought a new perspective to the principles of fiscal and monetary policy.

Rational Expectations and Monetary Policy Rules

As we have seen, a basic implication of the rational expectations equilibrium approach is that only unanticipated changes in the money supply affect real output. A further perspective on this issue can be obtained by considering the role of explicit monetary policy rules of the type discussed in Chapter 14.[6]

Consider an economy described by the dynamic aggregate supply and demand equations introduced in Chapter 16:

$$\text{Supply:} \quad \pi = \pi^e + \lambda(Y - Y^*) + u \tag{2}$$
$$\text{Demand:} \, Y = Y_{-1} + \phi(m - \pi) + v \tag{3}$$

The terms u and v are added to explicitly take account of shocks or disturbances that impinge on supply and demand respectively. We assume that they are not predictable

---

[5] The Lucas supply curve held so much attraction for many economists not only because of its striking implications, but especially because it was derived from an explicit microeconomic basis.

[6] For a more rigorous treatment of the material presented here, see Thomas Sargent and Neil Wallace, "Rational Expectations and the Theory of Economic Policy," *Journal of Monetary Economics*, April 1976.

in advance and average out to zero across time so that the best forecast that can be made is to set them equal to zero.

To provide a contrast with the rational expectations case, suppose the expected inflation rate is determined by simple adaptive expectations, that is $\pi^e = \pi_{-1}$. Then the aggregate supply function has the form

$$\pi = \pi_{-1} + \lambda(Y - Y^\circ) + u \tag{2a}$$

As we saw in Chapter 16, any disturbance will generate a cyclical adjustment path so that the economy takes time to return to full employment. We thus have two sources of variation in income. One is the *unsystematic* and unpredictable disturbances u and v and the other is the *systematic* variation generated by the structure of the model itself. The latter includes the effects of predictable changes in exogenous variables (m is the only such variable in the present model) and the adjustments generated in subsequent periods in response to a current disturbance. By assumption, the unsystematic disturbances cannot be offset by policy actions in the period in which they occur. However, the question remains whether the central bank could undertake corrective action in subsequent periods after a disturbance has been observed.

In general the information available to the central bank when it sets the rate of growth of the money supply, m, for the current period is the past behaviour of income and the inflation rate. For example, consider countercyclical policy rules of the form

$$m = \pi_{-1} - \psi(Y_{-1} - Y^\circ) + w \tag{4}$$

The rate of growth of money is set at a level that accommodates the inflation rate of the preceding period if income was at the full-employment level. If Y was above Y°, monetary growth is reduced; if Y was below Y°, monetary growth is increased. A third disturbance term, w, is added to allow for unpredictable factors that prevent the central bank from controlling the money supply without error. We now investigate whether the value of the parameter ψ can be chosen so as to eliminate the systematic component of the variation in income.

Substituting the rule (4) into the demand equation (3), we obtain

$$Y = Y_{-1} - \phi(\pi - \pi_{-1}) - \phi\psi(Y_{-1} - Y^\circ) + v + \phi w$$

Now if we set $\psi = 1/\phi$, the terms in Y_{-1} cancel out and this expression reduces to

$$Y = -\phi(\pi - \pi_{-1}) + Y^\circ + v + \phi w$$

Using the supply Equation (2a) to eliminate the terms in π, we obtain

$$Y = Y^\circ + \frac{1}{1 + \phi\lambda}[-\phi u + v + \phi w] \tag{5}$$

Equation (5) shows that with the appropriate choice of policy rule, the systematic deviations of income from full employment can be eliminated. The deviations of Y from $Y°$ reflect only the unsystematic disturbances.

The above case can be characterized as the extreme Keynesian case in which fine tuning is possible because the policy authority uses its knowledge of the dynamic structure of the economy to set policy while the public uses only naive extrapolations of the past to predict inflation.

Let us now contrast this with the rational expectations case in which we assume that the public uses all available information to predict inflation. A major argument for this approach is that adaptive expectations lead to systematic errors in prediction. As pointed out above, the model of Chapter 16 generates cyclical adjustment paths for income and inflation in response to a disturbance. Thus the prediction error follows a path during the adjustment that is predictable from the structure of the model. Why, then, is this information not used to eliminate this error?

This is precisely what is done in the rational expectations approach. The predictions are obtained by using the equations of the model with the disturbances set equal to zero, since these are the best predictions that can be made of the unsystematic terms. As shown in the appendix, the solution to the model in this case yields $Y^e = Y°$ for the predicted value of income and the actual value of income is given by

$$Y = Y° + \frac{1}{1 + \phi\lambda}[-\phi u + v + \phi(m - m^e)] \tag{6}$$

Equation (6) confirms the basic result discussed in Chapters 8 and 16 that changes in the money supply affect output only if they are unanticipated. Further, it shows the general result that under rational expectations, the variation in income is entirely unsystematic. In the model we are using, systematic variation in income can arise only if there are systematic errors in predicting the inflation rate as we have in the adaptive expectations case. In the rational expectations case, these systematic prediction errors are eliminated.

We conclude this analysis with a consideration of the role of policy rules in the rational expectations case. Suppose that the rate of monetary growth, m, is determined by a rule of the form in Equation (4) and that *the public knows that this rule is being used.* It follows that the term $m - m^e$ in Equation (6) will be simply equal to the unsystematic term in the rule, w, and Equation (6) will be identical to Equation (5). It follows that under rational expectations, income is independent of the choice of policy rule. This result is generally referred to as the *policy ineffectiveness proposition.*

On the other hand, it turns out that the inflation rate is not independent of the policy rule. As shown in the appendix, the solution for π is given by

$$\pi = \pi_{-1} + \frac{1 - \phi\psi}{\phi}(Y_{-1} - Y°) + \frac{1}{1 + \phi\lambda}[u + \lambda v + \phi\lambda w] \tag{7}$$

Since the coefficient on $Y_{-1} - Y°$ depends on the parameter ψ which characterizes the policy rule, the path of the inflation rate through time will depend on the choice of rule. This result is not surprising since it reflects the fact that the public takes the rule into account in its predictions of the inflation rate. If, for example, the rule implies an increase in the money growth rate for the current period, the expected *and actual* inflation rates will be increased so that real balances, and therefore income, will be unaffected by the (anticipated) increase in the money growth rate.

Equation (7) also illustrates the *Lucas critique* of econometric policy evaluation discussed in Chapter 14. If the relationship between the inflation rate and the lagged gap between income and full-employment income is to be estimated empirically, it must be recognized that the coefficient relating these two variables depends on the policy strategy being followed by the central bank. If an econometric model estimated from historical data is used to predict the effects of some different policy strategy without allowing for the influence of this on the model's coefficients, then incorrect predictions will be obtained.

Credibility

The importance of expectations regarding monetary policy in the rational expectations approach leads naturally to a concern with the credibility of policy. Individuals' reactions to current policy decisions depend on what they believe the current decisions mean about future decisions. Thus, believability of policy becomes crucial.[7]

Suppose the central bank announces its intention to reduce the growth rate of the money supply. If the public believes that the bank will follow through, the rate of wage increase will slow and it will be possible to reduce the growth rate of money without any significant output cost. Suppose the public does not believe the central bank. Then it is faced with the decision of whether to do what it said and create a recession, or not to do it, thereby avoiding the recession but losing credibility.

Indeed, it is even possible to see how under rational expectations individuals' beliefs can be self-justifying. Suppose a reduction in money growth is announced, people believe it will happen, and wage increases slow. Then the central bank reduces money growth, and the expectations are confirmed. Suppose people do not believe the central bank, and wages go on rising as before. Then, if the central bank fears a recession, it will not cut the growth rate of money, and the people are right again. This example illustrates the value of credibility.

Is there evidence that credibility — the extent to which people believe the government's policy announcements — does in practice affect the outcome of policies? In a famous paper, Thomas Sargent sought to establish that four of the hyperinflations of the 1920s, in Germany, Poland, Austria, and Czechoslovakia, ended quickly and at a relatively low unemployment cost because government policies were credible.[8] While

---

[7] See, for instance, Torsten Persson, "Credibility of Macroeconomic Policy: An Introduction and a Broad Survey," *European Economic Review*, 1988, pp. 519–32, and K. Blackburn and M. Christensen, "Monetary Theory and Policy Credibility: Theories and Evidence," *Journal of Economic Literature*, March 1989.

[8] Thomas J. Sargent, "The Ends of Four Big Inflations," in Robert E. Hall, ed., *Inflation* (Chicago: University of Chicago Press, 1982).

Sargent's evidence is extremely interesting, it is not conclusive, in part because it does not clearly show that the hyperinflations did end with relatively little unemployment.

Since credibility is so hard to measure, there is as yet no definitive evidence of its role in practice. That does not mean the concept is not useful, nor does it mean that the concept does not matter. Many governments and particularly central banks take explicit account of the effects of their decisions on their credibility, seeking to establish a reputation for toughness and steadfastness in the fight against inflation. That way they hope in the long run to be able to maintain low inflation without having to create recessions every time a supply shock hits the economy.

Economic Policy and Institutional Change

The approach leads also to an emphasis on institutional changes as ways of altering the behaviour of the economy. Members of the rational expectations school are less interested in what policy should be *now* than they are in ways of making it possible for policy to operate better in general. The quote from Lucas at the beginning of this chapter shows a general attitude toward attempts to predict the effects of a particular policy action. Members of the rational expectations school doubt that we know enough to predict how the public will respond in the the short run to a particular policy change, because the response depends on how the policy measure affects expectations. In the long run, however, the public will catch on to the effects of any policy change, and it thus becomes possible to predict the long-run effects of long-run policy changes. A member of the rational expectations school might support a legally enforceable require-ment to balance the budget, in part because this should have a very strong, predictable effect on expectations. In addition he or she may fear that policy makers not bound by rules may do anything, despite the fact that microeconomics might suggest a more sophisticated fiscal policy.[9]

Similarly, a rational expectations economist confronted with the inflationary expe-rience of the 1970s would argue that the best way to change the behaviour of the central bank is to change the institutional environment in which it works. Accordingly, such an economist is likely to support a monetary rule — for example, requiring the money supply to grow at 4 percent per year.[10]

---

[9] Robert Lucas, "Principles of Fiscal and Monetary Policy," *Journal of Monetary Economics*, January 1986, takes this position.

[10] You might wonder why members of the rational expectations school should care at all about monetary policy if they believe that (1) only unexpected changes in money affect real output and (2) the public's expectations eventually catch up with reality. The two assumptions seem to suggest that whatever the central bank is doing will eventually have no effect on real output. However, as we showed above, rational expectations does not imply that monetary policy is irrelevant to the behaviour of *prices*. Thus, members of the rational expectations school concerned about keeping inflation low can logically be in favour of a monetary rule that will prevent the average rate of growth of money from becoming high.

The Rational Expectations Equilibrium Approach, Monetarism, and Macroeconomics

There is considerable overlap between the policy views of monetarists and those of members of the rational expectations school. The similarity extends to the usually conservative views of policy held by members of both groups. There are, however, important differences between the monetarist and rational expectations approaches to macroeconomics. Monetarists are willing to assume that expectations may be systematically wrong and that markets are very slow to clear, whereas a member of the rational expectations school would not make such assumptions. Monetarism can be viewed as operating within the same framework and model as Keynesianism, while disagreeing over the relative importance of monetary and fiscal policy. The rational expectations school believes that the standard framework is fundamentally flawed and thus has developed the equilibrium approach, which argues that imperfect information is responsible for the business cycle. It thus offers a far more radical restructuring of macroeconomics than does monetarism.

Where will the rational expectations equilibrium alternative to conventional macroeconomics lead? It has already had a substantial influence on the way all macroeconomists think. First, rational expectations is widely used as a theory of expectations. Second, the sophisticated view of policy, in which responses to policy depend on the public's analysis of what policy measures will do to current and future behaviour of the economy, has been widely adopted.[11] The equilibrium approach, however, is more controversial than other components of the rational expectations view and seems to be inconsistent with the slow reaction of the economy to policy measures.[12]

20-3 Equilibrium Real Business Cycles

The proposition that only monetary *surprises* affect output was the subject of intense empirical research, which was noted in Chapter 8. At this stage, the evidence does not support the strong implication of the equilibrium approach that only unanticipated changes in the money stock affect output. This has led to two reactions. Some economists believed that better explanations would have to be found for the role of money in the business cycle. Others questioned the evidence linking money with the business cycle at all.

In particular, economists working on the equilibrium approach developed *equilibrium real business cycle* theory, the view that fluctuations in output and employment are the result of a variety of real shocks hitting the economy. They explained the

---

[11] The development of the rational expectations approach has led to much game-theoretical (the mathematical theory of games) research on policy. For an introduction, see John Driffill, "Macroeconomic Policy Games with Incomplete Information: A Survey," *European Economic Review*, 1988, pp. 533–41.

[12] See the discussion in the special issue of the *Journal of Money, Credit and Banking*, November 1980.

apparent link between money and output as a result of the money stock's accommodating movements in output. Thus money could be correlated with changes in output, but would not necessarily cause them.[13]

With monetary causes of the business cycle assumed out of the way, real business cycle theory is left with two tasks. The first is to explain the *shocks, or disturbances*, that hit the economy, causing fluctuations in the first place. The second is to explain the *propagation mechanisms*. A propagation mechanism is the means through which a disturbance is spread through the economy. In particular, the aim is to explain why shocks to the economy seem to have long-lived effects.

Propagation Mechanisms

Many of the mechanisms that real business cycle theory relies on to explain why a shock to the economy affects output for several years have already been discussed. Among these are inventory adjustments and changes in investment caused by shifts in profitability. These are part of anyone's theory of the business cycle.

The one mechanism that is most associated with equilibrium business cycles, though, is *the intertemporal substitution of leisure*. Any theory of the business cycle has to explain why people work more at some times than at others; during booms employment is high and jobs are easy to find; during recessions people work less.

A simple equilibrium explanation would be that people work more in booms because wages are higher. That way they would voluntarily be supplying more labour in response to a higher wage. (Remember that the equilibrium approach requires people to be on their supply-and-demand curves at all times.) However, the facts are not strongly in favour of that argument because the real wage changes very little over the business cycle. People are thus not obviously working more in response to higher wages.

The Keynesian or monetarist approaches explain these movements in output by saying that the demand for labour shifts as aggregate demand shifts, and that people may be unemployed in recessions because they cannot get work despite their willingness to work at the going wage.[14] In contrast, the equilibrium approach constrains itself

---

[13] This view is developed in a technically very advanced paper by Robert King and Charles Plosser, "Money, Credit and Prices in a Real Business Cycle Model," *American Economic Review*, June 1984. A nontechnical review is in Carl Walsh, "New Views of the Business Cycle," Federal Reserve Bank of Philadelphia *Business Review*, January–February 1986. Bennett T. McCallum, "Real Business Cycles," in Barro, ed., *Modern Business Cycle Theory*, provides a high-level review of this literature. See also Charles Plosser, "Understanding Real Business Cycles," and N. Gregory Mankiw, "Real Business Cycles: A New Keynesian Perspective," both in *Economic Perspectives*, Summer 1989, for a recent discussion of the topic.

[14] In some versions of the Keynesian model, including that of Keynes in the *General Theory*, it is assumed that firms move up and down the labour demand curve over the course of the business cycle (see the neoclassical labour demand curve in the appendix to Chapter 7). That implies the real wage would be higher in recessions than in booms. Since the real wage does not move much over the cycle, this explanation cannot be correct either. In the model developed in Chapters 8 and 16, the real wage is constant as a result of markup pricing, and employment changes with aggregate demand. Constancy of the real wage is a reasonable approximation to actual wage behaviour.

to assume markets are in equilibrium. The explanation for the large movements in output with small movements in wages is the following: There is a high elasticity of labour supply in response to temporary changes in the wage, or, as the argument is put, people are willing to substitute leisure intertemporally.

The argument is that people care very little about *when* in any given period of a year or two they work. Suppose that within a two-year period they plan to work 4000 hours at the going wage (50 weeks each year for 40 hours a week). If wages are equal in the two years, they would work 2000 hours each year, but if wages were just 2 percent higher in one year than the other, they might prefer to work, say, 2200 hours in one year, forgoing vacations and working overtime, and 1800 hours in the other. That way they work the same total amount and earn more total income.

This intertemporal substitution of leisure is clearly capable of generating large movements in the amount of work done in response to small shifts in wages, and thus could account for large output effects in the cycle accompanied by small changes in wages. However, there has not been strong empirical support for this view either.

Similar intertemporal substitution arguments have been advanced to explain fluctuations in consumption over the course of the business cycle. In this case the real interest rate is assumed to change, with individuals reducing current levels of consumption when the interest rate is high in order to take advantage of the higher rate of return on saving. Again, the evidence for this proposition is very weak.

Disturbances

The most important disturbances isolated by equilibrium business cycle theorists are shocks to *productivity*, or supply shocks, and shocks to *government spending*.

A productivity shock raises output in relation to a given level of input. Good weather and new methods of production are examples. Suppose there is a temporary favourable productivity shock this period. Then individuals will want to work harder to take advantage of the higher productivity. In working more this period, they raise output. They will also invest more, thus spreading the productivity shock into future periods by raising the stock of capital. If the effect of the intertemporal substitution of leisure is strong, even a small productivity shock could have a relatively large effect on output.

Increased government spending is another type of shock. To provide the extra goods the government needs, individuals will work harder if the real wage rises, and save more if the real interest rate rises. Thus we should expect an increase in government spending to raise the real interest rate and the real wage.[15]

There is less certainty in the real business cycle approach about the effects of a cut in taxes than about the effects of an increase in government spending. As we discussed in Chapter 15, the Ricardian view is that individuals recognize that a cut in taxes today is just an increase in taxes tomorrow, and that they therefore should not increase consumption when taxes are cut.

---

[15] Note that increased government spending raises the real interest rate in the *IS-LM* model, too, though there the crowding out is more of investment than consumption.

Summary

The equilibrium real business cycle approach is still a subject of intense research. Its goal of building macroeconomics on sound microeconomic foundations is surely widely shared. There is no doubt, too, that some of the mechanisms, such as inventory accumulation and investment dynamics, that underlie its explanation of the dynamics of the business cycle will form part of future business cycle models, as they have of past and current business cycle models. There is, however, room for doubt that the attempt to build business cycle models in which there is no role for monetary factors will be ultimately successful.

20-4 The New Keynesianism

Under the challenge of the rational expectations equilibrium approach there has been substantial research since 1973 that attempts to explain why wages and prices are sticky. We have already discussed in Chapters 8 and 16 the approach that builds on the existence of long-term and perhaps overlapping labour contracts to explain wage and price stickiness and inflationary momentum. Because the coverage in Chapters 8 and 16 is quite full, we shall not review that approach further, even though it is one major strand that attempts to account for wage and price stickiness even when expectations are rational.

More recently a *New Keynesian* school has developed.[16] The New Keynesians combine the Keynesian recognition that the economy does not adjust instantly and smoothly to shocks, including monetary shocks, with an insistence on building their explanations on microeconomic foundations. Among the leading New Keynesians are George Akerlof and Janet Yellen of Berkeley, Olivier Blanchard and Julio Rotemberg of MIT, Joseph Stiglitz of Stanford, Mark Gertler of Wisconsin-Madison, Ben Bernanke of Princeton, and Gregory Mankiw of Harvard.

New Keynesianism is built on three main microfoundations:

- efficiency wage theory

- the connections between monopolistic or imperfect competition and traditional Keynesian macroeconomic propositions

- the role of imperfect information in financial markets

We discuss the first two here.

---

[16] See Julio Rotemberg, "The New Keynesian Microfoundations," in NBER *Macroeconomics Annual*, 1987.

Efficiency Wages

As we have noted, the basic question to answer is why wages and prices do not move quickly to clear markets when there is unemployment. *Efficiency wage theory argues that wages are not cut because doing so reduces a firm's profits.*[17]

There are several explanations for this assumption. The simplest occurs in very poor countries, where individuals cannot feed themselves adequately unless they receive a reasonable wage. Cutting wages in such a country would reduce the physical ability of the workers to perform their tasks. Even if there were substantial unemployment, it would not pay an employer to cut wages because doing so would reduce profits as the efficiency of workers fell owing to poor nutrition.

Physical efficiency is not the problem in developed countries. Efficiency wage theory for such countries argues that firms pay above market-clearing wages in order either to attract the more efficient workers or to ensure that workers on the job do not shirk. The shirking version starts from the fact that it is often difficult to observe the amount of effort put out by workers. To create the right incentive to work, there has to be a benefit to having this particular job. To create the benefit, so that the worker really wants to keep the job, the firm pays above-market wages. Then anyone found to be shirking is fired and has to return to the labour market to look for a lower-paid job.

This view suggests that there may be two types of jobs — high-paying, desirable jobs that are difficult to find because the wage is above the market equilibrium wage and other jobs, at a lower wage, that are easy to find and for which firms can easily observe workers' effort. That description brings to mind such jobs as driving a taxi, in which there are almost always available positions, even when there is unemployment.[18]

Alternatively, there may simply be a social custom that wages are not cut. If workers whose wages are cut regard that as unfair and reduce their work effort in response, then wage cutting will not take place. This fairness argument, although it has the ring of truth, is not fully satisfactory because there is no explanation of how the custom developed.

Efficiency wage theory explains why some firms would want to to pay above-market real wages. Whether it can account for unemployment depends on the size and role of the secondary market and on whether there are always alternative jobs in that market that any unemployed person would take rather than remain unemployed. It is quite possible that many who are unemployed are waiting for primary market (high-paying)

---

[17] See Janet Yellen, "Efficiency Wage Models of Unemployment," *American Economic Review*, May 1984. For a more extensive examination, see Lawrence Katz, "Efficiency Wage Theories: A Partial Evaluation," NBER *Macroeconomics Annual*, 1986. Alan B. Krueger and Lawrence H. Summers, "Efficiency Wages and the Inter-Industry Wage Structure," *Econometrica*, March 1988, present evidence for the view that wage differentials in U.S. industry are more consistent with efficiency wage theory than with standard competitive theory that would ascribe wage differences to the characteristics of jobs and the people who hold them. For a related approach, see Assar Lindbeck and Dennis Snower, "Wage Setting, Unemployment and Insider-Outsider Relations," *American Economic Review*, May 1986.

[18] Sometimes the two types of jobs are described as primary and secondary, primary jobs being the better ones. This is the *dual labour market hypothesis*.

jobs. If so, efficiency wage theory can account for some unemployment. It is a further question whether such unemployment would vary cyclically, and particularly whether it would vary as monetary shocks hit the economy. To see whether this can be the case, we turn to possible causes of price and wage stickiness.

The Small Menu Cost Approach

There is a puzzling aspect of business cycle theories based on the assumption that wages are slow to adjust. Unemployment is a very serious problem creating large costs for society. Changing a wage or price is a relatively simple and apparently cheap matter. The payroll has to be reprogrammed, or a new price tag has to be put on. The puzzle is why these apparently small costs stand in the way of adjusting prices so as to get rid of unemployment.

The so-called *small menu cost approach* argues that small costs of changing prices can have large effects.[19] The argument is technical, but asserts that when firms set prices optimally, they lose very little by meeting increases or decreases in demand by producing more or less without changing prices. Then if there is some small cost for the firm of changing its prices or wages, a small shift in demand will not trigger a price or wage change. If firms do not change prices in response to shifts in demand, then the economy exhibits price (and/or wage) stickiness. The researchers in this area show that extremely small costs of changing prices can generate enough wage and price stickiness to give changes in the money stock substantial real effects.

Monopolistic Competition and Keynesian Macroeconomics

It is essential to the small menu cost result that firms be monopolistic competitors that set wages and prices, rather than taking them as given by the market. The key to understanding the small menu cost argument is this: *For a monopolist or monopolistic competitor, price is always above marginal cost.* If offered the opportunity to sell more at the current price, a monopolist will be willing to do so. Thus monopolistic competitors that find the menu costs of changing prices too high will nonetheless willingly sell more when the demand curve they face shifts, perhaps as a result of an increase in the money stock. Further, because price (which is equal to the marginal value of the good to the consumer) exceeds marginal cost, society benefits from the increase in output.

If firms were competitive, price would be equal to marginal cost, and firms would not be willing to increase output if price remained constant, even if the demand curve

---

[19] The simplest such model is N. Gregory Mankiw, "Small Menu Costs and Large Business Cycles: A Macroeconomic Model of Monopoly," *Quarterly Journal of Economics*, May 1985. A more complete model is developed in George Akerlof and Janet Yellen, "A Near-Rational Model of the Business Cycle, with Wage and Price Inertia," *Quarterly Journal of Economics*, Supplement, 1985.

facing the industry shifted.[20] Thus one major achievement of the new Keynesians has been the demonstration of a close link between imperfect competition on the microeconomics side and Keynesian propositions in macroeconomics, particularly the proposition that an increase in aggregate demand will lead to an increase in output.[21]

Coordination and Multiple Equilibria

Under imperfect competition, the profits of one firm depend on the actions of other firms; but, at the time one firm has to make its decisions about prices or output, it does not know with certainty what other firms will do. The actions of other firms are a matter of conjecture or expectations. These facts have two extremely important implications: First, there is inevitably *interdependence* among firms; they simply have to form expectations (or guess) about other firms' behaviour. Second, depending on what firms assume about other firms' actions, the economy may reach different equilibria. Some of these may be "good" equilibria, in the sense that output is high because everybody believes that everyone else also believes this is a good year; but it is also possible that firms form pessimistic views about other firms' actions and a "bad" or low production equilibrium results.

Multiple equilibria may also result from small menu costs. Consider many monopolistically competitive firms confronted by a shift in the demand curves facing them. Suppose that all but one of them chooses not to change the price charged for the firm's output, and consider the decision facing the last firm. If it increases its price, it will lose many customers; the marginal revenue from raising the price would be small, and hence would not outweigh the small menu cost. Therefore, if all but one firm does not raise the price, the last firm will not do so either.

Now suppose, instead, that all firms but one have raised their price. The marginal revenue the last firm faces is larger than in the previous case, and may therefore be larger than the small menu cost. Therefore, the firm would raise its price.

It follows that there may be two possible equilibria. Either all firms raise their price, or none does. In the first case we have a neoclassical or rational expectations equilibrium response to an increase in the money supply; in the latter case we have a Keynesian response. There may even be more possible responses.[22]

One way of viewing the possibility of multiple equilibria is that difficulties of *coordinating* responses to economic shocks may produce slow adjustment of wages and

---

[20] Robert E. Hall, "The Relation Between Price and Marginal Cost in U.S. Industry," *Journal of Political Economy*, October 1988, shows that price is above marginal cost for much of U.S. industry.

[21] The imperfect competition revolution in microeconomics took place at about the same time as the Keynesian revolution in macroeconomics, in the 1930s. Although many had argued that Keynesian macroeconomic propositions depended on the existence of imperfect, or monopolistic, competition, that link was not really established until recently. For a fully worked out model, see for instance Olivier Blanchard and Nobu Kiyotake, "Monopolistic Competition and the Effects of Aggregate Demand," *American Economic Review*, September 1987.

[22] This is shown by Julio Rotemberg, "The New Keynesian Microfoundations," *op. cit.*

prices. From the viewpoint of the firms taken as a group, the best response to an increase in the money stock may be for all to raise prices together. But they cannot get together to make that decision, so each will make its decision while having to guess what the others will do, and they may start off by not raising the price. Similarly, when there is unemployment, all firms together could reduce wages, but because of efficiency wages, it would not pay one firm to reduce wages if the others do not. Again, the problem of coordination prevents an instant return to a full-employment equilibrium.

The difficulty of coordinating responses to a shock points to one possible answer to the question with which this section started: Why, if unemployment has such large social costs, do firms not lower wages to reduce unemployment? The answer may be that no individual firm can do much about the unemployment problem. Acting in its own interest, it may not reduce wages, but if other firms would reduce wages at the same time, so would this firm.[23]

Summary

The New Keynesian ideas are still being worked out, and it is not clear whether they will succeed in providing a convincing account of the microeconomic foundations of Keynesian macroeconomics. The small menu cost notion in particular fails to convince many economists, but it does seem likely that efficiency wage theory, the role of imperfect competition, and the difficulties of coordinating responses to disturbances will play important roles in macroeconomics in the future.

20-5 Where Does It All Lead?

At the start of this chapter we asked why macroeconomics suffers from such rapidly changing opinions. The answer is that it does not. There has been an evolution from simple Keynesianism toward a more sophisticated approach, not a series of rapidly changing beliefs. Macroeconomics has evolved, and it now gives more weight to monetary factors and to aggregate supply, emphasizing the roles of both expectations and labour market institutions. The New Keynesianism reviewed in Section 20-4 does not lead to a significantly different overall view of the economy; rather, it should be viewed as attempting to develop microeconomic foundations for existing macroeconomics.

The rational expectations equilibrium approach does pose a more radical challenge to the standard way of viewing the economy, and it has already had a major impact on mainstream macroeconomics. As of now, it remains far from a major empirical

---

[23] Interestingly, the difficulty of coordinating wage reductions was mentioned by Keynes in the *General Theory* as one reason for wage stickiness.

success, though it has more theoretical appeal. Whether it will lead to the replacement of current mainstream macroeconomics with a new standard model remains to be seen, and time and evidence will determine that.

Box 20-1 Disequilibrium Economics and Post-Keynesian Economics

In the main text we developed the history of ideas as running from Keynesian economics to monetarism and the rational expectations equilibrium challenge, together with the New Keynesian response. However, two other strands of macroeconomics are sufficiently distinct and fruitful to deserve attention.

The Disequilibrium Approach

As early as the 1950s, economists recognized the implications of disequilibrium in one market for supply or demand in other markets. If workers cannot sell all the labour they wish at the going wage, and cannot borrow, how will this affect their consumption decision? If they cannot buy all the goods they wish at the going prices, how does this affect their supply of labour or their demands for money and other assets? If firms cannot sell at the going price all the output they would like to produce, how does this affect their demand for labour?[a]

The disequilibrium approach answers these questions by constructing a model of the economy that explicitly takes into account the *quantity constraints* on the decisions which households and firms face. Quantity constraints are present when households or firms cannot buy or sell all the quantities they wish at the going wages or prices. Central to the approach is the assumption that wages and prices do not move rapidly, and thus they leave markets in disequilibrium, which gives rise to quantity adjustments. These quantity adjustments in different markets are interdependent through the quantity constraints under which households and firms make their optimal decisions.

The most interesting contribution of the disequilibrium approach so far has been to influence empirical work. For example, studies of consumption pay close attention to the role of income and wealth, reflecting the possibility that individuals cannot borrow against future income, so that *liquidity constraints* affect spending behaviour. In studies of the labour market, the approach suggests the important distinction between "high-wage," or classical, unemployment on one side, and Keynesian, or "lack-of-demand," unemployment on the other.

This difference is illustrated in Figure 1. The figure shows the labour demand schedule, the marginal product of labour (MPN), with the real wage on the vertical axis and $\bar{N}$ as the full-employment labour supply. The full-employment real wage is $(w/P)_0$. Suppose the economy is at a point such as A, with real wage $(w/P)'$. At point

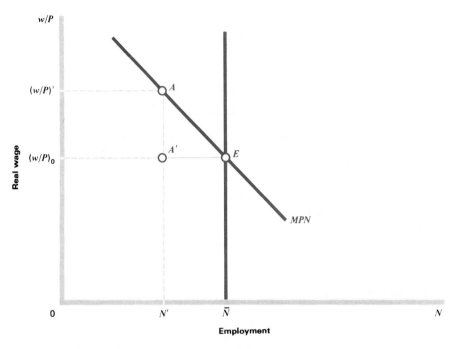

Figure 1   *Classical or Keynesian Unemployment?*

The schedule *MPN* is the marginal product of labour or the demand curve for labour. The full-employment labour supply is $\overline{N}$. At a real wage $(w/P)'$ there is "high real wage" unemployment because firms only want to hire a labour force of N', which falls short of the supply $\overline{N}$, but it is also possible that even at the lower wage $(w/P)_0$ firms only want to hire N' of labour because they cannot sell the output that would be produced by a larger labour force.

A, firms hire only an amount of labour N', which falls short of full employment because the real wage is too high. The economy suffers from *classical*, or *real wage, unemployment*. The cure is either a reduction in the real wage to $(w/P)_0$ or else productivity growth or increased investment that shifts the *MPN* schedule out and to the right and thus reduces unemployment.

Alternatively, suppose that the economy was at a point such as A'. Again there is unemployment, but this time the real wage is not the problem. Firms are not willing to hire more workers than N' because they cannot sell the output. Aggregate demand is insufficient to absorb more output than is produced by an employment level N'. Therefore firms do not hire more workers, and accordingly there is *Keynesian unemployment*. The cure, in this case, is not a cut in real wages but rather an expansion in aggregate demand through monetary or fiscal stimulus.

In both cases there is unemployment. In both cases it is unprofitable for firms to hire more labour than N'. In one case the problem is that labour is too expensive; in the other there is no market for the increased output. It is clearly essential to identify the kind of unemployment the economy faces before designing policy action.

This analysis was used in diagnosing the high European unemployment of the 1980s. There were many who argued that European unemployment in the early 1980s was classical, a result of too high a real wage. But a dose of Keynesian unemployment was added as policies turned restrictive from 1980 on. It would thus have taken both a decline in the real wage (or a sharp rise in productivity) and an expansion in demand to move back to full employment. As the decade closed, productivity growth and increased aggregate demand in Europe finally moved the unemployment rate back down.

Post-Keynesian Economics

Post-Keynesians are a diverse group of economists who share the belief that modern macroeconomics leaves aside or explicitly assumes away many of the most central elements of Keynes's *General Theory*.[b]

Five elements of this approach stand out distinctly. First, adjustment, just as in the disequilibrium approach, takes place primarily through quantity adjustment, not price changes. Indeed, price changes, where they occur, are often seen as disequilibriating. Second, the distribution of income between profits and wages plays a central role in affecting consumption and investment decisions. Third, expectations (Keynes's animal spirits), together with profits, are the chief determinant of investment plans. Fourth, institutional features such as credit constraints on households and self-finance by firms, as well as a financial structure involving credit creation in a pyramid, interact in shaping the business cycle and on occasion financial crises. Finally, unlike that of classical macroeconomics, the focus of post-Keynesian economics is on explaining why the economy does not work well. Several of these elements are of course shared with regular Keynesianism.

Post-Keynesian economics remains an eclectic collection of ideas, not a systematic challenge like, for example, the rational expectations equilibrium approach. The former has influenced economists in their research program, but the deliberate down-playing, indeed rejection, of individual rationality and maximization as a basis of behaviour by firms and households by post-Keynesians has kept the approach at odds with the mainstream of the profession. An attempt to bring macroeconomics into closer touch with microeconomics has been a major focus of the mainstream.

---

[a] The early reference is D. Patinkin, *Money, Interest and Prices* (New York: Row, Peterson, 1956), Chapter 13. The complete working out of these ideas can be found in R. Barro and H. Grossman, *Money, Employment and Inflation* (Cambridge: Cambridge University Press, 1976), and E. Malinvaud, *The Theory of Unemployment Reconsidered* (Oxford: Basil Blackwell, 1977), and *Profitability and Unemployment* (Oxford: Basil Blackwell, 1981).

[b] For an introduction see A. Eichner, ed., *A Guide to Post-Keynesian Economics* (White Plains, N.Y.: M.E. Sharpe, 1979), and the essays on post-Keynesian economics in the *American Economic Review*, May 1980.

If there have not in fact been frequent changes of opinion in macroeconomics, why does it still seem that way? It is because macroeconomic issues are important: Macroeconomics is both news and politically useful. Politicians look for economists with arguments that will support the politicians' positions. For instance, supply-side economists had an influential role in the Reagan administration because the American President wanted to cut taxes and needed professional support. No matter that the radical supply-side arguments were accepted by only a very small part of the profession; they provided at least some intellectual support for a policy that was based more on the President's ideology than on a detailed analysis of the potential effects of the tax cuts.

It is hoped that careful study will cumulate over the years into improved knowledge. Opinions, of course, change as new evidence accumulates, but genuine revolutions in thinking are rare. There was a Keynesian revolution in the 1930s and a significant shift toward monetarism in the 1950s and 1960s, which was easily accommodated by expanding the Keynesian framework. There may be a rational expectations revolution in progress. Even if it succeeds, it will build on much of the existing structure of macroeconomics. Even if it does not radically reshape macroeconomics, it will, nonetheless, make for serious changes in our understanding of the formation of expectations and the operation of economic policy. It has already set new standards in demanding that macroeconomics be based on microeconomic foundations.

The hope is that study of existing macroeconomics combined with the right degree of skepticism and questioning will make it possible for you to reach your own conclusions when the next brand of economics hits the headlines.

20-6 Summary

1. The rational expectations equilibrium approach to macroeconomics has two components. The first is a theory of expectations. It argues that people form expectations using all available information and do not make systematic mistakes. The second is the equilibrium approach. This assumes that markets are in equilibrium each period and attributes deviations of output from normal levels to imperfect information.

2. With adaptive expectations, a monetary policy rule can be used to eliminate systematic deviations of income from full employment. With rational expectations, policy ineffectiveness holds and income is independent of the policy rule.

3. The rational expectations approach to policy making emphasizes the credibility of policies as an important factor in determining policy success or failure. The approach views institutional reform as the main way to get better policy.

4. Equilibrium real business cycle theory denies any causal role for money in the business cycle. Rather, the cycle is seen as resulting from real shocks that hit the economy and are then distributed throughout it currently and also into future

periods by a variety of propagation mechanisms. The main real shocks are to productivity and government spending. The main propagation mechanism is intertemporal substitution of leisure and consumption. More standard mechanisms, such as inventory accumulation and investment in physical capital, also play a role.

5.   The approach to wage stickiness of Chapters 8 and 16 achieves one synthesis of Keynesian and rational expectations approaches by basing the slow adjustment of wages and prices to changes in monetary policy on the existence of long-term labour contracts.

6.   The New Keynesianism has accepted the challenge of the rational expectations equilibrium approach to develop microeconomic foundations for Keynesian macroeconomics. For this purpose it has built on efficiency wage theory and the small menu cost–monopolistic competition approach.

7.   Efficiency wage theories explain real wage stickiness as being a result of losses in productivity that would occur if firms cut wages. In combination with small menu costs, efficiency wage theory can account for sticky wages and prices as well as unemployment.

8.   The small menu cost–monopolistic competition approach shows that even small costs of changing prices may keep prices from changing. In that case, an increase in the money stock will lead to an increase in output. The approach also shows the close link between Keynesian macroeconomics and imperfect, or monopolistic, competition. It further shows that coordination difficulties may help account for the slow adjustment of the economy to shocks.

Key Terms

New classical macroeconomics
Rational expectations equilibrium
  approach
Lucas supply curve
Policy ineffectiveness proposition
Lucas critique
Credibility
Real business cycles
Propagation mechanism

Intertemporal substitution of
  leisure
Productivity shock
New Keynesianism
Efficiency wages
Small menu costs
Multiple equilibria
Disequilibrium approach

Problems

1.   Distinguish and define the two components of the rational expectations equilibrium approach to macroeconomics.

2. **(a)** In what ways is the monetarist approach discussed in the previous chapter closer to Keynesianism than to the rational expectations equilibrium approach?

    (b) In what ways is monetarism closer to the rational expectations equilibrium approach than to Keynesianism?

3. Suppose that people did not believe the Bank of Canada was serious about stopping inflation in 1980 and 1989. Can you then reconcile the subsequent recessions with the rational expectations approach? Explain. What do you think will be the effect of the inflation targets announced in 1991?

4. **(a)** Explain why, in the aggregate supply and demand model of Chapter 8, more work is done in booms than recessions.

    (b) Contrast this with the real business cycle explanation.

5. **(a)** Why, according to efficiency wage theory, are employers reluctant to cut wages?

    (b) Suppose there were always some jobs available at a low enough wage. Could efficiency wages still help explain why high unemployment can continue year after year?

*6. Explain why there appears to be a link between Keynesian macroeconomics and monopolistic competition, using the impact of an increase in the money stock on output as an example.

*7. Suppose the money stock is reduced. Explain why, if everyone could coordinate the reduction in his or her wages and prices, the economy would be more likely to move smoothly to a new full-employment equilibrium than if everyone had to guess what other people would do.

8. Evaluate the quote of Keynes with which this chapter begins.

9. In the introduction to this chapter, we note contradictory views on the budget deficit. One group of economists believes that large deficits cause high real interest rates and a balance of trade deficit. Another group believes that the budget deficit has no real effects. Going back to Chapter 18, trace the key point that leads to this difference of opinion. What is your opinion of this issue in light of Chapters 18 and 20?

Appendix   Solution to the Rational Expectations Model

Our model consists of Equations (2) and (3) in the text:

$$\pi = \pi^e + \lambda(Y - Y^\circ) + u \tag{A1}$$

$$Y = Y_{-1} + \phi(m - \pi) + v \tag{A2}$$

We first obtain the solution for the predicted values of income and the inflation rate by assuming that these predictions are consistent with the equations of the model. Thus we replace Y and π in (A1) and (A2) with Y^e and π^e, and substitute zero for u and v, since these are the best predictions of the disturbance terms:

$$\pi^e = \pi^e + \lambda(Y^e - Y^\circ) \tag{A3}$$

$$Y^e = Y_{-1} + \phi(m^e - \pi^e) \tag{A4}$$

It follows from (A3) that $Y^e = Y^\circ$, and, using (A4), π^e is given by

$$\pi^e = m^e + (1/\phi)(Y_{-1} - Y^\circ) \tag{A5}$$

Further, substituting $Y^e = Y^\circ$ into (A4) and subtracting (A4) from (A2), we obtain

$$Y - Y^\circ = \phi(m - m^e) - \phi(\pi - \pi^e) + v$$

Using (A1) to eliminate the term in $\pi - \pi^e$ yields

$$Y - Y^\circ = \phi(m - m^e) - \phi\lambda(Y - Y^\circ) - \phi u + v$$

or

$$Y = Y^\circ + \frac{1}{1 + \phi\lambda}[-\phi u + v + \phi(m - m^e)] \tag{A6}$$

This is Equation (6) in the text which gives us the solution for actual income, Y, as a function of the disturbance terms and the unanticipated part of the money growth rate.

We now assume that m is determined by the policy rule given by Equation (4) in the text:

$$m = \pi_{-1} - \psi(Y_{-1} - Y^\circ) + w \tag{A7}$$

We then have $m - m^e = w$ and Equation (A6) becomes identical to Equation (5) in the text. Since this equation does not contain the parameter ψ that characterizes the policy rule, we conclude that income is independent of the choice of rule.

To solve for the inflation rate, we substitute for π^e in the supply equation (A1), using (A5) to obtain

$$\pi = m^e + (1/\phi)(Y_{-1} - Y^\circ) + \lambda(Y - Y^\circ) + u \tag{A8}$$

Substituting the systematic part of the policy rule (A7) for m^e yields

$$\pi = \pi_{-1} + \frac{1 - \phi\psi}{\phi}(Y_{-1} - Y^\circ) + \lambda(Y - Y^\circ) + u$$

Using (A7) or equivalently Equation (5) from the text to eliminate the term in $Y - Y^\circ$, we obtain the following solution for π, which is shown in the text as Equation (7):

$$\pi = \pi_{-1} + \frac{1 - \phi\psi}{\phi}(Y_{-1} - Y^\circ) + \frac{1}{1 + \phi\lambda}[u + \lambda v + \phi\lambda w] \qquad \text{(A9)}$$

In contrast to the solution for income, this equation does contain the parameter ψ, so that the inflation rate is not independent of the policy rule.

CHAPTER 21 *Long-Term Growth and Productivity*

In this chapter we turn our attention away from the short-run problems of the business cycle to look at where the economy has been and may be heading in the long term. From 1870 to 1990, real income in Canada grew at an average annual rate of 3.8 percent. This trend rate is shown in Figure 21-1 along with actual real income. In per capita terms, the average rate of growth was 2.1 percent per year. With this growth rate, per capita income doubles every 33 years.

Table 21-1 shows that growth in Canada in the period from 1973 to 1983 was below the historical average. During that decade per capita real income grew at only 1.6 percent. At that rate, it would take 44 years to double.

To analyze the long-run behaviour of the economy, we focus on *trend* or *potential output*. We pose the following major questions: What determines the *growth rate* of potential output? Why does output grow over time and how fast? Will growth in the

Table 21-1 *Average Annual Growth Rates, 1870–1990*

	1870–1953	1953–1973	1973–1983	1983–1990
Real Income (%)	3.7	5.0	2.9	3.6
Per Capita Real Income (%)	2.0	2.9	1.6	2.6

Source: Same as Figure 21-1.

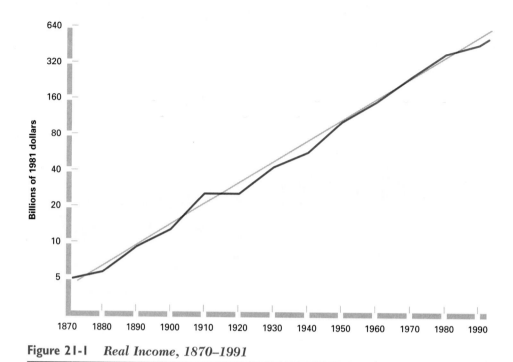

Figure 21-1 *Real Income, 1870–1991*

(*Source:* M.C. Urquhart, "New Estimates of Gross National Product, Canada, 1870–1926," in S.L. Engerman and R.E. Gallman, eds., *Long-term Factors in American Economic Growth*, NBER, 1986; Statistics Canada, 11-505, 13-201)

future be as high as it has been in the past? Will the economy maintain a trend of rising income per capita, as it has for the past 120 years?

In discussing the growth of potential output we are also posing the question: What are future levels of output likely to be? Even small differences in the growth rate of potential output cumulate over time to large differences in the level of per capita income and hence in the standard of living. With a growth rate of 2 percent per year, it takes 35 years for per capita income to double, but if the growth rate is only 1 percent, it takes 70 years to achieve a doubling of income per head. The growth rate of potential output is thus of central importance.

International comparisons of per capita income are presented in Table 21-2.[1] The first column shows per capita incomes in U.S. dollars in 1987 for the U.S., Canada,

---

[1] For historical international comparisons see Angus Maddison, *Phases of Capitalist Development* (London: Oxford University Press, 1982). The difficulties with comparing incomes across countries and a methodology for these comparisons are presented in Irving Kravis et al., *World Product and Income* (Baltimore: Johns Hopkins University Press, 1982). See, too, A. Bergson, "Comparative Productivity," *American Economic Review*, June 1987.

Japan, and several developing countries. The incomes are translated to a common base through an exchange rate between the local currency and the dollar (e.g., the yen in Japan and the peso in Mexico). There are two problems with this method: First, real exchange rates fluctuate a great deal, and thus the comparisons would look very different depending on the exchange rate used. Because of this problem, the exchange rate used in Table 21-2 is the average exchange rate for the period 1985–1987.

The second problem is more fundamental. Consider the data for India and the United States in the first column of Table 21-2. Per capita income in India is shown as $300. People literally could not live on such an income in North America, but on average Indians do survive. Thus, in terms of U.S. income, the Indian income level cannot be $300. It must be that incorrect prices (i.e., an incorrect exchange rate) are being used to compare per capita incomes in the two countries in the first column of the table.

The third column of Table 21-2 presents results of the *International Comparisons Project*, which uses a common set of prices to compare incomes across countries. Whereas the income data in the first row imply that per capita income in India is 1.6 percent of U.S. per capita income, measuring those incomes at the *same* set of prices suggests per capita income in India is 4.7 percent of that in the United States. However, that amount is still incredibly low (4.7 percent of U.S. 1987 per capita income is only $870), in fact far below the poverty line in the United States.

Table 21-2 shows that U.S. *growth* in per capita income is much lower than that of the other countries, but that its *level* of per capita income is much higher. However, if Korea, for example, maintains a high growth rate long enough it will ultimately catch up with and even surpass the U.S. level of income. Using the growth rates in Table 21-2, we can calculate that it would take less than 41 years to get there. That may seem to be a long period, but Japan did just that in the post–World War II period. In the past 40 years U.S. real income per capita only doubled, but that of Japan increased by a factor of more than 10. From that perspective some of the newly industrialized

Table 21-2 *Comparative Per Capita Income Levels*

	Per Capita Income 1987 (1987 $U.S.)	Growth Rate 1965–1987 (% per year)	Per Capita Income 1985 (U.S. = 100)
U.S.	18 530	1.5	100
Canada	16 000	2.5	75.0
Japan	15 760	4.2	71.5
Korea	2 690	6.4	24.3
Brazil	2 020	4.1	...
Mexico	1 830	2.5	...
India	300	1.8	4.7

Source: World Bank, *World Development Report*, 1989.

countries in Asia and Latin America may well get within reach of the old and established nations, such as the United Kingdom, Canada, or even the United States, within the next 30 to 50 years.

To answer questions about the long-run growth rate of output, we go back to fundamentals. With the unemployment rate constant, there are only two possible sources of growth.[2] *Factor supplies may grow, or the productivity of factors of production may increase*. This, in turn, raises the questions of what determines the growth of factor supplies and their productivity, and what the quantitative link is between growth in factor supplies and productivity, on the one side, and output growth, on the other.

There are two complementary approaches to these questions. One is *growth theory*, which models the interactions among factor supplies, output growth, saving, and investment in the process of growth. The other is *growth accounting*, which attempts to quantify the contribution of different determinants of output growth. The two approaches draw on a common analytical framework, which we now outline.

21-1 Sources of Growth in Real Income

In this section we use the production function to study the *sources of growth*. We show that growth in labour, growth in capital, and improved technical efficiency are the three sources of growth.

The Production Function

In earlier chapters we introduced the concept of a production function. The *production function* links the amount of output produced in an economy to the inputs of factors of production and to the state of technical knowledge. Equation (1) represents the production function in symbols:

$$Y = AF(K, N) \tag{1}$$

where K and N denote the inputs of capital and labour and A denotes the state of technology. The production function $AF(K, N)$ in (1) states that the output produced depends on factor inputs K and N and on the state of technology. Increases in factor inputs and improved technology lead to an increase in output supply.

The next step is to make these links more precise by looking at an expression for the growth rate of output. In Equation (2), which is derived in the appendix to this chapter, we show the determinants of output growth.[3]

---

[2] It is not essential for what follows that the average unemployment rate be the same as the natural rate; we make that assumption purely to simplify the exposition.

[3] Equation (2) applies when there are *constant returns to scale* in production; that is, increases in both inputs, in the same proportion, increase output in that proportion.

$$\Delta Y/Y = (1 - \theta) \Delta N/N + \theta \Delta K/K + \Delta A/A \tag{2}$$

$$\frac{\text{Output}}{\text{growth}} = \frac{\text{labour}}{\text{share}} \times \frac{\text{labour}}{\text{growth}} + \frac{\text{capital}}{\text{share}} \times \frac{\text{capital}}{\text{growth}} + \frac{\text{technical}}{\text{progress}}$$

where $(1 - \theta)$ and θ are weights equal to the income shares of labour and of capital in production.

Equation (2) summarizes the contributions of growth of inputs and of improved productivity to growth of output:

1. The contribution of the growth of factor inputs is seen in the first two terms. Labour and capital each contribute an amount equal to their individual growth rates *multiplied by the share of that input in income.*

2. The rate of improvement of technology, called *technical progress,* or the *growth of total factor productivity,* is the third term in Equation (2). The growth rate of total factor productivity is the amount by which output would increase as a result of improvements in methods of production, with all inputs unchanged. In other words, there is growth in total factor productivity when we get more output from the same factors of production.[4]

Example: Suppose the income share of capital is 0.3 and that of labour is 0.7. These values correspond approximately to the actual values for the Canadian economy. Furthermore, let labour force growth be 1.8 percent and growth of the capital stock be 4 percent, and suppose technical progress proceeds at the rate of 1.5 percent. What is the growth rate of full-employment output? Applying Equation (2), we obtain a growth rate of 4.0 percent (= 0.7 × 1.8 percent + 0.3 × 4 percent + 1.5 percent).

An important point in Equation (2) is that the growth rates of capital and labour are weighted by the respective income shares. The reason for these weights is that the importance to production of, say, a one-percentage-point change in labour differs from the same percentage-point change in capital, and that difference in importance is measured by the relative income shares of each factor. Specifically, if labour has a larger share than capital, output rises more when labour increases by, say, 10 percent, than if capital increases by 10 percent.

Returning to our example, if labour alone grows by 1 percent, output will grow by 0.7 percent, using the 0.7 percent income share for labour. If capital alone grows by 1 percent, output will grow by only 0.3 percent, reflecting the smaller importance of capital in production. However, if each grows by 1 percent, so does output.

This point — that growth in inputs is weighted by factor shares — turns out to be quite critical when we ask how much extra growth we get by raising the rate of growth of the capital stock, say by supply-side policies. Suppose in the example above, with everything else the same, capital growth had been 7 percent instead of 4 percent. Doing the calculations with the help of Equation (2), we find that output growth would

---

[4] There is a distinction between *labour productivity* and total factor productivity. Labour productivity is just the ratio of output to labour input, Y/N. Labour productivity certainly grows as a result of technical progress, but it also grows because of the accumulation of capital per worker.

increase to 4.9 percent, rising by less than a percentage point even though capital growth rises by three percentage points.

Increasing Returns to Scale

The result cited in the preceding paragraphs — namely, that if each input grows by 1 percent, so does output — holds only when there are constant returns to scale. If there are increasing returns to to scale, then a 1 percent increase in each input results in a greater than 1 percent increase in output. Whether there are increasing or constant returns to scale is a matter of fact, with much of the evidence suggesting that returns to scale are roughly constant. We now turn to the evidence.

Empirical Estimates of the Sources of Growth

The previous section prepares us for an analysis of empirical studies that deal with sources of growth. Equation (2) suggests that the growth in output can be explained by growth in factor inputs, weighted by their shares in income, and by technical progress. An early and famous study by Nobel prizewinner Robert Solow of MIT dealt with the period 1909–1949 in the United States.[5] Solow's surprising conclusion was that more than 80 percent of the growth in output per labour hour over that period was due to technical progress — that is, to factors other than growth in the input of capital per labour hour. Specifically, Solow estimated an equation for the United States similar to Equation (2) that identifies capital and labour growth along with technical progress as the sources of output growth. Of the average annual growth of total GNP of 2.9 percent per year over that period, he concluded that 0.32 percent was attributable to capital accumulation, 1.09 percent per annum was due to increases in the input of labour, and the remaining 1.49 percent was due to technical progress. Per capita output grew at 1.81 percent, with 1.49 percent of that increase resulting from technical progress.

The very large part of growth that is explained by technical progress makes that term really a catchall for omitted factors and poor measurement of the capital and labour inputs. Further work therefore turned quite naturally to explore this residual — that is, growth not explained by capital accumulation or increased labour input.

Perhaps the most comprehensive of the subsequent studies is that by Edward Denison.[6] Using data for the period 1929–1982, Denison attributed 1.9 percent of the 2.9

---

[5] "Technical Change and the Aggregate Production Function," *Review of Economics and Statistics*, August 1957.

[6] *Accounting for United States Economic Growth, 1929–1969* (Washington, D.C.: The Brookings Institution, 1974). See also Denison's *Accounting for Slower Economic Growth: The United States in the 1970s* (Washington, D.C.: The Brookings Institution, 1980); *Trends in American Economic Growth, 1929–1982* (Washington, D.C.: The Brookings Institution, 1985); and *Estimates of Productivity Change By Industry* (Washington, D.C.: The Brookings Institution, 1989).

percent annual rate of increase in real output to increased factor inputs. Output per labour hour grew at the rate of 1.58 percent, of which 1.02 percent was due to technical progress. Denison's findings thus support Solow's estimate that most of the growth in output per labour hour is due to technical progress.

The methods used by Denison have been applied to Canadian data for the period 1946 to 1967 in a study done for the Economic Council of Canada. Table 21-3 shows a breakdown of the contributions to growth of real output over this period. Out of an average rate of growth of 4.61 percent, 2.25 percent was estimated to be attributable to growth in factor productivity as a result of technical progress.

Technical progress explains almost half the growth in output, with growth in total factor inputs accounting for the other half of growth. Consider now the breakdown between labour and capital. Here increases in the labour force get a very large credit for their contribution to growth. Why? Is it because labour grows very fast? The answer is provided by Equation (2), which suggests that labour's growth rate has a relatively large weight because labour's share of income is relatively large. The counterpart is obviously the relatively low share of capital. Thus, even if capital and labour grew at the same rate, the fact that they have different shares in income — labour having a share of about 70 percent and capital having a share of about 30 percent — implies that labour would be credited with a larger contribution toward growth.

The remaining significant part of technical progress is *economies of scale*. This is a bit troublesome because we assumed away economies of scale in deriving Equation (2). In deriving that equation, we explicitly assumed constant returns to scale, but as the scale of operation of the economy expands, fewer inputs are required per unit output, presumably because we can avail ourselves of techniques that are economically inefficient at a small-scale level but yield factor savings at a larger scale of production.

The major significance of Denison's work, and the work in this area of others, including Nobel laureate Simon Kuznets (1901–1985) and J.W. Kendrick, is to point out that there is no single critical source of real income growth. The early finding by Solow that growth in the capital stock makes a minor, though not negligible, contribution to growth stands up well to the test of later research. Capital investment is certainly necessary — particularly because some technological improvements require

Table 21-3 *Sources of Growth of Real Output, 1946–1967*

Source of Growth	Growth Rate (percent per annum)	
Total factor input		2.36
Labour:	1.24	
Capital:	1.12	
Output per unit of input		2.25
Total output		4.61

Source: Economic Council of Canada, *Seventh Annual Review*, 1970, p. 93.

the use of new types of machines — but it is clear that other sources of growth can make an important contribution. Furthermore, since for most purposes we are interested in output per head, we have to recognize that we are left with only technical progress and growth in capital to achieve increased output per head. Here we have to ask: What are the components of technical progress? *Advances in knowledge stand out as a major source and point to the roles of research, education, and training as important sources of growth.*[7]

21-2 Potential Output and Productivity

When policy makers decide to use monetary or fiscal policy to bring the economy closer to full employment, they need to know where to aim. If the full-employment unemployment rate were 6 percent, it would not make much sense to use expansionary fiscal policies at a 5.5 percent unemployment rate. Thus we need measures of the full-employment unemployment rate and the corresponding level of *potential output* or *full-employment output*. The concept draws on the ideas of growth accounting to construct a GDP series that can serve as a benchmark for policy planning.

There are two steps in estimating potential output. The first is to estimate the production function, Equation (1), and the second is to estimate the full-employment levels of capital and labour and any other inputs that might be taken into account. For example, in the production function of the "MACE" model of the Canadian economy, constructed by John Helliwell at the University of British Columbia, three factors of production are taken into account. In order to estimate the impact of the energy crisis, the production function determines output of the energy-using sectors of the economy as a function of labour, capital, and energy inputs. This approach makes it possible to estimate the impact of the sharp increase in the price of energy in the 1970s.

Productivity Growth

Figure 21-2 shows an index of output per person employed in Canadian nonagricultural industries from 1961 to 1991. The marked decline in productivity growth after 1973 has been the subject of considerable interest and investigation. In a study undertaken by the Department of Finance, two factors were identified as being significant.[8] About one-quarter of the decline in overall productivity growth was attributed to a fall in productivity in the oil and gas industry. Output per person in this sector declined on average by nearly 10 percent per year over the period 1962 to 1973. Over the remainder of the 1970s, employment, particularly in the areas of exploration and drilling,

---

[7] A collection of useful papers on the sources of growth is contained in Edmund Phelps, ed., *The Goal of Economic Growth* (New York: Norton, 1969), and Dennis C. Mueller, ed., *The Political Economy of Growth* (New Haven: Yale University Press, 1983).

[8] Department of Finance, *Recent Changes in Patterns of Productivity Growth in Canada*, April 1980.

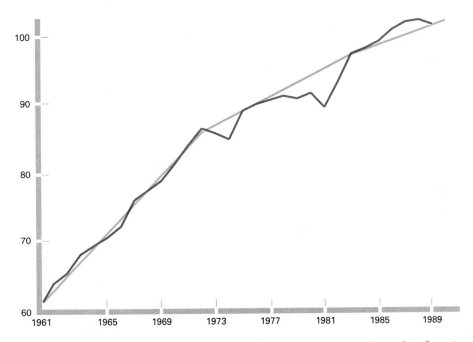

Figure 21-2   *Real Output per Person Employed in Nonagricultural Industries*

(*Source:* Department of Finance, *Quarterly Economic Review*, Annual Reference Tables)

grew rapidly, while output of oil declined and output of natural gas remained close to the 1973 level.

Another 25 percent of the post-1973 decline in productivity growth was attributed to a decline in the growth of the capital–labour ratio. Four other factors were examined but were found not to have had a significant impact. These were: (1) changes in the demographic composition of the labour force, (2) shifts in the share of employment from goods-producing to services-producing industries, (3) governmental pollution-abatement regulations, and (4) changes in average hours worked per employee.

Analysis of the productivity slowdown based on the MACE model referred to above provides a quite different perspective.[9] As indicated, this model focuses on the energy-using sectors, and Helliwell estimates that 30 percent of the decline in labour productivity between 1973 and 1982, relative to a steady growth case, is attributable to substitution of labour for energy. This represents, of course, a desirable response of producers to the sharp increase in the relative cost of energy.

---

[9] See J.F. Helliwell, "Stagflation and Productivity Decline in Canada, 1974–1982," *Canadian Journal of Economics*, May 1984, pp. 191–216. Very similar conclusions are reached in the recent Economic Council of Canada report, *Pulling Together — Productivity, Innovation, and Trade*, 1992.

According to Helliwell's analysis, the other major factor in the productivity slowdown was the low level of capacity utilization. This conclusion is particularly important for projecting into the future. It implies that if we are able to return to more normal utilization rates then we can expect the longer-term trend to growth of productivity to resume.

21-3 Output Growth and Supply-Side Economics

In the early 1980s, partly as a result of disappointment with slow growth and generally poor macroeconomic performance, *supply-side economics* (discussed in Chapter 15) attracted much attention. We now concentrate on the solid aspect, which argues that the level and/or the growth rate of output could be significantly increased through policies designed to promote greater efficiency, reduced regulation, greater willingness to work, and greater willingness to save and invest.[10]

In discussing full-employment output in earlier chapters, we took the labour supply to be given and independent of the real wage; similarly, we assumed a given stock of capital. However, the basic premise of supply-side economics is that capital and labour supplies are not given, independent of incentives to work, save, and invest. On the contrary, it is argued that the labour–leisure choice is strongly affected by the *after-tax* real wage and that the willingness to save and invest is likewise affected by the *after-tax* rates of return on assets. This perspective directs attention to fiscal policy as influencing factor supplies and hence the level and rate of increase of output.

Labour Supply

Households have to choose how much labour to supply. In practice that means choosing how many members of the family work and for how many hours per week or month. At first sight there appears to be little choice, since the typical job comes with a given number of working hours per week, but that is not quite the case once we take into account the possibility that more than one family member might work or the possibilities of working overtime hours or holding part-time jobs. Households' labour supply can thus vary in response to incentives.

The main determinant of labour supply is the after-tax real wage. Suppose it rises. Then some family members who had preferred to stay home may now be tempted into the labour force. For those already working, the real wage increase has ambiguous effects on labour supply. The *income effect* of the wage increase tends to reduce labour supply because it is now possible to work less and earn more, but because every hour

---

[10] On supply-side economics, see particularly Barry Bosworth, *Tax Incentives and Economic Growth* (Washington, D.C.: The Brookings Institution, 1984); Charles Hulten and Isabel Sawhill, eds., *The Legacy of Reaganomics* (Washington, D.C.: The Urban Institute, 1984); Laurence Meyer, ed., *The Supply Side Effects of Economic Policy* (Federal Reserve Bank of St. Louis, 1981), and Martin Feldstein, "Supply Side Economics: Old Truths and New Claims," *American Economic Review*, May 1986.

of leisure is now more costly, the *substitution effect* tends to increase labour supply. The outcome of conflicting income and substitution effects is thus a matter for empirical study. In addition, of course, higher participation in the labour force will tend to increase labour supply when the after-tax real wage rises.

Empirical Evidence

Jerry Hausman of MIT has shown in a number of studies that the household labour supply in the U.S. increases *significantly* in response to increased after-tax real wages.[11] This implies that changes in the tax structure that increase the after-tax real wage would increase labour supply and output. Hausman finds that the progressivity of income taxes reduces labour supply. The magnitude of the effect can be judged from the following experiment. Suppose the progressive income tax structure were eliminated and replaced by a flat 15 percent income tax which would lead to the same amount of revenue. What would happen to labour supply? Hausman estimates that total labour supply would rise by 5 percent. With an income share in the U.S. of 0.75, a 5 percent growth in labour supply would increase the level of full-employment output by 3.75 percent. This is certainly a nonnegligible gain, although the policy experiment — the move to a flat income tax — would be a major and controversial change in the structure of taxation.

Supply of Capital

The supply of capital represents the cumulation of past investment. The capital stock grows if additions to the stock more than offset the depreciation due to wear and tear and to obsolescence.

A supply-side point of view emphasizes the links between saving and investment. Recall that when the goods market clears and when net exports are zero, investment minus saving equals the budget surplus, or

$$I = S + (T - G) \tag{3}$$

Equation (3) shows that to raise investment, and thus growth of the capital stock, we require increased saving or reduced government budget deficits. Supply-side economics has focused on the incentives to save and invest. Supply-side economists argue that regulation has reduced the productivity of investment and that corporate and personal income taxes further reduce the rate of return eventually received by the savers who provide the funds needed to finance investment. If savers receive a lower rate of return as a result of taxation, say the supply-siders, they reduce saving, and therefore capital accumulation is reduced.

---

[11] See J. Hausman, "Labor Supply and the Natural Unemployment Rate," in L. Meyer, *The Supply Side Effects, op. cit.*; and Hank Aaron and Joe Pechman, eds., *How Taxes Affect Economic Behavior* (Washington, D.C.: The Brookings Institution, 1981).

For instance, consider an investment that yields 12 percent per year in real terms. That is, someone who undertakes the investment, costing $100 in year 1, earns $12 per year in real terms forever after (net of labour and material costs). If the income tax rate is 40 percent, the saver can at most earn, after tax, 60 percent of 12 percent, or 7.2 percent. As a result of taxation, the return to saving is substantially reduced. Accordingly, claim supply-siders, the higher the tax rate, the less saving there will be.[12]

What supply-side policies increase the yield on saving? There are a variety of means of exempting the return on saving from taxation. For instance, under the Canadian income tax system, contributions up to specified limits to a Registered Retirement Savings Plan are exempt from taxable income. Some argue for the complete exemption of savings from tax by replacing the income tax with a *consumption tax*. A consumption tax levies taxes only on consumption spending, not on income. Since the difference between income and consumption is saving, a consumption tax effectively exempts any amount that is saved from being taxed in the year it is earned, and thereby encourages saving.

There is considerable disagreement about how saving responds to changes in its return. There is not much support for the contention that increased after-tax rates of return to saving will *strongly* raise saving. Once again, we have two opposing effects: With increased interest rates, less saving is needed to ensure a given future income (say, for retirement). This effect (actually an income effect) reduces saving. At the same time, a dollar saved today yields increased future wealth and consumption and would therefore lead households to postpone consumption and increase saving (this is the substitution effect). The balance of effects is theoretically uncertain.

The empirical evidence does not settle the issue of whether changes in the after-tax rate of return affect the rate of saving.[13] Therefore policies that reduce taxes on saving as a means of generating more saving, capital formation, and growth have an uncertain effect on the economy.

Another line of argument questions the quantitative importance of policies to promote saving. We have noted that growth in capital receives a very small weight in determining output growth. Even if policies led to a 10 percent rise in the capital–labour ratio, output per head would only increase by 3 percent.

Regulation

Government regulation involves a tradeoff. Government regulations serve some social purpose (the environment, safety, conservation), but they also involve costs to firms that have to abide by them. Regulation therefore reduces business profitability. Policy

---

[12] See M. Boskin, "Economic Growth and Productivity," in M. Boskin, ed., *The Economy in the 1980s: A Program for Growth and Stability* (San Francisco: Institute for Contemporary Studies, 1980); *Economic Report of the President*, 1982 and 1983; and especially, Michael K. Evans, *The Truth about Supply-Side Economics* (New York: Basic Books, 1983).

[13] Gerald A. Carlino, in "Interest Rate Effects and Intertemporal Consumption," *Journal of Monetary Economics*, March 1982, reviews and extends the (ambiguous) evidence. See, too, Larry Kotlikoff, "Taxation and Savings: A Neoclassical Perspective," *Journal of Economic Literature*, December 1984.

makers are keenly aware that the tradeoff exists and therefore, rightly, focus on inefficient regulation and particularly costly (nonmarket) regulation as requiring review. That process has been under way for some time, but it would be a mistake to expect major growth in output from reduced regulation.

Budget Deficits and Growth

In Equation (3) we showed that private investment and capital formation will be higher when saving is higher and the government budget deficit is smaller.[14] Government budget deficits thus imply, other things being equal, a reduction in full-employment output growth. Government budget deficits absorb private saving — households buy government securities rather than the stocks or bonds that firms issue to finance their investment. Therefore, funds are diverted from growth toward other purposes. It is clear that if the only objective is to promote growth, the government should balance the budget or even run a surplus to free resources for investment. There is, however, a tradeoff between growth and the social objectives that may lie behind a budget deficit.

Evaluating Supply-Side Economics and Growth Incentives

The emphasis on increasing incentives to work, save, and invest is the valid core of supply-side economics. There are two questions here: (1) Will the proposed policies work, that is, increase future potential output? (2) If the policies do work, how far should we go in creating incentives to increase future potential output?

Policies to increase the labour supply by reducing taxes and policies to increase investment by reducing government budget deficits and providing investment subsidies would be effective in increasing potential output today and in the future. Thus supply-side policies are available, but we can also go overboard on such policies. If we are reducing government budget deficits while reducing other taxes, we are also reducing government spending. We could reduce government spending by getting rid of the post office, but most people would think it better to have higher taxes and a post office than lower taxes and no post office. Similarly, the government provides many useful services through its welfare programs — services that most people prefer to have — rather than aiming purely to maximize the level of investment.

Further, given government spending, and an economy at full employment, increases in saving imply reductions in consumption. Thus in supply-side economics we are trading off current consumption for future consumption. We are trading off the consumption of those now alive for the consumption of their children and children who come later yet. This process also can go too far. In the extreme, we (society) would not want to force the current generation to consume at a bare survival level just so

---

[14] To the extent that deficits are used to finance government investment, they, of course, do not reduce total investment.

their grandchildren can sit around their pools doing very little work while automated factories, made possible by a huge volume of past investment, produce a high level of output. Somewhere between not saving now and saving almost all of output, there is an optimal amount of saving to be done.

It is no easy task for society to decide what that optimal amount of saving is. Those who will be consuming in the future are not here to vote, because they have not yet been born, and those who are around now will have different views. Some may ask, as reportedly has Joan Robinson (1905–1984), the famous English economist, "What did posterity ever do for us?" Others may feel it is the duty of the parents to sacrifice for their children's sake. Ultimately the policy decisions that affect growth are settled politically.

21-4 Growth Theory

We turn now from empirical issues and the historical record to the theory of economic growth. The theory of economic growth asks what factors determine the full-employment rate of output over time. Growth theory is important because it helps explain both growth rates and why per capita income levels differ among countries. One of the central results of growth theory, for example, is the proposition that between two countries with the same technology and saving rates, the one that has the higher rate of population growth will eventually have lower per capita income.

We have already examined the sources of growth in Equation (2), where we showed that full-employment output growth depends on the growth in factor inputs and on technical progress. In this section we pursue the issue further to ask what determines the growth of factor supplies and what is the link to long-run per capita incomes or standards of living.

We take a rather simple formulation here by assuming a given and constant rate of labour force growth, $\Delta N/N = n$, and also that there is no technical progress, $\Delta A/A = 0$.[15] With these assumptions the only variable element left in Equation (2) is the growth rate of capital.

Capital growth is determined by saving, which, in turn, depends on income. Income or output, in turn, depends on capital. We are thus set with an interdependent system in which capital growth depends, via saving and income, on the capital stock. We now study the short-run behaviour, the adjustment process, and the long-run equilibrium of that interdependent system.

Steady State

We start by discussing the steady state of the economy. Here we ask whether in an economy with population growth and saving, and therefore growth in the capital stock,

---

[15] For further simplicity we also assume that the entire population works, so that the labour force and the population are the same.

we reach a point where output per head and capital per head become constant. In such a steady state, current saving and additions to the capital stock would be just enough to equip new entrants into the labour force with the same amount of capital as the average worker uses.

The idea of a steady state is this: If capital per head is unchanging, given technology, so is output per head; but for capital *per head* to remain unchanging even though population is growing, capital must grow at just the right rate, namely, at the same rate as population. More formally, if output per head is to remain constant, output and population must grow at the same rates, or $\Delta Y/Y = \Delta N/N = n$. Therefore, from Equation (2), setting productivity growth equal to zero, we have $0 = \Delta K/K - n$, or

$$\frac{\Delta K}{K} = n \tag{4}$$

Equation (4) states that in the steady state the growth rate of the capital stock is equal to the growth rate of population. Equivalently, in the steady state the amount of capital per head is constant.

We now show the steady state graphically in Figure 21-3. We put output per head on the vertical axis and capital per head on the horizontal axis. The production function,

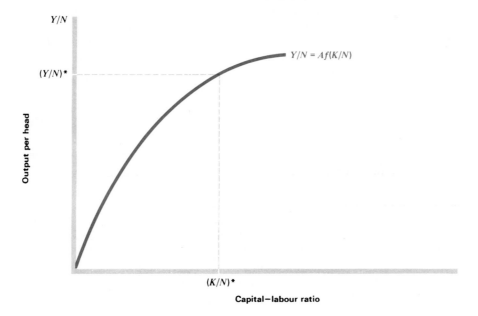

Figure 21-3 *Output per Head and the Capital–Labour Ratio*

The production function shows output per head as a function of the amount of capital per head, or the capital–labour ratio. The higher the capital–labour ratio is, the higher output per head is, but the increment to output from raising the capital–labour ratio grows progressively smaller as the capital–labour ratio rises.

which is central to understanding growth, exhibits diminishing returns to capital. As capital per head increases, so that workers use increasing amounts of machinery, output per head increases, but at a diminishing rate. Thus an increase in the capital–labour ratio is productive, but there are diminishing returns. In steady state, the economy settles down to a fixed capital–labour ratio $(K/N)°$. The production function shows the corresponding amount of output per head $(Y/N)°$.

Saving and Growth

We gain insight by examining the link between saving and the growth in capital. We are assuming there is no government. Accordingly, investment, or the gross increase in capital, is equal to saving. To obtain the increase in the capital stock, however, we have to deduct depreciation. Therefore the net addition to the capital stock is equal to saving less depreciation.

$$\Delta K = \text{saving} - \text{depreciation} \tag{5}$$

Two assumptions take us from (4) and (5) to a complete description of the steady state. In (5) we need to specify saving behaviour and to make an assumption about depreciation. We assume first that saving is a constant fraction s of income Y. Second, depreciation is a constant fraction d of the capital stock. Concretely, we might assume that people save 15 percent of their income $(s = 0.15)$ and that depreciation is at a rate of 10 percent per year so that every year 10 percent of the capital stock needs to be replaced to offset wear and tear $(d = 0.10)$.

Substituting these assumptions in Equation (5) yields

$$\Delta K = sY - dK \tag{5a}$$

or placing the right-hand side in Equation (4), we arrive at the following result that describes the steady state:[16]

$$sY = (n + d)K \tag{4a}$$

Equation (4a) states that in the steady state, saving (sY) is just sufficient to provide for enough investment to offset depreciation (dK) *and* to equip new members of the labour force with capital (nK). If saving were larger than this amount, net investment would be sufficiently large to make capital per head grow, leading to rising income per head. Conversely, if not enough were saved, capital per head would be falling and with it income per head.

---

[16] Placing Equation (5a) in Equation (4) yields $(sY - dK)/K = n$. By multiplying both sides by K and collecting terms, we obtain $sY = (n + d)K$.

The Growth Process

We next study the adjustment process that leads the economy from some initial capital–labour ratio over time to the steady state. The critical element in this transition process is the rate of saving and investment compared with the rate of depreciation, and population growth.

The argument is made easier by a bit of new notation. We define the amount of output per head as $x = Y/N$ and the amount of capital per head, or the capital–labour ratio, as $k = K/N$. This is simply notation and in no way changes our model.

$$k = \text{capital–labour ratio} = \frac{K}{N} \qquad x = \text{output per head} = \frac{Y}{N} \qquad (6)$$

Thus in terms of Figure 21-3 the vertical axis is labelled x and the horizontal axis k.

We now turn to the transition to the steady state. Note from Equation (2) that output per head will grow if capital per head grows and that capital per head will grow if saving is *more than sufficient* to cover depreciation of the capital stock and also to equip new members of the population with capital. This can be formalized by writing the change in the capital–labour ratio as follows:[17]

$$\Delta k = sx - (n + d)k \qquad (7)$$

The growth process can now be studied with the help of Equation (4a) and Figure 21-4. Here we reproduce the production function from Figure 21-3, writing output per capita as a function of the capital–labour ratio.

We have added the savings function, which, for each capital–labour ratio, is simply the fraction s of output. Thus, for any capital–labour ratio, say k_0, the corresponding point on the saving schedule tells us the amount of saving per head, $sx(k_0)$, that will be forthcoming at that capital–labour ratio.

We know that all saving is invested, so that gross investment or gross additions to the capital stock, in per capita terms, are equal to sx, given a capital–labour ratio of k_0. We know, too, from Equation (7) that the increase in the capital–labour ratio falls short of that gross addition for two reasons:

- Depreciation reduces the capital–labour ratio, and part of gross investment must be devoted to offsetting depreciation. In particular, if the depreciation rate is d,

---

[17] The percentage growth rate of the capital–labour ratio is equal to the difference between the growth rate of capital and the growth rate of labour, or $\Delta k/k = \Delta K/K - n$. Now using Equation (5a) to replace ΔK, we have

$$\frac{\Delta k}{k} = s\frac{Y}{K} - d - n = \frac{s(Y/N)}{K/N} - (d + n) = \frac{sx}{k} - (d + n).$$

Multiplying both sides by k yields Equation (7) in the text.

an amount dk is required as a depreciation allowance. For example, if the depreciation rate is 10 percent and the capital–labour ratio is 10 machines per person, each year the equivalent of 1 machine would depreciate and would have to be replaced; that is, 10 percent times 10 machines equals 1 machine that has to be replaced.

- Growth in the labour force implies that with a given stock of capital, the capital–labour ratio would be declining. To maintain the amount of capital per head constant, we have to add enough machines to the stock of capital to make up for the growth in population; that is, we need to invest at the rate nk.

It follows that we can write the investment required to maintain constant the capital–labour ratio in the face of depreciation and labour force growth as $(n + d)k$. When saving and hence gross investment are larger than $(n + d)k$, the stock of capital per head is increasing. If saving and gross investment are less, then we are not making up for depreciation and population growth, and, accordingly, capital per head is falling. We can therefore think of the term $(n + d)k$ as the investment requirement that will maintain constant capital per head and therefore, from Figure 21-3, output per head.

In Figure 21-4, we show this investment requirement as a positively sloped schedule. It tells us how much investment we would require at each capital–labour ratio just in order to keep that ratio constant. It is positively sloped because the higher the capital–labour ratio, the larger the amount of investment that is required to maintain that capital–labour ratio. Thus, with the depreciation rate of 10 percent and a growth rate of population of 1 percent, we would require an investment of 1.1 machines per head per year at a capital–labour ratio of 10 machines per head to maintain the capital–labour ratio constant. If the capital–labour ratio were 100 machines per head, the required investment would be 11 machines (= 100 machines per head times 11 percent).

We have seen that the saving schedule tells us the amount of saving and gross investment associated with each capital–labour ratio. Thus, at a capital–labour ratio of k_0 in Figure 21-4, saving is sx_0 at point A. The investment requirement to maintain constant the capital–labour ratio at k_0 is equal to $(n + d)k_0$ at point B. Clearly, saving exceeds the investment requirement. More is added to the capital stock than is required to maintain constant the capital–labour ratio. Accordingly, the capital–labour ratio grows. Not surprisingly, the increase in the capital–labour ratio is equal to actual saving or investment less the investment requirement and is thus given by the vertical distance *AB*.

In the next period, capital per head will be higher. Thus on the horizontal axis we draw an arrow showing k increasing. The line of argument here should now be evident. From Figure 21-4 it is clear that with a somewhat higher capital–labour ratio the discrepancy between saving and the investment requirement becomes smaller. Therefore, the increase in the capital–labour ratio becomes smaller. However, the capital–labour ratio still increases, as indicated by the arrows.

The adjustment process comes to a halt at point C. Here we have reached a capital–labour ratio k° for which saving and investment associated with that capital–labour ratio exactly match the investment requirement. Given the exact matching of actual

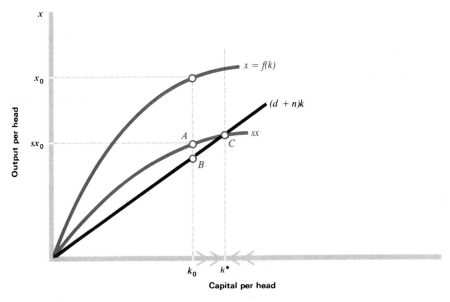

Figure 21-4 *Saving, Investment, and Capital Accumulation*

The saving function shows at each capital–labour ratio the part of income that is saved, sx. The straight line $(d + n)k$ shows the investment requirement. At low capital–labour ratios, saving exceeds the investment requirement, and hence output per head grows. Conversely, at high capital–labour ratios, saving is less than the investment requirement, and capital per head is falling. The steady-state capital–labour ratio is k^*, where saving is just sufficient to maintain the capital–labour ratio constant.

and required investment, the capital–labour ratio neither rises nor falls. We have reached the steady state.

We can make the same argument by starting with an initial capital–labour ratio in excess of k^*. From Figure 21-4 we note that for high capital–labour ratios, the investment requirement is in excess of saving and investment. Accordingly, not enough is added to the capital stock to maintain the capital–labour ratio constant in the face of population growth and depreciation. Thus, the capital–labour ratio falls until we get to k^*, the steady-state capital–labour ratio.

To review our progress so far:

- To maintain the capital–labour ratio constant, saving and investment have to be sufficient to make up for the reduction in capital per head that arises from population growth and depreciation.

- With saving a constant fraction s of output, we established that the capital–labour ratio moves to a steady-state level k^* at which output and therefore saving (investment) are just sufficient to maintain constant the capital–labour ratio.

- The convergence to a steady-state capital–labour ratio k° is ensured by the fact that at low levels of the capital–labour ratio, saving (investment) exceeds the investment required to maintain capital per head and therefore causes the capital–labour ratio to rise. Conversely, at high capital–labour ratios, saving (investment) falls short of the investment requirement, and thus the ratio declines.

Now we turn to a more detailed study of the steady-state equilibrium and the adjustment process. We note that the steady-state level of capital per head is constant, and thus the steady-state level of output per head is also constant. The steady state is reached when all variables, in per capita terms, are constant. This means that, in the steady state, output, capital, and labour all grow at the same rate. They all grow at a rate equal to the rate of population growth. Note particularly that the steady-state growth rate is equal to the rate of population growth and therefore is *not* influenced by the saving rate. (Recall that we are assuming no technical progress.) To explore this property of the steady state in more detail, we investigate the effects of a change in the saving rate.

A Change in the Saving Rate

Why should the long-run growth be independent of the saving rate? If people save 10 percent of their income as opposed to 5 percent, should we not expect this to make a difference to the growth rate of output? Is it not true that an economy in which 10 percent of income is set aside for additions to the capital stock is one in which capital and therefore output grow faster than in an economy in which only 5 percent of income is saved?

We show here that an increase in the saving rate does the following: In the short run, it raises the growth rate of output. It does not affect the *long-run growth rate* of output, but it raises the long-run level of capital and output per head.

Consider Figure 21-5 with an initial steady-state equilibrium at point C, where saving precisely matches the investment requirement. At point C, exactly enough output is saved to maintain the stock of capital per head constant in the face of depreciation and labour force growth. Next consider an increase in the saving rate. For some reason, people want to save a larger fraction of income. The increased saving rate is reflected in an upward shift of the saving schedule. At each level of the capital–labour ratio, and hence at each level of output, saving is larger.

At point C, where we initially had a steady-state equilibrium, saving has now risen relative to the investment requirement, and as a consequence, more is saved than is required to maintain capital per head constant. Enough is saved to allow the capital stock per head to increase.

It is apparent from Figure 21-5 that the capital stock per head will keep rising until we reach point C'. At C', the higher amount of saving is just enough to maintain the higher stock of capital. At point C', both capital per head and output per head have risen. Saving has increased, as has the investment requirement. We have seen, therefore, that an increase in the saving rate will in the long run raise only the level of output and capital per head, and not the growth rate of output per head.

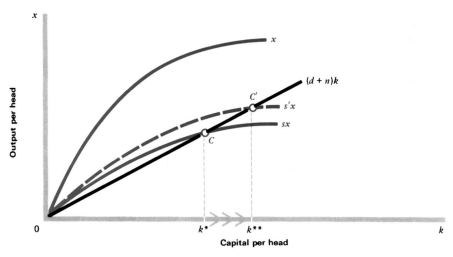

Figure 21-5 *An Increase in the Saving Rate*

An increase in the saving rate implies that at each capital–labour ratio a larger fraction of output is saved. The saving schedule shifts upward to $s'x$. At the initial steady state, saving now exceeds the investment requirement, and hence the capital–labour ratio rises until point C' is reached. An increase in the saving rate raises steady-state per capita income. The growth rate rises only in the transition from C to C'.

The transition process, however, involves an effect of the saving rate on the growth rate of output and the growth rate of output per head. In the transition from $k°$ to $k°°$, the increase in the saving rate raises the growth rate of output. This follows simply from the fact that the capital–labour ratio rises from $k°$ at the initial steady state to $k°°$ in the new steady state. The only way to achieve an increase in the capital–labour ratio is for the capital stock to grow faster than the labour force (and depreciation). This is precisely what happens in the transition process where increased saving per head, owing to the higher saving rate, raises investment and capital growth over and above the investment requirement and thus allows the capital–labour ratio to rise.

In summary, the long-run effect of an increase in the saving rate is to raise the level of output and capital per head but to leave the growth rate of output and capital unaffected. In the transition period, the rates of growth of output and capital increase relative to the steady state. In the short run, therefore, an increase in the saving rate means faster growth, as we would expect.

Figure 21-6 summarizes these two results. Figure 21-6*a* shows the level of per capita output. Starting from an initial long-run equilibrium at time t_0, the increase in the saving rate causes saving and investment to increase, the stock of capital per head grows, and so does output per head. The process will continue at a diminishing rate. In Figure 21-6*b* we focus on the growth rate of output and capital. The growth rate of output is equal to the growth rate of population in the initial steady state. The increase in the saving rate immediately raises the growth rate of output because it

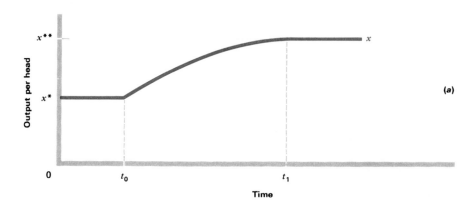

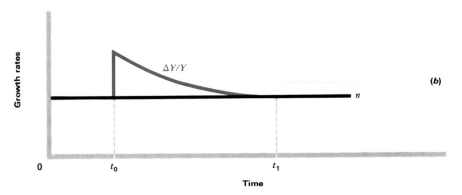

Figure 21-6 *The Time Path of per Capita Income and the Growth Rate of Output*

In panel (*a*), a rise in the saving rate leads to a rising capital–labour ratio and therefore to increasing output per head until a new steady state is reached. In panel (*b*), an increase in the saving rate raises investment above the investment requirement and thus leads to capital accumulation. Output growth rises temporarily and then falls back to the growth rate of population.

implies a faster growth in capital and therefore in output. As capital accumulates, the growth rate decreases, falling back toward the level of population growth.

Population Growth

The preceding discussion of saving and the influence of the saving rate on steady-state capital and output makes it easy to discuss the effects of increased population growth.

Box 21-1 Limits to Growth

There were fears in the 1970s that the world was rapidly running out of natural resources — not only oil, but also such commodities as copper, coal, and land (under the pressure of growing populations). These shortages, it was feared, would impose *limits to growth.*

Economists argued that price increases would cause people to conserve resources, that new technologies would develop, and thus that there was not too much to worry about. The use of energy per unit of GDP has indeed declined sharply since 1973, and so has the price of oil. Most other commodity prices have also dropped. The fear that growing populations put pressure on resources and cause environmental degradation has, however, increased since then, as tropical forests begin to disappear, and there is some evidence that the global climate may be warming.[a] Economic mechanisms could be used to modify the trend to global warming — for instance, by imposing taxes on the use of carbon fuels and making the proceeds available for the development of alternative technologies.[b] Resource limitations may nonetheless slow the rate of productivity increase.

---

[a] United Nations Environment Project, *World Resources 1988–89* (New York: Basic Books, 1989), and S. Schneider, "The Greenhouse Effect: Science and Policy," *Science*, February 1989.
[b] See W. Baumol and W. Oates, *The Theory of Environmental Policy* (Cambridge: Cambridge University Press, 1988).

The question we ask is: What happens when the population growth rate increases from n to n' and remains at that higher level indefinitely? We will show that such an increase in the rate of population growth will *raise* the growth rate of output and *lower* the level of output per head.

The argument can be conveniently followed in Figure 21-7. Here we show the initial steady-state equilibrium at point C. The increase in the growth rate of population means that, at each level of the capital–labour ratio, it takes a larger amount of investment just to maintain the capital–labour ratio constant. Suppose we had 10 machines per head. Initially, the growth rate of population is 1 percent and depreciation is 10 percent, so that we require per year 11 percent times 10 machines, or 1.1 machine, just to offset population growth and depreciation and thus maintain capital per head constant. To maintain the capital–labour ratio constant in the face of higher growth rate of population, say 2 percent, requires a higher level of investment, namely 12 percent as opposed to 11 percent. This is reflected in Figure 21-7 by an upward rotation of the investment requirement schedule.

It is clear from the preceding argument that we are no longer in steady-state equilibrium at point C. The investment that was initially just sufficient to keep the capital–labour ratio constant will no longer be sufficient in the face of higher population

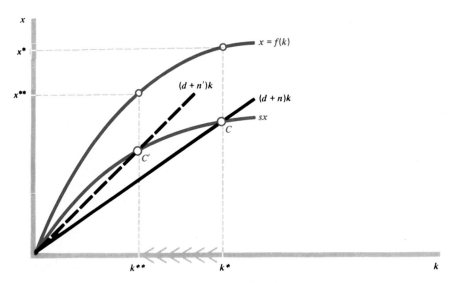

Figure 21-7   An Increase in the Population Growth Rate

Increased population growth raises the investment requirement, rotating the schedule upward to $(d + n')k$. At point C saving is insufficient to maintain capital per head constant in face of the more rapidly growing population. Capital and output per head decline until a new steady state at C' is reached. Thus an increase in the population growth rate reduces per capita income.

growth. At the initial equilibrium, the higher population growth with unchanged saving and investment means that capital does not grow fast enough to keep up with labour-force growth and depreciation. Capital per head declines. In fact, capital per head will keep declining until we reach the new steady-state equilibrium at point C'. Here the capital–labour ratio has declined sufficiently for saving to match the investment requirement. It is true, too, that, corresponding to the lower capital–labour ratio, we have a decline in output per head. Output per head declines from x° to $x^{\circ\circ}$.

The decline in output per head as a consequence of increased population growth points to the problem faced by many developing countries. Fast growth in population, given the saving rate, means low levels of income per head. Indeed, in poor countries one can trace poverty, or low income per head, to the very high rate of population growth. With high population growth, saving will typically be too small to allow capital to rise relative to labour and thus to build up the capital–labour ratio to achieve a satisfactory level of income per head. In those circumstances, and barring other considerations, a reduction in the rate of population growth appears to be a way of achieving higher levels of steady-state per capita income and thus an escape from poverty.

21-5 Summary

1. A production function links factor inputs and technology to the level of output. Growth of output, changes in technology aside, is a weighted average of input growth with the weights equal to income shares. The production function directs attention to factor inputs and technological change as sources of output growth.

2. Growth theory studies the determinants of intermediate-run and long-run growth in output.

3. The more rapidly the capital stock increases and the faster is technical progress, the faster per capita output grows. In Canadian history since 1870, output per head has grown at an average rate of 2.1 percent.

4. From 1953 to 1973, per capita real income grew at an average rate of 2.9 percent, but over the following ten years, the growth rate dropped to 1.6 percent.

5. Supply-side economics argues that the level and rate of growth of potential output can be increased by creating improved incentives for work, saving, and investment.

6. The concept of steady-state equilibrium points (in the absence of technical change) to the conditions required for output per head to be constant. With a growing population, saving must be just sufficient to provide new members of the population with the economy-wide amount of capital per head.

7. The steady-state level of income is determined by the saving rate and by population growth. In the absence of technical change, the steady-state growth rate of output is equal to the rate of population growth. An increase in the growth rate of population raises the steady-state growth rate of total output and lowers the level of steady-state output per head.

8. An increase in the saving rate transitorily raises the growth rate of output. In the new steady state, the growth rate remains unchanged, but the level of output per head is increased.

Key Terms

Production function
Growth accounting
Growth of total factor productivity
Limits to growth
Supply-side economics

Steady state
Sources of growth
Labour productivity
Technical progress

Problems

1. Which of the following government activities have effects on the long-term growth rate? Explain how they can do so.
   (a) Monetary policy
   (b) Labour market policies
   (c) Educational and research programs
   (d) Fiscal policy
   (e) Population control programs.

2. Discuss the role of government policy in raising (a) the supply of labour and (b) the supply of capital. How successful can such policies be?

3. Since 1973, the growth rate of productivity has sharply declined in most industrialized countries. List several of the factors that are responsible for this decline and discuss why the decline in productivity growth is an important issue.

4. Suppose the share of capital in income is 0.4 and the share of labour is 0.6. Capital grows by 6 percent, and labour supply declines by 2 percent. What happens to output?

5. An earthquake destroys one-quarter of the capital stock. Discuss in the context of the growth model the adjustment process of the economy, and show, using Figure 21-4, what happens to growth.

6. (a) In the absence of technical progress, what happens to output per head and total output over time? Why?
   (b) What is the long-run effect of the saving rate on the *level* of output per capita? On *growth* of output per capita?

7. Evaluate this statement: "The saving rate cannot affect the growth of output in the economy. That is determined by the growth of labour input and by technical progress."

*8. Suppose we assume a production function of the form

$$Y = AF(K, N, Z)$$

where Z is a measure of the natural resources going into production. Assume this production function obeys constant returns to scale and diminishing returns to each factor (like Equation (1)).
   (a) What will happen to output per head if capital and labour grow together but resources are fixed?
   (b) What if Z is fixed but there is technical progress?
   (c) Interpret these results in terms of the limits to growth.

*9. Use the model of long-run growth to incorporate the government. Assume that an income tax at the rate of *t* is levied and that, accordingly, saving per head is

equal to $s(1 - t)x$. The government spends the tax revenue on public consumption.
- **(a)** Use Figure 21-4 to explore the impact of an increase in the tax rate on the steady-state output level and capital per head.
- **(b)** Draw a chart of the time path of capital per head, output per head, and the growth rate of output.
- **(c)** Discuss the statement: "To raise the growth rate of output, the public sector has to run a budget surplus to free resources for investment."

10. Use Figure 21-4 to explore the impact of a *once-and-for-all* improvement in technology.
- **(a)** How does technical progress affect the level of output per head as of a given capital–labour ratio?
- **(b)** Show the new steady-state equilibrium. Has saving changed? Is income per head higher? Has the capital stock per head increased?
- **(c)** Show the time path of the adjustment to the new steady state. Does technical progress transitorily raise the ratio of investment to capital?

11. Discuss the statement: "The lower the level of income, the higher the growth rate of output."

12. Explain the catching-up hypothesis that asserts that the higher the level of per capita income, the lower is productivity growth. What factors do you think are responsible for this observed pattern?

Appendix   Properties of the Production Function

In this appendix we briefly show how the fundamental growth equation (2) is obtained. The material is presented for completeness; it is not essential to an understanding of the text.

We start with a production function that exhibits constant returns: Increasing *all* inputs in the same proportion raises output in that same proportion. Thus if we double all inputs, output will double. With that property the change in output due to technical progress and to changes in inputs can be written as

$$\Delta Y = F(K,N)\Delta A + MPK\Delta K + MPN\Delta N \tag{A1}$$

where *MPK* and *MPN* are the marginal products of capital and labour, respectively. We remember that the marginal product of a factor tells us the contribution to output made by employing one extra unit of the factor. Dividing both sides of the equation by $Y = AF(K,N)$ yields the expression

$$\frac{\Delta Y}{Y} = \frac{\Delta A}{A} + \frac{MPK}{Y}\Delta K + \frac{MPN}{Y}\Delta N \tag{A2}$$

Equation (A2) further simplifies by multiplying and dividing the second term on the right-hand side by K and the third term by N.

$$\frac{\Delta Y}{Y} = \frac{\Delta A}{A} + \left(K\frac{MPK}{Y}\right)\frac{\Delta K}{K} + \left(N\frac{MPN}{Y}\right)\frac{\Delta N}{N} \tag{A3}$$

We now argue that the terms in parentheses are the income shares of capital and labour. In a competitive market factors are paid their marginal product. Thus the term $N(MPN/Y) = wN/Y$, where w is the real wage. The right-hand side is recognized as the ratio of labour income to total income or the share of labour in income. Similarly, the term $K(MPK/Y)$ is the share of capital in income. With constant returns and competition, factor payments exhaust the total product. Therefore the shares of capital and labour sum to unity. Denoting the share of capital in income by θ and the labour share by $1 - \theta$, we arrive at Equation (2) in the text.

We note a further property of the constant returns production function. When returns to scale are constant, we can write the production function as follows:

$$Y = AF(K, N) = NAf\left(\frac{K}{N}\right) \tag{A4}$$

or using the notation $x = Y/N$ and $k = K/N$,

$$x = Af(k) \tag{A5}$$

This is the form used in the growth theory section of the text, where output per head is a function of the capital–labour ratio.

Glossary

Accelerator model of investment Theory that investment is proportional to the rate of change in output.

Accommodation Use of policy to offset a shock. For example, increase in money supply to prevent increase in interest rate when *IS* curve shifts out. *See also* Accommodation of supply shocks.

Accommodation of supply shocks Use of aggregate demand policy to maintain GDP when faced with a temporary dip in aggregate supply.

Action lag Period between the time a policy is chosen and the time it is put into effect.

Activist policy Policy that responds to current state of the economy.

Activists Economists who believe the government ought to use stabilization policy.

Adaptive expectations Expectations theory that expectations change gradually over time. *Contrast* rational expectations.

Adverse supply shocks Upward movement of the aggregate supply curve; the OPEC oil price increase is the classic example.

Aggregate demand Sum of all the purchases of final goods throughout the economy.

Aggregate demand curve Amount of goods demanded in the economy at a given price level.

Aggregate supply Total production of all final goods in the economy.

Aggregate supply curve Amount of goods supplied by firms at a given price level.

Anticipated inflation Inflation that can be predicted in advance.

Appreciation Increase in the value of a currency *vis-à-vis* other currencies.

Asset budget constraint A household's investments in different assets must add up to total wealth.

Automatic stabilizer Elements in the economy that reduce the impact of changes in autonomous spending on the equilibrium level of GDP.

Average propensity to consume (APC) Ratio of consumption to income.

Balance of payments Record of transactions of the residents of a country with the rest of the world.

Balanced budget multiplier The effect on GDP of equal increases in government expenditures and taxes.

Bank rate Rate of interest on advances to the chartered banks by the Bank of Canada.

Barro–Ricardo hypothesis Theory that the national debt does not contribute to net wealth because people recognize that the payment of interest and principal will require future increases in taxes. Named for Robert Barro and David Ricardo.

Beggar-thy-neighbour policy Attempt to increase domestic GDP at the expense of GDP in foreign countries.

Bond Promise by a borrower to repay a loan at a certain date and to pay interest in the interim.

Budget deficit *See* budget surplus.

Budget surplus Excess of government revenue over government expenditure. (Equals minus the *budget deficit*.)

Burden of the debt Costs imposed on individuals by the existence of the national debt.

Business cycle Pattern of expansions and contractions of the economy around trend growth.

Business fixed investment Expenditure on new machinery, equipment, and structures used in production.

Capital account Record of international borrowing and lending and purchases and sales of assets.

Capital mobility Ability of financial assets to flow between countries.

Cash reserves Notes and deposits at the Bank of Canada held by chartered banks. *See also* settlement balances.

Classical adjustment process Process by which the economy automatically moves toward internal and external balance through the effect of the trade balance on the domestic money supply.

Classical aggregate supply curve Vertical aggregate supply curve.

Classical case Vertical *LM* curve, resulting from the lack of an interest rate effect on the demand for money.

Clean floating Pure flexible exchange rate system in which central banks do not intervene. *Contrast* dirty floating.

Clearing system Process of settlement of the net amounts owing among the banks as a result of payments made by cheque.

Cobb–Douglas production function Production function with characteristics of constant returns to scale, constant elasticity of output, and unit elasticity of substitution between input factors.

COLA Cost of living adjustment clause in contracts that provides for increases in wages to match inflation.

Cold turkey policy Policy strategy of moving immediately to a lower rate of inflation.

Competitiveness *See* real exchange rate.

Composition of output Relative amounts of consumption, investment, and government expenditure making up GDP.

Consumer durables Consumer goods that yield services over a period of time; for example, washing machines.

Consumer price index (CPI) Price index that measures the cost of goods bought by a typical family.

Consumption Purchases of goods and services by households.

Consumption function Equation relating consumption to income.

Coordination of policies Policies agreed upon by countries to avoid undesirable spillover effects.

Credibility Extent to which people believe that the government will carry out its announced policy.

Crowding out   Displacement of some component of private aggregate demand by government spending.

Currency reform   Change in unit of currency; for example, replacement of the Israeli pound by the shekel.

Current account   Record of a country's international trade in goods and services.

Cyclical deficit   Portion of the budget deficit due to deviation of GDP from potential. *Contrast* structural deficit.

Debt-financed deficits   Budget deficits financed through sales of bonds to the public.

Debt management   Process of financing budget deficits and refinancing maturing debt.

Decision lag   Period between the time a disturbance is discovered and the time a policy is chosen.

Depreciation   (1) wear and tear on existing capital; (2) decrease in the value of a currency *vis-à-vis* other currencies.

Desired capital stock   Level of capital stock that maximizes profits.

Devaluation   Intentional reduction of the value of the domestic currency in terms of foreign currencies under a fixed exchange rate system.

Dirty floating   Flexible exchange rate system in which central banks intervene in exchange markets to moderate short-run fluctuations in exchange rates.

Discounted cash flow analysis   Valuation of a future stream of payments by applying a discount to future payments to allow for the difference in value between a dollar today and a dollar in the future.

Disposable income   Income available for the household to spend.

Dissaving   Negative saving, i.e., expenditure out of wealth.

Duration of spells of unemployment   Length of time an individual remains unemployed.

Dynamic consistency   Being tough when it hurts because you said you would earlier and you want people to believe you next time.

Dynamic multiplier   Response over time of aggregate demand to an increase in autonomous spending.

Econometric model   Set of equations used to make quantitative economic predictions.

Econometric policy evaluation critique   Criticism that current econometric models are inappropriate for studying policy changes because the policy changes themselves change the responses of economic agents.

Economic disturbances   Shifts in aggregate demand or supply, or money demand or supply, that cause output, interest rates, or prices to diverge from the target path.

Efficiency wage   Theory attributing wage rigidity to losses in productivity that would occur if wages were cut.

Endogenous variable   One whose value is determined by a set of relationships. *Contrast* exogenous variable.

Equilibrium income Level of income when aggregate demand equals the supply of goods.

Excess cash reserves Cash reserves held by chartered banks over and above the level required by the Bank Act.

Excess sensitivity of consumption Evidence that consumption has a larger response to current income than is consistent with the life-cycle–permanent-income theory.

Exchange rate Price of foreign currency in terms of domestic currency.

Exchange rate overshooting Short-run movement of the exchange rate beyond its long-run equilibrium in response to a disturbance.

Exogenous variable One whose value is determined outside the theory being used. *Contrast* endogenous variable.

Expansion *See* recovery.

Expectations-augmented aggregate supply curve Aggregate supply curve that includes the expected future price level as a major determinant of the current price level.

Expectations-augmented Phillips curve Phillips curve that includes inflationary expectations as a major determinant of the current inflation rate.

Expectations effect Long-run increase in nominal interest rate following increased growth rate of the money supply due to increased inflationary expectations.

Expenditure reducing (or increasing) policies Policies aimed at offsetting the effects of expenditure switching policy on aggregate demand.

Expenditure switching policies Policies aimed at increasing purchases of domestic goods and decreasing imports.

Factor cost Cost of goods net of indirect taxes. *See* market prices.

Factor shares Portion of national income paid to each productive input (labour, capital, etc.).

Final goods Goods sold to the final purchaser in contrast with intermediate goods that are sold to other firms for further processing.

Fine tuning Continuous attempts to stabilize the economy in the face of small disturbances.

Fiscal policy Government policy with respect to government expenditure, transfer payments, and the tax structure.

Fiscal policy multiplier Increase in aggregate demand for a one-dollar increase in government expenditure (or other change in autonomous demand).

Fisher equation The equation that states that the nominal interest rate equals the real interest rate plus the expected inflation rate.

Fixed exchange rate Exchange rate maintained at a given level by official intervention in the foreign exchange market.

Flexible exchange rates Exchange rate determined by supply and demand.

Frictionless neoclassical model Model of aggregate supply with flexible prices and perfect competition.

Full crowding out Total displacement of private spending by increased government spending. *See* classical aggregate supply curve and classical case.

Full-employment surplus Hypothetical budget surplus that would obtain with existing fiscal policy if the economy were at full employment.

GDP implicit price index Measure of the price level obtained by dividing nominal GDP by real GDP.

GDP, nominal Value of all goods and services produced in the economy during a given time period.

GDP, real Value of all goods and services produced in the economy using prices of some base year.

Government budget deficit *See* budget deficit.

Gradual adjustment hypothesis Theory that the change in the capital stock responds to the gap between the desired capital stock and the current capital stock.

Gradualism Policy strategy of moving toward a desired target slowly.

Gross domestic product (GDP) Total goods and services produced within the country using both domestic and nonresident factors of production.

Gross national product (GNP) The value of all goods and services produced by domestically owned factors of production.

Growth Increase in real GDP.

Growth accounting The theory of measuring the sources of economic growth.

Growth of total factor productivity *See* technical progress.

High-powered money *See* monetary base.

Hyperinflation Very rapid rate of price increase.

Imported inflation Inflation due to increase in domestic prices of imported goods following currency depreciation.

Income effect Increase in interest rate following initial drop (due to *liquidity effect*) after increase in money supply.

Income velocity of money Ratio of income to the money supply.

Incomes policies Attempts to reduce inflation by wage or price controls.

Indexation Automatic adjustment of prices and wages according to inflation rate.

Inflation Rate of increase of the general price level.

Inflation-corrected deficit Measure of the budget deficit adjusted for the reduction in the real value of government debt resulting from inflation.

Inflation tax Revenue gained by the government through increasing the money supply and causing inflation.

Inside lag Period between the time a disturbance occurs and the time action is taken.

Interdependence Interconnection between national economies linked through international trade.

Internal and external balance Internal balance occurs when output is at full-employment GDP. External balance occurs when the trade balance is zero.

Intertemporal substitution of leisure The extent to which temporarily high real wages cause workers to work harder today and enjoy more leisure tomorrow.

Intervention Sales or purchases of foreign exchange by the central bank in order to stabilize exchange rates.

Inventory cycle Response of inventory investment to changes in sales that causes further changes in aggregate demand.

Inventory investment Increase in stock of goods on hand.

Inventory-theoretic approach Money demand models such as the Baumol–Tobin model.

Investment Purchase of new capital, principally by the business sector.

Investment subsidy Government payment of part of the cost of private investment.

***IS-LM* curves** Goods market and money market equilibrium schedules.

J curve Curve tracing time path of the response of imports to exchange rate changes.

Keynesian aggregate supply curve Horizontal aggregate supply curve.

Keynesians Members of a school of economic thought who argue for active government stabilization policy. Alternatively, those who argue for fiscal rather than monetary policy.

Labour productivity Average output per worker.

Laffer curve Relation between tax revenue and tax rates, showing that tax revenue is maximized at a tax rate greater than zero and less than 100 percent.

Layoff Dismissal of an employee with a promise of a recall at a later date.

Life-cycle hypothesis Consumption theory emphasizing that consumers consume and save out of total life income and plan to provide for retirement.

Limits of growth Issue of whether resource depletion will eventually eliminate economic growth.

Liquidity A measure of the ability to make funds available on short notice.

Liquidity constraints Limitations on ability to borrow to finance consumption plans.

Liquidity effect Initial drop in interest rate following increase in money supply, due to movement in *LM* curve.

Liquidity trap Horizontal *LM* curve, due to extreme interest sensitivity of money demand.

Long-run aggregate supply curve Aggregate supply curve showing long-run tradeoff between GDP and the price level. Usually assumed to be vertical at full-employment GDP.

Lucas supply curve *See* expectations-augmented aggregate supply curve.

M1 Currency plus demand deposits.

M2 M1 plus personal savings and non-personal notice deposits.

Macroeconomic models Simplified formal models used to study and predict the behaviour of the nation's economy.

Managed floating *See* dirty floating.

Marginal product of capital Increment to output obtained by adding one unit of capital, with other factor inputs held constant.

Marginal product of labour Increment to output obtained by adding one unit of labour, with other factor inputs held constant.

Marginal propensity to consume (MPC) Increase in consumption for a one-dollar increase in disposable income.

Marginal propensity to save (MPS) Increase in saving for a one-dollar increase in diposable income.

Market clearing approach Theory that flexible prices clear all markets. *See* frictionless neoclassical model.

Market prices Cost of goods, including indirect taxes. *See* factor cost.

Markup Excess of price over cost (often assumed to be constant, as an analytical convenience).

Medium of exchange Asset used for making payments.

Monetarism *See* monetarists.

Monetarists Members of a school of economic thought emphasizing the importance of the money supply.

Monetary accommodation Use of monetary policy to stabilize interest rates during active fiscal policy operations.

Monetary base Currency plus deposits of chartered banks and other financial institutions at the Bank of Canada.

Monetary policy Use of money supply and interest rate changes to influence aggregate demand.

Monetary policy multiplier Increase in aggregate demand for a one-dollar increase in the money supply.

Monetary rule A rule setting the growth rate of the money supply.

Monetary theory of the exchange rate Theory emphasizing role of the money supply in determining the exchange rate.

Monetizing budget deficits Purchase of government debt by the central bank, indirectly funding the deficit by printing money.

Money (Money supply) Assets that can be used for making payments.

Money-financed deficits Deficits financed by increasing the monetary base.

Money illusion Incorrect interpretation of nominal changes in prices as indicating changes in relative prices.

Money multiplier Ratio of the money supply to the monetary base.

Multiple expansion of bank deposits Process by which a one-dollar increase in the monetary base leads to an expansion of the money supply by more than one dollar.

Multiplier Increase in an endogenous variable for a one-dollar increase in an exogenous variable; in particular, the increase in GDP for a one-dollar increase in government expenditure.

Multiplier uncertainty Uncertainty about effects of policy changes due to uncertainty about the value of the fiscal policy or other multiplier.

Mundell–Fleming model Model first proposed by Robert Mundell and Marcus Fleming that describes an economy with flexible exchange rates and perfect capital mobility.

National (public) debt Accumulation of all past deficits; total outstanding amount of government bonds.

Natural rate of unemployment The unemployment rate that is permanently sustainable given the institutions of the economy.

Net domestic income Total payments to factors of production.

Net exports Exports minus imports.

Net national product (NNP) GNP minus allowance for depreciation of capital.

Neutrality of money Proposition stating that equiproportional changes in the money supply and prices leave the economy unaffected.

New classical macroeconomists Economists who believe that the private economy is inherently efficient and that the government ought not to attempt to stabilize output and unemployment.

Nominal interest rate Stated rate of interest without any adjustment for inflation. *See* real interest rate.

Noninterest deficit *See* primary deficit.

Okun's law Empirical "law" relating GDP growth to changes in unemployment; named for Arthur Okun.

Open market operation Purchase or sale of government securities in exchange for money by the central bank.

Openness Extent to which the economy is involved with foreign trade as measured by the ratio of imports to GDP.

Output gap Difference between potential GDP and actual GDP.

Outside lag Time required for a policy change to take affect.

Overshooting Movement of an economic variable past its long-run value.

Peak High point of business cycle.

Permanent income Estimated lifetime labour income plus income earned on assets.

Personal income Income received by households.

Phillips curve Relation between inflation and unemployment.

Planned aggregate demand Total planned spending on consumption, investment, and government expenditure.

Policy dilemmas Conflicts between achieving two inconsistent targets; for example, *internal* versus *external balance*.

Policy rule Activist but nondiscretionary policy guide.

Political business cycle Theory that politicians deliberately manipulate the economy to produce an economic boom at election time.

Portfolio decisions Decisions on how to divide wealth among different assets.

Potential output Output that can be produced when all factors are fully employed.

Precautionary demand Demand for money held against uncertain expenditure needs.

Present discounted value (PDV) Value today of a stream of payments to be made in the future.

Price controls Government-imposed restrictions against raising prices.

Primary deficit The budget deficit, excluding interest payments.

Production function Technological relation showing how much output can be produced for a given combination of inputs.

Profit sharing System in which part of workers' compensation is a share of profits rather than an hourly wage.

Propagation mechanism Mechanism by which current economic shocks cause fluctuations that extend into the future.

Public debt *See* national debt.

Purchasing power parity (PPP) Theory of exchange rate determination stating that the exchange rate adjusts to maintain equal purchasing power of foreign and domestic currency.

q theory Investment theory emphasizing that investment will be high when assets are valuable relative to their reproduction cost. The ratio of asset value to cost is called q.

Quantity equation Price times quantity equals money times velocity.

Quantity theory of money Theory of money demand emphasizing the relation of nominal income to nominal money. Sometimes used to mean vertical LM curve.

Rational expectations Theory of expectations formation in which expectations are based on all available information about the underlying economic variable. Frequently associated with new classical macroeconomics.

Rational expectations equilibrium approach Theory that combines *rational expectations* with the *market clearing approach*.

Real balances Real value of the money supply obtained by dividing the money supply by the price level.

Real business cycles Theory that recessions and booms are due primarily to shocks in real activity, such as supply shocks, rather than to changes in monetary factors.

Real exchange rate Ratio of the price of imports to the price of exports.

Real GDP *See* GDP, real.

Real interest rate The real return on an investment obtained by subtracting the rate of inflation from the nominal interest rate.

Recession Period of economic weakness with declining GDP.

Recognition lag Period between the time a disturbance occurs and the time policy makers discover the disturbance.

Recovery Upward swing in the business cycle.

Rental cost of capital Cost per period of using a dollar's worth of capital.

Repercussion effect Feedback of domestic economic changes through foreign economies back into the domestic economy.

Required reserves Cash reserves held by chartered banks as required under the Bank Act.

Reserves *See* cash reserves.

Residential construction Investment in housing.

Revaluation Intentional increase in the value of the domestic currency in terms of foreign currencies under a fixed exchange rate system.

Seigniorage Revenue derived from the government's ability to print money.

Settlement balances Deposits at the Bank of Canada held by chartered banks and other financial institutions.

Short-run aggregate supply curve Aggregate supply curve showing the short-run relationship between GDP and the price level.

Short-run Phillips curve Short-run tradeoff between inflation and unemployment, holding anticipated inflation constant.

Small menu costs Theory suggesting that very small costs of changing prices and wages may lead to large amounts of price and wage rigidity.

Square-root formula Demand-for-money schedule developed in the Baumol–Tobin approach.

Stabilization policies Use of fiscal and monetary policies to smooth fluctuations in output.

Stagflation Simultaneous inflation and recession.

Standard of deferred payment Unit used in specifying contracts involving future payments.

Steady state State in which real (or real per capita) economic variables are constant.

Sterilization Open market purchase or sale by the central bank used to offset effects of foreign exchange market intervention on the monetary base.

Store of value Asset held to bridge the gap between receipt of income and expenditure.

Structural deficit Deficit that would exist with current fiscal policy if the economy were at full employment; also called full-employment deficit. *Contrast* cyclical deficit.

Supply-side economics School of economics emphasizing changes in potential GDP rather than aggregate demand.

Targets and instruments of policy The *target* is the variable policy is designed to influence. The *instrument* is the variable to be manipulated to change the target variable.

Technical progress Ability to produce more output with a given level of inputs; growth in total factor productivity.

Till money Currency held by chartered banks to meet demands of depositors.

Trade balance Exports minus imports.

Transactions demand Demand for money for making payments.

Transfers Payments to a household other than in payment for services; for example, unemployment insurance.

Transmission mechanism Process by which monetary policy affects aggregate demand.

Trend output *See* potential output.

Trough Low point of the business cycle.

Unemployment rate The fraction of the people in the labour force unable to find work.

Unintended inventory accumulation Increase in stocks of goods when firms' sales fall below the levels expected.

Unit of account Unit in which prices are measured.

Unit labour cost Cost of the labour required to produce one unit of output.

User cost of capital *See* rental cost of capital.

Value added Increase in value of output at a given stage of production; equivalently, value of output minus cost of inputs.

Wage and price controls Regulation of wages and prices by law rather than by supply and demand.

Wage push Demand for wage increases above inflation rate built into short-run Phillips curve.

Index

— — — — — — — — — — — *cut here* — — — — — — — — — — —

STUDENT REPLY CARD

Macroeconomics, Fourth Canadian Edition

You can help us to develop better textbooks. Please answer the following questions and return this form via Business Reply Mail. Your opinions matter; thank you in advance for sharing them with us!

Name of your college or university: _____

Major program of study: _____

Course title: _____

Were you required to buy this book? _____ yes _____ no

Did you buy this book new or used? _____ new _____ used ($_____)

Do you plan to keep or sell this book? _____ keep _____ sell

Is the sequence of chapters consistent with your course of study? If not, please indiciate the sequence you followed in your course.

Were there topics covered in your course that are not included in the text? Please specify:

— — — — — — — — — — · *fold here* — — — — — — — — — —

What did you like most about this text?

What did you like least?

Please add any comments or suggestions:

- - - - - - - - - - - - _cut here_ - - - - - - - - - - - ⌐
|
|
|
|
|
|
|
|
|
|
|
|
|
|
|
|
|
|
|
|
|
|
|
|
|
| _cut here_
|
- - - - - - - - - - - _fold here_ - - - - - - - - - - -|
|
BUSINESS
REPLY MAIL

No Postage Stamp
Necessary If Mailed
in Canada   7115

Postage will be paid by

Attn.: Sponsoring Editor, Business and Commerce
The College Division

McGraw-Hill Ryerson Limited
300 Water St.
Whitby, ON
L1N 9Z9
|
|
|
|
|
|
tape shut